BRITISH CAPITALISM AT THE CROSSROADS, 1919–1932

In the aftermath of the First World War British politics were subordinated to the goal of reconstructing a multilateral trade and payments system. This decision, as the author explains, must be understood as the result of the peculiar structure of British capitalism wherein mercantile and financial activity rather than manufacturing industry provided the core of wealth of the dominant community. For a decade Britain made a signal contribution to the restoration of multilateralism. But the price of leadership was increasing strain on the industrial community, and mounting antagonism against France and the United States for their unwillingness to cooperate on British terms.

With the world at a turning-point in 1928, British policy remained committed to reform through multilateral action, particularly once the Labour party resumed office. But the practical effect of policy was the opposite of that intended. Dogmatic opposition to all second-best alternatives helped drive all countries, Britain included, away from internationalism towards a narrow nationalism and economic protectionism. The account ends in 1932 when Britain embarked upon an active imperial policy while the rest of the world headed towards another war.

Using a wide range of primary sources, the author presents an account which integrates the economic, political, and diplomatic events of the period. Numerous broad issues such as the political influence of the City and the financial press, the operation of the gold standard and most-favoured-nation clause, the political impact of multinational firms, the League of Nations' contribution to economic cooperation and central bank relations are examined in detail. But attention is also paid to the role of individual bankers, industrialists, and statesmen, and institutions such as the Bank of England, the Bank of France, and the Federal Reserve Bank of New York, the Federation of British Industry, TUC, London Chamber of Commerce, NFU, Chatham House, and the Bank for International Settlements. The result is a radical new account of one of the most fateful eras of contemporary history.

BRITISH CAPITALISM AT THE CROSSROADS 1919–1932

A study in politics, economics, and international relations

ROBERT W.D. BOYCE

Lecturer in International History
London School of Economics and Political Science

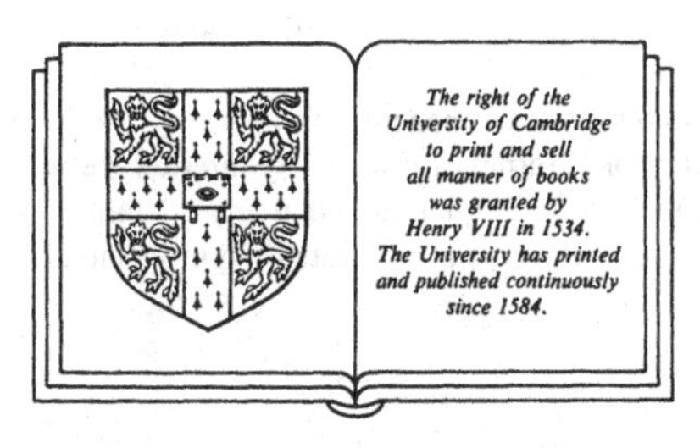
The right of the
University of Cambridge
to print and sell
all manner of books
was granted by
Henry VIII in 1534.
The University has printed
and published continuously
since 1584.

CAMBRIDGE UNIVERSITY PRESS

Cambridge
London New York New Rochelle
Melbourne Sydney

CAMBRIDGE UNIVERSITY PRESS
Cambridge, New York, Melbourne, Madrid, Cape Town, Singapore,
São Paulo, Delhi, Dubai, Tokyo

Cambridge University Press
The Edinburgh Building, Cambridge CB2 8RU, UK

Published in the United States of America by Cambridge University Press, New York

www.cambridge.org
Information on this title: www.cambridge.org/9780521124973

First published 1987
This digitally printed version 2009

A catalogue record for this publication is available from the British Library

Library of Congress Cataloguing in Publication data

Boyce, Robert W.D., 1943-
British capitalism at the crossroads, 1919-1932:
Bibliography.
1. Great Britain–Foreign economic relations.
2. Great Britain–Economic conditions–1918-1945.
3. Great Britain–Industries–History.
I. Title.
HF1533.B64 1987 337.41 86-23243

ISBN 978-0-521-32535-6 Hardback
ISBN 978-0-521-12497-3 Paperback

For my mother and the memory of my father

Contents

Preface

Richard Mayne, the writer and broadcaster, tells the story of a newly prosperous Italian couple who decided to purchase a dining-table: not just another mass-produced item this time, but something of quality, bearing the mark of traditional craftsmanship. On a drive through the Abruzzi, they came across an old cabinet-maker, and amidst the stacks of maturing timber in his workshop they explained their request. Some weeks later they returned and were proudly shown the product of the craftsman's labour. 'But,' they exclaimed, 'we asked for a square table. This one is not square, it's round!' The cabinet-maker nodded. 'Ah yes,' he replied, his hand fondly tracing the grain along the table's top, 'as I was making it, it became round'.

The present study began as an analysis of British external monetary policy in the 1930s, and became an account mainly of the 1920s. Archival research revealed that the explanation for policy decisions in the 1930s usually rested upon shorthand references to events in the earlier period. The issues had already been rehearsed, views clarified, and policy more or less settled. The earlier period offered the key to later policy, but it became clear that the analysis required extending in other directions as well. In the first place, monetary policy had to be placed within the broader context of domestic and economic decision-making. The economist may well advance theoretical knowledge by treating central bank or exchange rate decisions as discrete issues to be studied on their own. The historian who does so obscures the essential relatedness of issues within the political economy. In the second place, it was essential to go beyond Whitehall and Threadneedle Street to comprehend the sources of policy. The struggle over the return to the gold standard in the 1920s was part of a larger struggle to restore the political and economic conditions that prevailed before the First World War, both in Britain and the world at large. Besides the Treasury and the Bank of England, therefore, careful study was required of other institutions such as the Foreign Office and Board of Trade, the political parties and industrial, commercial, and agricultural pressure groups that set the climate in which decisions were taken, and beyond them the foreign powers whose cooperation was required for a successful outcome. By thus following the contours of the evidence, this study has also 'become round,' though whether the result justifies the labour is a matter for the reader to decide.

In the preparation of this study I have acquired debts to numerous individuals and institutions. The Economic and Social Research Council generously provided financial support for the bulk of the research work, while the London School of Economics and Political Science helped to defray the costs of several visits to foreign archives. Professors Donald Cameron Watt and Leslie Pressnell encouraged the project from the beginning, and Professor Kenneth Bourne and Dr Philip Cottrell read earlier drafts of the manuscript and offered much-needed advice. Mr A.J.T. Williams, secretary of the Bank of England, and Mr J.M. Keyworth, the curator, kindly allowed me to examine material in the Bank's archives. Mr Malcolm Evans of Morgan Grenfell & Company Limited, and Dr John Orbell of Baring Brothers & Company Limited generously opened their archives to me. Her Majesty the Queen graciously permitted me access to material in the Royal Archives at Windsor, and other holders of private papers including Lord Addison, Lord Croft, Lady Ford, Lord Kennet, Lord Melchett, the family of Sir Charles Addis, and Professor the Lord Stamp responded with similar consideration to my requests for access.

I am also indebted to MM. Werner Simon and Sven Welander of the Historical Collections of the League of Nations Library, Geneva, for introducing me to the League archives; Mlle. Alice Guillemain and her colleagues at the Ministry of Economy and Finance, Paris, for their unfailing kindness; Stephen Clarke and Carl Backlund of the Federal Reserve Bank of New York and M. Jean-Claude Desfretier of the Bank of France for extending such a warm welcome at their respective institutions; Everett and Josephine Case for so kindly affording me access to the Owen D. Young archives; John Barnes for allowing me to see the unpublished draft of the Amery diaries; and Elisabeth Barker for bringing to light the unpublished memoir of Bickham Sweet-Escott, now deposited in the British Library of Political and Economic Science. Others to whom I extend my thanks are Dr Angela Raspin and her colleagues at the BLPES for their assistance over the years; Dr Benedikt Benedikz of the University of Birmingham Library, and Dr Richard Storey of the Modern Records Centre at the University of Warwick Library for their friendly reception on my numerous visits; the Master,

Fellows, and Scholars of Churchill College in the University of Cambridge for permitting me access to the Hankey, Phipps, and other papers; and the librarians and archivists at the many other institutions where I pursued my research. I owe a special debt to Margaret Bradgate, Irene Leon, Nett Capsey, and Veronica Brooke for so cheerfully enduring the chore of typing successive drafts, and to Mrs Sheila McEnery of the Cambridge University Press for her sub-editorial help. But my greatest thanks go to Gudrun, Brynhildur, Steinunn, and other members of my family for lending their support over what must have seemed an inexplicably long time.

Abbreviations

ABCC	Association of British Chambers of Commerce
BB & Co	Baring Brothers and Co. Ltd.
BIS	Bank for International Settlements
BoE	Bank of England
BdeF, CG	Banque de France, Délibérations du Conseil Général, procès verbal
BT	Board of Trade
CAB	Cabinet
CEI	Committee of Economic Information
CEUE	Committee of Enquiry for European Union
EAC	Economic Advisory Council
EIA	Empire Industries Association
FBI	Federation of British Industries
FO	Foreign Office
France, MAE	France, Ministère des Affaires Etrangères
France, MF	France, Ministère des Finances
FRBNY	Federal Reserve Bank of New York
FRUS	United States Department of State, *Foreign Relations of the United States*
ICC	International Chamber of Commerce
ILO	International Labour Office
ILP	Independent Labour Party
ISTC	Iron and Steel Trades Confederation
JO	*Journal Official de la République française. Débats parlementaires*
LCC	London Chamber of Commerce
LN	League of Nations
MAF	Ministry of Agriculture and Fisheries
MGC	Morgan Grenfell & Co Ltd
NCEO	National Confederation of Employers' Organisations

NFU	National Farmers' Union
NUM	National Union of Manufacturers
PREM	Prime Minister's Office
RA GV	Royal Archives, papers of King George V
RVDI	Reichsverband der deutschen Industrie
SdN	League of Nations archives, Geneva
T	Treasury
TUC	Trades Union Congress
TWL	Thomas W. Lamont papers.

Introduction

Following the armistice in 1918 the British government took a series of decisions that reversed the wartime trend towards state regulation of the economy, protectionism, and Empire preference, and restored the country to its pre-war posture of economic internationalism. The decisions were taken swiftly and with little debate amidst the tumult of postwar events, but their consequences were tremendous. In the first place, the country's prosperity was made to depend vitally upon the reconstruction of the international trade and payments system. Secondly, domestic industry was again almost fully exposed to the strains of world leadership. Britain's contribution to postwar economic reconstruction, although obscured by the emphasis in recent accounts upon the contribution of private American interests,[1] was indeed impressive. But so too was the burden it placed upon the domestic economy and the opposition to economic internationalism that this eventually raised.

In the immediate postwar period public sentiment leaned strongly towards a general *retour en avant*. Domestic industry and labour, which were forced to shoulder the main burden of adjustment, were as yet poorly organised, and the war offered a convenient explanation for the difficulties they experienced. The return to the gold standard at the prewar parity of $4.86 in 1925 appeared briefly to re-establish disciplined control over the British economic system. But the immediate result in Britain was further deflation and acute industrial strife. In the meantime, shifts in industrial priorities and stiff overseas competition were making industrialists and trade unionists increasingly reluctant to accept the gold standard, free trade, and other internationalist policies. With the growth of mass production industry in the United States, the prospect of a highly organised Soviet empire in the east, and talk of an economic United States of Europe, numerous signs pointed towards the division of the world into mighty economic blocs. In these circumstances, rigid adherence to internationalism threatened to end in the country's isolation, and to many both on the right and the left the only practical solution appeared to rest with the economic organisation of the Empire. British bankers and statesmen renewed their efforts to promote reforms of the international trade and payments system after the return to gold, but with only modest results, while at home the debate over Britain's own economic future got under way in earnest. By the second half of 1928, when the system entered a new crisis, their efforts were obstructed by disagreements with the other major creditor countries and undercut by the ground-swell of domestic opposition to further sacrifices for the sake of international stability.

Briefly, under the second Labour government of 1929–31, Britain again attempted to lead the world back from the brink of autarky and chaos. But the government's dogmatic approach did little more than obstruct the second-best solutions advanced by other countries, and in little time the government was enfeebled by the same division that ran through the country as a whole. The financial crisis of 1931 placed British capitalism squarely at the crossroads. The Labour government sought to promote a diplomatic solution to the international crisis while pressing trade union supporters to accept further sacrifices. When little was accomplished on either front and a worsening run on the pound brought the government down, a new National government was formed with the avowed intention of imposing sufficient deflationary measures to restore international confidence in sterling. But by now savage cuts in public expenditure and foreign borrowing had little effect. The run on the pound intensified, and on 21 September 1931 sterling was driven off the gold standard. Thereupon the pressures so long accumulating for a break with economic internationalism became unrestrained; in a series of swift measures Britain adopted a posture of imperial protectionism. Commitment to this new posture, brief and incomplete as it was, signalled the end of an era for the whole world. Subsequent events were increasingly overshadowed by the threat of another war.

This is the story of Britain's efforts to provide leadership in international economic affairs in the years after the First World War: the successes, failures, and the domestic political struggle that lay behind it. In this account consistent emphasis is given to international monetary and commercial relations, and the role of the Governor of the Bank of England, Montagu Norman. Other accounts linking economics with diplomacy in the period have invariably devoted their attention mainly if not exclusively to the reparation–war debt issue. This is understandable since it undoubtedly occupied more of the politicians' and statesmen's time than any other international issue during the 1920s, and in a very real sense became the issue on which the fate of the Versailles settlement was made to depend. But having been made the subject of exhaustive attention by other scholars, it requires only summary treatment here.[2] In any case, it must be stressed that British statesmen regarded 'political' debts as merely one among many obstacles in the path of postwar recovery. Once the claims were reduced, currencies could then be stabilised, and with central bankers again in control of the international trade and payments system the remaining commercial and financial problems could be overcome. Norman, as head of the Bank, thus occupied a central place in the scheme. His initial successes in restoring the authority of the central banks in Europe and elsewhere and their subsequent failure to maintain stability are basic to the history of the time.

On the domestic stage the role of other institutions such as the employers' federation (FBI), the trade union organisation (TUC), and others such as the National Farmers' Union (NFU) and Empire Industries Association (EIA), along with the political parties and the press are also given prominence. Much of what occurred could be summed up as a clash of two constellations of interest. I have chosen to describe it in terms of a division between the industrial and the mercantile–financial communities. The term community will doubtless raise objections in some quarters for implying a coherence that scarcely existed. Where, it will be asked, was the demarcation line between the two communities or the contemporary awareness that such communities existed? These are serious questions, for which no simple answers can be given. In defence, it may be said that the most obvious abstractions often go unacknowledged: racism, sexism, deference, and English nationalism, for example.[3] As for community, the term is used to underline the fact that social relations, education, and religion as well as economic interests helped to define the increasingly sharp division over the country's economic destiny in the 1920s. As will be seen, by the latter part of the decade critics of economic policy frequently acknowledged a fundamental division in the country between the north and the south or southeast. Imprecise as it may be, community thus corresponds to a subjective reality of great significance in this period.

Twice in the early part of the century adverse international conditions had aroused support for a radical departure in economic policy: in the years of Joseph Chamberlain's tariff reform campaign and again during the First World War. The postwar years presented a third occasion for radical talk. Had the world slump been slower to develop, it seems at least possible that the fault-line dividing opinion within the country and each of the three major political parties might have produced a major realignment of forces and an enduring change in national priorities. As it was, the crisis resulted in a number of major concessions to domestic industry and a temporary abandonment of international initiatives, but also a fear of economic collapse which intensified class divisions and again obscured the demarcation between the two communities.

But this is not only a study of interests and institutions. Norman, as will be seen, was also an intensely interesting man whose actions were even more controversial than his biographers have allowed.[4] As well as Norman, numerous other men figure prominently in this account, some famous, some now obscure, a few deserving to be better known than they are now. The portraits of Sir Otto Niemeyer, Philip Snowden, Ramsay MacDonald, Winston Churchill, Sir Alfred Mond, Sir Arthur Salter, Norman, and certain others presented here are not perhaps flattering ones. Suffice it to say that conflict brings out the best and the worst in men. The interwar years were tense, trying times, dominated by fear of economic disaster and social upheaval. They were not in fact so unlike the present, which is one reason why this study may prove of interest to readers outside as well as within the academy walls.

1

The politics of economic internationalism

The century of economic internationalism

The hundred years between the battle of Waterloo and the start of the First World War was the century of economic internationalism in Britain. The policy of *laissez-faire*, whereby land, labour, and capital were left to the operation of self-regulating markets, attained its fullest realisation in the middle years of the century and thereafter declined.[1] Already, indeed, legislation existed on such matters as sanitation, food, and contagious diseases, child labour, hours and conditions of work, public libraries, prisons, and schools, and in subsequent decades further legislation was introduced to limit the impact upon society of market forces and maintain tolerable conditions of life.[2] Nothing, however, was done to alter Britain's relations with the rest of the world. Britain continued to treat the whole world as a single market, accepting the burden of adjustment to the ebb and flow of international demand and prices, and looking to international solutions to larger problems rather than resorting to protectionist policies.

Of the five main components of economic internationalism, three were accepted without controversy by the early years of the nineteenth century. Unrestricted capital movements, or free trade in capital as it was occasionally known, already existed and required no agitation. Restrictions on the emigration of skilled artisans were swept away in 1825.[3] And the ban on the export of machinery, already eroded by rapid technical change, was formally repealed in 1843.[4] Free trade on the other hand required a lengthy and exhausting campaign before the main objective of repealing the corn laws was attained in 1846. The fifth component, regulation of the currency and domestic credit on the basis of the international gold standard, was also established through banking legislation in face of diminishing opposition at about this time.[5]

The inclusion of the gold standard with the other factors may at first sight seem paradoxical. The others constituted the removal of restrictions upon the movement of factors of production; the gold standard, as modified in the nineteenth century, involved the establishment of the Bank of England's virtual monopoly of currency note issuing powers and its duty to intervene in the money and foreign exchange markets to ensure that sterling remained at its fixed parity with gold. But looking beyond the management of the gold standard to its practical functions, the reason for its inclusion is obvious. In the first place, it ensured confidence in the pound and contracts denominated in it, which facilitated international trade and commerce. Secondly, it enabled the Bank of England easily to draw in overseas funds when necessary by the operation of Bank rate, so that the exchanges could be kept steady without recourse to cruder measures such as tariffs, import quotas, rationing, or foreign exchange restrictions. Thirdly, by placing the note issue in the hands of a private institution, on the strict condition that all notes aside from a strictly limited fiduciary issue should be fully backed by gold, it removed the temptation for politicians to resort to the printing presses to pay for extravagant policies. The attractions of the last-mentioned function became steadily greater as democratic pressures on governments increased.[6] So important was the gold standard in the eyes of its supporters, in fact, that eventually most were prepared to jettison every other component of economic internationalism in order to maintain it.

The case for economic internationalism, at a time of rapidly expanding population, increasing food import requirements, and a near-monopoly of manufactured exports, was overwhelming, and in the 1850s and 1860s a broad consensus of support existed. But from the mid-1870s conditions sharply changed. A prolonged period of declining price-levels and sluggish trade intensified social conflict at home and strained relations with capitalist countries abroad. Trade unionism again became a force to be reckoned with. Socialism revived. Foreign protectionism also intensified, and major new industrial competitors emerged. One consequence was the rise of the Fair Trade movement in the 1880s, followed by the Tariff Reform movement, which in the aftermath of the Boer war became the first major challenge to economic internationalism.

Joseph Chamberlain, the Birmingham manufacturer and Radical-turned-Tory minister who dominated the movement, advanced an overarching formula for the regeneration of British capitalism. Scornful of cosmopolitan finance and convinced that Britain's very future as a world power demanded a strong industrial base, he called for a general tariff with substantial preferences for Empire goods. Thus protected, manufacturers would gain the advantage of assured Empire-wide markets, workers higher wages and state-supported welfare provisions, and the

British Dominions privileged access to Britain's huge market for foodstuffs and raw materials. In this way both the domestic and the external threats confronting Britain would be surmounted. The appeal of a revitalised British imperialism would serve to divert the growing threat of class war. Simultaneously the Empire would be forged into an economic bloc comparable in population, resources, and industrial production to Germany or the United States, and capable of bargaining with them from a position of strength.[7]

Chamberlain's vision captivated many within the Conservative Party. In May 1903 he resigned his cabinet post in order to be free to promote Tariff Reform, and within two years he had captured control of party policy. But the accumulated dissatisfactions of ten years of Tory government militated against his efforts, as did the revival of trade and resumption of modest inflation. Working-class voters could not be persuaded that 'you cannot be Free Traders in goods and not be Free Traders in labour', or to forego the 'cheap loaf', which was threatened by his plan to tax foreign wheat.[8] In January 1906 the Conservatives suffered a major defeat at the polls. Six months later Chamberlain himself was permanently disabled by a stroke. The Tariff Reform movement struggled on, but the party was henceforth careful to maintain its distance.

The second major challenge to economic internationalism arose during the First World War. Abruptly confronted with the fact that the country had become dependent upon Germany for numerous strategic goods, including dyestuffs, drugs, timing devices, and precision instruments,[9] and forced to expand munitions and agricultural production to the fullest possible extent, the state rapidly extended support to domestic industry. Official assurances were repeatedly given that the country would never again be allowed to become so economically vulnerable: strategic industries would be safeguarded, the ploughing-up policy introduced in 1916 to expand corn production would be maintained, and any import duties henceforth introduced would include an Empire preference to strengthen imperial ties.[10] But despite these assurances, and despite widely held fears of a 'war after the war' to regain shares of overseas commercial markets, the challenge was again remarkably short-lived.

In part this was due to the tendency to look back upon the pre-war years as a time of prosperity and social harmony, which if scarcely true was bound to seem the case after the calamitous upheavals of the war. There was also inevitably a widespread reaction after a period of unprecedented state intervention in the economy and escalating tax levies, and when the necessity for labour's cooperation in the war effort had come to an end. Yet even this does not fully explain the swiftness with which wartime plans for assisting trade were forgotten, or why alone of the European powers Britain should have accepted the sacrifices involved in restoring the gold standard at the pre-war parity. To understand this and the struggles of the 1920s, some appreciation is required of the extraordinary division in the country between its industrial and mercantile–financial communities, and the political advantages the latter possessed.

The industrial community

The industrial community, extending through the Midlands, the North, and the 'Celtic fringe', where the character of society had been profoundly affected by the industrial revolution, possessed two prominent social groups, the industrialists themselves and the industrial workers. By the early twentieth century each group had succeeded in impressing the other with its strength, and myths were common about their respective influence in the country as a whole.[11] But in fact as late as 1914 neither the industrialists nor the workers were sufficiently organised to formulate broad policies or exert more than occasional influence over the direction of national affairs. And though the war forced some organisational improvement on both sides, these were too new or too late to affect the crucial decisions in the immediate postwar period.

In the nineteenth century numerous local trade associations and employers' federations had come into being, but repeated attempts to create a national body representing industrial capital invariably foundered on the same rocks. Most sectors of industry were composed of competing firms, individualistic in outlook and too small to allow their owners time for much political activity. Manchester and Birmingham, respectively the capital of the basic export industries and the newer 'metal bashing' industries of the West Midlands, were too divided in outlook to cooperate effectively. The former favoured free trade, and so long as free trade prevailed there was little scope for collective action since even within the domestic market supply and prices lay beyond industrialists' control.[12]

The only organisation claiming to speak for the whole of industry was the Association of British Chambers of Commerce, which judged simply on the basis of membership seemed a most impressive body.In fact the association lacked funds, an adequate headquarters staff, and served as little more than a post office for communications among the local chambers which tended to go their own way. Some were predominantly industrial in outlook, but more were commercial; often it was the small merchant or professional man who found the atmosphere of their monthly meetings most congenial.[13] Sir Eyre Crowe, the leading Foreign Office authority on trade, was thus perhaps only slightly unfair to describe the association as 'really nothing more than a very incompetent debating society'.[14] During the 1920s the association boasted a membership of 'nearly 50,000 manufacturers and traders', and continued to describe itself as the voice of industry.[15] But in view of its disparate membership and the fact that the City-based London Chamber dominated the association's executive and published its main monthly journal, the association, when it spoke at all, was likely to reflect the views of commerce and finance rather than industry.[16] By this time two new 'peak' organisations representing specifically industrial capital had come into existence as a result of the need to coordinate production during the war.

The National Union of Manufacturers, set up in Birmingham in 1916, was able to claim a membership of 3,000 firms from every sector of industry by the later 1920s. But with exceptions these were small firms in the light engineering and motor industries, and the only NUM branches of real importance were those in Birmingham and London. The NUM did not suffer the Chamber of Commerce's problem of excessive heterogeneity, rather its opposite. Because of its narrow base of support and singleminded devotion to the cause of empire protection, it came to be regarded as a 'political' body whose views were so predictable as to be discounted in advance.[17]

The other peak organisation, the Federation of British Industries, was far more important. Also originating in Birmingham although soon relocated to London, the FBI was set up in 1916 with assistance from the Foreign Office at a time when concern about postwar trade competition was becoming intense.[18] The extraordinary conditions created by the war enabled the FBI to unite free trade Manchester with protectionist Birmingham and acquire the support of most of the large firms in the country. In 1917 its membership stood at 337 trade associations and individual firms. By 1920 this figure had reached 1,392, bringing the number of firms directly or indirectly affiliated to nearly 20,000.[19] The FBI could thus fairly claim to be the one truly representative voice of industry. Yet in practice its voice was usually muffled if not completely inaudible.

One reason was that the engineering employers, suspicious of delegating authority over wage settlements, created the National Confederation of Employers' Organisations in 1919, and made it a condition of their continued membership in the FBI that it should leave aside questions concerning labour. Another was that the FBI was unable to speak for agriculture – still the largest employer in the country – and indeed faced occasional opposition from the National Farmers' Union, which recognised that food production would be the last sector to receive protection from import competition and sought to bargain for reciprocal support from the manufacturers. A third and more important reason was that the leaders of the FBI felt it essential to speak for the whole of industry. Accordingly, where issues arose such as trade protection which divided members into opposing camps, they preferred to say nothing at all rather than cause dissension within their own ranks.[20]

The existence of Lever Brothers and Royal Dutch Shell by 1914 pointed towards the situation that has obtained since the 1930s when most sectors of British industry have become dominated by a few large firms, each with a broad product range and numerous operating divisions at home and abroad. In this situation the industrialist's role scarcely differs from that of the merchant banker, being largely devoted to the raising of capital, the negotiation of concessions for capital investment with domestic and foreign governments, and the allocation of funds among existing or new divisions according to prospective returns. With their headquarters mostly in or adjacent to the City, industrialists have become practically indistinguishable from, and often interchangeable with, financiers. Indeed, it is not too much to say that the mercantile – financial community has absorbed the industrial leadership, which now shares an almost identical educational, social, religious, and political profile.[21]

But in the 1920s these features were still largely in the future. The firms represented in the Federation's Grand Council, although larger than was common in the nineteenth century and large enough to free their managers from day-to-day responsibilities, were for the most part still small by present-day standards and simple in structure and product range. No hard and fast line divided industry and finance, it is true, and some industrialists shared the educational background and social standing of their City colleagues, but most did not. Many were engaged in family-run firms and even when rubbing shoulders with bankers or financiers at board meetings most of them continued to view the world essentially in terms of their own particular sector of industry. From the standpoint of the size and structure of firms, the 1920s were thus a critical decade for the promotion of policies in the interest specifically of industry.

Equally important was the fact that this was a time of serious decline for the old staple export industries, such as textiles, shipbuilding, and heavy engineering, while the electrical, chemical, and auto industries, making up what is sometimes called the second industrial revolution, were rapidly expanding, for it produced an important shift in priorities for industry as a whole. The new industries, being composed of relatively large firms with capital-intensive processes, were bound to look upon good labour relations and high and steady levels of production as more important than low wages and mere cheapness. Since their products and production runs demanded a more homogeneous market of high-income consumers, they were also more interested in the domestic and Dominions markets than with those of India and the less developed world or even Europe, where incomes were low in sterling terms and trade was obstructed by a multiplicity of tariff walls. Leaders of the new industries displayed a confident, impatient attitude towards the national policy-making process, and eventually a number of them disregarded the ever-cautious FBI to strike out on their own when the Federation failed to respond to their needs. But this happened only in the later 1920s, after years of mounting frustration.[22]

Developments in agriculture, a frequently overlooked sector of industry, also helped to make the 1920s a critical decade. Until the First World War, agriculture had been represented by several not very effective bodies. One was the Central Landowners' Association; another was the Central and Associated Chambers of Agriculture, which despite its claim to represent all three elements of the industry, the landowners, the tenant farmers, and the farm labourers, was also dominated by landowners. However, the prolonged decline in prices during the so-called Great Depression in the latter part of the nineteenth century had led to a marked increase in sales of land to tenant farmers who in 1908 formed their own organisation, the National Farmers' Union. The improvement in agricultural prospects at this time continued after the outbreak of war, which brought shortages in supply and promises of protection after the war. This and the continuing preference of landowners for portfolio assets sustained the shift towards owner-occupiers, who controlled 11 per cent of farms and farm land in 1913, over 17 per cent in 1921, and over 33 per cent in 1927.[23] It constituted the greatest change in land ownership since the Reformation, and was accompanied by an equally remarkable increase in NFU support. While membership of the Chambers of Agriculture declined, the NFU's rose from 21,000 at the outbreak of the war to 120,000 by 1929, justifying its claim to be the most authoritative voice of agriculture. Aggressive and independent, the NFU refused to be identified with any single political party, and was as a result a far more formidable body than the compliant organs it had all but supplanted.[24]

There were nevertheless strong countervailing pressures inhibiting the formation of a distinctive industrial view. On the one hand, differences within industry, particularly between sectors dependent upon domestic demand and others that relied upon overseas markets, continued to exist. On the other, industrialists, merchants, and bankers continued to join in common opposition to state encroachment upon the prerogatives of capital, tax increases, and the threat of socialism. The party structure was another inhibiting factor. Membership in the Conservative Party served to integrate industrialists into the country's elite structure, a process which, as will be seen, did more to turn industrialists into Conservatives than Conservatism into the party of industry.

Developments in the organisation of labour were in many respects analogous to that of the employers. Between 1913 and 1920, when demobilisation was completed, trade union membership doubled, from 4,135,000 to 8,348,000, before falling away to under 5 million by 1929. Meanwhile a wave of amalgamations resulted in the movement being dominated by a handful of large unions, including the Iron and Steel Trades Confederation formed in 1917, the Amalgamated Engineering Union in 1921, the Transport and General Workers' Union in 1922, and the National Union of General and Municipal Workers in 1924. Equally important was the restructuring of the Trades Union Congress, to which all the major unions were affiliated. With the creation of a General Council, comprising leaders of the main unions, and an increasingly professional secretariat, the TUC in 1921 ceased to be a mere association of unions and began to provide effective government for the movement.[25]

Two men soon came to dominate the General Council. One was Walter Citrine, a trim, methodical Liverpudlian who left the Electrical Trades Union to become Assistant Secretary of the TUC in 1924 and General Secretary two years later. The other was Ernest Bevin, the onetime Bristol carter who formed the giant Transport Workers' Union largely by his own efforts. A rough-featured man of massive, challenging bulk, Bevin was unrivalled as a champion of trade union interests. He was also Citrine's equal in intelligence, and although so unlike the bureaucratic Citrine as to be incapable of working with him, he shared his ambitions for the TUC.[26] Upon gaining ascendancy within the movement, both men began to take a serious interest in economic – as opposed to merely industrial – policy, and coincidental with their ascendancy the TUC began to retreat from a posture of confrontation with employers in order to join with them in devising a strategy for industrial growth. But the change was tentative and slow, owing to the deep-seated hostility to management that existed on the shop floor, the constant pressure from the Labour Party to leave to it sole responsibility for 'political' questions, and the TUC's sheer lack of experience in broad strategic thinking. Until the failure of the general strike in 1926 practically forced changes upon it, the TUC dealt almost solely with industrial issues, which offered little insight into the peculiar nature of British capitalism or the possibilities for a different economic strategy.

The Labour Party had begun its existence in 1900 with the anti-liberal objective of assisting the trade union movement in its struggle against the forces of the free market system. In 1918 its opposition to capitalism became explicit with the adoption of its first constitution, which called for 'the common ownership of the means of production, distribution and exchange'.[27] The constitution served to establish the party as *the* progressive force in British politics, but did little to underpin a radical economic strategy. For one thing the party's strongholds remained the great centres of export industry in the north and 'Celtic fringe', which had led it to endorse free trade in 1904.[28] For another, the principle of international working-class solidarity was strengthened by the war and reinforced the usual Cobdenite arguments for free trade. During the 1920s a growing number of party members, particularly from the trade union wing, reacted against the practice of exposing the country to world market forces and pressed for a return to the party's original interventionist objective. But it was difficult to fight policies so deeply imbedded in party tradition, and harder still in face of the altered structure of the party and composition of its leadership.

As the result of a series of decisions towards the end of the war, the Labour Party was transformed from a narrowly working-class party into a national one with substantial middle-class support. The change in the method of election to the National Executive Committee (NEC), initiated in 1917 by the trade unions in order to eliminate the influence of the Independent Labour Party (ILP), had the unintended effect of opening the way for a preponderance of career politicians and intellectuals.[29] Membership in the Parliamentary Labour Party (PLP) underwent a similar change. At the general election of 1918 some 49 out of the 57 successful candidates were sponsored by the trade unions; at the general election of 1922 the fraction fell to 85 out of 142, and in December 1923 to 101 out of 191.[30] The party still commanded the loyalty of the trade unions, but the creation of a National Joint Council in 1922 and other joint bodies suggested that there was now a gap to be bridged.[31] The decline in influence of the trade unions was matched by that of the ILP, whose *raison d'être* was largely undercut in 1918 with the decision to create local Labour parties, thereby providing an alternative means for middle-class and newly enfranchised women voters to join the movement.[32] The ILP remained the spiritual home of the party's most ideologically committed supporters, and a majority of Labour parliamentarians made a show of their militancy by belonging to it. But they no longer required the ILP as a base, and their membership meant little since their first loyalty was to the Parliamentary Party.

From the outbreak of war in 1914 the ILP had denounced the conflict as the product of imperialist rivalry and demanded a negotiated peace without annexations or indemnities. The initial result was to isolate the ILP from the trade union majority within the Labour Party. But it also had the effect of drawing towards the party a significant number of Liberals who had become disaffected by the direction of government policy; an accession with profound implications for Labour. An exceptionally well-educated, self-confident, and politically experienced body of men and women, the Liberal recruits soon found their way into positions of influence within the party, particularly in the fields of foreign and economic affairs where Labour had practically no experience. In 1918 the newly formed Advisory Committee on International Questions comprised Charles and Noel Buxton, Arthur Ponsonby, Philip Noel-Baker, Arthur Greenwood, Hugh Dalton, and H.N. Brailsford, all of whom except for Brailsford had been Liberals until the war. In deliberations on economic policy Dalton, Frederick Pethick-Lawrence, F.B. Lees-Smith, and Sydney Arnold played a consistently prominent role. None, however, felt required to alter his views in light of Labour's commitment to 'the common ownership of the means of production, distribution and exchange'.[33]

Like other Liberal economic experts, Pethick-Lawrence, a student of Alfred Marshall and winner of the Adam Smith prize at Cambridge, was attracted to Labour not least because of its support for a capital levy, a measure originating with fellow Liberals and whose main attraction was the promise of reduced taxes.[34] Dalton, the son of King George V's tutor at Windsor and scholar at Eton and King's College, Cambridge, was an authority on public finance. He was pleased with his notoriety as one of the left-wing 'bogeymen' of the London School of Economics, and profited by it to make a rapid ascent to Labour's National Executive Committee. Yet he found no difficulty working under the ultra-orthodox Professor Cannan, and not surprisingly, for the booming voice and overbearing manner aside, his contribution to economic debate was little more than orthodoxy got up in the language of moral concern.[35]

Most of the other former Liberals were distinguished by their lack of direct interest in economic issues, yet they were by no means uninterested. Virtual Cobdenites all, they were united in the belief that economic nationalism was the principal source of international conflict. The last war had been catastrophic; the next one, they were convinced, would bring anarchy, revolution, and the destruction of the existing social order. It was thus from profoundly conservative motives that they joined the socialists in the ILP to promote a just peace, an effective League of Nations, and a stable world order. But so far from contributing to a programme for socialism, they were a positive drag on account of their refusal to contemplate any compromise with internationalism. Perhaps none of this would have mattered had the party's leadership been clear-sighted in its objectives, but it was not.

Of the 'big five' who dominated the party during the 1920s, James Ramsay MacDonald was much the most imposing figure. Born the illegitimate son of a farm labourer in the Morayshire village of Lossiemouth, he had worked as a school teacher, clerk, and journalist before entering full-time into politics as the first secretary of the party in 1906 and from 1906 a Member of Parliament. Solidly handsome, eloquent, and blessed with a hard-to-place Scottish accent, he seemed one of nature's aristocrats. His decision to resign the leadership of the Parliamentary Party when the majority of his colleagues, going against agreed policy, voted to support the war effort in August 1914 had earned him a reputation for courage, uncompromising principles, and pacifism. His rhetoric and exegesis of socialist literature encouraged working-class voters to see in him a champion of radical reform. His open enjoyment of the higher forms of art and rural pursuits encouraged middle-class supporters to anticipate a just and humane socialism.

But behind the platform rhetoric was a man who seemed far more anxious to be accepted within the governing circles in which he moved than to cast them aside. Able and ambitious, his energies went into building up the party, a task for which his charismatic personality and opaque ideology were well suited. Yet in doing so he tended constantly to stultify debate on contentious issues. Exploiting the proud tradition of working-class solidarity, he urged followers to regard radical proposals as criticism of his leadership and to deal with them on this basis rather than on their merits. When pressed on policy, his habit was to suggest that the solution must await the advent of socialism. Sympathisers defended his behaviour as a demonstration of his suppleness and maturity, and as calculated to ensure maximum support for progressive politics. But to judge by his choice of reading material, his trust in the authorities of the existing capitalist order, and his refusal to encourage serious thinking about the means of transforming society, it is difficult to avoid the conclusion that he was hostile to the very idea of socialism. He was, as close associates were beginning to appreciate, a study in contradictions: champion of the common people, who disdained their company, preferring instead the company of the rich and well-born, leader of a party committed to extending democracy, who concentrated power in the hands of the Parliamentary leadership. His self-conscious awareness of his modest educational attainment made him a poor listener, just as his anxiety for respect made him jealous of his leadership of the party, reluctant to delegate authority, and disdainful of colleagues whose modest origins and social standing reminded him of what he had left behind. Uninterested in social reform, he turned his attention to foreign affairs, the traditional preserve of the conservative ruling class. As both Prime Minister and Foreign Secretary in the first Labour government, he was to display considerable diplomatic skill, although also more pleasure in exercising Britain's great power influence and disregard for small states, and less enthusiasm for the League of Nations than party followers were allowed to see.[36]

Philip Snowden, the party's leading authority on financial matters, appeared a very different sort of man. The son of a Yorkshire weaver, he had worked as a civil service clerk before entering Parliament in the 1906 election. Crippled in a cycling accident as a young man, his features gaunt and his frame supported by canes, he spoke and wrote with a caustic power that earned him the respect of friend and foe alike. He was the party's intellectual, a latter-day Saint-Just dedicated to the revolutionary transformation of Britain.[37]

Here too appearances were deceiving. Having entered the national political arena during the Tariff Reform controversy, he had taken up the cause of free trade with the zeal of a true believer. Not for him MacDonald's contrived attempt to stake out a distinctive position for the party, neither protectionist nor free trade but socialist; even during the 1920s he remained a vice-president of the Free Trade Union.[38] Frequently at the end of the war he railed against 'one of the most powerful and sinister monopolies in the country, one which has its grip on every branch of trade and commerce ... the Money Trust', and called for the nationalisation of the Bank of England and principal clearing banks. But a close examination of his remarks reveals that the demand had nothing to do with socialism and everything to do with the old-fashioned radical's hostility to trusts; in this case a trust that threatened to cause inflation and thereby undermine the nation's habits of thrift and hard work.[39]

His angriest Parliamentary performances were reserved for Budget debates.[40] Here was Snowden at his most impressive, at home amidst the ostensibly hard statistical facts of life. Yet his boastful demonstration that he had plumbed the mysteries of high finance betrayed, like MacDonald's indulgence in diplomacy, a suppressed sense of social inferiority. The actual target of his wrath was not the meanness of his governmental opponents but their tolerance for excessive public spending. Indeed, he placed greater faith in temperance then in state intervention as the solution to the nation's economic ills.[41] Despite angry talk of swingeing taxes on the rich, he hinted before the general election of 1923 that he would not implement the party commitment to a capital levy.[42] By then he preferred to move in society, encouraged by his wife whose social ambitions were notorious. Indeed, while he continued to appear the very soul of rectitude, she privately accepted in December 1923, when it seemed likely that he would soon become Chancellor of the Exchequer, 'some diamonds' from her friend Lady Rothschild.[43]

J.R. Clynes was representative of one sort of trade unionist in politics. Born in Oldham, Lancashire, he had risen through sheer hard work from the shop floor of a local cotton mill to the presidency of the giant General and Municipal Workers' Union. Briefly, until MacDonald re-entered Parliament in 1922, he was leader of the Parliamentary Party. A loyal member and able debater, he was however a colourless figure, whose outlook remained bounded by his working experience. He was prepared to confront questions of reform at the factory or industry level. But aside from an unreflecting faith in free trade and the League of Nations, the broader questions of political economy lay beyond him.

J.H. Thomas, General Secretary of the Railwaymen's Union, was representative of a very different sort. Jovial and deliberately down-to-earth, he affected pride in the fact that his education had been acquired in the 'University of the Streets', and displayed open contempt for the intellectualism of the socialist wing of the party.[44] He was the practical man, who approached politics the way he ran his union: like a business, for the benefit of its members. Once in office, he also showed himself to be an ardent imperialist, anxious to demonstrate that 'patriotism, love of Empire, service and duty are not the gift or monopoly of a class or a creed'.[45] This did not make 'our Jimmy' any the less popular in the party, for among rank and file supporters the crown and flag were potent symbols, and doubtless the great majority agreed with him that the working people having largely built the Empire, they could be trusted to run it. Few were aware that his ideological blindness had landed him in very questionable company, and that his drinking and gambling were becoming serious problems.

Arthur Henderson, the fifth of the 'big five', was the son of a cotton spinner, a Methodist lay preacher, and briefly an iron-moulder before turning full-time to trade union and political activities. That rare thing in politics, a popular and trusted bureaucrat, Henderson, or 'Uncle Arthur' as he was known in Labour circles, was an indifferent speaker and little-known outside the party. But inside he had become a virtual institution, as the secretary and chief organiser since 1912. During the war he accepted office in the government, the first party member to do so. In 1917, however, he came round to the view that a negotiated peace and a 'Federation of Nations' were essential for the future of the world, a conviction he held to thereafter. In 1912 he had joined the Fabians to become a 'socialist', a move prompted by the desire to qualify as a delegate to the Second International rather than allow the nomination go to a communist.[46] After the war he served as secretary of the Second International (renamed the Labour and Socialist International in 1923). But though he used the language of socialism when the occasion demanded, it meant little more to him than the brotherhood of working men. Socialism was internationalism and free trade. And 'Free Trade between the Nations', he explained, 'is the broadest and surest foundation for world prosperity and the best guarantee of a permanent Universal Peace'.[47]

The 2.4 million votes for Labour at the general election in December 1918 – up from 400,000 in 1910 – confirmed that the party had become a force in national politics. Yet in an important sense the party added nothing to the political strength of the industrial community; rather the contrary. It spoke the language of revolution, which was bound to frighten employers and encourage them to identify closely with other holders of wealth. Yet it remained incorrigibly conservative and blind to the contradiction of championing simultaneously internationalism and a planned domestic economy. Eventually, in spite of the party, trade unionists joined with employers in a tentative move towards a producers' alliance, but not before economic internationalism was restored at great cost to industry and the country as a whole.

The mercantile–financial community

Compared to the industrial community, the mercantile – financial community was far better placed to influence the making of national policy. Based on London and the home counties, the territory it embraced included a substantial amount of industry, for London was a major port and manufacturing town. Nonetheless its wealth derived chiefly from non-industrial or pre-industrial sources, such as landowning, public administration, soldiering, the liberal professions, and above all commercial and financial activity, and it was this combination of activities that gave the community its character and largely shaped its politico-economic priorities. London was huge: in 1914 it was as large as the next twelve cities in Britain combined.[48] It was also more than comparatively rich. According to the leading authority on the subject, 'it seems a plausible inference not merely that London possessed a larger total business income than all the chief provincial towns combined, but that its middle class was richer per capita and almost certainly more numerous'.[49] The commercial centre was the City of London, where more fortunes were made than in the whole of industry. Merchants and bankers required little in the way of physical plant and generally shunned ostentation, preferring to operate behind plain brass numberplates in an inverted display of success. In fact, the City 'by itself in every period and at every level of wealth was the single most important geographical unit, generally by several orders of magnitude over its nearest rival'.[50] A combination of factors had led the City to become a centre of international markets, dependent only slightly upon the nation's economic performance. With the integration of commercial and other forms of wealth, the mercantile – financial community also accepted the City's strong preference for political and economic internationalism.

As early as the Norman conquest the City wielded a powerful influence over the political fortunes of the country on account of its unique wealth.[51] Fortunes made in the City had long been translated into social position by merchants whose purchase of rural estates could be expected to pave the way into landed society for sons or grandsons. From the eighteenth century, however, links between City merchants and landowners became increasingly intimate. The revolution in finance, which saw the establishment of the Bank of England in 1694 and the issue of marketable government bonds, stimulated deposit banking and personal investment.[52] The agricultural revolution, which completed the transformation of farming into a capitalist enterprise, enriched the landowners and predisposed them to embrace the profit-making opportunities that occurred in the industrial revolution. The vast increase in public debt due to the Seven Years war, the American war of independence, and the Napoleonic wars resulted in the creation of a 'stock-and-bondholding aristocracy'.[53] Financiers, having raised nearly a billion pounds and managed the complicated arrangements for provisioning and paying the armies that brought victory over Napoleon, emerged with enhanced respect. In recognition of their services, several leading financiers were directly elevated to the peerage, an honour not extended to any industrialist until 1856.[54]

At the outbreak of the revolutionary wars in the 1790s, financiers in the lower Rhenish towns suffered a severe loss of business which led them to seize the opportunities opening up across the North Sea. Some of the greatest merchant banks date their London activities from this time, including Helbert Wagg, N.M. Rothschilds and Sons, William Brandt's Sons, Frederick Huth and Company, Frueling and Goschen, and Hambros.[55] After the wars the City confronted its commercial rivals with a combination of advantages including the wealth and experience of its merchant houses, the country's political stability, manufacturing lead, increasing import requirements, and security of its island position, the capacity of the Royal Navy to police its trade routes, and the wealth of commercial intelligence available through the Port of London. By the latter part of the nineteenth century London had become a remarkable assemblage of markets, for securities, money, bullion, commodities, insurance, and shipping, each overwhelmingly international in scope: 'the great money engine of the world' and the great clearing-house for its goods and commercial services. All the while the practice of transforming commercial and financial wealth into social position continued apace.[56]

Religious affinity played its part, for despite a popular image of the City as a cosmopolitan place crowded with Jews and other ambitious men of uncertain provenance, most City men were of English or Scottish stock and members of the established church; indeed, anti-semitism was as widespread in the City as elsewhere in the country.[57] Common church membership facilitated the integrating role of education. Here the principal agencies were the public schools, most of which were set up at a convenient distance from London during the nineteenth century, and the ancient universities of Oxford and Cambridge. Together they provided an education ill-suited to the technical problem-solving requirements of industry but well designed for the administrative, diplomatic, military, legal, or banking careers that awaited the sons of wealthy landowners and City men who largely made up their enrolment. As the century wore on the schools imbued their charges with increasingly uniform manners, values, and perspectives. And in the latter half of the century, after the principle of meritocratic recruitment was accepted by the civil service, they acquired a near-monopoly position as sources of recruitment to the higher or administrative grades and largely set the terms for educating the whole of the country's middle class.[58]

Nor was the process of social integration merely one-directional. By the 1840s a large fraction of the landed gentry had become directly involved in commercial or financial (but not industrial) activity or in the liberal professions, particularly the law. Declining rents, along with the imposition of estate duties and political agitation for changes in land tenure during the latter part of the century, accelerated the trend. Landowners, impelled to find other sources of income, took up directorships in the City. Some even began divesting themselves of land.[59] By the turn of the century earnings from agriculture had declined to 6 per cent of national income, while earnings from overseas commerce and finance rapidly mounted.[60] To an important degree these changes were reflected in contemporary shifts in party political allegiance.

The City, Whig since the time when it cast its lot with William III against a Stuart restoration, remained a bastion of Liberalism until the middle of the nineteenth century. But thereafter, once Disraeli removed the main objection to Toryism by abandoning trade protection and the Liberal Party adopted a number of Radical policies, a fundamental realignment took place. As late as 1872 all four parliamentary seats for the City were held by Liberals. In 1874 three of the four went to Conservatives, and subsequently, with two seats at issue, Conservatives were invariably returned and usually unopposed. The Liberal decision in 1886 to back Irish Home Rule caused most of the great Whig landowning families to break with the party and align themselves with the Tories under the Unionist banner. Nevertheless by 1900 finance had replaced landowning as the most important business interest among Conservative and Unionist MPs.[61] The parallel drift of industrialists away from the Liberals to the Conservative Party, drawn by the appeal of associating with their social superiors and the greater chance of acquiring honours, went some way towards a balance of interests.[62] This and the widening of the franchise, which required all parties to adopt programmes with broad electoral appeal, ensured that the Conservative Party did not become the captive of any single interest. But to an important degree both the Conservative and the Liberal Parties depended upon wealthy donors for their electoral campaigns even after the First World War, and the fragmentary evidence available indicates that the Conservative Central Office relied upon individuals in the City for up to three-quarters of its funds at election time.[63] No great significance need be attached to the financial link, except as an indication of the intimacy of Conservative–City relations. The City counted on the party to provide the climate of political stability essential for its role as the world's financial capital; the party in turn relied upon the City for financial advice and support. Some indication of the respect shown for City opinion is offered by the fact that at least two Coalition or Conservative Chancellors of the Exchequer in the postwar years owed their appointments in part to expressions of City preferences.[64]

From outward appearances the City has always invited the impression merely of a collection of markets, drawing together individuals with little more in common than the pursuit of self-interest. Of course some measure of competition existed and still exists in each of its sectors of activity. But in fact it has also possessed a corporate spirit and never more so than in the years surrounding the First World War. The specialisation of firms and the complexity of the business in which they engaged, such as the financing of a consignment of goods between third countries or the floating of a new company on the Stock Exchange, commonly involved them in a network of informal ties, often strengthened by interlocking directorships. And since much of their business as well as the commercial intelligence on which it depended was passed on through personal contacts, a club-like atmosphere prevailed, with the subtle threat of ostracism providing further assurance of a large measure of conformity.[65] Among the different sectors a recognised hierarchy existed, with the preeminent place accorded the merchant bankers and in particular the members of the Accepting Houses Committee such as Barings, Rothschilds, Hambros, Morgan Grenfell, and Lazard Brothers. It was from their boards that the Court of Directors of the Bank of England was chiefly composed. Deposit banking after the amalgamation boom towards the end of the First World War was concentrated overwhelmingly in the hands of the giant 'big five' joint stock banks, which also meant increased concentration in London. During the 1920s several of these banks became very heavily loaned to domestic industry and voiced dissatisfaction with the Bank of England's deflationary policy which undermined their clients' solvency. But despite their size they were excluded from representation on the Bank's Court until 1934, on the anachronistic grounds that their competition for deposits created a conflict of interest. By the same token industry was also unrepresented until 1928, when Sir Josiah Stamp was elected in order to allay mounting criticism of Bank policy. With this exception, the court continued to reflect the City's overwhelming preoccupation with overseas commerce and finance.[66]

Until the First World War the Governor and Deputy Governor of the Bank of England were elected from the Court of Directors for a two-year term virtually on the principle of 'Buggins' turn', without being expected to resign their positions in private firms. This reflected the dominance of London in the international monetary system and the ease with which the Bank managed the flow of funds across the exchanges. It also meant that the Bank remained intimately linked to the City without acquiring a distinctive spirit or outlook of its own. According to Walter Bagehot, the City was reluctant to leave the Bank in the control of one man for an extended period, since the enormous power in his possession might bring demands for a public say in his appointment.[67] But from the outbreak of war greater professionalism and continuity of direction became imperative. Lord Cunliffe was therefore retained in office until the end of 1917, and Montagu Norman, who became Governor in April 1920 remained in office for the next twenty-four years.

Montagu Norman was almost certainly the most extraordinary man ever to occupy the Governor's office at the Bank of England. The son of a banker and a descendant of Governors on both sides of his family, he had a conventional upbringing for someone from his milieu: Eton, one undistinguished year at Cambridge, a sojourn on the continent to learn German and French, war service in the South African campaign, a partnership in his maternal grandfather's firm, Brown Shipley and Company, and a seat on the Court of the Bank of England in 1907 at the age of thirty-six. The two distinctive features about his early years were the time he spent in the United States and the manifestation of deep psychological problems that were to trouble him for the rest of his life. As preparation for his career in merchant banking, his firm, which had close links with Brown Brothers of Boston, gave him the opportunity to travel widely in the United States and get to know the country well. The two years he spent there were among the most enjoyable of his life. He returned with a sound appreciation of American finance and a predisposition to work in close harness with American bankers. But he had also begun to suffer migraines and periodic nervous breakdowns, which led him on one occasion to seek the advice of Carl Jung in Zurich, and his intensely private manner contributed to a widening rift with his London partners. His resignation from the firm a few months after the war began left him free to 'devil' for Sir Brien Cokayne, the Deputy Governor of the Bank of England. The talent he displayed for central banking persuaded the Bank's inner committee of directors, the Committee of Treasury, to set aside their doubts about his suitability for office. In 1918, when Cokayne succeeded Cunliffe as Governor, he was elected Deputy Governor. Two years later Cokayne retired and Norman was elected in his place.

Norman, until then practically unknown in the City, soon attracted national attention. It was typical of City men to be reticent in public and coldly unreceptive to academic theorising, but in both respects Norman went to extremes. Secretive and almost inarticulate in public, his exaggerated efforts to avoid publicity had the opposite and perhaps unconsciously intended result. To those who sympathised with his ambitions, he seemed, with his soft broad-brimmed hat, cape, dark pointed beard, and sharply delineated features, the embodiment of the Bank's quiet authority. To his critics, the same features – 'More Montague than Norman', he once revealingly remarked of himself[68] – personified the arrogance of finance and the suspect cosmopolitanism of the City. His reluctance to allow colleagues into his confidence was to cause resentment at the Bank. For a time in the 1920s, senior directors showed their frustration by refusing to speak at the weekly meetings of the Committee of Treasury, and on several occasions attempts were made to remove him.[69] Nevertheless such was his authority within the Bank that he managed to ride out these storms and secure re-election every two years.[70]

By the end of the war the international monetary system had become severely dislocated. Norman, with the vision of London's pre-war greatness constantly before him, unhesitatingly accepted the Bank's duty to rebuild the system, using British expertise and a 'special relationship' with American bankers to coordinate access to their capital markets as a means of inducing general support. A host of problems confronted him, but his primary objective was to resurrect independent central banks in Europe, so that the discipline of the gold standard could again be effectively imposed in their respective countries. In the words of Emile Moreau, the Governor of the Bank of France between 1926 and 1930 and an astute of observer of Norman's activities,

> The economic and financial organisation of the world appears to the Governor of the Bank of England the major task of the twentieth century. His big idea would be the following. [The central banks] would succeed in taking out of the political realm those problems which are essential for the development and the prosperity of the nations: financial security, distribution of credit, movement of prices. They would thus prevent internal struggles from harming the wealth and the economic advancement of nations. These views are indeed doctrinaire, and without doubt somewhat Utopian or perhaps even Machiavellian.[71]

Norman's personal inhibitions and hostility to public interference in the Bank's operations made him appear disdainful of the press. Behind the scenes he used every means, including press contacts, to realise his 'big idea'.

In the years surrounding the First World War, the British Press experienced tremendous growth in circulation, encouraged by a new generation of proprietors whose overriding interest was commercial success.[72] The rise of the tabloid press and the reckless self-advertising behaviour of the leading proprietors, Lord Beaverbrook and Lord Rothermere, seemed a matter for regret in conservative circles.[73] Yet the City had little immediate cause for concern. Practically no one in the clubs and boardrooms of the capital, it seems, bothered to read the provincial papers.[74] And of the London papers on which informed opinion relied, most were controlled by 'sound' proprietors who left monetary and financial matters for City editors to examine. David Lloyd George's acquisition of a controlling interest in the *Daily News* in 1918, though controversial from a constitutional standpoint, made no perceptible difference to its Liberal internationalist viewpoint.[75] Sir William Ewart Berry, first Viscount Camrose, who acquired the *Sunday Times* in 1915, the *Financial Times* in 1919, and the *Daily Telegraph* in January 1928, had abandoned the Liberal Party for the Conservatives but remained a lifelong internationalist.[76] *The Times*, the most influential paper in the country, was purchased by Major J.J. Astor in the autumn of 1922 and placed under the editorial control of Geoffrey Dawson, a former editor and devoted liberal imperialist. Like most other editors of his generation, Dawson displayed a deferential attitude towards high finance, and when financial issues arose he relied for advice upon the merchant banker Robert Brand. Brand was an old friend from their days as members of Lord Milner's 'kindergarten' in South Africa; he was also Astor's brother-in-law, who had advised him during the purchase of the paper and proposed the reappointment of Dawson.[77] Although not formally connected with the paper until 1925, Brand regularly attended its board meetings, and on joining the board he was also designated 'Alternative Chief Proprietor'.[78]

The high Tory *Morning Post* was in many respects a very different paper. Lady Bathurst, who owned the paper until 1924, and the Duke of Northumberland, who headed the consortium of prominent Conservative supporters that purchased her interest, were both anti-semitic, anti-liberal, English nationalists, as was the *Post's* longtime editor, H.A. Gwynne. However, Gwynne also preferred to leave financial issues to a more knowledgeable writer, in this case Arthur Kiddy, the editor of the authoritative *Bankers' Magazine* who served as the paper's City editor. The result was an occasionally contradictory outlook on affairs, with the leader page brooding over Britain's decline in face of cosmopolitan influences, while the financial reports enthused about the merits of the international gold standard system.[79] The *Daily Mail*, the country's largest selling non-tabloid paper, reflected a similar division of responsibility. Rothermere, the proprietor, was deeply suspicious of all internationalist policies. But he usually reserved his own editorialising for the *Sunday Pictorial*, and left financial issues to be dealt with in the *Daily Mail* by Harold Cox, the City editor and a zealous internationalist.[80]

In an age when readers were as yet unaccustomed to seeing discussion of technical financial and monetary issues in the general press, and when no economics or industrial editors were employed, the opinions of City editors carried exceptional weight. Besides the *Morning Post*, St Loe Strachey's *Spectator* relied upon Kiddy to write the weekly City page; Cox wrote the City column for the *Sunday Times*. Norman afforded them occasional interviews along with the *Manchester Guardian's* Oscar Hobson and the distinguished City editor of *The Times*, Courtney Mill.[81] Like the others, Mill maintained a posture of critical independence towards the individuals and firms about whom he reported, while uncritically defending the City's commercial interests. Not infrequently, it seems, he allowed his column to become the vehicle for Norman's views.

Besides a generally sympathetic press, Norman and his allies in the

City were assisted in their cause by a number of new or recently formed organisations devoted to the encouragement of an internationalist outlook. Within Britain these included the Round Table, the Royal Institute of International Affairs, and the League of Nations Union; outside Britain there were the International Chamber of Commerce and the League of Nations itself.

The Round Table was established in 1909 by Lord Milner and his younger colleagues to promote the unity of the Empire, but had failed to come to terms with the Tariff Reform issue. By the end of the war those who favoured imperial protectionism, including Milner himself, were disillusioned with the movement and left it to be controlled by liberal imperialists. From time to time Robert Brand provided it with much-needed funds. He was its one authority on financial issues and a close friend of John Dove, who edited the monthly *Round Table* magazine.[82] The movement played only a modest role in the shaping of opinion, but among its contributions was the subtle one of diverting imperial sentiment away from aggressive economic policies.

The Royal Institute of International Affairs developed along somewhat similar lines. Founded in 1920, the Institute received Chatham House, the former home of William Pitt, as a gift from Colonel R.W. Leonard, the Canadian mining engineer and railway magnate. Leonard was chiefly interested in the promotion of imperial unity. At the same time as he made his donation, however, the Duke of Devonshire and the financier Sir John Power also made large donations, and a few years later the Bank of England covenanted a small sum which encouraged other City institutions to follow suit. The result was an amply funded and grandly housed centre for the promotion of interest in world affairs, located in St James's Square near most of the gentlemen's clubs. By bringing together leading diplomats, bankers, academics, and journalists, Chatham House helped to promote a common world view. And despite formal disinterest in the issues raised for discussion, the view was a consistently internationalist one.[83]

The League of Nations Union, formed in 1918 by the amalgamation of two organisations set up to promote a compromise peace and the creation of a permanent body for resolving international conflict, was a broad popular movement. Its membership came from all parts of Britain and at its peak in 1931 reached over 400,000. But its day-to-day running was overseen by Lord Robert Cecil, the patrician landowner and former Tory minister, and a handful of intellectuals. Cecil himself was motivated by two fears: that a world split into exclusive spheres of influence by the great powers would mean the inevitable disintegration of the British Empire, and the almost pathological fear that another war would end in revolution and the destruction of the existing social order.[84] But these fears were not unique to him. Indeed, it is likely that they informed the thoughts of most of the LNU's supporters.

The League of Nations itself performed an invaluable role in the promotion of political and economic internationalism. British postwar governments, finding their imperial defence forces dangerously overstretched and anxious to avoid any entanglements that might alienate the friendship of the United States or the Dominions, offered little more than lip-service to the League's peace-keeping efforts. But on the economic side of the League's activities unofficial British support was substantial. The first head of the League Economic and Financial Section was the former Cambridge economist, Walter Layton, and following him, Sir Arthur Salter. Salter, one of the 'new' civil servants in Whitehall who helped to organise the national insurance system before the war, was by his own admission a serious, colourless sort of person, but by all accounts an admirably efficient bureaucrat.[85] With his help the Financial Committee, set up in 1920, was largely dominated by its British members, and with occasional help from Layton he also saw to it that the Economic Committee, which began work when the major European currencies were restabilised, vigorously promoted internationalist policies. British involvement in League affairs was mainly intended to secure foreign support for internationalist policies, but the promise of effective results through the League also helped to sustain internationalism at home.

The initiative for creating a permanent International Chamber of Commerce came from American businessmen in 1919, although plans for such a body had been discussed at several international gatherings before the war, including one held in Paris in June 1914. At the organisational conference in Paris in 1920 a sharp difference of views emerged between French and Belgian representatives on the one hand and the British and American representatives on the other, with the former seeking an Allied industrial front to promote reconstruction on the basis of reparations and military sanctions, and the latter seeking to 'demilitarise' national economies and restore the market system. The conflict was only to be expected in view of the fact that the chambers of commerce on the continent were semi-official institutions which liaised closely with their respective governments and contained a strong industrial component, whereas those in the English-speaking world were private institutions dominated by merchants and bankers who jealously maintained their independence from the state. For several years this division remained apparent, but British representatives, exploiting the almost universal need for American credits and the numerous votes of the ex-neutral countries, asserted financial priorities over industrial ones and turned the ICC into an effective tool for promoting economic internationalism. The first of the three major congresses organised by the ICC between the wars was held in London in June 1921. Among the resolutions adopted, one called for re-examination of the reparations–war debt regime in light of its disruptive effects upon the international payments system, and another advocated out-and-out deflation in order to restore currencies to their pre-war parities with gold. Significantly, the chairman of the financial group that drafted the resolutions was Walter Leaf, chairman of the Westminster Bank and a future president of the ICC.[86]

The First World War did a good deal to increase temporarily the representation of industrial interests in Whitehall. A Ministry of Labour was created, numerous committees reported to the Board of Trade on the needs of specific industries, and briefly at the end of the war when the threat of social conflict was at its height, an industrial conference, suggesting a corporatist approach to government, gained intermittent life. No special ministry was formed to represent commercial or financial interests, but one was scarcely needed; for in a number of ways the most important ministries were already biased towards their internationalist priorities.

In the case of the Foreign Office and Diplomatic Service, the social origins of the personnel and strategic considerations mutually reinforced support for liberal imperialism. The clerks and diplomats, as officials in the one ministry of state required to make day-to-day decisions affecting the very future of the empire, were traditionally drawn from the highest strata of society. Formal entry examinations had been introduced in 1857, but the requirement of a personal recommendation from the Secretary of State – in practice his departmental advisers – limited the impact of the meritocratic principle upon the class character of the service, which was only slightly affected even after the First World War.[87] Even then virtually none of the officials had any but the remotest connection with industry: educationally they were unequipped to deal with its promotion, and they shared to the full the privileged classes' attitude of superiority towards those compelled to engage in 'trade' or descend onto the shop floor.[88] Banking and bankers, at least City bankers, were another matter: here class and professional interest made for a partnership. The bankers wanted free trade; so too did the Foreign Office officials. As Sir Eyre Crowe explained in his authoritative memorandum of 1 January 1907 on the basis of British foreign policy, Britain was bound to favour free trade on account of her dangerously vulnerable world empire and the need to 'strengthen her hold on the interested friendship of other nations'.[89] Similarly, since the officials were concerned solely with the maintenance of Britain's external influence, they naturally welcomed the prestige of a currency based on the gold standard and the capacity of City banks to provide loan capital for overseas use.[90]

During the war, when it seemed inevitable that the state must take a directing role in the struggle to regain overseas markets, several middle-ranking members of the Foreign Office proposed a new commercial intelligence department under the office's control.[91] Manufacturers had long been critical of the lack of support they received from the Foreign Office and Diplomatic Service, but they appreciated the prestige the diplomats possessed abroad and accordingly supported the Foreign Office's claim to monopolise representation abroad.[92] But the Board of Trade jealously guarded its own administrative territory, and with senior Foreign Office officials reluctant to fight for the privilege of promoting trade, the result was a compromise more favourable to the Board than the Foreign Office. The Foreign Office's commercial department, the outcome of another struggle with the Board a half century earlier, was wound up, and a new agency, the Department of Overseas Trade, was created, which reported to both the Board of Trade and Foreign Office though in practice operating as an adjunct of the Board.[93]

In the meantime, amidst the exigencies of war, the Board of Trade had acquired a bureaucratic empire, and at the war's end the Cabinet considered transferring to it the remaining machinery of blockade and converting it into a Ministry of Commerce such as existed in all the major competitor countries.[94] But the proposal failed to receive close attention, and many of the Board's responsibilities, including labour, transport, power, supply, and food , were soon hived off into separate ministries. What remained was a small establishment devoted to the restoration of Britain's traditional free trade relations with the rest of the world and dominated by three men. One was Sir Herbert Llewellyn-Smith, the Permanent Secretary until 1920 and for the next seven years His Majesty's Chief Economic Adviser, a post created for him as the chief British representative at the almost continuous international conferences on commercial relations. The second was Sir Henry Fountain, head of the Commercial Relations and Treaties Department, who like Llewellyn-Smith had begun work in the Board in the days of Queen Victoria. The third official was Sir Sydney Chapman, Llewellyn-Smith's successor as Permanent Secretary and Chief Economic Adviser. Chapman was a wartime recruit to government service, but as the former Dean of the Faculty of Commerce at Manchester University and author of a standard textbook on political economy, he too was thoroughly imbued with the internationalism of the pre-war era.[95] Under their combined leadership the Board saw little need for a Department of Overseas Trade, and it was soon orphaned by both its parents.

If the Board of Trade was the loser in the bureaucratic stakes, there was no question that it was the Treasury that came out the winner. As early as 1867 the Treasury's central role in the machinery of government had been acknowledged by according its head the special title of Permanent Secretary (rather than Under-Secretary) and a higher salary than other department heads. In 1919 the Permanent Secretary, Sir Warren Fisher, also became 'head of the civil service'. The practical effect was to strengthen the Treasury's influence over the whole of the civil service and increase the influence of the civil service over the decision-making process. Well before the turn of the century the civil service had acquired a fair measure of cohesion, due not least to the Northcote–Trevelyan reforms governing entry, which had resulted in recruitment for senior grades almost exclusively from the small elite that passed through the major public schools and proceeded to Oxford or Cambridge. But officials once appointed tended to remain within the same department and identify with its interests. Fisher energetically set about to change this, and using his influence as adviser to the Prime Minister on senior appointments and promotions he increased the circulation of officials among departments. Ministers, who had hitherto exercised a crucial influence over the career prospects of officials in their respective departments, retained only the right to veto Treasury appointments made in the Prime Minister's name. Officials in turn became less susceptible to their ministers' enthusiasms and rather more receptive to the Treasury's outlook.[96]

In the aftermath of the war the Treasury found itself with a vastly increased range of responsibilities, including exchange rate policy, external borrowing, reparations, and war debts.[97] Treasury officials, however, looked upon them as unfortunate but temporary obligations, to be set aside with the reconstruction of an international free market system.[98] Although socially a less exclusive group than their Foreign Office contemporaries, practically all members of the Treasury's key finance division were alumni of one or another of the better public schools and the Oxford classical school.[99] Nothing in their background predisposed them to consider the practical advantages of state intervention in the economy. Moreover, as top performers in the civil service entrance examination they possessed great confidence in their intellectual ability and their commonsense, non-theoretical approach to public policy. In practice they hewed with dogmatic tenacity to a simplified version of classical economics, which yielded what was known as the

Treasury view, namely that the state could do nothing to improve upon the allocation of resources through the market system. Perhaps as Lord Balogh has suggested, the formal elegance of classical economics had a special appeal to those trained in Platonic philosophy or pure mathematics.[100] At all events it provided a convenient rationale for their principal task as defenders of the public purse. The same task also made them strongly favourable to the discipline of the gold standard and thus the natural allies of the Bank of England.[101] The constant contact between officials of the Treasury and the Bank involved men of very similar background and outlook. Just how similar was underlined by the steady drift of Treasury men into lucrative positions in the City.[102]

The decision on economic internationalism

In January 1918 the Ministry of Reconstruction turned to the City for advice on postwar currency and exchange policy. A committee was formed with Lord Cunliffe, the Governor of the Bank of England, in the chair, and Sir John Bradbury of the Treasury, A.C. Pigou, Professor of Political Economy at Cambridge, and ten international bankers serving as members. Practically all the witnesses who appeared before the committee were likewise from the City, and of the twenty-one submissions received only one, from the FBI, was definably the expression of industrial opinion. Even at this point the FBI's advice differed markedly from that of City authorities. While accepting the desirability of returning to the gold standard, the Federation stressed reliance upon a strong trade balance rather than monetary expedients to bring the pound back to par, and warned especially against deflation while the burden of public debt weighed so heavily upon productive industry.[103]

The Cunliffe Committee ignored the Federation's advice; indeed, it suggested that the advice had never been given. As stated in the committee's report of August 1918, the first problem to be overcome was inflation, not the recovery of industry's place in world markets. 'Nothing can contribute more to a speedy recovery from the effects of the war, and to the rehabilitation of the foreign exchanges, than the re-establishment of the currency upon a sound basis'. In other words, priority must be given to restoring the gold standard, 'the only effective remedy for an adverse balance of trade and an undue growth of credit'. This was the opposite order of priority to that recommended by the FBI. Yet the committee not only asserted that it was in the best interests of industry, but suggested that it was also industry's preferred approach. 'We are glad to find that there was no difference of opinion among the witnesses who appeared before us as to the vital importance of these matters'.[104]

During the four months that followed the submission of the committee's report, the pressures of war ruled out any action on the subject, and the new government that took office in January 1919 was no better placed to act. A vast number of problems requiring their attention had emerged after the armistice. Moreover the Cabinet lacked a common vision. The Prime Minister, David Lloyd George, was at the height of his popularity and dominated the Cabinet, but faced arduous negotiations at the Paris peace conference. A Welshman of modest origins and a solicitor by training, he was a master of the platform and Commons debate, where his populist rhetoric had established him as a man of the left. But he was above all a manipulator, for whom policies were mere counters in the game of politics, and he showed no more commitment to post-war economic strategy than to any other issue. A few of his colleagues, such as Dr Christopher Addision, the wartime Minister of Reconstruction and postwar Minister of Health, counted on him to fulfill their electoral pledge to create a land 'fit for heroes to live in'. Others such as Andrew Bonar Law, the Canadian-born Glaswegian businessman who now served as Lord Privy Seal and Leader of the House, and Lord Milner, the former South African Pro-Consul and now Secretary of State for the Colonies, leaned strongly towards a policy of Empire protectionism. For the most part, however, the men who made up the government were of the Conservative or Liberal old guard: cautious men whose idea of politics had been firmly shaped in the years of 'normality' before the war.[105]

For the first six months of office the government's deepest concern was social unrest. Since the Bolsheviks had seized power in Russia in November 1917, revolution had spread through central Europe, nationalist agitation developed into armed struggle in Ireland, disturbances had broken out in India and the British treaty ports in China, and now at home industrial unrest reached a scale that caused Ministers to suspect a conspiracy and fear that the thin crust of civilisation might give way altogether.[106] Anxious to appease the working class, they set aside fiscal, financial, commercial, and monetary orthodoxy in order to hasten the revival of industry and employment. In February they agreed to postpone the removal of restrictions upon imported manufactures from outside the Empire so as to assist the reconversion of domestic industry to peacetime production.[107] In March they agreed to delay the balancing of the budget and maintain public spending as if the war had continued until the summer of 1919; to relax controls over domestic investment but maintain the embargo on overseas lending; and to remove the peg on the sterling–dollar rate and let the exchanges go. On 31 March the gold standard, suspended in 1914, was formally set aside until 31 December 1925.[108]

For another two years the spectre of Communism continued to haunt the Cabinet.[109] However, when the revolution failed to materialise after the first winter of disturbances, the fear receded and another danger came to the fore. This was inflation, which soared to an annual rate of 50 per cent in 1919, owing largely to the hasty removal of price controls, the new mood of optimism in commercial circles, and the opportunity for company promoters to borrow on the capital market for frankly speculative purposes. In May 1919 the Chancellor of the Exchequer Austen Chamberlain, presented his first postwar budget. The reduction of planned expenditure from £2,579 million in 1918–19 to £1,660 million in 1919–20, or 36 per cent, and the reduction in the annual deficit from £1,690 million to a mere £326 million made this one of the most deflationary budgets on record. But in the prevailing mood the decision to plan for a deficit of even £326 million, or some 60 per cent more than the total expenditure of central government in 1914, seemed inflationary enough.[110] A press campaign to end public 'waste' began, and Bank of England and Treasury officials bore down upon the Chancellor to raise interest rates and remove the barrier to foreign lending so as to allow the discipline of market forces to check the inflation and boom in stock market speculation.[111]

Chamberlain, now remote from the sources of radicalism that had inspired his Birmingham-bred father, easily fell under the sway of his advisers and anxiously echoed their warnings in Cabinet. For several months while the Prime Minister was occupied in Paris, Bonar Law and Milner managed to restrain colleagues from heeding Chamberlain's advice.[112] But by midsummer Lloyd George himself had grown uneasy at the chorus of complaints from financial authorities, and acquiesced reluctantly in a scheme enabling the Bank of England to move quietly but decisively, in Chamberlain's words, a 'step towards deflation'.[113] At almost the same moment, import controls were removed from all items except those singled out for special treatment.[114] And a few weeks later the Cabinet heard the Prime Minister declare that 'ruthless cutting down of expenditure was imperative', and call for the Treasury to coordinate a campaign of retrenchment.[115]

During the autumn of 1919 the Treasury bill rate and Bank rate rose sharply as a result of the Bank's deflationary action, and in December Chamberlain confirmed in Parliament the government's acceptance of the Cunliffe Report.[116] The first signs of a slow-down in the postwar restocking boom might have been discerned by now. But the mercantile – financial community had regained its nerve, making any warnings of a slump inaudible over demands to remove all remaining wartime controls and end public 'waste and extravagance'.[117] In April 1920 Bank rate was raised again to an almost unprecedented 7 per cent where it was to remain for a record twelve months.[118] Shortly afterwards, Chamberlain presented his second postwar budget. Expenditure was reduced by a further 30 per cent, and an actual net surplus of £231 million or 20 per cent was designated for debt redemption.[119] This and parallel action by the United States, along with an almost total absence of provision for assisting European recovery, was more than enough to end the boom, and a severe depression ensued.

During the next two years a few concessions were made to the objectives of imperial solidarity and safeguarded industries. Quota restrictions were placed on dyestuff imports, and 'key industries' such as chemicals, precision instruments, and wireless valves were protected by the Safeguarding of Industries Act of 1921, all of which included some imperial preference.[120] In December 1920 Austen Chamberlain, yielding to sustained pressure from Milner and Amery, promised £2 million per annum to assist emigration to the 'white' Dominions, and in the spring of 1922 an Empire Settlement Act was adopted confirming a long-term commitment to assist the relocation of 'British stock' within the Empire. But if the principle was conceded the financial commitment was left undefined in the legislation, and in the event it proved as small as the number of emigrants affected.[121] Meanwhile farmers, who had received a guaranteed floor price for corn in 1920, felt betrayed when the government hastily scrapped the guarantee once prices began to slide and the burden of a large subsidy threatened to unbalance the budget.[122] The only major industry to retain its wartime protection was the motor industry, and as the slump hit just when heavy reconversion costs were incurred, it was almost as badly affected as the rest.[123] The wartime promises thus were practically forgotten: very little was done to protect British industry or provide the Empire with men, money, and markets.

By these decisions the government established that Britain would rely upon an internationalist strategy for recovery. But for how long? The war had shattered international commercial and financial links, and temporarily destroyed many of Britain's most important Continental markets. As in other countries, it had also reduced the government's capacity to impose the burden of adjustment upon the domestic economy. And it had, albeit temporarily, transformed the traditional creditor/debtor relationship between Britain and the United States, and in strengthening New York had reduced the City of London's influence over money and capital flows. Recovery through the revival of international commerce and finance demanded leadership from Britain as never before. Almost inevitably this entailed awesome sacrifices, which placed enormous strain on the country's fragile politico-economic unity.

2

Crucified on a cross of gold

The economic consequences of the peace

The British delegation that Lloyd George led to the Paris peace conference in January 1919 had definite views on many issues but no very clear strategy to guide them. Lloyd George consistently fought against the extreme proposals advanced by the French delegation for severing the Rhineland from Germany and favouring the newly independent Poland with territory largely occupied by Germans. Yet during the recent general election he himself had encouraged expectations of massive compensation from Germany, and he allowed British representation on the conference committee on reparations to go to men who were known to hold extreme views. Reparations were initially intended to cover damage to civilian property directly in the path of war, but as this meant that France would receive the lion's share, British delegates insisted upon an extension of liability to include widows' and disability pensions, which meant a massive increase in claims. Lloyd George now sought to postpone a final settlement until passions had subsided, and seized upon a French proposal to avoid mention of a specific figure in the peace treaty; instead an Inter-Allied Reparation Commission would have until 1 May 1921 to prepare a definitive schedule of payments. This, however, created a very unsatisfactory situation. The French were encouraged to hold firm in their demands, which so annoyed the American President, Woodrow Wilson, that he threatened to quit the conference. Public hopes that Germany would pay the cost of the war were sustained. Germany was further demoralised and its economy placed under a cloud of financial uncertainty. Against his better judgment, Lloyd George had thus participated in what critics with some justice were to call the Carthaginian peace.[1]

By the spring of 1919 Allied proposals for drawing the United States into European financial reconstruction had been abruptly rebuffed. The French suggestion of pooling Allied war costs and reapportioning liabilities on the basis of ability to pay was rejected by Wilson's deputies in February. The proposal from the British Treasury representative, J.M. Keynes, for a large-scale lending scheme was turned down on 3 May. Four days later, with negotiations on the German treaty completed, British statesmen confronted the prospect of a prolonged crisis in central Europe. The civil war raging in Russia and the penal sanctions imposed upon Germany left little hope of economic recovery, which meant an inevitable delay in the restoration of British trade and likely intensification of the industrial unrest that now threatened the country's stability.[2] Even before the treaty was signed, therefore, British efforts at revision began, and continued at an almost endless series of conferences over the next few years, where British and French statesmen engaged in an exhausting test of wills.[3] The British pressed for reparation concessions without however going so far as to push the French into unilateral action to secure payment; the French pressed their claims on Germany, while hesitating before the risk of permanently antagonising their former British and American Allies.

A conference at Spa in July 1920 turned into a bitter confrontation between Allied and German heads of government, and succeeded only in settling the distribution of future payments: France would receive 52 per cent, Britain 22 per cent, Italy 10 per cent, Belgium 8 per cent, and the other Allies the remaining 8 per cent. When further delays in interim payment occurred, French troops on 8 March 1921 occupied the Ruhr towns of Düsseldorf, Duisberg, and Ruhrort. Two months later the Reparation Commission adopted the so-called London schedule of payments, setting the nominal total at 123 milliard gold marks (£6.6 billion) though indicating that the total expected payments would be 50 milliards. Reluctantly, in face of a threatened occupation of the Ruhr, the government of Joseph Wirth acquiesced, but after an initial cash payment further payment in cash or kind virtually ceased. While Germany seethed with anti-Western feeling, French authorities blamed British policy for inciting German non-compliance with the treaty, and in turn British authorities blamed French policy for prolonging the European crisis and delaying economic recovery. Both in their own way were right, but the stalemate was doing no one good. Inevitably, hopes of an early return to the gold standard were disappointed.

Industrialists and deflation

In the autumn of 1920 the Federation of British Industries received an invitation to submit a brief to the Brussels Financial Conference. The Cunliffe Report had become official policy in December 1919, but with prices spiralling upwards and the pound now below $4.00, leading industrialists were thoroughly apprehensive of restoring the pre-war parity through price deflation. They therefore turned down the invitation, 'lest [their] statement might disclose differences of opinion between the respective national representatives of this country and the Federation'.[4] By June 1921, with the Cunliffe Committee's recommendations being actively applied and industrial output falling faster and further that year than at any time in living memory, the FBI's credit and currency committee called for a new monetary inquiry. It should, they agreed, have the same terms of reference as the Cunliffe Committee, but this time its members must include representatives of industry and labour as well as finance, to ensure due consideration of the impact of future monetary policy upon trade and employment.[5]

With the approval of the Federation's executive committee, the President, Sir Peter Rylands, wrote to the Prime Minister. Rylands emphasised that he did not mean to criticise the Cunliffe Committee or suggest the rejection of the gold standard, which remained in theory the ideal system for Europe. But he wanted it recognised that conditions had drastically changed since the formal adoption of the Cunliffe Report eighteen months earlier. As he explained, European currencies were now so severely depreciated that no country could contemplate the sacrifice involved in returning to its pre-war gold parity, and industrialists on the continent openly opposed such a policy. In Britain the post-war rise in prices meant the need for far greater deflation than the Cunliffe Committee could have anticipated. And aside from any other effects, a substantial reduction in price-levels would make the already enormous burden of taxes upon industry simply 'intolerable'.[6]

The Federation's initiative brought no results. After a delay of nearly two months, Lloyd George, on Treasury advice, responded by denying the need for a new inquiry. Conditions, he claimed, had not changed since the adoption of the Cunliffe Report. Nor was the government following the advice simply of financiers. The same recommendations had been made in November 1918 by the Committee on Financial Facilities, 'which was largely composed of businessmen and widely representative of British industry', as well as by the experts assembled at Brussels in December 1920. In any case, now that the first signs of recovery were on the horizon it seemed to him unwise to create further uncertainty by reopening the question of monetary policy.[7]

Lloyd George's reference to the wartime Committee on Financial Facilities was important because it appeared to be an effective answer to the FBI's complaint that industry had not been consulted on the gold standard issue. In fact, however, it proved no such thing. The committee had comprised thirteen members, of whom five, including the chairman, were bankers. Of the rest, one was a senior Treasury official soon to turn banker, one a City accountant, one the President of the Chambers of Commerce, and one an official of the Office of Reconstruction. Only four were industrialists, and of them three were involved in arms manufacture or shipbuilding, the most internationalist sectors of industry. Moreover, the committee had reported after the first Cunliffe Report was published, which left it with little alternative but to endorse the latter's recommendations. The Treasury nevertheless regularly referred to the Committee on Financial Facilities Report and never failed to add that its authors were 'widely representative of British industry', in the effort to persuade wavering ministers of the popularity of an early return to the pre-war gold standard.[8] If the ministers were impressed, the FBI was not.

In October 1921 Rylands returned to the charge. Writing to the Prime Minister, he insisted that no man could reasonably deny that the inflationary boom and subsequent slump that took place after December 1919 had wrought great changes in Britain and indeed the whole world. How far the slump itself was due to the policy advocated by the Cunliffe Committee, he was not prepared to say, although a large body of expert opinion took the view that it had 'materially contributed to the condition now prevailing'. Suffice it to note, he added, that unemployment was greatest in the United States and Britain, the two countries where deflationary policies had been most vigorously applied. No country could singlehandedly recreate the conditions required for a return to pre-war parities; Britain's attempt to do so was seriously retarding her own recovery. On behalf of the FBI, therefore, he renewed his request for a new monetary inquiry.[9]

Rylands' request was again rejected. The depressed state of industry and severe unemployment had however already persuaded authorities of the need for an easing of monetary policy. Bank rate, after a record twelve months at 7 per cent, had been reduced a half per cent in April 1921. In June it was reduced to 6 per cent, and sterling, having recovered to nearly $4.00 that month, thereafter began to drift lower. In the circumstances, the Federation's leaders were content to let matters rest.

The British role in European financial reconstruction

The industrialists were not the only ones disappointed by postwar developments. Officials at the Treasury and the Bank of England had at first deemed their deflationary action 'wonderfully successful'.[10] Inflation was halted and wholesale prices rapidly declined. Unfortunately

American prices also declined nearly as far. Hence, after eighteen months, unemployment stood at 2 million or 16 per cent of the registered workforce at the end of 1921, and sterling remained far below par.

Initial efforts to restore financial stability on the continent had also proven ineffectual. In September 1920 Norman persuaded his predecessor, Cokayne, now Lord Cullen, Robert Brand, and Sir Robert Kindersley, chairman of Lazard Brothers and a member of the Bank's Committee of Treasury, to represent Britain at the Brussels Financial Conference. Largely on British initiative, resolutions were adopted calling upon governments to cease borrowing, curb expenditure, turn over control of monetary policy to wholly independent central banks, abandon exchange controls, and prepare for a return to gold.[11] The resolutions, like sermons against sin, afforded no room for objection among conservative opinion in Europe. But nowhere outside Britain did political conditions allow them to be applied.

During 1921 British reconstruction efforts were concentrated largely on Austria. The financial position of the country was nearly hopeless, having been cut off from its hinterland by the creation of independent Czechoslovakia, Hungary, and Yugoslavia, and left with an over-large bureaucratic apparatus, as well as being saddled with reparations, occupation costs, and charges for postwar relief. No less than eighteen countries held claims against the country, and practically all its assets were pledged against repayment. Norman, who was already involved through the Bank of England's controlling interest in the Anglo-Austrian Bank of Vienna, appreciated Austria's importance as the commercial nexus of south-east Europe, and sought to mount a rescue operation through the newly-formed League Financial Committee. But the scheme required the creditor countries to accept a lengthy postponement of payment, and though Allied representatives accepted the terms at a conference in London in March, objections were soon raised by Italy as well as the succession states, which were not prepared to cooperate until their own liability for part of the pre-war Austrian state debt was also removed. Presently Norman's attempt to associate the Federal Reserve Bank of New York in a rescue scheme also failed when the American government indicated its opposition even to semi-official involvement in European reconstruction. The delays intensified the political turmoil in Austria and accelerated the run on the schilling, which brought the economy nearly to a standstill. In December food riots occurred in Vienna, but for the time being no progress was possible.[12]

Lloyd George took the lead in convening a conference at Genoa in April 1922 with the purpose of speeding the pacification and recovery of Europe. The hope was to have a world economic conference involving

Russia, Germany, and the United States, as well as Britain, France, and other European countries, to arrange the reintegration of Russia into Europe using trade and financial inducements, and to ease Germany's reparation problem by assisting the promotion of commerce with Russia. It was a grandiose scheme, which collapsed when the United States refused to participate, the French dragged their heels on support for Germany and Bolshevik Russia, and the two outcast powers turned their backs on the conference to negotiate a bilateral treaty of cooperation at Rapallo. But it did at least provide another opportunity for British authorities to promote international monetary reconstruction.

As at Brussels eighteen months before, the resolutions adopted were British-inspired, this time chiefly the work of Ralph Hawtrey, Director of Financial Enquiries at the Treasury and its one trained economist. Once again they gave first priority to the stabilisation of currencies, establishment of independent central banks, and restoration of the gold standard. But whereas before no means were offered of avoiding the severe economic and social dislocation involved in returning to gold, the Genoa resolutions enunciated principles and procedures designed to reduce it to manageable proportions. One resolution called for the extension of the gold exchange standard: central banks should count as currency reserves not only gold but also foreign exchange which was itself backed by gold, thus increasing available reserve assets and world liquidity. Another resolution emphasised the need to coordinate national credit policies. A third endorsed the principle that central banks should aim at price stability as well as exchange stability. America's cooperation in the stabilisation of the purchasing power of gold was declared vital and its support was requested. The Bank of England was called upon to convene a central bankers' conference to draft an International Monetary Convention, setting out the basis of cooperation.[13]

The Genoa resolutions, though no more effective from a practical standpoint, marked a major advance from the orthodoxy of Brussels, and for the next ten years British authorities regularly referred to them in defending the decision to restore sterling to the gold standard. Norman had discussed the draft resolutions with Hawtrey before the conference, and subsequently took steps to convene a central bankers' conference.[14] No doubt he favoured the extension of the gold exchange standard, which meant the use of sterling as a reserve asset for many second-rank currencies and the maintenance of large foreign balances in London. Doubtless, too, he welcomed every inducement to central bank cooperation, which was of the essence of his plans. But it would be wrong to conclude that Norman's commitment to progressive monetary reforms was thereby established. The main innovation at Genoa was the endorsement of the principle of coordinated central bank operations for price-level stability as well as exchange stability – what was popularly known as a *managed* gold standard – a commitment which Norman seems to have looked upon with deep suspicion. Stable price levels were for him no more than a remote ideal: the importance of Genoa lay rather in its promise of an accelerated return to gold.

Shortly before the conference Norman wrote to Benjamin Strong, Governor of the Federal Reserve Bank of New York (America's nearest equivalent to a central bank), describing Hawtrey as 'a "leading light" of the Treasury [who] makes it his particular business to quarrel with the policy of the Treasury and the Bank of England'.[15] If Norman wanted Strong to support Hawtrey's guidelines for a managed gold standard, this was an odd way of going about it. Norman's own deputy at Genoa was Sir Charles Addis, Chairman of the London board of the Hong Kong and Shanghai Banking Corporation and a recently elected director of the Bank of England, who attended as adviser to the Chancellor, Sir Robert Horne. Although on friendly terms with Hawtrey, Addis regarded him as a dangerous radical on the monetary question. His own position had been made clear in his inaugural address as President of the Institute of Bankers in November 1921, when he denounced the suggestion of Professor Gustav Cassel, the economist E.M.H. Lloyd, Hawtrey, and others of restoring the gold standard by means of devaluation. He urged the return to the pre-war parity, however much deflation was required.[16] Shortly afterwards he sailed for China, and was still overseas when he received Norman's request to go to Genoa. His private reaction was, 'What a bore! And I really wanted a rest'.[17] He showed no enthusiasm for the possibility of reforms nor for the actual conference results.

In June Norman proposed a conference to leading foreign central bankers. Strong took fright at the thought of the United States being forced into a policy of inflation in order to maintain price and exchange stability with the spendthrift European countries, and responded negatively.[18] The Continental central bankers, who as yet refused to accept the need for currency devaluation, also displayed hostility towards the idea of a 'managed' gold standard. Norman was therefore obliged to shelve the conference proposal. If disappointed, it was not over the question of management, however, for he continued to deprecate Hawtrey's lack of realism on monetary policy.[19] Meanwhile he resumed unilateral efforts to rebuild the international monetary system.

Towards the end of 1922 assistance to Austria became possible when, with the country paralysed by the collapse of the schilling, foreign opposition to a League initiative was abandoned. Sir Arthur Salter, head of the League Economic and Financial Section, was despatched to Vienna to investigate and report back to the Financial Committee. The committee recommended an international reconstruction loan, subject to Austrian acceptance of a package of reforms including drastic public spending cuts and restitution of 'sound finance', and the assurance of full independence for the Austrian National Bank. Once adopted, a £25 million loan was arranged with the support of the Allied governments and private American bankers, and the Austrian economy immediately revived.[20] This was a major advance for Norman's plans and reflected great prestige on the Financial Committee, which henceforth played an important role in European reconstruction work.

From the outset the committee was recognised to be a British-dominated body. Its dozen or so members, chosen mainly for the weight they carried in their respective financial markets,[21] included two British nominees. One was Sir Basil Blackett, the Controller of Finance at the Treasury, who sat on the committee from its inception in October 1920 until 1922, when his place was taken by Sir Otto Niemeyer. The other was the financier Sir Henry Strakosch. In addition, Sir Arthur Salter served not only as secretary to the committee but also, in his capacity as liaison representative of the League, participated in the committee's deliberations. Strakosch, of central European origin, had begun his career in London as a foreign exchange dealer, and was now chairman of the Union Corporation, a holding company with extensive foreign investments particularly in the South African gold fields. He was also an authority on monetary issues, adviser to the South African and Indian governments, and almost certainly an associate of the London Rothschilds. During the 1920s he played an important though largely unseen role in international monetary relations, and the esteem in which Norman held him was central to the Financial Committee's success.[22] The committee's ability to promote reconstruction depended upon its ability to offer hard currency loans to the countries that approached it for help. Norman's cooperation was thus essential, for he controlled access to Europe's largest capital market and had the ear of most other important central bankers. As it happened, Norman found the committee almost perfectly suited to his requirements. It was dominated by 'practical' men rather than politicians or academic theorists, and offered a ready-made agency for promoting the restoration of central bank authority while avoiding the appearance of imposing Bank of England views on the distressed countries. It also provided an effective lever for prying loose the ex-enemy states from their burden of reparations – or as Norman preferred it, for putting economics before politics. The latter feature of the committee's activities became a source of resentment among French authorities and was to cost Norman dearly in the later 1920s. But in the meantime he exploited the committee with his customary zeal.[23]

In October 1923 Norman refused the Hungarian government access to the London market, insisting that it first secure the committee's approval on a plan for financial reform. This Hungary did, but when the committee agreed to the continuation of some reparation payments during the term of the reconstruction loan, he was infuriated. 'I wish we could have somebody's blood for the way the Hungarians have been treated', he wrote Bradbury in May 1924. He refused his crucial endorsement of the loan, and only after the British government and Treasury appealed to him to moderate his stance did he allow a tranche to be issued in London. A transfer clause was introduced enabling foreign payments to be suspended in the event of exchange difficulties, which served as a useful precedent for the Dawes Plan on German financial reconstruction.[24]

Two years earlier, in February 1922, the United States Congress instituted a World War Debt Funding Commission to negotiate terms for the repayment of wartime loans to its European allies. With isolationist sentiment running strong in America, the assumption of Congressional control over debts boded ill for those who believed that major American concessions were an essential element in a general settlement. Matters were scarcely improved when Arthur Balfour, in temporary charge of the Foreign Office, on 1 August 1922 issued a note to Britain's European debtors, advocating a general write-off of inter-governmental debts and supporting this with the assurance that Britain would claim from them only what was necessary to meet America's repayment demands on Britain.[25] Although this implied a sizeable writing down of British claims, Americans responded with anger at what seemed to them a British attempt to foist responsibility for European recovery upon the American taxpayer. But with Europe slipping into renewed crisis British statesmen were disposed to accept further sacrifices, as confirmed early the following year when terms for the funding of the American debt were adopted.

In response to the American request for debt negotiations, Stanley Baldwin, Chancellor of the Exchequer in the new Conservative government of Andrew Bonar Law, travelled to Washington in January 1923, taking Montagu Norman along as adviser. The Congressional Commission was authorised to accept funding of the debt over a period of twenty-five years at not less than 4½ per cent. Although this was scarcely satisfactory to the imperialist Bonar Law and leading members of his

Cabinet, the American Ambassador in London had encouraged hopes of more generous treatment. Norman moreover was extremely anxious for a settlement in order to remove this element of uncertainty overhanging sterling and strengthen the 'special relationship' he was developing with Benjamin Strong, his counterpart in New York. Norman quickly succeeded in charming Baldwin on the outward journey and impressing him with his view that 'almost any settlement now is better than none'.[26] In the event Baldwin accepted repayment on a 3 per cent basis for the first 10 years, requiring annuities of approximately £160 million, and repayment on a 3½ per cent basis for a further 52 years, requiring annuities of £180 million. The terms were considerably easier than the commission was formally authorised to grant, but were still regarded as dangerously onerous by Bonar Law and colleagues who accepted them with great reluctance. Norman, who shared in the criticism that ensued, may or may not have influenced Baldwin's decision; the Foreign Office, it should be noted, was almost equally anxious for a settlement in order to improve Anglo-American relations, which had been strained since Versailles.[27] But there is no doubt that Norman regarded the result as a major step towards the realisation of his 'big idea'. Ominously for him, it also brought a hardening of British attitudes towards further international 'sacrifices'. However, the issue was almost forgotten amidst renewed conflict over reparations.

By the spring of 1921 persistent German refusal to comply with Treaty obligations had led Lloyd George finally to join the French Premier, Aristide Briand, in threatening military occupation of the Ruhr. This brought German acceptance of the London schedule of payments on 11 May and an immediate payment of 1 billion gold marks (£50 million) to the Reparation Commission. But the balance of political forces in Germany did not allow the deflationary policies that were essential if such a transfer was to be effected without disturbance to the exchanges. Immediately afterwards the German mark slipped badly against foreign currencies, and on 14 December 1921 the German government requested a temporary moratorium on further payments. The frightening speed with which the mark was depreciating and annoyance at French attempts to secure preferential treatment through a revised schedule of deliveries in kind predisposed British authorities to favour a moratorium. Attempts to arrange an international loan for Germany broke down in June 1922, and in the next two weeks the mark fell by 60 per cent.[28] On 9 September a brief deferment of cash payments was agreed by the Reparation Commission. This did nothing to halt the collapse of the mark, however, and renewed efforts to find a solution only intensified French frustration at German non-payment.

On 26 December 1922 the Reparation Commission, by a three to one vote with the British member opposing, declared Germany in deliberate default. A conference of premiers early in the new year rejected Bonar Law's proposal for a four-year moratorium, and on 11 January 1923 French and Belgian troops marched into the Ruhr to secure reparations by force. What in Paris seemed a necessary assertion of national interests appeared from London as an attempt at French hegemony on the continent carried out at the expense of European reconstruction. 'Madness', was Norman's judgment of French policy.[29] In Germany the decision to support passive resistance despite dwindling revenues led the government to pay for services simply by printing money. Inflation accelerated, hastening the already depreciated currency to a rate of £1 = 40 billion marks and onwards to oblivion. Norman's hopes for an early return to gold, entertained in the aftermath of the Genoa conference, were dashed.[30] Stabilisation was out of the question until a reparation settlement could be reached and the uncertainties surrounding the German economy were removed.

Meanwhile Norman confronted difficulties from another direction when Strong in New York reacted to the prospect of renewed inflation at the end of February by raising his discount rate a half point to 4½ per cent, and in coordination with other Reserve Banks began open market operations to tighten market rates. By now the pound had recovered to $4.69½, barely 4 per cent below its pre-war parity, and Norman was determined to stop it sliding again. The difficulty, as he recognised, was that with 1.3 million unemployed and industrial recovery only just begun, any new monetary restriction was bound to attract criticism.[31] Briefly it seemed that American interest rates would go still higher.[32] The danger passed, but with sterling declining on the exchanges even before pressure began to be felt from the annual rundown of London balances to finance the autumn harvest overseas, Norman chose to act. Baldwin appealed to him on 23 June to refrain from doing anything to hinder recovery, to no avail.[33] Norman wrote to Strong, 'I trust we shall advance [Bank] rate to 4 per cent on Thursday, but you will realise that trade prospects do not make the change easy.'[34] And so it happened: the Committee of Treasury announced a rise in the rate from 3 to 4 per cent, and immediately the Bank faced criticism from several sources.

Domestic challenges to internationalism

At the July meeting of the FBI's executive committee, Col. O.C. Armstrong, a recent past-president and leading figure in the chemical industry, renewed the call for another monetary inquiry. As on previous occasions Forrest Hewit, director of the Calico Printers' Association, and a few other spokesmen for the older export industries indicated their support for the gold standard by expressing the view that industry was not competent to deal with the issues in question. But D.A. Bremner of the British Engineers' Association, and Sir Peter Rylands, the former FBI president and chairman of a family steel-making firm in Warrington, supported Armstrong's case. So too did Sir Alfred Mond, the former Liberal Minister and chairman of the chemicals firm Brunner Mond. 'The country had been living under Treasury theories of monetary policy, and he questioned their wisdom as they seemed to result in hampering trade and producing unemployment'. Sir Eric Geddes, chairman of Dunlop Rubber and the current FBI president, then proposed to hesitating members that they simply request a new inquiry with adequate industrial representation but without expressing a view as to policy. On this basis Armstrong's resolution was unanimously adopted.[35]

Voices from the advanced wing of the Liberal Party were also raised against the Bank rate decision. Hubert Henderson, editor of *The Nation* and one of the earliest critics of postwar monetary policy, took the occasion to declare that Britain must set aside indefinitely all idea of returning to gold until American cooperation on price stabilisation was assured; the country simply could not stand the dislocation of further gyrations in price levels.[36] A few weeks later his call to fellow Liberals to take up the question of monetary policy was answered when J.M. Keynes spoke to the Liberal Summer School on the advantages of adopting a consciously managed currency system.[37]

Keynes, a Cambridge economist who had served in the Treasury during the war and as adviser to Lloyd George at the peace conference, was one of the most brilliant men of his generation. His essay on the shortcomings of the Versailles Treaty, *The Economic Consequences of the Peace*, which contained devastating caricatures of Wilson and Clemenceau, had done much to strengthen revisionist sentiment in Britain after its publication in late 1919, and established his authority in political circles. An intellectual with practical experience in the 'real world', and an academic with a journalist's skill at publicity, he was also a committed Liberal reformer. During the 1920s he devoted much of his energy to the task of redefining the framework for maintaining the liberal capitalist system. The changed conditions facing Britain since the war made this essential, he believed, for *laissez-faire* policies were now impracticable, and in the absence of a constructive alternative, liberalism would be replaced by imperial protectionism or what was worse, socialism.[38] Despite his scorn for the right and left-wing alternatives, however, his approach reflected a similar preoccupation with class relations and pointed in the same broad direction. As he explained in numerous articles and essays, Britain must safeguard her independence and liberal society by retreating from extreme internationalism towards a more actively managed economy.

Britain, Keynes wrote, was no longer in a position to operate the gold standard for her own ends. The United States, possessing vastly larger bank deposits and metallic reserves, was bound to determine interest rates and credit conditions in the world, whatever the Bank of England attempted to do. By the same token Britain had lost her place as the world's leading manufacturer, which meant that overseas loans could no longer be expected to return automatically in payment for exports. It was at least as likely that they would simply result in claims for gold or foreign currency to purchase goods elsewhere, which would weaken sterling and force deflationary action at the expense of the domestic economy. For Britain to return to gold in present circumstances, therefore, would be tantamount to handing over control of the economy to American central bank authorities who, however well meaning, were unlikely to control the often wild price-level fluctuations that had been a feature of their country in the past; and Britain would face the constant risk of crisis and social upheaval. The only practical alternative was a currency system managed with the objective of a reasonable degree of price stability, and a policy of channelling savings away from overseas investment into domestic projects to stimulate employment and ensure social peace. As he explained in *A Tract on Monetary Reform* in October 1923, the old automatic gold standard was 'a barbarous relic'. Surely no one would contemplate again 'allowing the tides of gold to play what tricks they like with the internal price level, and abandoning the attempt to moderate the disastrous influence of the trade-cycle on the stability of prices and employment'.[39]

That autumn, with the international situation still too unsettled for action, future monetary policy remained a secondary but by no means forgotten issue. At the Imperial Conference in London in October a proposal for an Empire-wide paper currency standard received attention. The author of the proposal, J.F. Darling, was an imperialist who looked upon Lord Milner as his exemplar. To them it was self-evident that Britain's destiny was bound up with the Empire, and that in the absence of reciprocal ties the Empire would disintegrate under the centripetal force of attraction of rival empires. Darling was however no mere 'currency crank' but the former managing director of the Midland Bank, and his scheme attracted the sympathetic attention of several Dominion delegates. Hawtrey of the Treasury was called upon to muster every available argument in order to have it shelved.[40]

At practically the same time the Minister of Labour, Sir Montague Barlow, suggested publicly that the government might be obliged to set aside the rules of 'sound finance' in order to provide for the unemployed that winter. Barlow, the chairman of art auctioneers Sothebys, did not rank among senior Conservatives and initially his speech received scant mention in the press. But with the pound sagging on the foreign exchanges the City became nervous, and he was obliged to state that the government had no intention of resorting to inflationary policies.[41]

On 17 October, the day Barlow's statement appeared in the press, the FBI executive committee met to consider its position. Three months had passed since their latest request for a new monetary inquiry, and the government had not even shown them the courtesy of a reply. Rylands expressed annoyance at the City's way of surrounding the currency question with an aura of mystery and dismissing as a crank any industrialist who questioned present policy. Mond echoed Rylands' complaints and going further, asserted that on this issue industrialists and bankers had opposing interests. The United States, he pointed out, had abandoned deflation, and industry there was rapidly expanding on the strength of the purchasing power of high wages. Others including Bremner and Frank Farrell, President of the Silk Association of Great Britain and Ireland, which represented both the silk weaving and the fastgrowing rayon industries, endorsed Mond's remarks, and eventually the committee agreed unanimously to petition the Prime Minister for a new inquiry.[42]

The FBI's petition politely but unequivocally affirmed that industrialists were out of patience with the practice of leaving monetary policy for the City to determine. They accepted that their own outlook was also partial and disclaimed any special competence in the field, but were in no doubt as to its fundamental importance. None of the other measures being canvassed as a solution to the current depression, they affirmed, would have any result in the absence of a satisfactory monetary policy. They were equally certain that wherever the Cunliffe policy had been applied, the result was rapidly falling prices, economic dislocation, a severe check to exports, an increase in the real burden of internal debt, and substantial unemployment. Further, they warned against returning to the gold standard unless or until the other important trading nations committed themselves to similar action, or attempting to revalue sterling, which in view of existing pressures 'may impose an intolerable burden upon the producing section of the community'. For the time being policy should aim primarily at domestic price stability, though not at the 'abnormally low level' prevailing in the current 'severe depression, but at such an increase ... as normal trade activity would entail'. Future policy should be decided by a new inquiry comprising 'representatives of industry, commerce and labour as well as financial and economic experts', to ensure that trade, commerce, and employment were no longer dealt with in 'almost watertight compartments'.

The publication of the FBI's petition on 25 October coincided with a speech by Stanley Baldwin, Bonar Law's successor as Prime Minister, to the annual Conservative Party conference in Plymouth. Baldwin, anxious to dispel any suspicions still lingering from the Barlow affair, hastened to affirm his support for 'sound financial policy' and the return to gold. But no sooner was this said than he created new uncertainty by reopening the tariff controversy. Unemployment, he said, was the most serious problem facing Britain.

> I regard it as such. I can fight it. I am willing to fight it. I cannot fight it without weapons. I have for myself come to the conclusion that ... if we go on pottering as we are we shall have grave unemployment with us to the end of time. And I have come to the conclusion myself that the only way of fighting this subject is by protecting the home market.[43]

This was Baldwin at his simple best, and the conference cheered him to the echo. But among the party hierarchy the speech caused consternation. Bonar Law, whose fatal illness had led to Baldwin's elevation, had given a pledge at the previous general election that he would make no fundamental change in the nation's 'fiscal' policy without seeking a specific mandate, and Baldwin accepted that he too was bound by it. An early election thus became inevitable, before the arguments for protection had been clearly set out. Free trade supporters in Lancashire and the North were annoyed. So too were the die-hard imperialists like Leo Amery, Lord Beaverbrook, and W.A. Hewins, because Baldwin talked only of a national rather than an imperial trade policy. And even those who shared Baldwin's protectionist views were disturbed, for a defeat at the polls would clear the way for the Labour Party to take power and threaten the capitalist system itself.[44]

'Finance is the nervous system of Capitalism', MacDonald had written in 1921. 'Those who control Finance can paralyse Society ... If a Labour Government came to power, they could starve it. A financiers' counter-revolution would be more effective than a soldiers' one.'[45] Snowden frequently spoke in a similar vein and as recently as March 1923 had initiated debate in the House of Commons on replacing 'the capitalist system' by Socialism.[46] Enough indication had been given to persuade experienced observers that party leaders were not in fact bent on revolution. But could they be counted on to restrain their more militant followers? Or were they, as the *Daily Mail* warned, the Kerenskys of Britain: idealists who, having pushed open the door, would let 'the Reds rush in through it'?[47] The miners had just elected the firebrand A.J. Cook as their leader; left-wing candidates on the Clyde were threatening trouble. And what did the *New Leader*, the official journal of the ILP, mean when it called repeatedly for the nationalisation of the banking system and expansion of workers' purchasing power, if it did not mean printing money as in Russia and Germany?

It was these doubts that had overshadowed British politics since 1918 and became suddenly acute when the general election of 6 December 1923 reduced the Conservatives to a minority in Parliament and left Labour, as the largest opposition party, poised to take office. In the words of Winston Churchill, 'The enthronement [sic] in office of a Socialist government will be a serious national misfortune such as has usually befallen great States only on the morrow of defeat in war'. The *English Review* similarly declared, 'We stand now at a moment when the sun of England seems menaced with final eclipse. For the first time in her history the party of revolution approach their hands to the helm of the State not only, as in the seventeenth century, for the purpose of overthrowing the Crown, or of altering the Constitution, but with the design of destroying the very basis of civilised life.'[48]

The City, target of so much recent criticism, 'suffered fearfully from the forebodings of Labour or Socialism', Norman later admitted to Strong.[49] Norman evidently suffered as much as anyone, for on 14 January 1924 he advised City bankers without publicity that he was forthwith lifting existing restrictions on foreign lending.[50] Coming at a time when the pound was already at its lowest level since 1922 and falling fast, this was an extraordinary decision. The most plausible explanation is that it was taken to enable investors to escape Labour's dreaded capital levy. Not once but twice the City Conservative Association called on Baldwin to offer his support to Asquith, if he would form an anti-Socialist government.[51] Baldwin refused to enter a coalition, partly perhaps because his own rise to prominence was due to the breakup of the postwar coalition but also because senior colleagues feared the repercussions if Labour was refused the chance to form a government, while estimating that a minority Labour government would prove 'too weak to do much but not too weak to get discredited'.[52] A similar view prevailed in Liberal circles. Thus when Parliament met, Asquith joined Labour members to bring the Conservative government down. Labour members jubilantly rose from their benches to sing the Red Flag.[53] The flight from the pound sent the dollar rate down to \$4.20$\frac{5}{8}$. On 22 January, the day MacDonald visited Buckingham Palace to receive the seals of office, Norman commented to E.H.D. Skinner, his private secretary, 'This means the beginning of the end of all the work we have been doing.'[54]

The panic was short-lived. In his first audience with the King, MacDonald hastened to affirm that he had no intention of introducing a capital levy.[55] The following evening Norman paid a courtesy call on Snowden, now installed as Chancellor of the Exchequer. To his 'intense surprise', he discovered Snowden to be in awe of him and enthusiastic about his efforts to rebuild the international gold standard system. Snowden's own version of the encounter, although written years later, undoubtedly captures his feelings on the occasion. After 'the caricatures in the Socialist Press of the typical financier', he recorded,

> There came into the room a man so different! He might have stepped out of the frame of a portrait of a handsome courtier of the Middle Ages. It took but a short acquaintance with Mr Norman to know that his external appearance was the bodily expression of one of the kindliest natures and most sympathetic hearts it has been my privilege to know. It was said of a great statesman in the Victorian Age that he had the 'international mind'. How truly that may be said of the present Governor of the Bank of England![56]

Snowden, dazzled by Norman, was also ready to defer to Sir Otto Niemeyer, his chief Treasury financial adviser, who soon dominated him as completely as he did other Chancellors after the war. Niemeyer by all accounts was one of the most able men ever to enter Treasury chambers. Born in London in 1883 of German-Jewish stock, he attended St Paul's School and won a classical scholarship to Balliol where, working relentlessly, he earned a double first and beat Keynes into second place in the civil service examinations of 1906. Norman, who was to hire him away from the Treasury in 1927, once said that 'if he had Niemeyer's brain he would rule the world', a comment that was revealing both of Niemeyer's character and perhaps also Norman's daydreams. Emile Moreau, the French central banker, wrote of 'cet juif, froid et peu sympathique'. Per Jacobsson, a future head of the International Monetary Fund, observed: 'He has the worst Treasury manners'. Having reached the penultimate rung on the Treasury ladder in 1922 at the age of thirty-nine, he displayed his ability in the most overbearing Treasury fashion, which occasionally led him to ride roughshod over opponents and inconvenient facts alike.[57]

Shortly after the Labour Party took office the FBI renewed their request for a fresh monetary inquiry. Niemeyer's advice to Snowden summarised the orthodox case for pressing on with resumption and vividly illustrated his aggressive methods of persuasion. The FBI once again advocated priority for price stability over exchange stability. This, Niemeyer insisted, was unrealistic since in the absence of the discipline of the gold standard Britain must suffer runaway inflation – and as to the consequences of this, one needed only to consider the recent fate of the Soviet Union and Germany. It was true that relaxing monetary restraints and allowing the pound to slip might enable manufacturers to increase their profits temporarily, but food prices would also rise and soon force up wages at the expense of profits. To restore profit levels sterling would have to be further depreciated, and so the vicious circle would continue until sterling became worthless. There was in short only one approach to stability, not two, and its *sine qua non* was the return to gold. He therefore advised the Chancellor to dismiss the industrialists' 'confused and self-contradictory memorandum', while listing for him the advantages – though none of the disadvantages – of returning to gold at the pre-war parity.[58]

One advantage Niemeyer listed was the saving to be made on war debt payments to the United States once the exchange rate was restored to £1 = $4.86. He did not mention that it would undoubtedly be more difficult for Britain to earn dollars at the higher exchange rate. Perhaps inadvertently he also overstated the actual dollar requirements for the war debt, and made no comment at all about the impact of his deflationary plans on the vastly heavier domestic debt. Another advantage, he claimed, was lower Exchequer borrowing charges, since the alternative policy of 'inflation' would shake confidence in sterling and keep interest rates high. This was an arguable claim, but it was also nearly certain that the need to defend an overvalued exchange rate would require high interest rates as well. A third advantage was cheaper imports: a partial argument that overlooked the fact that a higher exchange rate would also make for greater import penetration, dearer exports, and balance of payments difficulties. A fourth advantage was the maintenance of Empire unity now threatened by the readiness of South Africa, Australia, and New Zealand to go their own way and return to gold without Britain. The spectre of the Dominions linking up to the dollar via the gold exchange standard was enough to make any British politician shudder, and it was to be regularly evoked by Niemeyer over the next twelve months. Some substance was provided when South Africa, much to Britain's annoyance, appointed a commission headed by the American economist Edwin Kemmerer and Gerard Vissering, President of the Netherlands Bank, which recommended an early return to gold. But the other Dominions were not in a comparable position. With little or no gold production and greater dependence on British markets, they were unlikely to act in advance of Britain whatever their preference.

In rebutting the FBI's case Niemeyer had treated their argument for price stability as a recipe for inflation. Then, having demolished this straw man, he insisted, as did nearly all financial authorities, that restoration of the pre-war gold parity would serve the interests of industry as well as of finance and commerce. Thus if Britain were to return to gold and undertake that small additional adjustment of wages and prices to make $4.86 the equilibrium rate, the Bank of England could again provide effective leadership for the international monetary system and the City could resume its role as the money engine of the world, enabling industry to thrive on the ensuing expansion of world trade. There was of course a good deal in this argument: the industrialists themselves accepted it in principle. But neither here nor at any other time did Niemeyer attempt to quantify the additional adjustment required or examine the difficulties of maintaining that equilibrium in such an unstable world. Instead he simply stressed and re-stressed the breadth of consensus that existed on the issue. Thus he claimed that there would probably be 'even less support for the apparent [sic] views of the FBI than there was in October', that Reginald McKenna, chairman of the Midland Bank, was the only banker who had opposed an early return to gold, and that even he had recently modified his views. Furthermore, he claimed, present policy had been unanimously endorsed not only by the bankers of the Cunliffe Committee but also by the Committee on Financial Facilities, which was 'widely representative of British industry'. In fact, McKenna had not modified his views.[59] Nor was he the only banker to stand out: Sir Christopher Needham, chairman of the Manchester and Liverpool District Banking Corporation, had also done so. And as for the claim that the Committee of Financial Facilities was 'widely representative of industry', this has already been shown to be false.

The capital levy discarded, MacDonald and Snowden proceeded to reassure sterling holders further by endorsing the recommendations of the Cunliffe Report and refusing the FBI's request for a new monetary inquiry.[60] But with sterling still more than 13 per cent below parity and Europe in crisis on account of the Ruhr occupation, a return to gold was for the time being out of the question. As Robert Brand, usually representative of City opinion, explained to a French associate in March 1924, only a dramatic rise in American price-levels could get the pound back to par. Further deflation in Britain, by adding to the burden of taxes, renewing pressure on wages, and fueling industrial unrest, was politically unacceptable. 'I do not believe myself that we can stand such a process.'[61] Hardly had the markets absorbed the shock of a Labour government, however, than another panic gripped the City. By June Brand had convinced himself that, heavy as the burden on industry might be, an early return to gold was essential.[62]

The Dawes Plan, the City, and sterling

The Franco-Belgian occupation of the Ruhr in January 1923 threw Germany into such a state of turmoil that almost any eventuality seemed possible. The government's support for passive resistance led to hyper-inflation, which wreaked havoc upon middle-class and working-class households. Separatist movements in the Rhineland revived, Bavaria drew away from Berlin's authority, and Fascist and Communist coups were attempted. Raymond Poincaré, the French Premier, whose decision it was to send in the troops, held out for two objectives: clear evidence of German willingness to pay reparations in future, and if Anglo-American agreement on a major adjustment of inter-governmental debts was not forthcoming, at least a British commitment to support the existing reparations regime.[63]

By 26 September he realised his first objective when the new government of Gustav Stresemann formally and unconditionally ended passive resistance. The following month diplomatic activity in London and Washington indicated that his second objective was in sight. On 13 October the British Ambassador in Washington invited American participation in a committee of experts to resolve the reparations problem.[64] American disillusionment with the peace-making process in 1919 had resulted in a determined avoidance of further political entanglements with the European powers. But the disastrous impact of the postwar slump upon American export trade served to remind administration officials of the importance of European stability, which with the Franco-German confrontation in the Ruhr seemed once more under grave threat. On 15 October the Secretary of State, Charles Evans Hughes, responded affirmatively to the British invitation, and called upon acquaintances in banking to serve on the expert committee.[65] Before the end of the year the membership and terms of reference of the committee were settled to Poincaré's satisfaction. On the face of it, his strategy seemed vindicated, but as some of his own advisers recognised, this was far from being the case.

Jacques Seydoux, the leading authority on Franco-German politico-economic relations at the Quai d'Orsay and one of the most sanguine supporters of the occupation in the spring, now saw no hope of retaining French control over the situation. Poincaré had all along avoided imposing his terms unilaterally on Germany so as not to jeopardise British and American involvement in the settlement. Anglo-Saxon involvement was now essential on account of the hard currency loan to Germany that all agreed was a vital part of any financial reconstruction scheme, and also on account of the sorry state of domestic finances which was forcing

France to look abroad for assistance. But clearly British and American financiers would insist on their own terms for such loans, rather than accepting terms that France laid down. As Seydoux recorded in December,

> There is no use hiding the fact that we have entered on the path of the 'financial reconstruction of Europe'. We will not deal with Germany as conqueror to vanquished; rather the Germans and Frenchmen will sit on the same bench before the United States and other lending countries. We will be given conditions, perhaps disarmament, evacuation of the Ruhr. Once engaged in the path, Poincaré will be unable to stop. Failure to procure the grand loan now would be catastrophic for our credit, the death blow to the franc. If Poincaré elects to change course, he must step down, for events cannot be stopped.[66]

Unfortunately for the French, Seydoux's prediction proved only too accurate. The experts who gathered at the Reparation Commission headquarters in Paris on 13 January 1924 elected Reginald McKenna to chair the Second Committee, charged with the task of devising means of inducing the repatriation of exported German capital, and the head of the American delegation, General Charles Dawes, to chair the more important First Committee on balancing the German budget and stabilising its currency. Dawes, an ebullient Chicago banker, had spent the latter years of the war in France and expressed strongly pro-French sentiments in his opening address to the committee. But his deputy, Owen Young, and the British expert, Sir Josiah Stamp, assisted behind the scenes by Sir Arthur Salter, dominated the committee from the start.[67] Despite Poincaré's previously stated opposition, they soon reopened the question of future levels of reparation payments, and ruled out 'productive guarantees' such as Allied control of state forests, mines, and railways in the Ruhr, on which he had insisted. On 9 April 1924 the experts submitted their plan to the Reparation Commission. Among its principal recommendations were the reduction of reparation payments to 1 milliard (billion) marks in 1924–5, with payments rising gradually until 1928–9 when the standard annuity would be 2.5 milliards, with possible increases according to an index of German prosperity; the introduction of a transfer safeguard clause to ensure that henceforth payments across the exchange would not threaten the stability of the mark; an international loan of 800 milliard gold marks (£40 million), to provide reserve assets for the new German bank of issue and help finance initial reparation payments; and the abandonment of all sanctions – Poincaré's *gages productifs* – to ensure the viability of the scheme. This was a far cry from Poincaré's wishes, yet the French experts had joined in giving the plan unanimous support and insisting that it must be integrally adopted.[68]

Despite French disappointment, British financial authorities were less than pleased with the result. At the beginning of the year Norman received a visit from Hjalmar Schacht, the new president of Reichsbank, whom he found much to his liking, and promised him massive assistance in order to strengthen German resistance to French pressure.[69] Stamp and his fellow expert, Sir Robert Kindersley, the chairman of Lazard Brothers, had pressed constantly for a greater reduction in the reparations annuity, to 2 milliard marks or at most 2.25 milliards. Norman and Treasury colleagues were disappointed that Stamp and Kindersley had finally accepted the 2.5 milliard figure. Privately they shared the view of the partners in J.P. Morgan & Co. of New York, who were to be called on to arrange the American tranche of the loan, that the burden on Germany was still dangerously excessive.[70] But in view of the absolute necessity of keeping the United States involved in European reconstruction they recommended immediate British endorsement of the plan and pressed Morgans to accept it.[71] The important question now was how to deal with a future suspension of payments: who would decide when a default occurred, and on the sanctions to be applied. A satisfactory answer was essential if the proposed loan was to be arranged and confidence in the German currency restored. Clearly major concessions would be required from France when statesmen met to examine the Dawes Plan at the diplomatic conference in London in July.

Between the completion of the Dawes Plan and the London conference, a general election in France brought the victory of the *Cartel des gauches*, a coalition of centre-left parties temperamentally more disposed to compromise than the *Bloc national*. The new Premier was Edouard Herriot, a *Normalien* and author of a study of Beethoven, who had cut short a promising academic career to enter politics before the war. Immediately upon taking up the reins of government, he made a display of his readiness to find a negotiated solution to the crisis in consultation with British authorities by visiting MacDonald at Chequers. Upon returning to Paris, however, he was greeted with criticism from all sides. Desperately, he appealed to MacDonald for a return visit, and by the time the London conference opened he was anxious to salvage some measure of French authority over the reparation settlement. To counter French demands, MacDonald called on Thomas Lamont, a senior partner in J.P. Morgan & Co., to indicate the bankers' terms for a loan. Norman, having earlier reassured the American bankers of the feasibility of the plan, now pressed Lamont to insist upon the most extreme conditions for arranging a loan, and Lamont, in some awe of Norman, agreed. Accordingly, a memorandum was drafted by Norman and accepted by the Morgan partners on 15 July, which affirmed that the bankers 'might require' authority over the appointment of the Reparation Agent and other key personnel, the removal of authority from the Reparation Commission, and the immediate removal of all French troops and 'interference' in both the Ruhr and the Rhineland.[72]

The immediate upshot was an angry confrontation between Lamont and Norman and Owen Young, who had returned to Europe to ensure the adoption of the Dawes Plan. Young sternly warned against conditions which made French cooperation impossible, and threatened to arrange the American tranche of the loan through a syndicate headed by Dillon Read & Co. if Morgans persisted in their obstruction.[73] Lamont, though doubtful that Morgans could be dispensed with, found his position impossible to maintain. Leaving aside the endangered profits from this major lending opportunity, such was the importance of implementing the Dawes Plan that the refusal of Morgans to cooperate at this point could spell disaster for the whole of Europe and bring the strongest reactions against the firm. He therefore reduced his conditions to mere recommendations when he spoke with Herriot, and tacitly accepted the conditions adopted by the conference which at any rate placed a British and American veto over Reparation Commission decisions and gave the loan priority over reparation payments.[74] Herriot in turn sought to demonstrate French authority by demanding a year's delay in the final withdrawal of French troops from the Ruhr. Primed by Norman, Snowden angrily intervened and threatened to reveal the Morgan conditions for issuing the loan, which might well have broken up the conference. Apprised of his intentions, Lamont warned Snowden against exposing his firm to charges of obstructing a settlement, and two days later the conference reached a successful conclusion.[75]

The Dawes Plan, if it did not go as far as British authorities wished, was nevertheless a tremendous victory for the internationalist cause. The likelihood of France again endangering Europe's stability over reparations was sharply reduced. Confidence in the German currency was restored, a massive volume of foreign funds – mostly American and British – began to flow in, and economic life quickly returned to normal. Above all, the bankers of London and New York at last seemed able to cooperate effectively in the promotion of European financial reconstruction. There was, however, an ominous aspect to this calling in of the New World to redress the balance of the Old.

During the Dawes negotiations Norman had sought to persuade the experts to place the new German currency on a sterling basis rather than gold, but failed to convince them that this was not a sacrifice in stability.[76] As a result, a situation was created where Britain's two great commercial rivals, the United States and Germany, would henceforth enjoy the benefit of fixed currencies denominated in gold while sterling fluctuated uncertainly on the exchanges. American foreign lending had greatly increased since the war. So far, most of it had gone to Latin America rather than Europe on account of continuing political and economic uncertainties. But with gold reserves of $4.2 billion – six times those of the Bank of England and nearly half the world's total monetary gold[77] – the United States was in a position to finance the rapid revival of German industry and trade. The prospect therefore arose that the expanding volume of international commerce made possible by the Dawes Plan would be transacted largely in dollars and marks rather than sterling, and bypass London altogether. A year earlier Norman and his closest advisers had been prepared to recommend that the Act of 1919 suspending the gold standard, which was due to expire at the end of 1925, should be extended to 1930.[78] Strong, visiting the Bank of England in April 1924, however, found senior directors in a state of 'consternation' at the thought of lagging behind Germany in currency stabilisation.[79]

Within the fortress-like edifice on Threadneedle Street only three men now participated to any degree in decision-making: Lord Revelstoke, the senior partner in Baring Brothers, Sir Charles Addis, and Norman. Indeed, only Addis and Norman were regularly involved, and relations between them were strained.[80] Addis, the son of a prominent Edinburgh Free Church minister and himself the father of thirteen children, had more than a touch of the patriarch in his manner. Sixty-four years old in 1924, he was ten years older than Norman and reluctant to accept the leadership of his less experienced colleague. One source of worry for Addis was the publicity being given to proposals by Keynes, E.M.H. Lloyd, and others for monetary experiments, such as abandonment of the effort to return to the gold standard in favour of managing the currency on the basis of a composite price index. This seemed to him dangerous talk, especially with Labour in office, and threatened to undermine permanently the City's place in world finance.[81] He was also increasingly anxious about the penetration of American finance into Empire markets and the likelihood that the Dawes Plan would increase American financial influence overseas.[82] Addis was one of the few men to whom Norman was prepared to listen, and he in turn found Norman captivating. But he was losing patience with Norman, who was too capricious for his methodical mind and far too cautious about measures to 'make the pound look the dollar in the face'.[83]

Addis, it seems, underestimated Norman's determination. Though Norman was too keenly alive to the need for friendly relations with the

United States to betray hostility in public, he fully shared Addis's apprehension at the speed with which New York had overtaken London as a capital market and his resentment at the way America managed to profit from Britain's difficulties. As he confided to his mother not long after the Dawes Plan came into effect:

> The only powerful agency [in Germany] is the Dawes machine which dominates German life; and the Dawes machine, while nominally and in form international, is in practice dominated by Americans. This suits me well as all these Americans are my friends, but its effects may be far-reaching. ... England is part of Europe: Europe has quarrelled: Europe has thus reached poverty and so far has kept dis-union alive within her: America is detached and has thus become rich. So Europe is the 'promised land' to America: to be possessed without even competition.[84]

He had tried and failed to have the new German currency linked to the pound rather than the dollar (via gold). Now when he wanted to place a large tranche of the Dawes loan in London, he found that a boom in new overseas issues was making this difficult. The one consolation was that a recession in the United States had begun to ease American interest rates, which tended to strengthen the pound.[85] Norman was as anxious as Addis to augment this effect, but with one eye on the Labour government and the other on the still unhealthy trade returns he rejected Addis's repeated calls for a Bank rate rise in favour of a more subtle approach. On 9 April, the day the Dawes Plan was published, he quietly reimposed a complete embargo on foreign lending, save only for League-sponsored reconstruction loans, as a means of strengthening sterling.[86] And on 16 April he took up the suggestion which Snowden, likely at his prompting, had publicly hinted at a few weeks earlier, of an inquiry into the question of amalgamating the wartime Treasury note issue with the Bank note issue, a step the Cunliffe Committee had called for *after* the return to gold.[87]

All this was welcome news to Strong. Like Norman, he regarded the gold standard as the first essential of a stable world trade and payments system. Like other American central bankers, he was also worried about the steady build-up of American monetary gold stocks. So far it had been possible to 'sterilise' excess imports by exchanging them for gold certificates, but this had reduced the interest earning assets of the Reserve Banks and the day was approaching when, unless something was done, there would be no means of stopping gold imports from creating inflation. He therefore had strong reasons for hastening Britain's return to gold, and in order to nudge sterling back to par he began efforts to close the gap between British and American prices. The New York discount rate was reduced a half point to 4 per cent on 1 May, to 3½ per cent on 12 June, and to 3 per cent on 8 August. The Federal Reserve Open Market Committee increased its assets.[88] And in May the Advisory Council of the Federal Reserve System published a sensational report affirming that the re-establishment of Germany on a gold bullion rather than a gold exchange basis would favour American trade and finance while undercutting the position of the City.[89]

Sceptically Keynes wrote that as Germany, after hyper-inflation, was certain to be a net borrower and likely to have precarious exchanges for the foreseeable future, the chances of it being a competitor of the City rather than merely a customer were practically nil. Hence, 'British industry may have reason to fear a flood of "reparation" exports. It is ludicrous for the City to tremble at the prospect of a stable gold mark.'[90] But there was more to it than that. The City was less concerned with direct German financial competition than with the establishment of German–American commercial links that by-passed London and reduced its entrepôt role. Immediately, the talk on Lombard Street was of monetary action to restore the pound to gold, and on 19 June Dr Walter Leaf, chairman of the Westminster Bank, issued a stern warning against further delay.

Hopes that modest inflation in the United States would be enough to lift the pound back to parity were, Leaf declared, a chimera and must be cast aside once and for all. The United States, as the Advisory Council's report affirmed, had no intention of letting its gold stocks get out of hand. Rather, they would use the gold to restore Germany, making her an even greater commercial rival than she had been before the war. Britain thus faced the awful prospect of:

> a combination between the dollar and the gold mark, between the credit resources of the United States on the one hand and German enterprise on the other ... a prospect which cannot be regarded without anxiety, so long as the pound is depreciated in the exchange markets of the world. To put it plainly, the depreciated pound would be squeezed out of world finance between the two great gold currencies, the dollar and the mark.[91]

He therefore urged an immediate 1 per cent rise in Bank rate.

Leaf, a noted classicist and elder statesman of the City, was not given to hasty judgments or sensationalism. But on this occasion, as he privately acknowledged, his aim was 'frightening the City'.[92] Sir Charles Addis and Sir Robert Kindersley echoed his call for dear money.[93] Brand now also accepted that Britain must return to gold whatever the cost to industry and employment. Arthur Kiddy of *The Bankers' Magazine* and *Morning Post* commented that Leaf's warning had come at precisely 'the psychological moment', and would no doubt be heeded by the appropriate authorities.[94] Courtney Mill of *The Times* also welcomed Leaf's intervention, adding that 'a number of thoughtful observers' had been thinking along the same lines for some time.[95] Kiddy's and Mill's knowing remarks were only too well-founded. Norman had in fact gone over Leaf's statement before publication and given it his full approval.[96] A letter from a 'well-known merchant' a few days later, asking if the damage to industry and employment prospects did not rule out an early return to gold, afforded Mill the occasion for a lengthy editorial which also bore all the marks of official inspiration.

Merchants, Mill complained – and it was clear that he meant not merchants but manufacturers – took only the short view, allowing their judgment to be influenced by 'the temporary disturbance of trade which a 10 per cent fall of prices would cause'. He deemed this insignificant compared to the great and permanent advantages of a lower price level and exchange stability. 'Merchants' favoured rising prices, whereas what was needed to restore prosperity were steadily *falling* prices. This was the true sign of large and increasing output; if proof were needed, one had only to look at Britain's experience during the second half of the nineteenth century when declining prices had been accompanied by rising wages and profits and unprecedented prosperity. As it was, Mill continued, the present level of the pound was disappointing. After the political uncertainties of the previous year the normal spring advance had been expected to send sterling high enough to ensure that it did not slip below $4.40 during the usual late summer and autumn period of demand for dollars to pay for cotton and other seasonal crops; but even now it was only $4.33. A higher Bank rate could therefore be expected soon. Employing one of the City's favourite metaphors, he explained: 'A rise in Bank rate acts like a medicine on the economic organism. Its purging effects may be unpleasant for the patient, but the purging is none the less necessary to bring the patient back to health.' If a 1 per cent rise brought sterling back to par, it would be 'very cheap at the price'. But if for any reason American prices stopped rising, 'we should have to face the fact boldly', and accept the need for stronger medicine.[97]

Earlier in the year several clearing bankers, with loan portfolios loaded with bad debt to industry, had expressed caution about active measures to restore sterling to gold.[98] Now Leaf's proposal caused a few other warning voices to be heard in the City. *The Economist* and *The Statist* reminded readers of the volatility of American price-levels and the dangers of pegging the pound without the assurance of American cooperation to minimise price fluctuations.[99] But the basic division of opinion lay not through the City but between the City and industry; and as pressure mounted for an early return the division became steadily more acute.

New opponents of deflation

Signs that the political left would not resign itself indefinitely to the view that relief of Britain's poverty and unemployment must await the pacification of Europe had begun to appear in the autumn of 1923 when the ILP formed a committee to examine problems of nationalising the banking system and operating it on socialist principles.[100] The committee, interrupted during the general election, was still working in June 1924 when the ILP petitioned the government for immediate action to stimulate the economy. The ILP submission laid principal emphasis on increased purchasing power through minimum wage legislation. Other recommendations included ratification of the Washington Convention on the eight-hour working day, aid to the Soviet Union, public investment in infrastructure development, and a fresh inquiry into the bearing of monetary policy on unemployment, trades cycles, and wage fluctuations, 'with a view to facilitating credits for industrial purposes and carrying through a policy of monetary stabilisation' – stabilisation, that is, of purchasing power and price-levels, not exchange rates.[101] The inspiration for the ILP petition came largely from H.N. Brailsford, editor of the London-based *New Leader*, and Tom Johnston MP, editor of the Glasgow-based *Forward*, who for some time had been striving to awaken readers to the fundamental importance of monetary policy.

In other contexts the two journals sweepingly condemned the capitalist system, but when it came to the question of gold they drew a clear distinction between industrial and finance capital. The former they associated with the workers' and national interest, the latter with a diametrically opposed cosmopolitan class. As they described it, the deflationary policy begun in 1920 was a bankers' ramp, designed to effect a vast transfer of wealth from the productive elements of society to the parasitic rentier class: 'one of the most colossal acts of robbery in British history'.[102] 'The manufacturers and the working classes get hit; the financiers do well.'[103] Johnston, betraying a frankly populist attitude and undisguised sympathy for the Empire, included the charge that the financiers were prepared to use the savings of British people to finance foreign competitors while starving the Empire of funds, and he was not above anti-semitic innuendo about their 'un-English' names.[104] Brailsford, too, could not resist some personalising of the issues and the drawing of a distinction between oppression by 'a native banking autocracy [and] the despotism of foreign bankers'. For the most part, however, his more mature journalism focussed upon the way deliberate monetary decisions, 'and not the working of obscure economic laws', contributed to Britain's mass unemployment.[105] Borrowing where useful, he included in the issue of 20 June an article by Keynes, 'Fear and the Business Man', on the damaging effect of falling prices on business confidence and the capacity of the central bank to control them. Two weeks later, amidst the stir created by Walter Leaf's declaration, he raised his own voice above 'the clamour of the City' to assert, without conviction, that it was 'unthinkable' for a Labour government to halt the economic recovery at last underway and create another slump simply in order to boost the pound.[106]

G.D.H. Cole, the Oxford don, was another left-wing critic of the gold standard. His contributions appeared regularly in the *New Statesman*, although one of his most widely quoted pieces appeared on 12 June in the high Tory *Morning Post*, where he caricatured the bankers and their Treasury acolytes as religious fanatics, ready to sacrifice industry on the altar of the 'great god called "Par"'.

Cole's article, followed the next day by a rebuttal from the veteran financial journalist Hartley Withers, highlighted the ambivalent outlook of the *Morning Post* towards a commitment to the gold standard, which was perhaps politically desirable but dangerously internationalist. The *Daily Mail* displayed a similar ambivalence, with the City editor, Harold Cox, urging the return to specie payment, while the leader pages thundered against another part of internationalist strategy, the Dawes Plan, for assisting the recovery of Germany, Britain's former enemy. Neither paper, however, gave prominence to the monetary question at this time. It was left for St Loe Strachey's *Spectator* and Leo Maxse's monthly *National Review* to put the radical right case against gold.

Strachey, once a Liberal, was still a free trader; Maxse had been a tariff reformer for thirty years. The *Spectator* appealed to an enlightened Conservative readership, the *National Review* to a much more deep-dyed backwoods variety. Yet both agreed that returning to gold would be criminal folly. The result would be to place Britain completely at the mercy of the United States, a power which displayed neither friendliness towards Britain nor the responsibility required for leadership of the international monetary system. Worse, it would add to industry's burdens, with the unemployment and unrest created playing directly into the hands of the Socialists and the Communists.

This was the warning they repeated in issue after issue, and Maxse, 'that lunatic Leo', as even friends called him, became caught up in the issue to the exclusion of almost everything else.[107] Before the war he had dwelt endlessly on the German threat; afterwards he remained anti-

German but substituted the United States as the most sinister threat to the Empire, and treated the gold standard question as a conspiracy to enslave Britain by the Jews of the City along with their German-Jewish confederates in New York.[108] Far-fetched as it was, the arrogance and carefully cultivated mystique of high finance invited this sort of black speculation. Moreover, to many on the right, Britain's postwar experience, including the 'sacrifice' of its farms and industries, the 'concession' of naval parity to the United States at the 1922 Washington Conference, the war debt settlement with the American 'Shylocks', and the Dawes Plan which promised a revival of German competition, required some explanation such as this. Maxse, though endlessly repetitive, wrote with the spiritedness of an angry man. And as Lord Milner's brother-in-law and a Vice-President of the London Conservative Association, he was taken seriously by a substantial fraction of the right.

One of the regular contributors to the *National Review* and one of the most anti-semitic was Arthur Kitson. An inventor of genius, he had worked for some years with Alexander Graham Bell in Philadelphia before the turn of the century. There he had met William Jennings Bryan, then crusading against the 'money-power' on a bimetallist platform. Converted to the cause, Kitson campaigned actively for him. Later he returned to England where he devoted an increasing part of his time and considerable fortune to currency reform.[109] His extreme anti-semitism almost certainly derived from Henry Ford, a hero to many British manufacturers of the day, whose newspaper the *Dearborn Independent* mounted a sustained campaign against 'Jewish finance' after the war.[110] Kitson himself was just one of dozens of 'currency cranks' agitating against the gold standard policy, and it seems doubtful that he helped his case by encapsulating basically reasonable criticism in an extreme conspiratorial view of the policy-making process.[111] Yet as owner of a successful engineering firm in Birmingham he attracted a modest following, particularly among members of the NUM, whose journal published his articles.[112]

Elsewhere signs of discontent among the 'producing classes' were also appearing. Several farming experts including the Ministry officials, E.E. Enfield and Sir Daniel Hall, had begun to awaken agrarian radicalism by explaining the current slump in prices in the context of monetary history.[113] Enfield, whose book on *The Agricultural Crisis* appeared in March 1924, accepted that a currency policy designed to stabilise price-levels was 'not yet near to being a political question in this country'. Probably this was so. The monetary issue had lain dormant too long to be revived easily, but it was not for want of trying. From January, the *Co-ordinator*, official organ of the Agricultural and Industrial Union, gave over its monthly issues wholly to the ominous consequences of the gold standard and the need to set it aside in favour of a managed currency linked to the price of wheat. Members of the Agricultural and Industrial Union were, it seems, usually members of the larger Central and Associated Chambers of Agriculture. Some indication of the popularity of their views was given at the quarterly meeting of the Central Chamber on 4 March 1924, when Charles Dampier Whetham, a landowner and former Cambridge don, received strong support for a resolution calling on the government to institute a new inquiry 'on which the interests of manufacture, agriculture and labour, as well as finance, are represented, to continue the consideration of monetary policy where it was left by the reports of Lord Cunliffe's Committee in 1918 and 1919'.[114]

At the meeting of the FBI Grand Council on 9 July Col. Armstrong drew attention to Leaf's call for an immediate Bank rate rise. Most members present agreed that the Governor of the Bank of England must be warned in the strongest terms against precipitate action.[115] Publication of the FBI's letter prompted the Association of British Chambers of Commerce to assure the Governor of its unconditional support and to deprecate attempts by outside bodies to influence the Bank's policy since 'such bodies cannot know the whole facts and necessities which are known to the members of your Court'.[116] The FBI considered responding to this implied criticism, decided against, and settled for a memorandum to the Governor restating their objections to the policy of deflating the economy for the sake of an early return to gold.[117]

If these warnings were heard within the Cabinet, there was no sign of it. The only member demonstrably alive to the issue was Snowden, and he only just restrained himself from endorsing the City view. Asked in Parliament by Tom Johnston if he realised that acceptance of Leaf's advice meant a renewed fall in price-levels and higher unemployment, Snowden replied evasively that opinions differed on the matter. However, he affirmed the government's commitment to the Cunliffe Committee's Report, and indicated that he would be guided by the Bank of England and his own Treasury advisers.[118]

The Treasury knights were not unaware of the price to be paid for returning to the pre-war gold parity by deflationary methods. Hawtrey, commenting on Leaf's proposal, pointed out to Niemeyer that it would 'produce another acute and serious unemployment crisis'. But he did not regard this as sufficient reason for holding back. More important was the maintenance of London as the financial capital of the world, 'for mercantile business tends to be transacted at the centres from which it is financed. The greatest factor in the material prosperity of this country is not manufacturing, important as that is, but *commerce*. The diversion of commerce to other centres is the severest loss to which we could be exposed'.[119] Senior Treasury officials had been shaken by the implications of the Dawes Plan for the future of sterling. They therefore wasted no time following up Norman's proposal for a committee to advise on the amalgamation of the two currency note issues.

The Chamberlain/Bradbury committee

The committee, known after its successive chairmen as the Chamberlain/Bradbury Committee, remains interesting more as an illustration of interest group influence than as a disinterested survey of informed opinion. Constituted almost precisely as Norman had recommended to Niemeyer,[120] four of the five members had been associated with the Cunliffe Committee: Lord Bradbury, Gaspard Farrer (a Baring Brothers partner), and Professor Pigou, who had been members of the earlier committee, and Austen Chamberlain who as Chancellor of the Exchequer had endorsed the committee's report. The fifth member was Niemeyer himself. At the first meeting on 27 June 1924, Chamberlain acknowledged that the question of note amalgamation was inseparable from the question of returning to gold and that Snowden would probably wish to have the committee's view on the latter question.[121] Norman and Addis, as the first witnesses, were present during these preliminary discussions, and thus had the advantage of knowing what was on their questioners' minds. But as neither Snowden nor Chamberlain was willing to advertise his interest in the resumption of specie payment while the Labour Party held office, the other witnesses were left to guess the committee's broader object and thus were ill-prepared to defend the interests they represented.[122]

The singlemindedness of the central bank spokesmen put them in an especially strong position. Norman, speaking first, left no doubt that he would do everything possible to bring an early resumption of specie payment. Three months earlier, he explained, he would not have thought it a realistic proposition; it was now 'a practical one'. Evidently he did not mean the pound was stronger or the British economy better able to stand the strain of supporting the principal currency of world trade and finance. Indeed, he admitted he was disturbed by the weakness of the pound. Rather he meant simply that London's position as a financial centre was being jeopardised by the strength of the dollar and the movement of Europe back to gold that he himself had encouraged. Unless something was done, the German mark might become within a few years 'a far more popular currency than the British pound'. Norman indicated that some of his fellow directors were nervous about returning to the gold standard amidst present international uncertainties. He also acknowledged in oblique fashion that industry was bound to resent the difficulties of adjusting to a 10 per cent rise in the exchange rate and the inevitable 'long period of dear money' that would follow resumption. To minimise industry's objection he recommended that the government should announce a 'fixed and immutable date' for returning to gold sometime well in the future, perhaps three years hence. This would be 'extremely valuable camouflage and appear far more reasonable than to fix a short date', for it would make the adjustment problem seem less acute, although in all likelihood the certainty of eventual resumption would immediately carry the pound to par and keep it there. Asked about the impact on industry, he encouraged hope that inflation in America would cut the adjustment in half. But later, to underline the need for decisive action, he advised the committee not to look for salvation through a rise in American prices, since the Federal Reserve authorities had the situation completely under control.[123] The zeal that led him to strike such contradictory notes was equally apparent when Addis took the stand.

Recent weeks had seen 'a remarkable change in public opinion, I mean in City opinion, with regard to the resumption of the gold standard', Addis affirmed. Nor, in his opinion, was it before time. Until recent years sterling had maintained its world role because, even with the cost of forward transactions to insure against exchange loss, it was cheaper to operate through the London market. However, in trade finance, 'a sixth per cent will go a long way before national sympathy'. As head of the Hong Kong and Shanghai Bank, he had 'grave misgivings' at the way Far Eastern trade with the United States, hitherto financed chiefly in sterling, was now financed almost wholly through 'gold dollar credits'. His bank alone was having to divert some $50 million a month in business. And, he warned, once traders got into the habit of dealing in dollars it became very difficult to persuade them to switch back to sterling. As a result, the banks involved had no choice but to transfer more of their acceptance and discounting business to New York.

Asked point-blank if Britain's own trade was affected by the developments he described, Addis replied, 'I don't think very much. I think the difficulty really is connected with London and its financial interests, the loss of commissions of various kinds. I should doubt if it affects very much the volume of trade.' Yet in explaining the 'sacrifices' required to get back to gold, he shifted his ground. Like Norman, he played down the difficulties for industry, pointing to the probability of rising

American prices, the readiness of much of the world to follow Britain's lead, and the likelihood of central bankers implementing the Genoa resolutions to prevent undue fluctuations in the purchasing power of gold. In any case, he added, echoing Courtney Mill's words, falling prices were good for the economy, as the latter part of the last century had shown, and far more conducive to social harmony than inflation. Even if Britain had to shoulder the full 10 per cent adjustment alone, 'I think it would not be too high a price to pay for the substantial benefit to the trade of this country and its working classes, and also, although I put it last, for the recovery of the City of London of its former position as the world's financial engine.'[124]

Industry failed to put its case across with anything like the same determination. Sir Felix Schuster, who appeared before the committee on 3 July on behalf of the Association of British Chambers of Commerce, claimed to be a spokesman for industry. Chairman of merchant bankers Schuster, Son & Company, he had been one of the first to call for immediate steps to restore a free market in gold after the appearance of the Dawes Report.[125] Now, in face of pointed questioning from the chairman, he insisted that in advocating resumption he represented not only financial and mercantile elements of the Chambers but also the nearly 50,000 manufacturing and trading members. Chamberlain seemed impressed.[126] But in fact Schuster had been asked to appear for the association by its president, Stanley Machin, and the chairman of its financial committee, Sir James Martin, both of whom were, like him, leading figures in the City and members of the Council of the Corporation of Foreign Bondholders.[127]

The FBI, the only industrial body to give evidence, had sought a preliminary interview with Chamberlain to find out more precisely what the committee were aiming at.[128] Chamberlain's response was so 'vague and unhelpful' that the idea of an interview was dropped.[129] But industrialists were fairly sure the question of returning to gold would be raised, although they were given to understand that returning at a devalued parity was 'not a matter which either the Treasury or the Bank of England were ... prepared to consider'.[130] They were also made distinctly uncomfortable by the hostility and derision with which City editors like Mill, Cox, and Kiddy treated their response to Leaf's advocacy of a higher Bank rate.[131] Anxious to be represented by someone who spoke the language of high finance, they therefore called on Hugh Chisholm, a former City editor of *The Times*, who was helping them prepare a separate brief on taxation policy. It proved an unfortunate choice. Appearing before the committee on 30 July, Chisholm summarised the arguments against precipitate action set out in an FBI brief submitted the previous day. But he minimised the differences between finance and industry, and at one point the chairman led him to say that industry's chief concern was stability of exchanges rather than prices.[132] It was left to McKenna and Keynes to make out a strong case against unilateral efforts to restore sterling to gold.

McKenna, the Chancellor of the Exchequer at the outbreak of war, had left politics after the break-up of the Asquith government in 1916 to become a director and in 1919 chairman of the Midland Bank. Immediately after the war he began to speak out against a deflationary monetary policy, arguing that this aggravated the problems created for industry by government extravagance.[133] Perhaps it was significant that he was Irish-born and a relative newcomer to the City. Perhaps joining the Midland Bank was also significant, for not only was it on the way to becoming the largest of the joint-stock banks but it was also the only one to eschew foreign or colonial affiliates in order to concentrate on domestic business. McKenna's predecessor, Sir Edward Holden, the former managing director, J.F. Darling, and Lord Milner, a director, were all prominent imperialists. In the early 1920s the Midland was not only the largest clearing bank in Britain, but arguably the largest bank in the world. The severe postwar slump by this time had confirmed the accuracy of McKenna's warnings and encouraged him to continue speaking out. Always a politician and always a showman, he wasted no time during his appearance before the committee in challenging the arguments of the City's international bankers.

The idea of deflating the economy to restore the exchanges when there were already over a million unemployed, McKenna described as: 'A pure dream ... absolutely out of the question ... perfectly absurd'. The Chancellor could cause 'infinite trouble, cause unlimited unemployment, immense loss and ruin, but he could not balance his budget while he was doing it, and he would have to borrow. Before he got our price level down 10 per cent he would be borrowing again because his revenue would not be coming in. He would be having to inflate before he got there'. Fears of sterling being supplanted by the dollar and gold mark seemed equally absurd. In the first place, the Dawes Plan linked the mark only nominally to gold: there could be no free gold market in Germany. Second, the attraction of the sterling bill derived from the size and cheapness of the London money market, not the behaviour of the exchange rate. Third, linking the mark to gold made it and the dollar, not sterling, the unstable currencies, because of the dangerous surplus of gold production. He was certain that the Americans were doing everything possible to induce Britain to return to gold so she would share the cost of sterilising surplus gold stocks and avert uncontrollable inflation. Hence, he told the committee, the obvious policy for Britain was to sit tight, wait for the Americans to 'make terms' – such as forgiving British war debts – allow the inevitable inflation in the United States to close the gap between their respective price levels, and meanwhile manage sterling solely with regard to domestic economic stability.[134] Keynes, who appeared before the committee the next day, was equally emphatic about the likelihood of American inflation and the need to sit tight.[135]

Bradbury was sufficiently impressed by the hope McKenna and Keynes held out of regaining parity 'within a very few months' without the necessity of deflationary measures to recommend this approach to his colleagues.[136] But if the committee were prepared to await American developments, Norman was not. The Federal Reserve, facing the onset of recession and anxious to avoid a repeat of the postwar depression, was already engaged in its first attempt at a deliberate easy money policy. Norman once more resisted repeated pleadings from Addis and City pundits to exploit this development and widen the gap in interest rates by raising his own Bank rate. But in a less publicised though almost equally effective move, he raised the cost of discounting bills nearly 1 per cent in July by tightening market rates.[137] The summer and autumn were normally a time of weakness for sterling, the banks were lending heavily to Germany, and the trade balance was steadily deteriorating. Yet with interest rates falling in New York and rising in London, sterling rose on the exchanges from $4.30 to 4.40 by late July. Thereafter other factors conspired to strengthen sterling. In August the London conference removed the political obstacles in the way of the Dawes Plan; six weeks later the £80 million Dawes loan was successfully issued, largely to American investors. Meantime bad harvests in Europe had begun to firm up agricultural prices and increase the earnings of the outer sterling-area countries. With American authorities anxious to finance the export of their own surplus farm production and renewed investor confidence in Europe, dollar lending also sharply increased, with a sizeable fraction of funds going temporarily into sterling securities in the expectation of an early return to gold. So strong was the upward momentum caused by these factors that even the renewed uncertainty of a general election merely slowed down the rise of the pound.[138]

At the annual Labour Party conference on 9 October, H.N. Brailsford, in the face of stony silence from Snowden and members of the National Executive, secured the passage of a resolution calling on the government to take up the monetary question and nationalise the Bank of England.[139] Immediately Lord Bearsted, Lieut.-Commander E. Hilton Young, Kiddy, and other voices from the City evoked images of Britain going the way of Russia under the Bolsheviks, her social order undermined by the debasement of the currency.[140] Already the political temperature had sharply risen that autumn amidst controversy over the government's indecisive treatment of J.R. Campbell, the editor of the Communist *Workers' Weekly*, whose arrest for incitement to mutiny ended with the charges being dropped. MacDonald's resignation over the affair brought the dissolution of Parliament and three weeks of electioneering in which the right-wing press made constant reference to the Campbell case, the recent granting of diplomatic recognition to the Soviet Union, and other issues designed to associate Labour in the public's mind with Communism. The campaign culminated three days before the election with the 'Zinoviev letter' in the *Daily Mail*. The letter, obviously a forgery and possibly furnished by the secret service, was a statement of directives for revolutionary agitation from the head of the Moscow International to the Central Committee of the British Communist Party, which the *Daily Mail* presented in the most sensational manner. Despite the scare tactics, sterling stood at $4.40 on 28 October, the eve of the polls. The following day the Conservatives won a sweeping 208 seat majority. With the threat of socialism thus removed and the assurance of a government sympathetic to the interests of the saving and investing classes, sterling rapidly rose towards par.

The gold standard restored

From New York, Strong had been pressing Norman since the spring to do more than merely rely upon the interest rate differential between London and New York to improve the sterling rate. On 4 November 1924 he wrote to Norman again. Besides enumerating the enhanced conditions for resumption, he now warned that inflation might soon force him to end cheap money in his market; thus Norman's only hope of regaining parity was by *force majeure*.[141] Norman needed no encouragement. Baldwin and the new Chancellor of the Exchequer, Winston Churchill, were sympathetic to an early resumption.[142] Therefore on 21 December, travelling in the name of his secretary Skinner, he sailed for New York on the *Caronia* with Sir Alan Anderson, the incumbent Deputy-Governor of the Bank, to discuss arrangements for the transition to gold with Strong and his American associates.

Arriving on 28 December, the British bankers spent the next week in the company of Strong and senior partners of J.P. Morgan & Co. The American bankers stressed the benefits Britain could expect from returning to the gold standard, although Strong also pointed to the factors that made such a commitment 'a real hazard'. Recent American foreign lending had been 'unusual – much the largest ever known', and could not be expected to continue at that level, Strong explained. Further, American claims on Europe would soon require annual repayments of at least $600 million, which would put further pressure on the European exchanges. There was also the problem of speculative price movements at home. The United States was a young country and financially a volatile one, whose monetary policy was bound to be geared primarily to domestic conditions. The most he could promise was that there would be 'no deliberate policy of deflation'. Britain should return, Russell Leffingwell of Morgans added, if, but only if, it was prepared to use Bank rate to defend its exchanges. Norman, however, was less concerned about the dangers of returning than of not returning: the encouragement this would give to the monetary radicals in Britain, and the resulting damage to sterling and the City. Strong's warnings only served to convince him of the need to act quickly, while suitable conditions lasted. He was satisfied to come away with the promise of a $200 million line of credit from the Federal Reserve Bank and a further $300 million from Morgans.[143]

In London it was Addis's turn to draw back from immediate action. The previous autumn he had become exasperated by Norman's refusal irrevocably to commit himself to an early resumption. Now alive to the dangers of relying upon American credits to maintain a free gold market, he spoke out in the Bank's Committee of Treasury against resumption until the pound had actually reached par and been held there for some time as a test of its solidity.[144] Finding that Revelstoke and Cecil Lubbock, the Deputy-Governor, shared his misgivings and that only Kindersley was confident about proceeding, he cabled a warning to Norman. 'The restoration of the Gold Standard should follow and not precede the conditions of trade appropriate to the maintenance of a stable exchange.'[145] Niemeyer now also felt misgivings at the degree to which Norman was prepared to make Britain beholden to America in order to get back to gold.[146] But Norman was not to be deterred. Press reports of his secret trip had encouraged the belief that action was imminent. Sterling, despite its underlying weakness, was trading near par. The City was enthusiastic. The only serious obstacle seemed to be the Chancellor, who belatedly had begun to have second thoughts.

Baldwin, casting about for someone to fill the Chancellorship the previous autumn, had tentatively selected Sir Robert Horne. But Horne, serving briefly as Chancellor in the Bonar Law government, had offended financial opinion by suspending the sinking fund and becoming the first Chancellor in modern times to introduce a protective duty in peacetime. Besides being a leader of the industrial group in the House of Commons, he had also displayed a critical attitude towards the gold standard in evidence to the Chamberlain/Bradbury Committee. Baldwin soon learned that the City would not welcome his reappointment and hastily abandoned the idea.[147] Looking elsewhere, he settled on Churchill.

The reasons for Baldwin's choice are not altogether clear. Having broken with the Conservatives over Tariff Reform in 1903, Churchill had only rejoined the party in 1923, which left many right-wing members resentful at his disloyalty and suspicious that he still hankered after a coalition with the Lloyd George Liberals. Perhaps Baldwin, thinking exclusively in political terms, decided it was safer to have Churchill inside the government than on the back benches, and worth offering him a senior post if it would bind him more firmly to the party.[148] Churchill had no direct experience in finance, which led senior officials at the Treasury and the Bank initially to imagine that he could easily be led.[149] They overlooked the fact that he had long experience of Whitehall's methods, and as co-author of the social reforms in the Asquith government and later as First Lord of the Admiralty he needed little reminding of the way the Treasury could dominate policy-making if not firmly resisted. Nor did they reckon on his acquaintance with two of the leading mavericks of the City.

One was the banker McKenna, Churchill's colleague in the Asquith Cabinet. On 27 January 1925 McKenna devoted his annual shareholders' address to the respective merits of a managed currency and a return to the gold standard, concluding in favour of the latter. This was surprising in light of the position he had taken before the Chamberlain-Bradbury Committee only six months before. But his argument now rested not on economic but political grounds, namely the discipline the gold standard imposed on governments and the confidence it inspired in the currency at home and abroad. 'So long as nine people out of ten in every country think the gold standard is the best, it is the best.'[150] Churchill found this 'a deliberately weak defence of the Gold policy', and on making inquiries learned that McKenna was still 'personally opposed to the Gold policy and regards it as unnecessary and unwise'.[151]

The other maverick was Lord Beaverbrook, whom Churchill had known well since before the war. A Canadian by birth, Beaverbrook had made a fortune in company promotion before coming to England in 1910 and entering Parliament as a Unionist the same year. He was a financier with close connections in the City. But he was a financier in the

American mould rather than the British, whose wealth derived from financing industry rather than from money market dealings, portfolio management, or acceptance business, and retaining the optimistic spirit of his native country his instinct was for economic policies aimed at growth rather than stability. Even before taking up residence in London he had been a passionate supporter of imperial unity, which, being a Canadian, connoted a certain *méfiance* towards the United States whose influence threatened constantly to envelop its smaller neighbour to the north. He was also a journalist, adept at presenting issues simply and boldly, and in 1925 owner of three London papers, the mass circulation *Daily Express* and *Sunday Express*, and the *Evening Standard*, the paper of the well-to-do commuter. Besides, he was a natural rebel who despite his wealth and title had always preferred to stand slightly outside the establishment, defending its interests while criticising its ways.[152]

Towards the end of January Beaverbrook met Churchill in the company of Niemeyer to outline the dangers of returning to gold in the present circumstances. To his fury, Niemeyer offhandedly dismissed his arguments.[153] The result was that on 28 January the *Daily Express* devoted its front page to an attack on the Treasury policy 'to favour City finance and the boosting of the pound up to the dollar level to the detriment of all the producing and selling classes', and singled out Niemeyer by name for special criticism.[154] The following day Churchill circulated to advisers a memorandum which, although described as 'largely ... an exercise', set out the dangers that Beaverbrook had in mind.

The gold standard question, Churchill wrote, could not be treated simply as a matter of concern to finance. 'The merchant, the manufacturer, the workman and the consumer have interests which, though largely common, do not by any means coincide either with each other or with the financial and currency interests.' If on returning to gold weakness on the exchanges forced up Bank rate, the effect on industry and employment would be 'very serious' and the Chancellor would face the brunt of the criticism. Was this not a good reason for hanging back, at least for another year? Churchill also noted that the United States seemed all too anxious to help Britain to return to gold, and asked if this was not a compelling reason for hesitating before embarking on such a venture. Beaverbrook laid particular emphasis on the danger of 'placing Britain under the heels of American finance', and Churchill, also a fervent imperialist, expressed deep misgivings about American motives.[155]

Niemeyer and Norman, in separate memoranda, vigorously countered Churchill's objections. Niemeyer, despite evidence to the contrary,[156] insisted that Britain's imperial interests demanded that she act now, if the Dominions were not to act without her and shift permanently into America's orbit. Norman advised the Chancellor to disregard industrial criticism. 'In connection with a golden 1925, the merchant, manufacturer, worker, etc., should be considered (but not consulted any more than about the design of battleships).' Strong's warnings notwithstanding, they encouraged hopes of American price stability and continuing high levels of foreign lending. Both advisers also stressed the desirability of reimposing the discipline of the gold standard now, while Britain and the United States had 'stable' non-socialist governments.[157]

On 12 February Churchill publicly affirmed his support for an early resumption,[158] but still he wavered. After listening to further warnings from the clearing banker F.C. Goodenough, who favoured gold but doubted that conditions justified early action, and from Beaverbrook and Keynes,[159] Churchill confronted Niemeyer again. Accusing him of failing to face up to what Keynes called 'the paradox of unemployment amidst dearth', Churchill bluntly suggested that adherence to Bank and Treasury advice had already resulted in a million and a quarter unemployed and seemed certain to lead to more.[160] Niemeyer stood the argument on its head, claiming that returning to gold was essential to the revival of industrial employment and pointing to evidence of industrial support for this policy – including the Report of the Committee on Financial Facilities, which was composed 'not primarily of bankers'.[161]

Within days Strong augmented his policy of open market sales by raising the discount rate, a clear signal that American price-levels could be expected to fall.[162] Norman followed suit by raising Bank rate – after New York, not before as Addis wanted – to minimise criticism of the Bank.[163] Criticism nevertheless issued from many quarters including the *Daily Herald*, the *Daily Mail*, the Manchester Association of Importers and Exporters, the NUM, and the FBI. The FBI warned Churchill of the folly of resumption while the currencies of two of Britain's major industrial competitors, Belgium and France, continued on their sharply downward course.[164] How many of these warnings Niemeyer allowed to cross Churchill's desk is not clear; some in any case arrived too late to influence his decision.[165] But even Norman now betrayed some misgivings about resumption, for no sooner did he secure Churchill's commitment than he once more suggested to Strong a central bankers' conference. Once again Strong cold-shouldered the idea: the Federal Reserve Bank was not prepared to enter into any foreign entanglement.[166]

In a last attempt to hear both sides of the question, Churchill arranged a dinner party on 17 March for his senior advisers and critics of an early resumption. Keynes, supported by McKenna, made out the opposition case, arguing that the price-level adjustment required to restore equilibrium was not 2½ per cent as the present exchange rate indicated and proponents of gold claimed, but more like 10 per cent; and therefore very stiff deflation could be expected, bringing more unemployment, labour unrest, and industrial contraction. Lord Bradbury, for one, did not dispute the claim. Instead he recurred to the City's bedrock argument, that 'the Gold Standard was knave-proof. It could not be rigged for political or even more unworthy reasons.' He was frankly reconciled to de-industrialisation.

It was very likely that contractions of the basic industries would have to be faced, but having lost the advantage of the flying start which we gained at the time of the Industrial revolution, we should have to do something of the sort anyhow, and the best future for this country therefore lay in preserving and even developing our international banking, insurance and shipping position, and into turning ourselves more and more into producers of the higher classes of goods in whose manufacture individual skill and workmanship was of greater moment than the employment of large numbers of operatives at repetitive processes – in other words, in those forms of enterprise where the man was more important than the machine.[167]

During the conversation, which continued into the night, McKenna was heard to say: 'There is no escape; you have to go back; but it will be hell.' The contributions of the others present went unrecorded, but they are not hard to guess. For aside from Keynes, all of those present were City or Treasury men.

Churchill was still not altogether persuaded of the soundness of resuming specie payment. The adjustment problem facing industry worried him, and although Norman had been persuaded to reduce his demand for American support credits from $500 million to $300 million, it disturbed him to have to rely on the United States at all.[168] The dinner had nevertheless confirmed his advisers' claim that 'responsible' opinion strongly favoured immediate resumption, and his own political position, as a still not fully accepted member of his party and a free trader in a largely protectionist Cabinet, militated against further resistance. The most he could hope to do was acquiesce in the gold standard while redressing the damage to the 'producing classes' by fiscal concessions. Two days later, over lunch at 11 Downing Street, he advised Norman of his intention to announce an immediate resumption the next month.[169]

At about 4 p.m. on 28 April Churchill announced Britain's return to gold standard at the pre-war parity in a preface to his first budget speech. The producing classes received a sixpence reduction in income tax and a £10 million reduction in supertax; the loss in revenue was to be made up by an increase in estate duty, designed to affect the rentier class. A silk duty, intended as a tax on luxury, was also introduced, and the McKenna Duties, which Snowden had removed, were reimposed in fulfilment of a Conservative election promise.[170]

'The voice of the timid and the critical have been heard, but the welcome given to Mr Churchill's announcement ... has been as nearly unanimous as anything in this country of free speech and thought can be expected to be.' Like almost every other financial journalist, the City editor of *The Observer* was too partisan to be a reliable judge of opinion.[171] Yet in light of reactions in Parliament and the industrial community his comment seemed accurate enough.

The *Daily Herald*, dwelling on the same aspect as conservative papers, announced in front page headlines the morning after the speech, 'Sixpence off Income-Tax: Lower Super-Tax'; the return to gold received only modest treatment on page two. This reflected the fact that the internationalists who dominated Labour Party discussion of financial issues had done practically nothing to anticipate the Chancellor's announcement. Not until the following day did the TUC–Labour Party advisory committee on finance and commerce meet and condemn it.[172] Opposition was also expressed within Labour parliamentary ranks.[173] But Norman in his efforts to minimise criticism had sought out Snowden, and was later able to explain to Strong that Snowden had put on a show of opposition in Parliament merely 'in order to prevent his Party moving a more damaging amendment; in this manner he helped us without substantially breaking with his followers'.[174]

During the second reading debate on the Gold Standard Bill on 4 May, Snowden introduced the opposition amendment condemning the government's 'undue precipitancy'. But he did so with a transparent lack of conviction, acknowledging that the decision was 'inevitable' and stressing his respect for 'those who know most about [this] abstruse, difficult and complex question'. Churchill chided him for his earlier advocacy of returning to gold and accused him of trying to have it both ways.[175] From the government benches a few voices were raised in apprehension at the Chancellor's decision, including those of Sir Frank Nelson, Sir Frederick Wise, Robert Boothby, and Sir Basil Peto.[176] The only outright opponent in the House, however, was Sir Alfred Mond, who insisted that he spoke for the FBI 'and other great groups of industrialists'. But Churchill disputed his claim to speak for industry, and with no one else to support him the Bill was approved without a division.[177]

Mond's lack of support was the result of several factors. In the first place, while respected as the country's leading industrialist, he was not liked by other industrialists on account of his German-Jewish origins and his reputation as a self-seeking and personally ruthless man.[178] Secondly, he was a Liberal whereas the main body of industrialists in Parliament, the so-called 'forty thieves', sat on the government benches.[179] Thirdly and most importantly, they faced a *fait accompli.* As they appreciated, it was one thing to oppose plans for the return to gold, but quite another to call for the decision to be reversed once it had been taken, with the inevitable exchange crisis and loss of national prestige that this would involve. In sum, the industrialists were as displeased with the decision as Labour, indeed rather more so. Their silence was not a token of approval. At most it was a grudging agreement to wait and see the result.

The Economist, congratulating Churchill and Norman, described the decision as a milestone in the history of economic affairs.[180] A contemporary authority has more accurately described it as 'a major historic error'.[181] With real interest rates (that is current interest rates plus price-level decreases or minus price-level increases) at an almost unprecedented 10 per cent for the balance of the decade in defence of an over-valued exchange rate,[182] the consequences were quite as bad as its critics anticipated – not the *mauvais quart d'heure* that Brand hopefully predicted.[183] Although a victory for internationalists, it proved to be a watershed in the history of internationalism itself. Subsequent reactions took many forms, of which dissatisfaction with the gold standard was only one, but all of which reflected an unwillingness to expose the domestic economy to further external pressures. In the struggle between those who regarded the strategic, social, and economic consequences of restoring the gold standard as too serious to contemplate and those who feared more the consequences of *not* returning, the latter had won. But the Bank of England did not gain the commanding influence over domestic economic conditions that proponents assumed was a concomitant of the gold standard. Henceforth it was constrained by the threat of domestic reactions and thus unable to provide decisive leadership at home or abroad. For the mercantile–financial community no less than industry, therefore, the next six years were destined to be a period of almost unrelieved crisis.

3

'Normalcy'

The Conservatives' dilemma

The main challenge confronting the Conservative government from its formation on 7 November 1924 was the heavy unemployment in the depressed export industries. The government commanded no less than 419 out of the 615 seats in the House of Commons; yet it was to prove almost wholly incapable of assisting industry or reducing unemployment, due to divisions within the Cabinet and the country.

Stanley Baldwin, Prime Minister for the second time, was before all else a politician, for whom politics were less a means to an end than an end in itself. For nearly twenty years prior to entering Parliament he had been a director of Baldwin's Ltd., the family-controlled iron, steel, and coal firm in Worcestershire. His father, in many ways typical of successful manufacturers of his time, had begun life as a Methodist and acquired a modest technical education at the Wesleyan College in Taunton; later, with his firm well established and his wealth secure, he abandoned Methodism for the Church of England and entered Parliament as a Conservative. His son was sent to Harrow, then to Cambridge. Spiritually it was a voyage from which he never returned, for having mixed with the scions of landed and financial wealth and tasted the pleasures of cultivated society, the life of a provincial industrialist held little appeal for him. Stolidity and a strong sense of filial duty kept him at it while his father lived. But on his father's death in 1906 he seized the opportunity to take over his Parliamentary seat, and embarked upon a political career. The ambiguity of his early years, however, remained very much in evidence.[1]

Like his father and most other West Midlands businessmen, Baldwin supported Tariff Reform. Yet it was not the vision of Britain as the industrial engine of a world Empire that inspired him, but that of an England insulated from the rest of the world and still largely rural. As Prime Minister in the 1920s, he liked to describe himself as an industrialist: a man who actually produced wealth and managed men. But he showed scant awareness of industrialists' problems and occasionally joined the bankers in deprecating their lack of enterprise.[2] On occasion he also called himself 'something of a banker'.[3] But his outlook tended to be more insular than the City bankers he so admired.

Speaking to the Royal Society of St George in 1924, he evoked one of his favourite images:

> the sounds of England, the tinkle of the hammer on the anvil in the country smithy, the corncrake on a dewy morning, the sound of scythe against the whetstone, and the sight of a plough team coming over the brow of a hill, the sight that has been seen in England since England was a land, and may be seen in England long after the Empire has perished, and every works in England has ceased to function.[4]

He was in short an English nationalist – English, not British – and positively hostile to internationalism. During the election campaign he accused the Labour government of 'following the unhappy will-o-the wisp called internationalism'. In Newcastle he explained to a large audience that, judging a tree by its fruit,

> the only fruits of internationalism that I have been able to perceive are the fruits of hatred and those fruits are poisonous. ...Internationalism ... can only lead to disaster.... It is very difficult for foreign nations to understand one another, and those who know least of them, of their history, language and culture, perhaps least realise those difficulties. Is it not true that, if everybody in a street tried to sweep someone else's doorstep, it would be the dirtiest street in Newcastle? (Laughter). Surely the wise thing is to make your own doorstep so radiantly beautiful that everyone else will desire to emulate it. (Cheers).[5]

Regarded from the standpoint of geography, it is noteworthy that no less than five members of Baldwin's Cabinet, including Baldwin himself, represented West Midlands constituencies. Yet looked at from the standpoint of family background, education, and source of wealth, the Cabinet resembled more the elite of the mercantile–financial community than spokesmen for the industrial community. Of the twenty-seven members between 1924 and 1929 (all men of course, no women), not one had attended a grammar school or anything so modest, whereas no less than twenty had attended one of the major public schools: Winchester (one), Rugby (three), Harrow (seven), or Eton (nine). Thirteen had gone to Oxford, seven to Cambridge, and one to Sandhurst. Thirteen owned substantial estates, among whom at least five could properly be described as members of the landed class. Baldwin aside, only two, Austen and Neville Chamberlain, owed their wealth directly to industry, and only one, Neville Chamberlain, had worked for any time in industry. That said, it is evident that they were also politicians first, alert to the outlook of industry as well as finance, while ready to place the welfare of their party before any particular economic interest. The only exception was Leopold Amery, the Secretary of State for the Dominions and the Colonies, who assumed the mantle of Joseph Chamberlain as the champion of the Tariff Reform. One of the Birmingham members, he was to become acutely impatient with his colleagues for their apparent indifference to the fate of manufacturing industry and the Empire. They in turn were to find his singlemindedness irksome.

In the aftermath of the 1923 election debacle, Baldwin had been constrained to renew Bonar Law's pledge that if returned he would not impose food taxes or a general tariff either directly or 'by the back door'.[6] A majority of the new Cabinet probably favoured protection, but some were strongly opposed, and there was not one of them who doubted the necessity for the pledge. The most the protectionists could hope for was that a modest increase in safeguarding duties would serve to educate the public to the advantages of a larger policy. In the meantime they accepted that the government's aim should be to restore 'normalcy' by a combination of modest social reforms and the economic policies that had served so well in the halcyon days before the war. Without a word of discussion they accepted the return to the pre-war gold parity. At Baldwin's urging, they also agreed to avoid confrontation with organised labour. The difficulty was that industrial peace and economic internationalism were virtually incompatible in the circumstances of the time.

The frustrations inherent in the government's position became evident almost immediately when, in fulfilment of an election promise, Edward Wood, the Minister of Agriculture, issued invitations to a conference to devise a policy for reviving the farming industry. The NFU's response was marked by bitterness at the disregard shown for the plight of agriculture by previous governments and deep scepticism towards the present one. The Union was prepared to accept the invitation, but reminded Wood that in 1923 Baldwin and the Prime Minister, Bonar Law, had frankly admitted that subsidies or protection were the only means of providing substantial relief, and requested an immediate assurance that this was still the Conservative view. Wood, able neither to confirm or deny it, reacted with annoyance at the NFU's intransigence. The refusal of the farm workers' unions to attend the conference provided a convenient excuse for dropping the idea altogether.[7] But this merely left the industry in its depressed condition and postponed confrontation with its leaders.

Relations were not improved by the government's decision to fulfil the commitment entered into by Baldwin's previous administration at the 1923 Imperial Conference and shelved when Labour took office, to impose new revenue duties on certain foodstuffs with the provision of Empire preference. Baldwin's election pledge ruled out the introduction of the actual duties, so instead the Dominions were compensated by the creation of an Empire Marketing Board, financed by an annual grant of £1 million to assist in the promotion and marketing of (non-competing) Empire produce in Britain.[8] This was scarcely satisfactory to Amery and fellow advocates of a large Empire policy, and British farmers were infuriated what while nothing was done for them, public funds were being spent to encourage the consumption of overseas produce. Wood, shaken by the criticism, told colleagues, 'I doubt whether any action by any government has ever excited more keen resentment among our farmers than this'.[9] Even more contentious was the government's handling of the safeguarding issue, which occupied debate for much of 1925.

Baldwin, while pledging not to introduce a general tariff, had promised during the election to provide efficient industries with safeguarding protection against 'unfair' foreign competition. Reference was made to a bill for this purpose in the first King's Speech, and the President of the Board of Trade, Sir Philip Cunliffe-Lister, in consultation with Baldwin, prepared a draft bill during the 1924 winter recess. But Churchill strenuously intervened, warning them that no amount of drafting skill could produce a bill that was not too narrow to be of any use or too broad to stop major industries such as iron and steel from making out a case for protection and triggering an avalanche of applications from other industries injured by the higher cost of steel. He therefore proposed that the application of the existing safeguarding act should be left in the hands of the Board of Trade, with new criteria laid down for the Board to use in assessing applications.[10] The Cabinet agreed to this course, and on 10 February the criteria were set out in a White Paper. Henceforth an industry seeking protection would have to satisfy an *ad hoc* committee appointed by the Board that it was of national importance and reasonably efficient; that competing imports were abnormally large by pre-war comparison, were sold below British manufacturers' costs, and caused serious unemployment; that competition was due to sweated labour; and that protection would not adversely affect any other industry.[11]

The criteria satisfied no one. Free traders were sure their vagueness was designed to allow a steady accretion of protection; protectionists were equally convinced they would prove an impassable barrier to all applicants; and farmers were disgruntled to find that their industry was not even eligible for consideration. The government thus came under pressure from several directions at once. The only consolation was that industry remained too divided to campaign effectively for stronger action, while the Labour Party was shown to have no credible alternative.

Labour, safeguarding, and Empire preference

Cunliffe-Lister, who opened the Commons debate on 16 February on the new safeguarding procedures, justified them primarily as a means of defending British workers against unfair foreign competition, reducing unemployment, and raising wages. But MacDonald, who introduced the Opposition motion of censure, refused to take the bait. The sweating issue was, he claimed, a red herring: an insignificant factor in foreign competition, which came mainly from the advanced industrial countries. If the government were serious about improving wages, they would support efforts to strengthen the ILO and ratify the 1920 Washington Convention on the eight-hour day. Britain had a moral obligation to join an international offensive against sweated production rather than merely taxing it or diverting it to third markets. And morality aside, unilateral British action might prove a dangerous precedent. Only recently, allegedly sweated conditions in Britain's own boot and shoe and cotton industries had been cited in Australia to support demands for protection.

Over the next hour MacDonald presented a catalogue of reasons for rejecting the proposed safeguarding procedures. It was an impressive performance, but as for Labour's policy he was less than precise. It was not protection, nor was it mere free trade, the Liberals' negative alternative. The most he would say was that, 'as between Free Trade and Tariff Reform, we are convinced that, with a policy of internal construction and a policy that would build up labour, the consumers, the mass of producers, on to a stronger and stronger position, by evolution of forces, Free Trade is preferable to Tariff Reform'.[12]

Other Labour speakers, including Hugh Dalton in his maiden speech, similarly dwelt on the theme that their party, while no less dissatisfied with *laissez-faire* than the government, had its own answer to unfair competition, namely 'the development of International Labour Conventions'.[13] But government spokesmen, having received numerous intimations of disillusionment with free trade within Labour's ranks, dwelt upon the inferior pay and conditions of foreign workers and pointed up the inconsistency between Labour's commitment to protect British workers from the evils of sweating at home and its refusal to take effective action against sweated products from abroad.[14] Their reward came when the Labour member Dr Haden Guest congratulated the government for presenting what was at least a concrete proposal and derided MacDonald for his negativism. 'You cannot feed the army of the unemployed on Free Trade pamphlets; you cannot feed them on hopes of a revival of world trade. Whether that revival is coming or not coming, it is certainly not a matter of the next few months, and the unemployed are men who live ... from day to day. ... Nor,' he added in pointed reference to MacDonald's decision to devote himself to external affairs during his term in office, 'with all respect, can you feed the unemployed on the achievements of foreign policy, excellent as these may be.' Guest acknowledged that policy-making was a matter for the party as a whole. But he for one refused to rule out safeguarding, and was sure that 'we want a very vigorous policy of development of the resources of the British Commonwealth of Nations, and that that is a very important and first step'.[15]

Guest, one of the new middle-class recruits to Labour and one of the few who had fought in the war, had no firm base in the party, and at the division he was the only opposition MP to vote with the Tories. Yet his criticism had touched a raw nerve in the party. Until the previous year the ILP had been uncritically internationalist, its proletarian and bourgeois elements united in their preoccupation with peace. Hopes for protection against the competition of sweated labour rested upon the Washington Convention calling for the normal working week to be limited to forty-eight hours, which had been adopted at a semi-official conference in 1920 and thereafter promoted by the ILO. The convention received an approving nod from practically every Western government, but once the postwar slump had ended and the threat of social upheaval was overcome, few of them were prepared to tie the hands of their employers. Even MacDonald's recent government, despite firm pre-election promises, moved with deliberate slowness on ratification and fell before taking the decisive step. Its failure to address the unemployment problem caused a reaction among more militant elements of the ILP, who turned to the interventionist tradition of the Labour movement while shrugging off their commitment to international solutions to social and economic problems. Guest's call for a review of party policy thus evoked a swift response from several prominent left-wingers.

One was Tom Johnston, the MP and editor of *Forward*. Another was John Wheatley, a fellow Clydesider and one of the few Ministers in the first Labour government to leave office with an enhanced reputation. A third was the veteran socialist George Lansbury, chairman of the Parliamentary Party's Commonwealth Group that Guest had helped create in 1924. With Wheatley in the lead, all three dismissed free trade and protection but reserved their strongest condemnation for free trade, which in Wheatley's words was 'outrageously anti-socialist'. For them the party's duty was to protect the living standards of British workers, whether the threat came from at home or abroad. Reliance on the ILO to level up conditions of labour among all of Britain's foreign competitors within the foreseeable future seemed to them a vain hope. What was needed was an immediate embargo on all sweated goods without waiting for international agreement.[16]

The meeting of the Parliamentary Labour Party on 3 March attracted wide interest when it became known that Guest intended to call for a reconsideration of the party's position on safeguarding. Guest duly raised the issue, but once he had tabled his resolution several speakers including Lord Arnold and the party secretary Arthur Henderson appealed for solidarity against any action that would play into the government's hands.[17] Guest's resolution was thereupon overwhelmingly rejected and an alternative executive resolution unanimously adopted. The resolution reaffirmed Labour's opposition to tariffs, but acknowledged the need to clarify the party's position on the sweating issue and called for a committee of party members, experts, and TUC representatives to produce a suitable formula.[18]

MacDonald, interviewed three days later, left no room for doubt that he wanted nothing more to be heard of the issue. Action against sweated competition was all very well in principle, he suggested, but how was sweating to be defined and would it work to the disadvantage of British trade in the more prosperous Dominions and United States markets? What then of Labour's policy? 'It is quite futile to discuss academic points as to fiscal policy under Socialism. All it is now necessary to say is that neither free trade nor protection are principles that hold good under any or every circumstance.'[19] However, after five years of depression and high unemployment in the main centres of party support, the question of trade policy could no longer be swept aside as easily as that. Wheatley and Johnston, despite places on the newly formed committee, continued their campaign for effective non-tariff protection, and indications that the left-wing of the party was moving in their direction appeared at the annual ILP conference in April. In an effort to avert confrontation between the Clyde-based protectionists and the ex-Liberal free trade elements, the ILP national administrative council presented its own scheme – unanimously accepted – including national import boards for wheat, meat, and essential raw materials as a means of stabilising prices at reasonable levels and eliminating profiteering by middlemen, the nationalisation of key industries, the total embargo of sweated imports, and the promotion of trade union activity abroad. Once more it was felt necessary to append a firm condemnation of both tariff protection and free trade. Yet the very fact that the ILP should now be directing serious attention to the regulation of trade was significant in itself.[20]

Equally significant was the decision of the TUC General Council not to participate in the Labour Party's inquiry into policy on sweated labour and instead proceed with a separate inquiry of its own.[21] This was mainly a reflection of the TUC's growing insistence upon an independent voice in policy-making, which had been given impetus the previous year when, in office, party leaders had shown themselves aloof from, even disdainful of, the trade union wing of the Labour movement. On the question of trade policy itself, the TUC had been wedded to free trade since its beginnings over fifty years earlier, and the certain opposition of the miners and textile and transport workers ruled out any reversal of policy. Yet there was also no doubt that trade union opinion was drifting away from free trade.

Workers in industries already protected by McKenna or safeguarding duties openly advocated the retention of the legislation, while others hoping for similar treatment began to speak out. Arthur Pugh, secretary for the 100,000 strong Iron and Steel Trades Confederation (ISTC) an organisation known for its protectionist leanings, gave a personal welcome to the government's safeguarding plans.[22] Trade union leaders in the Nottingham-based lace industry voted to support an application from employers for safeguarding.[23] Two widely publicised events gave a further fillip to trade union thinking: the establishment in Glasgow of an office of the Hugo Stinnes syndicate to promote the sale of Ruhr coal;[24] and news that the Furness Withy contract for five 10,000 ton diesel powered ships had gone to the Deutsche Werfte subsidiary of AEG in Hamburg.[25] On 1 March John Hodge and J.T. Brownlie, presidents respectively of the ISTC and the Amalgamated Engineering Union, gave notice to continental colleagues at a meeting of the International Metal Federation in Paris that British workers were not prepared to see their hard won, eight-hour day destroyed by the competition of sweated foreign labour. Both delegates professed hope for international acceptance of the Washington Convention and promised assistance to German workers in their current struggle with employers. But they wanted it known that there were already 'quite a lot of labour leaders' in Britain who were disillusioned with free trade and 'seriously considering whether protection would not after all be a cure for our unemployment problem'.[26]

Signs of movement on the fiscal question within Labour's ranks gave Baldwin all the more reason to avoid needless confrontation, and when an opportunity to demonstrate goodwill came on 6 March he was quick to seize it. That day, Frederick Macquisten, one of his own backbenchers, introduced a private member's bill designed to weaken the Labour Party by obliging trade unionists to 'contract in' rather than 'contract out' of the levy on their dues paid in to party coffers. Baldwin, with Cabinet approval, intervened to inform the House that the government believed in the justice of the bill but wanted it withdrawn in the interests of good industrial relations. 'Although I know that there are those who work for different ends from most of us in this House, yet there are many in all ranks and all parties who will re-echo my prayer: "Give peace in our time, O Lord."'[27] A more embarrassing situation arose two weeks later when Sir Nicholas Gratton-Doyle, another Tory backbencher, attempted to exploit divisions within the Labour Party by tabling a motion for the complete embargo of imported sweated goods. Government Ministers, unable to go so far as the motion advised, were obliged to sit through the debate in silence.[28] However, the persistence of opposition calls for support of international action to deal with the sweating problem encouraged the Cabinet to consider the possibility of efforts in this direction.

The recent Labour government having failed to ratify the Washington Hours Convention, the Conservative government's initial reaction was to leave it severely alone.[29] However, Lord Robert Cecil and the Minister of Labour, Sir Arthur Steel-Maitland, had become alarmed at the level of unemployment and frequency of strikes and lock-outs, and favoured the convention as a concomitant of Baldwin's appeasement tactics. Their hand was strengthened by reports that employers and trade unionists in both the engineering and shipbuilding industries were agreed on the desirability of official efforts to press foreign competitors into line on hours of work. Steel-Maitland thereupon took the initiative. Warning that Labour, if returned to office, would ratify the convention unchanged, and stressing its potential 'as a means of minimising foreign competition', he appealed to colleagues for time to investigate the possibility of negotiating modifications to make it acceptable to employers.[30] The Cabinet acquiesced, and during the next three years this became Steel-Maitland's chief preoccupation.[31] But in the meantime he was obliged to rule out immediate ratification on 9 April and again on 1 May when, as a show of international working-class solidarity, the Opposition made this the subject of Parliamentary debate.[32]

Labour, divided on protection, was equally divided on Empire preference, as became clear the following month. Differences surfaced at the meeting of the Parliamentary Labour Party on 10 June, two days before the Budget proposals for widening preferences on certain foodstuffs, tobacco, and wine were scheduled for debate.[33] A resolution calling on members to abstain was defeated, but only by six votes, and opinion was so sharply divided that the whips were taken off during the Commons debate. The result caused a sensation when it was confirmed that twenty Labour members had sided with the government and another twelve would have done so had they been able to attend.[34]

The Conservative press was exultant. 'Is it too daring to hope that Conservatism and Labour may ultimately find in Imperial Preference a common ground?' asked the *Daily Express*.[35] The *Sunday Pictorial*, the usual vehicle for Rothermere's personal views, confidently envisaged a time when Labour embraced Tariff Reform and on that basis Greater Britain rationalised her industry using mass-production techniques and reasserted her place as the leading world power. 'America has shown how that can be done without "sweating" the worker.'[36] Even the Liberal press gloomily accepted that, if the Conservatives exaggerated the significance of the vote, it nonetheless confirmed that the Labour Party could no longer be counted on to resist pressure for imperial protectionism.[37]

MacDonald, in an effort to minimise the event, dismissed talk of a rift in Labour ranks. All members, he insisted, were agreed on the need to remove taxes on consumer goods. The only difference was that some were prepared to accept half measures now while others insisted on the whole policy; and on the government's own estimate the reduction of duties in question would ease the burden on the consumer by £1.7 million annually.[38] But this was too simple. The Labour Party, like other free trade bodies, had always hitherto strongly opposed Empire preference. Like any other tariff advantage, so the argument ran, preferences tended to create vested interests and threatened difficulties with the Dominions when the duties themselves were removed. Worse, they involved discrimination against foreign countries, the most virulent source of conflict among nations. The previous year only five Labour members had refused the whip in order to support a Conservative motion calling for adoption of the preferences agreed upon at the recent Imperial Conference. Now not only were the rebels more numerous but they were also more outspoken.

During the Commons debate David Kirkwood, the former chief steward at the Beardmore Works and member of the Clydeside contingent which voted solidly with the government on this issue, justified his action by contrasting the high wage levels in the Dominions to the sweated conditions on the Continent. Then, turning to the internationalist arguments of his own front bench, he defiantly added, 'we are all out for universal peace. There is nothing to accomplish that better than cementing the British Empire.'[39] Wheatley and Lansbury, defending the rebels' stand, similarly explained that as socialists they sought the unity of all peoples, but being practical men they took the world as it came and accepted the Empire as a nucleus on which to build. This was an age of 'mighty combinations' of capital and people. 'Liberating' the Empire in present circumstances would be the worst kind of liberalism: anti-social and even anti-socialist; and could only result in more isolated political units and more intense competition among workers and nations. Just as socialists sought not to break up trusts but to transform them into assets for the whole community, so now they must adopt a progressive policy towards the Empire.[40]

Brailsford, Fenner Brockway, and other left-wing party members raised anguished cries at this 'new school of Socialist-Imperialism'. To them at least it was little short of scandalous for socialists to pretend that imperialism could be anything other than a concomitant of militarism and capitalism, to talk of the British Empire as if it comprised only the Dominions and not also India and African colonies where racist oppression and exploitation prevailed, or to imagine that discriminating in favour of Empire goods did not mean injustice to workers in Russia, Germany, and elsewhere. 'It is abandonment alike of the ethics and the economics of the Socialist movement.... It sweeps the Labour Party from its international foundations. Workers of all lands, unite!'[41] Yet even Brailsford, while holding fast to free trade, was casting about for an alternative economic policy in recognition of the fact that many of Britain's great pre-war markets such as India and China had been lost forever.[42]

The party's right wing was no less divided. While the leadership formally hewed to free trade, Guest joined Amery in launching the Empire Self-Supporting League,[43] and J.H. Thomas boasted of Labour's imperialism before the Corona Club.[44] The policy statement published in June 1925 devoted nearly a quarter of its space to Empire affairs. Awkward issues such as Indian self-rule and sweated conditions in the dependent territories were passed over in silence, while the proposal for bulk buying foodstuffs was treated as a purely British–Dominions issue.[45] On 27 July MacDonald opened the first British Commonwealth Labour Conference with a fervent denial of Tory claims to monopolise imperial sentiment, and again held out the bulk buying scheme as a socialistic form of imperial preference.[46] Snowden and the former Liberals defended free trade; but William Graham, who had been Snowden's assistant at the Treasury, wrote to Amery to propose talks on a large Empire policy. Recent conversations between Labour and Tory MPs on economic issues had been 'very impressive'. 'I believe that, on the basis of the Empire as a unit, we are much nearer to agreement than we imagine.'[47]

The looming confrontation over trade policy failed to materialise. In August the committee on sweated trades submitted its report calling for an embargo on sweated imports as defined by the Washington Convention, though with the sweeping rider that British action should be conditional on international agreement.[48] Shortly before the annual party conference in October, the executive forestalled criticism by transferring bulk buying from the Empire to the international section of the agenda.[49] Debate on economic policy at the conference passed off with only a moment of friction. Several speakers had dwelt on the need for an alternative to free trade or crude protection when Snowden demanded that the party call a spade a spade and acknowledge that as it opposed protection it favoured free trade. Johnston rose to protest that this gave a misleading picture of the party's policy, but delegates seemed barely interested and the executive's resolution was swiftly adopted.[50] For the time being all attention was focussed on the crisis in the coalfields.

The economic consequences of Mr Churchill

The origin of the coal dispute went back at least as far as the war, when exceptional demand for bunker and coking coal at a time of acute labour shortage led to the rapid exploitation of the richest seams. Subsequently, problems were compounded by the reduced level of international trade, increased industrial efficiency, and the trend away from coal towards other energy sources. British mine owners, reluctant to plough back profits into the modernisation of operations, were relieved of the necessity during 1923 by the Franco-Belgian occupation of the Ruhr, which caused a sharp decline in German production and windfall profits for British output. In the buoyant conditions of May 1924 the owners conceded a sizeable wage increase and the miners' longstanding demand for an eight-hour day. But after the Dawes Plan was introduced, continental production rapidly expanded and prices fell. Soon the owners were complaining that their operations were losing money, and in the spring of 1925 they announced their intention to reduce wages, with the threat of a lock-out if their terms were not accepted by the end of July. The miners were determined to hold onto their recently won concessions, and with the cry 'not a penny off the pay, not a minute on the day,' they rejected the owners' terms on 3 July. A serious coal stoppage seemed inevitable.

The mounting dispute drew criticism on several Ministers and in particular Churchill, who was once more made to feel the strains of office. In December he had tangled with colleagues over the safeguarding issue. In January his opponent had been the First Lord of the Admiralty, William Bridgeman, whose naval spending plans far exceeded the expenditure allowed for in Churchill's forthcoming budget.

The confrontation, diverted to a Cabinet committee in February, resumed in April, when Bridgeman threatened to resign and rumours circulated that Churchill was creating a crisis in order to make way for another Coalition government.[51] Eventually, on 22 July, the Cabinet patched up a compromise on naval spending.[52] But no sooner had this been accomplished than the TUC General Council announced its full support for the miners, thereby escalating the dispute in the coalfields into a threatened general strike. Repeatedly Churchill was accused of responsibility on account of his decision to return to the gold standard, thereby forcing up the exchange rate and pricing British coal out of world markets.

Beaverbrook, gleefully reminding readers that he had warned of just such an outcome before the return to gold, repeatedly attacked Churchill through his papers.[53] The FBI journal was equally critical, and Lloyd George, always ready to make political capital out of his opponents' difficulties, quoted both sources against Churchill on 10 July.[54] The next day, Churchill angrily denied any responsibility for the coal dispute. 'The Gold Standard was no more responsible than was the Gulf Stream.'[55] But as he well knew, if the return to the pre-war gold parity had not actually caused the dispute, there was no doubt that the 12 per cent rise in sterling between July 1924 and April 1925 in anticipation of the decision, and the fixing of the exchange rate at a time when the Belgian and French currencies were falling, had made an already difficult situation in the coalfields much worse. J.M. Keynes refuted his assertion about the irrelevance of the decision on gold in a series of articles entitled: 'The Economic Consequences of Mr Churchill', published in Beaverbrook's *Evening Standard* and afterwards under separate cover.[56] More prosaically but no less authoritatively, Sir Josiah Stamp added his dissent in an addendum to the report of the official inquiry into the coal dispute which appeared on 28 July. Two days later the FBI renewed its criticism.[57]

Criticism of Churchill was soon translated into pressure on Norman. Having restored the gold standard, Norman had looked forward to a period of dear money and a progressive reduction of the Treasury note issue in anticipation of the amalgamation of the two currency note issues, in order to strengthen sterling and enable London to play the leading role in international monetary reconstruction.[58] But exceptional quantities of gold from the Soviet Union, India, and South America were flooding the bullion market, and lower interest rates in New York were making it hard to justify a policy of dear money. Norman took Strong's advice and without informing Churchill began to accumulate dollars in New York and tuck them away in the Bank's accounts under 'other securities', so as to keep down the published weekly reserve figures.[59] But do what he could, the pound continued to appear strong.

On 21 July, Niemeyer, on Churchill's behalf, wrote to Norman, then on holiday in Europe with Strong, urging him to reduce Bank rate. British wholesale prices had fallen more than 7 per cent since the start of the year, Niemeyer pointed out, and the Bank had recently added £8 million gold to its reserves.[60] Norman rejected the appeal, but Churchill would not acquiesce and requested Norman to return to London for consultation. What passed between them is not recorded, but it seems that Churchill pressed Norman to reduce Bank rate immediately or at least just as soon as the coal dispute was settled, and Norman, without committing himself, indicated his willingness to act once the position was clearer.

The government, not yet ready to face a general strike, was encouraged to temporise by Norman's offer. As late as 29 July, Baldwin had ruled out any public subsidy as a means of buying off the confrontation. The next day, with Churchill's support, he secured Cabinet approval for a £10–15 million subsidy to enable wages to be maintained at current levels for another nine months while a permanent solution was arranged. Even then Norman held back. But Addis, who had urged a Bank rate reduction to ease the industrial postion at the Bank's Committee of Treasury on 26 July, renewed his call at the meeting on the 29th, and again privately to Norman on 4 August. Norman finally agreed. On Thursday 6 August, the Bank announced a reduction in Bank rate from 5 to 4½ per cent. Meanwhile the government faced criticism from its own supporters for backing down in face of trade union pressure and adding to industry's troubles by conceding the wage subsidy.[61]

Churchill's unease was apparent during the Commons debate on 5 August when questioned about Stamp's statement in the court of inquiry report. 'No responsible leader' had spoken out against returning to the gold standard, Churchill protested, and no one in either House had voted against the bill. As for Stamp, Churchill likened him to Lloyd George and Labour Party critics: one more Johnny-come-lately who, with no particular claim to authority on financial matters, had now suddenly caught 'currency fever'.[62]

Stamp immediately responded to this slur on his professional standing, in the columns of *The Times*. As he pointed out, it was His Majesty's government that had judged him competent to serve as Britain's expert on the Dawes committee on German currency stabilisation, and if Churchill cared to look he would find his repeated warnings against a premature return to gold in *The Times* and elsewhere since the beginning of the year. Nor had he claimed in the recent report that the coal crisis was due solely to the return to gold, as Churchill suggested, but rather that the additional burden of adjustment it caused had come at precisely the moment when the industry was least able to bear it.[63]

Mond, equally irate, complained in *The Times* about Churchill's remarks. Long beforehand, Mond reminded readers, he had warned that returning to gold meant reduced exports, unemployment, and serious industrial unrest. Raising the exchange rate left the employers no choice but to deflate costs, and as should have been obvious to everyone, trade unionists would not be persuaded that reduced money wages did not mean a reduction in real wages. Thus, he continued, Stamp was correct to place the emphasis on the monetary factor: his view was corroborated by Keynes and W.A. Lee, secretary of the mine owners' association. The press reflexively condemned the trade unions for their bloody-mindedness or the government for its pusillanimity.

> But once more the most fundamental cause which led to the crisis in the industry appears to have been entirely ignored.... It is fashionable at the moment to indict either the inefficiency of those who manage industrial concerns or to abuse the working man, and to appoint Commissions to inquire into the state of different industries. But as long as the currency policy of the country is directed without any regard as to how detrimental it may be to British industry it is useless to demand from either employers or workmen the solution of problems which are neither of their making nor over which they have any control.[64]

Stamp, Mond, and Keynes impressed many employers with their criticism of monetary policy, yet few were prepared to argue for radical change now. Confronted by an acute threat of labour unrest and civil strife, it was difficult to ignore assertions that the gold standard was a vital bulwark of the social order and defence against the destruction of private wealth. Thus Sir Peter Rylands bluntly attributed the crisis in Britain's basic industries to the fact that the financial interests, who dominated decisions on monetary policy to the exclusion of every other group, had seen to it that sterling was raised far out of line with the currencies of Britain's continental competitors. Yet he accepted that abandonment of the gold standard was 'unthinkable'.[65] The Lancashire mill-owner and Conservative MP for Stockport, Samuel Hammersley, complained of the way the banks oppressed the cotton industry, while repeating Bradbury's remark that the gold standard was 'knave-proof'.[66] At the annual meeting of the NUM in September the president, George Terrell, expressed annoyance at the Chancellor for disregarding his advice to consult industry before making his decision on gold, but left the matter at that.[67] The FBI, while declaring that recent events had fully borne out its warnings, dissociated itself from Keynes who was alleged still to advocate a managed currency, and merely claimed the right to be consulted in future.[68]

Reactions of the labour movement were broadly similar. The *Daily Herald*, having missed the chance to make something of Churchill's announcement of the return to gold, soon complained that the FBI had put the objections better than Labour's own spokesmen. 'Big business' appreciated that 'the Government's surrender to the bankers and the great financial houses' meant further wage cuts and more unemployment. 'Mr. Baldwin's way of securing industrial peace and Good Will!'[69] Yet now that the decision was taken, the *Daily Herald* took little further notice of the issue. Brailsford did what he could to promote interest in the *New Leader*, and in August a new critic came to the fore in the person of Sir Oswald Mosley, a young upper-class Tory defector with an incisive mind and a lust for power.

Speaking at the ILP summer school in Dunmow, Essex, Mosley set out the 'Birmingham proposals' for regenerating industry, while driving home the point that the gold standard was irreconcilable with a managed economy. Socialists, he insisted, must tear away the aura of mystery surrounding monetary policy and recognise that this was the factor upon which prices, employment, and everything else depended. 'A gold standard socialist is a contradiction in terms.'[70] Listeners offered him a respectful hearing, but his appeals were lost upon the rank and file of the labour movement. Few could grasp that besides individual commodities the value of money itself could be, and was, manipulated. For all but a few a capitalist was the employer who confronted them across the bargaining table. From the bottom it was hard to appreciate distinctions at the top, or appreciate that on an important if limited range of issues industrialists and workers had common interests: the hated Mond seemed scarcely different from the financiers of the City, especially when Mond's fellow employers were threatening a lock-out. Thus the annual TUC conference passed off without a single reference to the gold standard. The following week at St George's Hall in Liverpool the annual Labour Party conference again approved an executive resolution calling for 'public ownership of the Banking and Credit system'. During the debate a delegate from Doncaster acknowledged that workers had been 'about as much interested in this subject as they were in the nebular-hypothesis,' but insisted that this was changing in face of mounting evidence that the employers they negotiated with were merely the pawns of the bankers whose loans kept them afloat. Will Sherwood, President of the General Workers' Union, and Ben Tillett, the veteran dockers' leader, evoked the spectre of 'the great financial power, working in the dark, unseen and sometimes unrecognised by the organised workers'.[71]

But still there was no sign that anyone of influence in the Parliamentary party took the resolution seriously. With the growing estrangement of the ILP activists from the leadership of the Parliamentary party, the currency question remained ever more firmly in the hands of Snowden and the ex-Liberals who dominated economic policy-making. As for them, William Graham, Snowden's closest ally, boasted that they were 'if anything more orthodox than the orthodox,' and showed no inclination to act on conference resolutions where finance was concerned.[72]

The government was thus easily able to ride out the storm. Pressed by Niemeyer, Norman again agreed against his better judgment to reduce Bank rate, from 4½ to 4 per cent, which was announced on 1 October just before the Labour and Conservative conferences convened.[73] At the latter conference Leo Maxse introduced a resolution laying down the principle that 'our currency policy should take due regard of British industries'. But in keeping with tradition at such gatherings he refrained from polemics and, as he was bound to admit, the two recent Bank rate reductions had drawn some of the sting from his implied criticism. In an atmosphere charged with class conflict and the clamour for suppression of trade union power, the conference only wanted the issue out of the way. It therefore adopted his resolution without debate and moved on.[74] Subsequently Baldwin and the Conservative Central Office repeatedly underlined the necessity of the gold standard as a safeguard against subversion of the existing social order. And when on 3 November Churchill announced the lifting of the embargo on foreign lending, the gold standard was also credited with making this possible.

Free trade in capital

The informal loan embargo imposed by Norman in April 1924 had become a source of increasing discomfort to the Bank and the government since the return to gold. City financiers took the view that they had made sacrifices enough by following the Governor's directive, and now that the gold standard was restored, they were anxious to exploit the enhanced attractions of sterling to foreign borrowers.[75] British agents in South America complained of their inability to meet American competition since they could not offer financing for larger railway and industrial projects. As Norman put it, 'we all *hate*' the embargo.[76] But he was also aware that Britain's margin for foreign lending was very slim, and wished to avoid the criticism that was bound to occur if over-lending forced him to raise Bank rate so soon after returning to gold. He vented his frustration upon Australia and New Zealand, which, exempted from the embargo, had refused to heed his 'moral suasion' by moderating their borrowing demands in the period before the return to gold and were now, in his opinion, seriously over-borrowed. The Dominions were taking undue advantage of the 1900 Colonial Stock Act, which gave their loans trustee status in Britain. Norman loathed all loans made on political rather than commercial considerations, and particularly when they overloaded his market.[77]

Following unsuccessful efforts to persuade the New Zealand High Commissioner to reduce a prospective loan from £7 to £5 million, Norman on 11 May called on the Chancellor for support.[78] Niemeyer took Norman's part, and Churchill agreed to appeal to the Dominions for restraint. Amery however refused to transmit his message. Disappointed by the Cabinet's lack of enthusiasm for imperial action, thoroughly impatient with Churchill's economic liberalism, and also at odds with him on naval spending, he had no intention of collaborating with him in another blow to Empire solidarity unless forced by colleagues to do so. Churchill took the matter up in Cabinet on 10 June, armed with a letter conveniently supplied by Norman, stating that Dominions borrowing exceeded Britain's capacity to lend and warning that unless curbed it would force him to raise interest rates with all that that implied for industrial recovery.[79]

During the lengthy discussion Amery fought hard for the Dominions, arguing that Empire loans had the great advantage of being spent largely on British goods and therefore scarcely affected the exchanges. But Churchill could point to support from interests normally part of Amery's camp. Only that morning *The Times* reported Sir Alfred Mond's statement that industrialists 'took a different view from financiers as to the expediency of employing our resources for the granting of foreign loans'. Cunliffe-Lister pointed out that he had just come from a meeting of the Board of Trade's Advisory Council where industrialists expressed 'considerable apprehension ... as to the probable effects of Dominions borrowing on Bank rate'. In the end the Cabinet compromised, requesting Amery to send Churchill's telegram while agreeing to an inquiry into Britain's capacity to meet home, Empire, and foreign borrowing demands. An Overseas Loan Sub-Committee was soon appointed, with Norman in the chair and comprising Bradbury, Niemeyer, Stamp, and senior officials from the Board of Trade, Dominions Office, and India Office.[80]

Norman soon began negotiations with Australian representatives on a formula for limiting their demand on the London market. Agreement did not prove easy. The Australian state governments, possessing sovereign authority over borrowing, threatened to disregard the Commonwealth Loan Council if the proposed ceiling for new loans in the coming year was not raised from £40 million to at least £50 million, and Stanley Bruce, the Prime Minister, attempted to frighten British Ministers by warning that once Australia began to borrow in New York she might never return to London.[81] But Norman was now in a commanding position to 'teach the Dominions a lesson'.[82] Several recent Dominions loans had been poorly received on the market. No less than 80 per cent of the latest one, for New Zealand, had been left in the underwriters' hands. He was also aware that Bruce himself feared 'losing [the] London market permanently and only gaining New York when it suits *them*'.[83] Thus by the end of the month he secured agreement on a formula whereby the Commonwealth would be the sole borrower in New York, all the states would act together or not at all, and any loan issued in New York would be matched by a simultaneous loan in London on a ratio of approximately 80:20.[84]

Within Whitehall, Westminster, and elsewhere, talk of replacing free trade in capital with national or imperial restrictions increased during the summer. The Board of Trade, alive to Britain's growing dependence on Dominions markets and increasing American competition, advocated a policy of favouring Empire borrowers within the limits of British financial resources.[85] Amery echoed Bruce's warning about American influence, and both left and right radicals joined in support.[86] Mond called for the issue to be re-examined, 'not so much from the point of view of the Treasury and finance, but more and more from the point of view of trade and employment'.[87] An FBI pamphlet asked if the best alternative was home market development or 'a broad policy of Empire development based on a bold use of national credit, and a substantial movement of population from the UK to the Dominions'.[88] Keynes, in his *Economic Consequences of Mr Churchill*, also advocated a curb on foreign lending in favour of domestic investment.

Norman's committee decided otherwise. As late as 19 September, Niemeyer maintained that Britain's balance of payments left nothing to lend abroad.[89] But Norman, impatient at events, allowed City colleagues to know that he would not mind his hand being forced.[90] A petition from the clearing banks followed. Then, responding to the pressure, he informed the committee that he could no longer maintain the embargo merely through 'moral suasion'. Investors, anxious to acquire foreign securities, were increasingly exploiting the loopholes available, while those who had held back were losing patience. The stark choice was legal sanctions or removing the embargo altogether.

The committee were under no illusion that Britain could afford to resume foreign lending on anything like the same scale as before the war when, by their estimate, half the nation's annual savings or £200 million had gone abroad. Now there was at most £100 million annually available. They were also aware that current loan demands probably far exceeded this figure, but in the final analysis they were more impressed by the difficulties the City would make if they recommended legal sanctions than by any 'temporary' hardship inflicted on the domestic economy by letting the embargo go. As they pointed out, no criteria could be devised for governing access to the capital market that would satisfy all classes of borrowers. Besides, 'a strong body of opinion' regarded any such interference with the market as damaging to the 'national credit'. Even in the patriotic climate of the war legal sanctions had proven 'notoriously hard to administer' and a constant source of friction with financial institutions. They therefore rejected the idea of legal sanctions as well as policies of favouring industry by requiring loans to be 'tied' to export orders or giving priority to Empire loans, which they held to be open to the same objections. Domestic industry, they consoled themselves, had practically completed its reconstruction efforts, and in any case relied mostly upon its own resources for capital investment. As for the Dominions, they already had the advantage of the Colonial Stock Act which enabled them to borrow almost as cheaply as the British government itself. The only policy 'consistent with our traditions, with the general policy embodied in the gold standard', was free trade in capital. Now that the gold standard was restored, they saw no justification for not relying on this 'speedy, although perhaps drastic corrective' to overlending. Claiming that this was 'strongly advocated in both banking and industrial circles,' they made this their principal recommendation on 16 October.[91]

Amery made one last effort to secure priority for Empire borrowing, and from the Agent-General for Western Australia came renewed warning that the Bank of England was forcing his country into the American sphere of influence.[92] But Churchill refused any further consideration, and hesitated only long enough to ensure that Bank rate would not be forced up.[93] On 3 November, two weeks after receiving the report, he announced the lifting of the embargo to a large audience at the Hippodrome in Sheffield. Renewed lending, he affirmed, would stimulate the export trades, and to cheers, he added the assurance that the City could be counted on to give priority to loans intended mainly for the purchase of British goods.[94]

Economic internationalism restored

A month earlier the government confirmed its foreign policy when Sir Austen Chamberlain, the Foreign Secretary, joined delegates from

France, Germany, Belgium, and Italy in signing the Locarno treaties. Initiated earlier in the year when the Allied Control Commission revealed serious infractions of Germany's disarmament obligation and it seemed likely that France would press Britain for a new bilateral security agreement, the centrepiece of the treaties was the Rhineland Pact, whereby the signatories mutually guaranteed the frontiers between France, Belgium, and Germany. The treaties were not without value as an affirmation of the general desire for peace. But as events in 1936 were to confirm, Britain's obligations were more ambiguous than they appeared, and the absence of a military force in readiness to back them up spoke more loudly than words. Thus while Chamberlain favoured a British commitment to France, Amery, the champion of disengagement from Europe, regarded the Rhineland Pact in its final form as a personal victory.[95] Combined with the earlier rejection of the Geneva Protocol for strengthening the League of Nations' capacity to respond to aggression, Locarno confirmed the government's anxiety to retain good relations with the Dominions without, however, breaking with Europe and the tradition of upholding the balance of power.

A month later the government also clarified its trade policy. In his first budget Churchill reimposed the McKenna duties on motor cars and cycles, watches, clocks, and certain other items, which Snowden had removed in 1924. As nothing was added, the decision caused little stir. More controversial was the simultaneous introduction of duties on silk and rayon, which Churchill applied to offset a one shilling reduction in income tax and offset the advantage the rentier class received by the return to gold. Subsequently the government also supported a 'Buy British' campaign and merchandise marks legislation: both instruments of non-tariff protection and strongly supported by the FBI despite its formal neutrality on the fiscal question.[96] On the other hand, since the new rules on safeguarding procedure were introduced, every application save one, from the lace and embroidery industry, had been rejected, just as protectionists feared. The crucial question was whether the government would allow the application from four of the five main sections of the iron and steel industry (heavy steel, pig iron, wrought iron, and wire and related products), to be turned over in the normal way to an *ad hoc* committee of experts. If they did so they were likely to face the choice between opening the floodgates to applications from every industry affected by the higher cost of steel or rejecting the advice of their own experts.

Within the Cabinet Amery and Cunliffe-Lister strongly supported the application. Safeguarding the iron and steel industry, they argued, was especially desirable in present circumstances since it was both a major consumer of coal and a source of demand within the economy as a whole. But Churchill held firmly to the view that nothing could be more dangerous than splitting the anti-socialist vote by reviving Tariff Reform, and vigorously maintained that safeguarding steel was incompatible with Baldwin's pledge. Lord Salisbury, supporting him, warned of the dangerous precedent that would be created: employers in every industry would fall back on the government to bail them out rather than confronting the problem of excessive labour costs. Wood added the warning that farmers had long insisted on equal treatment with the manufacturing industry, and would become uncontrollable if steel received protection.

Divided, the Cabinet temporised by requesting the Committee of Civil Research to undertake a general inquiry into the state of the industry.[97] The findings as reported on 16 November were fully predictable: all four sections were severely depressed, imports were well up from pre-war levels, and safeguarding was the only practicable means of assistance available to the government. On the other hand, protection would mean higher steel prices, and while certain users such as the engineering and shipbuilding industries would probably acquiesce if the effect was modest, opposition could be expected from the shipowners and possibly other interests.[98] The Cabinet, thrown back on its judgement, briefly resumed debate. But there was nothing new to be said, and Amery aside, Ministers were reluctant to pursue the matter further. On 18 December they agreed that safeguarding, though economically justified, was politically unacceptable.[99] Three days later Baldwin frankly explained the decision in the House of Commons.[100]

The decision set the government's course for the balance of Parliament. The gold standard, free trade, unrestricted capital exports: it was the return to economic internationalism, albeit without enthusiasm and with certain modest concessions to domestic producers and the principle of Empire unity. But if this was normality in policy terms, in other respects the word scarcely applied to Britain. The 'intractable million', as Professor Pigou described the unemployment problem, persisted. Export trade, the other contemporary barometer of prosperity, also showed serious depression, and industrial unrest was more serious than at any time since 1920. As it happened, 1925 was the last year in which the political balance favoured internationalism: thereafter the erosion of support already evident threatened to become a landslide. The government, reflecting the division of opinion, found itself able to move neither forward nor back and henceforth remained almost completely immobilised.

4

Conflict over commerce

Global imperatives of the mass production age

Throughout the nineteenth century the vast economic potential of the United States was the subject of periodic fascination in Britain.[1] The First World War briefly demonstrated the reality of this power, when for four and a half years Britain's very existence hinged upon access to American financial and physical resources. Subsequently, the retreat of the United States into political isolation from Europe and the severe postwar slump diverted British attention towards developments closer to home. But by 1925, with British trade still depressed and American recovery in full swing, interest revived and Britons in large numbers journeyed across the Atlantic to see the New World for themselves.

Among those who made the journey there were inevitably some who sought the merely sensational features of American society: the high life of Manhattan, the low life of Chicago, and the phenomenon of Hollywood now in its first era as the film-making capital of the world.[2] But for those seriously concerned to understand the reasons for the remarkable prosperity of the United States the ultimate destination was invariably Detroit, to visit the Ford Motor Company's vast new River Rouge plant. In the case of Captain Victor Cazalet, a junior Minister at the Board of Trade, who gained a personal interview with Henry Ford, the resulting insight was touchingly naive. 'We began by discussing the Ford system,' Cazalet recorded. 'He attributes his great success to two things. A combination of certain mechanical inventions carried into execution under a particular system of organisation and production.'[3] With greater or lesser precision, however, the lesson carried back to Britain was invariably the same. The 'Ford system' represented nothing less than a revolution in economic affairs, in which the combination of rationalised mass production industry and vast homogeneous markets made possible high wages, low unit costs, and prosperity on a scale scarcely dreamt of before.

In November 1925 an FBI mission to the United States attracted wide attention when Colonel Vernon Willey, the president of the Federation and leader of the mission, described their findings to the press. As he put it, the United States was experiencing 'astounding prosperity' by reason of its new business philosophy of low profit margins and high volume production. Despite the extraordinary wage levels, prices were actually falling because the huge home market enabled industry to make rapid technical progress and pass on the economies to the customer. Willey thereupon set off on a speaking tour of FBI branches urging recognition of the need for 'collectivism' – amalgamations and cartel agreements – to secure maximum scale economies. As is clear from his public statements, the mission had been embarrassed at the way the American industrialists they met wrote off Britain as strike-ridden and technically backwards, and at the same time envious of the Americans' peaceful labour relations and boundless optimism about business prospects.[4]

Willey was head of a family wool textile firm and a free trader. But of British industrialists most outspokenly enthusiastic about the 'Ford system', the majority came from the new manufacturing industries. It was these industries after all which were in most direct competition with American exports and, being more capital intensive and more dependent upon home market demand than the older industries, they had more to gain and less to lose from the adoption of a high wage policy.

One such advocate was Sir Alfred Mond. In 1923, when rumours circulated that Lloyd George, on tour in North America, was so impressed by the prosperity he saw there that he intended to call for imperial protection on his return, Mond led the delegation of party stalwarts to meet him at Southampton in order to dissuade him from such an adventure.[5] Yet the following year Mond himself toured the United States and returned to report that the prosperity he had seen there made him feel like a pauper; in contrast to the situation in Britain, jobs were chasing men, not men jobs.[6] The impact of the experience was evident the following spring in his warnings against a premature return to gold, which he feared would rule out the conditions for industrial growth that now prevailed in the United States. It was also evident during a Commons debate in July 1925 when he called attention to the extraordinary increase in importance of the home market for British manufacturers and questioned whether this should not be welcomed and encouraged by a more selective approach to foreign lending rather than relying, as the government was now doing, upon the problematical quest for increased overseas markets.[7] Besides his lifelong association with the chemical industry, Mond was chairman of Amalgamated Anthracite, the largest mining syndicate in South Wales. Nonetheless at the end of July, just as his fellow mineowners were preparing a lock-out in order to enforce a reduction of wages, he prepared a talk for the Liberal summer school associating Britain's industrial plight with the deflationary effects of low wages.[8]

Sir Ernest Petter, a factory owner and pioneer engine builder, also attracted public notice during the winter of 1925 for stridently demanding a high wage policy. As part of a new 'social contract', involving agreement by the trade unions and merchants to abandon restrictive practices, government retrenchment, and 'protection bordering on prohibition', he advocated the raising of wages in the unsheltered industries back to parity with those in the sheltered trades. This, he frankly admitted, meant the almost certain downfall of the gold standard and, at least until British farmers expanded production, an increase in food prices. But, he insisted, these objections counted for nothing compared to the benefits to be gained, 'namely, real cooperation between employers and employees to secure maximum output, coupled with a general recognition that our industries – and with these I include our great industry of Agriculture – are of paramount importance to us'.

Colonel Willey's report had convinced him of the practicability of his approach. Indeed, so certain was he that, notwithstanding a long association with the Conservative Party, he was prepared to advocate the formation of 'a great National Industrial Party' if the government refused to heed industry's needs:

> I sincerely believe that we can achieve the same results as have been attained in the United States by the simple process of reversing our policy towards the skilled workers. I am convinced that within six months of the new policy being put into force we shall have cured unemployment, and restored peace and prosperity to our industries and our country, and this without dragging the country through the horrors of the bloody revolution which the counsellors of despair are preaching.[9]

This was not the last time Petter was to show his impatience with the Conservative leadership.

The right-wing press, although generally anti-American, presented enthusiastic accounts of the American economic miracle for the same reason. Capital and labour coexisted peacefully in America; the incipient class war confronting Britain was out of the question there. As the Very Rev. W.R. Inge, Dean of St Paul's – the 'gloomy Dean,' so called on account of his constant predictions of Red revolution – reported to *Morning Post* readers from the United States:

> I was glad to hear from all whom I have met, that 'Socialism in America is nearly dead'. There are plenty of serious social problems; but very few, except

among the low-grade immigrants from Europe, think of abolishing the private ownership of capital. One reason is that nearly every working man is a capitalist himself. ... But a more important reason is that the existing system, with all its faults, has been a magnificent success, bringing comfort, such as till lately was never thought of, to the homes of a hundred million people.[10]

Reports of this sort were common during the nine-month truce following the coal crisis of 1925. The extraordinary sales of *The Secret of High Wages: The New Industrial Gospel*, by two Cambridge engineers, Bertram Austin and W. Francis Lloyd, reflected the near-hysteria of the times.[11]

The Prime Minister, speaking in Sunderland on 27 January 1926, urged trade union leaders to consider why American workmen were so much better off.[12] When further interest was evinced among Conservative MPs, the *Daily Mail* took up the issue by financing a party of six trade unionists on a tour of American industrial centres.[13] Whether such a stunt had any effect on trade union opinion may be doubted; the Minister of Labour, Steel-Maitland, did not think so.[14] But he too was impressed with the apparent docility of American labour, and shortly after the general strike he secured Cabinet approval for an official industrial mission to the United States, comprising two trade unionists, two employers, and an independent chairman.[15]

Yet the appeal of the 'American system' was by no means restricted to the defenders of capitalism. Sir Oswald Mosley, having transferred his allegiance from the Conservative to the Labour Party, and temporarily out of Parliament, travelled to the United States in the winter of 1925 and again in 1926. As he later acknowledged, 'it seemed to me I was present at the birth of a new age. ... America had given me a vision, and I shall never forget the debt'.[16] The immediate result was to convince him that the next Labour government must devote itself to the promotion of 'mass production for a large and assured home market'. This was the rationale behind the 'Birmingham proposals,' which called for a reflationary monetary policy, radical tax reforms to ensure the increased purchasing power reached the workers rather than the rentiers in order to stimulate demand from the staple industries, and central planning to ensure that the goods were forthcoming to meet the demand.[17]

Similar proposals were advanced by H.N. Brailsford, A. Creech Jones, Frank Wise, and the Liberal economist John A. Hobson, whose formal statement, *The Living Wage*, appeared in March 1926 and provided the basis for 'Socialism in Our Time', a policy document adopted by the ILP at its annual conference the following month. The language was socialist, the demand for a high minimum wage constituted a challenge to employers, and MacDonald hastily rejected the scheme as 'flashy futilities' which were far too radical for a party dependent on middle-class support.[18] Yet the substance was far from being socialist, for *The Living Wage* explicitly rejected 'piece-meal nationalisation' as irrelevant to current problems and rested its under-consumptionist case squarely on the example of American success:

> The benefits of mass production cannot be realised to the full, because the purchasing power of the masses to consume fails to keep pace with the power of the machines to produce. The wrong division of the product involves in this way a limitation of its output. ... The recent experience of America confirms this diagnosis. Great national resources and high technical efficiency are only a part of the explanation of the present prosperity of the United States. Much is explained by the fact that the restriction of immigration and consequent scarcity of labour compelled the employers to resort to a policy of high wages. That gave them a vast home market and enabled them to develop in full the possibilities of mass production.[19]

The Labour left found it uncomfortable to applaud the success of the world's greatest capitalist country, and qualified their praise by pointing out that the United States suffered far more poverty, inequality, and discontent than bourgeois observers were prepared to acknowledge. But they were also aware of the hopeless inadequacy of existing Labour policy and anxious to present an alternative to the Communist Party's revolutionary call. Thus they cited the United States as the disproof of Marx's theories: as Brailsford put it, 'Henry Fordism,' not Marxism, was the future that worked.[20] And in articles such as Mosley's 'Is America a Capitalist Triumph?', and Brailsford's 'Can Capitalism Save Itself? The American Example', they accepted that the 'American technique' held out the promise of sufficient growth to eliminate poverty and unemployment. The crucial question was whether it would be applied by 'Labour with a Socialist purpose or by the progressive wing of Capitalism'. This, Brailsford affirmed, was the challenge *The Living Wage* was designed to meet. For if Labour continued to insist that nothing short of a complete transformation to socialism could restore the economy, 'capitalism may save itself for a generation while we are playing the day-to-day game of politics'.[21]

The nine-day general strike in May 1926 temporarily shattered hopes of creating a consensus for the 'American technique', and talk of shifting to a high wage economy swiftly declined in Conservative circles. Yet in other ways the American example made an enduring impact on British thinking. One was in the growing importance attached to industrial rationalisation, which became the most over-worked (and under-applied) term in politics for the balance of the decade. Another was in the continuing dissatisfaction with monetary policy, which increasingly came to be seen as an impediment to industrial recovery. A third was in encouraging speculation about new configurations of world power and Britain's place within them. The remarkable contrast with conditions in the United States strengthened arguments in Britain for a nationalistic policy of home market or Empire development. In turn these were reinforced by the apparent trend towards vast continental or regional trade blocs, which became the subject of intense speculation in Britain once signs appeared of concerted efforts to improve commercial relations in Europe.

Throughout Europe the First World War had intensified national feeling while leaving numerous territorial disputes unresolved. But it had also left a widespread horror of war, a desire to avoid a renewal of internecine conflict, and a deep sense of common loss. Europe, having squandered its manhood and much of its wealth, had torn up its political order and also, it seemed, handed over world influence to Bolshevik Russia and capitalist America. The defeat of the Red armies at the gates of Warsaw and the suppression of revolutionary movements elsewhere soon ended the threat from the East, which only began to revive after the announcement of the first five-year plan in 1928. In the meantime the American challenge grew more ominous: Europe, 'balkanised' and impoverished, appeared increasingly in danger of economic domination.

Between 1914 and 1919 the United States was transformed from a debtor of some \$3.7 billion to a creditor on a similar scale.[22] Yet its policies remained that of a debtor. Instead of promoting reconstruction of the international trade and payments system, it did little more than concede a reduction in interest on its wartime loans.[23] And instead of facilitating repayment, it adopted the Fordney–McCumber Tariff, the so-called 60 per cent tariff, which raised import duties to a height unequalled in American history or almost anywhere else in the developed world.[24] Meanwhile Herbert Hoover at the Commerce Department lent aggressive support to American manufacturers seeking foreign markets. American foreign investments, which reached a total of perhaps \$17 billion by 1930,[25] enabled the debtor countries to continue purchasing American goods. But this was plainly an unsatisfactory situation. European countries resented the lopsided character of trade relations with the United States and their increasing dependence on American loans. Even while the recycling of dollars continued, moreover, they appeared in danger of losing control over their industrial base to American multinational firms.

On the eve of the war probably fewer than 100 companies in Europe were American owned or controlled; by 1929 the figure exceeded 1,300.

Available statistics preclude categorical claims, but it seems likely that between 1924 and 1929, the years of greatest activity, American multinational firms expanded abroad faster than at any time before or since. Equally significant was the fact that practically all the expansion took place in the new industries, whose products were highly visible and popularly symbolised twentieth-century progress. These were the years when Remington, Underwood, and IBM business machines became a familiar sight in offices throughout Europe, Standard Oil signs went up on every highway, Goodyear and Firestone erected plants in Britain, ITT secured the contract for the Paris telephone exchange, and Hollywood films carried the message of American consumerism to practically every town and hamlet in Europe.[26] Until the Wall Street crash abruptly reduced the flow of direct foreign investment, there seemed no limit to it, and almost everywhere this 'invasion' caused worried talk. Britain was the chief target for American investment, but frustration was greatest in France where the impossibility of resolving the German problem alone and vulnerability over war debts and currency depreciation made Anglo-American finance virtually the arbiter of Franco-German relations.

In the aftermath of the Dawes Plan, France confronted an acute dilemma. Now that the reparations issue was partially resolved, the mark stabilised, and American capital was flooding into Germany, France could expect to see her present lead in postwar recovery give way before her demographically and industrially superior neighbour. The choice that presented itself was continued confrontation with Germany on steadily worsening terms, or an attempt to integrate Germany within the framework of a united Europe.

Almost from the day the Dawes Plan came into force on 5 October 1924 the French Embassy in Berlin began actively to promote a cultural and political dialogue.[27] Frenchmen also played a prominent role in organisations such as the *Union douanière européenne*, the *États-Unis des nations européenne dans les cadres de la Société des Nations*, known as *l'Initiative scandinave*, and the *League for European Cooperation*, which sprang up in the more hopeful climate created by the Dawes Plan and the Locarno treaties of 1925.[28] Edouard Herriot, the Premier and Foreign Minister, signalled the direction of French policy when he spoke to the Chamber of Deputies on 28 January 1925. Having warned foreign countries of France's determination to defend its national interests, he ended by asserting that his greatest desire was to see created a 'United States of Europe'. Europe was now merely a 'small canton of the world,' which must abandon some of its pride and combine its resources if it was to survive. The chamber was evidently impressed, for it voted overwhelmingly to have the speech placarded in every municipality in the land.[29]

Among other important developments at this time, the *Comité franco-allemand d'information et de documentation*, known as the Mayrisch committee after its moving spirit, the Luxemburg industrialist Émile Mayrisch, was established in 1925 with encouragement from the Quai d'Orsay.[30] The committee brought together leading French, German, Belgian, and Luxemburg industrialists as well as prominent journalists and other opinion-makers, and paved the way for the creation of the European Steel Cartel, the so-called *Entente cordiale d'acier*, in September 1926 with Mayrisch as its president. The Pan-Europa Society, created in 1922 by a young and enthusiastic Austrian, Count Coudenhove-Kalergi, was regarded with suspicion by the Quai d'Orsay on account of Coudenhove's possible *Mitteleuropa* ambitions and evident readiness to exclude Britain from European affairs.[31] Nevertheless Aristide Briand, the Foreign Minister, lent his name to the society in 1926 and nominated his closest political ally, Louis Loucheur, to head the French section, which included such notables as the Socialist Léon Blum, the arch-conservative Joseph Barthélémy, and a sub-committee of prominent industrialists and financiers.[32]

The Locarno treaties of October 1925 greatly encouraged hopes of closer collaboration between France and Germany. Briand and his German counterpart, Gustav Stresemann, were well aware of the ambiguous nature of their handiwork, which cast doubt upon their commitment to the general obligations of the League of Nations Covenant and left open the question of German territorial revision in the east. But they were content to see public hopes aroused. Thus at the signing of the agreements in London on 1 December 1925, Briand emotionally referred to them as 'the draft of the constitution of a European family within the orbit of the League of Nations ... the beginning of a magnificent work, the renewal of Europe, its investment with its true character by means of a general union in which all nations will be invited to participate'. Gustav Stresemann on the same occasion declared:

> We have a right to speak of a European idea; this Europe of ours has made the largest sacrifices in the world war; it is now threatened by the danger of losing through the effects of the war that to which it is entitled by reason of its tradition and development ... [A] community of fate binds us to one another. If we go under we go under together; if we would rise we cannot do so in conflict with one another, but only by working together.[33]

The following September, after their private meeting in the Swiss village of Thoiry, Briand was reported to have said in parting, 'If we do not hold together we shall be eaten up by foreign capital. ... Well, it is lucky we agree; if we did not, the American bankers would pull the shirts off our backs.[34] Nine months later Stresemann travelled to Oslo to receive the Nobel peace prize. There he spoke of the peoples of Europe drawing together 'in order to protect themselves from being overpowered and swamped'.[35]

How far either statesman believed his own rhetoric must remain a matter of doubt. Both represented divided governments, which required each of them to perform a delicate political balancing act simply in order to survive in office.[36] Following Locarno, Briand gave little practical support to the 'European idea', showing himself as jealous of French national interests as his rival Poincaré.[37] Stresemann, the former spokesman for German light industry and an imperialist, now the leading proponent of the policy of understanding (*Verständigungspolitik*) with Germany's former enemies, was regularly warned off the organisation of Europe by his conservative advisers at the *Auswärtiges Amt* who feared it would weaken the League of Nations and alienate Britain, both of whom were essential allies in Germany's recovery of power, while strengthening France and endangering the flow of American capital on which Germany now vitally depended.[38] Yet it seems that the First World War had left Briand convinced that France and Germany must bury their differences if Europe was to avoid American domination, and to some extent Stresemann shared his fears.[39]

Besides Stresemann the European idea appealed to many other Germans, particularly among the intelligentsia and parties of the centre and centre-left but also in business circles and parties on the outer fringes of politics. In November 1924 industrialists and bankers of the *Reichsverband der deutschen Industrie* (RVDI), the *Deutscher Industrie- und Handelstag*, and the *Zentralverband der deutschen Bank und Bankiergewerbes* agreed in principle on the aim of European unity and began joint investigations of methods for promoting European economic cooperation. That same year Edgar Stern-Rubarth of the Wolff News Service founded the *Zoll- und Wirtschaftsunion der europäischen Länder*, or the *Union douanière européenne*. In the spring of 1926 a German section of the Pan-Europa Society was created, with an impressive list of directors including Erich Koch-Weser, the leader of the Democratic Party, Joseph Koeth, the Deputy Minister of Economics, and as its head, Paul Loebe, the SPD Deputy and President of the Reichstag, who had just returned from a deeply affecting visit to the United States. Loebe, however, was a devotee of Franz Naumann's *Mitteleuropa* idea and an unrestrained advocate of *Anschluss* with Austria, which the Treaty of Versailles had declared unacceptable. Elsewhere in German industrial and political circles the European idea similarly vied with the still disturbingly strong appeal of an exclusive, German-dominated *Mitteleuropa*.[40] Nevertheless, on the far left the German Communists, toeing the Comintern line, called on workers to struggle for a 'Soviet United States of Europe'.[41] And on the opposite side of the political spectrum Adolf Hitler wrote in his *Zweites Buch* of the necessity for Germany to unite Europe under its domination; otherwise Germany would end up 'a second Holland or a second Switzerland,' for 'with the [Pan-] American Union a new power of such dimension has come into being as threatens to upset the whole former power and order of rank of the states'.[42] The means and the ends thus envisaged were wholly incompatible. But the fact that they all spoke of European unity suggested that it would soon appear on the political agenda.

European and Empire blocs

In Britain the prospect of a European bloc fitted nicely into the conceptual thinking of imperial protectionists, and seemed all the more plausible amidst the ominous difficulties at home. The prolonged threat of a general strike had created a kind of siege mentality, which was reflected in attitudes towards Britain's future and that of the world itself. Unemployment and trade union militancy evoked the spectre of spreading Communist influence among the working class. Comingled with fears of internal subversion was the nightmare of Britain isolated in a world of gigantic blocs while the Empire disintegrated in face of American economic penetration. As the Balfour Committee's compendious *Survey of Overseas Markets* in July 1925 confirmed, Britain faced a far more hostile environment than before the war. World trade had declined some 25 per cent since 1913, and if Britain's share was larger in 1924 this was due merely to Germany's temporary eclipse and could not be expected to last. Europe had decreased as a market for British goods, from 34 per cent in 1913 to 31 per cent in 1924, while the importance of the Empire had become correspondingly larger. But whereas Britain was commercially more dependent on the Dominions, they were becoming steadily less dependent on her. Even in India the lion's share of the postwar increase in import demand was being filled by American competition.[43]

Anxiety over these developments gave new impetus to demands for aggressive protectionist and imperialist policies. The National Union of Manufacturers opened their campaign for extended safeguarding on 23 July 1925 with a lunch for 250 businessmen in the Queen's Hotel in Birmingham. Leaders of the NUM, who resented the government's failure to consult them before issuing the safeguarding White Paper or returning to gold, refrained from criticising the government but made known their belief that it could not be trusted to carry out its mandate without sustained external pressure.[44] Shortly afterwards *The Free Trader* reported the creation of an Empire Self-Supporting League – 'one of the many protectionist organisations which has lately come into existence'.[45] Individually, few of them amounted to much: the League itself appears to have done little more than exhort housewives to 'Buy British'. But their numbers were significant, and the Empire Industries Association (EIA) which was formed in September 1925 from the amalgamation of the British Commonwealth Union and the Empire Development Union, two semi-moribund survivors of the Tariff Reform campaign, soon became a major factor in the revival of imperial protectionism.[46] Led by a banker, Herbert Cokayne Gibbs, first Baron Hunsdon, and supported by the industrial group of Conservative Members of Parliament, the British Empire Producers' Organisation, and spokesmen for the new industries, the EIA lobbied Ministers and petitioned the government at regular intervals. At the annual Conservative Party conference at Scarborough in October 1926, Sir Henry Page Croft and Patrick Hannon, the EIA's leading Parliamentary spokesmen, tabled the resolution criticising the government for its handling of the safeguarding weapon and demanding stronger action. The resolution was approved by acclamation.[47]

Amery, addressing an Empire function in London during the summer, painted a grim picture of British trade prospects, squeezed between a resurgent, protectionist Europe and a United States whose enormous productive capacity was outrunning domestic demand and overflowing into foreign markets. Britain's only hope, he warned, lay with the Empire, and since it had already allowed the United States to penetrate deeply into British markets the necessary first step towards real Empire cooperation was a 'declaration of economic independence from the United States'.[48] So certain was he of Britain's imperial destiny that he actively supported the Pan-Europa Society, despite Coudenhove's well-known belief that Britain's overseas commitments ruled out her participation in a united Europe. At the opening of the imperial conference in London that autumn he criticised Austen Chamberlain's survey of international relations as 'too flat in perspective and too much Europe' yet passing over in silence what Amery thought was the year's most significant event: the first Pan-Europa Congress, held in Vienna only a few days earlier.[49] At an informal lunch for Commonwealth delegates two weeks later Amery engaged in a heated debate with Churchill over Coudenhove's views as to whether Britain should be 'included in Europe or not'. Churchill, he found, was an 'out and out

European and regards the combination of England, France and Germany as the pivot of the world's peace. I strongly upheld the view that we were not European though a useful link between Europe and the new world outside.'[50]

During the next few years Amery made this his constant refrain in Cabinet, in Parliament, on platforms up and down the country, and on his world tour of Empire countries in 1927.[51] Nor was he alone. Robert Boothby, who had had his eyes opened by a visit to the United States in 1925,[52] joined three other young Conservatives, John Loder, Harold Macmillan, and Oliver Stanley, to write a study of the plight of British industry. Their principal theme was the deflationary impact of monetary policy upon domestic purchasing power and the need to provide markets adequate for the new scale of manufacturing production. 'The era of mass production is upon us. And mass production involves large economic units'. The United States, already a self-contained unit, was fast extending its control over Latin America. Europe was organising itself. The Soviet Union, another potential unit, was also attempting to establish in China the nucleus of a Communist-dominated 'Asiatic bloc'. As a result, the 'isolated position' of Britain was 'one of peculiar danger'. The authors admitted that an imperial customs union must still appear a Utopian dream, but professed to see evidence that Dominion statesmen were becoming aware that the imperatives of modern industry demanded nothing less.[53] As if to confirm their point, Stanley Bruce, the Australian Premier, repeatedly warned of increasing American and Japanese penetration of Empire markets in his effort to secure increased British preferences.[54]

At home, Alfred Hacking, Secretary of the Society of Motor Manufacturers and Traders, explained the now widely remarked upon failure of British firms to retain more than a small fraction of the Empire motor vehicle market as the consequence of the incomparably larger domestic market base enjoyed by their American competitors. Britain's only recourse was 'a United States of the British Empire ... as cohesive and self-contained as the USA'. Sir William Larke, Director of the National Federation of Iron and Steel Manufacturers, and Sir Hugo Cunliffe-Owen spoke out on similar lines, and so too did Sir Alfred Mond.[55] In January 1926 Lloyd George, in an attempt to reinvigorate Liberalism, unveiled a scheme for radical land reform. For Mond, who had already begun to speak out against European security commitments and in favour of closer Empire ties, this was the excuse he needed. He crossed the floor and immediately added his voice to the clamour for imperial protectionism from the Conservative back benches.[56]

In September 1926 Mond travelled to New York hoping to arrange a market-sharing agreement with the American and German chemical combines.[57] His efforts came to nothing, and on arriving back at Southampton he expressed his frustration at the way Americans dismissed Britain as inefficient, unstable, and hovering on the brink of revolution.[58] Nine days later he held a press conference to announce the formation of Imperial Chemical Industries (ICI) by the merger of all the major heavy chemicals firms in Britain. Instantly ICI became the largest firm in Britain. As he and Sir Harry McGowan, the former chairman of Nobel Industries and now ICI's managing director, explained, they had to merge in order to 'stand up to the foreign combines which were threatening to divide the world,' and they urged other British industries to defend themselves likewise.[59] Subsequently Mond exploited the publicity attending the event to carry his message to a wider audience.

Writing in the *Spectator* on 30 October, he described the world-wide phenomenon of 'continuously growing concentrations of interests and of industry' that threatened to leave Britain isolated between the United States and a countervailing European bloc, and called for a 'United Economic Empire'. A few weeks later he spoke to the Ladies' Imperial Club, setting out the stark choice of isolation or uniting with the Empire in order to confront the other great blocs on equal and more than equal terms. 'It would not be a question of negotiation, but of stating our terms.'[60] Speaking in Leeds he defined the goal as 'Free Trade within the Empire and tariffs against the rest of the world'.[61] As his extreme language suggested, he was certain time was running out for Britain in face of America's tug on Empire loyalties and the tendency of unemployment at home to breed revolutionary subversion. Several times he alluded to Mussolini's success in restoring order in Italy.[62] But his eyes remained firmly fixed upon the United States, whose economic system appeared to offer everything: employment, industrial peace, national greatness, and a stable capitalist order.

To economic internationalists the arguments for imperial protectionism were as spurious as ever. Nothing had altered the fact that Britain's external trade was divided in three roughly equal parts between Europe, the Empire, and the rest of the world. True, there had been a slight shift away from Europe towards the Empire, but this was temporary and offset by the fact that nearly 80 per cent of British re-exports went to Europe. In any case there was no hope now, if there ever had been, of drawing the Dominions into a unified trade bloc. As their high tariffs indicated, they were determined to build up separate manufacturing bases. Their tendency to trade relatively less with Britain and more with other countries was the inevitable consequence of growing maturity and the facts of geography.

Yet by the winter of 1925 even many of those who rejected the idea of an Empire bloc accepted the probability of eventual European economic unity. To be sure, they did not ignore the obstacles posed by a half century of Franco-German rivalry, the jealous nationalism, and the conflicting forms of government that made political integration so difficult to envisage. Nor did they minimise the obstacles in the way of economic cooperation. Europe's tariff walls were higher, more numerous, and vastly more complicated than before the war. In 1888 the German tariff contained some 400 items, in 1925 some 2,300; in 1892 the French tariff contained 1,500 items, by 1925 the figure had reached 4,000. Quantitative trade controls, practically unknown before the war were now commonly used. Trade relations were also far more unstable owing to the extremely short-term nature of existing treaty agreements. Before the war bilateral agreements of ten to twelve years were common; after the war all but 27 of the 180 agreements adopted were terminable within one year. And of major trading nations, France had still not returned to the principle of unconditional most-favoured-nation treatment: a matter of vital concern to countries like Britain which were not in a position to bargain for equitable treatment in foreign markets.[63] These were serious problems, yet if anything they encouraged internationalists to believe that changes must come. For they no less than their protectionist opponents accepted that the world was being transformed by the advent of large-scale, mass production industry with its demand for large and stable markets, and that Europe in self-preservation would be compelled to unite economically in response.

Ramsay MacDonald, always something of a weathervane of fashionable opinion, spoke of the growing awareness among continental politicians that 'unless in Europe they can create an enormous federation of Free Trade nations, there is not a single nation in Europe that can flourish in the industrial standard that it ought to occupy'.[64] The *Round Table* made the point more eloquently. Comparing relations between Europe and the United States with those of the Greek city-states and Augustan Rome, the journal asserted that Europeans were becoming intensely aware that however superior their culture, their divisions left them defenceless against domination by the larger power:

The economic tendency of the age is unquestionably in the direction of larger and larger units. Just as in industry the small factory has been overshadowed by the big industrial enterprise, so must the small national economic unit be eclipsed by the organised productive and financial power of a continent. The United States has already developed as a super-national power. Unless Europe can do the same, the doom of her economic pretensions is certain. The recognition of these facts is dawning on the Continent ... [T]he goal is still very far off ... But there are signs that a movement towards it has begun, which may prove the decisive issue of the twentieth century as the growth of democratic nationalism was of the nineteenth.[65]

The first indication of a general readiness to improve European commercial relations came in June 1925 at the third Congress of the International Chamber of Commerce in Brussels, when the semi-official chambers of the continental countries surprised observers by their unity of view.[66] It was not before time. Germany, having at last regained tariff autonomy on 11 January 1925, had swiftly augmented its tariff, revision of the French tariff was underway, German–Polish commercial relations had deteriorated into a state of virtual war, declining agricultural prices were forcing Austria and Czechoslovakia to raise import duties, and elsewhere the trend was the same.[67] A second hopeful sign appeared in September when Louis Loucheur, taking up the idea of an international economic conference proposed by the American financier Fred T. Kent at the ICC Congress and subsequently promoted by Sir Arthur Salter at Geneva, formally proposed it at the League of Nations Assembly. Alluding to the current negotiations for a Rhineland pact, he observed that while great efforts were being made to bring political peace to Europe, economic nationalism, the greatest source of conflict, was left completely unchecked. The Assembly responded with enthusiasm; the League's economic section was charged with the task of arranging a world conference.[68]

Loucheur's initiative marked an auspicious development in League affairs. Since the drafting of the Covenant, British hopes of using the League as an agency for restoring multilateral trade had been frustrated by French insistence that commercial policy was a matter strictly for national decision.[69] Now France was calling for League action and the other European member-states offered their support. But the fact that it was Loucheur who took the lead was enough to give British reformers pause. Loucheur, a wartime recruit to government, had earlier amassed a fortune organising the largest network of electrical distribution companies in France.[70] When he spoke of an economic United States of Europe, his idea was to unite it on the basis of industrial cartels or *ententes*. Probably his business experience predisposed him to this approach, and doubtless he appreciated how much France stood to gain from stabilising market shares after a period when the falling franc had enabled French industry to make deep inroads in neighbouring markets. But his approach was incompatible with free trade principles, and the very fact that he called on the United States and the Soviet Union to attend the conference in order to avoid misunderstandings and conflict strengthened expectations that France would seek to use the gathering to lay the foundations of an exclusive European bloc.[71]

The prospect of such an outcome led opponents of the British government's safeguarding policy to intensify their efforts, warning that any further move towards protection by Britain now would kill the European movement or at least drive it onto an autarkic path. As Walter Layton explained to a Manchester audience on 15 December 1925, 'Europe was at the crossroads, and the deplorable thing was that we were not there to encourage the right movement. ... That ... was the most deplorable tragedy since the war'.[72] Robert Brand used his influence with Geoffrey Dawson to see that *The Times* expressed a similar viewpoint.[73] Meanwhile Sir Arthur Salter in Geneva directed the organisation of a massive documentation to dramatise the problems of international trade and encourage the World Economic Conference, as Loucheur's proposal was known, to focus squarely on tariff reductions.[74] The bankers, Walter Leaf and Sir Alan Anderson, worked through the ICC to promote a 'European Trade League' with 'open markets on at least the same scale as those of the United States'.[75] And Norman continued his pursuit of monetary stabilisation, concentrating now on the Belgian, French, and Polish currencies.

With the Imperial Conference only a few weeks away, internationalists sought to deter protectionist action by holding a 'National Free Trade Congress' in Manchester on 29–30 September 1926.[76] The British Chamber of Shipping – 80 per cent of whose members' outward-bound cargo was coal, only about 4 per cent of which went to the Dominions – issued a warning to the government not to hope for concessions from the Dominions sufficient to justify jeopardising Britain's international trade.[77] More controversially, 'A Plea for the Removal of Restrictions on European Trade', bearing the signatures of 180 businessmen from fifteen different countries, was released in time to coincide with newspaper reports of the first day of the conference. *The Economist* hailed the document as the most powerful expression of European aspirations since the war and compared it with the London merchants' petition of 1820, which was commonly held to have signalled the start of the campaign for free trade in Britain. *The Times* recommended it to Dominion statesmen as a reminder of the importance to Britain of international and particularly European trade.[78] But the NUM and other protectionist interests cried foul, charging that this was a transparent attempt to bring European influence to bear upon imperial deliberations.[79] The manifesto had little practical result since the conference was given over almost exclusively to constitutional matters, but it did illustrate the kind of propaganda war taking place within Britain. As the NUM did not fail to point out, almost all the British signatories to the so-called businessmen's manifesto were in fact merchants and bankers rather than industrialists. Lloyd George dismissed it as a 'moneylenders' circular', and in due course its authors were revealed to be Arthur Bell, Sir Hugh Bell, Ernest Benn, and Sir Charles Mallet: the same City-based group that had organised previous bankers' manifestos.[80]

Walter Layton, recently named as a British delegate to the World Economic Conference, spoke at Chatham House on 8 February 1927 of the challenge the conference presented. America's amazing prosperity was creating widespread dissatisfaction in Europe with the '*morcellement*' of the continental market, and giving rise to talk of a customs union or at least the extended use of industrial *ententes* as a means of getting round the political difficulties of tariff reduction. Britain could only welcome European efforts to reduce trade barriers, but she could scarcely accept with equanimity a European customs union which favoured internal trade at the expense of extra-European countries or any other limited regional arrangements. 'Is the world to be divided in the future between three great economic units, Europe, the United States, embracing South America, and Britain and the Empire?' Obviously, he responded, Britain would be placed in an impossible predicament if she were forced to choose between Europe and the Empire.[81]

Internationalists like Layton directed their attention towards Europe and encouraged the view that France was the chief stumbling block to progress in multilateral trade reform.[82] If they mentioned the United States it was to point to the vast free trade area formed of the forty-eight states as the explanation for America's prosperity and an argument for liberalisation elsewhere. From their standpoint, France was responsible for the huge current account deficit in Anglo-French bilateral trade and for prolonging Europe's disarray by its alleged militarism and mania for security, its vindictive policy towards Germany, and its seemingly chronic financial and monetary mismanagement. At the same time they looked to a 'special relationship' with the United States as a vital reinforcement to Britain's global interests. Hence they preferred to minimise criticism of American policy while looking for signs of a turning point: another '1917', when the United States abandoned its economic neutrality in favour of active involvement in the reconstruction of the world economy.[83]

But if they were reticent others were not. A flood of literature had begun to appear including André Siegfried's *America Comes of Age* (1927), J. Ellis Barker's *America's Secret* (1928), and the Hon. George Peel's *The Economic Impact of America* (1928), some of it hostile, much of it sensational, and all of it devoted to the seemingly inexorable expansion of American economic power.[84] New sources of friction had also arisen including government subsidies to the American merchant marine, conflict over access to raw materials such as oil and rubber, American government plans to raise cotton prices by subsidising the cutback of domestic production, aggressive American foreign loan promotion, allegedly with loans tied to contracts for American goods, and serious disagreements over naval disarmament.[85] A thinly veiled anti-Americanism thus emerged in Britain as well as on the continent, the extent of which was indicated in the Commons debate on the Cinematograph Films Bill on 17 March 1927.

The bill, which offered a quota on foreign films and measures for reducing the distributors' hold over exhibitors, was intended, as Cunliffe-Lister frankly explained, to combat the Americanising influence of Hollywood films upon British consumer taste and their broader political impact upon the Empire. The President of the Board of Trade confirmed that Dominion representatives at the recent Imperial Conference had expressed deep concern that barely 5 per cent of the films shown in the Empire were British, and Conservative speakers used the debate to denounce 'the stranglehold of American monopoly interests'. This was largely predictable, but it was noteworthy that Labour speakers did not object to the government's aims despite their rejection of the bill. Several, including Arthur Greenwood and Lieut.-Commander J.M. Kenworthy, a recent defector from Liberal ranks, vied with Conservative opponents in deploring the effect of Hollywood upon British authority in the Empire and less developed parts of the world. Ramsay MacDonald in particular dwelt upon the dangers of showing American films that depicted 'white people' in sinful or demeaning activities to the non-white peoples of the Empire, 'people who, a few years ago, regarded us as being a dominant and ruling people'.[86]

On 3 May 1927 Sir Alfred Mond spoke to a gathering of Conservative MPs of his recent tour of European capitals. Everywhere, he claimed, business and political leaders agreed on the necessity for the economic unification of Europe:

> It was quite remarkable, and I should not have believed it if I had not come so closely into contact with it. The idea that you must form some economic union of European countries, some form of joint action in industry ... in taxation, in tariffs, and even further steps than that, in order to enable Europe to go on existing against the Continent of North America, is becoming almost axiomatic, almost a passionate faith.[87]

Mond's remarks were directed mainly against men like Layton who looked upon Geneva as 'the Mecca of the world' and anticipated that Europe would provide an expanding market for British goods. But it was too soon to tell whether the 'European minds' or Mond's fellow imperial protectionists were the more realistic in their anticipations.

Much would depend upon the World Economic Conference, which was scheduled to open in the Salle de Reformation, where the League Assembly met in Geneva, the following morning.

The World Economic Conference

The World Conference, a semi-official function, was attended by 194 delegates and 226 accredited experts from fifty countries including the Soviet Union and the United States. The British delegates, although nominated by the Board of Trade, were free to speak and vote in their personal capacity. The delegation comprised the ironmaster Sir Arthur Balfour, Sir Norman Hill, a prominent figure in the shipping industry, Walter Layton, Sir Max Muspratt, chairman of the British Chemical Manufacturers' Association and current president of the FBI, and Arthur Pugh, secretary of the ISTC and vice-president of the TUC General Council. At the opening session the president of the conference, M. Georges Theunis, announced to loud applause the appointment of Loucheur as first vice-president.[88] The British delegation held back, making no effort to secure the remaining executive positions. Nevertheless the British presence at the conference was pervasive. Besides the delegation and its accompanying experts from the FBI, the Chamber of Shipping, the Manchester Chamber of Commerce, and other bodies, Sir Eric Drummond and Salter attended as representatives of the League of Nations. J.R. Bellerby, a member of the ILO contingent, acted as a virtual member of the British delegation. Sir Herbert Llewellyn Smith, the recently retired Chief Economic Adviser to the government and a close observer of the Geneva scene as member of the League Economic Committee, attended at the personal invitation of M. Theunis. Walter Runciman, the shipowner and former Liberal Cabinet Minister, led the ICC delegation. The separate Dominion and Indian delegations also worked closely with their British counterparts. British influence could thus be exerted from several directions upon the progress of the conference and could check French-led attempts to promote narrowly European or nationalistic policies.[89]

During the first four days the conference remained in plenary session to allow a general airing of views on the current state of world economic conditions. The Russian delegate, notwithstanding lengthy criticism of the capitalist countries, affirmed his country's desire for peaceful coexistence and the normalisation of trade relations. The American delegate, however, refused to be drawn when Layton requested confirmation of his country's readiness to join in a general assault upon trade restrictions. Practically every other speaker, including the several British participants, dwelt upon the problems confronting Europe rather than the world as a whole, and time and again Europe's predicament was illustrated by reference to American prosperity.[90] No one disputed the need for action. However, differences soon emerged on the form that action should take.

Layton and Runciman accepted that in the circumstances complete free trade lay beyond the limits of the possible, but persisted in calling for the complete removal of all 'artificial' restrictions on trade. Loucheur on the other hand pointedly alluded to criticism of France as an 'ultra-protectionist' country from delegates whose own national tariff levels were high, and welcomed it as 'a sign of progress' that no one had come forward to propose general free trade. France, he declared in response to a Russian claim, did not seek to create a United States of Europe, which was economically as well as politically impracticable. Yet in almost the same breath he spoke of the necessity to create European-wide 'horizontal integration' or industrial ententes, and increase 'purchasing power' through higher wages and salaries, since only this way could Europe create an economic base competitive with the United States.[91] Confrontation began almost immediately the conference went into committee session.

On 9 May Daniel Serruys, director of the treaty department of the French Ministry of Commerce, presented a set of draft resolutions to the Commerce Committee.[92] Much of the case for 'economic disarmament' was unexceptionable. But his provision for tariff reduction rested on the principle of 'counterbalancing' duties: duties sufficiently high to offset 'more favourable conditions of production or a more advantageous regime of prices in the principal competing country'. This did not completely negate the principle of comparative advantage, since, as Serruys emphasised, a ceiling was set by the costs of the 'principal competing country', but it came perilously close to doing so, and as well raised the difficulty that estimates of production costs were highly problematical. The next day Layton spoke out, bluntly dismissing this section of Serruys' draft as 'impracticable and ... undesirable', and warning that British public opinion would likely turn to protection if it seemed that 'the other European countries had no intention of doing anything'.[93]

Layton's warning sent a shudder through the conference. Britain was still far and away the world's largest importer: she was the most important export market for France, Germany, Belgium, Denmark, Norway, Sweden, and Portugal (as well as the United States and many other overseas countries), and the second or third most important for practically every other country of Europe. Moreover in practically every case European countries were running very sizeable trade surpluses with

Britain, which they could ill-afford to lose.[94] The following day Loucheur spoke up in Serruys' defence. This time Runciman countered the arguments, supported by the chairman of the committee, M. Colijn, a former Dutch Premier whose views commanded respect among the low tariff countries of northern Europe.[95]

Thereafter progress was rapid. Serruys, having indicated France's decision to abandon her two-tier tariff system, involving a maximum schedule of duties or *tarif de combat*, and a minimum schedule accorded to foreign countries offering adequate reciprocal concessions, nevertheless held to the principle of reciprocity or conditional most-favoured-nation treatment in the matter of extending to third countries concessions made to a foreign country in bilateral negotiations. But breaking more sharply with previous policy, he called for the League to assume the task of investigating schemes for reducing tariff levels. And when on 12 May Layton presented an alternative set of draft resolutions, Serruys allowed the substantive items to stand, including endorsement of the most-favoured-nation clause in its 'widest and most unconditional form'.[96]

The Industry Committee, having first dealt inconclusively with rationalisation, took up international cartels on the 12th. British delegates were not of one mind on the subject. Industrialists in Britain, lacking the central organisations required for effective participation, were cool towards cartels but recognised that they were already widespread in Europe and accepted them in principle so long as they were strictly non-governmental arrangements.[97] Trade unionists opposed them and insisted at the least on public regulation and publicity.[98] Within mercantile–financial circles opinion was also divided. A few like Sir Alan Anderson favoured cartels as a means of by-passing tariff barriers, but for the most part they were regarded as a retrograde measure likely only to stabilise trade at present levels and nullify the value of most-favoured-nation commitments.[99]

In the event the cartel idea proved far less popular than at first seemed likely. Delegates from several of the smaller countries including Finland, Norway, and Switzerland were either flatly opposed to it or at least seriously disturbed by its implications.[100] The German delegate poured scorn on its value as an agency for trade liberalisation and economic peace. The Swedish delegate spoke up for consumer interests. Several trade union and ILO spokesmen insisted upon public regulation and formal safeguards for employees: precisely the sort of interference employers' organisations rejected. Assisted only modestly by British delegates, the committee brushed aside the idea, accepting that international cartels were a fact of life, though not necessarily a desirable one, and calling for the widest publicity of their activities.[101]

This agreed, the only other question outstanding was the future economic organisation of the League of Nations. Here too opinion among British delegates was divided. Pugh, in line with the pre-conference recommendation of the TUC and Labour Party, advocated keeping the conference in being as a semi-permanent body to promote international economic cooperation and guard against the recrudescence of imperialist rivalries. But the other delegates held to the view that this would only weaken the authority of the League Economic Committee on which Britain was strongly represented.[102] During the final stage of the conference sharp differences emerged between the majority British position and French, German, and labour representatives. In the end the latter gave way and the final decision was passed on to the League where British influence was likely to prevail.[103]

Leaders of internationalist opinion in Britain, anxious to avoid raising false hopes beforehand, were with good reason pleased at the conference results. The French cartel approach to trade relations had been decisively rejected. The conference strongly condemned existing tariff levels in Europe, and barring the abstentions of the Soviet Union and Turkey unanimously adopted a series of resolutions along conventional free trade lines.[104] But whether it was the 'amazing success' claimed by *The Nation* or the 'landmark in economic history' as *The Economist* asserted was another matter.[105] Although practically every independent country had been represented at the conference, governments were not bound by the results. The American delegation had been especially emphatic that its actions did not commit Washington to anything. The Europeans remained doubtful of progress without the cooperation of the United States, the world's largest exporting nation. Moreover, Britain itself was becoming an obstacle on account of the growing uncertainty over its future commercial policy.

Deepening divisions over free trade

Despite some improvement in productivity in the years after the post-war slump, the dominant feature of the British economy remained the depression in the older export industries and resultant high levels of unemployment. As *The Times* commented early in 1927, the unsheltered industries had already gone through 'five years of the most intense depression they had ever experienced' before the calamitous general strike in 1926, which was 'the blackest of black years'.[106] The brighter climate of affairs that marked the start of 1927 faded with the slow-down of economic activity in the spring. The same pattern occurred in 1928, and in 1929 the only difference was that the down-turn began in June, several months later in the year. With wholesale prices continuing their downward trend and real interest rates standing well above 10 per cent, the inevitable concomitant was mounting pressure for assistance to industry, in particular for import protection.

During the first half of 1927 agriculture was again at the centre of attention. By this time domestic food production had fallen below the level reached in 1914, and far below that reached in 1918, with arable land going out of production at the rate of 200,000 acres a year. The government's White Paper on agriculture in 1926 had been a frankly negative document, and Walter Guinness, Irwin's successor as Minister of Agriculture, acknowledged that the industry was 'in low water'.[107] Trouble came to a head early in 1927 when the *Daily Mail* took up the farmers' cause in a determined way.[108] In May, Sir George Courthope, chairman of the 200-strong Conservative backbench Agricultural Committee, introduced a motion at the quarterly meeting of the Council of Agriculture for England, censuring the government for failing to honour its election pledges to maintain food production and rural employment, and calling for the extension of safeguarding to the industry.[109] The NFU, in recognition of the government's electoral predicament, had held back on the protection issue until now. But NFU leaders were known to be intensely jealous of the government-sponsored council, their rival for authority within the farm community, and certain to become more outspoken if the council proceeded to act.[110] The council duly adopted Courthope's motion by a margin of thirty to fourteen.[111] Thereupon the NFU called on county branches to ginger up local MPs, and repeatedly criticised the government for failing to honour its pledges. According to one source, feelings against the government reached 'white hot' temperatures among farmers that year.[112]

The second half of the year was marked by renewed controversy over safeguarding for iron and steel, which began with the application from the heavy steel-makers in July.[113] A few months later, the *Morning Post* led off a concerted campaign to build support among workers in the industry and other interested parties.[114] The applicants' request for reconsideration rested mainly on the claim that market conditions had been radically altered by the depreciation of the French and Belgian currencies. There was no doubt that this was so. Between 1924 and 1927 steel imports had risen from 2.4 to 4.4 million tons. As the campaign got underway, moreover, it became evident that other interests with an important stake in the future of the industry were becoming seriously concerned at its plight. South Wales tinplate manufacturers, an export-oriented group who had hitherto opposed protection, now made no move to dissociate themselves from the campaign. The British Engineers Association also ceased its opposition, and indications appeared of a similar change of attitude among employers in the shipbuilding and mining industries.[115]

The Balfour Committee on Trade and Industry, whose final report appeared in March 1929, affirmed that 'there is no strong and general trend of organised commercial opinion in favour of any material change of national tariff policy'.[116] But perhaps this was only to be expected. The committee, as constituted by the first Labour government, was strongly biased in favour of commercial as opposed to industrial opinion.[117] The FBI, industry's largest representative body, remained silent on the fiscal question. Privately, the President, Sir Max Muspratt, accepted that industry was 'going through a transition stage', that there was 'a growing feeling' that Britain could no longer afford to be the only free trade country in a protectionist world.[118] Publicly, the Federation preferred to say nothing for fear of losing its claim to speak for the whole of industry – and largely for this reason was increasingly by-passed by employers during the latter half of the decade.[119] Industrial opinion did remain divided over protection, but all the evidence points to growing support; and this was as true of organised labour as of employers.

In 1923 the decision of the employers in the woollen and worsted industry to break with their free trade tradition and seek safeguarding had been a contributory factor in Baldwin's fateful decision to go to the country for a mandate on protection.[120] On that occasion and in 1925, when the employers again made application for safeguarding, the trade unions concerned chose to stand aloof. But between 1923 and 1928 woollen imports (mainly from France) doubled to more than 40 million square yards, and unemployment in the industry rose above 25 per cent.[121] A movement within the 200,000-strong National Association of Unions in the Textile Trades to support safeguarding was headed off by Philip Snowden and other Labour MPs in the West Riding in January 1928.[122] But in the autumn similar efforts failed: trade union delegates meeting in Bradford on 1 December voted to collaborate with employers in a joint safeguarding application, to stop the industry from declining further.[123] This was followed a few weeks later by a formal request from Arthur Pugh, Secretary of the Iron and Steel Trades Confederation, to the Prime Minister for an impartial inquiry into the plight of the steel industry. The protectionist leanings of the confederation, although evident for many years, had hitherto been held in check by the opposition of the South Wales unions. Now, despite the absence of any specific mention of safeguarding in Pugh's letter, there could be no doubt that this was the intended objective.[124]

The government stood fast. Guinness, backed by the Cabinet, restrained the backbench agricultural committee from joining in the Council of Agriculture's agitation.[125] During the summer, he, Baldwin, and other Ministers spoke in rural constituencies, appealing to farmers to 'look truth in the face': to recall that the 90 per cent of the population living in the towns would not tolerate food taxes and that the 2 million women voters added to the rolls at the next general election posed an additional barrier; to recognise that their problem was a world-wide one, and bear in mind that a Conservative defeat meant the return of the Liberals or Labour, both of whom were preparing wild land nationalisation schemes.[126] In July 1928 and again the following spring Cunliffe-Lister turned down the steel-makers' safeguarding application by referring to Baldwin's statement of 21 December 1925 in the Commons.[127] Early in 1929 the Cabinet rejected Pugh's request for an inquiry and suppressed the report of the safeguarding committee, which found in favour of the woollen and worsted industry, until after the general election due later in the year.[128]

Perhaps there was no choice. In view of existing divisions in electoral opinion and among the interests represented within the party itself, the government could have acted otherwise only at great risk. But there was a price to be paid for rejecting the repeated appeals from industry. The Conservative rank and file, which overwhelmingly endorsed resolutions for extending safeguarding at every annual conference, displayed increasing dissatisfaction with the government's performance; the EIA, NUM, NFU, and the various backbench committees similarly became harder to appease. Within the Cabinet itself acrimonious differences between free traders and protectionists led to repeated threats of resignation by Amery and Churchill, and spilled over into public feuding in the summer of 1928.[129] Between 1925 and 1929 only nine of the forty-nine industries that applied for safeguarding protection were successful.[130] As none of the successful applicants was of major importance, protectionists had reason to be disappointed. Torn as it was, the government showed scarcely more willingness to align itself with internationalist opinion, however. Indeed, its contribution to trade liberalisation efforts during the latter part of the decade was strictly of a negative kind.

Retreat from leadership on the commercial front

At the quarterly meeting of the League of Nations Council on 16 June 1927, Stresemann proposed that the League should give its strongest endorsement to the World Conference resolutions. Belgium, Czechoslovakia, and Germany had already affirmed their unreserved support, and other countries represented on the council including France appeared ready to do the same. But from the chair Sir Austen Chamberlain coolly referred to his government's 'first but rather hasty study' of the resolutions, and made it clear that Britain was not prepared to lend them her full support. Stresemann did not hide his disappointment, but as unanimity was required the council had to settle for an anodyne resolution commending the conference report to all governments.[131]

The diplomatic conference, convened under League auspices at Geneva in October 1927 for the negotiation of an international convention abolishing import and export 'prohibitions', further illustrated Britain's negative role. Within Europe the use of embargos, quotas, and licensing and barter arrangements, or as they are now known, quantitative trade controls, had been widely resorted to for the first time in a century during the recent war. As a means of husbanding scarce foreign exchange reserves, their value was incontestable. But from the standpoint of multilateral trade relations they constituted a highly undesirable innovation, for they involved the freezing of trade into rigid channels, and since no means of allocating market shares could fail to affect exporting countries differently, the result was discrimination in one form or another and the practical nullification of most-favoured-nation commitments. Calls for their removal had thus begun almost immediately after the Armistice, the 1922 Genoa Conference among others declaring them 'one of the gravest obstacles to international trade'.[132]

Britain had much to gain and little to lose from an all-embracing agreement. Her only imports regulated by quantitative controls were dyestuffs. The Anglo-German commercial treaty moreover ruled out further resort to such restrictions, and through the operation of most-favoured-nation agreements this self-denying ordnance extended to practically the whole of Britain's import trade. France on the other hand maintained extensive controls, and in eastern and southern Europe their use was still widespread.

At the conference, however, it soon became clear that agreement would depend upon Britain's willingness to make a contribution. France, having agreed to abandon her embargo on the import of dyestuffs as part of the recent commercial treaty with Germany, now sought the removal of Germany's restrictions on coal imports which were keeping up the price in Germany and reducing the value of reparations in kind. Several other delegations had come determined to press France to abandon export controls on scrap iron. The Swiss delegate had instructions to oppose an exception for British dyestuffs. The German delegate insisted that for political reasons coal import restrictions could not be abandoned without some reciprocal benefit, the only worthwhile one being removal of Britain's dyestuffs quota. When therefore, Sir Sydney

Chapman, the British delegate, was obliged to insist on an exception for dyestuffs, the result was stalemate. A convention was adopted which Britain was the first to ratify. But since most countries made their ratification conditional upon the adherence of certain other countries, its future remained very much in doubt.[133]

Another exception Britain insisted on before the convention was drafted covered veterinary and phytopathological restrictions on agricultural imports, collectively known as sanitary restrictions. During the 1920s such restrictions had become widely used, or rather misused, on the continent as economic and even political weapons, and in the latter part of the decade efforts were made under the auspices of the International Institute of Agriculture in Rome to devise regulations governing their use. But despite the importance of agricultural trade in Europe and the improvement in commercial relations that could be expected to follow from removal of contrived sanitary restrictions, the Ministry of Agriculture vigorously resisted British participation in a negotiated solution.[134] The Ministry argued that Britain's insular position provided her with unique possibilities for maintaining high sanitary standards, and being the only major food importing country she would be forced to accept wholly inadequate restrictions if the matter was left to international negotiation. This was perhaps true, but it was apparent that the Ministry's demand for a free hand had as much to do with domestic pressures as international ones. British farmers, denied the straightforward protection promised them during the war, pressed for the maximum extension of sanitary restrictions, and through the NFU put their case much more forcefully than before. The Ministry, without much believing in the effectiveness of new restrictions, repeatedly gave way out of a desire to avoid the blame for any sanitary problems that might arise.[135] Among goods embargoed or severely restricted from entry in the 1920s were live animals, fresh meat, hay, cherries, and potatoes. In terms of Britain's total import bill their value was modest and consumers had little difficulty finding substitutes, but practically all of them fell with particular force on France. French peasants, who were also becoming better organised, demanded a negotiated settlement of their grievances, and when this was refused the cry of Perfidious Albion became intense.[136]

The increasing use of sanitary restrictions was only one source of growing Anglo-French commercial friction. Viewed from London, Britain appeared to be a free trade nation struggling for survival in a protectionist world. But viewed from across the Channel the situation appeared very different. In the first place Britain's postwar duties, if limited in number, were generally applied at *ad valorem* rates so high as to be almost prohibitive. Secondly, practically all of them materially affected French trade and several of them fell directly upon old-established industries concentrated in one or a few towns, such as the silk trade in Lyon which faced a duty of 56 per cent by 1927, the lace-making industry of Morez, and the leather glove industry of Grenoble and Millau.[137] Thirdly, in order to meet inflated Exchequer requirements, Britain had greatly increased the range and level of revenue duties, some of which, such as those on tobacco, spirits, and wines, constituted a serious barrier to French trade. British authorities denied that revenue duties were protective since they applied mainly to goods not produced at home, and where goods were domestically produced they faced an equivalent excise duty. But this argument had been rejected at the World Conference on the grounds that all import duties discouraged trade or caused substitution with non-dutiable goods. Nor did it help Britain's case that the 'equivalent' excise duties were not always equal in value to the revenue duties, or that the Conservative government had increased the element of imperial preference.[138] Comparing revenue obtained from import duties – albeit a misleading basis for comparison – Britain actually seemed not only more protectionist than before the war but substantially more so than France herself.[139]

French authorities regarded their own contribution to international commercial relations to have been substantial. For some years preparations had been under way to revise the pre-war French tariff to make up for the loss of protection and revenue due to currency depreciation. A tariff bill was eventually tabled in 1927, but hardly had it appeared when on 17 August the Franco-German commercial treaty was signed and the bill was set aside. The treaty, popularly known as the economic Locarno, involved numerous changes in the French tariff and an overall increase in the level of duties. Yet compared with the tariff revision already planned, the result was a substantial lowering of duties. Moreover, it confirmed France's abandonment of the old two-tier tariff and acceptance of the principle of most-favoured-nation treatment.[140]

The treaty however came at a time when British traders were already disturbed at the worsening of the Anglo-French balance of trade. For many years before the war France had consistently earned a surplus from trade with Britain, but whereas in the five years 1909–13 the surplus averaged £12.2 million per annum, during the three years 1925–27 it exceeded £37.5 million, added to which tourist receipts also greatly increased and almost wholly in France's favour.[141] The explanation for the worsening bilateral balance rested chiefly with Britain's over-valued exchange and the depreciation of the franc; the French tariff was in fact scarcely more protective in 1927 than in 1913.[142] But British traders were concerned with the consequences not the causes, and seeing French duties abruptly raised against British goods simultaneous with French concessions on items of importance to German competitors, they pressed the Board of Trade to seek redress through diplomatic channels.[143]

As instructed, Lord Crewe, the British Ambassador in Paris, delivered a note of protest to Briand on 12 January 1928. Britain, he pointed out, was France's best customer, and two-thirds of French goods, equivalent to more than the whole of Britain's exports to France, still entered Britain free of duties. Not only was the recent rise in French duties in flagrant violation of the spirit of the World Economic Conference, but there was 'a growing feeling amongst traders' in Britain against 'the present fiscal system' in view of the evident refusal of European countries to make any concessions except through the process of tariff bargaining which Britain under free trade was unequipped to carry out.[144]

The French response, although conciliatory, reflected the very different perception of trade relations as seen from Paris. Crewe was reminded that, as a result of currency depreciation, French duties on some of the largest items of British trade were lower than they had been for years. For instance, the duty on coal, which represented fully half of British exports to France, was fully 66 per cent below the pre-war level, while duties on textiles were on average 20–30 per cent lower than two years before. Additionally, certain of Britain's specific grievances concerning duties on textile, agricultural, and other machinery had been met either as a unilateral concession or as a result of concessions contained in treaties recently negotiated with Switzerland and Belgium which were automatically extended to Britain by reason of her long-standing most-favoured-nation privileges. On the other hand, Crewe was reminded of outstanding French grievances and the existing invitation to negotiate a new commercial treaty.[145]

Cunliffe-Lister anticipated that France would gain more than Britain from negotiations and refused the offer, preferring instead to rely upon France's interest in maintaining British political and economic goodwill.[146] A few weeks later, however, Churchill announced in his fourth Budget a further large increase in revenue duties on wine with a corresponding increase in imperial preference.[147] Goodwill, such as it was, thus became another victim of the self-imposed deflationary pressures on the Exchequer.

British commercial relations with other leading continental countries were scarcely better. German dissatisfaction with Britain had existed since the adoption of the Dyestuffs Act and increased with the reimposition of the McKenna duties, the silk and rayon duties, and certain of the safeguarding duties such as those on fabric gloves. At meetings between representatives of the FBI and its German equivalent, the RVDI, in 1926 and 1927, complaints from the British side about German protectionism evoked equally strong complaints in response.[148] In March 1928 Sir Ronald Lindsay, the British Ambassador in Berlin, took up the question of German tariff protection at the Wilhelmstrasse. He was politely but firmly told that dissatisfaction in Germany at recent British fiscal changes was such that the existing Anglo-German treaty would probably be denounced at the earliest opportunity.[149] A week later Sir Ronald Graham, the Ambassador in Rome, reported a similar story. Responding to his complaints about Italian restrictions on coal and other imports, officials at the Palazzo Chigi described the strong dissatisfaction in Italian business circles at British commercial policy and practically ruled out any concessions.[150]

The previous year at the World Economic Conference European delegates had shown their determination to reverse the 'balkanisation' of the continent and meet the American challenge by endorsing unilateral, bilateral, and multilateral initiatives on tariff reduction and other means of liberalising trade. But their virtual unanimity on ends masked a basic disagreement on means. While British delegates urged the unconditional or automatic provision of most-favoured-nation treatment whatever the method of approach, Jacques Rueff, attending the conference on behalf of the League Economic Section, informally promoted a limited regional pact among the continental countries.[151] Was this not what was intended by the endorsement of multilateral initiatives? And was it not obvious that so long as the United States refused to participate in collective action, this was the only way of making progress? Left unanswered by the conference, these questions soon came up at the League Council where they were turned over to the Economic Committee for clarification.[152]

By coincidence the chairman of the committee at this time was Daniel Serruys. A Belgian by birth and as a young man one of Europe's leading Byzantine scholars, he had been recruited into the French civil service during the war, where he soon became known as the ablest commercial negotiator in the business.[153] The Franco-German commercial treaty, his greatest achievement, marked France's acceptance of the most-favoured-nation principle. But this did not mean that henceforth France would extend similar treatment to all countries as of right. On the contrary, having signed the German treaty, France deliberately withheld most-favoured-nation treatment from the United States until certain grievances were removed.[154]

Bilateral Franco-American trade before the war had been roughly in balance, but during the war and throughout the 1920s the balance shifted heavily in favour of the United States.[155] One reason was the passage of the eighteenth constitutional amendment instituting prohibition in the United States in 1919, which fell with particular force on French export trade.[156] Another was America's postwar emergency tariff and the 1922 Fordney–McCumber Tariff, which raised American duties to an all-time high, affecting 52 per cent of British exports, 64 per cent of European exports as a whole, and fully 72 per cent of French exports owing to the fact that many were deemed to be luxuries.[157] French dissatisfaction, coloured by the United States' withdrawal into isolation and insistence upon war debt repayment, remained intense. The withholding of most-favoured-nation treatment brought repeated protests and eventually retaliation. The Mellon–Bérenger debt funding agreement went unratified by France. Early in 1929 French tax law was modified with the two-fold aim of discouraging further American direct investment in French industry and increasing the liabilities of American firms already operating in France by an amount roughly equal to French obligations under the Mellon – Bérenger agreement.[158] Serruys thus knew only too well the related problems raised by the most-favoured-nation principle and American economic nationalism.

The deliberations of the Economic Committee which commenced in March 1928 soon confirmed that French anxieties were widely shared on the continent. As Dr Ernst Trendelenberg, Serruys' German counterpart in the recent treaty negotiations, explained, all the European countries shared a common procedure for tariff-making whereby changes were arrived at through a process of bilateral negotiations, the results then being extended to third countries sharing most-favoured-nation rights. The one exception was Britain, which shared with the United States a policy of autonomous or non-negotiable tariff-making. With Britain balanced between free trade and protection, the United States intensely protectionist, and neither prepared to negotiate with other powers, how could Europe hope to arrange improved trade relations? 'It was in that quarter that the chief difficulty lay.'[159]

Britain, lacking bargaining instruments, had long made most-favoured-nation treatment the cardinal feature of her trade and navigation treaties,[160] and in committee deliberations Sir Sydney Chapman insisted that the World Economic Conference had endorsed the extension of such treatment without reference to other factors.[161] But the seven members of the nine-man committee who came from continental countries as firmly disagreed.[162] While sharing his desire for trade liberalisation, it seemed obvious to them that the conference had not confirmed most-favoured-nation treatment as a natural right, since otherwise there could be no inducement to participate in the multilateral conventions that were advocated. Further, notwithstanding America's support for the most-favoured-nation principle, they were not prepared to exchange, in Serruys' words, 'an open door for a closed door'.[163] Eventually a formula was drawn up recommending that an exception should be made from the operation of the most-favoured-nation clause for 'plurilateral conventions of a general character and aiming at the improvement of economic relations between peoples', provided that they were open to all countries to join on equal terms and had the approval of the League of Nations. But out of respect for the sanctity of contracts it was left to individual countries to modify their treaty obligations so as to allow for such plurilateral conventions through the normal process of bilateral negotiation.[164] Meanwhile the necessity for collective action was becoming rapidly more urgent.

In May 1928 the League of Nations Economic Consultative Committee, set up to monitor progress in the application of the World Conference resolutions, expressed cautious optimism about the direction of commercial relations over the previous twelve months. Protectionism in Europe, rising dangerously at the time of the conference, had been virtually halted, and taking into account the Franco-German treaty, which both parties agreed would have been politically unacceptable in the absence of the conference, and the Prohibitions Convention, there were grounds for claiming that 'on balance' European trade relations had shown 'some improvement during the year'.[165] But by May 1929 the committee was obliged to warn that progress had been halted and unless immediate action was taken a new era of protectionism was almost certain. The decline in commodity prices, now endangering the economic stability of countries in eastern Europe and overseas, was one source of difficulty. More important, the United States was threatening to create new difficulties for the rest of the world by increasing its already massive tariff wall.[166]

Britain now had nothing to offer. Talk of Britain resorting to protection made European countries all the more anxious to avoid offending her by joining in discriminatory schemes, but beyond that it merely added to the uncertainty overhanging commercial relations. British members of the Consultative Committee urged a new appeal for tariff reductions. Louis Loucheur bluntly responded that the situation was 'dominated by the question of the relation between Europe and America'. Until this was solved further tariff reduction was out of the question.[167]

Here then was the irony of British postwar history. Leaders of the mercantile–financial community, in pushing too vigorously for a return to the policies of 1914, had overreached themselves. In the effort to 'make the pound look the dollar in the face', they had intensified the difficulties facing industry and magnified the challenge of American economic expansion. As a result, the consensus between the two communities on economic internationalism, which had prevailed for most of the preceding century, was again shattered. The government, mirroring the conflict, vacillated over commercial policy and retreated from the opportunity to reassert Britain's traditional role as leader of the free trade world. As the following chapter describes, the same developments also effectively undermined Britain's leadership of the international monetary system.

5

The scramble for gold

Churchill, Norman, and the industrial crisis

By the end of 1925 Montagu Norman's 'big idea' was still far from realised. Britain had returned to the gold standard with unexpected ease: none of the credits arranged in New York had been required, and following Britain's lead some thirty other countries had also returned to gold.[1] On the other hand, Norman had found himself with far less autonomy over the management of credit and currency than he expected, and his hopes of a 'special relationship' with the American central bank authorities had also received a severe knock. In August he had been pressured by the Chancellor to reduce Bank rate in order to help resolve the coal dispute.[2] Facing renewed pressure in September, he looked for a rise in the New York discount rate to forestall the need for action, but found that Benjamin Strong was unable to act against the mounting speculation in his securities markets because of Washington's determination to assist the financing of American crop exports.[3] Norman lowered his rate, but no sooner had he done so than Strong warned him to expect a rise in the New York rate.[4] Norman peevishly complained about this inopportune development and requested Strong to hold off for three weeks while Churchill considered the Norman committee's recommendation to remove the embargo on long-term lending.[5] But, with speculation in New York drawing balances from London and forcing the Bank to sell gold in defence of the exchanges, the writing was on the wall. By December the gold losses had reached £13 million, sending reserves below the Cunliffe Committee's recommended minimum of £150 million. Norman now had no choice. Late on Wednesday 2 December he called at the Treasury to leave word that the Bank's Committee of Treasury would announce a higher Bank rate after its meeting the next morning.

Churchill responded angrily to the news. Having just lifted the foreign loan embargo, he had good reason to expect charges of favouring the City at the expense of industry, which now faced higher borrowing costs. Feeling betrayed by his advisers and convinced that the gold standard was little more than a bankers' ramp, he telephoned the Governor on the morning of the third, 'protesting against the proposed increase and threatening to state in the House of Commons that such increase had been made without his having been consulted and against his wishes'. In the event Norman proceeded with a full 1 per cent Bank rate rise and Churchill did not carry out his threat. But thereafter Norman found himself under greater pressure than ever, with Churchill making their weekly meetings an occasion for tirades against his advice and 'the evil effects of the Gold Standard'.[6]

As the government's nine-month subsidy to the coal industry came to an end in the spring of 1926 and the threat of a general strike revived, Churchill's frustration remained intense. While preparing his Budget speech, he suggested to his private secretary that Niemeyer might contribute a paragraph on the first year's experience back on gold along the lines: 'At any rate our prosperity, such as it is, stands on an absolutely sound foundation. Having deliberately thrown ourselves out of a top storey window, we have at least the assurance that we can start fair again from the pavement.'[7] But such bitter sarcasm was reserved for the corridors of the Treasury. When he came to deliver the speech on 26 April he again spoke like a true believer, stressing the value of Britain's seven-year struggle to get back to $4.86. With domestic price-levels now fully adjusted to the new exchange parity, he affirmed, the return to gold meant an annual £5 million saving on commodity imports from the United States, £750,000 on the American war debt, and 'tens of millions' on foreign investments. Bank rate was no higher than the year before returning or on frequent occasions before the war, and almost certainly would have been lower but for the folly of the miners' strike. The cost of living was down seven points, which meant a corresponding rise in real wages. The exchanges with all the great gold-using Dominions had moved in Britain's favour and were now in close normal relation with one another. But most importantly, 'we stand to-day on a basis of reality. ... We may not be soaring in the clouds, but there is at least firm ground under our feet.'[8]

For the time being, amidst the acute tension engendered by the general strike, which erupted on 4 May 1926, this seemed to be almost the last word in the debate. In February James Maxton, the Parliamentary leader of the Clydeside ILP, had introduced a private member's bill to nationalise the Bank of England; it was quickly set aside, then quashed on procedural grounds.[9] The FBI discouraged members from criticising the gold standard by pointing out that for the present there was no likelihood of securing majority support against it.[10] Some indication of the depth of unease was given by the fact that behind the closed doors of the London Chamber of Commerce members of the Financial Section debated the question of abandoning the gold standard at two sessions during the winter of 1925–26, before reaffirming support for it.[11] But the only development of consequence was the appearance of a revised edition of Lord Milner's *Questions of the Hour* late in 1925, a few months after the author's death.

Milner, upon leaving public office in 1921, had accepted directorships in several City-based firms including Prudential Assurance and the Midland Bank, and the Rothschilds' nomination as chairman of the mining company Rio Tinto.[12] But in his case at least, being in the City was not the same as being of it, for as his notebook revealed, his outlook remained that of a pre-war Tariff Reformer, with all his hostility directed against the 'plutocrats' who pulled the strings behind the government. As he saw it, the plutocrats or 'Moneyed Interest' had waged a successful campaign against the command economy which had proven so effective during the war, then continued pressing for cuts in public expenditure. Interested solely in the value of their paper securities and blind to the social consequences of retrenchment and monetary deflation, they had crippled productive industry and destroyed hopes of a new social order based upon patriotism and class harmony. His only consolation was that eventually the situation would become so desperate that workers and employers even in the older export-oriented industries would recognise the need for trade protection. At that moment, with industry and agriculture united, 'the real fight will begin – the parties being Productive Industry on the one hand, and the Moneyed Interest on the other'.

Milner's book, to judge by the frequency of reference to it in the next few years, had an important influence in industrial and farming circles, where sympathy for imperial protectionism was already strong. To take one example, Sir Ernest Petter, the automotive engineer, as late as July 1925 blamed Britain's industrial troubles on excessive wage levels in the sheltered trades and the absence of import controls.[13] After reflecting upon Colonel Willey's FBI tour of the United States and Milner's criticism, he cast aside his deflationary critique and pointed instead to the pernicious role of finance. Besides protection, he now advocated a social contract involving labour, capital, and the state, and the abandonment of the gold standard if this was necessary for the restoration of social peace and the revival of the economy.[14] The retired banker J.F. Darling carried Milner's message to a receptive audience of the Manchester Association of Exporters and Importers.[15] incent Vickers, a director of the armaments firm Vickers Ltd, which was just then being rescued from bankruptcy by the Bank of England, may also have been influenced by Milner's criticism when he confronted Norman at the annual shareholders' meeting of the Bank in 1926, warning him that 'henceforth I was going to fight him and the Gold Standard and the Bank of England policy until I died – (and well I remember the words of his reply!)'.[16] Subsequently Vickers used his influence within the Central Chamber of Agriculture to promote interest in the currency question and provided backing for the economist and fellow Milnerite, J. Taylor Peddie, to create the British Economic Federation, which was intended as the nucleus of a producers' alliance against the economic internationalism of high finance.[17]

But it was not until early 1927 that the tension created by the general strike abated sufficiently for widespread complaints about the working of the gold standard to be heard. The event that triggered the revival was Reginald McKenna's address to the annual shareholders' meeting of the Midland Bank, in which he contrasted America's 'great and increasing prosperity' with Britain's 'six years of trade depression and unemployment of almost unparalleled severity'. This, he suggested, was largely explained by the superior working of the American Federal Reserve System, which was far more responsive to industry's credit requirements than the Bank of England, and he ended by calling for a thorough-going inquiry into the Bank's operation.[18] Hitherto, industrialists who were disturbed by the effects of monetary policy had been reluctant to expose themselves to the derisive rejoinders of the City editors or offend the bankers on whose credit they so heavily depended. But now, with a recognised authority saying exactly what was on their minds, they seized the opportunity to applaud his remarks.

On 17 February the president of the Bradford Textile Society wrote to Churchill, pointing out that he was an active speaker for the Conservative Party and warning that unless McKenna's call for an inquiry was quickly heeded the government would be wrecked. 'The present condition of industry is largely due to our financial policy, and growing numbers feel the results of the Cunliffe Committee's recommendation should come under review, particularly as the Committee excluded both industry and labour.'[19] On 15 March D.A. Bremner forwarded to the Chancellor a resolution unanimously passed by the council of the British Engineers' Association, welcoming McKenna's 'courageous speech' and strongly endorsing his call for an exhaustive inquiry into 'the theoretical basis and practical technique of our credit and currency system including the position of the Bank of England as the central institution and custodian of our monetary resources'.[20] That same month Rear-Admiral Beamish, a die-hard Tory, submitted to Parliament a petition for a monetary inquiry containing over 28,000 signatures and the names of fifty-one local authorities.[21] And on 30 April the FBI journal *British Industries* printed what was to be the first in a series of articles blaming the return to the gold standard for most of industry's troubles, and warning that unless something was done about the imminent shortfall in world monetary gold, conditions could only get worse.[22]

Just what the petitioners expected from an inquiry must remain a matter for speculation. Most, it seems, shared McKenna's view that the Bank of England's tight money policy was due to Norman's excessive caution rather than sterling's weakness, and that emulation of the Federal Reserve System would enable the Bank to expand the money supply without jeopardising sterling's link to the gold standard. If so, they were almost certainly wrong. But the important point was that industrialists increasingly objected to a monetary system that made domestic credit conditions dependent on the vagaries of world gold production, international price levels, and the impact of purely financial transactions on the exchanges. And a monetary system that did not expose domestic credit to international forces was not properly a gold standard at all. Hence, ill-conceived as it may have been, industrial criticism represented a potentially radical challenge to the gold standard – as the central bankers appreciated only too well.

In 1925 British wholesale prices had fallen 10 per cent. But contrary to Churchill's assurance that the price-level adjustment was at last complete, wholesale prices fell another 7 per cent in 1926 and continued to fall every year thereafter until 1933. Despite his public assurances that the gold standard provided a 'basis of reality', meaning security from the depredations of socialist finance, privately he continued to betray deep unease about the social and economic consequences of gold. Amery, agitating constantly for trade protection, took to advocating a 'Gold Exchange Duty'.[23] As he pointed out, returning to gold had involved raising the exchange rate, increasing borrowing costs, inflating the real burden of public and corporate debt, and increasing taxation, all of which handicapped industry in its struggle against foreign competition. Churchill, while not prepared to admit it to Amery, found the criticism unanswerable. Behind the walls of the Treasury his disparagement of policy became constant. When Niemeyer attempted to defend it, Churchill paraphrased Amery in reply.

As Churchill put it, British governments had faithfully submitted to the views of their financial advisers, and restored sterling to its pre-war parity. The national credit had been improved and the cost of living reduced. But the cost had been enormous: 'bad trade, hard times, an immense increase in unemployment, involving costly and unwise remedial measures, attempts to reduce wages in line with the cost of living ... [and] fierce labour disputes arising therefrom, with expense to the State and community measured by hundreds of millions'.

To sum up, the financial policy of Great Britain since the war has been directed by the Governor of the Bank of England and distinguished Treasury permanent officials who, amid the repeated changes of Government and of Chancellors, have pursued inflexibly a strict, rigid, highly particularist line of action, entirely satisfactory when judged from within the sphere in which they move and for which they are responsible, and almost entirely unsatisfactory in its reactions upon the wider social, industrial and political spheres.[24]

Churchill was known on occasion to test policies by throwing out to advisers the anticipated challenges of critics, but this was more than mere rhetorical sparring. Years later he still spoke bitterly of Norman for so smoothly drawing him into 'the biggest blunder of [my] life'.[25] And when, shortly after the above complaint, Niemeyer announced that he was leaving for a senior post at the Bank of England, Churchill was outraged, regarding this as a personal betrayal, even perhaps part of a long-planned conspiracy.[26] But by now no option seemed open to him. To admit that the decision to return to gold had been a mistake, after all the troubles that had followed, would almost certainly bring down the government and end his career there and then. Even to admit doubts would instantly shake confidence in the pound and draw criticism from every quarter. With no choice but to brazen it out, therefore, he replied in June 1927 to a call from the Labour benches for a monetary inquiry by insisting once more that the monopoly of wisdom on such matters rested with high finance, and that if McKenna and Keynes were dissatisfied with present policy, they stood alone. 'I think those are the only two names of eminence in the financial world which can be quoted against the orthodox policy which His Majesty's Government are pursuing.'[27] This may have been true, but the hopes of the same 'financial world' of restoring sterling to its place as lynch-pin of the international gold standard were already proving chimerical. For Norman's dream of forging an alliance of the world's central banks was at this moment turning into a nightmare.

Norman, Moreau, and the Poincaré miracle

At the time of Britain's return to gold, the depreciation of the French and Belgian francs, though worrying to industry, had been merely an annoyance to Norman and his colleagues, whose immediate task was facilitated by the influx of refugee capital from the continent. Briefly during the summer of 1925, Norman envisaged a major international operation simultaneously to stabilise the two francs and the lira. When this hope faded, he remained ready to chance his arm on separate Belgian and Italian operations. However, in the autumn he set aside plans to help the lira when he discovered that the Bank of Italy deferred on matters of importance to the Fascist state. Strong and the Morgan bankers appealed to him against a doctrinaire position on what seemed to them a secondary matter. But Norman held it to be of the essence of the gold standard that central banks should operate it free of political pressure, and for more than a year refused to budge.[28]

In the meantime the Morgan bankers in New York withdrew from a proposed credit to the Bank of Belgium, having decided that recent financial reforms did not go far enough to ensure budgetary or balance of payments equilibrium. This time it was Norman's turn to protest. Fearing that the fate of the whole scheme for European monetary stabilisation hung in the balance, he pointed out that the Belgian authorities, at great risk to themselves economically and politically, had succeeded in divorcing their currency from the French franc in the effort to return to a gold basis. And whatever the remaining shortcomings in Belgian finances, these would be more than offset by the tonic effect on the whole of Europe of Belgian stabilisation. But despite his repeated appeals and his offer to double his own participation in the credit, he could not persuade the Morgan men to change their minds, and since American capital was essential, nothing further could be done. This was a severe blow to the Bank of Belgium, which had nearly exhausted its foreign exchange reserves in the vain endeavour, and a serious setback for the principle of central bank cooperation. Subsequently the Belgian, Italian, and French currencies continued on their downward slide.[29]

In May 1924, when the *Cartel des gauches* took office in France, the franc, the 'Germinal franc', stood at 60 to the pound, although the legal fiction of its pre-war gold parity of 25.22 to the pound was maintained. Thereafter, governments came and went, each one committed to restoring the national finances, and each one divided over the choice of taxing wealth or current production and consumption, or unable to overcome similar divisions in the Chamber. By January 1926 the franc stood at 129 to the pound. By July it had plunged to 240, and with no solution in sight seemed set to sink lower. The speed with which the scene was changing, with the virtual failure of the Ruhr occupation, the collapse of hopes for a painless solution to the question of who would pay for the war, the recovery of Germany, the change of parliamentary complexion, and the now seemingly irreversible decline of the franc, intensified political conflict and created an atmosphere of hysteria. Some Frenchmen suspected the existence of a financiers' *mur d'argent* designed to make government by progressive parties impossible; others suspected an Anglo-American plot to enforce demands for repayment of war debts or simply to reduce the exchange value of French goods. American and British tourists felt the menacing hostility of Parisian crowds. Well-to-do Frenchmen sent families and movable assets out of the country. The Palais Bourbon was besieged by angry demonstrators, while Marshal Pétain and other reactionaries spoke grimly of the need for a dictatorship.[30]

Then suddenly what became known as the Poincaré miracle occurred, when on 21 July the *Cartel des gauches* collapsed, clearing the way for a government of national union under the wartime President, and the flight from the franc ended on the assurance of tough financial reforms. At almost the same time Belgium experienced a similar change of fortune when the financier–statesman Emile Francqui took office with emergency powers. This time the reforms were sufficiently drastic to justify a renewed effort to stabilise the currency, a task made much easier by the firmness of the French franc. With Norman in the chair, central bankers gathered in London to prepare the arrangements, and on 25 October Belgian authorities returned to a gold exchange standard. The success of the operation, in which French and German central bankers worked side by side with British and American colleagues, inspired Norman to describe it as a 'miracle' and to hope for rapid progress towards his larger goal.[31] Unfortunately for Britain the parity chosen for the new 'belga', a mere seventh of the old rate, sharply undervalued it against sterling. An even more serious problem arose from the stabilisation of the French franc.

Towards the end of July 1926 Norman called at the Bank of France to meet the new Governor, Emile Moreau. Moreau was impressed by the Englishman's elegance and charming manner, but doubtful of his good will.[32] A member of the elite corps of *inspecteurs des finances*, Moreau had spent twenty years as Governor of the Bank of Algeria before taking up his present post in June. But he remained a provincial, returning to his family estate near Montmorillon in the Poitou whenever possible and continuing to serve as the local mayor.[33] Little travelled and unfamiliar with foreign languages, he was an outsider in the world of international banking, and, a political appointee himself, listened sceptically to Norman's advice on the need for his total independence from the French state. To Moreau, Norman himself, so far from being politically independent, was an agent of British imperialism, a view almost certainly shared by the regents who dominated the *Conseil général* of the Bank of France, such as Baron de Rothschild, Baron Hottinguer,

Jacques de Neuflize, Félix Vernes, and François de Wendel. Intensely nationalistic and deeply anguished by the predicament in which France had been placed by the weakness of the franc, they regarded Norman with some justice as an ally of Germany and enemy of France.[34]

At the time of the Dawes Plan negotiations, Norman had manipulated British and American financial resources to strengthen Germany's hand while weakening France's. Subsequently, while Germany flourished on the strength of a stable currency and massive Anglo-American commercial credits, the Bank of England refused to assist France until terms were agreed on the repayment of war debts.[35] In 1925 Germany exploited its new-found strength to offer financial assistance to Belgium in exchange for the return of Eupen and Malmédy, and to France in exchange for the immediate evacuation of the Rhineland and revision of the Dawes Plan including agreement on the reparation total. Only a few weeks before Norman called on Moreau, Stresemann renewed his proposal of financial assistance to Poland in exchange for territorial concessions. Briand favoured the German terms for a settlement with France, which became the basis for his private conversations with Stresemann at Thoiry in September, but Poincaré resisted agreement and Moreau immediately lined up with him.[36] It was with these developments in the immediate background that Moreau found Norman reluctant to ease terms on the outstanding balance of the 1916 credit from the Bank of England, and insistent that Poland and Yugoslavia should seek reconstruction loans through the League Financial Committee. Moreau interpreted this as a thinly veiled attack on French interests. France, in an effort to offset the reduction in control over Germany, was actively strengthening relations with friendly east European countries. A mutual security pact with Roumania had recently been added to defence treaties with Poland and Czechoslovakia, and in 1927 a new treaty was signed with Yugoslavia. But now, it seemed, Norman planned to use the League Financial Committee to draw France's allies into the British sphere of influence. Moreau, having helped to 'liberate' France from Anglo-American financial bondage, reacted to the new challenge by adopting a posture of undisguised hostility towards the committee. His undeviating aim was henceforth to rebuild the franc to an unassailable position, enabling France to resume its pre-war lending role and thereby resist British encroachment on vital French interests.[37]

Norman's second meeting with Moreau, in February 1927 in Paris, was no more satisfactory than the first. Discussion of the terms for renewal of the 1916 credit, which occupied most of their time, ended with Moreau indicating he would prefer not to renew it at all but pay it off and repatriate the gold deposit. The credit, originally amounting to

£72 million against a gold deposit of £24 million, now stood at £33 million and the gold deposit at £18 million. Norman doubted that Moreau had the necessary sterling resources for repayment, and feared his intervention in the foreign exchange market. Moreau suspected that Norman had expended the gold deposit in the effort to shore up sterling. Discussion of financial assistance to Poland further underscored their differences. Turning to more general matters, Norman expressed anxiety at the spread of American influence overseas, not least through direct investments, and spoke of the vital necessity for Europe to unite in self-defence. Moreau was aware of Norman's preoccupation with the American challenge. But he was more worried by Norman's own apparent design for domination of the continent, and receiving no satisfaction on the issues at hand looked forward to the opportunity to cut the Bank of England down to size.[38]

Once the flight from the franc had been halted, Moreau initially sought a revaluation to provide some justice to France's beleaguered *rente*-holders. He was however determined to move in his own time, to avoid a fiasco like Belgium's premature attempt at stabilisation and what he regarded as Norman's blunder of enfeebling the British economy for the sake of financial prestige. By December the franc was again above £1 = 120 and signs of a crisis appeared in the French motor industry. Moreau intervened in the foreign exchange market to halt any further appreciation, pegging the franc at about 120, one-fifth its pre-war value. Taking domestic and international factors into account, this may well have been close to equilibrium rate. But it was not obvious at the time, and in the absence of any clear declaration of official intentions, pressure for further appreciation was inevitable. The French economy, despite the cloud of financial mismanagement that obscured it, had been functioning at a brisk pace, and export trades, benefiting from the fall in exchange rates, had been faring particularly well. For investors, yields on French *rentes* were high and equity prices on the Bourse were low. Moreover, Rothschild, de Wendel, and certain other authorities had given public encouragement to the idea of returning to the old parity, and Poincaré was known to be sympathetic to revaluation. Speculators did not have to believe in the return to the Germinal franc to recognise that holding francs on the chance of appreciation was now a virtually risk-free gamble. The announcement in April 1927 that the Bank of France had repaid the credit from the Bank of England and regained the £18 million gold deposit further bolstered expectations of revaluation. Besides the increased demand for francs due to the favourable balance of payments and increased internal circulation requirements, speculative purchases also sharply increased.[39]

Moreau's efforts to hold the *de facto* rate led him to accumulate foreign currency holdings, which rose from £10 million in December 1926 to more than £110 million by May 1927. He held the bulk of these funds on deposit in the markets from whence they had come. But since, as it seemed to him, this merely fuelled the speculation by cushioning its effects on the markets involved, he decided to convert some of these balances into gold in order to force up interest rates in the offending markets and interrupt the speculative activity. In mid-May he requested Strong to sell $100 million of his dollar balances for gold. At the same time he began to sell sterling balances in London for dollars, and requested Norman to convert a total of £20.5 million of sterling into gold for his account. Norman was infuriated by what he regarded as Moreau's interference in his market, and after several sharply worded exchanges, Moreau agreed to suspend his gold buying until Norman could suggest another way of halting the speculation. A meeting was arranged for 27 May in Paris.[40]

The meeting began with Moreau denouncing the operations of speculators in London and New York, and Norman equally determinedly challenging the rationale for Moreau's recent actions. While it was true that much of the speculative franc buying was transacted through London, Norman explained, most of it was on Dutch, German, or other foreign accounts. It seemed most unfair to him that Moreau should punish London simply on account of the efficiency of its markets, which made it the largest repository of foreign short-term balances, and particularly that he should do so by taking advantage of the fact that London was the only free gold market in Europe. In any case, putting pressure on the Bank of England could serve no useful purpose. Since there appeared to be no down-side risk in holding francs, speculators in London would not be deterred by somewhat higher interest rates, and those operating from New York would be completely unaffected. Indeed, Moreau's recent decision to exchange sterling balances for gold had merely increased the prestige of the franc and its attractiveness to speculators. Rather than tightening rates in London, Moreau should ease rates in Paris and in other ways encourage the absorption of 'hot money' into constructive activities within France and abroad. Finally, if France would not stabilise the franc formally, she should at least announce firmly that speculation would not be allowed to have any influence upon exchange rates.

Norman then proceeded frankly to describe his own predicament. Since returning to gold he had attempted to increase his control over his markets by a policy of moderately dear and tight money. Moreau's repayment of the wartime credit had enabled him to reduce the fiduciary note issue by £4 million. However, in response to mounting criticism of the Bank's deflationary policy he had been obliged to cut Bank rate by half a per cent, and to raise the rate now would cause 'a riot'. Every bank in Britain was loaned up to the hilt to industry, and it was imperative for him to minimise borrowing costs. When he thought of 'the suffering, the unemployment, and social repercussions' a higher Bank rate must cause, he hesitated to act. Moreau had converted £5.5 million sterling into gold and indicated his intention to raise the total to £20.5 million. The impact, Norman warned, would fall not on the supply of credit in London, but on the proportion of reserve cover for the pound. If Moreau persisted, he would force Britain off the gold standard.

Moreau was by no means chastened by Norman's criticism. He remained convinced that his decision to convert his sterling balances into gold was no more than the normal prerogative of a depositer in a gold standard centre. If Norman's complaints did anything, they merely underlined for Moreau the risks that Britain had taken in stabilising the pound in 1925 on such a slender margin of reserves, and the necessity of accumulating substantial gold reserves – a *masse de manoeuvre* – before attempting to stabilise the franc. However, Professor Charles Rist, the Deputy-Governor of the Bank of France, held strongly that Britain must be allowed to remain on the gold standard in the interests of world stability, and the report of an encounter later in the day between Pierre Quesnay, Moreau's youthful chief of research, and Harry Siepmann, Norman's adviser on European central bank relations, also pointed to the need for caution. The Bank of France had claims of £70 million on London, but the British Treasury had unconsolidated war debt claims of £600 million on the French Treasury which, Siepmann warned, would be presented if the Bank of England were further embarrassed. Moreau agreed that in the circumstances his London balances were too dangerous a weapon to be used.[41]

The meeting thus did nothing to bring Norman or Moreau around to one another's point of view, but it did presently yield a kind of truce. Strong, who had repeatedly warned Moreau that to force Norman into a higher Bank rate would create a situation of 'great danger, which would react on all of us', volunteered to sell Moreau £1.5 million in gold on earmark in London, thereby reducing Moreau's claim on British gold. Norman himself tightened market rates somewhat and encouraged Hjalmar Schacht of the Reichsbank and other continental central bankers to do likewise. Ten days later, on 7 June, Quesnay brought to London Moreau's proposals for a *modus vivendi*. Among other things, Moreau offered to reduce his discount rate so as to create a 'new atmosphere' in Paris with regard to borrowing and discourage the inflow of foreign funds. Secondly, while not prepared to increase his sterling balances, he agreed to drop plans for any further conversion of sterling into gold. Norman for his part agreed to seek buyers for £20 million of Moreau's sterling balances over the following six months.[42]

In the first week of July 1927 Strong convened an informal gathering of central bankers, attended by Norman, Rist, and Schacht, at his Long Island home, to discuss ways of easing the strain on London of international money movements. Rist reaffirmed the Bank of France's readiness to play its part and accepted Strong's offer to buy £12 million of its London balances in exchange for earmarked American gold.[43] By now, however, the problem of French pressure on sterling had receded before the larger problem of deflationary price trends caused, at least in part, by the defensive reactions of European central banks in face of their ominous losses of gold cover to the United States. Independently, Strong decided to reduce his rediscount rate at the first opportunity and persuade Federal Reserve Board colleagues to collaborate in a policy of easy money, to assist Europe as well as combating the looming domestic recession.[44] With European borrowing rates up and American rates down, the Bank of France selling foreign exchange spot and buying back forward in order to limit the volume of liquid funds in Paris, and American banks lending abroad short and long-term funds on an unprecedented scale,[45] sterling strengthened and remained comfortably above gold export point for the balance of the year. But it was scarcely a satisfactory situation. The Bank of France was building up vast claims on London and other foreign centres which it was patently reluctant to maintain. Moreover, European monetary stability was now acutely vulnerable to any interruption in the flow of dollar credits.[46] Thus Norman remained in the humiliating position of existing on the suffrance of the French whom he detested and the Americans whom he feared.

Global political pressures on Britain

As in international monetary relations, so too in the broader sphere of external affairs, the mid-1920s found Britain constantly over-stretched and vulnerable. In September 1920 the Bolshevik régime in Russia had signalled its ambitions in Central Asia by staging a congress of the 'enslaved popular masses' of the East at Baku on the Caspian Sea; thereafter Afghanistan, India, and China became prime targets for subversion.[47] As it happened, Bolshevik efforts in India came to almost nothing; Comintern leaders privately dismissed the party established there in 1925 as a 'pseudo-Communist party'.[48] Nevertheless the threat seemed real enough at the time, not least because it coincided with the advent of Mahatma Gandhi's mass movement against British rule. Gandhi called off his campaign of passive resistance after an incident in 1922 when twenty-one policemen were killed, but terrorism continued on a small scale, and the nationalist Congress party led by Motilal and Jewaharlal Nehru gained wide support among the Indian people. In retreat, Britain sent out the Simon Commission in 1927, the first in a series of attempts to appease moderate Indian opinion through constitutional reform. Briefly trouble threatened again in Ireland until agreement on the demarcation of the Northern Irish border was reached in December 1925. More serious difficulties meanwhile arose in Egypt. While granting Egypt formal independence in 1922, Britain reserved control over communications, defence, and the protection of foreign nationals, which made her the target of attack from supporters of Saad Zaghloul, leader of the nationalist Wafd party. Here, too, Britain's response was to negotiate constitutional changes, but now that nationalism had reached the stage of a mass movement purely formal change was inadequate, and sporadic violence continued.

In China the mobilisation of the masses was also well advanced, and here Communism and nationalism were clearly linked. Russian advisers took charge of training the nationalist Kuomintang forces in 1923, while local Communists organised large numbers of urban workers in trade unions. In May 1925 long-simmering hostility towards British imperialism erupted during a strike in Japanese textile mills in Shanghai, China's largest port and industrial centre. A confrontation between demonstrators and British police in the city's international settlement resulted in the shooting down of thirteen Chinese. A general strike was organised in all the major cities, British goods were boycotted, and Hong Kong, Britain's chief far eastern base, was blockaded for several months. In 1926 open conflict threatened when General Chiang Kai-shek's Kuomintang army and its Communist allies set off from Canton on a northern campaign which brought them within six months to the Yangtse, the main artery through Britain's sphere of interest. British authorities, despite the obscurity of the situation and American hostility, chose to appease the Canton régime, and in March 1927 Kuomintang troops entered Shanghai.[49] Barely four months later Britain found herself seriously at odds with the United States over the issue of naval parity.

In 1921–22 the Washington conference had produced an agreement for limiting the total tonnage of capital ships, the ratio for the major powers, Britain, the United States, and Japan, being 10:10:7 respectively. British authorities deeply regretted the passing of the two-power standard whereby the Royal Navy was maintained at a strength equal to its two nearest rivals, and the replacement of the Anglo-Japanese Alliance with an anodyne Four-Power Treaty (Britain, the United States, Japan, and France) guaranteeing the status quo in the Pacific, but had acquiesced in order to forestall a costly and dangerous arms race with the United States. On 20 June 1927 representatives of the three major Pacific powers again met in Geneva for the purpose of extending the Washington agreement on capital ships to subordinate categories of warships. Unfortunately prior consultation had been minimal, and American delegates caught their British counterparts off guard by advancing a formula which completely failed to meet Britain's strategic requirements. Britain faced the task of policing enormously long imperial and commercial sea-lanes, which required a numerous fleet, whereas the United States, with more limited overseas interests, was disposed to accept a smaller number of ships with greater weaponry. To make matters worse, the chief American naval expert, Rear-Admiral Hilary Jones, was a 'big navyite' and openly anti-British; nothing British delegates could do would persuade the Americans that equality in face of unequal security requirements demanded something more than simple numerical parity.[50]

The confrontation in Geneva, lasting from late June to early August and unrelieved by British diplomatic initiatives in Washington, evoked intense anti-American sentiment within the Cabinet. Following upon United States' refusal to support the new order established by the Versailles Treaty, pressure to end the Anglo-Japanese Alliance, the adoption of the highly protectionist Fordney–McCumber Tariff, stiff terms for repayment of war debts, and aggressive support for American foreign commerce, Ministers saw in the current negotiations further evidence of hostility towards the British Empire. Most outspoken was Churchill, who, despite his own recent efforts to reduce naval spending plans, led the opposition to equality on American terms. Acceptance, he warned, would leave Britain helpless to resist American designs on the Empire. Although he hoped colleagues would continue to reassure the public that war with the United States was unthinkable, 'Everyone knows that this is not true.'[51] Lord Robert Cecil, the government's adviser on League of Nations affairs and a delegate at the Geneva conference, appealed for an agreement. He did not doubt that war with the United States was possible. Where he differed was in his belief that such a war must end in the destruction of everything the Conservative Party held dear: the Empire, capitalism, and the existing social order. As he wrote to Churchill, 'I regard a future war on a big scale as certainly fatal to the British Empire whether we win it or lose it, and probably also to British civilisation.' Churchill, however, had his way, and when the conference collapsed Cecil embarrassed the government further by resigning.[52] Thereafter Anglo-American relations remained at a low ebb for the balance of Parliament.

Relations with France were no better. French security and reparation demands continued to be regarded in Britain as the chief obstacles to European appeasement, while in France resentment continued at Britain's aloofness from the Continent, the Locarno treaties notwithstanding,[53] and British financial assistance to the former enemy states, which forced the pace of Franco-German rapprochement. Paris actively promoted the 'European' idea, and in a number of little-publicised but practical ways France consolidated relations with Germany. Industrial cartels proliferated with official encouragement from both countries.[54] Reparations in kind received favourable tax treatment in France and were even relied on by the army.[55] The Franco-German commercial treaty of August 1927 involved a wide-ranging adjustment of French duties in favour of German trade, partly at the expense of third countries including Britain.[56] As Briand and the Quai d'Orsay saw it, France was obliged to come to terms with Germany before the economic, demographic, and military advantage turned decisively in Germany's favour. Yet they remained deeply suspicious of German ambitions, and were anxious to draw in Britain as a permanent counter-weight in the European balance.

Jacques Seydoux, recently retired from the Quai d'Orsay, explained the French point of view with admirable clarity in a prominent article in *The Times* in March 1928. Britain, he wrote, had shown an obsession with the balance of power and the prestige of sterling since the war. As a result she had hastened German recovery while weakening her own industrial base, and allowed herself to become unreasoningly hostile to France by exaggerating France's purely transitory strength. France regretted Britain's policy towards Europe, but hoped she would eventually recognise the need for direct involvement in the maintenance of continental stability. The fact was,

> France and Germany cannot do without Great Britain; but Great Britain needs them both. The peace of Europe and of the world demands that any Franco-German *entente* on the economic plane should have as its corollary a still closer *entente* between France and Great Britain; for if France desires to be on good terms with Germany, she desires to be on still better terms ... with Great Britain.[57]

Instead of a continental commitment, Britain offered only lectures at Geneva and elsewhere on the need for peace, financial discipline, and free trade. It was ironic but scarcely surprising that, according to John Dove, the widely travelled editor of the *Round Table*, Austen Chamberlain, the one francophil in the Cabinet, should have become 'the best abused man in Europe'.[58]

Towards a domestic producers' alliance

Monetary deflation meanwhile continued to exacerbate divisions within Britain. Bankers, economists, journalists, and even the Prime Minister dwelt on the shortcomings of industry: its individualism, failure to rationalise, and inadequate marketing technique.[59] Industrialists, having suffered the injury of deflation, found these insults extremely hard to take. After some especially slighting remarks by a banker on the management of the older industries, in January 1928, Vincent Vickers complained to the *Morning Post* of 'the continual hurling of stones upon their depressed condition from the lofty pinnacle of banking circles'. The new industries, or most of them, at least had the advantage of import protection and exceptional demand. But all industries were waiting to see some benefit from the sacrifices imposed on them for the sake of the 'Credit of the Country'. 'And it is only the consciousness of the great dependence upon the banking community, and their hope of favours to come, that has (so far) prevented the older industries from giving full vent to their opinions.'[60]

Similar exasperation coloured the editorial comments of the journal of the electrical manufacturers (BEAMA), a leading new industry, a few months later. Dismissing charges of inefficiency, the journal described as, 'fantastic', claims by certain financiers that returning to gold had helped industry to weather the 1926 crisis – when the return to gold had actually been the cause of the crisis. 'The reasoning here is like that of a surgeon who considers an operation successful which has unfortunately killed the patient.'[61] At about the same time Sir Alan Smith, chairman of the Engineering Employers' Federation, turned his notoriously hard gaze towards the banking profession in response to a trade unionist who had quoted optimistic forecasts by a banker as justification for higher wages.

> Now I think that, as a cardinal principle, if you want to know anything about industry, never go to a bank manager. A bank manager may be able to make his dividends, not on the prosperity of industry, but on its adversity. ... He is by reason of his position, perhaps the least capable of giving a fair, reasonable and correct interpretation of the trend of industry and commerce in this or any other country.[62]

Among farming organisations the main source of controversy was the alleged contradiction between government support for wage boards and opposition to price supports. Endorsement of McKenna's call for a new monetary inquiry only just appeared as the fourteenth and final item on a petition sent by the Council of the Central and Associated Chambers of Agriculture to the Prime Minister in July 1927.[63] The Commons debates on agriculture on 20 December 1927 and 29 February 1928 indicated even less interest in the currency question. On the other hand, certain farm authorities, including Arthur Amos, Charles Dampier-Whetham, Sir Daniel Hall, and Lord Bledisloe, Parliamentary Secretary to the Minister of Agriculture, publicly linked the farmers' plight to the deflationary impact of the gold standard, and Thomas Williams, the president of the NFU, quoted Bledisloe's comments during a bitter attack on the government at the union's annual meeting in January 1928.[64] A paper by Dampier-Whetham on 'The Effect of Monetary instability upon Agriculture', delivered at the March meeting of the National Farmers' Club in Westminster, evoked a response which indicated that the currency question was, if not yet at the forefront of farm issues, well on the way to becoming so.

Dampier-Whetham dwelt in a careful, scholarly way with the experience of British agriculture since the Napoleonic Wars, identifying the long-run course of prices and prosperity with changes in the world stock of monetary gold. Pointing to the now widely held expectation of a serious shortfall in gold production and the failure to follow up the 1922 Genoa resolutions, he expressed his fear that governments would simply wait in hope of an internationally agreed solution to the problem of world deflation until unemployment became so serious that they were forced to act. Unfortunately, belief in an unrestricted market for gold was 'an article of faith in the City of London. It facilitates foreign trade, and enables London, as a financial centre, still to look New York in the face. And so the heretic, who points out that these undoubted benefits are offset by certain disadvantages, gets a scant hearing in financial circles.'

With the deference practically every layman still displayed when publicly referring to the affairs of high finance, the chairman described Dampier-Whetham's subject as 'rather an intricate one and perhaps beyond the usual purview of farmers'. But the discussion that followed was reminiscent of debates during the 'hungry forties' in the bluntness and sheer anger of contributions from the floor. The Essex farmer who seconded the vote of thanks to the speaker, reflexively acknowledged his 'absolute incompetence to deal with the task'. Thereupon he launched into a lengthy and bitter denunciation of 'the financial policy of Governments, whatever their political faith, and of the City of London [which] appears to be entirely in favour of the merchant and importer ... and against the producer,' and amidst applause concluded by suggesting the reintroduction of bimetallism. Speaking next, a Hampshire farmer described how, having lost a great deal of money in arable farming at the end of the war, 'it made me wonder whether there was a cause other than increased supply'. He agreed with Keynes, the gold standard was a 'relic of barbarism'. His own branch of the NFU had discussed the question several times and he thought every farmer would support McKenna's call for an inquiry into 'the Bank Charter of 1844,' which he was sure was the root cause of the problem. The financiers, though never ceasing to tell farmers to cooperate, economise, and so on, naturally discouraged discussion of the basic issue.

> We are told it is a very difficult subject, but it is not so very difficult. I believe that people who are responsible for monetary policy are very anxious for us to believe that it is a difficult question (laughter), and want it left to them. The other side of the picture is that, while all producing industries are in the doldrums, financiers and banks have been remarkably prosperous since 1920 (Hear, hear.) The Bank of England shares, I believe, have risen from £150 to £265, and all banks have 16 or 18 per cent dividends this year. How many of you have made 16 per cent? Have you made 5 per cent this year? You would be very lucky if you did so. I believe they are quite happy that we shall remain in ignorance of the importance of this question of monetary policy (Hear, hear).

Lord Bledisloe, though also admitting 'some temerity' at broaching the subject, affirmed his agreement with previous speakers. The monetary influence lay at the root of their troubles, 'not the various causes which are so often made public in Parliament and elsewhere'. He therefore proposed that they publish their speeches in a pamphlet for circulation throughout the rural community, and volunteered to share the cost. The meeting ended with praise from a Suffolk farmer for Lord Milner's perspicacity in seeing that 'we are approaching a new political alignment in which the division in future will lie between the producer and the financier.'[65] The next day the Council of the Central and Associated Chambers of Agriculture directed its policy committee to examine and report on Dampier-Whetham's address.[66]

Bledisloe, a large landowner and Tory backbencher, was also a professionally trained and thoroughly dedicated farmer, which perhaps distinguished him from many others of his social standing. The decision of postwar British governments to abandon agriculture to world market forces had struck him as folly. So disturbed was he that when MacDonald offered him the agriculture portfolio in the first Labour government, he was sorely tempted to take it. Labour's commitment to Socialism held him back, but in the aftermath of the general strike he was more dissatisfied than ever. How many other large landowners shared his enthusiasm for monetary reform can only be guessed at. But there is no doubt that most shared his belief in the necessity of a numerous and prosperous rural population, for strategic reasons, as a market for manufactured goods, and above all as 'a bulwark against Bolshevism'. And certainly there were many who agreed that if, as seemed evident, protection was not politically feasible, *something* must be done to ease the plight of the nation's wealth producers.[67]

Prompted by Bledisloe, Milner, and others, the idea of a producers' alliance, dormant since the collapse of Tariff Reform in 1910, now began to revive. Peak organisations such as the FBI, NCEO, and TUC offered no lead, their membership being too broadly based to coalesce around a coherent strategy and their administrative heads too jealous of their authority to encourage a common front. Instead new bodies appeared including Peddie's British Economic Federation and Kitson's Economic Freedom League, no one of which exerted any measurable influence but which together were sufficiently numerous to serve notice on the older bodies of the dangers of inaction.[68] In the winter of 1925–26 the Empire Industries Association attempted to widen its base by drawing in members of the labour movement. The negotiations came to nothing when the trade unionists and Labour MPs involved were unable to muster a significant number of followers.[69] Nevertheless they were a portent, and the negotiations between the NUM and NFU in the spring of 1928 were part of the same trend. Since its founding in 1908 the NFU had opposed protection for manufacturing until or unless agriculture received the same treatment and warily kept its distance from industrial groups. But pressure from the rank and file was such that when the NUM promised to discuss common action if the NFU formally adopted protection as its policy, the Council of the NFU was obliged to reverse its initial position and accept the invitation once the NUM in turn accepted the principle of safeguarding for all or none.[70]

The Mond–Turner conference, the first occasion in British history when industrial capital and labour met *en bloc*, does not on the face of it bear comparison with the other initiatives. The principal motive for a producers' alliance had always been the desire to replace economic internationalism by an aggressive national–imperial policy. The Mond–Turner conference, which sprang from a mutual desire to avert a repetition of the events of 1926, was ostensibly concerned with problems related to rationalisation, that is with industrial revival within the existing economic framework. Nonetheless support for a new national policy was only one step away, as the composition of the conference and its first interim report indicate.[71]

The employers' group taking part, though claiming to be representative of industry, was in fact comprised almost wholly of men from the largest firms in two sectors. The first, the new industries, was represented by, among others, Sir Herbert Austin, Sir Hugo Hirst, Sir Edward Manville, Sir Josiah Stamp, Sir Samuel Courtauld, and the chairman Sir Alfred Mond; the second, steel, by Lord Aberconway, Sir Henry Bond, Sir Arthur Dorman, Sir Robert Hadfield, Mr Mannaberg, and Sir Peter Rylands. Almost all were committed protectionists and no less than seven of the twenty-four sat on the Council of the EIA.[72]

The TUC, representing labour in the conference, was still formally internationalist, as confirmed by the joint Labour Party–TUC submission to the World Economic Conference entitled 'Factors Affecting the Peace of the World'. Yet the TUC conference in September 1927, where readiness for direct talks with employers had been signalled, offered the strongest evidence yet that organised labour was disillusioned with its present course and casting about for new directions. Aside from encouragement for the conference itself, one indication was contained in the strong approval for the executive's call to break off contact with Russian trade union representatives, refuse the affiliation of the Communist-backed National Minority Movement, oppose the holding of a joint congress of the Amsterdam and Moscow Internationals, and in other ways draw back from the principle of international working-class solidarity. Another was given by the adoption of resolutions calling for inquiries into the problems of sweated imports, foreign dumping, and tariff restrictions, and the dangers posed by the growth of cartels and trusts under the control of international finance. A fourth resolution introduced by the Transport Workers' leader, Ernest Bevin, calling upon the General Council to support the economic unification of Europe, offered the clearest indication of the drift in trade union opinion away from pure internationalism.

Bevin, whose presence dominated the hall, reminded Congress that he had been a member of the official mission sent the previous year by Steel-Maitland to investigate the reasons for America's prosperity. He did not want it thought that he believed American capitalists were superior or more benevolent than capitalists anywhere else. But he did acknowledge that he had been thoroughly impressed by what he had seen and was captured by the vision of forming a comparable economic bloc wherein Britain would gain the same scale economies now realised in the continent-wide American market. The previous speaker, Ben Tillett, had dwelt on the efforts of capitalists to organise the European economy on the basis of trusts. Why, asked Bevin, should the labour movement not take up the challenge of organising Europe in the interests of the workers? Just as the United States had proven 'a veritable El Dorado' for the impoverished Europeans who had gone there, so

Europe itself, by uniting, could meet the demands of the millions of poor who remained.

I am a little bit of a dreamer; I think it is necessary ... to inculcate the spirit of a United States of Europe – at least on an economic basis, if we cannot on a totally political basis. ...Cast your eye over Europe with its millions of underfed, with its millions of people with a wretchedly low standard of living. We can have mass production, we can have intensified production, and we must direct the consuming power in order to absorb that mass production [by] the millions of people in [Eastern] Europe, whose standard of living is not far removed from the animal, and whose standards are capable of being raised 1,000 per cent, by bringing together their productive capacity in return for the craftsmanship of our own Western Europe.

From the floor, critics did not mince words in condemning this proposed break with internationalism. As J.B. Figgins of the Railwaymen put it, Bevin was indeed a dreamer, but his encouragement of 'European exclusiveness' guaranteed the nightmare of 'greater imperialism.... There could only be one economic unit, an economic unit of the world.' The miners' leader A.J. Cook similarly warned, 'this resolution ... cuts right across our whole idealism, built up in the early days for forming an all-embracing international'. In a more practical vein, he pointed out that Britain's interests extended far beyond Europe, and urged that TUC efforts be concentrated upon eliminating sweated production in the coal mines of India, in Australia, and elsewhere, through international wages and hours agreements. Jack Jones MP, a GMWU delegate, however, defended the resolution, and pointing to the trend towards larger economic units dismissed the old internationalists as the new isolationists. On a ballot the resolution was adopted by a margin of 2,258,000 to 1,464,000.[73] Victory added to Bevin's rapidly increasing stature within the TUC. And at the meeting of the General Council on 23 November it was Bevin who moved the motion to prepare a reply to the employers' invitation for talks.[74]

Significantly the first issue dealt with by the Mond–Turner conference was monetary policy. Neither side had originally intended to dwell upon it: the employers alone included reference to the subject in their draft agenda, and then only as the last of twenty items.[75] But under strong criticism from opponents of the conference, both the employers and trade unionist supporters were anxious to demonstrate its usefulness, and upon the initiative of W. Milne-Bailey, secretary of the trade union committee, they turned to monetary policy as an issue on which they could largely agree.[76] The specific issue in question was the amalgamation of the wartime Treasury currency notes with the Bank of England note issue, a step called for by the Cunliffe and Chamberlain/

Bradbury Committees and expected to be announced in the Chancellor's budget speech on 24 April. Both employers and trade unionists feared that such action would be tantamount to a reduction of the fiduciary issue and result in further deflation.[77] Hence on 13 April they submitted a memorandum to the Chancellor pointing to expert predictions of an imminent world shortage of monetary gold and requesting him to suspend action on note amalgamation until a full inquiry was made into 'the best form of credit policy for this country'. The memorandum referred to the hope of implementing the Genoa resolutions on economies in the use of monetary gold, regulating its distribution, and preventing undue fluctuations in its purchasing power. Returning to the prewar automatic gold standard, it claimed, was 'now generally recognised' to have been the cause of short- and long-term price instability which seriously dislocated national development and 'gave rise to grave social and industrial ills'. Once again, criticism was directed against the automatic functioning of the gold standard, though in practical terms this meant nothing less than a rejection of the gold standard itself.[78]

At the Treasury, P.J. Grigg passed the memorandum on to Churchill with the comment, 'important and rather inopportune'.[79] For some months the Treasury and the Bank had been quietly preparing legislation for note amalgamation. Fearful that Parliament might start an inquiry into the Bank's operation or demand radical changes 'à la McKenna, etc.,' they had been hoping to avoid publicity until the bill could be rushed through the House in May.[80] The appearance of the memorandum, as Courtney Mill acknowledged, caused 'some furious thinking' in the City.[81] Always the City's loyal servant, Mill himself had done what he could to minimise publicity. On his advice, *The Times* rejected a lengthy article on the subject by Keynes. Then when Brand intervened to insist upon publication, on the grounds that the paper's reputation was at stake, Mill had it placed as obscurely as possible amidst the estate advertisements.[82] Commenting on the Mond–Turner call for a public inquiry, Mill professed to see no objection so long as it was carried out 'by people competent to make it'. But almost in the same breath he deplored the idea of throwing 'our monetary affairs ... into the melting pot', and virtually equated such a course with the advocacy of inflation.[83] If industry was unhappy with monetary policy, he added a few days later, it should have spoken up before Britain returned to the gold standard. 'Industry did not protest against that action, and obviously there can be no going back now.'[84]

This was too much for Mond, who wrote to *The Times* complaining of being 'misunderstood or misrepresented' there and by every other organ of the City. As he put it, the whole country from the Prime Minister on down was anxious that peace be restored between Capital and Labour; but there was really no point in trying so long as monetary policy ensured an indefinite continuation of industrial disputes, unemployment, and depression. 'It is perfectly useless for people to repeat the parrot cry of inflation whenever and wherever any attention is directed to the necessity of financial and currency reform. Currency systems exist for the benefit of the country and not the country for the benefit of a currency system.'[85] With the encouragement of FBI officials, Sir Peter Rylands, too, fired off an angry letter to *The Times* repudiating Mill's claim that industry had passively acquiesced in the return to gold.[86] Within a few weeks the FBI, NUM, and electrical manufacturers expressed support for the memorandum; and several elaborate petitions, printed by the British Stable Money Association and bearing the names of many leading figures in the cotton textile, engineering, and mining industries, were submitted to the Prime Minister in support of the view, 'that the root cause of our difficulties is to be found within the monetary system, and ... that a committee of inquiry should be appointed forthwith to inquire into the operations of the Bank of England as governed by the Bank Charter of 1844'.[87] Nevertheless when Churchill duly confirmed plans to amalgamate the note issues and debate took place in Parliament, the effect was to create the same misleading impression of capitalist solidarity confronted by a radical left-wing challenge that had been the feature of the debate in 1925 after the return to gold.

As on the earlier occasion, Snowden led off for Labour on 14 May, calling for the Bank Notes Bill to be set aside until a monetary inquiry could be carried out, while making it as clear as possible that he personally had no complaints with the present management of policy. 'I have no desire at all to see a central bank under political interference', he reassured the Commons.[88] Other Labour speakers, including the former Liberal, Frederick Pethick-Lawrence, and Hugh Dalton, also stressed the national rather than class or sectional interests that moved them to demand an inquiry.[89] But Edward Grenfell, the senior Conservative member for the City of London and one of Norman's oldest friends, did his best to ginger up Conservative back bench support for the bill by reminding the House of the dangers of delay:

> We must remember that when first the Bolsheviks came into control in Russia, they saw the value of depreciating and destroying all faith in the currency, and they spared no pains to do so. They felt sure that, in order to produce anarchy, the destruction of all faith in the currency would be more helpful than anything else.[90]

Pethick-Lawrence urged the industrial members on the government benches to break their silence and confirm that a more flexible currency system was not the demand merely of wild men. They would, he taunted them, become known not as the forty thieves but the forty fools if they did not join Labour on this question. Mond rose once, but Churchill had already approached him privately to discourage confrontation,[91] and when Steel-Maitland stood up to claim the Speaker's attention Mond left the House without speaking.[92] The nearest thing to criticism from the employers' standpoint came from the cotton mill-owner Samuel Hammersley. Speaking on behalf of the export trades, Hammersley asserted a fundamental conflict of interest between bankers and industrialists and expressed concern that the present banker-dominated directorate of the Bank of England meant inevitably a bias towards deflation. At the same time, he welcomed the recent addition of Sir Josiah Stamp to the board, and he quite accepted Grenfell's warning about the dangers of leaving the note issue for a future Socialist government to manipulate.[93] Braving the censure of party whips as well as colleagues from the financial community once more proved too much for industrial spokesmen. The House divided along party lines, resulting in a comfortable majority of 229 to 107 for the bill. This was an important tactical victory for internationalism. The irony was that it coincided with the virtual breakdown of central bank cooperation and the onset of a new crisis in which the Bank of England came under pressure from two directions at once.

Central bankers in conflict

For two years central bankers had been uneasily aware that the widespread movement back to gold they themselves had encouraged, and the restrictive policies subsequently required to defend metallic reserves, had contributed to the deflationary trend of world price-levels. Rist, speaking with Strong in August 1926, confirmed that this was worrying him, and indeed one reason for Moreau's reluctance to allow the franc to rise beyond 120 to the pound seems to have been the fear that France might be caught with rising prices in a period of generally declining price-levels. Strong on this occasion dismissed the problem. If, as Rist said, world industrial output increased faster than the supply of new monetary gold, he could see no cause for worry since gold was also being used more efficiently as the basis of credit.[94] But the following year Strong admitted privately that he too was worried. The central bankers who joined him on Long Island in July 1927 had made the question of their responsibility for world deflationary pressure one of the main topics for discussion. While avoiding any definite conclusions, Strong explained to an American colleague, 'the general feeling was that to some extent arguments could be advanced in support of this charge. My feeling has been that further price declines will make the issue one of vital importance to banks of issue and I am anxious that we in this country should have a good alibi.'[95]

Norman had been worried about the deflationary effects of a world gold shortage at least since the hearings of the Royal Commission on Indian Currency and Finance in the winter of 1925. On this occasion three authorities, Joseph Kitchin, the Managing Director of the Union Corporation, Professor Gustav Cassel, and Sir Charles Addis, presented evidence that gold production would fall short of the 3 per cent annual increase in liquidity required to meet the expanding needs of world trade. Norman agreed in principle to the restoration of the gold standard in India, but so anxious was he of additional competition for existing gold stocks that he persuaded Strong to join him in arguing the case for the gold exchange standard before the commission.[96] Since then, commodity prices, whose earlier rise had meant strong foreign exchange positions for countries in the outer sterling area and facilitated Britain's return to gold, had declined markedly, bringing heavy borrowing pressure on London from Australia, New Zealand, and the other commodity producers. The possibility of a breakdown of the reparations regime also loomed because Germany had not succeeded in restoring a trade surplus since the adoption of the Dawes Plan, and Norman as well as Schacht expressed his worries on this score at the Long Island conference.[97] On top of this had come Sir Henry Strakosch's warning. Speaking privately with Norman in June 1927, Strakosch painted a grim picture of central banks forced into competition for metallic reserves, rising interest rates, restricted credit, price deflation, countries such as Austria and Roumania (in which he had a close interest) with heavy foreign debt burdens, forced to choose between savage retrenchment or abandoning the gold standard and risking runaway inflation, and a generalised world crisis. Norman, who knew and respected him, was deeply impressed.[98]

Norman, like other central bankers of his day, preferred the solidity of a gold specie or at least a bullion standard, but he accepted that in the world as he found it there was no alternative to the gold exchange standard. The main advantage was that the smaller central banks, by using foreign exchange to supplement metallic reserves, were able to stabilise their currencies and meet expanding currency requirements without putting an intolerable strain on the international monetary system. The main disadvantage was that a pyramid of credit was erected upon the metallic reserves of the central banks at the centre of the system, which could potentially throw great strain upon them. This, however, did not seem an overriding objection. Before the war the Bank of England had succeeded in managing the world's credit with only slender metallic reserves. It had done so practically unaided then; the crucial factor now was active cooperation from the other leading central banks. Moreau was a problem, but Norman remained hopeful that Strong would provide the support needed to keep the system functioning.

Despite evident differences at the Long Island conference, Strong had eased interest rates in a show of solidarity and continued to assist with the disposal of French sterling deposits.[99] Barely three weeks after the conference he risked political censure by arranging for an American to join the League Financial Committee: Jeremiah Smith, a Boston lawyer closely associated with Brown Brothers, who had overseen the 1924 stabilisation loan to Hungary.[100] Meanwhile he continued to press for joint action to stabilise the Italian lira. In this case it was Norman who had been holding back on account of the Bank of Italy's lack of independence. He now reluctantly accepted that 'in Italy no one is independent', and on 12 December 1927, Bonaldo Stringher of the Italian central bank joined Norman and Strong in London to begin negotiations. A week later a stabilisation credit was arranged through Morgans, Barings, Rothschilds, and Hambros, and on 22 December the lira was formally restored to the gold standard. Once again the Norman–Strong partnership appeared in good working order. Strong, a divorcee with grown-up children and in chronically bad health, normally travelled alone to Europe where Norman took charge of him in a solicitous, mothering way. Their friendship, if mutual, was however decidedly more intense on Norman's part, and appears to have blinded him to the fact that Strong was not, and could not be, equally devoted to the quest for world monetary order.[101]

On 25 November 1927 Strakosch called on Norman again to warn of the need for concerted action to halt price deflation.[102] Three days later Norman wrote to Strong:

> Perhaps the chief uncertainty or danger which confronts Central Bankers on this side of the Atlantic over the next half dozen years is the purchasing power of gold and the general price level.... This is a very abstruse and complicated problem which personally I do not pretend to understand, the more so as it is based on somewhat uncertain statistics. But I rely for information from the outside about such a subject as this not, as you might suppose, on McKenna or Keynes, but on Sir Henry Strakosch. I am not sure if you know him: Austrian origin; many years in Johannesburg ... full of public spirit, genial, helpful ... and so forth. I have probably told you that if I had been a Dictator he would have been a director here years ago.... This is a problem to which Strakosch has given much study and it alarms him. He would say that none of us is giving it sufficient attention.[103]

If Strong agreed, he proposed to invite Strakosch to join them in Algeciras where they planned to vacation together in late January 1928.

Strong's reply revealed how far the pressure of events was forcing them apart. To ease the strain on European central banks, stimulate the American economy, and facilitate the export of American farm surpluses, he had reduced his discount rate in August 1927. The trouble was, as he realised at the time, this gave the wrong signal to the securities and real estate markets, which already attracted an excess of speculative funds.[104] The resurgence of speculation also intensified the already mounting criticism of the Federal Reserve System's handling of monetary policy. The prolonged decline in commodity prices had reawakened monetary radicalism in the mid-west, and the campaign for a new policy giving priority to price stability now being mounted by economists, businessmen, farm spokesmen, and trade unionists was rapidly gaining support in Congress. As in the days of William Jennings Bryan, the complaint was raised that the nation's real wealth producers were being strangled by a lack of credit while eastern bankers allowed vast credit resources to be diverted into brokers' loans.[105] Complaints were also raised in Europe and especially Britain that the United States was absorbing an unreasonable amount of the world's gold stock and 'sterilising' it rather than allowing it to serve as the basis for additional credit.

Strong, seriously ill and increasingly a prisoner of domestic opinion, reacted by retreating into a steadily more nationalistic posture. Defending his record of past contributions to European financial recovery, he began to stress the need for European solutions to European problems, and voiced concern at the extent to which his own position was threatened by European interests. Privately he encouraged Parker Gilbert, the Reparations Agent in Berlin, to set in train a new reparations settlement in order to strengthen the European payments system.[106] To Norman he complained that so far from having too much gold he scarcely had enough, in view of the more than $1 billion that foreign central banks held on deposit in America for which payment in gold might be demanded at any time. The possibility of such demands forcing him to impose penalty rates of interest to defend his reserves, thereby causing a major international crisis and bringing down the wrath of his critics at home, became a recurrent nightmare for him.[107] Thus when he met Strakosch in London in December he did not mince words in rejecting his views. 'What I told him appeared to shock him', Strong later reported to Norman. It was, in brief, that so far as he was concerned there was no general shortage of monetary gold, and that the gold exchange standard should be wound up rather than extended further. Strong told him, 'I much preferred to see the central banks build up their actual gold metal resources in their own hands to something like orthodox proportions, and adopt their own monetary and credit policy and execute it themselves.'[108] What he did not say was how the central banks could hope to acquire those gold stocks without aggravating the deflationary problem he had earlier acknowledged to be of such danger to the system.

The example first of Britain, then the United States, beset by the problem of unstable short-term balances left an enduring impression upon French observers.[109] After their own experience of severe financial instability, nothing further was required to convince them of the need for metallic reserves of orthodox proportions. As it happened, the element of rivalry that arose between Paris and London further prejudiced them in this direction. With the recovery of the franc and the prospect of stabilisation once the parliamentary election in June 1928 was out of the way, French statesmen, the directors of the big Paris banks, and Moreau himself looked forward to the development of the Paris financial market. For strategic as well as commercial reasons, their *grand dessein* was to turn it once more into a major lending centre, exerting through access to its resources the sort of influence on the Continent that London exerted in the Dominions and elsewhere. This strengthened their intention to return to the gold standard in a manner 'la plus classique et la plus stricte'.[110] It also predisposed them to regard the gold exchange standard as a weapon in Norman's hands for undercutting their influence in Europe, and hence all the more undesirable.

The immediate source of contention was the decision of Roumania and Yugoslavia late in 1927 to seek help in stabilising their currencies. Norman made it known that acceptance of the League Financial Committee's supervision of the financial reconstruction programmes would be a condition of raising any loan in London.[111] Besides the political neutrality of the Geneva organisation, Norman was probably now more anxious than ever to see that currency stabilisation was not accompanied by an increased demand for gold, and counted on the Financial Committee to ensure that the currencies were placed on a gold exchange standard with sterling substituting for gold as their basic reserve asset. As a London banker, whose outlook was shaped by the pre-war world when sterling and gold were used almost coextensively, the promotion of sterling as a reserve asset was hardly exceptionable since it appeared to serve not merely Britain's interests but that of the international monetary system itself. But to Moreau, who aspired to establish a regional role for the franc, Norman's internationalism was nothing more and nothing less than an inflated form of British imperialism; an imperialism moreover based upon the sleight-of-hand application of the gold exchange standard, which enabled Norman at one and the same time to shore up his own feeble currency by insisting upon the deposit of foreign reserves in London, and to place his own officials in control of the foreign central banks through the agency of the League Committee.[112] As Roumania and Yugoslavia were part of the French security system, Moreau adopted the view that France must take charge of their financial reconstruction. This in turn was unacceptable to Norman, for whom the introduction of alliance politics into international monetary relations was simply anathema.

When Poland had sought to stabilise its currency in the spring of 1927, Moreau succeeded in barring the path to the League Financial Committee only to find the stabilisation loan taken over by a consortium of aggressive, second-rate American banks.[113] He had been offered no part in the stabilisation of the lira, which was arranged through the Bank of England in December 1927 with the help of a $75 million loan from Morgans and several London houses. He was thus already losing patience when Norman pressed ahead on the Yugoslav and Roumanian schemes with only a transparent attempt to maintain the fiction that the League was actually in charge.[114] Peter Bark, chairman of the Anglo-Austrian Bank, a wholly-owned subsidiary of the Bank of England, handled negotiations for the Yugoslav loan, while representatives of the consortium of London merchant banks led by Rothschilds which was to provide the funds held their meetings at the Bank, and Bank officials advised the Yugoslav government on the revision of statutes of its central bank. Schroders was given charge of the consortium for the Roumanian loan, and Niemeyer, now a Bank of England official, participated in the negotiations, although the pretense was maintained that he did so solely as a member of the League Financial Committee.[115]

Henri Pouyanne, the French Financial Attaché, called on Norman on 28 January 1928 to warn him off the Yugoslav scheme.[116] When this produced no satisfactory result, Moreau approached Poincaré to obtain his support for a showdown. Moreau's highly coloured account of Britain's financial imperialism, carried on under the guise of impartial League initiatives and facilitated by her ability to draw almost at will upon American financial resources, evidently impressed the premier. As a counter-strategy, Moreau proposed an all-out effort to sever London's 'special relationship' with New York, draw countries of vital importance to French security clear of League control, and pressure Norman into an agreement on spheres of influence in Europe. Poincaré, according to Moreau's account, eagerly agreed: Moreau should go to London armed with his enormous sterling balances, 'to offer Norman war or peace'.[117]

Two weeks earlier, Norman despatched Niemeyer on a tour of Washington, Boston and New York in an effort to persuade leading American bankers of the crucial role being played by the League Financial Committee in European reconstruction work and discourage them from supporting any scheme which did not bear its imprimatur. If the trip accomplished anything, however, it was merely to make Strong uneasy about British attempts to draw him into a politically-charged European issue.[118] Meanwhile Moreau arrived in London to present his demands, and finding Norman too ill to see him, put them to the Deputy-Governor, Cecil Lubbock. Moreau affirmed that the Bank of France was determined to manage the Yugoslav and Roumanian reconstruction schemes and expected the consortium of French and American banks being organised by Jean Monnet, the former French diplomat now associated with the American bond house Blair & Co., to provide the Roumanian stabilisation loan. Lubbock, hopeful that Niemeyer had succeeded in his mission, was confident that Monnet's efforts would come to nothing once it became clear that the main British and American banks were unwilling to cooperate. He therefore equivocated, affirming that the Bank of England would look at schemes outside League auspices but of course reserve the right to judge each one on its merits. Moreau left satisfied that he had an agreement. As he understood it, future European reconstruction schemes would be arranged directly between the Bank of England and the Bank of France, and French experts would be allowed to join supervisory teams at the central banks where schemes already operated. The next day, however, Norman appeared back at the Bank, took Lubbock severely to task for conceding to Moreau the principle of non-League schemes, and proceeded to advise Roumanian officials to accept the authority of the League Financial Committee.[119]

Moreau was infuriated to learn that Norman had returned to Threadneedle Street even before he had reached Dover, which he took as proof of Norman's deception. Immediately he sent Rist and Quesnay to New York to undo Niemeyer's work.[120] Their version of events corroborated other reports reaching Strong that bankers and politicians on the continent were coming to see him as a collaborator in Norman's efforts 'to establish some sort of dictatorship over the central banks of Europe'.[121] Moreover he began to suspect that Norman was trying to use him as a catspaw in his intrigues against French control of the Roumanian stabilisation loan. Coming at a time when domestic criticism of Federal Reserve policy made him anxious to avoid any appearance of entanglement in European politics, this was more than he could tolerate. He rejected Norman's advice to refuse support for the Monnet consortium, and instead offered it his encouragement.[122]

In the closing months of 1927 Norman faced a new and prolonged struggle to retain his tenure at the Bank. His predecessor, Sir Brien Cokayne, now Lord Cullen, along with Kindersley and certain other members of the Committee of Treasury argued for a return to the prewar system of electing the Governor on a rotating biennial basis. Norman chose to see it simply as a contest between the older directors who wished to turn back the clock and his younger allies who appreciated the need for more professional management to cope with the dangerous uncertainties of the postwar world.[123] But Norman's own arrogance, secretiveness, and unwillingness or inability to delegate authority contributed in no small way to his difficulties. Even Sir Charles Addis, Norman's strongest supporter, advised compromise in face of the 'general concensus (sic)' among directors on the Bank's Court in favour of Norman's retirement, and eventually it was agreed that he should go by April 1931.[124] Exhausted from stress, Norman left the Bank on 17 February 1928, and after returning for a few days the next week to deal with the Roumanian affair, sailed for Madeira to recuperate.[125] His predicament was however all the more acute when he returned on 11 April. The Mond–Turner report, which appeared the very next day, triggered renewed criticism of monetary policy within the industrial community, culminating in the FBI's endorsement of the call for a public inquiry. Shortly afterwards Moreau demanded a settlement of the Roumanian issue and insisted that Norman should come to Paris.

Neither man was more than formally polite, neither altogether candid when they met in Moreau's office in the rue de la Vrillière on 27 April. Moreau denied any hostility towards the League Financial Committee, which was scarcely true. He insisted nonetheless that the Monnet consortium would handle the Roumanian loan: there was no turning back, and he expected the Bank of England to lend its support. Norman demurred, pointing out that Roumania was in default on its 1913 loan and barred from listing on the Stock Exchange. There was a nice irony in this argument since it was practically the same as the one that Pouyanne had earlier used to warn Norman off lending to Yugoslavia. Moreau took Norman's objection as a mere excuse and warned:

> If the Bank of England were to refuse participation [he] would regard it as an unfriendly act and as confirming the suspicions which it was possible to entertain about the motives and methods of the Bank of England, not only in this but also in other questions. He would then have no further regard to the interests of the Bank of England and would always act with an eye solely to the advantage of the Banque de France.

This, as Norman appreciated, was a threat to present the Bank of France's £150 million sterling balances for payment in gold, an act which would force Britain off the gold standard. He indicated that he might support the Monnet scheme if given a week to straighten matters with the Stock Exchange Committee and Council of Foreign Bondholders.[126] On 4 May he confirmed his support on certain conditions, 'in the interests of central bank solidarity'.[127]

In mid-May Strong sailed for Europe, significantly leaving London off his itinerary. Norman intercepted him at Cherbourg to explain why even now he did not want to touch a Roumanian scheme outside the purview of the League, but failed completely to win back Strong's support. To Strong neither Britain nor France had any claim to dominate European monetary relations, and all of Norman's talk of upholding principles and procedures for financial reconstruction through the League Financial Committee seemed merely elaborate fig-leaves for British ascendancy. Through Walter Stewart, an economist seconded from the Federal Reserve Bank of New York to the Bank of England, he was well-informed about Norman's activities. He knew, for instance, that the Yugoslav reconstruction scheme, which was to have been a League responsibility, had been taken over completely by the merchant bankers who met in the Bank of England, and that in return for a promise of loans of up to £50 million the Yugoslav government had committed itself to deal exclusively with the British consortium for the next ten years. In fact it was only when Stewart insisted upon informing them that the Bank's own Committee of Treasury learned of the Yugoslav negotiations and dissociated the Bank from the deal. In light of this knowledge, Strong reacted sharply to Norman's evasiveness and described his behaviour towards Moreau as 'stupid beyond belief', especially considering that Moreau's sterling balances hung like a 'sword of Damocles' over the Bank of England. The loss of Strong's support was the severest blow yet to Norman's ambitions and the strain again showed. Looking 'a bit frightened ... and very much confused by the position', he gave Strong the impression that he feared his fellow directors might demand his resignation.[128] Shortly afterwards he suffered another nervous breakdown and sailed to South Africa for a three month rest.[129] In the meantime the question of an international inquiry into monetary policy introduced a new source of embarrassment for all the central bankers.

Central bankers and the approaching crisis

The first serious proposal for an international inquiry into gold and price-levels originated with Sir Henry Strakosch. At his meeting with Strong in December 1927 he proposed that the League of Nations Financial Committee should undertake the task, then present its findings to the central banks for their practical application. Strong made it clear that he wished to avoid a formal conference of central banks and would have nothing at all to do with one if it implied acceptance of the Genoa resolutions. So far as he was concerned, central bank policy was strictly a matter for the central banks: he had no intention of providing a forum for the likes of Keynes, Cassel, or his fellow countrymen John Commons or Irving Fisher, founder of the American Stable Money Association,[130] who were encouraging the public in the quite unrealistic belief that the Federal Reserve system could effectively regulate domestic price levels in the interests of full employment and production. The only useful functions to be served by a League investigation now, he suggested, were the collection of reliable banking statistics and the improvement of techniques for central bank operations in gold.[131]

Absent from the Bank on 22 February 1928, Norman was saved from confrontation with Moreau, but was also away when the Committee of Treasury blackballed the Jewish Strakosch from a seat on the Bank's Court.[132] Whether Strakosch heard what transpired remains unclear, but it was perhaps no coincidence that thereafter, with Norman away, he ceased to look to the Bank for leadership in international monetary reform and instead channelled his efforts through the League. In May he produced an elaborately documented memorandum entitled, 'Monetary Stability and the Gold Standard', spelling out the grave dangers of allowing an artificial shortage of gold to cause a further fall in commodity prices, and sent it to Sir Arthur Salter with the request that he place the topic on the agenda for the next quarterly meeting of the League Financial Committee.[133] Just at this time Strakosch, in collaboration with Walter Layton, the editor, was organising a consortium of City bankers to buy control of *The Economist*.[134] It was probably therefore at Strakosch's instigation that Layton submitted a resolution to the newly formed League Economic Consultative Committee recalling 'the fears entertained by the Genoa Conference of the dangers that might arise from undue fluctuations in the purchasing power of gold', and recommending that the League take up the problem. On 19 May the resolution was adopted.[135]

The next week Salter travelled to Paris to see if Strong could be persuaded to support a formal inquiry. The Economic Consultative Committee resolution, as he pointed out, spoke not of stabilising price levels but only of checking undue fluctuations, which was a much more modest ambition. Strong was unmoved. The House of Representatives had been debating a price stabilisation bill and the Senate Banking and Credit Committee was debating the Federal Reserve Board's responsibility for excessive speculation when he left for Europe. In his absence the Federal Reserve Board had cautiously reversed policy by raising the discount rate in stages from 3 to 5 per cent and tightening money by selling $500 million of government securities. Unfortunately this failed utterly to halt speculation which surged ahead fuelled by brokers' loans, and succeeded only in dampening legitimate business and depressing commodity prices. He thus ruled out a central bankers' conference, which would pit him, the only 'real creditor', against the rest and arouse American suspicions of foreign dictation. A purely technical League inquiry was less objectionable, but only if undertaken by sound men such as Stewart, Rist, Burgess, or perhaps Harvard's Oliver Sprague: not Stamp (Salter's suggestion) and definitely not 'mere theorists' such as Keynes, Cassel, or Fisher.[136] Meanwhile in London the British Stable Money Association, supported by Strakosch and Stamp, petitioned the Prime Minister to begin an inquiry into monetary policy.[137] Early the following month Strakosch set off for the Financial Committee meeting. At this point an important split appeared within the leadership of the British financial community.

As Strakosch, Norman, and most other authorities, British and foreign, privately agreed, a grave problem had arisen over the international distribution of reserve assets and the tendency of commodity prices to decline. Beyond that, however, there was no agreement on what should or could be done. Strakosch took the view that as Britain was the least able of all the monetary powers to retreat into a nationalistic posture, it was incumbent upon her to take the lead in publicising the problem and pressuring foreign central bankers to join in collective action. In particular, he sought support from American bankers since the tradition of monetary radicalism in the United States made them susceptible to public pressure; together Britain and America could practically make policy for the world. However, to the more cautious Norman and his allies the approach of serious trouble made it seem all the more dangerous to draw public attention to monetary matters. As they saw it, the capacity of central banks to respond vigorously to signals from the gold and exchange markets was crucial to the maintenance of the gold standard and international order itself. Hence to encourage the public to believe that the central banks could stabilise prices, particularly just when they seemed set to fall farther, was to invite an outcry if credit restrictions became necessary, and to revive socialistic demands for the nationalisation of the banks. Whatever was to be done – and it was not at all clear what was feasible – it must be done by the central banks themselves and completely away from the public view. As Norman wrote to Strong in the spring, 'I am sceptical as to how far it would be practicable and how far it would be wise for the Central Banks to admit in any way that they can regulate prices through their gold and credit policies ....'[138] Accordingly, when Strakosch put his case for a League inquiry to the Financial Committee on 4 June 1928, he faced opposition from an unexpected source. The Dutch and German members offered their support, but along with Comte André de Chalendar, the French member, Sir Otto Niemeyer adopted an attitude of complete reserve.[139] The most Strakosch could obtain was an acknowledgement of the problem and a request to the League Council to consider what to do.[140]

Thereafter the battle for reform was fought on both the international and home fronts. In Paris on Monday 25 June, Salter called on Moreau to discuss possible League action. But as this was the day the franc was restored to the gold standard (at £1 = 24.21 francs), it was scarcely the best moment to raise the subject. Moreau looked forward to divesting himself of his foreign exchange balances and building up an unassailable metallic reserve position. His worry was inflation, not deflation. British calls for an inquiry seemed to him merely an admission of weakness and an attempt to shift Britain's burden of adjustment onto other countries: the opening gambit in an attack upon his dearly-earned reserves. Salter's visit merely put him on his guard. The following day he called on Strong, now staying near Paris, and secured his agreement on joint opposition to an inquiry.[141] Two weeks later, with Strong staying just across the border from Geneva at Evian-les-Bains, Salter organised a lunch for him to meet colleagues in the League Economic and Financial Section. This time Salter attempted to persuade Strong to cooperate by stressing 'the growing menace of public opinion' in Britain, which made it essential to seek ways of halting deflation. Partly on account of the Bank of England's excessive secretiveness, Salter explained, British authorities now faced widespread demands for a reconsideration of monetary policy: the recent FBI resolution showed just how strong these demands had become. But above all they had to think of the upcoming general election and the danger of a Labour government being returned, this time armed with radical plans to take over the Bank of England in order unilaterally to stabilise the purchasing power of gold. If the League Financial Committee went ahead with an inquiry and the central bankers refused to consider its results, the latter would become the target for acute criticism.

Salter's arguments were as ineffective with Strong as they had been with Moreau. Strong came away from the lunch impressed by the degree to which British personnel dominated the whole economic side of the League, but not by the quality of Salter's assistants, whom he dismissed derisively as university men: 'a bunch of men who were out of a job, were seeking a job, and were rather determined to get one by attending to our business for us'.[142] He had already begun to line up the principal European central bank governors against an inquiry, and was soon able to confirm the support of Schacht of Germany, Vissering of the Netherlands, Bachmann of Switzerland, and Franck of Belgium, as well as Moreau. But as he wrote to Stewart at the Bank of England the day after Salter's lunch, the obvious person to head off the League Financial Committee was Governor Norman.[143]

That summer the troubles facing the international monetary system became acute. The previous year the system had been sustained by reduced interest rates in the United States, relatively higher rates in Europe, and a vast outpouring of dollar loans. American foreign lending averaged $135 million a month in 1927 and rose to $172 million a month in the first half of 1928, but thereafter, as the Wall Street boom began its great ascent, dollars ceased to flow abroad while foreign funds flowed in, drawn by the speculative profits and call loan rates of 9 per cent and more. During the latter half of 1928 American foreign lending fell to a monthly average of $63 million, and with the same influences operating in 1929, total foreign lending amounted to only $790 million, less than half the figure for 1928. This dramatic decline in capital exports was reflected in American gold reserves, which fell by $500 million between April 1927 and June 1928, then rose by $280 million over the next sixteen months.[144]

The growing world dollar shortage was serious enough; to make matters worse, France placed intense pressure on the system at the same time. By June 1928 when the franc was stabilised, the Bank of France had accumulated foreign exchange balances of £203 million and gold reserves of £237 million as well as commitments to buy forward another £89 million in foreign exchange. Over the following eighteen months its gold reserves rose to £341 million.[145] The Bank disclaimed any large-scale selling of foreign exchange, asserting that the gold imports were due mainly to the free play of market forces.[146] But in fact almost all the increase was accounted for by the Bank's policy of allowing its forward contracts for foreign currency to expire and taking payment in gold; some £87 million in foreign exchange was disposed of in this way between June 1928 and June 1929. And even this understates the impact upon sterling. For as the Bank ran down its sterling assets, it increased its dollar balances; the actual decline in sterling assets during the twelve month period amounted to some £97 million.[147] Together France and the United States increased their official gold holdings by over £140 million, or twice the annual world production of gold for these years.[148] Moreover, already by the winter of 1928 Wall Street had drawn in some £400 million in European funds, according to Norman's estimate, much of which was offset by the run-down of London sterling balances.[149]

The position facing Norman on his return from South Africa was thus desperate. He had succeeded through a policy of dear money in building up his own reserves, which reached a record £173.9 million in September 1928.[150] However, in doing so he had also exacerbated public hostility to the Bank, and now that hopes for a trade recovery in the spring had again dissolved before the prospect of sharply rising unemployment, a further increase in Bank rate was certain to raise a storm of protest.[151] On 8 August the three-month bill rate was increased to stave off Bank rate action,[152] but the writing was on the wall – unless, of course, the Federal Reserve Bank of New York could bring Wall Street under control. As Norman pointed out to George Harrison, Strong's deputy, 'You will realise that our proposals are like spitting against the wind if your Call Money continues round 8%.'[153] Unfortunately Strong's death in October weakened the New York bank's influence within the Federal Reserve System, and the other regional banks resisted the discount rate hike that might have curbed the speculative boom before it was too late to avoid a subsequent crash.[154] In the circumstances Norman saw no choice but to sit tight, while doing what he could to remain on friendly terms with New York in the hope of influencing Harrison to act.

In November, not long after *The Economist* published Strakosch's memorandum on gold as a special supplement, Norman began actively to discourage plans for a League inquiry. On the fifteenth he invited Salter to lunch at the Bank, and on the twenty-third he called in Strakosch for a chat.[155] Salter, who now had a general mandate from the League Council to proceed, presently advised Strakosch of the need to modify their plans if they were ever to secure any cooperation at all from the central banks. He recommended approaches to Sprague and Rist, who was about to retire from the Bank of France, to join the inquiry to ensure that the central bank viewpoint was represented. He also recommended limiting the terms of reference in the first instance to the non-contentious question of future gold supply and demand, leaving policy questions to be introduced once the inquiry began.[156]

On 14 December the League Council endorsed the call for an inquiry into 'the causes of fluctuations in the purchasing power of gold and their effect upon the economic life of the nations'.[157] Norman continued to stand firmly with his central bank colleagues. He called in Sir Basil Blackett to mention that he had nominated him to the Bank's Court and to request him not to join the inquiry or speak publicly on the subject of gold.[158] Meeting at the Bank of France in February 1929, Norman, Moreau, Schacht, and Stewart agreed to pressure members of the Financial Committee to postpone the appointment of the Gold Delegation, as it was now being called, and meanwhile to set up a private committee of their own to take over the study of the gold question.[159] Now that the League Council had twice unanimously approved the principle of an inquiry, Norman's side-tracking efforts came to nought, and Rist and Sprague agreed to join the delegation. But the chances of such a body doing anything to influence French or American policy seemed more than doubtful.[160] And with the Bank of England's gold reserves falling again below the 'Cunliffe minimum' in December 1928, forcing Norman's hand on Bank rate, criticism of the gold standard in Britain reached unprecedented levels.

'Is the Financier a Parasite?' *The Economist* in July 1928 firmly answered its own question in the negative.[161] 'Industry Crucified on a Cross of Gold?'. *The Commercial* employed the impeccably orthodox talents of George Schwartz of the London School of Economics to dismiss the claim.[162] But the fact that such questions should be raised at all was indication enough that there were many who thought otherwise.

Beaverbrook's *Express* newspapers, having made only occasional reference to monetary policy since 1925, now resumed their slashing attacks on financiers and the Bank of England.[163] The FBI journal, *British Industries*, referred monthly to the basic monetary causes of industrial difficulties.[164] In September the Labour Party Executive forestalled criticism from the ILP at the forthcoming party conference by publishing a supplement to its new policy document *Labour and the Nation*, deploring the effects of deflation and calling for an inquiry into monetary policy.[165]

Speaking to the Bolton Economic League the next month, Sir Josiah Stamp warned that 'all the industrial goodwill and all the Christianity in the world' would not stop Britain declining to the rank of a second-rate nation unless the purchasing power of her currency was stabilised.[166] Almost immediately, Cecil Hilton, the Conservative member for Bolton and a prominent local businessman, spoke out in Parliament against the government's readiness to allow industry to go to the wall for the sake of monetary orthodoxy.

I say as a good Conservative and supporter of the Government they have lost caste in Lancashire... What does it matter to the lads and lassies of Lancashire how much gold is in the Bank of England?... This gold standard is a fetish... It should not rule Lancashire; it should not rule England.[167]

Party whips and eventually the chairman of the local Conservative association were enlisted to restrain Hilton from further embarrassing the government.[168] Stamp took an early opportunity to disclaim the suggestion that any country, except possibly the United States, could hope single-handedly to solve the problem of declining gold prices.[169] The incident nonetheless pointed to the fact that Lancashire, once a bastion of monetary orthodoxy, was now a hotbed of radicalism. With most mills still not paying dividends since incurring increased debt during the brief postwar boom, feeling against the banks was particularly strong among industrial employers. And with practically nothing to gain from tariff protection, it was natural that their attention should turn to monetary and financial reform.[170]

In December, BEAMA, the electrical manufacturers' association, issued a stinging attack upon the Bank of England for operating in a manner that favoured finance at the expense of industry.[171] This was not the first time that BEAMA had levelled its charges, but it was the first time they had received wide notice in the national press.[172] Hardly had the stir died down when, on 7 February 1929, the Bank of England announced a 1 per cent rise in Bank rate, to 5½ per cent, the highest it had been since 1921. With that, the whole of the industrial community erupted in anger.

The *Daily Express* joined the *Daily Herald* in declaring the decision 'the complete and final condemnation of the gospel of deflation, dear money, and the exaltation of the paper value of the pound over the practical needs of British industry', and accused the bankers of leaving industry 'at the mercy of Wall Street speculators' for the sake of sterling's international prestige.[173] Spokesmen for the NUM, FBI, and Manchester Chamber of Commerce greeted the news with expressions of unconcealed annoyance.[174] Farm leaders renewed their demands for assistance, claiming that they were indeed being crucified on a cross of gold.

At the annual meeting of the NFU a few weeks earlier, speaker after speaker had pointed to the impossible predicament created for them by the government, which had on the one hand forced prices down by returning to gold, while on the other hand had held up labour costs by retaining the 1924 Agriculture Wages Act. With arable farming reduced almost a million acres below the 1914 level and declining, opposition to the Conservative Party was threatened at the next general election, and there was even talk of independent farm candidates.[175] Similar feelings dominated what *The Times* described as the most important agricultural conference in recent memory, which the Agricultural and Industrial Union convened to advertise the farmers' plight within the nation's capital.[176] Early the next month the Conservative backbench Agricultural Committee petitioned the government for a subsidy on home-grown wheat. The committee acknowledged protection to be politically impracticable and passed over monetary reform in silence. But like the NFU, its demand was framed in the form of compensation for deliberate policies inimical to the industry.

On the one hand Monetary Policy has depressed prices, while on the other Legislation has increased costs. Both causes are the outcome of *State* action. Small wonder that the arable farmer is being crushed between the upper and nether millstones.[177]

Policy alternatives for the second Baldwin government

For the government, economic discontent continued to be, as it had been practically from the moment of taking office, the all-consuming problem. But what was to be done? Amery aside, Ministers accepted that the current state of public opinion ruled out anything much more in the way of safeguarding. All could agree on the desirability of public retrenchment, but effecting substantial economies was as usual easier said than done. It was a similar story with industrial rationalisation. Several times Ministers discussed the possibility of promoting the amalgamation and modernisation of firms in the iron and steel and cotton industries, but while agreeing on the desirability of action they drew back, reluctant to interfere with private capital. Bankers seemed the proper agents for any new initiative, and it was left to them to take the responsibility.[178] Emigration was another regular topic on the Cabinet agenda, but here the necessary cooperation of the Dominion governments was not forthcoming.[179] Steel-Maitland continued to hope for the adoption of the Washington Convention on working hours as a means of reducing foreign competition in the basic industries, and got so far as initiating international negotiations to harmonise interpretations of its operative clauses. But the NCEO, the employers' confederation, threatened the government with the direct consequences if it proceeded to tie their hands in this fashion. Steel-Maitland did not abandon the idea, but found himself unable to devise a new formula that would meet with the employers' approval while retaining any practical value.[180]

In the winter of 1927 Churchill had come forward with a scheme for reviving industry without recourse to protection: by removing two-thirds of the rates burden upon manufacturing firms and what remained of rates still levied on farms. A great deal of time and effort were expended in the elaboration of the scheme, and doubtless it was of value to industry. But it also created serious difficulties for Neville Chamberlain, the Minister responsible for local government, and in the final analysis it did nothing to reduce the overall burden of taxes on the country or to stimulate demand. Moreover, as a political initiative it was of doubtful value, first on account of the difficulty of making electoral capital out of such a complicated fiscal issue, secondly because the next general election was bound to take place before the end of 1929, hence before the scheme could get properly under way.[181]

Another possibility which never quite reached the Cabinet agenda was a policy of requiring that the proceeds of foreign loans issued in Britain should be spent in Britain. Amidst mounting evidence that the United States and France engaged in 'tied' lending,[182] spokesmen for British industry became increasingly critical of the City's indiscriminate lending activity. The Bradford Chamber of Commerce took special exception to a loan to the City of São Paulo, where a large cotton industry built with British capital and run by Lancashire men was even now demanding tariff protection against British exports.[183] The electrical manufacturers complained that a mere £10 million of the £36 million loaned by the City for overseas electrical projects between 1926 and 1929 had been spent on British equipment.[184] Similar complaints appeared in right-wing and left-wing journals,[185] and Keynes, whose call for foreign lending controls was incorporated in the Liberal *Yellow Book*, renewed his campaign in the *Nation and Athenaeum*.[186]

By 1929 indications had begun to appear that the City would not be averse to informal guidelines for tying foreign loans, so long as they were applied with tact and discretion.[187] The Department of Overseas Trade became enthusiastic, and the Foreign Office lent its support in the hope that if a way could be found to increase foreign lending without adversely affecting the balance of payments Britain might be able to withstand the onslaught of American trade competition and maintain her influence abroad.[188] The Office prepared a memorandum proposing the removal of the 2 per cent stamp tax on bearer bonds (the usual form of foreign issue) so as to stimulate borrowing, along with the adoption of guidelines for ensuring that British industry reaped the benefit. Sir Austen Chamberlain agreed to circulate the memorandum to Cabinet colleagues. But the Treasury, getting wind of the scheme, intervened and insisted on its withdrawal.[189]

The Treasury maintained an ambiguous position towards foreign lending controls. On one recent occasion Treasury officials objected to any encouragement of overseas loans on the grounds that the balance of payments could not stand the strain. On another they reverted to the old argument that tying loans could serve no useful purpose since sterling claims must ultimately be redeemed in British goods.[190] But there was no doubt that they resented Foreign Office encroachment on their administrative territory, and the latter department had to be content to interview Norman on this and related issues. The meeting highlighted the incomprehension that had been allowed to develop as the result of Norman's secretive methods and insistence upon total political non-interference. Norman was annoyed at Chamberlain for failing to support him in his struggle with Moreau over the Roumanian reconstruction loan. Chamberlain did not understand why Norman should have insisted so firmly that Roumania must go through the League Financial Committee. Norman evidently failed to appreciate the difficulty of mobilising diplomatic support for the Schroders consortium when other British financial houses had signed up with Monnet's Franco-American group. This made him all the more ready to dish the hopes of the Foreign Office for tied foreign lending. As he explained, if British manufacturers were unable to hold their place in foreign markets, it was chiefly because they were unenterprising and too 'individualistic' to rationalise their operations. The solution was certainly not to tie foreign lending to export orders, which would only handicap the City and reduce the quality of its loans. He was prepared to cooperate in such a scheme only if the government was prepared to guarantee the loans, which he knew Chamberlain was bound to refuse.[191]

Steel-Maitland at last raised the possibility of a change in monetary policy in the wake of controversy over the Bank rate rise. He suggested to Ministerial colleagues a committee of inquiry composed of industrialists with experience of finance, men such as Melchett, Dudley Docker, Weir, and Hirst.[192] But the proposal got nowhere. The previous June Churchill had angrily denounced the gold standard in Cabinet, and had come close to doing so in Parliament when asked if he approved of the recent Bank rate rise.[193] But the Treasury leapt to the Bank's defence, and Churchill, alive to the dangers of stirring up controversy over the issue in an election year, agreed that no good could come from a new inquiry.[194] Even Amery accepted that, regrettable as it might be, the decision on gold had been taken and there was no turning back.[195] But the general feeling of frustration was manifestly evident. Britain, depressed and in decline, appeared to be the victim not only of fate but of the irresponsible behaviour of certain other countries with a smaller stake in the international economy. It was all the more annoying that the same countries should also appear to be faring so well.

French prosperity and the American challenge

France, forced to relocate industry during the war and construct anew in the devastated departments of the north after the Armistice, had (with the reincorporation of Alsace and Lorraine) regained her 1913 level of economic activity by 1924, and increased output by another 30 per cent to three times the depressed level of 1919 before the end of the decade, a rate of growth unsurpassed even by the United States.[196] Such progress had not gone completely unobserved in Britain, but until 1926 the reality of the situation was obscured by the chaos of French public finances and the weakness of the franc.[197] The stabilisation of the currency, however, removed this distorting prism and ensured wide attention for the annual report by Robert Cahill, the Commercial Counsellor at the Paris Embassy, when it was published in October 1928.[198]

Among many other startling developments, Cahill pointed out that in 1913 Britain had produced four times as much pig iron and three times as much steel as France; in 1928, for the first time, French production of both items exceeded Britain's. France, he claimed, had also made 'astonishing progress ... in her engineering output' and in practically every other industrial sector. Her finances had undergone a 'complete transformation', her balance of payments showed an 'immense advance in visible exports' and a 'marked growth of invisible exports'. Unemployment, according to official figures at least, was down to barely a thousand, and several million Spaniards, Portuguese, Italians, and others had entered the country in response to the demand for labour. Englishmen, already convinced that France was the author of much of their difficulties, found this hard to take. As *The Times* observed on Cahill's report, 'one might conclude that the real devastated area was the whole field of British trade, and that we and not France and Belgium were the worst victims of the war'.[199]

But as before it was American economic growth and overseas expansion that attracted greatest attention. Now ahead of Britain in manufactured exports, British observers including Sir Robert Horne, Anthony Eden, and William Graham accepted that the day was coming when the United States would find its domestic market for mass produced goods 'saturated', whereupon it would launch a concerted drive to capture overseas markets.[200] In 1927 and 1928 American foreign lending doubled that of Britain. The portfolio component of the investment was regrettable only for what it said of Britain's decline, and was otherwise to be welcomed. But the direct foreign investment was deeply worrying. Stimulated by inflated equity prices on Wall Street, which made it easy for American 'multinational' firms to raise new capital or offer attractive share exchange terms, it was increasing at an almost exponential rate. For a short time the whole of Empire and European industry appeared in danger of being bought up by American firms.

In the early 1920s rivalry between British and American oil companies over the acquisition of foreign drilling rights had led to excited talk of an oil war. Fears that American reserves would last only a few more years prompted the State Department to support American producers in their efforts to obtain shares of the British-controlled Persian and Mesopotamian fields, and the Foreign Office to urge a policy of appeasement. Little more was heard of the issue after 1923 because of cartel agreements among the firms and rising production which resulted in an oil glut by the late 1920s.[201] Meanwhile, however, another source of conflict arose with the introduction of the Stevenson rubber scheme in 1922 for restricting exports of rubber from the two main producers, the British colonies of Burma and Malaya. The scheme was intended to safeguard long-term supply, which was endangered by the collapse of prices following the war and postwar slump. But American tyre manufacturers, who purchased over two-thirds of world production, angrily denounced Britain's exercise of monopoly control. A sharp rise in rubber prices in 1925 brought matters to a head, and thereafter output restrictions were progressively lifted until the autumn of 1928 when the scheme was wound up.[202] But hardly was this problem removed when others came to the fore. Their very number was indicative of the challenge the United States presented to a defensive, discomfited Britain. What made them particularly disturbing was that nearly all involved the new industries or resources on which they depended.

Among the most important developments in the resource sector was the announcement late in 1928 of a merger of Mond Nickel and International Nickel, which together produced over 80 per cent of world output. Prior to the merger International Nickel had been re-registered in Canada, doubtless to minimise adverse publicity, although it was known still to be controlled from New Jersey. To judge by the new board of directors, British and American interests were finely balanced. But it was significant that the post-merger firm was called simply International Nickel: there could be little doubt who had been merged into whom.[203]

Early in 1929 British electrical manufacturers publicly complained of their inability to meet American competition on account of discriminatory copper prices. Copper Exporters Inc., the Brussels-based subsidiary of an American mining consortium which controlled over 90 per cent of world copper production, was exploiting its near-monopoly position to raise prices to distressing heights, but owing to American antitrust laws, raising them only to overseas customers.[204] Just as complaints became general, the American Smelting and Refining Corp. bid for control of N'Changa Copper Mines, one of the richest properties in Rhodesia. In this case a British counter-bid was successful.[205] But in most other instances American capital proved irresistible. In June, Lautaro, the British-owned firm which dominated the Chilean nitrate industry, conceded control to the Guggenheim interests of New York. In this case access to American technology as well as finance was decisive.[206]

More widely remarked upon was the progress of the world 'war' waged by Ford and General Motors for domination of overseas markets. In November 1928 Ford revealed plans for a European manufacturing centre at Dagenham, which on completion would have an annual output of 200,000 vehicles, equal to the total current output of the whole of the British industry. The new share offering on the London Stock Exchange presented the first opportunity ever to invest in the company that symbolised American world supremacy in mass production industry, and those fortunate enough to secure a participation soon made enormous capital gains. For this the City could be pleased, but for British manufacturers it was scarcely cause for rejoicing. Both the American giants had recently set up assembly plants in Japan, and one of them was reported in Parliament to be planning a large-scale manufacturing operation in Australia.[207] Shortly after the Dagenham news, General Motors, which had purchased Vauxhall Motors in 1925, acquired Weyman Motor Bodies in Britain, and Adam Opel A.G., the largest and most modern manufacturing firm in Germany. In turn, Ford announced plans to increase the capitalisation of its German and French subsidiaries prior to expansion, and arranged free port privileges in Constantinople for an assembly plant to supply the eastern Mediterranean market.[208] By 1929 British motor manufacturers, insofar as they exported at all, exported almost solely to Empire countries, and even here they controlled barely a tenth of the total market, practically all the rest being in American hands.[209] American producers, assembling locally to avoid heavy import duties and gain the advantage of imperial preference in other British markets, had already made Canada a private preserve. Australasia, the market for fully a half of British exports, now seemed set to disappear the same way. With British manufacturers already experiencing a decline in the rate of growth while their American competitors surged ahead, it was small wonder that the future of the industry should become a topic of almost constant debate in Parliament and the press.[210]

Equally controversial were the developments in the communications and electrical industries. After years of negotiations and uneasy collaboration between British and American firms, the spreading world influence of Radio Corporation of America (RCA) and the even larger International Telephone and Telegraph (ITT) led the British government to convene an imperial wireless and cables conference in 1928 to consider the security and other issues at stake. The chief recommendation of the conference was the fusion of Empire communications facilities, including all private and government-owned cables, Marconi Wireless, and the British state-owned radio service, to form one large private corporation under the direction of a committee on which the Empire countries were represented. Legislation was swiftly adopted, and in 1929 Cables and Wireless began operations under the chairmanship of Sir Basil Blackett, the former Treasury official and finance member of the Viceroy's Council of India.[211]

Concern over the electrical industry occurred at the same time, in the first instance over the large number of generating and distributing companies in England being acquired by Samuel Insull's Chicago-based Utilities Light and Power Company. The Cabinet's attention was drawn to this development in March 1928, and at the Prime Minister's request the Committee of Economic Information (CEI) undertook an investigation.[212] The CEI soon assured the Cabinet that vital national interests were not endangered but accepted that the situation required watching.[213] There the matter rested until early 1929 when Utilities Light and Power acquired the entire common stock of the Greater London and Counties Trust, which controlled the seven chief British power-generating companies, operating on a monopoly basis in ninety-five cities, as well as the Edmundson Electric Company.[214] In order to forestall opposition, the former Conservative Lord Chancellor, Lord Birkenhead, was hired as chairman of the all-British board of London and Counties. But in February press reports confirmed that Birkenhead's company was merely a subsidiary of the American firm.[215] Questions were asked in Parliament as to whether foreign control meant foreign managers, orders for foreign equipment, and expensive American loans. Colonel Ashley, the Minister of Transport, and Birkenhead offered assurances to the contrary.[216] But a few months later Birkenhead's firm again came in for hostile publicity when it added Midland Counties Electric and the Shropshire, Worcestershire and Staffordshire Electric Power Company to the sixty British operating subsidiaries under its control.[217]

On the manufacturing side the news was dominated by the take-over battle for the General Electric Company (GEC). The American General Electric Corp., which had long controlled Thomson-Houston, increased its hold on the British industry during the later 1920s by acquiring large holdings in Metro-Vickers Electrical, Edison Swan, and Ferguson Pailin, leaving GEC the only important firm still in British hands. Sir Hugo Hirst, the chairman of GEC and an ardent imperialist, attempted to forestall an American take-over in August 1928 by depriving all foreigners of voting rights in the firm. When nevertheless large blocks of GEC shares continued to change hands on the New York curb market, he announced plans for a new issue of voting shares restricted to British nationals.[218] The London-based financial press condemned this 'notorious proposal', this 'financial Bolshevism', claiming that it would destroy London's reputation as an international financial capital and bring reprisals against British overseas holdings.[219] At this point Norman intervened.

Norman sympathised with Hirst's objective, and indeed may have encouraged him in his initiative, but he could not condone discrimination aimed directly against American investors. Governor Harrison warned him that the Guarantee Trust of New York, which had issued certificates against some £50 million of British securities, would reconsider its investment policy if Hirst proceeded with his scheme, and Norman was not prepared to add this to London's difficulties.[220] Hirst withdrew his share offering at the last moment. At the GEC annual meeting a few months later, nevertheless, he was able to point with satisfaction to other firms which had taken similar patriotic action.[221] Numerous British-owned firms had indeed altered their articles of association or were planning to do so, in order to forestall American takeover attempts, among them Imperial Airways, Marconi International Marine, Rolls Royce, Fairey Aviation, the Burmah Corporation, the Rubber Plantations Investment Trust, and the Buenos Aires and Pacific Railway.[222] Meanwhile Norman attempted to interest the London banks in forming a consortium to purchase control of British overseas banks and other firms in danger of falling into American hands. Nothing came of the idea. The banks were heavily loaned, and whereas the soundness of the overseas investments was being affected by the decline in commodity prices, the bull market in New York made it easy for American purchasers to offer generous prices.[223]

Baldwin, Neville Chamberlain recorded in the aftermath of the disastrous 1927 Geneva naval conference, 'has got to loathe Americans so much that he hates meeting them'.[224] Subsequently Anglo-American relations were further strained when in July 1928 it was revealed that Britain and France had secretly negotiated an arms limitation agreement. Inevitably Americans treated it as a cynical arrangement, giving France free scope to maintain her huge land forces in return for accepting British naval force levels, while leaving the United States out of consideration. The American administration reacted with unmistakable annoyance, big navyites renewed their agitation for expansion; and the

American and British press again raised the spectre of war.[225] Two weeks after the November presidential election, the Foreign Office warned the Cabinet that Anglo-American relations were more unsatisfactory than at any time since 1920. 'Except as a figure of speech, war is not unthinkable between the two countries. On the contrary there are present all the factors which in the past have made for war between the states.'[226]

Throughout the autumn Anglo-American relations and related questions of naval disarmament, belligerent rights, and a possible arbitration treaty remained almost constantly on the Cabinet agenda. Churchill, again the most outspoken opponent of appeasement, issued grim warnings of American designs for naval supremacy. 'Once that condition has been established, the centre of the British Empire will have been undermined.'[227] But the discussions had an air of unreality about them, for aside from Churchill and a few naval officers no one was prepared seriously to contemplate open conflict. As Esmé Howard, the British Ambassador in Washington, explained to Baldwin, there was simply no alternative to appeasement since war was certain to mean at the very least America's absorption of Canada and the West Indies, the break-up of the Empire, soaring food prices, and overwhelming opposition from the British public.[228] The Foreign Office similarly advised the Cabinet against such dangerous thoughts. Britain confronted 'a phenomenon for which there is no parallel in our modern history – a state twenty-five times as large, four times as wealthy, three times as populous, twice as ambitious, almost invulnerable, and at least our equal in vital energy, technical equipment and industrial science'.[229] Even Amery felt bound to accept the need for appeasement until Britain placed herself in a position to counter the 'American menace' by organising the Empire into a bloc of comparable size and strength.[230] It was therefore with great relief that shortly after the presidential election Baldwin received a personal assurance from William Castle, the Assistant Secretary of State, that the victor, Herbert Hoover, was not ill-disposed towards Britain. Baldwin took an early opportunity to issue a public affirmation of his desire for improved relations, and by the spring of 1929 informal negotiations for a new naval agreement began to make headway.[231]

Yet this did nothing to remove the fundamental source of the British fears and frustration, namely American economic expansion, which seemed now more threatening than ever. Hoover, as Secretary of Commerce during the previous eight years, had become known as the chief architect of this expansion, and during the campaign he had exploited this reputation by speaking of his readiness to increase government support for merchants and manufacturers seeking opportunities in foreign markets.[232] His landslide election victory thus appeared in Britain and elsewhere in Europe as an ominous sign.[233] And his decision to tour Latin America in the interval before taking office was interpreted as the first step towards the organisation of the Americas into a single trading bloc.[234] To make matters worse, early in the new year Congress indicated its readiness to increase the already massive American tariff, and not simply by raising duties on agricultural imports as Hoover had promised during the election campaign, but by increasing protection for manufactured and semi-manufactured goods as well.[235]

Esmé Howard, despite fervent advocacy of appeasement, accepted as a certainty the imminent 'saturation' of the American consumer market and a subsequent battle for export markets.[236] The Foreign Office, relying on reports from Howard and diplomats in Latin America, was also prepared to believe the worst. Hoover, it warned the Cabinet, could be expected to interpret his election victory as a mandate to coordinate America's industrial, financial, transport, and diplomatic resources in order to capture the overseas markets needed to absorb domestic overproduction. 'Under Mr Hoover, who is no friend of this country, we may expect a rigorous and ruthless "drive" by the United States for the capture of new foreign markets especially in South America. This is clear from the evidence which has reached the Foreign Office from all sides.'[237] Sir Austen Chamberlain, who readily endorsed the Foreign Office warning, volunteered his own opinion that Britain too must 'rationalise' her resources if she was to withstand the American onslaught. Sir Arthur Balfour, chairman of the recently completed inquiry into industry and trade and an old acquaintance of Hoover's, firmly believed that he would immediately start 'an economic offensive against us all the world over'. Sir Victor Wellesley, the Foreign Office's leading authority on politico-economic affairs, remained sceptical that the United States was as yet sufficiently organised to mount such an operation, but Cunliffe-Lister, hearing Balfour's remarks, acknowledged his own anxieties:

> American export organisation is very thorough and has unlimited finance. If they break down it will probably be on quality and the too aggressive manner of their salesmen – not in organisation or finance. But they are not likely to break badly even on the former ... My only hope is that Mr Hoover will be equally offensive to the Dominions and that if Australia and Canada find their food products taxed, they will retaliate on US goods.[238]

Hoover in his inaugural address on 4 March 1929 went out of his way to repudiate foreign claims of American 'imperialism'.[239] Three days later, however, Baldwin sought out Ramsay MacDonald to warn him to be vigilant in the event that he was returned to office at the next general election. 'The American money power is trying to get hold of some of the natural resources of the Empire. They are working like beavers.' Tom Jones, the Cabinet secretary to whom Baldwin related the conversation, advised against the tactics of 'Hugo Hirst and some other financiers,' because of the danger of reprisals against British overseas holdings. 'The PM was inclined to agree,' Jones recorded, 'but dreaded American control. He has been talking to the Governor of the Bank of England.'[240]

According to André de Chalendar, the French Financial Attaché in London, the City even more than political or naval circles was jealous of its international position and anxious about American expansion.[241] This was probably true. Norman and his associates found it expedient to avoid any public expression of concern, but betrayed intense frustration in private.[242] To cite just one example, John Baring, first Baron Revelstoke, whom Norman relied upon for advice, privately 'lamented the tremendous power of the US, and ... the sad position necessarily occupied by Great Britain, who, in spite of their loss of blood and treasure since 1914, find themselves ground under the iron heel of the insolent wealth of a Trans-Atlantic people who must be considered the greatest profiteers that the world has ever seen'. Lord Tyrrell, the Ambassador to France, to whom Revelstoke confided these observations, fully agreed.[243]

Norman, faced with New York borrowing rates that now soared on occasion to 20 per cent, appealed to Harrison time and again for decisive action to stem the speculation on Wall Street before the whole of Europe was forced off the gold standard.[244] When it became apparent that Harrison's hands were tied by opposition to dear money from Andrew Mellon, the Secretary of the Treasury, Adolph Miller, the Chairman of the Federal Reserve Board, and mid-western Board members, Norman travelled in secret to Washington in an effort to persuade the Board to act. The trip was in vain: the board, unused to meeting foreign bankers, found him arrogant and rejected his 'demands' for sharply higher interest rates.[245] In New York he angrily warned Harrison and the Morgan partners that their inaction would bring the roof down on all their heads.[246] Returning to London he called on Sir Edward Grenfell to lend his support in gingering up his New York colleagues.[247] Shortly afterwards he travelled to Paris to urge on the work of the Young Committee on reparations, and meeting J.P. Morgan Jr there he thoroughly disturbed him by warning that the various countries his firm had helped back to gold would collapse unless something was done quickly.[248]

The American bankers privately accepted they were facing a 'world credit crisis', but counselled patience. Harrison, they explained, required time to bring the Fed round to his views.[249] But Norman could not wait, nor could he do much on his own. A Bank rate rise now was almost unthinkable since it would seriously damage the prospects of the Conservatives being returned at the approaching general election.[250] And assistance to the German, Hungarian, Danish, and Italian central banks, all of whom had made direct or indirect approaches for credits, would do little good since, as he explained to Harrison in May, their need was for dollars; sterling credits would merely transfer more pressure onto the London exchanges.[251] With no help forthcoming, Norman reimposed a partial ban on foreign lending, singling out loans to public authorities while allowing 'reproductive' loans to continue in order to minimise the damage to the City.[252] But another unpopular Bank rate rise was becoming unavoidable, and privately he railed against America's lack of financial leadership.

The government was similarly immobilised. For two years its imperial protectionist supporters had subjected it to intense pressure; so much so that Liberals accepted the probability of another tariff election.[253] Yet Ministers still doubted that a mandate for protection was possible. They therefore shunned the one policy that most of them believed would aid the economy while defending the return to gold, a policy some now regretted. The gold standard was an essential safeguard against socialist misrule and just as important to industry as it was to finance, Baldwin and Churchill affirmed in major campaign speeches.[254] All issues became weapons in the political struggle, but the defensive tone of the speeches only served to underline the element of conflict that existed between the industrial and mercantile–financial communities. Having influenced the behaviour of the Conservative government, this basic fault-line proved equally important to the second Labour government which took office in June.

6

The second Labour government at The Hague

For most of 1929 international relations were dominated by the attempt to put reparations on a sounder footing and shore up the international monetary system by the creation of the Bank for International Settlements. This combined initiative derived mainly from the growing apprehension in British and American banking circles about a possible world crisis. Events soon showed that their fears were well-founded. But existing criticism of the banks made them reluctant to draw attention to the need for monetary and financial reform. And even those politicians who described themselves as internationalists displayed a marked reluctance to accept further 'sacrifices' for the sake of world stability. The frustrations of a decade of reconstruction had left the world dangerously short of leadership.

Stamp, the Young plan, and the BIS

The Dawes Plan had scarcely been drafted when British experts began to look forward to a further, more radical revision of the reparations regime. Norman warned of the need for revision at the meeting of central bankers on Long Island in July 1927,[1] and shortly afterwards Strong took up the matter with Parker Gilbert, the Agent-General for Reparations, whose annual report on 10 December 1927 advised the reopening of the issue. With reparations rising to the standard Dawes annuity of 2.5 milliard marks in 1928–29 and German foreign commercial borrowings rapidly mounting, Gilbert foresaw a foreign exchange crisis before the end of the decade. The solution he envisaged included the removal of the payments transfer safeguard in order to enforce some discipline on Germany, and the adoption of a final and specific settlement in place of the open-ended commitment of the Dawes Plan.[2]

Official British reactions were initially unfavourable. Since the issue of the Balfour note of 1 August 1922, Britain accepted the desirability of writing down reparations so long as war debts were also reduced at the same time,[3] and British experts accepted that it was only a matter of time before the crisis Gilbert anticipated actually occurred. But they were also convinced that until the Dawes Plan was shown to be unworkable and the United States accepted the integral link between war debts and reparations, any attempt to revise reparations alone would only result in the reimposition of excessive claims on Germany or reductions solely on Allied account. In neither case would Britain's national or international interests be served.[4]

British opposition continued until October 1928 when, with Germany and France agreeing to reopen the question and Gilbert offering assurances that future German payments would be sufficient to cover Allied war debt obligations, Churchill reversed his stand.[5] Action might be premature and unlikely to produce the complete and final settlement that Gilbert hopefully described. Yet Churchill was persuaded after a closer look at the figures that there was no hope of ever gaining cover for Britain's 'arrears' – some £200 million paid to the United States before any reparation or Allied war debt payments had been received – and so long as future payments to America could be assured there were obvious advantages to reopening the question now. The French were anxious for a settlement which would provide a basis for prepayment by means of a 'mobilisation' loan, the Germans for one which would remove the various controls over their economy required under the Dawes Plan and provide the *quid pro quo* for an immediate evacuation from the Rhineland of Allied troops who were scheduled to remain there until at least 1935. Besides being a gesture of solidarity to France and Germany, Britain's support for revision would strengthen her hand in pressing for an early evacuation of the Rhineland, which was a source of tension in Europe, and French ratification of the Churchill–Caillaux war debt agreement negotiated in 1926.[6] At Churchill's request the Cabinet agreed to reopen the reparations issue on 29 October.[7] Shortly afterwards an expert committee drawn from the interested countries was appointed.

The British expert on the committee was Sir Josiah Stamp, seconded by John Baring, first Baron Revelstoke: an excellent choice as events were to prove. Stamp, the chief draughtsman of the Dawes Plan, was closely familiar with the issues at stake and, as President of the Royal Statistical Society, possessed the sort of mind that thrived on juggling annuity schedules, which was an essential part of the committee's work. Perhaps equally important was the fact that he was a deeply religious man.[8] Baptist by upbringing, Methodist by choice, he had come to regard price instability as the chief enemy of social harmony and a threat to the very moral basis of society. The expectation of further deflation with its inevitable cost in social injustice was what had led him to speak out against Britain's premature return to gold in 1925. For the same reason he had subsequently become a leading member of Irving Fisher's Stable Money Association.[9] And on joining his fellow experts at the Hotel Georges V in Paris on 11 February 1929 he immediately sought to make a virtue of necessity by using the reopening of the reparations issue as an opportunity to strengthen the international payments system. Stamp's driving energy and zealous manner occasionally tried the patience of his foreign colleagues. But what he lacked in finesse was largely made up for by Revelstoke, an older and more subtle man with thirty years' experience in the cosmopolitan world of merchant banking. When Revelstoke suddenly died midway through the committee's proceedings, Stamp received assistance from Sir Charles Addis, an able man who had the advantage of being Britain's representative on the Reichsbank board, but who was less tactful than Revelstoke.

The committee's first decision was to elect Owen D. Young, the senior American expert, to the chair. As with General Dawes five years earlier, European delegates hoped this sort of flattery would encourage Americans to recognise their country's integral responsibility for solving the war debt–reparations tangle. Young at least required no persuading on this score. A Wall Street lawyer and veteran of the Dawes Plan negotiations, he appreciated that American war debt claims were bound to affect European reparation demands, however strongly Washington denied their formal connection. But he was dogged from the outset by Hoover's incoming Republican administration, which nervously interpreted his every step towards a new settlement as a victory for the wily Europeans.[10] And perhaps because he was involved in two of the most dynamic new industries of the twentieth century, as president of General Electric and co-founder of RCA, he saw no reason for deep concern about the state of the world economy. Whereas Stamp was convinced that the day was rapidly approaching when Germany's continuing trade deficit and mounting external debt made reparation payments on anything like the present scale impossible, Young confidently looked to expanding world trade to solve the problem.[11] He thus found Stamp tiresomely pessimistic, with his insistence upon a radical writing down of German reparations and improved transfer safeguards.[12] Independently of one another, nevertheless, the two men were instrumental in shaping what became known as the New or Young Plan.

For ten weeks the committee did little more than dispute the amount Germany could in future be expected to pay. Schacht, the German expert, who had come with exaggerated hopes of revision and was anxious for his reputation in right-wing circles, refused to discuss the continental creditors' proposal for an average annuity of 2.4 milliard marks, but also refused to offer a figure of his own and provocatively suggested that German acceptance of substantial obligations would depend upon a drastic re-writing of the territorial clauses of the Versailles Treaty. Emile Moreau, representing France, showed his impatience by talking menacingly of further military action against Germany and threatened to walk out of the conference until Young called his bluff. Thereafter he was reduced to displays of bad temper.[13] On 18 February Stamp sought privately to reason with Schacht but came away empty-handed. On 5 March Young sent in J.P. Morgan and Thomas Lamont to do battle with him. Morgan, a simple and nearly inarticulate man, was used to giving orders, not negotiating among equals or arguing the toss with jealous nationals like Schacht. He returned from the confrontation in a state of virtual breakdown.[14] Only slight progress had been made when in the last week of April German foreign exchange losses threatened the country with renewed currency chaos.

The main cause of German currency weakness was the Wall Street boom, which had driven money market rates to 20 per cent and acted like a magnet for liquid funds throughout the world. For Germany this meant a steep decline in new investment, a slump in economic activity, budgetary problems for the government, and a sharp run-down of the commercial banks' inner reserves. As the banks relied on foreign short-term borrowings for some 40 per cent of their resources, the evidence of their predicament was adding to the pressure on the mark.[15] Other factors also played their part, such as reports of a breakdown in the Paris negotiations and rumours of politically–inspired withdrawals of French deposits from Germany, which although untrue seemed only too plausible in the circumstances.[16] Schacht encouraged the rumours and deliberately aggravated the crisis in the hope of obtaining drastic concessions from the creditor powers.[17] The crisis brought matters at the conference to a head, though not with the results that Schacht desired.

Late in April leading German bankers privately dissociated themselves from Schacht's aggressive stance, and through Charles Mitchell of the National City Bank offered Young their support. Young called upon them to warn Schacht that further German borrowing in New York would depend upon a satisfactory reparations settlement.[18] Young also put pressure on the French through Morgan, who warned Poincaré that 'if a settlement was not reached there was no use of their coming to his firm as the American fiscal agent of France for credits', either now or in the future.[19] And early in May when Schacht reported that the Reichsbank's reserves had fallen dangerously low, Young, with Governor

Harrison's approval, warned him to expect no assistance from the Federal Reserve Bank until definite progress had been made in the reparations talks.[20] Under strong pressure from the German government as well as the bankers to accept the compromise figure of 2,050 million marks that Young put forward, Alfred Vogler, the Ruhr industrialist who had been Schacht's second, resigned. But Schacht now reluctantly agreed.[21] And Stamp, hitherto his strongest supporter for a lower figure, also affirmed his agreement.

Nothing had altered Stamp's view that German reparations should be radically reduced for the sake of long-term international financial stability. But as he admitted to Young, British Ministers were prepared to agree to almost any settlement Young proposed rather than jeopardise the recent improvement in Anglo-American relations, and in view of the ominous state of world finances he too regarded agreement on reparations as absolutely essential.[22] German municipalities and firms owed well over £100 million to City institutions. If these credits should become frozen, British banks would be left insolvent, interest rates would be forced still higher, and the whole of the British economy would suffer. Thus despite the absence of any concessions from the continental creditors, France, Belgium, and Italy – the Latins, as he called them – he was prepared to work within Young's annuity figure. As he later explained:

> It is impossible now for any real financial crisis in Germany to be localised. … Lord Revelstoke was particularly apprehensive and felt that it was worth paying a very high price indeed to avoid such a contingency. … We held to the position that we could not be led into a deadlock with these consequences merely because of the lesser apprehensions of our Latin colleagues.[23]

For Young, agreement on the new average annuity meant that the experts' major task had been accomplished, but for Stamp the equally large problem of allocating reparation shares still lay ahead. Moreau and the Belgian and Italian experts, Emile Francqui and Alberto Pirelli, took the view that as Germany had punctually paid instalments of the Dawes annuity since 1925, further payments could be expected unless Germany deliberately chose to interrupt them. If Britain was determined to see Germany's burden lightened, it was Britain that must accept the corresponding reduction in receipts.[24] Stamp appreciated that any reduction in Britain's share of receipts as laid down at Spa in 1920 was bound to be seized upon by critics at home. To his credit he managed to devise a formula which came so close to satisfying British interests that initial reactions to the new plan were generally favourable.

Stamp's approach was to draw a clear distinction between reparations due in 'the period of reality, viz. the next ten years', and those due in 'the distant future'. Recognising that they constituted 'totally different planes of reality and probability', he set out to improve the likelihood of payments in the first period by writing down Britain's nominal claims in the second. As an inducement to the 'Latins' to cooperate, he initiated a shift in negotiations from distribution on the basis of the Spa percentages to coverage of the creditors' war debts on a year-to-year basis. True, this meant a reduction in Britain's Spa percentage and a definite abandonment of any hope of coverage of the so-called arrears, but this was a purely nominal sacrifice. The new schedule provided Britain with constant war debt coverage: no surplus in the long term, but no deficit in the near term either. Indeed the practical effect was actually to increase Britain's receipts during the period 1929–39 and decrease them only in subsequent years. The present value of the overall 'sacrifice', calculated on a 5½ per cent basis (the present Bank rate, which was uncommonly high) and expressed in terms of a flat rate annuity, was 48 million marks or £2.4 million a year. But as there was no question of any reduction in receipts until the 1940s, when few seriously expected the reparations regime still to be functioning, there was, in Revelstoke's words, 'no sacrifice at all'. Besides serving Britain's interests, the new schedule was also more favourable to Germany than appeared at first glance. German payments were reduced from the present rate of 2.5 milliard (billion) marks to an average of 2.05 milliards. Disregarding the escalator clause that linked the Dawes annuity to an index of German prosperity, this was only an 18 per cent reduction. However, payments started at the lower figure of 1.7 milliard marks, or 32 per cent below the standard Dawes annuity, and rose only gradually to the new 'standard' of 2.4 milliards after thirty-seven years. The new schedule had the additional merit of linking reparation receipts with war debt outpayments 'to the full, or at any rate, up to the maximum point that, in the present temper of Washington, it is politic to do'.[25]

A second modification in the distribution arrangements, made at Stamp's suggestion,[26] divided the payments schedule into two annuities. The first, the 'unconditional' annuity, amounted to about one-third of the total, which was to be paid whatever Germany's economic condition. The second, 'conditional' annuity was postponable for two years at Germany's request. France was to receive £25 million of the £33 million of the unconditional annuity. On the basis of these assured payments France intended to issue one or several reparation loans for public subscription, thereby gaining prepayment of her claims and tying German reparation obligations more closely to her general commercial credit-worthiness. Despite the apparent subordination of British claims to those of the French, Stamp willingly acceded to this arrangement. In the first place, prepayment of reparations was no part of British policy and hence the legal fiction of 'unconditional' payments was unobjectionable. Secondly, Britain's position was safeguarded by the requirement that in the event of a two-year postponement of the unconditional annuity, France must provide a guarantee fund of £25 million, sufficient to compensate Britain and other creditor countries for their relatively small share of the continuing unconditional payments. In the event of further postponement the whole question of distribution could properly be reopened.

British interests were more closely affected by other features of the plan, Stamp believed. Efforts had been made to reduce the Dominions' share of the annuity along with Britain's. These had been defeated despite the fact that the 'Americans clearly had no sympathy for the Dominions' claims, and merely regarded it as a political situation'. Additionally the growing menace of payments-in-kind had been substantially checked.

By the fourth Dawes year (September 1927–August 1928), some 1.04 milliard marks or over 40 per cent of reparations were being paid in kind. Italy, lacking domestic fuel sources, had relied on South Wales for 67 per cent and Germany for 7 per cent of its coal imports before the war. But by 1929 Italy was taking 97 per cent of her payments-in-kind from Germany in the form of coal. Hence, despite increased postwar consumption, British coal exports to Italy stood nearly one-third below the 9.4 million ton level reached in 1913, whereas German exports were up 3.5 million tons over the same period. The Fascist state exerted informal pressure on private purchasers to buy reparation coal, according to Board of Trade sources. The Italian state railways, which had long depended on British supplies, were now importing the whole of their 3 million ton annual requirements from Germany and not even allowing British merchants to compete for the business.[27]

France, the largest recipient of reparations in all forms, had also taken active steps to facilitate payments-in-kind. Municipal works projects in which at least 20 per cent of the cost went for German deliveries received interest rate subsidies from the state. German machinery privately purchased for the devastated regions benefited from a 40 per cent reduction in import duty; purchases for the armed forces or *équipement nationale* paid no duty at all. During the fourth Dawes year payments-in-kind to France amounted to 478 million marks, or 72 per cent of all German exports to France.[28] In fact, even this understated the problem, for where large projects were involved the provision of some German machinery often meant that *all* the machinery had to be purchased from Germany in order to be compatible.[29]

Within the Treasury the simple view prevailed that payments-in-kind were of no special importance because all reparations required Germany to earn foreign exchange and hence all reparations involved competition for British trade and commerce.[30] This might be good text-book economics, but as Stamp recognised it bore scant relation to the real world. Britain was Germany's chief competitor in the export of coal and manufactures. To the extent that German reparations were paid in these goods, British trade would correspondingly suffer. Aware that the Board of Trade was under intense pressure from colliery owners, industrialists, merchants, and trade unionists for the elimination of payments-in-kind, he fought hard for concessions.[31] In the end he secured agreement that they should be reduced immediately by a half, to 540 million marks per annum, and eliminated altogether after ten years.

Stamp was satisfied that the Young Plan met Britain's immediate objectives. German payments were reduced, if not enough then at least as much as could be hoped for in the circumstances. British outpayments were covered. Payments-in-kind were reduced to 'the lowest possible point'. The American connection was highlighted by the close parallel between the reparation payment schedule and American war debt claims.[32] The addition of a proposal for a new international bank persuaded him that reopening the reparations question had proven to be a fortunate decision. As he explained to the Cabinet:

> The institution of the Bank of [sic] International Settlements will have, we believe – in its by-product of European cooperation in the control of gold – something of far greater value to civilisation and particularly to British interests than the whole of reparations and debts. What one thinks of the importance of the Bank from this point of view depends entirely upon the seriousness with which one regards the present uncoordinated and uncontrolled forces which settle our fate through the fortuitous value of a single metal.[33]

The idea of an international bank had been in the air since the previous summer when members of Gilbert's office raised the question of handling the Reparation Commission's functions after it was wound up.[34] It thus came as no great surprise when Schacht and Francqui both suggested a new international institution in separate conversations with Young on 22 February. Schacht, anxious to minimise the impact of reparations on Germany's foreign exchange position, envisaged a credit-creating agency that would increase liquidity on the basis of reparation deposits and thereby facilitate the expansion of world trade and German trade in particular. Francqui, who had played a key part in Belgium's postwar reconstruction, was less specific and mentioned only a trustee role for the proposed institution.[35] Young seized upon their idea in the hope that this might provide a way of 'depoliticising' reparations and inducing the Germans to cooperate in reaching a settlement. At his request, American banking experts were called in from London and New York to assist in the drafting of a scheme. As the European currencies weakened against the dollar, J.P. Morgan, Lamont, Revelstoke, Schacht, and Moreau, all of whom were in Paris, nervously encouraged their efforts.[36]

The plan set out by the American experts envisaged three ways in which the proposed Bank for International Settlements (BIS) would provide 'an elastic element between the payments to be made by Germany and their distribution', safeguard German stability, and increase the chances of uninterrupted payments to the creditor countries. When the transfer of the unconditional part of the annuity posed difficulties for Germany, it would discount German bills against foreign exchange in its reserves. In the event that transfer problems threatened to interrupt payment of the conditional part, it would take the mark deposits the German government was obliged to make and reinvest them in Germany to sustain the domestic economy, then borrow in third markets against the security of these investments and use the proceeds to pay the conditional reparations. It would also market warrants entitling holders to German deliveries in kind, and help finance complementary capital investment projects. Besides these functions the bank would take on certain others created by the new reparation scheme. It would manage the reparation bond issues anticipated by the Latin countries; take charge of assessing German requests for temporary suspension of the conditional part of the annuity, ensuring that decisions were based upon objective financial criteria and free from political bias; and serve as trustee for the £25 million deposit required from France in the event of suspension of conditional payments.[37]

Stamp, who drafted the section on the proposed bank in the Young Plan,[38] incorporated the experts' main recommendations. However, in his version reparation functions assumed only secondary importance. Instead its principal function now was to turn the liability of large international capital transfers into a means of expanding world trade and payments. The bank would undertake 'intermediate credit operations' without distinction for nationality. It would act as a clearing house for transfers of inter-governmental debts and monetary gold. It would act as a lender of last resort to member central banks. In sum it would 'contribute to the stability of international finance and the growth of world trade ... opening up new fields of commerce, of supply and demand ... and augment and perfect existing arrangements for carrying through international settlements'. The bank would be capable not only of intervening in the event that postponement of reparation transfers became imperative, but of 'forestalling circumstances which might of themselves lead to a transfer postponement'. The report concluded:

In the natural course of development it is to be expected that the Bank will in time become an organisation, not simply or even predominantly concerned with the handling of reparations, but also with the furnishing to the world of international commerce and finance important facilities hitherto lacking. Especially it is to be hoped that it will become an increasingly close and valuable link in the cooperation of Central Banking institutions generally – a cooperation essential to the continuing stability of the world's credit structure.[39]

That Stamp was correct in regarding international monetary stability as the chief problem confronting the world was fully borne out by events in the next few years. Nothing would have been more valuable than an institution capable of creating liquidity quickly and in large quantities to make up for the acute dollar shortage in Europe, and enable governments to avoid the politically intolerable adjustment measures required to maintain exchange stability. But could the BIS possibly fulfil the divergent, not to say conflicting, aims that Stamp envisaged for it? Almost from the outset signs appeared that it could not.

Shortly after the appearance of the American experts' proposals, Pierre Quesnay, Moreau's assistant, expressed strong reservations about the larger discretionary functions of the proposed bank. As he indicated, France would be glad of an institution to assist in commercialising reparations by placing the bond issues that were planned. But it had no intention of allowing anyone to exercise broad discretionary powers over the transfer of reparations and certainly not in order to stimulate German trade competition.[40] Nor was France alone in resisting a large scheme with credit creating powers.

Towards the end of April, Stamp and Sir Charles Addis, who had replaced Revelstoke, found the French and American experts united in opposition to gold-backed foreign exchange for the BIS's reserves and insistent upon gold. French hostility to the gold exchange standard was well known, but the British experts even at this point seem not to have fully appreciated the hostility of American bankers to any scheme that threatened to create further credit 'inflation', and it was only with difficulty that they managed to secure agreement that the composition of reserve assets should be left to the discretion of the Bank's management.[41] To make matters worse, on 16 May Henry Stimson, the American Secretary of State, announced that the Federal Reserve Bank of New York would have nothing to do with the proposed bank.[42] The decision was of doubtful legality, but there was no getting around the fact that the Hoover administration had decided to take no chances with domestic opinion by accepting contact between the Federal Reserve Bank and a reparations agency. Before the end of June, arrangements were made for a syndicate of American commercial banks led by J.P. Morgan & Co. to be represented on the BIS board. But this was scarcely a substitute for central bank involvement. Given a willingness to do so, central banks could treat BIS deposits as reserve assets, a procedure which opened up enormous possibilities for the avoidance of payments crises and control of international price-levels. On the basis of commercial support only, the BIS could not hope to do much more than its institutional backers could do on their own.

Public interest in the work of the Young Committee had been aroused in April when Snowden launched a vigorous attack on the Conservatives' feeble handling of the reparation issue and promised that given the responsibility he would not be content to see 'my country and my people bled white for the benefit of other countries who are far more prosperous than ourselves'.[43] Press comment indicated a widespread feeling that Britain had made concessions enough on inter-governmental debts,[44] and Churchill, with one eye on the forthcoming general election, affirmed that he would not tolerate a disproportionate reduction in British receipts.[45] Snowden continued to dwell on the reparation issue, making it the main topic of his election campaign.[46] But no other politician followed his lead. To judge by press reactions to the experts' report, signed in Paris on 7 June, a week after the election, the British public was, in the words of *The Economist*, 'almost passionately anxious to see the whole business settled once and for all'.[47]

The BIS proposal evoked a wider range of views than any other aspect of the plan. Critics on the far left and die-hard right professed to see in it the work of cosmopolitan finance.[48] Industrialists complained to the Board of Trade that German competitors appeared likely to be the main beneficiaries.[49] *The Bankers' Magazine* voiced the concern of some in the City when it welcomed the acknowledgment of the need for closer central bank relations but deplored the creation of 'some kind of super-bank' which might impair London's pre-eminence as 'the banking and financial centre of the world'.[50] Keynes on the other hand welcomed the experts' report, less for the reparations revision which did no harm but hardly went far enough to warrant the effort expended, than for the BIS proposal which stood just a chance of developing into the 'nucleus for the super-national Currency Authority which will be necessary if the world is to enjoy a rational monetary system'. Most of the national press echoed this view.[51] Journals such as *The Observer*, the *Morning Post*, and the *Yorkshire Post*, which had earlier denounced further British sacrifices, now joined in welcoming the experts' report.

Similarly, the TUC-controlled *Daily Herald*, and the Rothermere and Beaverbrook papers, having given prominence to the issue in the spring, did not bother to comment on the experts' report or display further interest in the question until events at The Hague conference attracted their attention. The new Labour government, so far from being pushed into intransigence by an aroused public or press, could thus count on broad support for a policy of accepting the Young Plan and going from there to promote substantive economic cooperation. That it chose not to do so reflected more than anything else its lack of a coherent strategy.

The internationalism of the second Labour government

For the Labour Party the years between its first and second terms of office were a time of almost constant effort by the left-wing as well as elements of the right to break free of the immobilising combination of political and economic internationalism, which left so little scope for easing the plight of industry. The party leadership displayed an equal determination to avoid debating the issues and to rely upon high-flown generalities in place of a plan of action. *Labour and the Nation*, the policy document adopted at the party conference in the autumn of 1928, vividly illustrated the shortcomings of this approach.

Repeatedly the document affirmed that a Labour government would replace the anarchy of the market system with a scientifically planned economy. 'Capitalism' was 'bankrupt', and André Siegfried, the political scientist, was quoted to the effect that Britain's problems derived from 'the inability of her rulers to realise that the nineteenth century has come to an end'.[52] Yet with equal emphasis it affirmed unqualified support for internationalism. Labour would work through the League of Nations to promote arbitration, conciliation, and disarmament. It would support the extension of the League's economic functions, ratify the Washington Hours Convention, seek an international solution to the problem of gold-price instability, and in true Cobdenite fashion 'abolish ... obstacles to commerce' in the interests of world prosperity and peace. 'In foreign affairs, the Labour Party stands for the view that the vital interests of the world, whether economic or political, are the common interests of all peoples.'[53] How were the goal of a planned national economy and internationalism to be reconciled? It was virtually certain that intervention in the economy could not succeed without *some* insulation from external influences, *some* restrictions upon the international movement of capital and goods. The document did not say, and it was clear that senior Ministers in the new government had devoted little if any thought to the matter.

Although MacDonald did not act as his own Foreign Secretary as in 1924, he still sought to perform on the stage of great power diplomacy, and with preparations already under way for a naval disarmament agreement with the United States he insisted upon retaining authority over Anglo-American relations.[54] He was not interested in the dismal science of economics. His sole concern was to obtain an agreement with the United States, and he had neither the time nor inclination to deal with the more intractable economic issues confronting the government. Arthur Henderson, whom he neither liked nor respected, became Foreign Secretary.[55]

At the end of the war, Henderson had joined in protests against a punitive peace, arguing that it would perpetuate the 'economic antagonism which contributed so largely to the general causes of the present European conflict, and would lead inevitably to a bitter and devastating repetition'.[56] Yet in his presidential speech to the Labour and Socialist International in 1928 he referred briefly to the economic problems facing the world, then added that 'they are as dust in the balance at the present juncture in comparison with the vital issues of armaments and war'.[57] Like others of the Radical–Liberal tradition he was devoted to the cause of peace and took for granted that free trade was an essential component, but otherwise he regarded economic and political issues as essentially distinct areas of competence. It was a naive view and a dangerously inadequate one. Recent experience had demonstrated that the peace of Europe depended upon its economic stability, not the other way round. The only thing to be said for it was that it fitted nicely with the economic views of William Graham at the Board of Trade and Philip Snowden at the Treasury.

Graham, an earnest, industrious Scotsman, had been Snowden's junior at the Treasury in 1924 and remained somewhat in awe of him.[58] Snowden, now 64 years old, was more remote from the trade union and radical elements in the party than ever. Since first holding office, he and his wife had been swept into the country house circuit, and, whether cause or effect, he betrayed increasingly open abhorrence of the 'irresponsible' ideas promoted by the left. A former chairman of the ILP, he resigned his membership in 1927, explaining publicly that it was redundant now that the Labour Party had adopted a 'definite Socialist basis', while privately complaining that ILP policy was 'drifting more and more away from ... evolutionary Socialism into revolutionary Socialism', a charge not even hyperbolically true.[59] The previous year he had again spoken in Parliament of the 'grip upon Government by national and international finance', which made 'the public ownership and control of banking and credit absolutely essential'.[60] Yet when the general election drew near he announced to Labour supporters that the time for nationalising the banking system was 'not ... yet ripe', and in words scarcely bettered by the *Daily Mail* warned of the vast arbitrary power a government would possess if it was allowed to control the banks.[61]

MacDonald did not hesitate to form another government dependent upon Liberal support, and chose practically all his Ministers from the right-wing of the party. He had, *The Economist* commented, 'spared Cheltenham and the City from alarm'.[62] At the first meeting of the Parliamentary Party after the general election he declared that it would 'show the country ... that it knew how to govern'.[63] Policies, however, and not simply competent administration were urgently needed to deal with Britain's already acute unemployment problem and the looming threat of an international economic crisis brought on by the vastly disruptive bull market on Wall Street and a gratuitous increase in American protectionism. For six months the log-rolling process triggered by Hoover's campaign promise of further protection for American farmers had been under way in Washington. Hopes of improved Anglo-American relations and the general election diverted attention in Britain during the spring. But on 28 May, two days before polling day, the House of Representatives approved a bill that sharply increased import duties on both agricultural and industrial goods.[64] Such action, at a time when the United States was already running a huge balance of payments surplus with the rest of the world, the *Chamber of Commerce Journal* angrily exclaimed, 'out-Herods Herod'.[65] The news came too late to affect the outcome of the British election, but gravely affected international relations in the months that followed.

Already numerous signs existed that France would take the lead in organising European resistance to the American challenge. In April the Paris press carried reports of a proposed alliance of European motor manufacturers to resist the 'Transatlantic enemy'.[66] In May the French Socialist Party appealed to the United States 'to consider whether it is possible, wise and without danger to civilisation and the economic life of the world to compel Europe to export for a long period of years large quantities of gold, while it is subjected by the United States to the competition of an output having lighter charges and protected by high tariff walls'.[67] Following news of Congressional plans, the *Confédération générale de la production française* and the *Association nationale de l'expansion économique* published a joint letter condemning American tariff plans and raising the spectre of retaliation, while the 500 presidents of the French Chambers of Commerce similarly condemned the behaviour of the United States and called on the French government to 'emerge from its neutrality and enter into such negotiations with other European nations as may be necessary to defend Europe from the economic point of view'.[68] Elsewhere in Europe the talk was the same.

Signor Olivetti, representing Italian employers at an ILO conference in Geneva, accused the United States of 'preparing for the economic conquest of the world', and called on Europe's workers and employers to set aside their differences and unite against the American threat.[69] Stresemann, returning from a League Council meeting in Madrid where he had held secret conversations with Briand on the future of Europe, affirmed before the Reichstag that the central problem of the day was no longer Germany's isolation in Europe but 'one of Europe as a whole in fee to the power of the United States'.[70] At the fifth biennial congress of the International Chamber of Commerce which opened in Amsterdam on 8 July the corridors buzzed with talk of resistance, and the Belgian national committee received strong encouragement for their proposal of European-wide cooperation.[71] Three days later Briand announced his intention to speak at the League Assembly in September on the subject of European federation. It was time, he explained, to build upon the framework of lasting peace provided by the Locarno Treaties, apply the lessons of the United States' success, and equip Europe to face the consequences of American tariff policy.[72]

In Britain Lord Beaverbrook was among the first off the mark, with the call for an Empire Free Trade 'crusade' in the *Sunday Express* on 30 June. Simultaneously fascinated by the United States and disturbed by its power, he seized the opportunity to exploit the unease within the Empire and Conservative circles. In private he admitted that the Dominions were unlikely ever to accept complete free trade with Britain.[73] Nevertheless he favoured the simple formula of Empire Free Trade, which suggested something quite different from the failed idea of Tariff Reform, and welcomed the difficulties it caused for the Tory leadership. Baldwin, whom he held in contempt for failing to take up the Empire preference and food tax issue in 1923, was in a vulnerable position after the election defeat. By pitching his appeal in the boldest terms, Beaverbrook sought to leave him no choice besides endorsing the crusade or opposing it and losing the backing of the party.

Within days the struggle over Conservative Party policy began. Neville Chamberlain, speaking to an EIA lunch on 4 July, declared that all past pledges had now expired and that the party's Empire and industrial policies would be completely reformulated. He had however spoken without knowledge of Beaverbrook's appeal, and to his intense annoyance was forced to issue a statement denying any association with

Empire Free Trade.[74] His idea was to move cautiously, make tariffs only part of a broader programme, negotiate preferential agreements with the Dominions, and ensure a mandate for food taxes by demonstrating the advantages of reciprocal trade within the Empire. Beaverbrook's formula was 'pure mischief-making': far too ambitious and calculated merely to put the Dominions on the defensive.[75]

Meanwhile during the Commons debate on the King's speech, the feud between Churchill and Amery erupted in angry confrontation. Churchill described Labour's election victory as the result of dividing the anti-socialist vote and warned that a Tory commitment to protectionism would ensure Labour's hold on office for years to come. Amery, suspecting Churchill of angling for another Coalition, rounded on him. The Conservatives' defeat was due to their failure to offer the working people of Britain an inspirational alternative to socialism, he responded, and called for a bold Empire policy.[76] Amery found himself unsupported in the shadow Cabinet and in danger of expulsion.[77] But behind the scenes he joined with Melchett in organising a new industrialists' pressure group.[78] Signs of a back bench revolt also appeared when Sir John Ferguson, the Conservative candidate in the Twickenham by-election, announced his conversion to Empire Free Trade and numerous MPs braved Baldwin's censure by supporting his campaign.[79]

The Labour government came under pressure from several directions as well. Sidney Webb, now Lord Passfield, the Dominions and Colonial Secretary, advised Cabinet colleagues on 2 July that the Canadian government would seek a bolder policy of imperial preference to offset the anticipated loss of trade with the United States, and was sounding other Dominion governments on the subject.[80] At practically the same moment Stanley Bruce, the Australian Prime Minister, issued a similar call. 'The American output,' he warned local businessmen, 'would soon exceed the consumptive powers of the home market, and an attack on overseas markets was inevitable. The resulting flood would be tremendous, disastrous.'[81] Before the end of July numerous Parliamentary questions were tabled, some calling for representations against the proposed American tariff increases, others for joint resistance with European countries.[82] Conservative Members angrily denounced government plans to remove the safeguarding duties along with their Empire preferences at this crucial juncture. And critics on both sides of the House demanded an inquiry into monetary policy, in light of growing pressure on the pound from the Wall Street boom.[83]

The government barely hesitated before affirming that Britain's world interests demanded improved relations with the United States. Hence, despite the already one-sided character of bilateral trade, Graham rejected the call for representations against intensified American protectionism – making Britain the only important trading nation to raise no protest. By the same token he also repudiated any suggestion of associating Britain with a European alliance to resist American economic aggression, and only at Foreign Office urging refrained from antagonising Briand and French opinion by openly deprecating the idea of European federation.[84] Snowden in turn conceded the possibility of an inquiry into monetary policy, but denied absolutely any idea of tampering with the gold standard.[85] The effect of the pressure was nonetheless to throw the government on the defensive. If international diplomacy was to solve Britain's problems, it would soon have to show results. Snowden in particular was determined to demonstrate Labour's capacity when the diplomatic conference on the Young Plan convened at The Hague.

Whitehall and the Young Plan

Within Whitehall senior officials strongly favoured acceptance of the Young Plan as it stood. Summing up the Foreign Office view on 17 June, Orme Sargent of the Central Department affirmed that the advantages of accepting it and the costs of rejection were both so great as to rule out any serious British challenge. Labour's policy of promoting European peace required the immediate evacuation of all Allied troops from the Rhineland, a step France had promised to support so long as agreement was reached on reparations. Stresemann, whose moderate leadership Britain sought to support, also depended upon an agreement: failure to agree and reversion to the Dawes Plan would produce a serious financial crisis in Germany, undermine his position, and give new life to the nationalists with their schemes of 'defiance, revenge and rearmament'.[86]

Lord Tyrrell, the Ambassador in Paris, added his voice in support of the plan. As he explained, France had suffered acutely from financial difficulties since the war. Unlike Britain, which had substantial war debt claims, France had only reparation receipts to cover her war debts. She needed the fiction of large and certain payments to consolidate her position. By the time the Hague conference convened, France would have ratified the British and American war debt agreements committing her irrevocably to payment, something she had refused to do for three years in the absence of definite coverage from reparations. She was prepared to do so now not only because of the $400 million she would otherwise forfeit to the United States, but also because the new plan offered the possibility of a commercial bond issue providing prepayment of reparations. To reopen debate on the Young Plan would throw the whole of French finance into turmoil and raise the spectre of renewed deficits and inflation, creating a politically intolerable situation.[87]

The Foreign Office also pointed out that the Italians would strongly resist any attempt to claw back their increase in receipts. If they seemed to be the largest beneficiaries from the plan, it was partly out of recognition that their reparation claims on the remnants of the Austro-Hungarian Empire were worthless. More importantly, the United States government would also be annoyed if Britain made difficulties at this stage. Despite official aloofness, the efforts of Gilbert, Young, and the other American experts were being closely watched in Washington. Charges that Britain had upset their plans for petty and selfish motives would almost certainly be taken badly and reduce the chances of a naval agreement.[88] The authors of the Young Plan had declared their work indivisible. The Foreign Office held that the financial objections must be 'absolutely overwhelming' to warrant insistence upon modifications.[89]

Two days later Sir Warren Fisher, Permanent Secretary of the Treasury, and Sir Richard Hopkins, Controller of Finance, advised the Chancellor that the financial objections were by no means overwhelming and also advised acceptance of the plan. Fisher was sure that the continental countries had played their usual 'shabby tricks' on Britain. But he pointed out that at least Britain's future payments to the United States were covered, the Dominions' position was safeguarded, and the Americans, who would be conceding an even larger percentage sacrifice than Britain on claims arising from the postwar occupation of Germany, would be able to boast that they had again settled a European problem too contentious for the Europeans themselves. This in itself was sufficient reason for acceptance.

> Our relations with the USA are the one international interest that is fundamental to our welfare (and indeed to world peace). ... I hate the idea of being swizzled ... by the Dagos ... but I account this as nothing compared with the faintest risk of stultifying ourselves in our endeavour after rapprochement with the United States of America.[90]

Hopkins, the only civil servant who left no doubt that he actually understood Stamp's accomplishment, stressed that talk of British sacrifices was utterly hypothetical. It was true that Britain stood to lose perhaps £2 1/4 million per annum and the French, Belgians, and Italians stood to gain an annual £273,000, £592,000, and £1,795,000 respectively, but only if one assumed that reparations would be paid for the full fifty-nine years of the plan – and who accepted that assumption? Assuming they lasted even twenty years, Britain's 'sacrifice' would be only £580,000, and calculated on an interest rate below 5 1/2 per cent the 'sacrifice' would practically vanish. Acceptance of the plan meant superior coverage for Britain's war debt payments over the next ten years, which was what mattered. Rejection meant a severe financial crisis in Germany and inevitable repercussions in London, as well as all the blame for the consequences. He could thus see every reason for unqualified acceptance, especially as, 'There are at present no indications of a public opinion forming itself in any quarter in this country against the plan, such as there would have been if the plan had made a substantial sacrifice to France'.[91]

The day after Fisher and Hopkins reported to the Chancellor, the French Financial Attaché in London reported to Paris that the British Treasury anticipated more controversy over the constitution of the BIS than over the reparations plan itself, which seemed as good as settled.[92] Unfortunately for him, this was not so. Two months earlier when Snowden had stirred controversy over the reparations issue, Frederick Leith Ross, the Deputy Controller of Finance, had made known his opinion in the Treasury that Stamp had been completely outmanoeuvred by the Latins and that it would be far better to stick with the Dawes Plan than accept the new arrangements including the proposed BIS, which had no practical value. Subsequently he had been absent from the Treasury, recuperating from a perforated ulcer, and it was not until after his colleagues had offered Snowden their views that he returned to resume his criticism.

Leith Ross stood one rung below Hopkins and two below Fisher on the Treasury ladder of seniority. But Fisher, when not engaged in his duties as Head of the Civil Service, devoted himself to the work of the Committee of Imperial Defence, and Hopkins, a recent recruit from Inland Revenue, was not yet able to assert his views with confidence on matters such as reparations. Leith Ross on the other hand was an expert in international financial affairs; indeed, since the departure of Bradbury, Siepmann, Blackett, and Niemeyer for the City, he was the only senior Treasury man with any experience in this field. For ten years he had attended the almost continuous European reconstruction conferences, the circus as fellow experts called them, and was used to asserting his views at the highest level. He was also a combative man, rather proud that his brilliant career at Oxford had ended abruptly on account of unruly behaviour, and that he usually managed somehow to thread his way out of the tight spots that his impetuosity landed him in. Additionally, one suspects, he was feeling miffed at being passed over for Hopkins' position.[93] At all events, he again denounced Stamp's craven surrender to the continentals, dismissed the Foreign Office case for acceptance of the Young Plan as 'rather tendentious', and advised the Chancellor to stand fast on a number of alterations.[94]

This was precisely what Snowden wanted to hear, and the proposal for British strategy at the forthcoming conference which he circulated to Cabinet colleagues a few days later displayed the aggressive slant of Leith Ross' pen. Britain, Snowden complained, had 'poured out [her] financial resources unstintingly' during the war only to be treated afterwards as 'the milch-cow for every European need'. Against more than £1,200 million loans to the Allies (excluding the Soviet Union) and over £260 million subsequently repaid to the United States, Britain had received a mere £35 million. Further sacrifices might be justified for a final settlement, or if other Allies made equal sacrifices. But the Young Plan was unlikely to last more than a few years, and France, who owed Britain £600 million in war debts, was to receive most of the unconditional annuity and after paying war debts would have a £35 million annual *solde* or surplus. Moreover, this surplus would be added to 'the immense foreign exchange resources which are already at the disposal of the French authorities, and which have already been on more than one occasion a menace to the economic situation in this country'. Italy, whom the previous government had relieved of six-sevenths of her war debt, would come away with an annual gain of nearly £2 million. But while France, Italy, and Belgium were to receive increased shares and Germany's burden was to be lightened, 'we are asked to take a smaller share of such payments as are received from Germany, and to take them from the unsecured portion of the annuities, and the net result of these sacrifices will simply be that at the next stage of the negotiations we will start so many points lower down the scale'.

Snowden declared the Young Plan proposals 'outrageous' and 'quite impossible to accept ... involving as they do an annual average loss of about £2,400,000 and a capital loss of £37,500,000'. Nor did he profess to see any reason to refrain from demanding changes. Churchill had already stated that the British government was not bound by the experts' work; and what was the point of the forthcoming conference if not to examine their work in a critical spirit? Other powers would probably also seek modifications. Poincaré, for instance, had indicated his intention to reduce the powers of the proposed BIS. In Snowden's opinion, the political repercussions of a firm policy were much exaggerated. Other powers were too anxious for agreement to allow a breakdown over Britain's claims. And if a breakdown did occur it need not affect the other issue in question, evacuation of the Rhineland, for there was nothing to stop Britain from unilaterally withdrawing her own troops. Britain should therefore keep the political and financial questions separate, accept the new basis of German payment, and stand firm for three changes: restoration of the Spa percentages, a larger share of the unconditional annuity, and reduction of payments-in-kind to the same extent as the cash payments. In the event of a breakdown, the other countries would doubtless attempt to throw 'the whole responsibility ... on our shoulders,' but the British government would have no difficulty letting the people know the 'true facts'.[95]

The records of the Cabinet meeting of 17 July state only that the question of policy at the forthcoming conference led to 'considerable discussion', without revealing the points raised. It would be interesting to know if Snowden was challenged on any of his own 'somewhat tendentious' arguments. Did anyone, one wonders, point out that it was unrealistic to talk of separating political and financial questions, when the very essence of French and German policy was to keep them bound up together? Or that Britain's Rhineland policy, which had for its aim the pacification of Europe, would not be satisfied by the unilateral withdrawal of British troops? Was someone prepared to correct the impression that diplomatic conferences were intended as occasions for conflict, or that in the present case any other power would demand fundamental changes in the experts' plan? Did anyone point out that France's larger share of the unconditional annuity did not, except in a purely nominal sense, mean greater priority or security of payment? More fundamentally, was it pointed out that on Snowden's own assumption as to the likely duration of the Young Plan there could be no talk of sacrifices at all; that indeed on any sharply reduced period of payments *Britain stood to gain* from the basis of distribution designed by Stamp?

Almost certainly the answer is no, at least so far as the latter questions were concerned. Even those who favoured unqualified acceptance of the Young Plan, including Henderson's professional advisers, spoke of sacrifices, as if Britain was actually foregoing some £2½ million a year in budget revenue, which was just not the case. If Snowden was ignorant of 'the true facts,' the rest of the Cabinet was almost certainly equally so. The discussion, one may surmise, revolved around the political risks of Snowden's approach and ended by his seemingly unanswerable claim that Britain's finances as well as her international self-respect could not stand any further sacrifices. Significantly, the only document formally circulated at the meeting was Snowden's memorandum. The Cabinet fully endorsed its recommendations, subject only to the proviso that before allowing negotiations to break down the British delegation should confer with the Prime Minister.[96] Snowden, to Henderson's intense annoyance, was nominated head of the British delegation.[97]

Snowden and the defence of British interests at The Hague

The first Hague conference, which lasted from the 6th to the 30th of August, became little more than a struggle between Britain and the other principal reparation recipients over their respective shares, and can therefore be summarised briefly. On the opening day Snowden announced that he accepted the terms of Germany's future obligations but required the restoration of Britain's share of payments, a larger share of the unconditional annuity, and a reduction in payments in kind before he could accept the balance of the scheme; and thereupon the confrontation began.[98] At the plenary session the following day Henri Chéron, the French Minister of Finance, took issue with Snowden's claim that he was under no obligation to accept the experts' report. The fact that they were officially nominated and given a wide mandate placed an obligation on all governments to accept their unanimously agreed results, Chéron stated, and with the support of Senator Antonio Mosconi of Italy and Paul Hymans, the Belgian Foreign Minister, he demanded that the plan be accepted 'in its entirety as one indivisible whole, without alteration'.[99]

Later that day Pierre Quesnay along with Pirelli and Francqui, the chief financial advisers of the three opposing delegations, called on Leith Ross, Snowden's principal assistant, to warn that if British demands were not dropped the French government would have the Bank of France convert its sterling balances to gold and transfer them to Paris. Leith Ross estimated that French assets in London amounted to perhaps £240 million, withdrawal of even a fraction of which could force sterling off the gold standard. But he assumed that the Bank of France would not allow such a calamity, and ordered the 'blackmailing party' to leave. Their bluff called, nothing happened.[100] That summer, sterling reserves fell well below the 'Cunliffe minimum' for the first time in the year and gold flowed to Paris. Suspicions were voiced in the City of French political machinations, but the timing of the gold movements indicated other factors at work. For one thing sterling was weak against practically all the major currencies, not just the franc. For another, gold exports to Paris amounting to £12.4 million took place during July and the first week of August, that is while the French were still counting on British cooperation, whereas during the week of 8–14 August, after the confrontation began, gold movements were slight. The following week sterling again moved below gold export point to Germany and France, and between 15–30 August, £5.3 million gold was lost to France in a small, steady outflow. But here again sterling was weak against other currencies as well, and gold losses to France continued through

September when French foreign policy again called for British friendship.[101] Although the French themselves sometimes encouraged the idea of carefully orchestrated financial manoeuvres there is little evidence that anything so Machiavellian ever took place, and indeed on this occasion the Bank of France was deeply embarrassed by the unwanted inflow of gold.[102]

The confrontation at the conference resumed at the first meeting of the financial committee on 8 August. Chéron repeated his argument for unqualified acceptance of the plan. Snowden reiterated his demands, adding to the undoubted annoyance of his audience that British claims had the special merit of deriving from a war she had entered 'not in her own interests ... not because any of her material interests were endangered [but] in support of treaty rights and ... in defence of the safety and security of other nations'.[103] He further claimed that the other creditors had broken a promise by tampering with the Spa percentages at Paris, until Pirelli forced him to retract the accusation. Encouraged by Treasury advisers, he accused Chéron of a 'grotesque and ridiculous' interpretation of the Young Plan benefits at the second meeting on the 10th. Chéron, whose obesity made him the butt of much humour in Paris, was sensitive to such remarks, which he took as a personal insult. An apology from Snowden the next day was required to bring him back to the conference table.[104]

MacDonald attempted to intervene. Fearful from the outset of Snowden's intransigence, he had been pressed to restrain the Chancellor by General Charles Dawes, the new American Ambassador, and by Thomas Lamont, the Morgans partner.[105] Norman, on his return from the United States, joined MacDonald and Lamont in Edinburgh to warn that a breakdown at The Hague could result in the collapse of the gold standard.[106] MacDonald cabled a warning to Snowden, but it was mistakenly sent *en clair*, and Snowden demanded a message for release to the Press to re-establish his credibility at the conference.[107] To MacDonald's suggestion that Lamont cross to The Hague for discussions, Snowden curtly replied this was 'not necessary'.[108]

Snowden, who had no experience of diplomacy, seldom travelled abroad, and lacked the negotiating practice of his trade unionist colleagues, was evidently carried away by the impact of his abrasive House of Commons debating style on the other delegates at the conference. In his simple way he imagined he was acting in a proper internationalist spirit. For him, what was good for Britain was also good for the world and vice versa, from which it followed that when France, Italy, or Belgium advanced claims that were unacceptable to Britain it was not so much a matter of conflicting national interests but of the foreigner's crass selfishness and morally inferior behaviour. But this refusal to accept the legitimacy of foreign viewpoints revealed him to be a nationalist and a very rigid nationalist at that. He admitted as much when, taking a break from the conference, he noticed the Union Jack on the standard of his official car and commented to his secretary, 'I have been a pacifist, I am an internationalist, but somehow or other, whenever I see that flag in a foreign country, I become incredibly imperialist'.[109] It seemed not to occur to him that, unlike the Commons, all the major countries represented at the conference had to agree on the results and be able to secure ratification in their respective parliaments.

For another week Snowden remained in his hotel suite, refusing to negotiate and simply waiting for the others to meet his terms. On Monday 19 August, after all concessions had been rejected as insufficient, advisers to the British delegation were requested to prepare appreciations of the political and financial effects of a breakdown, and the Prime Minister was warned to expect this eventuality. The following day Louis Loucheur, a member of the French delegation, offered 50 per cent of Britain's Spa percentage on behalf of France and Belgium. This too was rejected. Stresemann appealed for recognition that a breakdown would spell disaster for Germany and the world. Briand offered only two alternatives: a return to the Dawes Plan or the Young Plan as it stood. Snowden dismissed Stresemann's warnings about the fragility of the German economy, and lectured the others in their moral duties. Britain's demand was not simply for £2 million per annum, but for 'the observance of international agreements. Nothing was more important in international relations than that there should be no default on solemn engagements.'[110]

By Thursday 22 August, Snowden had again brought the conference to the brink of collapse, having rejected an offer presented by Henri Jaspar, the Belgian Prime Minister, for 60 per cent of Britain's claim, and demanded a final offer in writing the next day.[111] Henderson at this point intervened. Out of patience with Snowden's inflexibility and annoyed at Graham, the third ministerial delegate, for privately agreeing that Snowden was 'pushing things dangerously far', while meekly siding with him at their daily meetings, Henderson now spoke out in the strongest terms, demanding that Snowden contact MacDonald before allowing the conference to break down.[112] For several days telegrams were exchanged across the Channel. Snowden requested MacDonald to convene the Cabinet in The Hague.[113] Ministers in London proposed instead that Snowden or colleagues return for consultations. Snowden ruled this out on account of the delicate state of the conference. The idea of a meeting was set aside and Snowden was asked to carry on, but not to insist on full satisfaction of his claims.[114]

Subsequently MacDonald attempted to outflank Snowden with the help of Sir Maurice Hankey, the Secretary to the Cabinet and Committee of Imperial Defence, who was serving as both secretary to the British delegation and Secretary-General of the conference. On the first occasion Hankey declined the suggestion that he should secretly approach Loucheur to indicate Britain's terms. A former Marine officer who shared the Navy's disdain for Continental commitments, he was enjoying the demonstration of British firmness too much to 'spoil Snowden's game'.[115] But finally on the 25th, with Snowden still refusing to negotiate and the conference again lurching towards breakdown, Hankey urged MacDonald to appeal directly to Snowden for a settlement.[116] MacDonald's telegram arrived the following day, with the warning that the break-up of the conference would be hard to justify when over half of Britain's claim had already been met, and that already elements of the press were turning hostile.[117] The warning had an immediate effect. For the first time since the conference began Snowden did not merely reject the offer presented that evening but responded with a proposal of his own. With Jaspar acting as mediator, offer and counter-offer were then exchanged until at 1 a.m. on the 28th agreement in principle was reached.[118]

With a settlement of the percentages question, other outstanding issues were soon resolved. Graham, who had already received concessions on payments in kind, secured during the final bargaining an Italian commitment to purchase 1 million tons of British coal at best British prices for three years.[119] Henderson was equally successful. From the first meeting of the political committee on 8 August Briand had affirmed his willingness to cooperate on an early withdrawal of troops from the Rhineland, subject only to a definite settlement of the reparations question. Once reached, the completion date for the withdrawal of French troops was agreed, outstanding differences over occupation costs were left to the financial experts, and on 31 August the Foreign Ministers quickly and amicably completed their work.[120]

Snowden returned a hero. A 'wildly enthusiastic reception' greeted him at Liverpool Street station.[121] The *Daily Herald* hailed his triumph. *The Statist* called him the first British statesman since Palmerston fearless enough to tell foreigners to 'go to the devil'. An invitation was soon extended to visit the Royal family at Sandringham. Presently Snowden and MacDonald (for his efforts to secure a naval agreement with America) received the freedom of the City of London.[122] Certainly within his own terms Snowden had been successful. He had gained back 83 per cent or a nominal £2 million per annum of Britain's share of reparations which Stamp had 'sacrificed'. Additionally he had won an increase in Britain's share of the unconditional annuity from less than £900,000 to £2,750,000, a substantial order for British coal, and certain other concessions. In a radio broadcast on 2 September he was thus able to contrast his own stout defence of British financial interests with the 'quixotic generosity' of past governments, which had made them 'the milch cow of Europe'. And he could add righteously, 'Beyond this, and of far greater importance, was our assertion of our international rights and our determination that international rights should be respected.'[123]

But Snowden's reckoning, albeit widely shared, was scarcely realistic. On the one hand, the only financial gain of any real significance was the £5 million lump sum addition from reparation payments during the transition period between the Dawes and Young Plans. The nominal £2 million annual gain, which Snowden had made such an issue, would not actually involve any payments *until the 1940s*, beyond the period of reality as Stamp had said. On the other, account must be taken of the risks that were run. Even after Snowden had been offered 60 per cent of his demand, Leith Ross had urged him to hold out for at least 80 per cent and if necessary let the conference break down, in other words risk a crisis over a nominal £480,000 per annum. Outlining the possible consequences, Leith Ross described a freezing of sterling loans in Germany, the failure of City banking houses, a run on the pound abetted by French withdrawals, and the collapse of the gold standard. This he stressed was 'the extreme case' and unlikely to occur.[124] All the same it was extraordinary that any such risk should have been contemplated for the small, indeed, trivial, objective in view.

In addition Snowden had courted the risk of public censure and only just managed to escape. On the left, H.N. Brailsford had once again demonstrated his gifts as a journalist by speaking out in criticism of Snowden's readiness to endanger European stability for 'a shilling a head'.[125] It is true that other journals of the left did not follow his lead. But several influential journals of the centre, including *The Nation and Athenaeum*, *The Observer*, and *The Economist* expressed strong reservations about his diplomacy.[126] *The Times* had intended to issue a firm warning against obstructiveness shortly after the conference began. It held back because of Treasury assurances of a successful outcome, but was later approached by Norman's colleague Addis who suggested that a warning shot should be fired across Snowden's bow.[127] Several times Stamp received attention in the press for his criticism of Snowden's narrow-minded approach to the reparation question, and *The Bankers' Magazine* spoke out in Stamp's defence.[128] Midway through the conference *The Statist* commented, 'it is certainly significant that no serious criticism of the Young Plan made itself known through our organs of public opinion until Mr Snowden made his characteristic stand against the additional sacrifices which it demanded from Great Britain'.[129] Snowden, in other words, had created the necessity for a diplomatic victory. Later he was to claim that after two days at The Hague he knew there would be no breakdown over his demands.[130] His actions confirm he believed no such thing.[131] One is left to imagine the reception awaiting him in London had his gamble not paid off.

In the end Snowden succeeded, as Brailsford and other critics pointed out, because Stresemann had agreed to assume an additional burden. This was modest enough in purely financial terms, but it ran directly counter to Labour policy and created difficulties for German defenders of the policy of 'fulfilment'. Besides jeopardising other central objectives of foreign policy, Snowden also threw away the opportunity to make the conference a display of European solidarity and instead transformed it into a confrontation which, if unspecific in effect, contributed to mutual hostility.[132] Nor, despite his repeated claims, was respect for international rights and agreements enhanced. On the contrary, if Snowden's activities accomplished anything, it was to illustrate to his own countrymen just how little respect there was abroad for Britain's 'rights' or her contributions to world leadership and how self-seeking the European states really were. Dalton commented, there was something odd in a Labour Chancellor returning to 'rapturous applause from the worst elements in England'.[133] It was a measure of the frustrations of a decade of zealous adherence to internationalism that Snowden, a true believer, should have succeeded only in arousing nationalist and imperialist sentiment from his one venture in international diplomacy.

The Bank for International Settlements

The BIS plan, held in abeyance during the conference, again received attention when the organisational committee began work at Baden Baden in October. By this time however all momentum for a large institution with powers to create liquidity had gone. Snowden showed little interest in the plan and left it to his Treasury advisers to decide on Britain's official interest. They in turn had quite abandoned hope of seeing a real international reserve bank created, and now merely insisted upon further restricting the operations of the BIS that might draw business from London or intensify pressure on the world's monetary gold stock. The one positive contribution they looked for from the bank was in drawing American central bankers closer to European affairs and accelerating their 'education' as to the integral link between intergovernmental debts and international monetary stability.[134] For this reason they were content to leave the development of the plan to Norman and his colleagues at the Bank of England.

During the initial stage of deliberations in the early part of the year it seems that Norman had been persuaded by Schacht to look upon the bank plan as a valuable means of reducing the dimensions of the reparations problem. But like Schacht he also quickly became disillusioned when France and the other continental reparation recipients resisted the idea of allowing the bank any latitude in the handling of reparation funds.[135] He did not in any case share Stamp's anxiety about the need for international monetary reform. Although seriously disturbed by the weakness of sterling and other European currencies, he continued to believe that all would be well if only central bankers were sufficiently independent of national political control to be able to work in close harmony with one another. His one concern about the development of the bank plan was thus not its powers but its complete independence, 'beyond the reach of Governments';[136] and in this respect his outlook harmonised nicely with American banking representatives.

Towards the end of August, Lamont complained to Snowden that interested governments seemed ready to destroy the non-political character of the proposed bank by making it 'more of an adjunct of the Treasuries ... a new and glorified Reparations Commission'. If that happened, he warned, the BIS would not provide the central bank cooperation that the Bank of England so badly needed.[137] Like Norman, Lamont sought a politically independent bank. The difficulty was that the reparations it was designed to handle belonged to governments, which required Treasuries to exercise some control over their handling. That was not all. In November the Americans announced that they would have nothing to do with the bank if it handled war debt payments to the United States.[138] This ruled out the clearing operations involving reparations and war debts on which Stamp had set some store, as well as obscuring the link between them which the European countries had been anxious to demonstrate, and for a moment it seemed that the French would lead a general withdrawal from the organisation committee.[139] Norman's nominees on the committee, Addis and Walter Layton, were too anxious for American participation to complain. But what after all was left? As a Treasury report put it, the committee had whittled away the bank's potential to the point where it would merely 'receive the creditors' money and honour their cheques up to the amount of their balances, and will do no more'; it had removed 'every trace of the elastic element which the plan contemplated'.[140]

Continuing hopes – and fears – that the BIS might eventually become an important institution led to a prolonged dispute over its location and some wrangling over posts. Eventually Basle was selected as the least objectionable centre, and an American was given the chairmanship.[141] The institution that opened its doors for business on 17 May 1930 was not the central bankers' bank that Stamp had envisaged but Norman's central bankers' club; an exclusive club to be sure, but also remote from the problems besetting Britain and the world.

Between early June, when the Labour government took office, and the start of The Hague Conference in August, gold drained steadily from the Bank of England, as the pull of Wall Street drew funds from Europe and forced balances in London to be run down. In mid-July Snowden rejected any idea of abandoning the gold standard. By 6 August, the day the conference opened, however, the Bank's reserves were down to £140 million, £10 million below the 'Cunliffe minimum'.[142] Norman was forced to contemplate a higher Bank rate, a temporary increase in the fiduciary issue, even suspension of the gold standard.[143] Public pressure for action was also mounting.

In the last week of July the TUC petitioned the government to heed the Melchett–Turner conference call for an inquiry into monetary policy.[144] The FBI repeatedly demanded similar action.[145] At almost the same moment Samuel Hammersley, the Lancashire mill-owner and Tory MP, convened a 'producers' conference', which appealed to the Prime Minister not merely for an inquiry into the working of the gold standard but its suspension. As the delegates explained, industry was fed up being sacrificed to the interests of finance, especially as across the Atlantic America was demonstrating it had 'found the key to industrial prosperity. The whole of the national economy of that country is directed to continuously decreasing the cost of production per unit of goods manufactured, thus enabling her to maintain the payment of high wages, and increase purchasing power.' They were also convinced that immediate action was necessary because increasing American pressure on the international balance of payments was bound to force the Bank of England into further deflationary action just to defend the present exchange rate. While not denying the importance of the City's 'invisible' earnings, officially estimated at £65 million per annum,[146] they saw no reason to suppose that, so long as monetary policy was intelligently handled, all this would be lost with the suspension of the gold standard. 'But in any case the commissions earned are infinitesimal when compared with the more substantial profits that could be earned from the development of the nation's potential productive power. The expense of maintaining a free gold market, the burden of which – a high Bank rate – is carried by industry, is too great for this country to bear unless we reconcile ourselves to becoming a second-class or third-class industrial power.' The appeal was signed by representatives of twenty manufacturers' organisations, including the two leading cotton spinners' associations, the Society of Motor Manufacturers, the Machine Tool Trades Association, the British Wool Federation, The Silk Association, the Manchester Association of Importers and Exporters, the Cable Makers Association, the Society of British Gas Industries, the National Council of the Pottery Industry, the Sheffield and Perthshire Chambers of Commerce, the National Union of Manufacturers, and the Federation of Grocers' Associations, as well as sixty-three prominent industrialists and members of the farm community.[147]

It was no coincidence that this appeal for a way to 'maintain the payment of high wages' should have come in the midst of a lock-out in Hammersley's own cotton industry. There is however no evidence that the Prime Minister paid it any attention. An entry in his diary two weeks later records with obvious self-satisfaction, 'dealt with cotton' – by persuading the workers to accept a 6¼ per cent reduction in wages.[148]

Norman meanwhile held off raising Bank rate so as not to embarrass Snowden and in the hope that a successful outcome at The Hague would improve the tone of the London and other European financial markets.[149] But the conference, if important for what it did not do, contributed nothing to the solution of the great dollar shortage facing Europe. Norman, unable to hold off longer, raised Bank rate another full point to 6½ per cent on 26 September. The outcry was unprecedented. Lord Aberconway, the ironmaster and Liberal peer, termed it another 'heavy blow' to industry 'for the benefit of the bill brokers of the City'.[150] Lord Melchett, in a prominent article entitled 'Unemployed – By Order of the Bank!', in Beaverbrook's *Sunday Express*, repeated the charge and called outright for the abandonment of the gold standard.[151] At the annual TUC conference a few weeks earlier, Ernest Bevin had spoken out strongly against the operation of the gold standard, and a resolution ascribing industrial difficulties to monetary causes and calling for a thorough-going government inquiry was adopted.[152] Shortly after this event, the annual Labour Party conference at Brighton held an emergency debate on financial policy.

Norman, growing anxious, urged Snowden to say nothing at the conference that would encourage hopes of a monetary solution to Britain's problems. He need not have worried on this score. Taking the floor to defend the Bank rate rise, Snowden pointed angrily to the 'orgy of speculation in a country 3,000 miles away'. But while conceding an official inquiry into the relationship between finance and industry, he warned against hopes of any solution except by 'international cooperation', through the new BIS, for instance.

The speech was well received, and Herbert Morrison, the conference chairman, quickly stepped in during the subsequent debate to halt an ILP attempt to secure reference to 'a system of national control' in the inquiry's terms of reference.[153] A relieved Norman wrote to congratulate Snowden on his speech.[154] According to the *Daily Telegraph*, Snowden's proposed conference was simply a means of doing nothing, and with the promise of wide terms of reference and a membership that would 'command public confidence', there was no question but that this was his intended purpose.[155] Yet it was scarcely satisfactory to say that Britain must rely on international cooperation, in particular through the BIS, when little had been done to make the BIS an effective agency, when The Hague conference had been made an occasion for bitter dispute, and when the world economy was literally falling to pieces.

7

Free trade: the last offensive

Labour's search for an international strategy

Arthur Henderson, speaking to reporters at The Hague on 31 August 1929, stated that the conference just ended had 'opened up a new era. For the first time since August 1914 it can be said that the war era is really ended.'[1]

Henderson's elation was understandable if not altogether warranted. The Hague conference had concluded successfully after more than three weeks of bitter confrontation over Snowden's demands. An ostensibly final reparation settlement had been adopted. Germany was freed of the humiliating controls on her economy that had been part of the Dawes Plan. More important, the departure of Allied troops from the Rhineland would be advanced from 1935 to the spring of 1930. At the Tenth Assembly of the League of Nations, about to open in Geneva, Henderson planned to sign the Optional Clause committing Britain to accept arbitration in all justiciable disputes, a step he hoped other powers would follow, bringing nearer the day when international conflict would be restricted to the submission of contending legal briefs to the Permanent Court of International Justice.[2] Negotiations with the United States on a naval arms limitation agreement had progressed to the point where MacDonald would soon visit Washington for talks with President Hoover. Within three months of taking office the Labour government had gone some way towards realising its foreign policy objectives, and demonstrating that, as MacDonald had promised, it 'knew how to govern'.

As with other postwar governments, the litmus test of the second Labour government's success, however, would be its capacity to deal with unemployment. So far, Ministers had done nothing to realise the vague assurances in the King's Speech of schemes 'for the improvement of the means of transport ... the depressed export trades ... My Overseas Dependencies ... agriculture ... the fishing industry', for emigration, the cotton, the iron and steel, and the coal industries.[3] The only thing they were specific about was what they were not prepared to do. They would not depart from the principles of sound finance. They would not tamper with the gold standard. They would not allow the drift towards protectionism to continue; at the first opportunity protective duties as well as revenue duties on foodstuffs would be removed. They would rely completely on an internationalist solution to Britain's problems. All the signs existed of an economic crisis of global proportions, as the result of soaring American interest rates, declining commodity prices, and a swingeing increase in the American tariff, yet the government possessed no plans for improving international economic relations.[4] Not until the eve of the Tenth League Assembly was an initiative formulated, and then it was inspired chiefly by the desire to present an alternative to Briand's proposal for European federation.

Within Britain news that Briand would speak on this topic at Geneva had received a widely mixed reception. The *Morning Post*, confident that nationalism was the supreme political reality in Europe, bracketed it with Locarno as another of Briand's quixotic crusades.[5] Others on the right, captivated by the idea of an era of vast politico-economic blocs, found nothing remarkable or implausible in it. Amery, long an enthusiast of European unity, welcomed it.[6] Beaverbrook and Melchett spoke as if a United States of Europe was almost a reality already.

Internationalist opinion was also divided. *The Commercial*, although critical of the American tariff bill, rejected both British and continental proposals for an organised reaction. Empire Free Trade it dismissed as frivolous, the Briand proposal as a dangerous provocation. 'It would divide the world into three great fiscal groups which could hardly hope to live at amity with one another.'[7] *The Statist* and *The Economist* saw Empire Free Trade as impracticable and undesirable, but treated the suggestion of European economic unity with sympathy. *The Statist* looked for improvement of continental trade and decreased dependence on tariff protection by the extended use of industrial cartels.[8] *The Economist* spoke of European unity as inevitable. 'The tendency of modern times is towards greater political and economic aggregations.' The journal did not hesitate to rule out British participation in a European federation in view of her greater commitments elsewhere, but welcomed the initiative and dismissed any suggestion that it was inspired by rivalry with the United States or posed any difficulty for Britain. So confident was it, that Patrick Hannon, the Conservative MP from Birmingham, charged the editor with 'an attempt to camouflage the reason' for interest in a United States of Europe, which was 'the ultra-protectionist policy of the

United States', and for failing to explain the serious consequences for British trade, which made it vital to organise 'a United States of British countries' in self-defence.[9]

In contrast, the *New Statesman* denounced Briand's initiative as at best a cynical French manoeuvre to steal the limelight at Geneva, at worst an attempt to recreate the old *bloc continental*, this time against the United States.[10] The *Daily Herald* was equally hostile. To its leader-writers a united Europe, and especially one united by France, represented nothing but danger to the authority of the League of Nations and world peace.[11]

The Labour government shared the *Herald's* dislike of France and its faith in free trade and the League of Nations, and gave no encouragement to Briand's scheme. But MacDonald was preoccupied with Anglo-American relations, Henderson, Snowden, and Graham with The Hague conference. Thomas, Lord Privy Seal and Minister responsible for employment, was busy setting up committees and talking with officials and businessmen about job creation schemes before breaking off to visit Canada in an attempt to drum up orders for British goods. Despite the vital importance of international trade relations to the government's future, the only members prepared to give any time to the questions that Briand's initiative at Geneva was certain to raise were the two junior Ministers at the Foreign Office, Hugh Dalton and Philip Noel-Baker. Fortunately for them, officials in the Belgian Foreign Ministry were equally worried by the precariousness of the Labour government and the danger that Britain might lapse into protectionism, a situation disastrous for their trade and foreign policy, which relied upon British involvement in Europe to save them from domination by France or entanglement in another Franco-German conflict. At their urging, Paul Hymans, the Foreign Minister, accepted the idea of a tariff truce, and hearing this the British Ministers persuaded Graham to adopt the proposal as his own.[12]

Regionalism versus internationalism at Geneva

The most impressive feature of the Tenth Assembly was the recognition by practically every European delegate of the precarious state of commercial relations, and the vital importance of a sound economic underpinning for the maintenance of world peace. At the same time the polite, cautiously worded speeches revealed fundamental differences over appropriate action. Briand's long-awaited speech came on 5 September. Proudly acknowledging association with the age-old idea of European union, utopian as it might seem, he spoke of the desirability of forging 'some kind of federal bond' in Europe. Beyond this he offered nothing specific, but he seemed to have no doubt as to the order of priorities. 'Obviously' the association would be 'primarily economic, for that is the most urgent aspect of the question'.[13]

The Assembly had to wait four days for Germany's reaction on account of Stresemann's desperately bad health. On the morning of the 9th, however, he managed to affirm Germany's qualified support for Briand's initiative. He could not endorse the idea of a United States of Europe or any grouping of European states directed against the United States or the Soviet Union. But he applauded Briand's vision and offered Germany's support for closer European economic cooperation.[14]

The British reaction had been indicated by MacDonald in his address to the Assembly on 3 September. Peremptorily echoing the general concern for 'economic disarmament' as well as military disarmament, he mentioned Briand's forthcoming pronouncement and assured the Assembly that Britain would support any scheme that contributed to 'economic freedom'. But, he added, as if to distinguish between practical action and vague aspiration, 'This Assembly, however, must face the problem of tariffs.'[15]

Following shortly after Stresemann to the rostrum, William Graham, the first British economics minister to speak at Geneva, made even less effort to hide his hostility. 'Far be it from me ... to throw cold water upon any plan which is designed to bring European nations more closely together, either in the political or economic field. We shall, however, gain nothing ... if we are not perfectly frank and candid with one another in reviewing the difficulties which may be involved.' Taking up Stresemann's reference to the danger of inter-continental rivalry, he added his own warning about plans, whether based on preferential tariff arrangements or cartels, trusts and the like, which involved discrimination against extra-European countries:

> I am perfectly satisfied that if, for reasons which on the surface might appear to be sound, we in Great Britain or any other country embarked upon a policy of discrimination, we should be untrue to all that is best in the economic work of the League of Nations; such a policy might, from the economic standpoint, generate that friction which would manufacture war between the nations – war which it is our express purpose in this League to make certain will never recur. Do not let the note of discrimination enter this controversy.[16]

Graham's positive advice, so befitting his unassuming personality and free trade faith, was to seek progress through a number of small steps. More than forty international conventions on economic, social, and transit problems had already been prepared under the auspices of the League and merely awaited a sufficient number of ratifications to be brought into force. Graham looked to them to reduce the levels of non-tariff barriers to trade. In addition he urged that the League Economic Committee's inquiry into the coal industry be followed up by a European-wide agreement on wages, hours, and conditions of work, to end the anarchy currently reigning in the industry. Finally he offered a 'concrete proposal': a two or three year tariff truce, to provide a breathing-space for implementing a programme of multilateral tariff reductions.

That day Briand was host to European delegates at a lunch at the Hôtel des Bergues, where he tried to anticipate objections to his federation proposal. To fears that a European organisation would draw interest away from the League and undermine its authority, he assured his audience that he had deliberately chosen Geneva to introduce his proposal so that it would develop within the atmosphere of the League. Article 21 of the League Covenant envisaged regional ententes, and a European federation would be just that. As to the suggestion current in some quarters that his motive was to organise Europe against the United States, he solemnly vowed that he would rather abandon the idea altogether than allow it to take on this character. His own information was that the United States favoured the proposal, recognising that a new era of prosperity in Europe was to everybody's advantage. He was prepared to believe that if a start could be made on a common approach to European economic problems, there would soon be recognition of the need for more comprehensive agreements on such things as labour and social policy and eventually for 'political solidarity'.

During the ensuing discussion Stresemann and Henderson reverted to the objections to an initiative involving only the European countries. Stresemann, with great politeness and emphatic agreement on the unsatisfactory state of European trade relations, dwelt upon the necessity to avoid any action that might undermine the authority of the League. Henderson expanded Stresemann's remarks and added a warning of his own against the danger of appearing to organise Europe against another power, be it the United States or the Soviet Union. If the European states really wanted to demonstrate their unity, he concluded, apparently unaware of the irony in his advice, they should join in ratifying the Washington Hours Convention. Other delegates had fewer reservations about Briand's proposal, however, and everyone appeared to share the view that some action was urgently needed on the economic front. Eventually all present joined in inviting Briand to prepare a memorandum outlining his proposal for consideration by their governments, then to collate their views in a report to the League's Eleventh Assembly a year later.[17]

Four days later in the Second (Economic) Committee of the Assembly, Hugh Dalton and Louis Loucheur, on behalf of Britain, France, and Belgium jointly introduced two resolutions. One called for further investigation of conditions of work in the coal industry in anticipation of the ILO conference on coal scheduled for June 1930. The other, on concerted economic action, embodied Graham's proposal for a two-year tariff truce, but stressed the tariff disarmament measures that the truce was expected to make possible.[18] This seemed to disprove any conflict between Graham's and Briand's initiatives, yet the distinction between limited regional measures and the universal 'free trade' approach to commercial relations could not simply be wished away.

Dr Hendrikus Colijn, the Dutch Minister of State, welcomed the resolution on concerted economic action. Like others from the liberal trading countries of northern Europe, he was extremely anxious to keep in line with Britain and apprehensive of Briand's proposal. Yet he did not completely rule it out. The dismal failure to implement the resolutions of the World Economic Conference was provoking strong reactions, and although a low tariff bloc in Europe might prove impracticable, 'In view of the present poverty of ideas none must be lost'.[19]

M. Stucki, the Swiss delegate, also welcomed the resolution on concerted economic action, but warned that it could not succeed until the question of most-favoured-nation treatment was squarely faced. Supposing, he suggested, a group of states agreed on mutual tariff reductions, but found that a large protectionist and aggressively exporting country called, say, Arcadia, refused to make reciprocal reductions, yet insisted upon the full benefit of the tariff reductions agreed on among the other countries by reason of its most-favoured-nation treaties. 'It was unlikely that the States would be disposed to accept this fool's bargain.' Stucki pointed out that in two days time a Franco-Swiss commercial treaty would come into force which made specific exception for concessions granted within the framework of 'plurilateral conventions' as laid down by the League Economic Committee. The next step, he said, was for the Economic Committee to make up its mind about the treatment of countries – such as Arcadia – which refused to participate in approved conventions or to act within their spirit.[20]

From another standpoint Rudolf Breitscheid, the German *rapporteur* of the Second Committee, warned against hoping for too much from the tariff truce. It might merely 'stereotype' the existing situation, leaving some countries excessively protectionist and others over-exposed to foreign imports. It might also tempt some countries to raise tariffs in anticipation of an international agreement.[21]

Breitscheid at least accepted the principle of a tariff truce; F.L.

McDougall, economic adviser at the Australian High Commission in London, did not. As he explained with some impatience, the tendency in Geneva and London was 'to suggest that the League of Nations stood for a definite economic policy of free trade and further to suggest that tariffs imposed for protective purposes were against international ideals'. Yet the fact was, practically every League member employed tariffs for protective purposes. He also felt that the League should recognise that there was a distinction to be made between the mature European nations and the 'younger overseas nations': the latter required tariffs to protect their infant industries. By this time the slump in commodity prices was causing serious difficulties for the overseas nations, and delegates from Canada, India, the Irish Free State, South Africa, and Persia indicated support for McDougall's view.[22] Most of the European delegates, however, seemed favourable to the resolution on concerted economic action, and it was forwarded to the Assembly on 23 September 1929, where it was adopted without dissent.[23]

At the end of the Assembly, then, both the British and the French initiatives had received tentative approval. Perhaps after all they were not incompatible. It was conceivable but unlikely. Although Briand had studiously refrained from defining his means or ends, the thrust of French thinking at every level in recent years had been towards the organisation of Europe as a third force in the world, between the Soviet Union and the United States. Perhaps optimists like Salter and Layton of *The Economist* were right to believe the desire for trade expansion was such that European states would join in a progressive reduction of trade barriers, creating trade, not merely diverting it. Even then Graham and his officials would take some persuading that it should be condoned. They could accept customs unions as a legitimate exception to the most-favoured-nation principle, the sheet-anchor of British commercial policy, but any regional arrangement short of this was simple discrimination. On the other hand support for the British-inspired resolution to halt the slide into protectionism was limited. Was there any possibility of either initiative succeeding?

The third Prohibitions conference

The resolution on concerted economic action called upon League and non-League countries to indicate to the Secretary-General their willingness to participate in a diplomatic conference to conclude a two to three-year truce, with subsequent negotiations for the relaxation of trade barriers. On the basis of replies received, the League Council would decide whether to convene a conference about the end of January. Thereafter bilateral or multilateral negotiations would be undertaken; finally a second conference would be held to examine and if necessary supplement the negotiated agreements. For the Labour government the realisation of this programme was of critical importance. There were, however, other resolutions prepared for the Second Committee and adopted by the Assembly whose success or failure was bound to reflect upon the climate of commercial relations. These called for three conferences: to negotiate a convention removing administrative barriers to the activities of foreign nationals and firms; to standardise instruments of credit; and to remove remaining obstacles to the application of the Prohibitions convention. The latter was of considerable importance in its own right as well as a test of the government's ability to influence international commercial relations.[24]

Following the first Prohibitions Conference in 1927, twenty-eight of the thirty-five countries represented, including Britain, France, and the United States, signed a convention banning quantitative restrictions on trade within six months from the day it was brought into force. The terms and the duration of the convention were subjects of a second conference the following summer. There it was agreed that the convention would come into force for five years commencing 1 January 1930, so long as a minimum of eighteen unconditional ratifications were received by the League three months beforehand. Already several signatory countries had betrayed their reluctance to forego instruments of quantitative control by reserving their right to employ them 'in extraordinary circumstances', and by insisting on exceptional treatment for certain goods. When the deadline came on 30 September 1929 only sixteen European countries plus the United States had deposited ratifications, and eleven of these were conditional on the unqualified support of one or several other countries.[25]

When the third Prohibitions Conference opened in Paris on 5 December 1929 it was apparent that the main stumbling block to further ratifications was the trade war between Germany and Poland, which had continued almost uninterruptedly since 1925.[26] Germany had made its ratification conditional on Polish and Czech ratification but maintained an exception for coal. Poland refused any commitment while neighbouring countries imposed quantitative restrictions on imports or exports of coal, iron and scrap iron, and by means of contrived sanitary restrictions on imports of livestock and animal products. Dr Colijn, president of the conference, was unable to persuade the eleven countries which had made their ratification conditional on those of Germany and Poland to drop these conditions. To isolate the problem he asked the German and Polish delegates to request their governments' permission to accept the convention against all contracting countries except each other. Meanwhile the conference temporarily adjourned.

Sir Sydney Chapman, representing Britain, and Sir Arthur Salter, attending on behalf of the League of Nations, were enthusiastic about Colijn's initiative. The previous month the conference on the treatment of foreign nationals and firms had collapsed in total failure. Bringing the Prohibitions convention into force would go a long way to restore confidence in collective action, whereas another failure would be damaging to international trade relations and seriously prejudice the tariff truce conference in the new year. The French were trying through diplomatic channels to persuade Germany and Poland to cooperate; Chapman, Salter, and Sir Henry Fountain, head of the Commercial Relations and Treaties Department of the Board of Trade, appealed to the Foreign Office for similar action.[27]

By this time French diplomatic action had been followed by German acceptance of Colijn's formula, making a British *démarche* in Berlin unnecessary.[28] In Warsaw on 12 December, Erskine made strong representations to M. Zaleski, the Foreign Minister, but Zaleski refused to budge. As he explained, Poland's trade balance was already dangerously weak, the Russian market remained closed, and the tariff war with Germany continued unabated. While the Czechs exempted coal and the French scrap iron exports from the convention, Poland stood to gain almost nothing by ratifying the convention.[29]

When the Prohibitions Conference resumed the following day, Colijn tried to persuade delegates of the six unconditionally ratifying countries – Britain, Finland, the Netherlands, Norway, Portugal, Sweden, and the United States – to bring the convention into force among themselves, hoping other countries might follow later. Chapman was agreeable, the others were not. Some declared it too risky to renounce instruments of protection for a period of years when the continent's leading industrial nations retained their freedom of action. Others pointed out that most-favoured-nation obligations made it impossible to limit their commitment this way.[30]

Colijn then put forward a draft protocol which obviated the question of ratification altogether. By this document signatory countries would accept the spirit of the convention as of 1 January 1930, and the obligation to remove all quantitative restrictions not specifically exempted within six months of that date. Countries with conditions not met on 30 June would be freed of their commitment to the convention; remaining countries could withdraw at the start of any of the four subsequent years.

This, with minor amendments, was the protocol adopted on 19

December.[31] Seventeen countries, including most of the important European trading nations, signed and Finland and Sweden were expected to do so. It was a makeshift whose value would only become clear in June. But despite the British government's deep interest in the convention, it was reluctant to take further action. Poland was unlikely to modify its position so long as serious differences with Germany existed, and any appeal to Germany or other countries to modify their exceptions threatened at once to reopen the thorny question of Britain's exception for the import of dyestuffs.[32]

The unemployment problem

The Labour government's role in supporting the Prohibitions convention, if ill-fated, was at least uncontroversial. Foreign tariffs, not quantitative restrictions, were the main cause of complaint among British manufacturers, and tariff protection their usual demand. By the time the convention became binding on Britain in July, some objections were raised to a commitment not shared by other major trade competitors.[33] But until then the level of criticism was slight compared to that which arose over the tariff truce proposal as the preparatory conference drew near.

Until mid-autumn the government defended its record by reference to several accomplishments in external affairs. None in fact amounted to much. The Hague conference produced nothing not available before. The signing of the Optional Clause was one of those legalistic gestures which eventually made inter-war diplomacy a by-word for ineffectualness. The restoration of friendly relations with the United States was already advanced when the government took office and MacDonald's visit to America in September was little more than a show of goodwill.[34] In October another objective was realised when Henderson completed negotiations for recognition of the Soviet Union. Except for the latter, the government received a remarkably good press for its handling of foreign affairs. But popularity could not thus be indefinitely sustained. Unemployment remained the most pressing problem.

Thomas proved himself almost immediately unfit for the task of devising any solutions to the unemployment problem. An alcoholic and *habitué* of the House of Commons members' bar, his self-conscious awareness of his working-class origins and lack of education had found expression in an exaggerated vulgarity and open scorn for the intellectuals on the left of the party. All these characteristics now became strikingly apparent. Within weeks of his becoming 'Minister of Unemployment', the waspish but observant Beatrice Webb recorded widespread dissatisfaction with Thomas among his fellow Ministers. He was, she wrote on 28 July 1929, too 'rattled' to consult his colleagues or concentrate on proposals, 'and when not under the influence of drink or flattery, is in an abject state of panic about his job'.[35]

Three other Ministers had been assigned to help Thomas on a somewhat ill-defined basis. George Lansbury, First Commissioner of Works, was regarded as MacDonald's one concession to the left in a Cabinet dominated by the right. An idealistic and even brave man, he was also an emotional rather than intellectual adherent to socialism. Tom Johnston, Under-Secretary of State for Scotland, was taken more seriously. The editor of *Forward*, the ILP's leading weekly journal, and the most 'responsible' of the Clydeside MPs, he was regarded as one of the coming men in the party. Sir Oswald Mosley, Chancellor of the Duchy of Lancaster, was harder to place. Since joining the party seven years before, he had been pleased to be regarded as a member of the left. At the same time he kept clear of the proletarian element led by James Maxton, which had captured control of the ILP in 1925, and he went out of his way to cultivate MacDonald's friendship. Intelligent, deeply serious, handsome, eloquent, and still only thirty-two years old, he seemed destined to rise much further.

A more unlikely combination it would have been hard to find, and suspicions were aroused that MacDonald's motive in appointing them was to keep them busy disputing with one another: 'dogs were to be kept busy eating dogs', as Johnston put it.[36] But they had more in common than appeared at first sight. All three had demonstrated their impatience at the notion that Britain's prosperity depended on the revival of the basic export industries. All three had expressed radical criticism of the monetary and financial system: Johnston's *Forward* and *Lansbury's Labour Weekly* had opposed the return to the gold standard, and Mosley and the latter journal had both called for its abandonment.[37] All three were opponents of economic internationalism and advocates of an active home market development policy.[38]

Hardly had they received their appointments than Mosley began to prepare a scheme, which he circulated for comments before the end of the year. As in the 'Birmingham proposals' he had drawn up four years earlier, he now advocated abandoning the 'fetish of exports' in favour of development and management of home market demand. To promote this he proposed a £200 million home development loan, while calling also for a radical restructuring of the Cabinet system and central government in order to carry through the managerial decisions.[39] The startling political reforms aside, there was nothing in Mosley's proposals that was completely new. In the months before the 1929 general election

Lloyd George had called for large-scale borrowing and an expanded public works programme.[40] Even Sir William Joynson-Hicks, the right-wing, anti-labour Home Secretary in the recent Conservative government had suggested going into the general election with a modest scheme of public works financed through borrowing.[41] By now a sizeable minority of economists and politicians accepted that exceptional conditions required exceptional measures, whatever the dictates of 'sound finance'. Yet the great majority almost certainly still found the idea of spending the country's way out of the depression utterly perverse: a temporary palliative, but one that would create worse difficulties in the future. If this was true of economists and politicians it was even more true of the financiers and industrialists whose investment decisions determined the employment prospects for the vast majority of the population. As Lloyd George had committed the Liberals to a large-scale loan and road-building scheme, it seemed possible to push the necessary legislation through Parliament. But quite aside from lack of enthusiasm among the Asquithian wing of the Liberal Party and resistance in business circles, Labour Ministers had to be persuaded of its soundness. And what were the chances that Thomas would understand it or Snowden approve it? Equally important, what was the likelihood that MacDonald would contemplate such a scheme, bearing in mind his anxiety to provide 'responsible' government?

Thomas, after six weeks in Canada as Britain's 'commercial traveller', returned home empty-handed on 18 September to face growing criticism in Parliament and the press.[42] Desperate for something to show and completely unable to appreciate the views of his ministerial assistants, he turned to Montagu Norman in the hope of mobilising the City's massive resources in aid of industrial rationalisation. Norman, it seems, responded with alacrity, no doubt only too glad to appear to be helping, in view of the hostility towards the Bank of England in Labour circles. He was alive to the fact that the ability of the private sector to bring about its own recovery would be the most effective discouragement to state intervention.[43] And of course if there was business to transact the City wanted the commissions.

Thomas' gratitude was apparent in his speech to the Manchester Chamber of Commerce on 10 January 1930. Thinking perhaps of himself as well as the country, he defiantly asserted that Britain was not 'down and out'. Then to the obvious delight of his audience, he affirmed that Britain must export to live, that government interference was no solution to industry's troubles, and that 'There was too much tendency in this country to be spoon-fed'. He referred to charges that finance had become the enemy of industry in order to deny them. He wished it known that he appreciated 'the sagacity, single-minded effort, integrity and wisdom of the Governor of the Bank of England in steering this country through its present period'.[44]

It was obvious that Thomas was not now, if he ever had been, able to appreciate that resting the government's hopes for a solution to unemployment on the City was naive, even ironic. The City attached only one condition to its offer of financial support for industrial rationalisation projects: that they should be commercially sound investments. But it was this one condition that made nonsense of the whole idea. Bankers had *always* been interested in commercially sound investments. The whole problem was that the sectors of industry responsible for most of Britain's postwar unemployment offered practically no such opportunity.

MacDonald himself took a tentative step towards responsibility for a solution on 1 December 1929 by holding the first of several lunches at Downing Street, with leading industrialists, economists, and civil servants, to plan for an 'economic general staff'. MacDonald had been drawn to the idea during his first period in office and later it reappeared in party literature as an integral part of proposals for a scientifically managed economy. What he expected to gain from such a body is not clear. Almost certainly he himself had no clear idea, although probably he hoped to be told how industry could stand on its own legs in competition for world trade. Industrial rationalisation was the constant theme of the preliminary conversations.[45] The formation of an Economic Advisory Council (EAC) was confirmed by Treasury minute on 27 January 1930, and on 12 February MacDonald divulged the names of those involved. The secretary of the council was to be the Liberal economist Hubert Henderson. The fifteen members included two Labour economists, two Liberal economists, two trade unionists, two directors of the Bank of England, two industrialists, two bankers, a leading City accountant, an agricultural expert, and a spokesman for the Cooperative Societies. The Liberal Leslie Hore-Belisha spoke for many on both sides of the House when he asked the Prime Minister if he had left anyone out: 'The only person I had in mind was Uncle Tom Cobley.'[46]

Like Thomas's trust in the City, MacDonald's trust in a 'think tank' as heterogeneous as this was utterly ill-conceived. For it to be any use as a planning or directing body, its members would have to agree on the objectives of economic policy, which of course they did not. As constructed, it was bound to replicate existing differences within the country. Individual members produced some very able discussion papers, but the only result was to generate more noise and less useful intelligence, more disagreement, more delays, and less likelihood of any departure from the government's extreme internationalist policy.

Time was not on the government's side. The steep rise in unemployment during the winter before taking office had been followed in the spring by a return to 1928 levels and briefly some improvement on them. But fluctuations of this kind had been common throughout the 1920s, and before any trend could be confirmed a new decline set in.[47] By December 1929 total unemployment stood at 1,304,000, some 30,000 more than at the same time the year before, and more than 200,000 above the previous year. Nor was this the only cause for apprehension. Bank rate stood at 6½ per cent, higher than at any time since the grim postwar slump. The Wall Street crash in late October raised the prospect of easer credit, but the international monetary system was seriously malfunctioning and desperately needed reform. Equally ominous was the trend towards protectionism in the United States, Europe, the Dominions, and around the world. By the fourth quarter the collapse of primary product prices was fully apparent. This meant imports were cheaper, but the countries most seriously affected were also among Britain's best customers. Britain's rural community was also in acute distress. Scarcely surprising, then, was the sense of crisis that pervaded political discussion.[48] Added to this was the outcry from industries benefiting from the McKenna, safeguarding, and silk duties, now threatened with the loss of protection. The TUC was becoming increasingly agitated by talk of rationalisation and disarmament, both of which spelt more jobs lost.[49] The government was clearly fumbling in its attempt to come to grips with the problem. And if the Conservatives were not bearing down harder it was only because they were wrangling over the direction their own party was to take.

The collapse of free trade support

While Parliament was in recess little had been heard of Empire Free Trade. The quiet was broken in late October as the new Parliamentary session was about to begin.[50] Beaverbrook was again first off the mark with a penny pamphlet outlining his policy for emulating the United States, that 'Empire consisting of forty-eight different units', and an orchestrated campaign in his several newspapers.[51] Others followed closely behind.

Rothermere mobilised his own press campaign for wholesale safeguarding. On 12 November the council of the British Empire Producers' Association endorsed Melchett's resolution, which referred to 'the tendency towards large economic units' elsewhere in the world and called upon the government to offer the Empire a lead.[52] Two days later a new propaganda body, the Empire Economic Union, was announced. The inspiration of Amery and Melchett, the Union brought together leaders of the new industries, such as Sir Herbert Austin, Sir Hugo Hirst, and Sir Harry McGowan, along with industrialists with a special interest in Empire trade – Sir Hugo Cunliffe-Owen of British–American Tobacco, Sir John Ferguson of Liptons, Dr A.E. Humphreys, chairman of the Flour Milling Employers' Federation, and Sir Benjamin Morgan, chairman of the Sugar Federation. Their aim was Empire Free Trade, or 'as near to it as we can [get]'.[53] Less ambitious but equally interesting was a study group comprising bankers, Conservative politicians, and civil servants, which met at the home of Sir Basil Blackett. Amery led discussions at the second meeting on 28 October with a talk on his favourite theme of the British Empire as an economic unit and its relation to other economic blocs, actual or potential. Most of those present seem to have agreed that the imperatives of mass production were the determining factor in world politics, that the threat of American production outrunning domestic markets was a real one, and that formation of such entities as a 'Pan-European union' was only a matter of time. As Blackett put it, 'The formula of the future was Marxism transposed – Industrialists of the world unite, and woe to national producers who refuse to organise in advance!'[54]

Amery during these weeks seemed to be everywhere at once, agitating and speaking in the Empire cause, along with Hannon, Page-Croft, and a few other back-bench colleagues. Conservative opinion shifted rapidly in their favour. At the annual Conservative and Unionist conference at the Royal Albert Hall on 21–22 November, resolutions calling for the wholesale extension of safeguarding and Empire economic unity dominated debate, and support for both was overwhelming. Baldwin was obliged to heed the mood of the conference. He thanked Beaverbrook for advancing the Empire cause, and in words Beaverbrook himself might have used stated that:

> we stand once more at the cross-roads. This is an age of great combinations. The United States was welded together even in the lifetime of the older ones among us by the arbitrament of war. People talk in Europe today of a United States of Europe. Our progress depends on our capacity to visualise the Empire, the Dominions and Colonies alike, as one eternal and indestructible unit – (cheers) – for production, for consumption, for distribution ...[55]

Thereafter a steady jostling went on between Beaverbrook, Baldwin, and Amery. Beaverbrook continued his 'crusade' for Empire economic unity. Baldwin paid lip service to it but shied away from the duties on foodstuffs that Beaverbrook demanded.[56] Amery urged Beaverbrook on, while appealing to Baldwin for concessions in the interests of party solidarity. In January 1930 Baldwin retreated to a broad extension of safeguarding but no food taxes,[57] in March to the old idea of a referendum on food taxes.[58] A year earlier this would have placed him in the vanguard of party opinion; not now. The party and the country had moved on so rapidly that his changing stance surprised no one and won him little praise.

Neville Chamberlain, with Sir Philip Cunliffe-Lister and Sir Samuel Hoare, meanwhile took charge of policy planning at Conservative Central Office. They rejected Amery's claim that a United States of Europe was already on the horizon; otherwise their outlook was much the same. They saw no hope of a boom in world trade. The spread of industrialism, and the rise of new industries which operated profitably only at or near full capacity, persuaded them that all countries would insist on protecting their domestic markets. They anticipated in Europe an *ad hoc* process of bilateral and multilateral tariff and commodity agreements which would improve trade among participating countries but would involve the elimination of most-favoured-nation rights except as a negotiated benefit. The United States seemed certain to implement a major tariff hike and, reaching saturation point in the domestic market for manufactured goods, campaign vigorously to capture overseas markets. The only bright spot they could find was intra-imperial trade. It already accounted for 42 per cent of British exports and probably nearer half of manufactured exports. Judging by the growth of foreign, and particularly American, exports to the Dominions and India since the war there seemed to be tremendous scope for substituting British goods. They believed the opportunity for action had arrived. Nationalism in the Dominions was running strongly in their favour. If nothing was done to exploit it, or worse, if Britain spurned the Dominions by reducing preferences and entering into a tariff truce agreement with the European countries, they might well 'make their own arrangements without us, and ... preferences may diminish and vanish'.[59]

In the first week of January 1930 this prospectus was put to the 'six wise men', businessmen who had agreed to advise on party policy. Five of the six endorsed it, including Sir Kenneth Stewart, chairman of the Lancashire Cotton Corporation, and Edward Peacock, the Baring Brothers partner and director of the Bank of England. The only dissenter was Sir Alfred Lewis, head of the Furness Lines, who explained with a trace of embarrassment that he was bound to put the internationalist position of the Chamber of Shipping.[60]

In the circumstances the government's internationalist approach to trade reform was bound to come in for intense criticism. Graham, who intended to lead the British delegation to the 'Preliminary Conference with a view to Concerted Economic Action', was anxious that it should be called by its proper name so as to keep in the forefront the objective of reducing foreign trade barriers. To his regret, officials and critics alike called it the tariff truce conference. Many charged it would 'stereotype' existing trade relations and make Britain the 'dumping heap of the world'. The Empire Industries Association, the NUM, and the National Federation of Iron and Steel Manufacturers all spoke out strongly against the truce.[61] Their opposition was as predictable as the support of the merchants and financiers of the Free Trade Union. More surprising, however, was the opposition of organisations which only a few years before had endorsed the results of the World Economic Conference. The executive council of the Association of British Chambers of Commerce, the national committee of the International Chamber of Commerce, the European and United States section of the Manchester Chamber of Commerce, and the FBI all came out against the truce, the last-named complaining to Graham that it was the first time in many years a government had committed the country on a matter of such importance to industry and commerce without prior consultation.[62] *The Times*, which had taken a strong internationalist stance as recently as the general election, also swung sharply around. In a lead article it condemned the truce for threatening to stabilise a situation already prejudicial to Britain and 'entangling' the country in a European economic alliance just when a free hand was needed to develop imperial economic relations.[63]

If that were not enough, indications mounted that the European countries were no longer willing to support the truce. The Italian government's reply to the invitation to attend the truce conference stressed that acceptance implied no commitment whatever to the results.[64] France, a co-sponsor of the proposal, now also seemed to be turning her back on it. Early in January Lord Tyrrell, British Ambassador in Paris, reported protests against French participation in the truce by a number of pressure groups including the Chambers of Commerce and the National Association for Economic Expansion.[65] France did agree to attend, without reservations, the conference set for 17 February, but indications were that the French delegates had no intention of accepting any agreement along the lines of Graham's objectives.[66]

On 28 January Tyrrell reported to Sir Robert Vansittart a secret warning from Daniel Serruys of efforts by Louis Loucheur to promote Franco-German economic relations to the exclusion of Britain.[67] Serruys was now a director of merchant bankers Lazard Frères and Citroen, chairman of the League Economic Committee, and member of the French delegation to the tariff truce conference. There was no question that he was well informed. At a second meeting Serruys elaborated on French hopes for a strictly European solution to current economic problems, chiefly by means of industrial rationalisation and cartel schemes and possibly tariff preferences. Speaking as a private citizen he described to Tyrrell the exasperation in official French circles at the way British officials dogmatically insisted upon universal free trade as the only solution to Europe's problems.

As he had now been asked to come out into the open, he would say that the manner in which we consistently advocated this theory and thought we could teach it to the French, as at one time our financiers like Bradbury had thought they could teach the French their methods of finance, created the most deplorable impression. If anything had turned French opinion against the tariff truce it was the clumsy interventions of Salter [and] the Free Trade 'épouvantails' who were constantly paraded by British delegations at Geneva.

In Serruys' opinion neither the British theory nor the French theory could carry the day at the moment. What ought to be done was to talk in a free and friendly manner. Perhaps the French had been wrong in talking too much to the Germans. But it was so difficult to talk with British officials. Many of them did not seem able to understand the continental theory or talk the continental language, and Serruys quoted Chapman in this connection. Fountain was better. But we ought to talk, to see each other's difficulties and the matters on which it was possible *through Geneva* – and Serruys was very insistent on Geneva – to make progress.[68]

Two days later Tyrrell reported 'warnings' from 'two reliable sources' – almost certainly Serruys and Alexis Léger, chief of the political and commercial division of the Quai d'Orsay – 'to the effect that if we seriously consider that our proposals for a tariff truce have the least chance of acceptance, we are completely deceiving ourselves'. According to his sources, France had taken soundings in European capitals and found 'quasi-unanimity against acceptance of a tariff truce'. France was opposed chiefly for agricultural reasons: a bill had been tabled in the Chamber of Deputies proposing a wide range of tariff increases. Pierre-Etienne Flandin, Minister of Commerce and head of delegation, was reportedly anxious for the closest contact with Graham. But, Tyrrell added, his informants 'insisted on the fact that the French government is definitely decided to organise Europe economically and my feeling is that they have already received considerable encouragement from other countries including certainly Germany'.[69]

Board of Trade officials were already well aware of French interest in regional arrangements. They had ignored the French before, and ignored them now.[70] Instead they requested the Foreign Office to make the strongest efforts to ensure the League Council agreed to a conference at the earliest possible date.[71] They then armed Graham with a memorandum asking the Cabinet's authorisation to accept the draft truce convention.[72] Presenting his case to colleagues Graham admitted that 'influential bodies in many countries are opposed to the proposal', and there was bound to be serious opposition at home if the conference made no plans for subsequent tariff reductions. But he remained convinced that the truce was in Britain's interest so long as France, Germany, and Italy also joined.[73]

In Parliament Graham faced a number of hostile questions. In reply to one he was obliged to admit that eight countries, including Finland, Germany, Italy, and Poland – he omitted Australia, Canada, and India out of imperial susceptibilities – had prepared or implemented tariff increases since the truce proposal was first put forward.[74] With protectionism advancing at this pace, the prospect of arranging any sort of truce was slim indeed.

The first tariff truce conference

The Preliminary Conference with a view to Concerted Economic Action opened at Geneva on 17 February 1930, attended by delegates from thirty countries. As Graham noted, more than half were headed by government Ministers, 'an unprecedented development in League economic conferences'.[75] He might also have noted that only eight of the thirty had full powers to sign a convention.[76] Moreover only three non-European countries were represented. The United States sent only an observer. And aside from an openly unenthusiastic Irish Free State delegate, the Commonwealth stayed away.

Count Carl Moltke of Denmark, elected president of the conference, opened by referring to 'the special difficulties which Europe was called upon to face and a conviction, confirmed by the United States of America, that the lack in Europe of a large market in the modern sense of the word was in direct contradiction with our twentieth-century conception of essential requirements of large-scale production and commerce'.[77] Paul Hymans of Belgium spoke of Europe on the brink of a tariff war, and warned of the need for 'economic disarmament'. Herr Schmidt, the German Minister of Economic Affairs, recalled Stresemann's advocacy of European economic cooperation. Graham warned of the 'crude, and I think dangerous ideas of self-sufficiency and economic isolation', now gaining currency, and appealed for agreement on tariff reductions. Merely stabilising tariffs at present levels would be 'frankly disastrous'.[78]

But thereafter differences of view became obvious. The Danish and Dutch delegates gave their complete support to the truce and non-discriminatory tariff reductions. The Czech delegate, however, raised the question of reconciling tariff reductions with most-favoured-nation commitments to non-participating countries. M. Madgearu, the Roumanian delegate, pointing to the example of the United States, called for regional arrangements 'as the first stage towards the establishment of European economic unity'.[79] M. Bottai, the Italian Minister of Corporations, followed with a general attack on multilateral trade negotiations and on the truce proposal in light of the present inequality of tariff levels and the refusal of non-European countries to participate. The Hungarian delegate deprecated the tendency to consider only tariff barriers when agrarian countries faced others at least as onerous. 'I need only mention veterinary and phytopathological regulations.' M. Gautier of the French delegation then announced that France would present her views on the truce and the 'creation of a European market' as soon as possible. But he could say nothing more now. The Tardieu government had fallen the day before the conference began, and as yet no replacement had been formed.[80]

On the morning of the 21st the conference divided into two committees, the first dealing with the draft truce convention, the second with subsequent 'concerted economic action'. Graham addressed the first committee, again appealing for a comprehensive truce. Britain, he said, looked for a minimum of exceptions and reservations, and of course expected to see all such agreements applied on a most-favoured-nation basis, 'unqualified and as widely extended as possible'.[81]

Graham now found himself in the embarrassing position of being obliged to demand an exception of his own, for fiscal or revenue duties. One of Labour's election promises had been the restoration of the 'free breakfast table', by removing the various duties on consumption goods that weighed so heavily on the working class. But on account of the world slump now under way Snowden faced difficulties in balancing his forthcoming Budget and, free trade convictions notwithstanding, was in no position to forego this source of revenue. Graham explained that revenue duties were not protective because they applied almost exclusively to goods that Britain did not produce, and therefore constituted only a nominal exception to the truce. The European delegates were not impressed. The World Economic Conference and the League Economic Committee had already concluded that no distinction between revenue and protective duties could be made.

The fundamental question, however, was the position of participants in a truce *vis-à-vis* non-participants: whether the most-favoured-nation principle should apply on an unconditional basis or only conditionally, if suitable concessions were agreed. Aside from Britain and the low tariff countries of north-west Europe, most were very reluctant to extend the benefits of the truce on an unconditional most-favoured-nation basis, or to enter into a truce at all while other important trading nations stood aside. On the 24th the Japanese delegate announced that he could not commit his country unless 'neighbouring countries, such as the United States, China, India and Australia', did so as well.[82] On the 27th the Italian delegate called for a looser formula requiring only the prolongation of existing treaties. The next day Serruys, acting head of the French delegation, bluntly dismissed the draft truce as 'unthinkable' in present circumstances. Did Serruys speak for France? As the new Tardieu government had only just been formed and he was not a permanent official, it was far from clear. Bitter argument immediately broke out. The Board of Trade's Sir Sydney Chapman, standing in for Graham, feared the conference would collapse and hastily moved adjournment of the committee.[83]

Chapman by now was convinced that Britain must modify her objectives. Other countries were not prepared to accept her position on revenue duties, and at least some, he believed, would be only too glad to see the conference wrecked by British action. He therefore proposed to call for exceptions to the truce to be listed, to submit the shortest possible British list, and to ask that the truce last only eighteen months from 1 October 1929, so that Snowden would have his hands free before the 1931 budget. Graham and Snowden readily agreed.[84]

Serruys' objection to the truce was more serious, but from private conversations Chapman believed the French were prepared to enter into a more modest agreement. This would distinguish between countries such as France which normally consolidated duties by treaty, and those like Britain which retained autonomous control over duties. The former would have to maintain consolidated duties unchanged, and alter unconsolidated duties only after due notice and an opportunity for representations from other countries. The latter would be barred from making any changes, but retain the right to withdraw from the truce if their representations were not satisfactorily answered. In practice this would tie up the protectionist countries reasonably well. It was the look of the thing that was unfortunate: Britain would appear to tie both her hands while the protectionist countries tied only one.

Chapman meanwhile was kept busy defending British interests in the second committee. On 1 March a sub-committee appointed to examine means of improving economic relations between the agricultural and industrial countries of Europe reported in favour of a 50 per cent tariff preference for European wheat. Chapman and the Italian, Signor Ciancarelli, gave their full backing to the Dutch delegate who insisted, despite appeals from Madgearu, the committee chairman, upon registering an explicit objection.[85] In turn Chapman objected to the sub-committee's reference to negotiations for a veterinary convention, until Serruys offered a compromise formula proposing mere discussion about a convention.[86] With Stucki's support Chapman succeeded in modifying another recommendation calling on creditor countries to increase foreign lending.[87] Again on the 3rd, controversy arose over the most-favoured-nation question when the sub-committee appointed to deal with it presented a divided report.[88] On the 4th, Chapman was obliged to insist on less specific reference to the phytopathological convention signed in Rome in 1929, which Britain had no intention of signing.[89] Then, having succeeded in removing most of the objectionable proposals, he found the greatest difficulty in securing some reference to future tariff reductions in the draft programme for subsequent concerted action.

At last on 7 March, Flandin, again Minister of Commerce in the new Tardieu government, arrived in Geneva. After consulting with the Belgians and Germans, he presented a new truce proposal to Chapman. It followed the general outline of the earlier one, but instead of barring changes in consolidated duties it merely barred the denunciation of existing treaties. This did little to reduce its value. If bilateral treaties could not be denounced this would prevent one party putting pressure on another to accept higher duties, and Britain could still abandon the truce if her representations against increases in foreign duties were ignored. It appeared even more one-sided than before, but Chapman advised Graham to accept it while he made further efforts to improve it.[90]

At a private meeting with Flandin on 9 March, Chapman pressed for the stabilisation of consolidated duties so as to improve the appearance of the proposal. Flandin firmly refused, although as a gesture of good will he offered to make the obligations less binding on Britain as well. In the conference Chapman had been disturbed to find Flandin almost silent on the question of subsequent tariff negotiations, and he now pressed for a commitment that France would participate. Flandin was willing, but reminded Chapman that there were other obstacles to trade that France would want to discuss, in particular veterinary and phytopathological restrictions. The rural vote was important in France, and British use of these restrictions had aroused intense dissatisfaction. 'You should know the French preoccupation', Chapman wired Graham. 'If we refuse even to discuss these things France and other countries besides would refuse to discuss tariffs and give this as a reason... Personally I should doubt whether we shall get much out of tariff negotiations directly though indirectly their effect should be to make protectionism more difficult.'[91]

During a one-day Commons debate on 4 March, Graham struggled to correct the impression that the truce plan would merely stabilise tariffs at existing levels or entangle Britain in a European bloc. 'That was not the idea at all.' With Liberal support, the division left the government with a comfortable majority at the end of debate.[92] But after Flandin spoke at the conference on the 8th, criticism increased. Even the *Manchester Guardian* declared against accepting the truce formula, which would last from 'All Fools Day 1930 to All Fools Day 1931.'[93]

The formula was weak, one-sided, and an 'irreducible minimum', Graham told the plenary session in Geneva on 14 March. But so long as it was not further 'weakened in any particular, however small,' he indicated Britain would accept it.[94] Provision for exceptions, the last obstacle, was confronted the next day in the first committee. Because long lists of exceptions had been submitted, Flandin proposed that only those items for which existing legislation already provided a permanent exception should be approved. However, when on the 18th a French delegate announced that this formula encompassed the *loi de Cadenas*, a law reserving to his government the right to extend unlimited protection to practically every item of agricultural production, the reaction was immediate. The Luxembourg and Belgian delegates requested an exception for a similar list, the Greek delegate for tobacco and wine, which constituted 80 per cent of Greek exports. M. Stucki requested that the Swiss list should read 'same as French *loi de Cadenas*'. Colijn thereupon proposed the total suppression of the relevant article in the convention, and eventually a simple formula along the lines originally proposed by Flandin was adopted.[95] On the 22nd the second committee completed its work on the protocol for subsequent concerted action.[96] Two days later a final plenary session closed the conference.

The convention embodying the truce and signed by eighteen countries differed fundamentally from the draft convention with which the conference began. Tariff increases were not now ruled out. Countries that normally consolidated duties through bilateral treaties, which included most of Europe, were required only to prolong existing treaties and give opportunities for representations before increasing duties. Instead of a two to three-year truce commencing on 1 October 1929 the convention called for a truce of one year commencing 1 April 1930, and as ratification was open until 1 November 1930 the truce was in fact of only six months duration. Nor could Graham hope for tariff reductions to follow. The protocol on subsequent action merely called for responses to a questionnaire on the best means of fulfilling the 1927 World Economic Conference resolutions.[97] Moltke was only speaking the truth at the final session when he said the success of the arrangements depended not on legal prescription but the spirit in which they were applied.[98]

Graham, 'bombarded' with hostile questions on his return to Parliament, defended the truce convention as less satisfactory than hoped for but still 'a valuable document'.[99] No one was happy with it. Flandin on his departure for Geneva had deprecated 'a brutal suppression of tariffs, which would produce far greater catastrophes than benefits', and reaffirmed France's commitment to 'the enlargement of intra-European trade'.[100] At almost the same moment the United States Senate ended seven months of debate by passing the Smoot–Hawley tariff bill.[101]

8

The challenge of regionalism

The tariff truce conference in February–March 1930 was the last major initiative of the second Labour government in its effort to maintain an open world economy. Thereafter, aside from two or three minor forays, it adopted a defensive posture, appealing for 'economic disarmament' while obstructing or rejecting proposals that failed to meet its standard of internationalism. To some these were noble efforts to protect the British Empire and world peace, but they contained more of the tragic than the heroic. For it was becoming increasingly apparent that the alternative to regional or other second-best solutions to the crisis was not an open world economy, but economic nationalism with strong overtones of autarky and political extremism. Besides, as fast as the government beat back challenges to economic internationalism abroad, the domestic basis of support for its policy gave way to demands for salvation behind national or imperial tariff walls.

The Briand plan

In March 1928 Jacques Seydoux's reference to a Franco-German entente had led Sir William Tyrrell, then Under-Secretary of State at the Foreign Office, to comment, 'M. Seydoux is chasing a mirage of longstanding, viz. that economics in the case of France and Germany will overcome race antagonism.'[1] This reflected the Foreign Office's conviction that German attitudes had changed little since 1914. If scarcely friendly towards France, the Foreign Office did not share the francophobia of the Bank of England, the Treasury, and other centres of internationalism. At the same time the tendency of British diplomats to treat industrial and commercial affairs as outside and decidedly beneath their range of competence led them to underestimate the breadth of support for economic cooperation among European businessmen and politicians. Thus when Henderson requested briefing on European federation following Briand's announcement of plans to raise the subject at the Tenth League Assembly, the Foreign Office prepared a memorandum which suggested that the European movement was little more than the inspiration of one man, Count Coudenhove-Kalergi.[2] As for him, Tyrrell had written, 'I know Coudenhove: he is a thoroughly impractical theorist.'[3] All the same, the Office had good reason to suspect German intentions.

On 3 October 1929 Gustav Stresemann died. In the last years of his life he appeared to have moved a long way from narrowly nationalist objectives, towards cooperation with France on an economic scheme for Europe. His death thus robbed Germany and Europe of leadership at a particularly fateful moment. High interest rates and declining capital investment had already created serious budgetary problems for Germany when the Wall Street crash on 24 October caused panic in financial markets, drove up unemployment, and widened the yawning budgetary gap. The immediate result was to confront the coalition government led by Hermann Müller with the impossible dilemma of imposing the deflationary measures required to maintain confidence in the mark and losing the support of Müller's own SPD, or of maintaining unemployment insurance and other welfare provisions at present levels and losing the support of the deputies of the bourgeois People's Party. Müller resigned on 27 March 1930, and three days later Heinrich Brüning, the right-wing leader of the Catholic Centre Party formed a government which, lacking a majority in the Reichstag, depended for its authority on the decree powers of President Hindenburg. Brüning saw little prospect of reopening the reparations question, and relied upon a policy of severe deflation to improve Germany's relative position and maintain himself in office. He had not, however, reckoned on the furious campaign of both left- and right-wing extremist parties against the Young Plan, which they chose to single out as the primary cause of Germany's acute economic plight. And he was soon drawn into the schemes of nationalists within the Foreign Ministry.[4]

The Foreign Minister since the autumn of 1929 was Julius Curtius, who had been Minister of Economics since 1926 and Stresemann's collaborator at the Hague Conference. He stoutly defended the Brüning government's decision to ratify the Young Plan against attacks from the Communist Party (KPD) and the new Nazi–Nationalist alliance. But beyond this he displayed little of his predecessor's strength of character or political vision. As his chief adviser he chose Bernhard von Bülow, who held a watching brief over Briand's federation proposal, rather than Carl von Schubert, Bülow's superior at the Wilhelmstrasse and Stresemann's closest collaborator. Bülow regarded Briand's scheme as little more than a trap for imprisoning Germany within a French-dominated Europe. Instead he sought an active policy of extending German influence to the south and east, thereby undercutting French influence and isolating Poland, which depended upon Czechoslovakia and Austria as outlets for its coal and agricultural production. A *Mitteleuropa* policy would be popular with important elements of German industry, especially the coal and steel interests of the Ruhr.[5] It would also, Bülow hoped, contribute to the realisation of *Anschluss* with Austria and major frontier adjustments at Poland's expense. Curtius, interested in the economic and the political advantages, had already discussed the possibility of a customs union with Johann Schober, the Austrian Chancellor, in February 1930. Schober was interested, and Brüning, who harboured a deep-seated hostility towards 'imperialistic' France, fell in with the scheme. France and her allies, however, were bound to see a customs union with Austria as a prelude to *Anschluss,* which had been proscribed by the Treaties of Versailles and Saint-Germain, the Geneva Protocol of 4 October 1922, and other international instruments. It was a dangerous game, which Brüning could not reasonably hope to win.[6]

Tyrrell had begun to alter his sceptical view of Franco-German relations soon after he became Ambassador to Paris in 1929. He was persuaded that the French were sincere in wanting to avoid difficulties at the first Hague conference in order to make it an occasion for demonstrating European solidarity.[7] Like most British statesmen, he was captivated by the supple, sardonic, and quick-witted Briand. The violent opposition to the Young Plan that arose in Germany soon after its publication had unsettled French politics, which had moved to the right since the 1928 elections. But he was impressed that Tardieu should choose to retain Briand as Foreign Minister in his new government after Briand's own government was defeated at the end of a stormy debate over the reparations–Rhineland evacuation agreement struck at The Hague.[8] Early in 1930 he learned on good authority that the agreement which brought a temporary halt to the commercial conflict between Germany and Poland was the result of French pressure on Warsaw. He could not confirm reports of Franco-German conversations on economic relations, but he was prepared to say that 'the Germans here seem to be hand in glove with the French at the moment, and the intimacy of their relations constantly surprises me and would probably very considerably startle people in London'.[9]

According to Daniel Serruys, one of Tyrrell's main sources of information, French statesmen were of two minds about the direction their foreign policy must take. Some, including Loucheur and Alexis Léger, Briand's *chef de cabinet*, argued that France must join with Germany in promoting 'the federalisation of Europe on the economic basis of the organisation of production, rationalisation, etc.' They believed immediate action was imperative now that France had agreed to evacuate the Rhineland, and when the future was so uncertain. Both Germany and Italy were beginning to show serious interest in extending their influence in central and eastern Europe, and an eventual German-Italian-Hungarian alliance was not beyond the bounds of possibility. With Germany dominating *Mitteleuropa* and the United States dominating much of the rest of the world, France appeared in danger of becoming isolated. They regretted the impossibility of working with Britain, but her dogmatic insistence on free trade made her seem 'hopeless'. The Europe they envisaged would be organised behind 'some kind of tariff barrier which would be erected to [Britain's] disadvantage and still more to that of the United States'. By creating protected markets for agricultural and industrial goods they hoped to draw the revisionist countries into their scheme. Serruys claimed that Loucheur and Léger had persuaded Briand to follow their advice. He doubted that their plans were clearly worked out or that they appreciated the difficulty the most-favoured-nation question would create. Nevertheless he was, or claimed to be, impressed by the degree of encouragement they had received from influential sources in Germany. France, he advised, was approaching a crossroads of major historical importance, and the direction she took would depend critically upon the support she received from Britain.

Tyrrell suspected that Serruys' revelations were inspired at least partly by the desire to frighten Britain into a more cooperative spirit at the forthcoming tariff truce conference. Still, most of what he said was corroborated by Léger and the rest corresponded well enough with Tyrrell's understanding of France's predicament. It seemed logical that France would want to consolidate relations with Germany now that the settlement of the reparations and Rhineland issues had 'infinitely' reduced sources of friction between them, and when the future was so fraught with danger. He was also confident that practically all Frenchmen wished Britain to play a more active role in European economic affairs, in view of their inferiority to Germany in this respect. Accordingly, he urged that Henderson and Graham should be informed of the critical state of Franco-German relations and advised to heed Serruys' appeal.[10]

The Foreign Office's request for views on Briand's federation proposal yielded more sceptical reports from envoys elsewhere. Sir Ronald Graham, Ambassador in Rome, ruled out Italian participation while relations with France were so strained. He accepted that Italy was casting about for a new foreign policy and ready to turn almost anywhere for support: perhaps to Germany, perhaps even the Soviet Union. Their preferred solution, he had 'no doubt at all', was 'a European one', in which Britain actively participated as a counter-weight to France, but Rome assumed that Britain would 'pretend she does not belong to Europe, but can concentrate on the Empire and the United States'.[11] Sir Horace Rumbold, Ambassador in Berlin, disputed Tyrrell's claim that Franco-German differences had been 'infinitely' reduced. The German minorities question continued to present a number of intractable problems involving Danzig, the Polish Corridor, Upper Silesia, the Czech Sudetenland, and Austria. Besides, as Schubert had told him, Germany was not prepared to enter any arrangement that brought her into confrontation with the United States, the Soviet Union, or Britain. In Rumbold's words, 'Britain would have to lose a great deal of prestige before Germany would entertain the remotest thought of an alliance with any European country or countries if such an alliance were to arouse serious annoyance in London.' Nevertheless with unemployment soaring and less inspired leadership at the Wilhelmstrasse, he anticipated that economics would dominate German politics for the forseeable future. 'The Germans', he wrote Henderson in mid-March, 'have a natural predilection for all kinds of combines.' In the deepening crisis he expected them to look ever more intently for economic cooperation with Britain, the United States, or even France.

> [Germany] is ceasingly striving to find additional markets for her exports, and may well see in some such economic federation of Europe as would permit of customs concessions to German goods being made, without necessarily involving similar concessions to America and England on the ground of most-favoured-nation terms in commercial treaties, an excellent method of achieving her ends.... [I]t is quite clear that Germany stands to gain enormously by the reduction of European customs barriers and by increased freedom of communication and transit, which would mean to Germany, occupying the central position in Europe, much what the sea meant to English commerce in the middle of the 19th century.[12]

During the spring of 1930 France intensified efforts to ensure a sympathetic German response to Briand's forthcoming memorandum on European federation. A Franco-German Chamber of Commerce was established in Paris.[13] In March the *Comité d'études pour l'union douanière européenne* canvassed support for its objective from Chambers of Commerce throughout Europe.[14] A strong French delegation, including former Premier Painlevé, Loucheur, and Serruys, attended the second Pan-Europa Congress when it opened in May at the Hotel Kaiserhof in Berlin.[15] All the while, as Rumbold reported, 'the French Embassy in Berlin continue as before to make a parade of cordial relations, not only with literary and artistic, but with political and official circles here'.[16]

Tyrrell repeatedly urged a sympathetic British response to Briand's proposal. By now wholly sympathetic to the French point of view, he was certain that Britain's interest no less than France's lay in active involvement in European affairs.[17] But if he was well-disposed towards the idea of a French-led European federation, officials in London were not. The Board of Trade went out of its way to reassert the supreme importance of the most-favoured-nation principle for British trade. Certain exceptions the Board could accept: where there were complete customs unions, or where preferential links existed between countries bound together by geography or long historical association, as in the case of Spain and Portugal, Portugal and Brazil – or the countries of the British Empire. But the 'so-called United States of Europe plan', in the Board's view, was not a customs union but a body of states giving each other special customs preferences against the rest of the world, and should therefore be 'strenuously resisted as cutting at the root of British most-favoured-nation policy, and not as being a minor derogation from it'.[18]

Early in May Briand expressed the hope of discussing his federation plans with Henderson when the Foreign Secretary passed through Paris on his way to the League Council meeting in Paris. The Foreign Office advised against discussions until Briand's intentions were clearer, and Henderson readily agreed. The London naval conference was near to agreement on limiting auxiliary ships, the issue that had so severely strained Anglo-American relations when negotiations at the Geneva naval conference in 1927 collapsed, and Henderson attached far more importance to disarmament and Britain's special relationship with the United States than the question of European federation, which was too closely associated with France for his liking. During informal conversations at the Quai d'Orsay Briand sought to assure him that his scheme conformed to the principles of the League of Nations and safeguarded the sovereignty of participating countries. Henderson promised to examine it carefully but underlined his concern 'that there would be nothing in the scheme which would give it even the semblance of being directed against the United States of America'. Briand assured him 'there was nothing of the kind and that this consideration had been very much present in his mind throughout'.[19]

Briand's 'Memorandum on the Organisation of a System for European Federal Union' was circulated to interested governments on 17 May 1930. Its appearance coincided with the Quai d'Orsay announcement that all conditions had been met for putting the Young Plan and the BIS into full operation and that the evacuation of the Rhineland would be completed by 30 June 1930, with the opening of the second Pan-Europa Congress in Berlin, and with Serruys' paper on a United States of Europe at the eighth session of the Mayrisch Committee in Heidelberg.[20] Despite the impeccable timing, however, the contents of the memorandum proved a serious disappointment to many of its recipients. For whereas at the Tenth League Assembly Briand had spoken of economic cooperation as the most urgent need, the 'economic problem' was now clearly subordinated to the 'political problem'. The memorandum identified the tangle of customs barriers interlacing Europe as the main obstacle to industrial growth and employment creation, the basic 'source of both political and social instability', and 'the most serious obstacle to the development of all political and judicial institutions on which the foundations of any universal organisation of peace tend to be based'. European countries were asked to pledge themselves to the principle of federal union, the economic objective being given as 'the establishment of a common market'. But discussion of the means of economic collaboration was restricted to a few generalities, and more space was devoted to questions of security. In his desire to obtain Britain's support, Briand had chosen to downplay the economic side of the scheme. Unfortunately for him this had the result of reducing its appeal to other countries without altering British views.[21]

Over the next two months European envoys watched closely for indications of Britain's response to the memorandum. A number of the Baltic and Scandinavian states as well as Belgium, Austria, and certain others intended to support Briand's initiative. Britain's participation as a counterweight to France and Germany was however widely regarded as essential to any European organisation, and to all inquiries the Foreign Office responded with total silence. This was interpreted (correctly) as hostility, which further prejudiced support for the scheme.[22]

The author of Britain's initial draft reply was Alan Leeper, First Secretary in the new League of Nations and Western Department and one of the few members of the Foreign Office who knew much about the European movement. He accepted the importance of American economic expansion as both an example and a threat to Europe, and repeatedly differed with colleagues over the probability of an eventual European bloc.[23] He had no illusions about the difficulties this would create for Britain. To remain both 'in and out' would probably be impossible, and to go 'in' would mean a break with the Dominions. But as he saw little chance of a coherent bloc being formed in the near future, he was more concerned to avoid compromising Briand's influence in France: 'an old and valued friend of this country ... almost alone among French politicians he has in recent years consistently shown himself a good European, the friend of peace, and of the improvement of international relations'. Leeper therefore prepared a reply to the memorandum which, without fully committing Britain to Briand's scheme, expressed sympathy with its objectives.[24]

This, however, was unacceptable to Henderson's political advisers, Philip Noel-Baker and Lord Robert Cecil. They agreed that the division of Europe into twenty-seven contending national units was unfortunate, and that Britain stood to gain from a united, prosperous, and peaceful Europe. But Noel-Baker, a professor of international relations from the LSE and a Quaker, warned Henderson of the danger that a European organisation – the Assembly, Council, and Secretariat that Briand proposed – presented for the League of Nations. '[I]t could not fail in practice to be a dangerous rival.'[25] Cecil, the former Tory Minister who had been brought in to the Foreign Office to advise on League of Nations affairs, sounded an equally disturbing warning. If the scheme got off the ground, 'it would add strength to the Pan-American movement and might increase the Asiatic feeling which already exists'. The scheme was fraught with danger: 'Even if we keep out of a European group, could Canada hold aloof from an American or India from an Asiatic group? It seems very doubtful. The British Empire would be part of all these groups geographically and economically, and their existence without the co-ordinating system of the League would be a seriously disintegrating influence on the Empire.'[26]

Henderson was impressed by these warnings and by the concurrence of Sir Arthur Salter, an economic authority. Salter, writing from Geneva, dwelt on market requirements for modern mass production industry, 'the actual waste involved in the present small units, [and] the dangers resulting from the great disparity between the great unit of the United States and the small ones of Europe'. But he assured the Foreign Secretary that all this had been recognised at the Tenth League Assembly: that was the meaning of the tariff truce and the concerted economic action now being devised at League headquarters. Hence Briand's scheme was irrelevant, a threat to the League, and an incitement to the creation of other exclusive blocs. Still, in view of the seriousness of the European situation, he recommended that Britain not try to kill the movement, but to use it for her own ends. This meant insisting it be under the control of the League and, working within it, mobilising support for European cooperation along lines 'compatible with the essentials of the "universal" interest'.[27]

Salter's argument struck precisely the right note with Henderson, who called for Leeper's reply to be redrafted.[28] Being completely ignorant of economic affairs, it seems he never doubted Salter's argument that the European movement could be diverted from limited regional economic cooperation to universal free trade goals without destroying it. Nor could he appreciate the annoyance certain to be felt by Serruys and others in Paris when they saw references to the ILO conference on working hours in the coal industry and preparations for concerted economic action as evidence of the effectiveness of the League of Nations. For by the time the British reply was sent the coal conference had collapsed, and in French opinion League-sponsored economic action had always been a non-starter precisely because, being based on the unconditional most-favoured-nation principle, it required the cooperation of countries outside Europe as well as inside.

In Germany the prospects for the Weimar Republic had seriously deteriorated since the winter. With soaring unemployment, political violence again became widespread, and the Nazis secured major gains in the Saxon Diet election of 22 June 1930. The following week the last French troops left the Rhineland, 'seen off' by a massive Nazi–Nationalist demonstration at Cologne while the Brüning government refused any gesture of gratitude. The German reply to Briand's memorandum was prepared at the Wilhelmstrasse by Bülow, now Secretary of State, and Erich von Weizsäcker, his equal in aggressive nationalism. Aside from a suggestion of economic cooperation in certain unspecified areas, it was a thoroughly negative document, reflecting their hostility to France and the European status quo. From this distance it is impossible to say whether any other reply was ever possible. Absence of serious debate in the Cabinet suggests there was not. But from the outset it was assumed that hostile responses from Britain and Italy would effectively kill the plan. Thus the form of the reply was decided almost exclusively with domestic considerations in mind.[29]

Tyrrell continued to press for a sympathetic reply. Over lunch with Tardieu on 24 June, the French Premier repeatedly spoke of 'the grave economic crisis which the whole of Europe was facing,' and the need for the closest possible cooperation between France, Germany, and Britain.[30] Later, Tyrrell reported a direct appeal from Briand for a sympathetic reply, whatever the qualifications.[31] A sharp exchange between Briand and Grandi, and demands for a tougher foreign policy from right-wing critics in the French Parliament, led Tyrrell to write to Henderson personally 'to renew my appeal to do everything you can to strengthen Briand's position'.[32] No one in London was prepared to listen. A Cabinet committee comprising MacDonald, Henderson, Snowden, Thomas, and Graham was set up on 28 May to consider Britain's reply. It met only once, on 14 July, a day before the deadline Briand had set for replying, with neither Thomas nor Snowden present. The committee perfunctorily accepted the Foreign Office draft.[33] On 16 July the Cabinet, after the briefest discussion, did likewise, and it was thereupon handed to M. de Fleuriau, the French Ambassador.[34] Significantly, it was one day late.

The emerging censensus on imperial protectionism

That a British 'socialist' government should condemn Europe to face its worst economic crisis in modern history without any practical means of cooperation, for the sake of free trade, a special relationship with the United States, the exemplar of unregulated capitalism, and the maintenance of the British Empire, was not a little ironic. It was doubly so since it happened at precisely the moment when British public opinion turned away from internationalism to seek salvation within an exclusive Empire bloc.

The previous September at the annual Trades Union Congress, a minor sensation had occurred when Ben Tillett, in his presidential address, warned of advancing American financial imperialism and the growth of protection throughout the world, and called for efforts to unite with Britain's kith and kin overseas in the economic organisation of the Empire.[35] Tillett, now 69 years old, a zealous anti-Communist and advocate of industrial collaboration, might not be representative of the trade union movement as a whole, but after the disillusionment with free trade in the past decade, his speech was not the source of embarrassment if would have been a few years earlier. During the winter of 1929–30 controversy over the direction of the Conservative Party dominated the news to such an extent that the fiscal question seemed merely a matter of intra-party feuding. It was of course much more than that. In every sector of the country, including organised labour, evidence accumulated of a conviction that the Empire offered the only hope for future trade, and that the Imperial Conference in the autumn might be a unique opportunity to establish closer economic links.

Support for imperial protectionism among industrial employers found expression in the intensified activities of the NUM, the British Empire Producers' Organisation, Melchett's Empire Economic Union, and the Parliamentary lobbying group, the Empire Industries Association. By January 1930 even the FBI's ever-cautious director, Sir Roland Nugent, had begun to describe himself as an 'economic nationalist'. It was not a question of the theoretical advantages of internationalism or nationalism, he wrote a Manchester member. It was simply 'whether it is *possible* to be international when everybody else insists on being national; and ... whether, if one persists in being international too long, one may find that one's chances of becoming national and saving something from the wreck may have gone'.[36] Even more striking was the evidence of change within sectors of the country hitherto committed to internationalism.

During the winter the various Chambers of Commerce had opposed the tariff truce because it would merely freeze the status quo without reducing tariff levels. The Twelfth Congress of Empire Chambers of Commerce, which opened at the Guildhall on 26 May, heard aggressive speeches from Lord Melchett and Sir Arthur Shirley Benn of the London Chamber, and ended by calling on the forthcoming Imperial Conference to draw up plans for 'effective economic cooperation between the various parts of the Empire ... and, ultimately ... the economic union of the whole'.[37] On the 28th the Free Trade Union opened a two-day conference in London, but it was overshadowed by the news, leaked to the *Daily Express* and *Daily Mail* and given headline coverage, that the TUC was about to issue a document endorsing Empire Free Trade. The General Council, clearly embarrassed, promptly denied the claim, adding that the paper in question was merely for discussion.[38] But this was not the whole story. Twice during May representatives of the TUC and the FBI exchanged views on submissions to the inquiry into monetary policy now under way and to the forthcoming Imperial Conference. They had been pleasantly surprised to find themselves agreed on the need to expand inter-imperial trade by, among other things, improving the machinery for coordinating policy. What was needed, Sir James Lithgow, president of the FBI, stated was 'an economic organisation for the British Commonwealth... parallel with that of the League of Nations'[39] – the sort of machinery the Labour government was presently to oppose for Europe.

The discussion paper was the first report of the General Council's Economic Committee, which had been set up the previous year at the suggestion of Ernest Bevin. The committee accepted that 'economic theory condemns the general policy of tariffs', but held that recent developments had reduced internationalism to 'isolationism' and the time had come for a policy of 'expediency.... It would, indeed, seem that the formation of more limited groups is a necessary first step towards the more comprehensive unity.' Of the possible alternatives, the committee ruled out participation in a European bloc on grounds of excessive competition in manufacturing, shortages of raw materials, and coolness in some European capitals to British membership. An Anglo-American bloc was ruled out because the Americans were able and apparently determined to dominate the Pan-American region alone.

The 'most practicable group' appeared to be the countries of the British Empire, which should be united into a coherent bloc. To avoid friction between the groups, the committee recommended extending the 'scope and influence' of the League of Nations, but this was offered only in passing. It accepted that economic internationalism as promoted at the World Economic Conference and the tariff truce had failed, and a radical change in policy was necessary.[40]

Three months earlier Beaverbrook and his Empire Free Trade crusade had joined with Rothermere to form the United Empire Party.[41] Baldwin complained that this would divide the imperialists and prolong the Socialist government, but quickly made terms. It was agreed that if Dominions concessions warranted taxing foreign foodstuffs entering Britain, a referendum would first be held, and on 4 March Baldwin announced this to a packed meeting of Conservative Party members at the Hotel Cecil.[42] He did not like committing himself so far, however, and Beaverbrook became infuriated at his equivocations. In April, Neville Chamberlain, apparently in hope of securing a new agreement with Beaverbrook, secured the resignation of J.C.C. Davidson, the party chairman and one of Baldwin's intimates.[43] Beaverbrook, however, was not to be so easily appeased: nothing less than a commitment to food taxes would satisfy him now. In May he mounted a concerted campaign in his newspapers against a referendum and against Baldwin and all other party leaders who refused to accept food taxes. To restore order in the party a special meeting was held on 24 June at Caxton Hall.

By now industry had moved decisively in favour of protectionism. A poll carried out by the Leeds Chamber of Commerce in early June confirmed that barely 7 per cent of over 500 members who replied supported free trade.[44] Another poll by the Manchester Chamber of Commerce found that nearly a quarter of the 2,000 members replying favoured a general tariff and another half favoured a broad extension of safeguarding. Even in Manchester, home of free trade, little more than a quarter of the businessmen remained faithful to the cause.[45] The transformation was reflected within the Conservative Party. Lord Derby, the 'King of Lancashire' and hitherto the most hostile critic of the Tariff Reform element, was seen in conclave with Beaverbrook on the eve of the Caxton Hall meeting. So too were Derby's son Oliver Stanley, Harold Macmillan, and other younger men of the party, as well as several dozen of the backbenchers associated with the EIA.[46]

Baldwin opened the meeting with an attack on Beaverbrook and Rothermere, accusing them of trying to dictate to the party. This evoked thunderous applause, but there was obvious lack of enthusiasm at the announcement that there would be no change of policy 'in the present circumstances'. A resolution endorsing his position was followed by one from Colonel Gretton, representing some forty rebels, which would have accorded the leader 'a free hand' on food taxes. Many were dissatisfied with Baldwin's uninspired leadership and would gladly have accepted Gretton's resolution were it not for the damage to party unity. After a speech by Sir Robert Horne, leader of the Conservative industrial group in the House and a Beaverbrook stalwart, indicating dissatisfaction with present policy but warning against any action that would undermine party leadership, Baldwin's support was assured.[47] Hardly had the situation been stabilised, however, when a remarkable event upset it once more.

On Wednesday 2 July, some twenty leading City bankers and financiers met at Hambros Bank to draft a manifesto for a new trade policy. Like the trade unionists a few weeks before, they did not want it thought that they had lost faith in free trade as an ideal basis for commercial relations. But in similar fashion they referred to the 'bitter experience' of the four years since the previous bankers' manifesto, when hopes for a reduction in European trade restrictions – and as in 1926 only European restrictions were mentioned – had gone completely unrealised. In the present crisis, they accepted, Britain must fall back on the Empire.

> While we retain the hope for an ultimate extension of the area of Free Trade throughout the world, we believe that the immediate step for securing and extending the market for British goods lies in reciprocal trade agreements between the nations constituting the British Empire.
>
> As a condition of securing these agreements, Great Britain must retain her open market for all Empire products, while being prepared to impose duties on all imports from all other countries.[48]

When news reached the press late on Thursday, the reaction was tremendous.

For a hundred years the City had been prepared to throw its weight behind internationalist policies: 'A free market for money and a free market for goods.' The manifesto did not mean that the City had abandoned economic internationalism; its interests were far too widely dispersed for that. But it recognised the need to shore up the domestic economy if the City itself was to survive as the leading financial capital of the world. Trade protection was the price the City was prepared to pay to maintain sterling as a world currency. Signatories included directors of merchant bankers Helbert Wagg, Guinness Mahon, Morgan Grenfell, Baring Brothers, and Hambros; directors of the Prudential and Royal Guardian Assurance Companies; several directors of the Bank of England including Sir Alan Anderson, the former chairman of the Chamber of Shipping and a well-known free trader; and the chairmen of the five main clearing banks, among them the former Liberal Chancellor of the Exchequer, Reginald McKenna. A counter-manifesto by Sir Hugh Bell, Ernest Benn, and Sir Charles Mallett, organisers of previous manifestos, contained a far less impressive list of supporters and merely confirmed the importance of the other document.[49] The influence of the City in the mercantile–financial community and on business and political opinion in the country as a whole was such that no government could disregard its views. Amery, with good reason, wrote to Baldwin that they had been given 'the biggest leg up since 1903'.[50]

The Times, which had mocked Beaverbrook and Rothermere on forming their new party and lost no opportunity to point out the Dominions' opposition to Empire Free Trade, had got no further than advocating a modest revenue tariff on manufactures on the morning the bankers' manifesto appeared.[51] The next day it was emboldened to advocate full-scale negotiations with the Dominions including the offer of food taxes, and dismissed the 'already extinct' proposal for a referendum. The *Daily Telegraph* and the *Morning Post* also dropped their reservations about food taxes. The *Round Table*, having cautiously accepted protection in June, now took a more forthright stand.[52]

On 7 July, Baldwin, Neville Chamberlain, and other members of the Shadow Cabinet agreed on a motion of censure condemning the government's doctrinaire rejection of food taxes and calling for a policy of safeguarding against 'unfair foreign competition', and negotiation of reciprocal Empire trade agreements.[53] Baldwin still had to be coaxed into going this far, and now exasperated colleagues almost beyond endurance by his refusal to state outright that he accepted in principle the use of taxes on foreign foodstuffs as an instrument to induce the Dominions to open their markets to British exports. His preference for import quotas seemed like an evasion, and the Rothermere–Beaverbrook press again treated him with contempt.[54] The talk among Conservatives was of his replacement by someone more vigorous, perhaps Sir Robert Horne or better, Neville Chamberlain.[55] Chamberlain was furious with Beaverbrook over the breakdown of an agreement about rival candidates at by-elections, but almost as annoyed at Baldwin.[56] Austen Chamberlain also dwelt on Baldwin's faults: his 'dull egotism and vanity. What is to be done in face of such blind self-complacency?'[57]

The Liberal Party suffered, if anything, even more of a jolt by the collapse of support for free trade. At its summer school at Oxford in the first week of August the fiscal question dominated discussion. E.D. Simon, a Manchester machinery manufacturer and Member of Parliament, pointed out 'the tremendous revulsion of opinion' against the maintenance of free trade in a protectionist world. 'Our export trade has gone wrong. It is fading away – bleeding to death.' He claimed that the limits of direct taxation had been reached. Was not this a compelling case for a 10 per cent revenue tariff? The annual £70–80 million it brought in would be worth one shilling in the pound in direct taxation and provide assistance to the export industries. C.G. Renold, another Mancunian, made a similar appeal, calling on Liberals to 'get away from the Free Trade slush'. He decried free trade as being based solely on exchange advantages, ignoring entirely the prior question of production. Surely, he argued, Britain could never compete with the United States until the modern mass production that was required received the protection of the home market.[58]

This was the first time free trade had come in for criticism by Liberals at a Liberal gathering. The majority were not prepared to abandon the faith just yet, but the idea of a free inquiry received broad agreement. As for Lloyd George, reports circulated that he had an open mind on the subject.[59] Speaking on 1 September and several times during the autumn, he defended free trade, but his iconoclasm was too well-known for any statement of his to carry conviction.[60] Signs of an anti-Lloyd George group, led by Sir John Simon and comprising perhaps a third of the fifty-nine Liberals in Parliament, also multiplied during the autumn, indications being that it would accept protection rather than Lloyd George's adventuresome spending schemes, and join in a working alliance with the Conservatives.[61]

For trade unionists as much as Liberals, free trade was part of a whole set of ideas, political and moral as well as economic. It was bound up with fear that protection spelt monopoly profits, taxes on the necessities of life, advantages to the rich at the expense of the poor. It was integrally linked to the principle of international working-class solidarity and long-held assumptions about the threat of economic imperialism to world peace. But by the 1930 TUC conference, held in Nottingham the first week in September, practical advantage took precedence, and with it the 'socialist' rationale for protection that Tory imperialists had vainly appealed to since the days of Joseph Chamberlain. John Beard, head of the farm workers' union and that year's chairman of the General Council, had been campaigning for agricultural protection since the winter of 1929. He assured delegates that the trade union movement would never seek 'all-round Protection', but added defiantly:

> Our unions were formed to prevent so-called free trade in labour. As Trade Unionists and Socialists we believe in interference with the so-called 'immutable economic laws'. We believe in the regulation and conscious control of economic factors and economic forces,' to use the words of our Report. ... Expediency

in the broadest sense of that term must be our guide, and not some abstract principle which may have no relation to the actual facts and problems with which we are faced.[62]

The following day Ernest Bevin defended the Economic Committee report in a debate that lasted through the morning and most of the afternoon. Strenuous arguments were put up against it: that opposition in the Dominions made talk of Empire economic unity unrealistic, that it was contrary to the principle of working-class solidarity, that it offered a sure formula for conflict with the United States. The Miners' Federation spokesman promised to fight it 'tooth and nail'.

Bevin responded with a balanced appeal for expediency and socialist interventionism. Britain could not create 'world federation' alone or ignore the fact that recent efforts in this direction such as the World Economic Conference and tariff truce scheme had badly failed. 'From my point of view, I regard the last war, and possibly the next war, as struggles for spheres of influence and the domination of raw materials. … You cannot read about the tour of Mr Hoover in South America without realising the motive that was behind that tour for a pan-American development.' He strenuously rejected the claim that the report was a surrender to capitalist extremists: it was 'a departure from the old method of leaving to the City of London the operation of the old monetary and free trade *laissez-faire* system'. Free trade was incompatible with 'the organisation of industry under public ownership'. He insisted that nothing, not excluding tariffs, should be ruled out in the search for recovery. Delegates, mindful of the calamitous rise in unemployment, adopted the report by a vote of 1,878,000 to 1,401,000.[63]

Three weeks later the results of an FBI survey of its members were collated. Of the 72 per cent who returned a definite reply, less than 5 per cent favoured 'the existing Free Trade policy'.[64] Freed from the fear of offending the membership, the Grand Council began to link up with other employers' and farm groups to promote protection. Conversations were held with TUC representatives, after which Lord Lithgow, the FBI president, submitted a joint statement to the government, asserting 'the paramount importance they attach to all possible steps being taken to increase Commonwealth trade', and warning that the Imperial Conference now less than a week away might be the last opportunity for doing so.[65] For the first and only time in its history, the FBI ventured into mass political action by joining the Empire Industries Association in a campaign to promote imperial protectionism.[66]

The only remarkable thing about the FBI's sudden burst of activity was that it took so long in coming. As staff members were uncomfortably aware, the Federation had been increasingly by-passed by the larger, more aggressive employers since the mid-1920s, and was now being ignored in favour of Beaverbrook's party, the EIA, the EEU, and Sir William Morris's newly created National Council of Industry and Commerce.[67] The policies of the Morris group differed little from the others, but two features set it apart. One was the preponderance of employers from the new industries in the founding committee: men like Sir Woodman Burbridge of Harrods and Sir Frederick Richmond of Debenhams stores, Dr Henry Dreyfus of British Celanese and Lord Melchett and Sir Harry McGowan of ICI, Sir Hugo Hirst of GEC and Sir Felix Pole of AEI, Sir Ernest Petter, Sir John Thorneycroft, and Morris himself. The other was the intensity of their demands for action and open impatience with political parties and Parliament itself. While politicians clung to their outworn theories, industry was going to the wall, and normally peaceable, patriotic workmen were being driven to Bolshevism, Morris told a press conference on 19 September 1930. It was time to stop the rot, put politics aside, and let practical men take charge of restoring prosperity. 'We have in England the best workmen in the world. They are screaming for a leader. During the past decade we have suffered from a system of government that has not helped, but hampered, industry.'[68]

Others besides Morris were coming to the conclusion that the country could not afford the luxury of party government in its present economic state: H.A. Gwynne of the *Morning Post,* Sir Edward Grigg, the ex-Colonial Governor, J.L. Garvin of *The Observer,* R.H. Brand, and other proponents of Lloyd George's brand of right-wing social democracy – as well as, privately, Lloyd George himself.[69] Now the industrialists were saying it with all the bluntness of ten years' accumulated frustration. At the organisational meeting on 25 September, Morris's call for a strong government led one guest to propose instead 'a strong man'.[70] It was no coincidence that less than two weeks before in the German Reichstag elections, Hitler had suddenly leapt to international prominence.

Labour and protectionism

The Labour government was subjected to the same pressures. With unemployment abruptly rising once more, an ominous tendency towards protectionism abroad, and industry demanding action, MacDonald and Thomas had begun to grumble audibly early in 1930 about Snowden's dogmatic stand, and let it be known that, in their opinion, free trade had had its day.[71] Sir Arthur Balfour, the Sheffield steelmaker and one of the men MacDonald had called in to advise on forming an economic advisory council, wrote to Conservative leaders in mid-January that they might well 'see the Labour government chasing out Mr Snowden and one or two others and then suggest tariffs as the only cure for unemployment'.[72] There was no likelihood of this happening yet, however. Thomas had Norman's promise of support on which to rest his hopes, and MacDonald was busy as chairman of the Naval Disarmament conference, which opened in London on 21 January and continued until 22 April, and had yet to hear from his council of experts.

In fulfilment of the government's promise to 'make farming pay', Noel Buxton, Minister of Agriculture, had announced plans in October 1929 for a private and informal conference of farmers, farm workers, and landowners.[73] Prior to the election, Labour had made great play with proposals for import boards and domestic marketing boards as substitutes for protection. Both were intended to cut out the allegedly exorbitant profits of the middleman, the former for the benefit of the consumer, the latter for the farmer. Neither proposal had been seriously examined. Had they been, it would have been clear that their appeal rested on exaggerated notions of the profits to be squeezed out of the handling trade. Import boards during the war had proven to be unwieldy and a source of constant friction with foreign suppliers. Marketing boards had more to recommend them, but neither offered an answer to the central problem facing the industry. Arable land had been going out of production at the rate of 200,000 acres a year since 1921, and there was now a dangerous glut of cereals on the world market. Nothing would save agriculture from acute and growing distress except steps to insulate it from declining world prices. And the terms of the conference – 'a fair return to the farmer and an adequate wage to the worker, together with the maximum use of the land for productive purposes, *while not increasing the price to the consumer*' – ruled this out.

The conference brought no result. Having met nine times between 17 January and 21 March 1930 and spent dozens of hours in deliberation, delegates agreed to recommend either a national wheat and flour board with sole power to purchase from abroad and the duty to buy a fixed percentage of home-grown wheat at a fixed price, or the requirement that millers buy a fixed percentage of domestic wheat at a fixed price. But the government had meanwhile set up another inquiry composed of millers, Treasury officials, and politicians, which caused the delegates angrily to abandon their deliberations.[74]

The second inquiry was also virtually fruitless. Intended to examine a departmental proposal for a home wheat marketing board with quotas on imports,[75] MacDonald included for its consideration a proposal of his own for a 'registration fee' on imported cereals, the proceeds to be used to subsidise domestic production. Snowden was 'staggered' at MacDonald's suggestion. 'You do not change a food tax by calling it a registration fee instead of an import duty.'[76] To him it was incredible than anyone, and particularly a Labour leader, should think of registration fees, quotas, import boards, tariffs, or any other form of interference in the market for foodstuffs. All of them meant restrictions on supply and hence increased prices, a burden on the consumer, and inflation, and once conceded would open the floodgates to demands for protection from other industries. So far as he was concerned the debate had ended in 1846 and there was nothing more to be said.[77] After nine frustrating sessions members of the inquiry 'chose to admit their inability to make any recommendations'. A 'substantial majority' favoured assistance to cereal growers, but within the limits of their instructions could not agree on the means. This left the Cabinet with only a minor scheme for agricultural marketing boards, which were virtually irrelevant to the growing distress in the farm community. Ministers therefore requested Buxton and Snowden to see if a home wheat quota could not be instituted without 'any appreciable charge on public funds'.[78]

As late as January 1930 Buxton held to the view that British agriculture must await an international solution to the problem of falling prices.[79] But with huge unsold surpluses from the 1929 cereal crop in Canada and the United States overhanging the market, prices plummeting, and vast rallies of farm workers, farmers, and landowners organised around the country to advertise the plight of arable farming, he swiftly altered his view. By April he had received assurances of support for a home wheat quota from Sir Robert Hutchinson, the Liberal spokesman on agriculture, and Sir George Courthope, leader of the Conservative agricultural group in the Commons. His departmental advisers strongly favoured a home wheat quota; Hubert Henderson, secretary to the Prime Minister's new Economic Advisory Council, also favoured it. He therefore set aside his internationalism in favour of the socialist case for market intervention. It was true that a quota would mean some benefit to the producer at the expense of the consumer. But was this not 'the general idea of Trade Unionism, which is to see that the producer has a first charge on the product of his labour?' Moreover, was there not a reasonable hope that with an active agriculture policy Labour could win the rural seats which were essential for a clear majority in the House?[80] Faced with unyielding opposition from Snowden, Buxton appealed to colleagues for support. Thomas responded, but MacDonald, despite his obvious sympathy for agricultural protection, refused to intervene.[81] Since the Prime Minister's support was essential, the wheat quota proposal was set aside for the time being. As this was only the first of several occasions when the Primer Minister advanced protectionist proposals only to fall silent, leaving the field to Snowden, his motives deserve consideration.

In economic affairs, as in many other respects, MacDonald's outlook was hardly distinguishable from that of a moderate Tory MP from the home counties. He knew nothing about monetary policy, and holding bankers of the City in awed respect, relied on them to provide guidance.[82] He deplored 'poor law and dole' socialism and sneered at the middle- and upper-class supporters of the Labour movement for promoting what seemed to him irresponsible and impracticable schemes of state assistance.[83] The one solution to industrial difficulties he could appreciate was protection, as he acknowledged regularly through 1930; but he was not prepared to fight for it.

The reason, it seems obvious from his diaries, was that far more than issues, far more than policies or his Party's welfare, MacDonald, the illegitimate farm labourer's son from Morayshire, was concerned to gain acceptance among 'responsible' society. Perhaps no document has revealed, unintentionally, more of its author's inner motives than this voluminous hand-written record. Its one constantly recurring theme at this period is the great responsibility cast upon the author's shoulders, the failure of colleagues to measure up to his expectations, the embarrassment they caused him, their lack of loyalty to him. For MacDonald, what mattered was not relieving agricultural distress or reducing unemployment, not doing at all, but being, being Prime Minister, which enabled him to set aside the sham battle for socialism, the pretend conflict with the parties of capitalism, and assume the more congenial role of defender of the Crown, the Constitution, and the British Empire. His emotional need was to stand in the middle, to include and be included in the widest possible spectrum of society and opinion. Hence the alacrity with which he embraced the notion of Parliament as a Council of State, of an Economic Advisory Council uniting every interest, and an all-party approach to unemployment. Hence, too, his ease in the company of Stanley Baldwin, that stolid symbol of Tory paternalism, and his intense dislike of Lloyd George, whose iconoclasm and restless search for new ideas threatened to destroy the symbols of order to which MacDonald was so attached.

In the same context, one can understand his extraordinary tolerance for even the most incompetent and obstructive of colleagues. Thomas he knew to be an alcoholic and 'more and more a wreck'.[84] Yet, having made the mistake of appointing him to the most critical post in the government, he insisted on keeping him there. By the same token he realised that Snowden was an obstacle to practically any form of economic action. Yet he did nothing to force his resignation, much as he wished him to go.[85] He was constantly annoyed at colleagues for advancing proposals that threatened the harmony of the Cabinet, as any proposal among such a divided group was bound to do. As he described them, they were all socially ambitious and lacking in 'decision, initiative, drive and a conception of the wide issues' – all of course except himself.[86] He placed small value upon any ideas they advanced. Uncomfortable among them, he preferred the company of his immediate family or his many rich and well-born acquaintances, and particularly the women among them both. Lady Londonderry, to whom he was most closely attached at this time, was the wife of a prominent Tory politician and mine-owner and an active anti-socialist campaigner in her own right.[87] Politics were avoided when he was in such company, but to seek consolation in the elegant surroundings of his political opponents only further reinforced his predisposition to a cautious, conservative path.

All this was shown in his handling of the slow-developing crisis over Mosley's memorandum on unemployment policy, which had begun in January 1930. Mosley submitted his scheme, with the general endorsement of Lansbury and Johnston, and on 3 February the Cabinet passed it on to a committee chaired by Snowden.[88] No committee chaired by Snowden was likely to give much consideration to proposals so daringly unorthodox, and it was submitted to the Treasury and Ministry of Transport for evaluation. After a suitable delay, they returned a thoroughly negative verdict. Snowden, presenting their report to Cabinet on 9 May, dismissed the idea of 'shovelling out public money merely for the purpose of taking what must inevitably be a comparatively small number of people off the unemployed register to do work which is not more remunerative and much more expensive even than unemployment'. What was needed was to maintain confidence within the business community, 'and we must therefore avoid all schemes involving heavy additions to budget charges or grandiose loan expenditure'.[89]

Meanwhile predictions for unemployment put it at 2 million by the end of the year, and the government had come up with no solution. The Cabinet procrastinated, set up another committee under Thomas to reconsider the memorandum, and allowed opinions to be aired for another ten days. Then, when rumours of ministerial dispute began to circulate publicly, MacDonald in a summary manner brought deliberations to a close. It is clear that he had never seriously contemplated supporting Mosley's plan. His opinion was summed up in the comment, 'Mosley would get away from practical work into speculative experiments. Very bad impression'.[90] In January his one concern had been to see that Mosley did not embarrass Thomas by upstaging him.[91] In May it was to see that the memorandum was buried as quietly as possible.

But Mosley had no intention of allowing his work to be passed over in such a cavalier manner. Despite MacDonald's appeals, he resigned from the government, presented his scheme to the Parliamentary Labour Party, and insisted on putting it to a vote. Party members, under notice that the government would resign if the scheme was adopted, displayed their loyalty by rejecting it.[92] But many rank and file members were deeply troubled by the government's lack of policy. One by-election had gone badly for them on 6 May, another on 29 May. The radical core of the ILP was in full rebellion: fifteen had abstained from voting at the end of the unemployment debate on 19 May, leaving the government with a majority of merely fifteen on the division. The TUC's *Daily Herald* treated Mosley's resignation with undisguised sympathy.[93] The government survived a Conservative motion of censure on 28 May for their mishandling of unemployment, but Mosley's had been the outstanding speech, while MacDonald's and Thomas's were unimpressive.[94] Three days later MacDonald received a letter from sixty Labour members calling for Thomas's resignation.[95]

MacDonald had decided earlier, just as the crisis was breaking, that he would take personal charge of the unemployment problem, and in a Cabinet reshuffle despatched Thomas to the Dominions Office. Perhaps there, he recorded in his diary, Thomas might regain 'his equilibrium'.[96] He also revived the idea of a Council of State by calling for an all-party conference on agriculture and unemployment. With the appeal of protectionism dramatically confirmed in recent by-elections, Lloyd George had no wish for an early general election and accepted the invitation. Baldwin, encouraged by the same trend, stayed away. MacDonald reluctantly embarked on a two-party conference.[97] But what was there to talk about? He had indicated that he would not accept safeguarding, nor would the Liberals. Lloyd George still advocated a big scheme of public works financed by borrowing, but while only Snowden said so out loud, practically no one in the Parliamentary ranks of the Liberal or Labour Party believed in such an approach. It was good election material and useful as a whip to beat the government, but when it came down to it, almost no one was prepared to deny the need for business confidence and balanced budgets. 'All this humbug about curing unemployment by Exchequer grants,' MacDonald wrote to Walton Newbold with uncommon forcefulness on 2 June, 'is one of the most superficial and ill-considered proposals that has ever been foisted upon the Party'.[98] MacDonald himself had no proposals to discuss. The only direction he could see was towards protection.

On 30 May H.D. Henderson completed the draft of an 'Industrial Reconstruction Scheme', calling for a temporary 10 per cent revenue tariff in order to finance prospective deficits in the unemployment insurance fund and subsidise industrial rationalisation.[99] This followed logically from the position he and other progressive Liberal economists had adopted during the 1920s. He had opposed the return to gold except in conditions that precluded deflationary pressure on the domestic economy. He had joined Keynes and other members of the Liberal Industrial Inquiry in advocating the diversion of investment funds from overseas to domestic projects. As editor of *The Nation* he had startled readers in January 1930 by denouncing Snowden's plan to remove the McKenna and other duties when industry was already in enough difficulty.[100]

Besides offering a means of meeting the prospective deficit in the 'dole' and stimulating industrial rationalisation, which many Liberals continued to hope would be the long-term solution to Britain's economic problems, Henderson's scheme included a one-third preferential rebate on Empire imports, which provided a material contribution to imperial solidarity. It was, as events confirmed, precisely the formula that many in the broad centre of the political spectrum were looking for: a simple, practicable alternative to grandiose but dubious schemes such as Mosley's or Lloyd George's. The memorandum was put on the Cabinet agenda for 4 June. It was not discussed, but as the assistant secretary of the Cabinet recorded, 'Henderson's bombshell must have been in everybody's mind.'[101]

Three weeks earlier Arthur Henderson, at Graham's urging, had raised the subject of multilateral tariff negotiations as a matter of urgency at the quarterly meeting of the League Council in Geneva.[102] All Graham's hopes for a truce now hung by a thread, and so far there was no programme of 'concerted economic action'. To set an example for other signatories, Graham placed Britain's ratification of the truce before the Cabinet on 24 June. The Cabinet was not prepared to give the same uncritical support as in the new year, however: too much had happened since then. Dr Christopher Addison, the former Lloyd George Liberal and Buxton's successor as Minister of Agriculture, and Clement Attlee, Thomas's successor, were again pressing for a home wheat quota.[103] Despite Graham's appeal, ratification was refused.[104]

Thomas, recovering his spirits if not his equilibrium, announced in the Commons two days later that the government would go into the Imperial Conference in September with a free hand, and for the next few weeks there was reason to believe this was so.[105] Thomas himself, over drinks in the Commons bar one may presume, encouraged rumours of agreement among ministers that Labour would exploit the rising tide of protectionist sentiment in the country by negotiating with the Dominions an ambitious scheme of trade preferences, thereby winning Beaverbrook's support and leaving the Tories high and dry. He told a Conservative member that the Cabinet had discussed tariff plans and everyone was in favour except Snowden and Graham. A 'way out' was being found for Graham, who could justify his reversal of position by reference to the report on the steel industry he was preparing and by Labour's obligation to protect British workers. Snowden was the only serious obstacle, 'and if he won't come in he may have to be thrown overboard'.[106]

Thomas, if shamefully indiscreet, may have been exaggerating only a little. Certainly to Conservatives, desperately impatient with their own leader and clamouring for a 'free hand' themselves, it seemed only too plausible an account. Recently Graham had in private given the unmistakable impression of being ready at least for agricultural protection.[107] Their own soundings corroborated Thomas's claim that on a free vote 70 per cent of Labour MPs would support safeguarding.[108] It seemed obvious that Labour would try to respond to the new mood in the country.

No Minister contradicted Thomas's statement in the House, which he repeated on 4 July – the day after the appearance of the bankers' manifesto – in an even more emphatic manner. Speaking at the opening of the Colchester Civic and Empire week, he described the Imperial Conference as an opportunity 'for free and unfettered discussion on all aspects of the unemployment problem', and suggested that its theme might be 'the rationalisation of the Empire'. Then, evoking the image of the Empire as a united force in a world of self-contained blocs, he stated: 'Everything the United States possess today in material wealth and resources is possessed within the ambit of the British Empire.'[109]

Once again the crucial question was MacDonald's position, and once more he seemed ready to offer decisive leadership. During the summer he approached Snowden with a three-point programme designed to secure a Labour majority at the next election: a commitment to maintain social services, a forward policy on unemployment, and a 10 per cent revenue tariff. Snowden learned that MacDonald and Thomas were canvassing other Cabinet members, warning that by the following year the financial position would be so bad that the only alternative to a revenue tariff would be a heavy increase in direct taxation.[110]

In a speech at Crystal Palace on 12 July, MacDonald dismissed Empire Free Trade as impracticable, but echoed Thomas's claim of entering the conference with a free hand. Meanwhile in the Colne Valley, Snowden was denouncing protectionism, which he blamed for much of the world's ills.[111] Four days later the Tories moved censure of the government's dogmatic adherence to free trade. Snowden spoke out defiantly, and in a sentence that could not have been better calculated to infuriate opponents on both sides of the House, declared that the government would bar nothing from discussion at the conference, but would approve nothing in the nature of food taxes or general protection. MacDonald by his own admission made 'one of the worst speeches in House I ever made. Said what I did not want to say and did not say what I wanted. Very annoyed but was worn out and my head would not work.'[112]

Several times in the next few weeks MacDonald seemed almost ready to act. Despite his earlier refusal to support Buxton on the wheat quota, he indicated that he still favoured agricultural protection when the campaign for a quota resumed in Cabinet in the summer. Attlee as his first task as Lord Privy Seal had examined the plight of the cereal growers and soon reported that unless something was done 'a very awkward situation will arise, worse than that over the Mosley memorandum'.[113] Addison accepted the need for both import boards and quotas and tried energetically to persuade his colleagues.[114] In mid-July an EAC committee chaired by the Liberal Sir John Simon came down firmly against any permanent protection for agriculture but disagreed about temporary, emergency measures.[115] Snowden followed this by circulating a paper setting out the objections to favouring the farmer at the expense of the consumer.[116] MacDonald was nevertheless tentatively prepared to call for protection when the EAC met on 24 July. Speaking after Addison and Keynes who warned that the coming harvest would send prices lower still, he asked if they should not erect 'a sea wall to protect our acres'. His idea was not 'crude protection', he insisted, but a temporary five-year quota offered on condition that farmers 'rationalised' production.[117]

On 25 July a Cabinet committee chaired by Addison reported in favour of a home wheat quota, 'pending the working out of the full party policy of an Import Board'.[118] But in Cabinet next week, Ministers retreated from any commitment to import boards, at least until the Imperial Conference had studied the question. They accepted that quotas were open to serious objection, and postponed further discussions until the autumn.[119] Thus another round went to Snowden. And where was MacDonald during the battle? The records are not explicit, but his biographer accepts the likelihood that he simply 'lay low'.[120]

Snowden, the victor, stated government policy on 1 August before the House rose for the summer. Besides confirming plans to introduce a marketing bill, he held out the prospect of agreement at the conference on 'bulk purchase, import boards and stabilisation of prices'. Offering this as the reason for saying nothing on the cereal question, he promised that as soon as conference decisions were known, 'the Government will undertake whatever practicable steps can be devised to put cereal growing in this country on an economic foundation'.[121] This was scarcely candid. Largely due to his own efforts, the Cabinet had backed away from the alternatives he mentioned. In his opinion there was *no* economic foundation for cereal growing in Britain: market forces dictated that farmers should get out of it and go into beef-raising, or dairying, or some other activity.[122] It was indicative of the feeling on both sides of the House, to say nothing of the farm community, however, that he should have chosen to obscure government policy in this way.

Graham, heartened by this, renewed his request for authorisation to ratify the tariff truce. 'No one,' he took it, 'proposed now to put on a tariff in connection with agriculture or anything else.' He urged Cabinet to appreciate the dangers of further delay. British delegates to the League Assembly would be in a very embarrassing position if they could not support a convention they themselves had promoted. The subsequent tariff negotiations would be doomed before they began, and the government's 'whole policy' would be destroyed. Graham soon discovered he had misjudged the occasion. With MacDonald in the chair, Snowden absent, and just seven Ministers present, Graham was no match for Addison and Thomas, who objected to the truce 'from the point of view of Agriculture and Industry ... from that of the coming Imperial Conference, [and] in view of probable difficulties with the next Budget'. To ratify would be to rule out even a revenue tariff, which would depress industry further. Besides, if Britain did ratify, she would be practically alone, to judge by present indications. Ratification was refused, and MacDonald advised Graham to make clear in Geneva that Britain must see some advantage from tariff reduction negotiations before she entered the truce.[123]

During the next three weeks rumours abounded of official interest in a tariff. The *Daily Herald* reported that Henderson's revenue tariff scheme was on the agenda of Ministers preparing for the Imperial Conference. J.L. Garvin of *The Observer* predicted that the outcome of the Liberal–Labour talks would be agreement on a revenue tariff, with Snowden being forced to resign.[124] MacDonald may have done something to encourage such speculation. To Charles Dawes, the American Ambassador, who visited him in Lossiemouth, 'he indicated that it would not be difficult for him, if he deemed best, to reach agreement upon [a tariff] policy with Stanley Baldwin'.[125]

But as always, MacDonald shied away from decisive action. Having broken off his holiday to attend the two-party conference in London on 28 August, he immediately flew back to the peace and quiet of Lossiemouth. As a result, Snowden, the deputy Prime Minister, chaired the Cabinet meeting on 2 September to consider Graham's third request for ratification of the tariff truce. MacDonald had written to Thomas to see 'that the full significance of ratification, before we know what is really going on in Geneva, will be thoroughly considered,' and to Graham and Snowden to the same effect.[126]

Graham revealed deep apprehension about his own position at the now imminent League Assembly. He was sure 'our position at Geneva would be undermined and would become quite impossible economically if we refused at this stage to ratify'. Thomas followed with a vigorous argument against ratification and indicated equal concern about the Imperial Conference, now barely five weeks away. To foreclose all options on trade policy before the conference would be 'disastrous,' he warned them. It would 'give the Dominions the opportunity of putting the responsibility for the failure of the conference on to His Majesty's Government' – when his career as Dominions Secretary, it went without saying, would end as disastrously as his previous one as Minister responsible for employment. Graham, however, found an ally in Henderson, who was also about to leave for Geneva, and sought a declaration that the government 'had no intention of changing the traditional Free Trade Policy of the Labour Party'. Snowden also spoke out. Britain faced a simple choice: to ratify and await tariff reduction negotiations; or to refuse ratification, face the certainty of being blamed for the breakdown of the truce, and make a tariff war inevitable.

> With regard to the argument that the Government should keep their hands free so as to be able, if necessary, to impose import duties in the next Budget, he, the Chancellor of the Exchequer, wished to make it quite clear that whatever the position might be, such a proposal ... was out of the question.... The national honour was at stake ... the only thing to be done was to ratify the Convention and to enter as quickly as possible on the negotiations; if these were successful the Government would be entitled to great credit, and if they failed no responsibility would rest on the Government.

Snowden's speech ended the discussion. By a vote of eight to two the Cabinet gave Graham the authorisation he sought.[127]

A different result would have required the Prime Minister's intervention, something more explicit than the advice in his letter. There was no doubt of the importance of the decision, despite Graham's claims to the contrary. Graham pointed out that any changes in fiscal policy accepted at the Imperial Conference or elsewhere would have to await introduction in the April budget, and the government could be free of its commitment to the tariff truce by 1 April 1931; ratification therefore placed no new constraint on policy. But this assumed normal procedure in distinctly abnormal times, and tying the government's hands for eight months at present levels of unemployment was a large concession to precedent. The decision was also bound to discourage consideration of alternatives to free trade, and placed the onus on the advocates of internationalism to produce results, making them all the more opposed to regional economic arrangements, as the Eleventh League Assembly soon showed.

Sounding the international note at Geneva

When Briand circulated his memorandum on European federation, his aim was to secure endorsement of the principle in the hope that, once accepted, there would be a willingness to confront the practical measures involved. Britain had virtually destroyed these hopes, first by discouraging him from exploiting fully the appeal of regional economic cooperation, then by holding back her reply, and finally by submitting an unmistakably hostile reply. Other countries, seeing Britain's evident dislike of the scheme, gave similarly discouraging responses. The result was to add to the pressure mounting against Briand in France. With the Reichstag election set for 12 September and unemployment fast rising, a new stridency entered German politics. The withdrawal of the last French troops from the Rhineland in June had been followed immediately by a provocative Nazi rally in Cologne and an intense campaign against 'enslavement' to reparations. Briand's right-wing critics at home saw in the replies one more proof of the wrong-headedness of his Locarno policy, which only encouraged revisionism.[128] He battled on for the federation scheme, agreeing to open the Assembly with a report of his investigations of European support, to be followed by Henderson explaining 'the position of my Government, especially having regard to our peculiar relationship with the Dominions and India'. In a last attempt to win support for the principle of union he convened a meeting of European delegates prior to the Assembly.[129]

At this meeting on 8 September, Briand told delegates that, as no country had rejected his proposal outright, they should agree to a declaration in principle. Further, they should accept the proposal from Poland of a League committee for European affairs. Henderson immediately and bluntly intervened. He rejected Briand's interpretation of the replies, consequently his recommendations, and called on him to present his report without elaboration to the Assembly. The German Foreign Minister, Curtius, supported Henderson. Briand, discouraged and annoyed, threatened to abandon his project altogether, and only with difficulty was persuaded to present a unanimous but anodyne resolution on future cooperation.[130]

Last minute attempts to overcome British objections were made by Eleutherios Venizelos, the Greek Prime Minister and a keen supporter of European unity, and by René Massigli, the French diplomat responsible for League affairs. Massigli advised Cecil that all the European delegates were saying to him, 'Agree with the English and nothing else matters to us, we will do what you like.'[131] He still hoped that Henderson with Briand would prepare a resolution to set up a European committee which would leave appointments to the Europeans instead of the League, and give them a clear mandate for action. Cecil had recently reported to MacDonald that 'all over the Continent it is admitted that Briand's proposals have no chance unless we support them'. But he was not prepared to offer Massigli encouragement.[132]

Briand, presenting the European resolution to the League Assembly, gamely affirmed his 'great satisfaction' with the 'unanimously favourable' replies to his memorandum.[133] But he convinced no one and failed to capture the imagination of his audience as he had done on previous occasions.[134] A resolution endorsing a 'scheme for collaboration among European governments' was presented in the name of forty-five countries. In this form there were no objections, and on 23 September, European delegates elected Briand chairman. He proposed the title '(League of Nations) Committee of Enquiry for European Union', suggested the League be asked for secretarial assistance, and adjourned the committee until January.[135]

In the deepening economic depression almost every delegate to the Assembly spoke of the desperate need for some sort of collective action. The Dutch delegate, M. van Blokland, appealed for a renewed commitment to the resolutions of the World Economic Conference. If something was not done to stop protectionism, he warned, even free trade nations 'may also be obliged to throw themselves into the insensate struggle'. The Danish delegate, Dr Peter Munch, spoke of the 'disastrous tendency' towards economic nationalism, which was fomenting class war, endangering world peace, and threatening to discredit the League. On behalf of Switzerland, Holland, and six other countries of northern Europe, he asked the council to accelerate 'an international settlement of the problem of the most-favoured-nation clause'. Nothing was more vitally important, he said, than 'that the economic anarchy at present prevailing in Europe should be replaced by a rational organisation... either in the form proposed by M. Briand or in some other form within the framework of the League'.

The Austrian Foreign Minister, Dr Schober, suggested that Briand's objective might best be approached by merging smaller groups, each to be formed on economic criteria and including one uniting the agricultural exporting countries of eastern Europe with industrial exporting countries. Hitherto a supporter of Briand's scheme, Schober was now pointing towards an *Anschluss* with Germany, and within a few days German and Hungarian delegates had endorsed his remarks.[136] But Henderson devoted his speech to an impassioned appeal for disarmament and support for the General Act of Arbitration, Conciliation and Judicial Settlement, which, he announced with great pleasure, Britain intended to sign. And Graham, who addressed the Assembly on the 13th, renewed the call for universal free trade. It was time to 'sound the international note in economic relations, and in order to promote recovery, to beat down those barriers which separate us and which prevent that true cooperation'. He announced Britain's decision to ratify the tariff truce and outlined her hopes for multilateral tariff negotiations on certain specific commodities starting with textiles and machinery. As to Briand's scheme, he remained silent.[137]

In the week before the Assembly, representatives of Bulgaria, Czechoslovakia, Estonia, Finland, Roumania, and Yugoslavia had met in Warsaw to try to work out a solution to the agricultural problem.[138] The industrial countries were faring badly enough; the agricultural countries were in dire straits. Between 1929 and 1930 the price of bacon had fallen 15 per cent on the international markets, that of maize 22 per cent, and wheat 42 per cent. Between 1930 and 1931 bacon fell another 37 per cent, maize by 56 per cent, and wheat by 51 per cent.[139] This was disastrous for the poor, troubled countries of eastern Europe. With the Soviet Union again a grain exporter and huge stocks accumulating overseas, the only solution that seemed at all feasible was to induce the industrial countries of Europe to absorb surpluses by a modest reduction in overseas imports. To do this required intra-European preferences.

When the League Assembly's deliberations shifted to the Second (economic) Committee, the question of preferences came to the fore. The Roumanian Foreign Minister, M. Madgearu, spoke for the Warsaw countries. He called for a redefinition of most-favoured-nation rights to facilitate regional arrangements and exceptions, including a temporary preferential agreement among European cereal exporting and importing countries. Belgium, Germany, and Austria expressed cautious sympathy. So did Flandin, but his difficulty was that France was practically self-sufficient in agricultural products, whereas Germany was not, and for strategic reasons France feared any preferential arrangement that placed her east European allies in a dependent relationship with Germany. He warned against a policy based on the crude division of Europe into agricultural and industrial countries. With a nod towards Britain he also deprecated a single-minded preoccupation with tariff reduction. What was needed was a pragmatic approach, with due consideration to non-tariff barriers such as the contrived use of sanitary restrictions.[140]

The Dominions, India, and Holland denounced Madgearu's proposal for League-sanctioned trade discrimination. Miss Susan Lawrence, representing Britain on the Second Committee, insisted on principle above all, and joined the Dominions in condemning Madgearu's solution: 'such discrimination as is suggested is altogether opposed to the root principles of the League'. At the same time, without naming the British Empire, she defended exceptions to the most-favoured-nation clause 'between countries which have had long political associations'.[141]

For two weeks the Assembly was a battleground, with Madgearu at the head of the east European delegates leading charge after charge in an effort to get modification of the most-favoured-nation clause to accommodate regionalism, only to meet an immovable British presence.[142] Eventually every issue was decided in Britain's favour. If there was to be further action on Briand's scheme it would take place under the supervision of the League and its British Secretary-General, Sir Eric Drummond, an opponent of regionalism.[143] The Second Committee did not endorse the Warsaw objectives. The problems of European cereal surpluses and non-tariff protectionism were relegated to subordinated places on the agenda of the next Conference on Concerted Economic Action, set for November. The League Economic Committee was left to carry on its interminable wrangling over the nature and application of the most-favoured-nation clause.[144]

The British delegation could be pleased that it had imposed 'the international note' over limited, regional approaches to Europe's problems. But was it a victory? As before, British delegates betrayed a Eurocentrism as extreme as their opponents, identifying world problems exclusively with European protectionism, while ignoring the protectionism of the United States and the Dominions as well as the dilemma their own non-cooperation posed for Europe. Unlike their friends from the low-tariff countries of northern Europe, they showed no appreciation of the fragility of European society, or the grave threat to international peace that the economic crisis was creating. They seem not to have known that Germany was already making discreet approaches to east European countries in pursuit of hegemony in Europe, although the behaviour of Germany, Austria, and Hungary should have put them on their guard. Four days into the Assembly came news of the German election. The Weimar coalition parties had fared poorly, the Communists had done well and the Nazis sensationally well, increasing their seats from 12 to 107. Little was known about Hitler, but there was no doubt that he represented some form of extreme nationalism. With developments like these, it was a question whether Henderson's preoccupation with disarmament, arbitration, and conciliation was not a grand irrelevancy, and whether Europe could afford to await Graham's international solution.

'This is the eleventh year I have attended the Assembly,' M. Osusky, the Czech delegate to the Second Committee, observed, 'and it is the first time that I have been present at a discussion coloured by such black pessimism in regard to economic problems.'[145] Flandin spoke bitterly of the doctrinaire and hypocritical attitude taken by 'certain' countries – it was obvious he had in mind the Anglo-Saxon countries – which was paralysing constructive action. They persistently demanded tariff reductions heedless of the fact that other countries could not contemplate such reductions without the assurance of other sources of revenue and stable markets. While insisting that everyone uphold the most-favoured-nation clause in its unconditional form, they maintained their own preferential arrangements or simply closed their doors to foreign goods. 'The nations,' he warned, 'have not forsworn the sword as an arbiter of international justice merely in order to replace militarist by economic imperialism, which is no less dangerous to the peace of the world.'[146]

Stalemate at the Imperial Conference

The main subject of the Imperial Conference which opened in London on 1 October 1930 was the proposed Statute of Westminster, placing relations between Britain and the Dominions on a new constitutional footing. All the controversial issues had been settled, however, and it was the economic side of the conference which dominated.

Thomas and later Snowden had allowed the impression to stand during the summer that Britain, if opposed to 'a crude subsidy or protective tariff', would give a sympathetic hearing to proposals from the Dominions for a preference in the huge British market for foodstuffs, including 'bulk purchase, import boards, and stabilisation of prices'. The Dominions were not dissatisfied.[147] Addison repeatedly encouraged British farmers to hope that import restrictions were on the way: 'The Free Trade System ... was dead as Queen Anne.'[148] He proposed instead a system of import boards, first for wheat but eventually for other products. By this one instrument the country would be able to regulate imports so as to ensure a stable market for domestic growers, enter into bulk purchase agreements, and extend Dominions suppliers some preferential treatment. This proposal came before the Cabinet in mid-September, when Snowden's vigorous objections led members to acknowledge serious difficulties.[149] And when on 24 September the Cabinet discussed reference to a cereals bill in the forthcoming King's speech, Snowden ruled out both import boards and a domestic price quota as incompatible with their publicly declared opposition to 'crude subsidies and protectionism'.[150] MacDonald recorded that Thomas, who opened the conference talks on economic issues, 'did not do very well ... not adequately prepared'.[151] It was not Thomas who was inadequately prepared, it was MacDonald's government that had failed to provide him with a coherent brief.

Difficulties began at once. R.B. Bennett, the Canadian Prime Minister, offered Britain and the other Empire countries 'a preference in the Canadian market for a like preference in theirs', based upon 'a ten percentum increase in prevailing general tariffs, or upon tariffs yet to be created'. The offer was modest, to say the least. On a 25 per cent tariff it meant only a 2.5 per cent preference, which would do virtually nothing to facilitate access to the highly protected Canadian market.[152] As an inducement for Britain to adopt 'food taxes' it was patently inadequate. But it was an offer, and was accepted by Australia, New Zealand, and South Africa. Britain was thus in the position of having to accept it or propose some alternative if she was to avoid charges of wrecking the conference. Next morning the Cabinet agreed that the offer was inadequate, but beyond that could decide on no positive action.[153]

For the next four weeks the falsity of the government's position was betrayed in the bad temper and awkwardness of the Ministers. On 9 October, Snowden not only rejected Bennett's offer but went on to lecture the Dominion Prime Ministers in his usual haranguing style. According to MacDonald he advised Bennett to cultivate economic relations with the United States as Canada seemed unable to help herself, and claimed that he actually welcomed the dumping of Russian goods – one of Bennett's chief worries – since it meant British consumers paid less. 'One of the [Canadians] said he would give the Chancellor $5,000 to go and make that speech in Canada for his party interests, but would pay the same amount to keep him at home in the interests of goodwill between Canada and ourselves.'[154] Thomas, worried that the conference would bring him further discredit, desperately sought to appease the Dominion delegates, yet succeeded in offending Nicolaas Havenga, South Africa's Finance Minister, to the point where he threatened never to put a South African loan on the London market again.[155] MacDonald devoted himself to smoothing troubled waters, but displayed his unease by first refusing to meet an NFU delegation, then abusing them in an interview with the *Daily Herald*.[156]

By 24 October it was evident that the economic committee, which the British had suggested as a delaying tactic, was taking its work seriously and would shortly recommend a British quota for Dominion wheat. MacDonald asked the Cabinet to be allowed to accept it, but they procrastinated.[157] By the 27th Thomas was in a state of panic, convinced the conference would be 'shipwrecked' unless progress was made in the next few days. The Canadians and Australians were expecting a quota, and everywhere in the Empire people were expecting practical results. Thomas warned his colleagues that if they now announced that a quota was unacceptable, the Dominions would conclude that Britain had been 'fooling them for the last fortnight', and the reaction would be incalculable. If colleagues would not accept a quota, they must at least offer to maintain existing preferences until next year's conference in Ottawa. This seemed to him only common sense since he could not believe that in the foreseeable future Britain could afford to lose the revenue and protection of existing duties.[158]

Graham by now leaned towards a quota, consoling himself that this departure from free trade would not involve any increase in prices and so escape the label 'food tax'. Bullied by Snowden, however, the Cabinet decided to maintain 'a non-committal attitude'. Token concessions such as broadening the activities of the Empire Marketing Board and an assurance on existing preferences were left to an *ad hoc* committee of senior Ministers.[159]

At one point Snowden threatened to resign rather than commit himself to existing duties. Next day he stood out alone against Thomas, Graham, Henderson, and MacDonald. During the lengthy and heated exchange he spoke out scornfully against an agreement to 'give up something to people who have never given us anything, but, on the contrary, had put up tariffs against us', until corrected by Henderson, who pointed out that they were not talking of a unilateral offer but a reciprocal one, requiring Dominions agreement to maintain their own preferences. Snowden insisted 'he would never agree' to renounce his constitutional responsibility for taxation. Graham and Thomas warned of the tremendous blow to Labour's electoral standing if the conference broke down. Snowden said the government could point proudly to its resistance to food taxes – which were not under discussion. A stronger Prime Minister would have found it easy to force Snowden's resignation in a confrontation like this, and would not have hesitated, knowing it would be welcomed by a large section of the party. But although MacDonald recorded his exasperation with Snowden and readiness to accept his resignation, he now let others argue the case for concessions.[160] Eventually Snowden agreed to maintain existing preferences for three years or pending the outcome of the next Imperial Conference, so long as he could add the wholly vitiating qualification that the offer was subject to Britain's right to fix her budget from year to year.[161]

For another two weeks the conference dragged on amid bickering and bad feeling. When the economic committee's report appeared on 11 November, the British delegate offered only to study it. Henry Stevens, the Canadian Minister of Trade and Commerce, accused the British of 'bad faith', and demanded that they legislate.[162] MacDonald, warning of the ugly mood that was developing, hinted that he would accept the report, but with Snowden rigidly opposed to acceptance the Cabinet would not budge without stonger leadership than this. MacDonald resigned himself to blaming Graham for getting them into such a predicament.[163] Three days later, the conference ended with the substantive issues referred back to the governments for examination.

Economic internationalism had won another victory of sorts. Britain had drawn back from joining the hypocrisy of the Dominions, who sought precisely the discriminatory regime within the Empire they so vehemently objected to in Europe, but this was the most that could be said for it. Like the stand taken at the eleventh League Assembly, the price paid was an intensification of the general mood of frustration and despair. Nor did it contribute to multilateralism, for if it obstructed the path towards a restrictive Empire bloc, it did nothing to slow the trend towards narrower economic nationalism.

The second tariff truce conference

Prospects for the second Conference on Concerted Economic Action, scheduled to open in Geneva on 17 November 1930, were bleak. By 1 November, the deadline for notifying acceptance of the tariff truce, only eight states had deposited their instruments with the League: Belgium, Britain, Denmark, Finland, Latvia, Norway, Sweden, and Switzerland – 'the good boys of Europe', as Sir Sydney Chapman called them. Luxembourg subsequently did so, and the French Chamber of Deputies voted on the 13th to authorise ratification. But Flandin preceded the division with an assurance that he would not enter into tariff reduction negotiations until he had guarantees against indirect protectionism.

From the first plenary session of the conference it was clear the truce convention lacked sufficient support to be put into force. Chapman, under instructions to reserve Britain's position in the absence of

German, French, and Italian ratification, had to join the other ratifying states in requesting a postponement. The period of ratification was therefore extended to 25 January 1931, when another conference was scheduled to review the progress of concerted economic action.[164]

A 'British Committee', set up to examine Graham's proposal for multilateral negotiations on duties on specific goods, soon confirmed that this approach was, as Chapman reported, 'dead'. A Dutch proposal, supported by the Austrians, Belgians, Danes, Norwegians, and Swiss, called for the division of participating countries into those with autonomous tariffs and liberal commercial policies, and those with negotiated tariffs and protectionist policies, with the former agreeing to maintain the truce only if the latter heeded their requests to reduce or consolidate specific duties detrimental to their trade. As no better alternative was in sight, Chapman requested and received Graham's permission to accept it.[165] But once again nothing had been done actually to reduce tariff barriers. Again Chapman was forced to register his opposition to preferences for east European agricultural goods within Europe, which were strenuously promoted by M. Manoulescu on behalf of Roumania, Hungary, and Yugoslavia, and with the support of Bulgaria and Poland. And again M. Elbel singled out 'the veterinary restrictions imposed by Great Britain on French cattle and meat', as a prime example of the non-tariff barriers which would have to be removed before France could contemplate tariff negotiations. Shortly afterwards Colijn closed the conference with an appeal for active support of the forthcoming bilateral negotiations, warning that otherwise free trade countries would be forced into protection and a tariff war would be inevitable. The conference, a Foreign Office official commented, was 'altogether ... one of the most unsuccessful ever held'.[166]

The second tariff truce conference did not end the government's single-handed assault on protectionism, but it did end all reasonable hope that anything could come of it. The only practical result was to provide a target for the derision of government critics. At the end of the year Graham's Parliamentary Secretary was obliged to confirm in the House that no less than thirteen participants in the original tariff truce conference had now raised their tariffs.[167] The temptation for the government to renounce internationalism so as to ease the strain upon industry and the budget was nearly overwhelming.

The crisis within the parties

The debate on the General Council's trade policy report had been the highlight of the annual TUC conference at Nottingham in September

1930. A month later the highlight of the Labour Party conference at Llandudno was the debate that began with Mosley's speech. Since the mid-1920s when they had visited the United States and seen the growth potential of a mass production–mass consumption economy, Bevin, the author of the TUC report, and Mosley had progressed intellectually along similar paths. Mosley now welcomed the TUC report and proceeded to recast his formula for a managed capitalist system within the framework of a united Empire. The Empire: here surely was the proper basis for developing the 'American system' on an American scale! His speech at Llandudno, which placed as much emphasis on imperial protectionism as on reflation, was well received, and failed to obtain the conference's approval only because party loyalty kept delegates from thus censuring the executive. This was made plain when Mosley was re-elected to the executive and Thomas was voted off.[168]

This was only one example of the unprecedented volatility of party politics. Baldwin had dropped all idea of a referendum, but Beaverbrook roughly rejected his plea to be allowed the unchallenged leadership of Conservative opinion.[169] As Beaverbrook reminded him, opinion had moved a long way since the Hotel Cecil speech in March and now required open advocacy of food taxes.[170] Baldwin called a special meeting at Caxton Hall on 25 October and found his parliamentary position safe enough. Rank and file opinion was another matter. Public opinion was demonstrated the same day in the results of the Paddington by-election when the Beaverbrook candidate defeated the Conservative.[171]

The Liberal Party was in even greater disarray. Badly divided before the general election, the party was now shackled to a government that failed to take any resolute action to deal with the slump, and to Lloyd George and his grandiose unemployment policy. By the autumn of 1930 the party was split three ways. One group, led by Sir John Simon and including practically all members who sat for rural constituencies, was moving rapidly towards alliance with the Conservatives. Another, led by Sir Herbert Samuel, hewed closely to the old formula of free trade, retrenchment, and reform. As for Lloyd George, he professed continued faith in free trade, a bold programme of public works, and readiness to prop up Labour while pushing it to a more progressive policy, but it was always hard to be sure of his real intentions.[172]

Divisions within the Labour Party were now also evident. The ILP moved steadily towards outright opposition to the government over its failure to deal with unemployment. An ILP amendment to the King's speech on 28 October, criticising the government for its refusal to implement a socialist policy, received the support of 13 members, a small fraction of the more than 200 Labour MPs, but enough to alarm a minority government, particularly since the ILP was traditionally the custodian of the party's socialist conscience.[173] Another potential breakaway group was coalescing around Mosley. Soon after the Labour Party conference rumours circulated that Mosley had approached Henderson to lead a revolt against MacDonald.[174] In December, Mosley with sixteen other Labour MPs issued a manifesto declaring their faith in his Empire-wide design.[175] So far there was no open break, but it was obvious that patience with MacDonald was wearing dangerously thin.

Conflicting demands of party loyalty and the economic slump were the source of tension in all three political parties. On the Conservative side, Beaverbrook with Rothermere's support embarrassed Baldwin and threatened to drive a permanent wedge between the leadership of the party and its followers. During the autumn Beaverbrook was seen in the company of Mosley and Lloyd George as well as Sir William Morris and spokesmen for the die-hard right.[176] But in spite of their hostility to the present leaders, neither Beaverbrook nor his right-wing supporters ever gave up hope of rejoining a suitably reformed Tory Party. The only exceptions were perhaps the industrialists surrounding Morris, men like Sir Ernest Petter, whose disgust with the Conservative leaders was such that they no longer trusted in Tory support. Others, encouraged by the trend of recent by-elections, each favouring the most extreme exponent of protectionism, anticipated changes within the party.

More problematical were the individuals who were disillusioned with the internationalism of the Labour and Liberal Parties but not persuaded by the larger claims of imperial protectionism. The two-party talks in the summer had produced nothing concrete but ended any approach through large-scale public works projects, 'relief work,' as MacDonald insisted on calling it. The revenue tariff scheme that Garvin reported does not seem to have been mentioned. On the other hand a committee of economists, created at Keynes's suggestion in the EAC, agreed by four to one on the need for some kind of protection, with three of the four – H.D. Henderson, Stamp, and Keynes – favouring a 10 per cent revenue tariff.[177] MacDonald circulated their report to Cabinet on 24 October.[178]

By now the urgent need for some kind of action was being constantly borne in on the government. Sir Arthur Balfour, the steel-maker, wrote to MacDonald in early October, warning him that the country was 'on the verge of a debacle', and calling for 'some form of Coalition Government' and a 10–20 per cent tariff on all manufactured imports 'as a matter of revenue and necessity'.[179] A few days later the King sent a message to his Ministers, advising them to heed Balfour's warning.[180] MacDonald attended a private dinner arranged by the Liberal peer and friend of the King, Lord Mottistone, and including Lloyd George, Churchill, Reading, and Horne, to discuss the possibility of a national government. No record of the conversations was kept, but this much is clear: all those present were dissatisfied with the existing party system and hankered after a new right-wing social democratic coalition. Almost certainly they would have agreed on retrenchment and a revenue tariff as the basis of policy.[181] A few weeks earlier Churchill had boldly declared for precisely this programme.[182] And it was probably what lay behind Lloyd George's remark a few days later in Parliament that both free trade and protectionism were beside the mark.[183]

Through the autumn and winter MacDonald referred to this formula again and again. In spirit he had already abandoned the Labour Party, blaming it for indecision, incompetence, and failing him in the great task of governing the country. He talked freely of his readiness to help form a national government,[184] and betrayed an increasing unwillingness to fight for policies within the Cabinet: if it would not do the sensible thing and 'both economise and put on duties', he was not responsible for the consequences.[185] In fact, one Minister after another raised the possibility of turning away from internationalism: Lansbury, Hartshorn, Attlee, even Graham.[186] But there was no leader to mobilise them. With unemployment rising above 2.5 million and a serious budget deficit in prospect, there was only drift.

After yet another discussion about unemployment early in the new year, Cabinet Ministers consoled themselves that, 'The present crisis was probably due to the faulty system under which the whole world was working, and no Government could be expected to bring any marked alleviation within twelve or eighteen months'. It is a measure of their demoralisation that the last item on the agenda that day was 'the large unsatisfied demand in domestic service ... the Minister of Labour stated that the number of persons available for this form of employment was being increased every week'.[187]

9

The gold standard undermined

For most of the second Labour government's period in office, June 1929 to August 1931, controversy over the gold standard remained in the background. One reason was that the explosion of interest in the fiscal question dominated the political world to a degree unequalled since 1906. Another was Snowden's announcement of a full-scale inquiry into banking and finance as they related to industry. The problem was not thereby removed, however. Violent capital and gold movements continued to disrupt the exchanges, and deflationary pressure on the domestic economy became more acute than ever. Much of the resulting frustration went into demands for trade protection. But it also sustained – despite the enduring myth to the contrary – a seething dissatisfaction with the gold standard within the industrial community, and even among mercantile elements of the City, which threatened to erupt into uncontrollable opposition. It was not surprising that the years of the slump were also marked by intense activity within the financial community to allay public criticism of the gold standard, and to ease the deflationary strain on the domestic economy through reform of the international monetary system.

The Macmillan committee

Critics of the gold standard appreciated only too well that the findings of a committee of inquiry would have little to do with objective truth and a great deal to do with the composition of the committee. The Cunliffe Committee, which had recommended the return to gold, had been composed almost entirely of City bankers. Subsequent petitions for a new inquiry made a point of stressing the need for proper representation of industrial capital and labour. When Snowden, in a gesture of appeasement to critics of the gold standard, announced at the annual Labour Party conference in October 1929 a committee 'to investigate all aspects of banking, financial and credit policy',[1] the FBI and other producer groups at once requested representation. Snowden brushed them aside.[2]

Of the fourteen members of the committee, seven represented financial or mercantile interests: the bankers Lord Bradbury, Robert Brand, Reginald McKenna, Cecil Lubbock, and A.A.G. Tulloch; the City-based company director, J. Frater Taylor, and the Sunderland coal merchant, Sir Walter Raine. Two were economists: Maynard Keynes, a progressive, and Theodore Gregory, staunchly conservative. Industry was represented by only one member, Lennox Lee of the Manchester-based Calico Printers' Association, and labour by one, Ernest Bevin. The remaining members were Walton Newbold, a journalist and briefly, years before, a Communist MP, Sir Thomas Allen, the leading figure in the Cooperative movement, and the chairman of the committee, H.P. Macmillan, former Scottish Lord Advocate and (non-political) Advocate-General in the first Labour government.

'Is Walter Newbold's appointment a joke?'[3] The *New Leader*'s rhetorical question summed up Newbold's standing among socialist intellectuals. Although no longer a Communist, he still fancied himself a theorist of the left. He wrote in reference to Brand, 'We represent respectively those twin-born foes, the international issue houses and the Marxian Socialists'.[4] Yet his 'Marxian Socialism' placed him wholly on the side of the international issue houses, in opposition to the reactionary nationalism of the trade union and employers' representatives. This, and the fact that he was a 'passionate MacDonaldite', may explain why he was preferred to more able men as the token left-winger on the committee.[5]

The surprise of the committee was Bevin, who displayed a deeper insight into the problem than any of the others. It seems that, after the poor performance of the first Labour government and the failure of the general strike, his visit with the official mission to the industrial United States had produced a quantum leap in his thinking. The experience was in the nature of a revelation, leaving him convinced of the boundless potential of a managed capitalist system on the mass production–mass consumption model. His clear-headed interventions during the committee proceedings went far to make up for the inadequate industrial representation. But it was a constant struggle, not least because of the open hostility of the chairman.

Macmillan was no economic expert, but he knew the function the committee was supposed to serve. As he explained,

> It is obviously undesirable that anything that this Committee does should disturb the *status quo* ... we do not want to reopen any topics which may be con-

sidered for the moment closed. One of the things we all want to do is to maintain the stability and confidence of the financial world ... I think what we say in our Report about the gold standard might be very brief indeed.[6]

This, of course, suited the bankers only too well. In Bradbury's words, 'If we do that, I think we have got rid of the most troublesome basic part of our Inquiry'.[7]

That still left a number of important issues, but on every one Macmillan left no doubt where his sympathies lay. The Bank of England, he noted, had recently come in for a good deal of harsh criticism. Some had even suggested 'that the Bank ought almost to be a representative body upon which all sorts of interests shall be represented, and so on. Well, I do not think we are likely to recommend that.'[8]

When Keynes took the lead in private, informal sessions on the options available, Bevin made his radical outlook known. Keynes had raised the possibility of going off the gold standard only to dismiss it as being too dangerous, at least until every other remedy had been tried. Bevin objected. He was sure the return to gold had been fine for the City and an unmitigated disaster for the rest of the country. This being so, he found it wholly unacceptable that the committee should deliberately refuse to 'go to the root of the trouble'.[9]

From this point Keynes began to get impatient with Bevin. It was true that prices had fallen considerably since the return to gold in 1925, but the decision had been taken, and he could not believe any responsible person would seriously advocate breaking faith with creditors by going back on it: 'the consequences of that might be too appalling to contemplate'. The cost of devaluing, according to Keynes, would be prohibitive, not only because of the loss on foreign investments – 10 per cent of £2,500 million or £250 million – and the moral obligation to compensate all *bona fide* holders of short-term funds in London – amounting to another £50 million – but more important, because of the great and enduring damage to Britain's credit. At all events, 'the powers that be were simply not prepared to listen to such advice'.[10]

Keynes's ascendancy over the other members of the committee was apparent from the outset because of his command of the subject and his ability to translate technical issues into simple terms. If he sometimes caused a frisson by the frank way he discussed the social implications of the alternatives, his point of view was easily acceptable to most of the members. One option he advanced was an agreed reduction of incomes through a sort of 'National Treaty' organised by the government, and including rents and profits as well as wages. Bevin, immediately appreciating the immense practical difficulties, asked if this would not produce at least as much disturbance as devaluation. Keynes shrugged it off with the comment that it all depended upon the spirit in which it was carried out.[11]

Another of his suggestions was trade protection, to improve the balance of payments and at the same time reduce real wages, restore profits in the sheltered industries, and increase the investment and employment opportunities within the domestic economy. Gregory was sceptical of the argument for abandoning free trade, but Raine and McKenna concurred and Brand was coming round to the same view. Bevin, also a free trader, accepted the case for temporary protection for iron and steel in return for an industrial commitment to rationalisation.[12] Keynes's third recommendation was to end free trade in capital by discriminating in favour of domestic investment. This was greeted by silence from the bankers. A fourth remedy, the promotion of international monetary reform, to reverse the trend of falling prices, evoked a readier response.

What was needed, Keynes explained, was a coordinated reduction of discount rates to make borrowing and investment more attractive, and an agreement on a simultaneous reduction of central bank reserve requirements so that a larger credit structure could be built on the existing reserve base. Beyond that he looked for general endorsement of the gold exchange standard, concerted encouragement of investment and capital development, and eventually the pooling of gold reserves at the BIS. While it was desirable to involve as many countries as possible, only two were really necessary, the United States and France. The deflationary price spiral was now affecting them almost as seriously as Britain, and making them more 'internationally minded'.[13]

Keynes's reasoning was sound enough. His error was in the wild optimism of his time scale: American authorities did not come around to accept monetary reflation for another two years, the French for six. Hopeful talk of an international solution to the slump was just what the committee wished to hear, however. It avoided radical alternatives, and left responsibility for the monetary and financial system in the hands of the bankers themselves.

The Agricultural and Industrial Union, promoted by Taylor Peddie and drawing support from a number of domestic producers' organisations, submitted a brief in January 1930 which called for 'a national paper currency'.[14] The Manchester Association of Importers and Exporters recommended the return to a floating exchange.[15] Arthur Kitson, speaking for his own small Birmingham-based Economic Freedom League, urged the immediate suspension of the gold standard.[16] J.R. Bellerby, formerly of the ILO and about to take the chair of economics at Liverpool University, gave similar advice.[17] The ILP condemned 'the policy of monetary deflation', which for nine years had 'put the prestige of the City in international finance before the needs of industry and of employment'. The most pressing need was an expansion of domestic purchasing power, best realised through active monetary reflation, with the cooperation of central banks in the creditor countries, 'but if it demanded the stabilisation of the exchange value of sterling at a figure somewhat lower than the present level, then this necessity should be faced'.[18]

These were by definition the 'currency cranks'. When they came before the committee in person they met with cold scepticism. If they provided written briefs, these were never mentioned in later private sessions. Another obstacle tended to distort the picture. Spokesmen for the financial community by and large appeared in a private capacity, whereas spokesmen for industry appeared on behalf of representative bodies, whose opinion tended towards the lowest common denominator. Industrial spokesmen did not want to go beyond their briefs and the committee did not want to pursue any radical line, so the result was to understate the degree of opposition that existed to the gold standard.

For the FBI, Sir Roland Nugent, and the FBI's chief economist, Roy Glenday, drafted a submission which underlined the impact on industry of the gold standard, and advocated the promotion of international monetary reform, with a clear warning to other major creditor countries that in the absence of world reflation, Britain would soon be forced to abandon internationalism in favour of a nationalist–imperialist policy. The majority of Grand Council members had no difficulty accepting this in principle, but were reluctant to offer any specific recommendation on banking or monetary reform.[19]

Sir Peter Rylands recalled how, as President of the FBI, he had been 'pilloried' by the financial pundits for warning against a premature return to gold. While only too pleased to say 'I told you so', he refused to believe they could now turn back. He was devoting all his energies to the protectionist campaign of the FBI's rival, the NUM.[20] Sir Edgar Sanders, a company director with African and shipping interests, took strong objection on free trade grounds.[21] Lord Lithgow, the Clydebank shipbuilder and FBI President-elect, objected as an internationalist. Naively he saw the Macmillan Committee not as a means of protecting the gold standard from radical attack, but as a stick with which the Labour government intended to beat the bankers and divert public attention from the need for further wage cuts and retrenchment. He believed the draft submission played into the government's hands by supporting the claim that monetary policy had been the main cause of postwar industrial difficulties.[22] There was also a serious practical problem: all of the industrialists were dependent on bank borrowing. Not one of them was prepared to appear before the committee to be questioned about his own experience, for fear of queering relations with his banker.[23]

The most Nugent and Glenday could do when they met the committee on 15 March 1930 was to present the first part of the report as official, the second as their personal view. 'You have had industry under a terrible strain just about as long as it can stand. I have never known people so depressed', Nugent told them.[24] While the most attractive solution was an international conference to overcome the maldistribution of gold stocks, which was starving the world of liquidity, he hoped that unilateral, national action would not be ruled out. He suggested tied foreign lending, or a discriminatory tax favouring domestic over foreign investment, or a tariff.

> Suppose you could really convince the authorities of the Bank of France and the Federal Reserve Board and the other important monetary authorities of the world that the alternative was a definite national policy in this country, with all that that implied, you might persuade them that they had better have the devil they know than the devil they do not know.[25]

After strong pressure from some of the most active members, including Bremner of the Engineers' Association and Forrest Hewit of the Calico Printers' Association, a wider survey of opinion within the Federation was carried out.[26] The results were available when Nugent and Lithgow appeared again before the committee. Nugent submitted that the foreign scramble for gold caused industry's severe shortage of credit. Lithgow contradicted him: industrial difficulties had nothing to do with finance or monetary policy but with the failure of British industry to compete with the United States and the rest of the world. The solution lay in severe cost cutting, rationalisation, tax reductions, and so on. Nugent had the last word, however. According to the FBI's survey, industrialists generally favoured a 'national credit policy'.[27]

The General Council of the TUC shared the FBI's dissatisfaction with the operation of the gold standard, but, without Bevin, none of the others felt competent to confront the experts. Their first submission offered little more than a survey of postwar economic conditions.[28] Only after the annual conference in September was a second, more pointed, submission prepared. The TUC objected to unrestricted foreign lending when domestic industry required capital investment. Even more, it objected to any attempt to adjust to falling prices by forcing down wages. The only result would be industrial strife and further social injustice, by throwing the whole burden of adjustment on one section of the community. Experience in the cotton and coal industries had shown that foreign competitors would respond by further cuts, thus diminishing total purchasing power and accelerating the downward price spiral.

> We say quite definitely that there is no solution along this line, but only a grave worsening of the present situation. Against such a policy we would throw the whole of our resources and power, believing that a lowering of the standard of living of the workers would be a grave disservice to British industry and a disaster of the first magnitude for the whole of our people.[29]

The only solution was reflation on a world scale. The government should give full backing to the League Gold Delegation, but second-best solutions might be necessary: a general tariff, or devaluation.

The only expression of agricultural opinion the committee heard came from the Central Landowners' Association. It is difficult to know if their cautious comments were any more typical of the farm community than the outspoken ones Sir Josiah Stamp encountered when he spoke at the Farmers' Club in February 1931. The Landowners blamed rural depression on the gold standard system, but fatalistically accepted that nothing could be done without international agreement.[30] Stamp prefaced his remarks by saying that farmers would be surprised to hear that gold had anything to do with their difficulties. Politely but firmly he was told that farmers would not be surprised at all. And to his embarrassment, several participants in the ensuing discussion held that, on his own interpretation of events, the obvious solution was devaluation or outright suspension of the gold standard.[31]

The Association of Chambers of Commerce continued the pretence of speaking for manufacturing industry in its submission to the committee. The association denied charges that credit was unavailable 'for any reasonably profitable business', looked to the restoration of profitability through further reductions in domestic wage costs and taxation, and in other respects held to a narrowly orthodox line.[32] Two authentic voices of industry offered very different testimony, however.

E.L. Peyton, deputy chairman of the Austin Motor Company and spokesman for the Birmingham-based NUM, was an enthusiast for Kitson's radical monetary theories. None of the anti-semitic, conspiratorial element emerged during his interview with the committee, but the radicalism did.

> We naturally very much object to the gold standard, which forces the banks to vary their lending rate. You borrow money at 5 per cent., and because America may come and borrow a few million pounds up goes the Bank Rate, down come our securities, and our credit is restricted by the bank, and we find ourselves having to dispense with employees when otherwise we would have carried on.[33]

Like most witnesses, Peyton gave an approving nod to international monetary reform, but his main concern was different: 'the prosperity of this country is absolutely wrapped up with the purchasing power of the people. If you have one and a half million on the dole, how can they buy anything?' To stimulate industry he advocated protection, and to ensure adequate credit he looked for a separation of 'the domestic currency and banking from foreign banking'.

Taylor Peddie in June presented the views of the Master Cotton Spinners' Associations. He too condemned the operation of the gold standard and advocated insulation of the domestic economy from international banking business. What was needed was 'a differential discount rate' to favour domestic borrowers, 'an exclusive national policy for Great Britain.... In other words, the external movements of gold should cease to affect the internal level of prices.' Macmillan cautioned Peddie to bear in mind that the committee had to make recommendations acceptable to the government and with due regard to the stability of the money markets. Peddie, the Milnerite, appealed to Macmillan to recognise 'the very much greater danger that if no change is recommended the breakdown will be extremely serious'. Britain's financial stability rested on trade, but the failure of the monetary system to provide adequate purchasing power was creating conditions for revolution in China, Russia, Mexico, and now too in Europe. Even for Britain, 'the only thing that could avert disaster would be the adoption of a more elastic currency system'.[34]

As Peddie's testimony on behalf of the cotton masters indicated, Lancashire businessmen were now thoroughly infected with monetary radicalism. Henry Clay, professor of economics at Manchester University and shortly to take up a post at the Bank of England, had been jolted a few months earlier when speaking at a meeting of the Manchester Chamber of Commerce to which members of the Joint Committee of Cotton Trades Organisations had been invited. His subject was the return to the gold standard, which he summed up as necessary and beneficial to industry as a whole, though perhaps requiring unforeseen adjustments for the export industries. Not one of the participants in the ensuing discussion supported his view. One called for the outright abandonment of the gold standard. Another, a prominent Burnley employer and chairman of the Joint Committee, advocated devaluation. Clay, caught off guard, retreated from economic to political argument. He refused to admit the 1925 decision had been wrong, but added that even if it was it could not be reversed, since 'the position of London would be immediately affected as a money market'. As for devaluation, 'One had to balance the losses of other interests against the gains of industry'. But as the final speaker summed up, it was surely unacceptable that the country as a whole and industry in particular should be sacrificed for the financiers of the City.[35] Afterwards the chamber undertook its own inquiry, and on 15 September petitioned the Prime Minister for urgent action to end the deflationary spiral caused by the malfunctioning of the gold standard, calling on the government to take as its 'guiding principle, that the well-being of British Industry is of more vital importance to the people of this country than any financial consideration'.[36]

The Gold Delegation's first interim report

Such strong dissatisfaction intensified differences within the City. Governor Norman represented one faction whose chief concern was to avoid anything that might damage confidence in the pound or raise false hopes that Britain could maintain exchange equilibrium without harsh deflationary action. Called before the Macmillan Committee in March 1930, he was an unwilling witness.[37] He referred to the unfortunate consequences of the Belgian and French decision to stabilise their currencies at exceptionally favourable parities after sterling had been restored to its pre-war parity, and to the continuing scramble for gold. But despite persistent questioning by Bevin, he refused to acknowledge any link between the return to gold and subsequent unemployment: a rise in Bank rate had little effect outside the money market, and if it had, the impact was 'relatively small compared with the advantages to the external position'.[38] As Keynes pointed out, this was sharply at variance with the role of the Bank rate as described by the Cunliffe Committee. It also contrasted with the tenor of Norman's earlier complaints to Moreau of the Bank of France. But it fitted with international bankers' claims that British industrial difficulties were to be explained by the over-lavish provision of unemployment benefits and excessive trade union power. As Walter Stewart, an American adviser to the Bank of England, told the committee, 'It is very easy in circumstances of this kind, I think, to find the fault lying abroad. My own conviction is that the state of British industry has imposed a heavy strain upon British finance.'[39]

The other faction wanted to emphasise the causal link between the economic slump, falling prices, and the malfunctioning of the international monetary system, hoping that American and French authorities would be either converted or embarrassed into joining Britain in price-level stabilisation. This was the unspoken aim of the forty-five bankers, City editors, economists, and civil servants who made up the Chatham House study group which met between December 1929 and February 1931.[40] Sir Josiah Stamp was one of the more active members of the group, speaking and writing on the gold problem.[41] Sir Henry Strakosch, as little known to the general public as ever, continued to play an influential role behind the scenes. He appeared before the Macmillan Committee in May 1930, and in July *The Economist* printed his written submission as a special supplement.[42]

This was well timed. After the Wall Street crash the previous autumn, pressure on sterling had abated, enabling the Bank of England to rebuild gold reserves from £131.7 million to £163.6 million, well above the Cunliffe minimum, and to reduce Bank rate from 6½ per cent to 3 per cent by 1 May 1930.[43] Hardly had cheap money returned, however, than the Bank began once more to lose gold to France. The initial cause was demand for the heavily oversubscribed offering of French shares in the BIS, the very institution intended to reduce such disturbances.[44] The closing of subscriptions on May 16 brought only temporary relief; between May and August the Bank of France gained over £20 million in gold, most of it from London. France had thus gained £65 million within a twelve-month period, over £200 million since *de facto* stabilisation in 1926, and the inflow showed no sign of diminishing.[45] Strakosch's warning thus seemed only too apt.

At the first session of the Gold Delegation in August 1929, with the support of Sir Reginald Mant of South Africa and Professor Gustav Cassel of Sweden, Strakosch had tried to proceed at once with proposals for stabilising gold price levels. The Dutch, French, Italian, and American members flatly refused; their instructions were merely to examine and report on 'the causes of fluctuations in the purchasing power of gold and their effect on the economic life of the nations'.[46] None of them saw any good coming of the inquiry, and only with strong support from Salter did Strakosch secure their agreement to meet again in June 1930.[47]

During the second session Strakosch faced the hostility of Professor Oliver Sprague, the American representative, soon to become Montagu Norman's chief expert adviser, as well as that of several continental members.[48] In the end he managed to get approval of an interim report, limited to the question of prospective supply and demand for gold but embodying the core of his argument. It affirmed that a shortfall in gold supplies could be expected soon to aggravate the slump by forcing credit restriction and further depressing commodity prices. It also referred to the enormous accumulation of gold stocks by the United States and France – £111 million between them during 1929 alone – and suggested this was neither necessary nor desirable. Finally it offered some remedies, including the elimination of all domestic circulation of gold coins, concentration of metallic resources at central banks, reduction of legal reserve minima by treaty, and adoption of the gold exchange standard by countries yet to stabilise their currencies on a gold basis.[49]

Drafting the report was one thing; persuading central bankers in Paris and New York to accept it was another matter. They were clearly annoyed at the criticism of their gold holdings, and opposed publication of the report. Strakosch's effort to embarrass them they put down as merely another attempt to relieve Britain of the necessity to bring her prices into line with foreign competition.[50] Moreover, all signs pointed to rejection by the Bank of England.

The City editors who could be trusted to reflect the Governor's viewpoint, had given Strakosch's memorandum in *The Economist* a cold reception. Strakosch, unaware of the extent of Norman's hostility to his efforts, called at the Bank to urge him to abandon 'neutrality' on the gold question and use his influence in the BIS to see that the Gold Delegation report received careful consideration. Norman, just back from South Africa, said he had not read it, but even if he agreed with it, he could not take an independent position but must 'merge his views' with those of the BIS's board. Strakosch found this extraordinary. So far from merging their views with the board's, the French and American members had insisted that it virtually boycott the Gold Delegation.[51] Strakosch's arguments, however, had no effect: Niemeyer, who now shared his view of the seriousness of the problem, was in Australia; and Norman continued his posture of neutrality.[52]

Manchester and the gold standard

If Norman had had his way, nothing more would have been heard of the gold problem. But in face of the outflow to Paris – the 'golden river' as one newspaper put it[53] – as well as falling price levels and the growing threat of dear money, demands for action persisted. The result was to intensify the confrontation between those who agreed with Strakosch, and those who, whether they agreed or not, were not prepared to lend encouragement to monetary radicalism. Publicly, in the press and after dinner speeches, and privately, behind the closed doors of the Macmillan Committee, the Prime Minister's EAC, and the Cabinet, the struggle continued. Most officials and Ministers lined up on the side of authority to ward off pressure on the Bank of England and to silence debate. But no sooner was one challenge met than another arose.

At the Treasury an international initiative to relieve sterling was first mooted in May 1930, when Leith Ross as secretary to the Macmillan Committee received a copy of Strakosch's memorandum. He called it

> a very lucid summary of the view that the recent fall in international prices is primarily caused by the hoarding of gold, i.e., by withdrawing gold from the countries which use it as the basis of credit expansion. While I would not agree

that the recent drop in prices is solely due to this cause, it is very hard to resist the conclusion that this is one of the primary factors of the position.[54]

There were two common explanations of the flow of gold from London to Paris. One, from observers as different in outlook as George Glascow of *The Observer*, Paul Einzig of *The Banker* and the *Financial News*, and Francis Williams of the *Daily Herald*, was that the French deliberately encouraged it in order to enfeeble Britain and enable France to dominate Europe.[55] The other, favoured by most other commentators, was that it resulted from a primitively organised and poorly managed Paris financial market. Those who held the latter view believed that France had returned to gold at a rate that seriously undervalued the franc. This stimulated the demand for francs, which the Bank of France was unable to meet because of legal constraints on its open market operations, and which the commercial banks met by the cruder method of importing gold for conversion into francs. The absence of a developed cheque clearing system aggravated the problem. So did French reluctance to apply their surpluses to foreign lending, and the build-up of idle balances. Since the 'Poincaré miracle', successive governments had maintained annual budget surpluses. These, plus tax revenue accumulated between autumn and spring, plus sums allocated to the sinking fund agency, had reached 5 billion francs (£40 million) by the spring of 1930 and were rapidly rising. By leaving it on deposit at the Bank of France the effect was to 'sterilise' some £15 million in gold reserves, which had a deflationary impact on France and the rest of the world.[56]

Leith Ross was convinced that the gold movements were not due to deliberate policy, and even caused embarrassment in Paris. British press criticism nonetheless seemed to him no bad thing if it helped the Bank of England to persuade French authorities to undertake reforms. At MacDonald's suggestion, he submitted a memorandum, based on Strakosch's case against American and French hoarding, to the Bank for consideration. To his surprise he found that the Bank 'dissent strongly from the diagnosis at the beginning, and accordingly disagree with many of the objectives suggested as likely to remedy the situation'.[57] The Bank ascribed Britain's troubles to her failure to bring down costs in line with world prices, and held that this and only this would restore the position. Leith Ross was not persuaded, but he accepted the Bank's authority over monetary policy and fell in with its view. Replying to MacDonald, he reversed his earlier claim that economists agreed on the central importance of monetary causes of the slump, asserted brazenly that 'the Cambridge group of economists' who did so were chronically inconsistent and prone to offer extreme remedies, such as abandoning the gold standard, and discouraged any hope of progress in international monetary cooperation.[58] During the next few months he supported the Chancellor and Governor in their holding action against the insurgents.

In April 1930 Keynes had attempted to broaden the scope of the EAC to include the question of monetary reform and the diversion of loanable capital into home market investment, until Snowden intervened. As jealous of his control of financial policy as he was hostile to Keynes's experimentalism, Snowden flatly opposed such a step on the grounds that it would constitute a challenge to the Macmillan Committee.[59] At the seventh EAC meeting on 24 July, he claimed that businessmen were attaching less importance than before to monetary considerations as an explanation of the slump, and cited the latest bulletin of the National City Bank of New York. But as Keynes and Stamp must have been aware, the editor of the bulletin, Dr Benjamin Anderson, so far from being a typical businessman was a notoriously conservative economist and one of the most strenuous defenders of the 'automatic' gold standard.[60]

A petition from the Manchester Chamber of Commerce in September, calling for action on monetary reform, prompted Leith Ross to prepare two draft replies. One offered non-monetary explanations for the prolonged depression in the export industries, adding that the government could do no more to improve the operation of the gold standard until it heard from the Gold Delegation and the Macmillan Committee. The other merely referred to inquiries in progress. Snowden chose the simpler one, claiming that the petition deserved no more. 'It has failed to attract any real public interest and it would be a pity to revive it. It would be fatal if Lancashire were led to suppose that a change in monetary policy offered them a cure for their troubles.'[61]

Snowden, never one to allow reality to interfere with his convictions, was contradicted by the widespread comment the petition attracted in the national press and the almost constant stream of criticism of gold that issued from Lancashire. A few weeks later Lord Marley, a Junior Minister at the War Office, circulated a memorandum quoting Strakosch, Stamp, and the Lancashire petition, and pressing for national as well as international action on the monetary front.[62] MacDonald, prompted by an outraged Snowden, showed that he too could adjust the truth to suit himself. Upbraiding Marley for encroaching upon Snowden's turf, he stated that the Macmillan Committee was doing all that could humanly be done to expedite matters. 'This subject has been frequently mentioned in the Cabinet.... If you had known all the facts, you would not have worded your reference to that Commission (sic) in the way you have done.' Marley, as MacDonald appreciated, could not know all the facts. If he had, he would have known that neither the

Macmillan Committee nor monetary policy itself had ever once figured on the Cabinet agenda.[63]

In the committee, Macmillan himself found all the talk of falling prices incomprehensible. If the cost of living declined, was this not a good thing? And if it was a problem, was the solution not simply to reduce wages and taxes by cutting down those lavish welfare payments which made for 'rigidities' in the British cost structure? Committee members obliged him to accept that the impact of the fall in prices should be central to their report. But Bevin was still alone in arguing that there was any practical alternative to domestic price deflation or coordinated central bank action.[64]

The outlook was not propitious. On 7 November Keynes, summarising the findings of the EAC's Economists' Committee, predicted an indefinite slump in prices and warned against hoping for international reflationary action. The continental press generally treated the Gold Delegation Report as 'the result of British intrigue aimed at hiding the weakness of the gold position of this country'. Keynes's one hope now was that another really bad winter would force American bankers to recognise the need for coordinated reflation; together Britain and the United States were powerful enough to do what they liked. Bevin and G.D.H. Cole, hitherto an opponent of tampering with the gold standard, suggested that devaluation might become necessary, but Snowden would not hear of it. He was equally opposed to any form of international initiative: 'Even the publication of the Report of the Gold Delegation had ... done incalculable harm in the United States and France, where it was regarded as a conspiracy by this country'.[65]

Later that day in the Macmillan Committee Bevin continued to tangle with Keynes over relying solely on an international solution to price deflation. Keynes was prepared to consider any interim means of maintaining payments equilibrium – tariff, quotas, a national treaty on wages, profits, and rents, foreign lending restrictions – anything but suspending the gold standard, which was too drastic to contemplate. Bevin found this perverse: 'In all our discussions we seem quite willing to face an industrial upheaval or a decrease of wages; but we are simply terror-stricken at touching the rentier, or the value of the pound'. Round and round they went. Keynes stressed the importance of Britain's mercantile–financial activity. Bevin objected to singling out wages for attack and urged removal of 'the monetary straitjacket' in order to expand purchasing power. Briefly a chink in the wall of opposition appeared when Lord Bradbury, standing in as chairman, said that, faced with the choice of a tariff or devaluation, he would choose devaluation.[66] This was not surprising since the Liverpool-based Williams

Deacons Bank, of which he was a director, was overloaded with bad debts to local industry and was in very serious trouble.[67] At later meetings Bevin proposed the same solution, but Macmillan cut him short with heavy sarcasm.[68]

Anglo-French financial conversations

The previous April Keynes had warned the EAC that, given the improbability of an export-led recovery, there were only two alternatives. One was import substitution through protection, the other was 'productive and useful home capital development'. There was nothing else except a 'policy of inactivity in the hope of some favourable development turning up in the outside world'.[69] This was perhaps true, though he himself had actively discouraged devaluation or abandonment of the gold standard. But the government turned its back on the two alternatives, and since monetary relations remained in the hands of Governor Norman, any British initiative for international monetary reform was practically ruled out. This could be inferred from the pronouncements of Norman's mouthpiece, Courtney Mill of *The Times*, who repeatedly deprecated monetary explanations of the crisis, reported approvingly the views of continental critics of monetary reform, and dismissed the interim Gold Delegation Report as fundamentally misconceived.[70]

Yet surprisingly, something did turn up towards the end of the year. Since 1929 French bankers and statesmen had grown steadily more uncomfortable at the anger aroused in London by the one-way flow of gold to Paris. As they saw it, the movement reflected the normal operation of the gold standard: France's balance of payments was strong, Britain's was weak. Britain was simply trying to have her cake and eat it too: inflating her cost structure by excessive outlay on the 'dole', yet maintaining pretensions of being the financial capital of the world. From all accounts Britain was dangerously over-lent, so much so French authorities were surprised she had remained on the gold standard until now; meanwhile most of Europe's funk money sought refuge in Paris.[71] French authorities also took British anger as a sign of frustration at the re-emergence of Paris as a rival financial centre. Since the stabilisation of the franc a number of steps had been taken to enhance Paris' international role: in April 1930 plans were approved for the creation of an acceptance bank; the stamp tax on securities was reduced; the tax rate on foreign loan interest was brought into line with the rate on domestic loans; and the Treasury had recently relaxed regulations governing the listing of foreign securities on the Paris Bourse.[72] Plans for Paris aside, French authorities had particular reason for abhorring

British schemes for 'inflation' now. The great improvement in France's financial position brought about through the 'Poincaré miracle' had at last been swallowed up by rising prices at home and collapsing prices elsewhere. The Wall Street crash had brought an immediate downturn in the luxury goods trade and tourism, and the 1930 harvest was a disaster. For the present France seemed an *île heureuse*, free from the economic troubles around her. But the first signs of domestic hoarding were evident, and there was little doubt that the onset of a balance of payments deficit would soon end the present gold inflow.[73]

All the same, they agreed something must be done. Hitler and the Nazi Party had devoted the whole of their election campaign during the summer to the claim that Germany's plight was due to the crushing burden of the Young Plan, and obtained huge gains at the polls. This had led Brüning to reassert his authority by adopting an openly hostile attitude to reparations as well. As a result, French authorities became all the more anxious for Britain's friendship. They hoped for a common stand against any suspension of payments while Germany was able to pay, and for Britain's support in refusing to pay war debts to the United States in the event of a German suspension.[74] Thus two weeks after the German election, Briand warned the French Treasury of the unfortunate political consequences of the gold movement from London to Paris.[75] Treasury officials first tried to justify their financial policy through diplomatic channels.[76] When this brought no result, Premier Tardieu took matters into his own hands by informing *The Times'* Paris correspondent in confidence that he was anxious to find an amicable solution to the gold problem.[77]

Leith Ross, who had discussed the issue with Jacques Rueff, the French Financial Attaché, was under no illusion that British and French points of view could be easily reconciled.[78] For instance, Tardieu suggested a loan to the Bank of England rather than a change in Bank of France policy, a measure which British officials regarded as no solution at all. But an exchange of views was better than nothing. Leith Ross therefore supported the proposal for a meeting of British and French Treasury experts in Paris, taking it for granted that Norman would wish to have parallel conversations with Clement Moret, Moreau's successor at the Bank of France. Again Leith Ross laboured under a misapprehension.

Norman could not say that he would not assist the Treasury in their efforts to promote reform, but after his brutal confrontations with Moreau during the previous five years he had no intention of requesting French assistance or cooperation. In Paris in early December he paid a courtesy call at the rue de la Vrillière to meet the new Governor. Moret, a former Treasury official, was well disposed towards Britain and had already begun to make small purchases of sterling to ease pressure on the franc–sterling exchange. He now proposed several joint initiatives to strengthen the pound, but to his bewilderment he found Norman unwilling to discuss any of them.[79] Norman might agree with British critics that French monetary and financial policy required improvement, but he would not compromise London's prestige by suggesting it. A loan would only make him more beholden to the French, which was out of the question; and he feared that even conversations with French authorities would enable the Labour government to put off the unpleasantness of setting its own house in order. Professor Sprague, now serving as Norman's expert adviser, indicated as much to Leith Ross when he 'emphasised the desirability of not appearing to ask favours from the French and doubted the wisdom of palliatives which might conceal the true position and delay radical remedies'.[80] Leith Ross was left to hope that Norman would follow up any agreement reached between British and French Treasury officials.

In January and February 1931 Leith Ross with his assistant David Waley met three times with Louis Escallier, Directeur du Mouvement des Fonds, the Directeur-Adjoint Jean-Jacques Bizot, and Rueff. At the first meeting the British experts presented the case for French action to reduce the deflationary impact of their financial system by open market operations to ease the shortage of francs in Paris, or if this was not feasible, by putting into circulation the huge idle government balances at the Bank of France, and by efforts to increase foreign lending. The French experts listened patiently, and without conceding anything on the main point at issue, encouraged hopes of a compromise solution.[81] On 2 January, just as the conversations got underway, the Bank of France reduced its discount rate. The move was welcomed in the City, as well it might have been, since Moret had wanted to raise, not lower, the rate in order to warn French businessmen of approaching difficulties.[82] Governor Harrison of the Federal Reserve Bank of New York, however, had pressed Moret to assist London, and Briand, Tyrrell learned, had insisted upon the reduction as a contribution to better Anglo-French relations.[83]

At the second round of talks two weeks later, Escallier stressed the amount of discounting already carried out by the Bank of France, but held out no hope for an active open market policy. He agreed to do what he could to reduce the idle official balances. Foreign lending seemed to him a more intractable problem. French investors had burned their fingers badly when the Bolsheviks repudiated the Tsarist debt, and even if they could be persuaded to lend abroad again, there were practically no sound borrowers. As for short-term lending, the bill market needed time to develop. He suggested investor confidence would be increased if new issues were repayable in a choice of currencies. This was unwelcome to London, however, for fear that such issues might become a conduit for drawing off London balances and thus adding to sterling's weakness.[84]

Soon after this meeting there were further indications of French good will. Early in June 1930 shortages in London had obliged the Bank of England to make payment only in bars of standard (0.916 2/3) fineness, no longer in fine (0.995) gold on which the Bank of France insisted. The result was that bars from London had to be refined before delivery in Paris, reducing the sterling–franc gold export point from about francs 123.89 to 123.45, creating delays, and undermining confidence in sterling. On 16 January 1931 the Bank of France agreed to accept bars of standard fineness.[85] A few days later Bizot arranged the listing of several additional foreign securities – mostly 'kaffirs', or South African gold stocks – on the Paris Bourse.[86] The following week the French representative on the League Gold Delegation withdrew his objection to publication of the delegation's second report, though not to its submission to the BIS.[87]

The report was again an interim one, not the final and definitive study for which Strakosch and Leith Ross had hoped. Nevertheless, despite the cautious language and repeated references to the discipline required of gold standard countries, which reflected French influence, its central argument was unmistakably British. The gold standard was said to be 'not a fixed and rigid mechanism', and did not function automatically. Countries that sought to replace foreign exchange reserves with gold or accumulated more gold than their exchange levels required were criticised, rules were laid down for reducing domestic demand for gold, and central banks were called on to accept lower level reserve requirements. While debtor countries were advised to deflate in order to remain sound borrowers, creditor countries were declared to have a 'correspondingly greater' obligation for the maintenance of the system, by sustaining their foreign lending at a level approximating to 'their net active balance on income account'. All in all the report, while too brief to convince the sceptical and too technical to be widely read, represented a small victory for the British advocates of international monetary reform.[88]

Leith Ross, confronted by Escallier's assertion that legislation to widen the range of securities eligible for discount at the Bank of France was politically impossible, and that a sizeable increase in French foreign lending was simply unfeasible, warned French officials at their second meeting that he would make the reduction of official balances at the Bank of France the test of their sincerity.[89] This was understandable: the balances had risen from 5 billion to 14 billion francs (£114 million) in under a year.[90] In response, Bizot on 2 February confirmed plans for an important discounting operation in British Treasury bills and for paying out 1 billion francs against a maturing bond issue.[91] When Leith Ross expressed disappointment at the modest total, Escallier assured him there were plans for a loan conversion which was likely to absorb most of the remaining balances, and if necessary further action would be taken to absorb them.[92]

But that was as far as they got. Leith Ross in his forthright way told colleagues that if Britain wanted France's cooperation on monetary policy she must be prepared to cooperate with France on the reparations–war debt question, including support for a common front against the United States if Germany carried through its recent threat to halt reparations. Sir Richard Hopkins, mindful of the dangerous exchange and budgetary situation that would arise from a suspension of reparations, agreed, and Vansittart indicated that the Foreign Office might not object. Norman, however, did. Claiming that the German position had 'considerably improved' in recent weeks, thus removing any likelihood of a suspension of payments, he opposed a commitment to the French.[93] His information conflicted sharply with reports from Sir Horace Rumbold, the Ambassador in Berlin, who warned that the economic situation in Germany was extremely bad and was playing into the hands of the Nazis and Communists.[94] Snowden nevertheless endorsed Norman's advice. Leith Ross was left to resume the argument for changes in French monetary and financial policy without being able to offer the one thing the French were anxious to obtain.

All that Leith Ross could do was to keep insisting that France should cease her constant pressure on world gold stocks. As often, he was told that if Britain wanted to safeguard her currency reserves, she need only follow normal practice and raise Bank rate. Vainly he protested,

> To suggest restrictions of credit in Britain as a cure for the present situation was like suggesting decapitation as a cure for the toothache. Our whole object in wishing to avoid the gold movement to France was to obviate the need of restricting credit which must be the consequence of a continued outflow. By restricting credit we would draw gold from other parts of the world. Our own position would be protected, but the economic crisis throughout the world would be accentuated.[95]

Their exchange, though friendly, brought them no closer to agreement. The communiqué issued after their third meeting merely affirmed that the officials would 'keep in touch'.

The *Financial Times* described the City as 'bitterly disappointed' at the lack of concrete results, though other sources indicated less concern.[96] As luck would have it the end of the talks coincided with a temporary upturn in economic conditions. French gold reserves, which had increased every week since May 1930 from a vast 42 billion francs to an even vaster 55.6 billion (£455 million), had abruptly stopped growing two weeks earlier. And for the first time in several years world commodity prices stopped falling and began to rise. Briefly, very briefly, it seemed possible that recovery was on the way.[97]

Devaluation or deflation

The previous November signs of disillusionment with the gold standard had begun to appear even within the City. Lord Bradbury's privately expressed views have already been mentioned. Lord D'Abernon, financier and former Ambassador to Germany, spoke to the Liverpool Chamber of Commerce on 14 November 1930, describing the decline in prices as the basic problem facing the world. A negotiated agreement among the creditor powers, he suggested, was the proper solution, but if it were found that the gold standard needed modification or could not be operated because of obstructive action by certain countries, 'it should not be difficult to devise measures which would bring relief'.[98] Talk of remonetising silver and bimetallism also surfaced in the press.[99] And on 20 November, Lord Herbert Scott asked Norman to meet a delegation from the London Chamber of Commerce to discuss the calamitous slide of world commodity prices.[100] Norman had good reason to insist on strictest secrecy before agreeing, for when they met, Scott, with representatives mainly from the mercantile element within the City, bluntly warned that 'within a measurable space of time, the industrial and commercial community will be ... starting agitation for a revision of our financial policy', and when that time came they would be among the agitators.[101] Norman remained unresponsive. At further meetings Norman indicated his willingness to consider a modest scheme of trade protection, but could not contemplate monetary experiments.[102] The merchants might doubt the necessity of the gold standard as a check to government spending, he did not. In turn he warned Snowden that the fate of the gold standard depended upon the government's readiness to face retrenchment.[103]

Snowden responded by warning the Cabinet on 7 January 1931 of the grim prospects for the coming budget and the perilous weakness of the exchange. Confidence in sterling must be quickly restored if foreign holders of the vast short-term balances in London were not to take flight and send sterling into the abyss. With one hand he held out the prospect of 'a reexamination of monetary policy throughout the world', with the other he assured them they must accept retrenchment; they could not hope to persuade other countries to participate in such a re-examination while Britain was unwilling to put her own house in order. As taxation had reached the point of diminishing returns, there was no choice but a drastic cut in spending.[104]

Three weeks later Lord Grey and Walter Runciman called for a national campaign in favour of government retrenchment, and the next day a crowded meeting in the City's Cannon Street Hotel was held with Norman's old friend Edward Grenfell, MP, in the chair and the financiers of the Free Trade Union on hand. 'Friends of Economy' thereupon came into existence.[105] This was followed two days later by a Treasury memorandum to the Royal Commission on Unemployment Insurance, warning that continued public borrowing to cover deficits in the scheme 'would quickly call in question the stability of the British financial system'.[106] On 11 February the House debated a Conservative motion of censure accusing the government of destroying the economy by its excessive spending. The Liberals, not wishing to bring down the government, put forward an amendment proposing a non-partisan 'economy committee' to identify targets for spending cuts, and Snowden responded Janus-like to this offer. First he indicated he would set up the committee as a way of shelving the problem, then warned of the calamity awaiting the country if its finances were not restored to a sound basis, leaving little room for doubt that he was bent on reducing social benefits, including the 'dole'.[107]

The surprise of the debate was Lloyd George, in a speech as shocking to Labour and Conservative front benches as Snowden's had been to his own back benches.[108] He urged the government to set its face against deflation and embark on a large-scale public works programme. Snowden, he charged, was in the pocket of the City, and the City was always reactionary, always out of touch with industry, and 'wrong every time' in its advice to governments. Recalling his own experience as Chancellor before the war, he described how he had been 'received by City magnates with frigid and flopping silence, as if they were a row of penguins in the Arctic Ocean'. They had engineered a flight of capital to scare him off social reform. 'Neither I nor Mr Asquith took any notice of them. We went on with old age pensions and with insurance.' He promised to be the government's strongest supporter if they followed the same path, though he must have known this was almost inconceivable under Labour's present leadership.[109]

Snowden's speech brought the final Mosleyite split. On 20 February

Mosley and five other MPs made up their minds to leave the Labour Party, and a week later announced the formation of the New Party.[110] Meantime the 'Currency group', a small body of Labour MPs formed the previous summer, circulated a memorandum to the PLP calling on the government to consider every alternative before touching social benefits. Greatest hope rested on an international conference convened by Britain to remove the incubus of reparations and war debts from the world trading system. But other solutions were mentioned, including currency devaluation: the gold standard was not 'sacrosanct'.[111] The ILP also published a list of alternatives: war debt revision, heavier taxes on the rentier class, a reduction in sinking fund payments, capital export controls, easier credit for industry, and abandoning the gold standard.[112] The government nevertheless set up the economy committee with Sir George May, a retired City insurance executive, in the chair and four of the six remaining seats filled by businessmen nominated by opposition parties.[113] A call for sharp reductions in public spending could thus be expected. The 're-examination of monetary policy throughout the world' never came.

International schemes for reviving demand

For over a year Keynes, Strakosch, Stamp, Layton, and other advanced defenders of the gold standard had looked for signs that France and the United States would join in a common policy for halting the downward slide of world commodity prices. The French had at last agreed to discuss it, but American cooperation was seen as the more important, and the only indication of American support for international action was regarded by Treasury and Bank officials more as an embarrassment than an opportunity.

Sir William Clark, High Commissioner in Ottawa, reported on 4 February 1931 that Hoover had invited Premier Bennett to inform Britain of his willingness to 'co-operate to the utmost' if Britain would convene a conference on silver. Bennett also promised his cooperation.[114] British officials saw in this initiative merely support for mining interests in the United States and Canada who were suffering like every other group from world depression. According to the producers, the decline in the price of silver had severely reduced the purchasing power of China and other silver standard countries. By raising its price through a combination of restrictions on Indian sales, re-coinage, and possibly a form of bimetallism, the tremendous markets of the east could be restored. British officials with good reason rejected this. Simply to raise the price of silver would be disastrous for the countries that used it for their currency and countries that traded with them, for it would raise their exchange rates, reduce exports, and force them to cut back imports. Leith Ross advised that a conference on silver alone could only embarrass Britain by forcing her to take a position between India, a major holder of silver, and Canada, a major producer.[115] Snowden agreed, and Clark was advised to tell Bennett so.[116]

Reference to the American proposal and British reply in the Cabinet on 4 March evoked some dissatisfaction at the absence of any initiative, but no decision was reached.[117] Later that day MacDonald asked the American Ambassador to inform Secretary of State Henry Stimson that he was 'turning his thoughts to some big international move to try and straighten out the present deplorable economic conditions of the world', and would welcome an exchange of views.[118] There is no sign that he devoted further time to the issue, nor did the American administration show any further interest in a silver conference or any other international action.[119]

Another question raised in February was that of tying foreign loans to British export orders. The Foreign Office took the initiative, as it had three years earlier, because of the contribution loans made to British influence abroad.[120] This time the Treasury did not stand in the way, but took the matter up with the Bank of England.[121] On Addis's advice, Sir Ernest Harvey, the Deputy-Governor, flatly rejected the proposal. Repeating the old free trade in capital argument, he told Leith Ross that tied lending would in the long run destroy London's reputation as an international capital market and would 'deprive the British manufacturer of the valuable stimulus to competition in reducing costs, scrapping obsolescent plant, and in adapting products to the needs of foreign customers'.[122] Urged on by Vansittart and Hopkins, as well as manufacturers, Leith Ross called on Harvey 'to see that the question was seriously examined'.[123] But nothing further was done.

What came to be known as the Kindersley or Norman plan, was meant to revive capital exports from the United States and France, through a lending institution in a neutral market. This would raise up to £50 million capital through bond issues in the creditor countries for relending to foreign governments and firms, and do so on such a scale that investor risk would be spread through a wide portfolio of securities.[124] Unfortunately the French saw this as an attempt to use their money to shore up Germany and British investments in Germany, and the Americans suspected any plan to place their funds under international control. Norman presented the plan at the February meeting of the BIS board. Luther, the Reichsbank President, who not long before had been forced to secure a 119.5 million mark (£6 million) credit from foreign banks, was enthusiastic. Moret was cool.[125] Leith Ross got a similar response when he mentioned the plan during the third round of Anglo-French Treasury talks. Kindersley promoted it in New York, and Norman appealed to Harrison for support. If relief was not given to the countries of central and eastern Europe, he warned, they might well turn in desperation to the Soviet Union, which was now embarked on its first Five-Year Plan.[126] At the March and April meetings of the BIS the plan secured unanimous support in principle. But as French and American funds were not forthcoming this meant nothing, and the plan soon dropped from sight.[127]

Another international lending scheme devised by the Belgian financier Emile Francqui was promoted at the BIS in April.[128] Governor Moret again raised objections to a scheme that involved foreign control over French funds. Embarrassed by the appearance of constant obstruction, however, he persuaded the reluctant regents of the Bank of France to allow him to organise a consortium of the five leading French commercial banks to engage in foreign lending at medium term (six months to five years). The Treasury-controlled Caisse des Dépots et Consignations agreed to discount the consortium's bills up to a total of 500 million francs (£4 million), and the Bank of France agreed to discount the Caisse's notes. Moret hoped for the formation of a similar consortium of the 'big five' clearing banks in London, so each could participate in the other's business.[129] Unfortunately the Austro-German customs union crisis began before the scheme progressed beyond the preliminary stage, and got no further once the financial crisis erupted in Austria.

The twelfth EAC meeting on 12 March 1931 was dominated by Keynes's call for a revenue tariff. Whatever initiative Britain took, he explained, a balanced budget was needed to ensure confidence in the pound and a respectful hearing for the country's views. Hence the need for a tariff. Graham resisted on free trade grounds, MacDonald and Sir Sydney Chapman referred to the difficulties of implementation, and once again the meeting ended without agreement.[130]

At the thirteenth meeting on 16 April, Lord D'Abernon spoke at MacDonald's invitation.[131] The thrust of his remarks was that, as further deflation was socially and politically unacceptable, Britain must appeal to other creditor powers to join in a coordinated policy of reflation. Again the experts disagreed and the Ministers showed no inclination to act. MacDonald noted that unofficial soundings abroad indicated no support for another international conference, and echoed Keynes's warning that foreigners might treat Britain's initiative as a sign of weakness, with inevitable consequences for sterling. Bevin, with Citrine's support, once more called for reconsideration of the gold standard, but

Sir Alfred Lewis, the banker, reacted with 'horror', and Keynes, stressing the damage its abandonment would cause the City, advocated that other 'more plausible and less dangerous expedients' be tried first. After another twenty minutes of inconclusive discussion, MacDonald affirmed that all 'practical suggestions' would be considered by the Cabinet, and closed the meeting. The EAC's thirteenth meeting was also the last during the lifetime of the government.[132]

A few weeks earlier a by-election had been held in St George's, Westminster, known as the safest Tory seat in the country. With the Conservative Party still in disarray, Beaverbrook supported Sir Ernest Petter as the Empire Crusader candidate, and it seemed he might win without a fight. At the last minute the Conservatives put up Duff Cooper. He was young, personable, and eloquent; Petter was none of these things, and he made the mistake of allowing Baldwin's leadership and the Indian question to overshadow unemployment, the one subject with which he was qualified to deal.[133] The result was a victory for Cooper, for Baldwin, and the Party managers. Beaverbrook acknowledged defeat and wound up his Crusade.[134] Thereafter the Conservative Party, on Chamberlain's directions, set the tariff question aside to wage the now massive campaign for retrenchment.[135]

In these circumstances Professor Sprague delivered several strongly worded speeches on the need for a drastic reduction in British price levels. Central bankers saw no alternative; Britain must bring the cost of her manufactures into line with agricultural prices, which meant reducing them 30 per cent or so, he gloomily affirmed. Without the leadership to carry this out 'then there could be nothing in the future for this country but a slow decline – or, if one generalised for the individualistic Western world, a slow decline relative to the possibilities of the competing regime which was being developed in Russia'.[136]

Coming from an official of the Bank of England, especially one with an American accent, Sprague's warning provoked a strong and mostly angry reaction. At H.D. Henderson's urging, MacDonald wrote to Norman for his assurance that Sprague did not speak for the Bank.

> You will readily understand that to the practical politician and to the practical businessman alike this is a policy almost of despair. ... Every reduction in wages and prices involves tension and many of them will only take place after bitter resistance. ... Is it surprising therefore that there is a growing feeling amongst all classes that as the value of money in terms of goods does both change and fluctuate, efforts should be made to reduce the relative value of money rather than that of goods?[137]

Men such as Gustav Cassel, Blackett, Stamp, Hawtrey, T.E. Gregory, D'Abernon, 'and many others', MacDonald continued, rejected Sprague's view that nothing could be done through monetary policy. Even in these difficult times, was there not some means of advancing in this direction? Norman in reply dismissed these authorities as mostly 'orators or debaters with little or no actual experience of Central Banking', and defended Sprague as an outstanding economist who had simply used blunt words to express deeply held convictions.[138] MacDonald apologised for troubling Norman: 'I am constantly being bothered in this matter, and it is a subject which I have never really studied and therefore know nothing about'.[139]

Soon afterwards, Keynes returned from America where he had gone as soon as his duties on the Macmillan Committee were fulfilled. Contrary to Sprague's speeches, he had found central bankers in New York and Washington decidedly progressive on reflationary policy. While not 'as confident and whole-heartedly adherents of the so-called "monetary" school as, for example, I am myself', nonetheless 'they lean very decidedly to that side of the fence'.[140] In confidence he had shown them an advance copy of the Macmillan Report, and on those parts concerning the need for coordination of central bank policy to ensure price-level stability they were entirely sympathetic and ready to cooperate. Unfortunately their views were well in advance of the commercial bankers. Even they were coming to see further liquidation as suicidal, but obviously American support for reflation would take some time to materialise.

By then, however, no time remained. The spreading financial crisis had brought the collapse of the Vienna-based Kreditanstalt, sending shock waves throughout Europe. The reichsmark was threatened with collapse. Sterling temporarily strengthened with the inflow of refugee capital, but the forward rate was already showing ominous weakness.[141] MacDonald thanked Henderson on 29 June for sending the extract from Keynes's report. 'The point', he added despairingly, 'is that whilst something permanent is being devised the house will be down about our ears and everyone agrees that that would be a disaster, the repercussions of which no one could foresee'.[142]

10

The Austro-German customs union crisis

In 1929 the chief issue confronting the Labour government was reparation revision, along with high and rising interest rates. In 1930 it was the drastic fall-off in world trade and upsurge in unemployment. Now in January 1931 it was the budget question that came to the fore. The government was committed to providing for the poor and unemployed, and obliged to maintain confidence in the pound by balancing the budget: objectives that were becoming harder to reconcile in face of the rising social security payments and dwindling revenues caused by the world slump. At this time renewed efforts were made to devise collective solutions for Europe's deepening politico-economic crisis. Britain, however, stayed on the sidelines, her politicians immersed in party conflict, and the public unaware of the role open to her to play in events across the Channel. Within Whitehall such awareness dawned gradually, but differences over political and economic priorities nullified attempts to provide anything but further obstruction.

Britain versus European preference schemes

Early in January Alexander Loveday, head of the League financial section, informed Sir Frederick Leith Ross that the Little Entente states intended to propose a system of intra-European preferences at the next session of Briand's Committee of Enquiry for European Union (CEUE). Leith Ross was sure Britain would insist on full most-favoured-nation treatment. Loveday, who attached 'a good deal of importance' to the proposal, warned that this would be a mistake. If Britain insisted on it so would the United States, and the proposal would never get off the ground. Instead, he suggested that Britain simply demand to share European preferences on account of her free trade policy. As Leith Ross pointed out, this was a matter for the Board of Trade – and the Board had no intention of condoning European preferences.[1]

The second session of the CEUE – the first, the previous September, had been purely formal – opened in Geneva on 16 January with speeches on the disastrous impact of the economic slump. Briand, who spoke first, stressed the fact that no country had succeeded in escaping, and drew the moral that Europe must 'unite in order to live'.[2] No one disagreed; the question was *how* they were to unite. At once differences emerged.

Dr Colijn and Arthur Henderson insisted that it was for Europe's high tariff countries, who had not so far applied the resolutions of the 1927 World Economic Conference, to reverse their policies. As Henderson put it, they must halt their build-up of 'economic armaments' and avert the threat of 'a general European tariff war' by supporting the bilateral negotiations on which the fate of the tariff truce now depended.[3] M. Marinkovich, the Yugoslav Foreign Minister, angrily disagreed. If the 1927 resolutions had not been put into effect 'it was because it was not possible to put them into effect'. The fact was, they took no account of 'political and moral issues'. Europe's agrarian states could remove their customs barriers to the exports of the great overseas producers like Canada and the Argentine, 'provided they sacrificed four-fifths of their population'. To him, Henderson's free trade paradise was no more appealing than the Soviet Union's Five-Year Plan, 'with this difference perhaps, that you do not shoot the population, but starve them'. He believed the only practical approach was one which enabled the east European countries to dispose of their cereal surpluses and restore the equilibrium between the agrarian and industrial halves of the continent. Strict adherence to the most-favoured-nation principle would have to be abandoned. The size of the surplus, which represented at most 10 per cent of Europe's needs, seemed scarcely large enough to warrant complaints from the New World. But unless such action was taken, the agrarian countries would be forced to retreat into autarky and close their markets to the industrial products of western Europe. The extra-European countries had demonstrated their unwillingness or incapacity to help, so Europe must help herself. He therefore endorsed the call for bilateral negotiations – provided the most-favoured-nation principle was dropped.[4]

During the next few days other delegates took positions between the two. Belgium's Paul Hymans urged general support for the tariff truce scheme. Faced with the threat of Britain retreating behind an imperial tariff wall, and looming confrontation between France and Germany, Belgium desperately supported all initiatives with any prospect of halting Europe's slide into chaos and war. In December she had joined other northern countries in signing the Oslo Convention, an open-ended agreement committing signatories to mutual tariff reductions.[5] Besides the tariff truce, Hymans referred to the potential of international cartels and an approach to the European cereals surplus problem along the lines suggested by Marinkovich.[6] The German Foreign Minister, Julius Curtius, pointing to Germany's 4½ million unemployed, also supported both bilateral negotiations and preferential arrangements.[7]

Eventually the commission agreed to set up several sub-committees: one on the disposal of Europe's existing grain surplus, another on future surpluses, and a third to draft plans for an international agricultural mortgage corporation. It also called for support of the bilateral negotiations associated with the tariff truce. But no substantive decisions of any kind were taken, and at British and Italian insistence the commission agreed to invite the Soviet Union, Turkey, and Iceland to participate in future deliberations where they concerned Europe as a whole, which was certain to make decisions of any kind more difficult.[8]

Towards the end of the session the British Ambassador in Moscow sent to London an article from *Izvestiya* which alleged that 'England does not relish the establishment of a French hegemony in Europe; she wishes to open the doors of the conference so widely that only meaningless noise will issue from them'. This, as the diplomat Alexander Cadogan acknowledged, 'does not go very far beyond the bounds of "fair comment"'. Besides Alan Leeper, however, there were at least a few at the Foreign Office who betrayed increasing discomfort at this posture. It was not that they felt strongly about economic issues, which remained remote from them, but they could not ignore signs that Europe's economic plight was giving rise to political extremism which threatened to undermine peace. Nor were they happy to see Britain continually acting as the chief obstruction to regional cooperation when continental countries so persistently sought relief in this direction.[9] The Foreign Office was soon to alter its policy, but not before further awkwardness over representation at the CEUE meetings in Paris.

On 10 February André Tardieu took pains to stress to Poliakoff, *The Times* correspondent, the importance France attached to the forthcoming cereals conference.[10] The Steeg government had just fallen as a result of its failure to ease the burden on French farmers. The new Laval government was obviously concerned to succeed where its predecessor failed, and Tardieu was particularly anxious as Minister of Agriculture and President-Designate of the conference. Scarcely less important were the strategic implications of the economic crisis in eastern Europe. Starting with Roumania and Yugoslavia, Germany had begun to hold out bilateral preferential trade agreements to the countries there. If they were not to fall into the German embrace, France must find some outlet for their surpluses.

The Board of Trade advised against British participation altogether. It seemed probable that agreement would be sought on derogations from the most-favoured-nation principle and perhaps an undertaking not to buy Soviet wheat. Britain would be forced to refuse, and then no doubt be blamed for the failure of the conference. The Ministry of Agriculture and the Dominions Office sided with the Board. But at the Foreign Office Leeper protested that the Board was not being realistic in attempting to obstruct intra-European preferences. The Dominions would no doubt continue to raise objections, but as Mr McDougall, the economic adviser to Australia House, had admitted to him a few days earlier, 'the Dominions' protest ... was illogical and could not be indefinitely maintained considering that they were asking for preferences from *us*, a point M. Marinkovich has made much of'. France, Germany, and Italy might well agree to offer preferences to eastern Europe in return for concessions for their manufactures. Leeper was more convinced than ever that 'sooner or later ... we [will] have to choose between Europe and the Empire', and that the Board's policy of trying to have both would prove useless. The Board had suggested that at most a Paris Embassy junior should attend in the capacity of observer. Vansittart disagreed: 'We need not give the show away to that extent'. Dalton was in accord. 'Visible non-cooperation is never the right policy for us, who are always urging foreigners to cooperate, through the League or otherwise, for common ends. I should have preferred the familiar figure of Sir S. Chapman to be present. He is perfectly capable of stone-walling and "observing".' Chapman and Tyrrell attended for Britain.[11]

The conference on present surpluses went as the Board had anticipated. Two resolutions were adopted, one calling on all countries, whether normally purchasers of Danubian wheat or not, to purchase as much as possible, the other, to reserve part of their maize and barley import requirements for the produce of that region. The British reserved their support, as did Belgium, Denmark, Iceland, Holland, and Sweden.

At the conference on future surpluses, in spite of pressure from east European countries for immediate action, Tyrrell and Chapman insisted on prior consultation with overseas grain producers and 'devoted our attention to securing that the report should be as non-committal as possible'. But confrontation had merely been postponed. If, as seemed likely, the overseas countries ignored the call to attend the conference at the International Institute of Agriculture in Rome on 26 March, Britain's hand would be forced.[12]

At the second Conference on Concerted Economic Action or tariff truce conference the previous autumn Graham, desperate to keep the tariff truce proposal alive, had agreed to pursue bilateral negotiations as a test of support for trade liberalisation. The Board of Trade had issued detailed proposals to seven consenting states, requesting reductions of 25 per cent on certain protective duties and the consolidation of others. But Britain offered nothing in return, making a response unlikely, and bringing down on Graham increasing Conservative criticism. On 9 February it was admitted in the Commons that thirteen European countries had raised duties against British goods since the first tariff truce conference. The next month the Secretary for Mines, Emmanuel Shinwell, conceded that since June 1929 when the government took office, no less than twelve countries in Europe and ten overseas had made tariff changes of 'some general importance to British trade'.[13] Graham, on the defensive, assured a Conservative questioner that success in the bilateral negotiations was a condition both for reconvening the truce conference and Britain's adherence to the truce.[14] He soon had cause to regret this statement. Sir Eric Drummond, the Secretary-General of the League, announced the reconvening of the truce conference for 16 March, before the bilateral negotiations were even underway. Graham desperately sought a postponement, but Drummond was convinced this would do no good. Countries which had ratified the truce had succeeded in doing so only at the cost of bitter controversy, which they would not wish to see renewed.[15]

The second session of the second Conference on Concerted Economic Action in Geneva lasted barely two days. Twenty-four European countries were represented, but only twelve had deposited ratifications: Britain, Belgium, Estonia, Denmark, Finland, Greece, Holland, Latvia, Luxembourg, Norway, Sweden, and Switzerland. A survey of intentions soon revealed no others could be expected. The German delegate offered hope of ratification if British and French support were certain, but Elbel, the French delegate, practically ruled this out, and Chapman devoted his efforts to persuading others to keep the convention alive while postponing its application. It was a hopeless task and by the end of the first day Chapman was obliged to accept defeat. After consultation with Graham, Chapman joined other signatories in denouncing the convention.

Colijn, speaking at the final plenary session on the 18th, regretfully confirmed that no progress had been made in implementing the World Economic Conference resolutions since their adoption in 1927. He hoped the countries would not avail themselves of their freedom on 1 April. Then perhaps the CEUE meeting in May might find some means of revising the truce. It was a hope offered without optimism to a deeply sceptical audience.[16]

The collapse of the tariff truce, though long anticipated, was a serious blow to the government's economic strategy. It meant the end of one road, and there was no sign of readiness to start on another. The Cabinet committee on agricultural policy, formed in December under Clynes, the Home Secretary, on 20 February recommended a wheat quota, even though this might set a precedent and involve 'a slight increase in the price of bread'. However, MacDonald and Snowden belatedly added Alexander and Pethick-Lawrence to the committee, doubtless aware that they would object to this implicit 'food tax' and abandonment of free trade.[17] At the Cabinet on 4 March MacDonald confirmed that Snowden, recovering from a prostate operation, also opposed the quota. Despite the acknowledged urgency of the situation a decision was put off until Snowden could be present.

That same day the Cabinet postponed a decision on steel. Bruce Gardner of the Securities Management Trust, one of Norman's creations, had prepared rationalisation plans which were now available, and 'the Cabinet were impressed with ... the very critical state of the Iron and Steel Industry'. Though Graham warned that delay was 'dangerous', Ministers pointed out that the plans raised serious difficulties. On one hand they scarcely sufficed to bring down prices into line with foreign competition, which in 1930 sold nearly 3 million tons in Britain, compared with domestic exports of 3.25 million tons. On the other, the amalgamations they called for would leave 'considerable regions derelict and workless'. The Cabinet therefore agreed that Graham should hold further talks with Gardner and representatives of industry, and draw up a memorandum 'setting out the possible alternatives to a tariff'.[18]

The following week the EAC took up the question of trade policy as dealt with in the economists' report. Keynes summarised their case for a 10 per cent revenue tariff. First, there was 'a large intractable mass of unemployment associated with dislocations between costs and world prices ever since the post-armistice boom'. Second, there was a tendency for Britain to 'lend abroad more than could conveniently be financed'. The economists agreed on the need to improve the trade balance by increasing exports. However, the majority were doubtful that this could be done without intense wage and price cutting among industrial nations. Hence they accepted the alternative method, of curbing imports. Keynes believed that for political reasons it would be essential to treat imported foodstuffs and manufactures separately, but was prepared to consider any means, including single-industry duties, import quotas on agricultural products, and reciprocal preferences, just so long as they were expedient.

During discussion, Graham opposed reciprocal preferences since these would 'entirely destroy the most-favoured-nation clause'. Keynes agreed, but argued that this was no loss. 'He believed the adherence of this country to that clause worked against reciprocal reductions in the tariffs of other countries by tending to prevent foreign countries agreeing to give one another special preferences.' Chapman denied the charge, giving the traditional justification that it at least ensured Britain of whatever tariff concessions were offered elsewhere.

About the iron and steel industry, MacDonald said that while he agreed with the trade unions that the rationale for free trade was 'completely gone', a revenue tariff would not save steel. As to a solution, opinions varied as widely as ever. Bevin, Thomas, Keynes, Stamp, and Lewis all agreed that protection was necessary. But Bevin would make it a condition that the industry be nationalised, Lewis disagreed because this would frighten off investors, and Thomas supported him. Graham was afraid steel-makers would use protection as a substitute for rationalisation, and would also give rise to irresistible demands for protection elsewhere. Keynes was prepared to support Bevin's demand for state participation if that was the only way to rationalisation. 'The case was urgent, and the gravest danger was that of doing nothing.' Still MacDonald avoided a decision. Industry leaders had been requested to get together and produce a reorganisation scheme within 'a short period.... If, at the end of that period, no agreement had been reached, the Government would have to consider the situation.' And on that indecisive note the discussion ended.[19]

Spokesmen for the steel industry flatly refused to carry through the agreed rationalisation without assurance that the heavy investment required would be profitable. Britain, the only free market left in the world, was the victim of increased dumping, and state financial assistance and tariff protection were both needed. Graham explained this to the Cabinet on 22 April. Eventually Ministers authorised him to explain to Liberal leaders the urgent need for action including perhaps a public corporation to carry out the rationalisation programme, but not to enter into any commitments.[20]

In mid-April Snowden circulated his views on the proposed wheat quota. Once wheat received assistance there would be demands from coal, steel, and other industries; he saw no reason to alter his view that this would be folly. 'It would completely identify us with the Beaverbrook–Conservative programme. It would receive the strong opposition of the Liberals and it would split our own party from top to bottom.' In other words, political suicide.[21] The Cabinet discussed the wheat quota without reaching a decision.[22] The EAC again took up the revenue tariff question, again inconclusively, but already an element of unreality pervaded the council's deliberations,[23] and during the remaining life of the government, no further meetings of the council took place. MacDonald chaired a new Cabinet trade survey committee, but as its name suggested, the committee made no attempt to settle on a policy, despite the economic storm now clearly visible on the continent.[24]

The Austro-German customs union crisis

The storm had broken suddenly on 19 March, the day following the collapse of the tariff truce conference, when plans were revealed for a customs union between Austria and Germany. Spokesmen for the two countries strenuously insisted that their scheme was purely economic, initiated only after years of support for international trade liberalisation, and in Germany's case, at least, there was considerable substance to the claim. Germany had fully backed the recommendations of the World Economic Conference, supported the tariff truce proposal, and, despite suffering severely from the world slump, had (so far) resisted preferential schemes in Europe. But there were too many signs that Brüning had embraced a *Mitteleuropa* policy for claims of a purely economic motive to be taken seriously, and in France, Poland, and the Little Entente countries the scheme was seen – rightly – as a first step towards the shattering of the French alliance system and German dominance of southern and eastern Europe.[25] The authors of the scheme included an invitation to other countries to join, suggesting it would contribute towards Briand's quest for a united Europe. Opponents of the scheme saw this as a none-too-subtle means of avoiding legal objections based on the Treaties of Versailles and Saint-Germain and the Protocol of 4 October 1922, which forbade the abandonment of Austrian independence. That other east European countries were likely to grasp the opportunity to gain unobstructed access to the 60 million consumers of the German market made the French all the more determined to oppose it. Lingering hopes of a peaceful, constructive, European solution to the German problem thus abruptly faded, and Briand himself faced humiliation. Only a few weeks earlier he had dismissed the possibility of *Anschluss*. Now his nationalist critics derided him for his blindness to German realities and denounced his 'idealism'.[26]

In Britain the press initially welcomed the scheme as a contribution to trade liberalisation.[27] Within official circles, however, opinion was deeply divided. Law officers, called in to advise on Austria's treaty commitments, concluded that the plan was probably illegal. Notwithstanding the safeguards it provided for Austrian institutions, the sovereignty of Austria was certain to be compromised by a merger of its economy with the vastly larger German economy. The difficulty was in proving this before the fact in a court of law.[28]

Board of Trade officials viewed things differently. They discounted the political motive and focussed on signs that it was the product of prolonged frustration at the failure of multilateralism. From this narrowly economic standpoint they could see no grounds for objection. They accepted that full customs unions were legitimate exceptions to the most-favoured-nation principle, and hoped the plan marked a step away from the postwar balkanisation of the European economy. In William Graham's words, 'it would in my view be a very short-sighted policy to oppose such a Union from an economic standpoint'.[29]

Supporting evidence came from two Ambassadors. Sir Horace Rumbold in Berlin affirmed that German policy was guided chiefly by fear of economic collapse and the conviction that the reorganisation of European trade had become essential. '[I]n business and banking circles in Berlin ... the chief topic of conversation has been the menace represented by the progress made by the Soviet Union in carrying out the Five Year Plan, and the necessity of some serious effort being made by the European countries to put their house in order before Soviet economic pressure becomes too strong.' This and the fear that Austria might make an arrangement with her other neighbours were, he believed, the main reasons why Germany had brought the scheme forward now. Although the timing was unpropitious, he was of the opinion that Britain should not stand in the way of such a natural and long-sought solution to Austro-German relations.[30] Sir Eric Phipps in Vienna reported conversations with several Austrian authorities, all of whom stressed the economic logic of the scheme and the sincerity with which the invitation was extended to other countries to participate.[31]

Nevertheless officials at the Foreign Office were not prepared to contemplate the scheme. Its economic merits were doubtful, since the common external tariff was expected to be at the higher German level, and according to the conventional wisdom of the day a customs union was scarcely suitable to countries whose trade was competitive rather than complementary. But it was the political objections that were overwhelming, for nothing could be better calculated to antagonise Franco-German relations and endanger European peace than this economic *Anschluss*. As Orme Sargent, head of the Central Department, told the Foreign Secretary, the question was thus not whether to accept the scheme but simply how to kill it. An unfavourable judgment from the Permanent Court of International Justice would only arouse frustration in Germany and Austria and revive the declining Nazi movement at Brüning's expense. A favourable or suspended judgment would jeopardise Briand's position, and stimulate France to create a rival continental bloc. Reported French plans to join the Union were a 'great step forward' in the direction of Briand's goal of European federation, but extensive preferential arrangements would be involved. 'This would not suit our book at all, for we would have in self-defence to demand in each case most-favoured-nation treatment, and it is highly probable that this demand of ours would at once kill the whole thing.' Yet it would not do for Britain simply to oppose this alternative as well, and be charged with 'placing our narrow selfish ends in the way of European federation'. There was only one solution: Britain must devise 'a scheme of our own'.[32]

The first proposal for 'a scheme of our own' came a few days later from Philip Noel-Baker. Noel-Baker was impressed by Brüning's apparent acceptance of Stresemann's fulfilment policy, Germany's increasing dependence on export trade, and her loyal support for Graham's tariff truce efforts. He also thought it significant that Germany's request to the CEUE to examine the customs union scheme had been sandwiched between a reference to the failure of the tariff truce convention, and a call 'to discuss once more the possibilities of a better exchange of goods in Europe which would arise from agreements on preferential tariffs'. Since both Austria and France were also anxious to resolve the crisis by some form of collective action, he felt sure the moment for a breakthrough on the trade front had at last arrived.

He believed the simplest approach was across-the-board tariff reductions in progressive stages, 'e.g. 25% in favour of all other countries which agree to make similar reductions'. The advantages to continental countries seemed to him obvious: each would retain its relative position *inter se* while gaining advantages *vis-à-vis* non-participants. He saw no reason why the Board of Trade could not make satisfactory arrangements to participate, perhaps agreeing not to raise duties for, say, three years, or simply securing most-favoured-nation rights without obligation to share in the common external tariff. 'The advantage to British exporters of a 25% reduction in tariff levels in Europe would in itself be so considerable that an understanding not to impose further tariffs for a fixed period of time would not prove to be a difficult Parliamentary obstacle. In any case the political advantage of securing a settlement of the present European crisis would almost certainly ensure acceptance.'[33]

A second proposal, for a 'passive policy', was put forward by D.L. Busk, a junior at the Foreign Office. This was not 'a scheme of our own', but the means by which Britain could obstruct the Austro-German scheme. By taking up the German request to consider it in the CEUE,

Busk believed it would be temporarily halted, and could quickly be shown to be unworkable except, if at all, as a bilateral agreement. If it also allowed time for French feelings to cool and the Germans and Austrians to retreat amidst involved, technical discussion, it would have served its purpose. However, if the Germans and Austrians persisted at their game, Britain had two trumps. She could insist on most-favoured-nation rights under the Anglo-Austrian Treaty, and since Austria was already nervous about lowering barriers against German exports, this was probably an adequate deterrent. If not, there were the legal objections under the 1922 Protocol.[34]

In conversation with Ronald Campbell, the British Chargé d'Affaires in Paris, Alexis Léger, Briand's *Chef de Cabinet*, bitterly reproached the 'small clique of pre-war officials at the Wilhelmstrasse, headed by von Bülow', for pulling the customs union scheme out of its pigeon-hole and 'after brushing it up and adapting it to present conditions' pushing it onto the weak-willed Foreign Minister, Curtius. Nevertheless he told Campbell that the French cabinet had agreed upon a constructive policy for improving European relations, rather than hardening them further. France would turn over the question of Austria's right to enter the customs union to the International Court of The Hague. Meantime she would promote 'something which would prove of real assistance in the economic sphere to a considerable number of states'.[35]

On 22 April M. Arnal of the economic section of the Quai d'Orsay, called on Sargent to outline these proposals. He admitted candidly that an Austro-German customs union would act as a powerful magnet to all the east European agricultural countries. In response, France was preparing a scheme whereby the six leading grain importing countries of the Continent – Austria, Czechoslovakia, Germany, Italy, Switzerland, and France – granted preferences to the grain exporting countries of eastern Europe. So as not to encourage increased production these would be limited in scope and duration, and would exclude the Soviet Union. France hoped other importing countries would not demand a *quid pro quo*, but if Austria had to concede counter-preferences they would be extended to all countries enjoying most-favoured-nation rights. France was confident that, because of the 'comparatively small amount of grain which the scheme involves', overseas grain producers would not make difficulties. As for Austria, France proposed unilateral preferences from the protectionist countries of the continent. Germany's needs seemed to be financial rather than commercial, so a special effort would be made to arrange a loan or credits. She would also probably want to participate in a major development of cartel agreements which France intended to encourage.[36]

The following day Dalton took the chair at an inter-departmental meeting to consider Britain's options. Sir Henry Fountain and Sir Sydney Chapman, the Board of Trade representatives, favoured accepting the customs union as it stood. Leith Ross from the Treasury and Foreign Office officials pointed to the disastrous effect the scheme was already having on political relations and on confidence in the financial markets, and firmly ruled this out. Fountain thereupon advocated a passive policy. A Foreign Office spokesman warned of the danger of relying on a negative verdict from the International Court, especially as Czechoslovakia might decide to join the scheme under economic necessity. Leith Ross agreed that it would be best to put forward a scheme of their own. As his colleague Waley put it, the German request to the CEUE for an examination of the scheme stated as clearly as possible, 'Give us a general tariff reduction scheme and we'll chuck the Austrian affair'. The French proposal was no answer: it offered nothing to Germany while calling on her to grant preferences to east European countries, in face of certain opposition from her own farming interests and her treaty commitment to the Soviet Union. Moreover, despite talk of financial assistance, it was clear the Paris market was unwilling to commit long-term funds to Germany and equally clear that Germany did not want to become more vulnerable to French pressure by accepting short-term credits.

Fountain openly condemned the French scheme. As Britain did not export grain she would not be directly affected by the 'bribe' to east European countries, but she did export flour to the Continent: nearly £1 million in 1929 and £4 million in 1925. Certain smaller luxury trades such as hat manufacturing were also likely to be adversely affected if Austria received the 'bribe' of unilateral preferences. Even more than this was the principle at stake, as he explained with exemplary clarity:

> Once an exception of this sort, however apparently insignificant, is admitted, it is difficult to see how we could resist demands for similar exceptions in future. Other countries than Austria may have to be bought off by similar methods, and a preference to some of these countries might be of very real practical disadvantage to us. Whilst countries with general tariffs have at least some bargaining counters which they can use to protect their own interests abroad, Great Britain is dependent solely on her right to most-favoured-nation treatment, and once this right goes we are defenceless. It is, of course true that high tariffs impede our trade, but it cannot be gainsaid that differential tariffs which place us at a disadvantage with our competitors and third markets would be infinitely more disastrous.

Mr Clutterbuck of the Dominions Office wanted it known that his Ministry took a similar view. The French scheme was completely unacceptable to the Dominions, who could not be expected to abandon their most-favoured-nation rights to make it workable.

Having ruled out the French scheme, the committee turned to Noel-Baker's alternative. But it was immediately clear that the same objection applied here too, and the committee quickly passed on to Busk's 'passive policy'. It was agreed that Germany and Austria should be informed that their customs union scheme compromised British most-favoured-nation rights, damaged disarmament prospects, European cooperation and financial markets; and Britain might raise legal objections as well. The French would have to be told of Britain's opposition to their counter-proposal. And in light of reports that Austrian manufacturers were already beginning to shiver at the prospect of exposure to unrestricted German competition, it was further agreed that 'no opportunity should be lost of adding to the difficulties which, in the eyes of the Austrian Government, already stand in the way of effecting the proposed customs union'.[37]

During the next week steps were taken to put the passive policy into operation;[38] yet nothing was finally settled. Henderson had briefed the Cabinet on the legal aspects of the crisis, but there had been no discussion of the economic alternatives.[39] Pressure mounted: German and Austrian spokesmen endeavoured to persuade British representatives of the purity of their motives, and the French pressed their alternative scheme. Others, British as well as foreign, argued insistently for a bold step to forestall a Franco-German confrontation and save Europe from a deeper crisis.[40] Outside Whitehall, indeed outside the Foreign Office, little was known of these developments, but within the Foreign Office the pressure for an active policy became intense.

On 17 April, George Thelwall, Commercial Counsellor at the Berlin embassy, reported a conversation with Dr Ritter, head of the economic department at the German Foreign Ministry. Ritter had described his 'complete disgust with the abortive conversations at Geneva concerning tariff reductions and the removal of trade barriers'. He hoped the customs union would eventually form the nucleus of a broad European bloc. French opposition made immediate action impracticable and Germany was prepared to await the outcome of deliberations by the League Council. At all events, he concluded, 'Germany had done something to set matters in motion so far as commercial relations in Europe were concerned'. This struck Thelwall as significant because it confirmed suggestions from other quarters that Germany was 'more anxious to get something done with regard to economic co-operation than to force through the present scheme'. Rumbold, the British Ambassador, agreed. 'It appears to reveal ... a willingness for a renewed discussion about economic arrangements in Europe.'[41] Sargent, minuting the report on the 24th, regretted that it had not arrived before the inter-departmental meeting the day before; it confirmed that Germany would not only 'pose as a "good European" at Geneva', but while offering to drop the customs union, would insist upon a substantive alternative programme. 'In fact she will try and force us to adopt an 'active' policy – far too active, no doubt, for the liking of the Board of Trade.'

Four days later Sargent received the report of conversations between Pinsent of the Treasury, Loveday of the League of Nations, and the French officials François-Poncet and Bizot. Loveday expressed cautious optimism with developments. News of the Austro-German scheme had disturbed the political atmosphere, but there seemed to be 'many influences which approve of it', and he expected several other countries, including Roumania and Hungary, would be drawn to it. France seemed 'unwilling to risk a pitched battle and a division of Europe into two camps', and it seemed to him likely that Austro-German compromise and French counter-offers would produce agreement on a broad programme of trade liberalisation based on tariff preferences. The key question, he believed, was Britain's attitude, which he feared even now would be governed by the Board of Trade's dogmatic insistence on the most-favoured-nation principle. '[I]f a European preference "Union" on these lines is worked out we ought to bless it on condition that, so long as any other country that can show it treats the "Union" countries as favourably as they treat one another, that country should obtain the same preferences from the Union. (N.B. This differs from m.f.n. in stipulating reciprocity of a kind, and would give Great Britain the benefits while excluding the USA)'.

The Rueff plan

François-Poncet took a similar line, convinced that 'the British frontal attack on tariffs had always been doomed to failure', and that Britain ought to join in the 'indirect attack' of the French programme. France was prepared to forge a rival bloc in the last resort, but would make a determined effort to develop an alternative for the whole of Europe, and 'looked anxiously' for British cooperation. Like Bizot, he stressed the importance of implementing the international agricultural mortgage lending scheme as a complement to the French programme.[42]

Late in April Montagu Norman met Emile Francqui, the Belgian financier-statesman, who was convinced that news of the Austro-German scheme had so unsettled opinion in Europe that 'by hitting while the iron is still hot' it might be possible for the British government to take the lead in a bold plan; he hoped that Britain would propose that 'the whole of Europe (excepting Russia presumably) should be invited to consider the possibility of introducing free trade throughout Europe.... The Belgian Government would certainly welcome such a proposal and... he personally believed that not only Germany but a large number of European countries would at once give their support.' Norman was tantalised by Francqui's proposition, and urged Leith Ross to take it up.[43]

At the same time Sir Eric Drummond warned the Foreign Office of a serious clash with France unless British economic policy was quickly modified. He did not want to deal with the Austro-German customs union merely in terms of treaty rights and obligations, which would tend to confirm the reputation of the League as a narrow legalistic body.

> Frankly I am a little unhappy that we are unable to accept any constructive proposals. We object to the Austro-German business. We object to the French scheme for helping the agricultural countries, and to what is proposed by France to aid Austria. That will not place us in a very pleasant position, and it is no good thinking we shall be popular as a result.... We shall be looked upon by many as blocking European reconstruction, and by France and her allies as playing a definitely German game.... Further I am not quite sure we are wise to rely so entirely on the Most-Favoured-Nation treatment business. There is already a movement on foot to denounce the Commercial Treaties containing that clause, and I very much fear that a completely negative result of the approaching discussions will strengthen that movement, and then we shall be faced with a very unpleasant situation.[44]

Foreign Office officials were well enough aware of the obstacles to anything but the present 'completely negative' policy in the light of the positions adopted by the Board of Trade and Dominions Office at the inter-departmental meeting. The Dominions Office followed up with a report of the Rome wheat conference. There Argentinian, Canadian, and Australian delegates rejected any suggestion to relax the most-favoured-nation principle to ease the plight of the Danubian cereal producers. As they argued, 60 per cent of their crops were exported compared with 16 per cent of the Danubian crop. Hence they were the worst victims of the international crisis and could scarcely be expected to sacrifice markets.[45]

On 2 May the Board of Trade forwarded the report of a meeting in London between F. Vanlangenhove, Secretary-General of the Belgian Ministry of Foreign Affairs, and Chapman and Fountain. Vanlangenhove, speaking for the states signatory to the Oslo Convention – Denmark, Holland, Norway, Sweden, and Belgium – urged British support for the convention. They had agreed to consolidate their schedules of customs duties within the convention, to work for a progressive lowering of duties, and to extend the convention to any other country which agreed to align itself with them through the reduction or mere consolidation of duties. The existing member states, although small, carried on an important fraction of world trade, and Vanlangenhove expressed confidence that by 'the force of attraction' other states would be drawn into this low tariff area. He also admitted his anxiety for rapid results, since the protectionist tendencies of Belgium's larger neighbours were stifling much of her trade.

Vanlangenhove's invitation presented Britain with the opportunity to join the low-tariff nations of continental Europe in a programme calculated to save them all from a narrower, more nationalistic economic policy, while providing the world with a practical lead. For all but one of the Oslo treaty countries Britain was the chief export market and chief source of (net) foreign earnings. This and the looming prospect of Britain turning away from Europe in favour of an exclusive Empire bloc had been among the crucial factors in their decision to adopt the treaty. For the same reason Britain occupied a sufficiently strong position to set her own terms for membership. It is at least imaginable that the government could have seized the opportunity, justified its actions by reference to the failure of universalist initiatives and to the League Economic Committee's advocacy of derogations from most-favoured-nation treatment for plurilateral conventions of an open-ended and liberal character, and secured the support of the Liberal Party for its action.[46] With Britain in, Germany would probably have entered, and the rest of Europe would then have followed. But in the event, the Board of Trade refused even to contemplate such a possibility.

Without reference to Graham, let alone the Foreign Office or the Cabinet, Chapman and Fountain dismissed Vanlangenhove's appeal. 'It was pointed out to him that the proposal for derogations from most-favoured-nation treatment was one which did not at all commend itself to His Majesty's Government.... The commercial policy of His Majesty's Government, as was well known, was based entirely upon most-favoured-nation treatment, and their position would be gravely imperilled by any inroads upon this principle.' Nor, they added, could Britain possibly agree to consolidate duties in respect to one group of countries, since, through the operation of the most-favoured-nation clause, the advantage would be automatically extended to other countries, thereby removing their incentive to pursue tariff negotiations.[47]

This policy was the subject of discussion on 6 May at the Cabinet meeting, where the Foreign Office memorandum in Henderson's name was circulated. The memorandum disparaged the 'risky and ungrateful policy' of obstructing foreign initiatives, and acknowledged that all the likely alternatives involved preferential arrangements in conformity with 'the new interpretation of most-favoured-nation treatment given two years ago by the Economic Committee'. Britain's choice lay between an alternative policy at the cost of introducing 'a certain elasticity' into the most-favoured-nation principle, and possibly some difficulties with the Dominions over their exclusion from European preferences, or of being condemned 'rightly or wrongly for making a general system of tariff reduction impossible'. Henderson, it seemed, stood for 'elasticity'. He intended to begin by offering his services as an honest broker between France and Germany in an effort to bring them to an agreement on economic cooperation. But ultimately Britain could not remain disinterested:

> If Great Britain is to use the present opportunity to cooperate in building up some measure of European economic union, she will be required to make certain sacrifices, otherwise she runs the risk of being held responsible for having brought to nought the joint efforts of Europe to replace the dangerous Austro-German customs union by some progressive scheme for the economic union of Europe.[48]

The Cabinet discussion which greeted Henderson's proposal was one of unrelieved suspicion and hostility. There was opposition to any compromise of the most-favoured-nation principle, to the French idea of promoting industrial cartels, to the concession of special treatment of the Austrian trade, and to Noel-Baker's suggestion of freezing British tariffs for a period of years. Henderson, ignorant of the economic implications of his own brief, was confused by the welter of criticism he had raised. Defensively he said his purpose had been merely to acquaint the Cabinet with the various proposals that might be raised in Geneva. Then, unaware or forgetting that his brief covered discussion of economic programmes at the CEUE meeting *before* the League Council, he assured them that, as the council met for only two days, he did not anticipate any attempt to reach a decision on these matters, but 'if a Committee were set up on the economic aspects of the question' he could work with Graham and consult the Cabinet again. The Cabinet were satisfied. Relieved of the need for choice, they granted Henderson 'discretion on matters of detail', while asking him to refer back on matters of principle.[49]

If the Cabinet evaded the hard choices placed before them, the French government could not, and repeatedly it appealed for British cooperation. On 2 May, Rueff had called on Leith Ross with a new outline of counter-proposals. This differed little from that which Arnal had presented earlier, and Leith Ross told him of the objections raised at the inter-departmental meeting.[50] Two days later de Fleuriau communicated the same proposals to Vansittart, who likewise indicated objections, particularly lack of inducements for Germany.[51] Next, Rueff invited Leith Ross to the French Embassy, where he admitted that his government also had doubts about the practicability of their counter-proposal but were determined to find some alternative to the customs union scheme acceptable to Britain. France appreciated the special difficulty posed by the Dominions, but was it not possible for Britain to join a European economic union if certain safeguards were first received? The two he had in mind were that, so long as Britain maintained free trade, she would be assured the benefits of European preferences without obligation to participate in them; and that all such preferences would be created by reductions in internal European tariffs rather than increases in external tariffs. The important thing was to confront the crisis by an adequately large response. Leith Ross agreed with the last comment, and Rueff departed hopeful that with these provisos Britain would acquiesce in the French scheme.[52]

Meanwhile in Paris Tyrrell spoke with Robert Coulondre, director of commercial relations at the Quai d'Orsay, and learned of additional concessions the French had incorporated into their scheme. Besides holding out to Germany the promise of better financial facilities, France was prepared to encourage international industrial cartels and provide facilities for their successful operation. Now too France would raise no objection if, in return for granting preferences to east European wheat, Germany was offered reciprocal preferences for her own manufactured goods. France was prepared to threaten Germany with 'economic warfare' if it proceeded with the customs union scheme, and would warn Germany of the need to choose between driving Britain into protectionism or ensuring her cooperation with Europe on the basis of the French programme. France remained committed to a policy of cooperation, Coulondre assured Tyrrell, although he was bound to admit neither the German press nor government showed much interest in reciprocating.[53]

That day and the next the French Chamber of Deputies debated the customs union scheme. Bitter words were spoken about Germany's deceitfulness, and from benches on the right came complaints of Briand's feebleness in allowing the crisis to occur at all. Briand, as he had done so often before and was now doing for the last time, rose on the final day and in a long, eloquent speech appealed to the Chamber to support him in a policy of peace and reconciliation based on 'un plan effectif de solidarité européenne'. Whatever their real motives, Germany and Austria were prepared to discuss alternatives at the CEUE meeting in Geneva, and France would not be isolated when she met them. Briand assured his audience he was working in the closest cooperation with the British Foreign Secretary, and France's eastern friends could always be counted on for support. The Chamber responded by approving the government's policy by the comfortable margin of 430 to 52.[54] Later, Leon Blum, just returned from a meeting of the Socialist International at Zurich, told Tyrrell that, according to his German friends, the Brüning government could be expected to put up a sham fight for the customs union scheme, but that to all intents and purposes it was already dead. 'This he hoped would give an opening to promote Briand's scheme for a more general economic cooperation among the Continental states.'[55]

By now Rueff's latest proposals had had their desired effect within the Foreign Office. Two documents drafted by Sargent make this clear. The first set out all the objections to the French proposals.[56] The second, prepared a few days later and after Rueff's second meeting with Leith Ross, advanced all the arguments in favour of the proposals. The unique feature of Rueff's latest scheme, and the one which would overcome Britain's chief objection, Sargent claimed, was that it assured Britain most-favoured-nation privileges merely on condition that her present free trade regime was maintained, with no commitment on future policy. Britain's imperial and world position ruled out an active role in promoting the scheme, but if these conditions were accepted, Sargent could see no good reason to oppose it. He thought it desirable to invite countries outside Europe as well as inside to participate, to avoid 'the appearance of being organised as against Soviet Russia on the one hand and the United States of America on the other. Only if they refuse to participate would they then be subject to the discrimination to be meted out to non-participants.' He expected the Dominions would not join even if they were invited, but instead demand most-favoured-nation rights and raise the 'strongest resistance either singly or in cooperation with the United States'. This was why Britain could not initiate the scheme, but 'if it were put forward by some other government and if it contained all the safeguards required by His Majesty's Government ... and if generally it was shown to be advantageous to Europe both politically and economically, then we certainly should hesitate before vetoing the scheme merely because it might be inconvenient to the Dominions'. This, Sargent wrote, was the conclusion he had reached after consulting the Treasury, the Board of Trade, and the Dominions Office.[57] In his rush to complete the paper he had consulted them, but only in a casual way by telephone. Nonetheless Vansittart initialled it on 11 May, and Henderson carried it to Geneva next morning.

The first difficulty for British delegates to the CEUE meeting arose over the proposed international agricultural mortgage corporation. This had originated at the second tariff truce conference, was actively supported by France and her east European friends, received the approval of the League Council in January, was shaped by experts appointed by the Financial Committee, and further elaborated by a CEUE sub-committee on agricultural credit.[58] The Treasury, represented on the sub-committee by Walter Smith, strongly favoured the scheme as a means of inducing French capital exports and reviving the depressed economies of eastern Europe. The Foreign Office favoured it because France attached so much importance to it, and they saw serious danger in refusing all cooperation with her in devising an alternative to the Austro-German customs union. Admittedly the £120,000 required from Britain for the corporation's £5,000,000 reserve fund would annoy farmers in Britain and the Dominions. But the Ministry of Agriculture had indicated this was not an insuperable problem, and to British statesmen the importance of European stability justified the political embarrassment involved.[59] Henderson, arriving in Geneva on 14 May, learned from Smith that the scheme was now completed, a charter had been drafted, and other countries were waiting to see if Britain supported it; with British support the scheme would be implemented, without it the scheme had no future. Henderson cabled Snowden that if there were no objections he would announce Britain's support at the forthcoming CEUE meeting.[60]

That evening Vansittart was obliged to warn Henderson of difficulties. He had learned that Graham and Dr Christopher Addison, the Minister of Agriculture, would 'refrain from offering opposition', and Snowden was ready to acquiesce in the £120,000 participation, but that Thomas, worried by effects on the Ottawa conference which might further damage his reputation, opposed participation until British policy could be thoroughly reviewed. Since this was obviously impossible in the absence of the Foreign Secretary, Vansittart hoped to secure a decision at a meeting of the Prime Minister, Chancellor, and Dominions Secretary.[61]

'This matter surprises me', was MacDonald's comment on receipt of Vansittart's request for a meeting. Although under discussion for some time, the scheme had never been raised in Cabinet, he said, and he knew nothing of it until Thomas mentioned it the previous day. 'This is an issue of first class importance and should have been brought before the Cabinet when Walter Smith reported, and papers sent to me immediately. It cannot be decided between departments.'[62] MacDonald was too anxious to avoid criticism from British and Dominions farm interests to contemplate any positive action.

On Saturday 16 May, Sir Edward Harding, Permanent Under-Secretary at the Dominions Office, wrote to Vansittart and Thomas wrote to MacDonald, objecting to Sargent's brief for Henderson on the Rueff scheme. In his rush to complete the brief and anxiety to see Britain play a constructive role in Europe, Sargent had encouraged the impression that the Dominions Office was prepared to accept the Rueff scheme with suitable safeguards, which emphatically it was not. On the contrary, it saw the scheme as an extreme danger to Britain's relations with the Dominions, the United States, and the rest of the non-European world, no matter what safeguards were offered. It was undoubtedly true that Britain could effectively block the scheme by insisting on most-favoured-nation treatment. What was equally true was that if Britain did not block it, all the efforts of Canada, Australia, and other Dominions to defend their own most-favoured-nation rights would be disregarded by the Europeans, who would denounce the relevant commercial treaties. As a result Britain would be held responsible for the exclusion of Dominion goods from European markets. To put the country in this position, as Sargent appeared ready to do, seemed to Harding wholly unacceptable, and particularly so when Britain had just announced her intention to strengthen economic ties with the Empire at the approaching Ottawa conference.[63]

Thomas denounced the Rueff scheme and the international agricultural mortgage plan with equal vigour. The first failed to recognise Britain's role as head of the Commonwealth and a world power. 'By all means let us find, if we can, an alternative solution to the Austro-German Customs Union proposals (sic), but surely our Imperial position will be impossible if we rush into support of proposals which discriminate against the Dominions and in fact force us to choose between Europe and the Empire.' Britain's refusal to support the recommendation of the recent conferences on European grain surpluses, he noted, had been enthusiastically received 'in Canada especially'. But he was also concerned about domestic criticism. The government, despite promises, had done nothing to relieve the plight of British farmers. If they were now to participate in an agricultural mortgage scheme to assist Continental producers when they had nothing to offer those at home or in the Empire, they would 'surely [be] playing into the hands of our opponents'.[64] Put bluntly, Thomas, like MacDonald, was insisting that lack of initiative in one area of policy demanded inactivity in another.

Even had the Ministers hoped to resolve the question when they met at Downing Street the following Monday it is unlikely they could have done so. The implications of any alternative were immense. But they were only anxious to procrastinate, and their work was made easier since the Foreign Office, unaware that Thomas would call for discussion of the Rueff scheme, was represented by Dalton who had not read the brief Sargent had prepared for Henderson. He was 'much embarrassed' and quite unable to defend the Foreign Office view. Thomas, supported by Graham, thus had his way without difficulty, and Henderson was cabled to hold off all commitment to the Rueff and mortgage schemes.[65]

Henderson's primary task of shelving the customs union scheme was by this time fulfilled. The collapse of the Kreditanstalt, Austria's largest commercial bank, a few days before the League Council meeting, had thrown that country into a major crisis. In consequence, as Henderson later told Tyrrell, the Austrians seemed to have 'no stomach for further fight'. When Schober called on him on the 14th he had put Britain's objections to the scheme with such force that Schober immediately informed his German friends that Austria would not proceed with it, and had stood firm despite their strenuous efforts to persuade him to change his mind. Next morning Henderson went to the station to greet Briand who had just suffered a humiliating defeat in the presidential election. At the opening session of the CEUE a few hours later, with Briand in the chair, Henderson went out of his way to praise Briand for his efforts at international cooperation. A private meeting with Briand and the German and Italian Foreign Ministers, Curtius and Grandi, proved amicable enough and Henderson succeeded in persuading Briand to allow general discussion, including reference to the Austro-German scheme, to proceed in the CEUE in advance of the council meeting.[66]

Curtius led off next day with a defence of regional approaches to trade liberalisation, and of customs unions as a means of attaining this goal without jeopardising the most-favoured-nation principle; Germany was prepared to exchange views on forming a customs union with any interested country. Briand called for a broad-based programme of commercial reforms in lieu of narrow, potentially divisive arrangements such as the Austro-German scheme.[67] A paper was then circulated outlining France's legal, political, and economic objections.[68] Grandi repeated Italy's scepticism towards broad multilateral solutions and in particular the French idea of industrial cartellisation; Italy wanted respect for the most-favoured-nation principle and the tariff truce convention. François-Poncet followed with an explanation of the French counter-proposals. Schober then brought the meeting to a close by describing Austria's dilemma because of the most-favoured-nation principle, and ended with an assurance that his government would give the French proposals sympathetic consideration.[69]

At the opening meeting of the League Council on Monday, 18 May, Henderson led off by calling for the Austro-German scheme to be sent to the International Court at The Hague and requesting the Austrian government to take no further action until the court had decided on the scheme's legality. Schober agreed, and after Briand and Curtius had had a chance to state opposing views on the legal question, Henderson's proposal was accepted without dissent.[70]

His next step was to discourage unacceptable alternatives. On 19 May, the second day of the CEUE session, he appealed emotionally for an end to defeatism and a start on tariff reductions, to draw Europe back from the brink of utter disaster. Nothing in the League's record had been more 'strikingly successful' than its economic and financial work from the Brussels financial conference in 1920 to the agricultural mortgage scheme 'just completed', Henderson assured his audience.[71] The following day, however, when the draft of the mortgage scheme was presented, Henderson awkwardly referred to 'certain particular difficulties' in the way of British participation, and asked for time to allow his government further consideration.[72]

On the 21st the Swiss delegate, M. Motta, presented the report of a sub-committee set up at Henderson's suggestion to recommend the basis for an economic programme from the alternatives at hand. The report followed the lines of the French proposal, and Henderson immediately protested. He 'put in, on behalf of my government, a most emphatic reservation'.[73] Instead, a series of resolutions was adopted calling for the creation of yet more CEUE committees, but nothing in the way of substantive action.[74]

Sir Robert Vansittart, in the second of his 'old Adam' memoranda, warned the Cabinet on the eve of the League Council meeting of the need for a 'concrete policy' to meet the new, more threatening situation in Europe. The sharpened conflict between the 'haves' and the 'have nots' which, he wrote, was the outstanding feature of the past year, had led Britain to attempt pacification by the 'comfortable exertion of "influence"'. He suggested that repeated invocation of the name of the League and its principles was simply not enough: Ministers must recognise that this was only too reminiscent of Britain's pre-war posture, which European countries had condemned as insular, or downright hypocritical. Ministers must also understand the unparalleled gravity of the crisis. Economic desperation was fomenting political extremism, which in turn made the economic problem more intractable. Just as Hitlerism in Germany and Fascist bellicosity in Italy were essentially 'symptoms of an economic disease', so too the customs union crisis was a manifestation of the same affliction on the body politic.[75]

Vansittart's advice, albeit general and embedded in an over-long and agonisingly over-written paper, was sound enough. But in the circumstances it was idle to expect it to have any effect. Britain now leaned decisively towards imperial protectionism, so much so that it could scarcely have joined in a European preference arrangement or a low-tariff area without cogent and effective leadership, something it manifestly lacked. Ministers were hopelessly divided on trade policy, with Thomas at one extreme committed to imperial protectionism, Snowden at the other unwavering in his stand on free trade, and the others arrayed between. Vansittart's Foreign Office colleagues, in accepting that a new posture was possible, had allowed themselves to lose sight of domestic political realities.

The Cabinet merely 'took note' when his paper came before them on 20 May.[76]

11

The collapse of economic internationalism

In his effort to diffuse the Austro-German customs union crisis in April 1931, Arthur Henderson had encouraged fellow statesmen in Europe to rely on an international solution to the growing economic troubles afflicting the continent. He assured them that the working party of the CEUE would provide a lead when it met in Geneva late in June. Understanding little about economics and even less about the inspiration for the CEUE, it seems unlikely that he had any clear idea of what it might accomplish, unless that the British representative might convert the others to free – or at least freer – trade by preaching against the sin of protectionism. In that case Walter Layton was an appropriate choice for the assignment.

Layton, editor of *The Economist* and stalwart internationalist, consented reluctantly to go to Geneva on 24 June, believing that the continental countries were economically nationalist beyond redemption. For all his much-vaunted intelligence sources, he was unprepared for the intense interest shown by continental representatives in entering into regional or bilateral customs unions to counter the drift towards autarky. The Northern countries as well as Austria, Germany, and more cautiously France, all indicated their willingness to grant Britain and other free trade countries most-favoured-nation treatment within their respective projects. 'The point which interested everybody was the relationship between any such project and Great Britain.' Layton was equally impressed by the Francqui plan for promoting international lending, which he seemed to know little about beforehand. But this too remained merely a good idea when the committee adjourned until 18 August.[1]

How far Layton was prepared to go to endorse regional economic schemes was in any case by no means clear. He seems to have accepted that these regional arrangements would be customs unions, with complete elimination of internal trade barriers as the distant goal. Although customs unions were accepted as a form of free trade, the initial stages were bound to involve participants in preferential tariffs, the very thing Britain strenuously opposed. By and large internationalists like Layton were frozen in their tracks, aware that the world slump was imposing intolerable strains upon Britain, but unwilling to compromise the principles of internationalism for fear that, once started, there could be no turning back. The report of the Macmillan Committee, drafted by Keynes, was typical in this respect.

According to the report the slump was the trough of a trade cycle, albeit one of 'quite unusual dimensions', aggravated by special factors. The first was the selection of exchange parities by countries 'groping their way back to gold', which bore no consistent relation to respective price levels. These new parities had favoured the trade position of certain countries, notably Belgium and France, producing a maldistribution of monetary gold. The second was the reparations–war debt settlement wherein France and the United States were net beneficiaries, similarly redistributing monetary gold to London's disadvantage. Before the war London had provided firm and consistent leadership for the international financial system. Now there were three centres, New York, Paris, and London, and a 'dispersion of initiative and responsibility' because of the shift in lending power since the war. Until 1914 London had provided a steady flow of investment capital and trade finance, as well as the necessary insurance and other entrepôt services. In recent years New York and Paris, lacking the same experience, had used their lending power 'only spasmodically'. The result was an acute liquidity crisis which affected Britain as severely as other countries.

Nonetheless, the report continued, Britain depended too heavily on trade and commerce and the proceeds of past investment to think of abandoning the gold standard and throwing the international monetary system into chaos. The cooperation of France and the United States was needed in a major operation to reflate world prices and revive trade. Together the central banks of the three major creditor countries could lead the world to recovery, but the report warned that time was running out. Within Britain the prolonged depression had stirred 'a spirit of self-consciousness' which was leading to rejection of *laissez-faire* principles in favour of 'management of the life of the people', and in particular to rejection of the gold standard. 'At no time since the ... historic disputes which followed the Napoleonic Wars ... has the monetary organisation of our country been the subject of so much criticism as in recent times.' Change in attitude and the conditions causing it thus pointed towards Britain's departure from the gold standard – unless France and the United States awoke to their responsibilities soon. The transfer of gold from debtor to creditor countries at an annual rate of £70 million was evidence of 'how little margin there is left'.[2]

Just how remote coordinated reflation might be was revealed even before publication of the report, when Keynes visited the United States. There he found Governor Harrison and colleagues in New York sympathetic to the idea, but unhopeful of educating their less international-minded colleagues in interior centres to the immediate need for reflation.[3] On 1 July the question of the British government's attitude to the report was raised in Cabinet. Snowden conceded that they would be pressed to announce their intentions, but added that 'as it had taken two years to compile they had a good answer for not making an early reply'. He said the Treasury was preparing a commentary and invited Ministers to await its completion. At the Cabinet on 15 July MacDonald asked if the time had not come to form a committee to consider the report, which had been published two days earlier. Again Snowden referred to the Treasury commentary in preparation, and they let the matter rest. At the final Cabinet on 30 July before Parliament rose for the summer, the question of the report was merely 'continued on the Agenda Paper'.[4] But by now the financial crisis had spread to London, distracting attention from all but the most immediate issues.

The continental financial crisis

The continental crisis began on 11 May in the wake of the confrontation over the Austro-German customs union scheme when the Österreichische Kreditanstalt, a Rothschilds house, was revealed to be virtually bankrupt. The implications for eastern and southern Europe were extremely serious, for the bank had an interest in no less than 60 per cent of Austrian industry and assets throughout the Danube basin.[5] The City also had reason to be deeply worried. It was largely at British urging that Austria had undergone reconstruction under the auspices of the League Financial Committee in 1922, thus becoming the model for similar operations elsewhere. Moreover, the City had poured funds into Austria, largely through the Kreditanstalt. The intimacy of the City's involvement was indicated by the fact that no less than three British directors sat on the Kreditanstalt's board, Niemeyer, Strakosch, and the Russian-born Peter Bark;[6] and according to Siepmann, the Bank of England itself had £7 million tied up in the Kreditanstalt.[7] Yet it was not the loss of British investments or prestige in Central Europe that worried Norman most, but rather the future of capitalism in the region. So seriously did he take this threat that he disregarded the advice of his friends at Morgans in New York, who urged him to defend the sanctity of contract by insisting that the Kreditanstalt deal with its creditors on a strictly individual basis. As he explained to George Harrison, such was the extent of the Kreditanstalt's commercial holdings that if private help was not fully mobilised, the Austrian government would be forced to assume control, thereby transforming the country into a semi-socialist state. And if Austria was not propped up, neighbouring countries might be driven into the same impasse.[8]

Norman's first step was to help set up a creditors' committee under the chairmanship of Lionel de Rothschild, to steady fundholders and forestall a self-defeating rush of withdrawals.[9] Next, he secured the agreement of his fellow BIS directors to a three-month 100 million schilling credit for the Austrian National Bank, offered on 30 May. The Austrian government, with this breathing-space, turned to the one financial market replete with funds, calling on the Banque de Paris et des Pays Bas to underwrite a 150 million schilling loan. For a few days arrangements proceeded smoothly, but as the full extent of the Kreditanstalt's losses was revealed and the schilling came under increasing pressure, the French bankers drew back. They demanded a guarantee from their own government to cover them against loss, and some participation by London houses. Although these were already overcommitted in Austria, they felt obliged to participate on a small scale in order to shore up their interests. But the French government set two pre-conditions on its guarantee: that Austria submit to foreign supervision of her economy, as the League Financial Committee had demanded in the past of states in distress, and that she also renounce any intention of proceeding with the customs union scheme.

Already delays had dissipated any good effect earlier assistance may have had on market confidence, and on Sunday 14 June, Niemeyer warned Norman from Vienna to expect a complete Austrian internal banking moratorium the next day. Norman persuaded Austrian officials to postpone the announcement, then spent Monday and Tuesday searching the City for houses willing to buy or place additional Austrian paper. Finding no takers, he had the Bank of England advance 150 million schillings which the Austrian National Bank needed desperately to replenish its reserves. It was too late. The French had delivered their terms like an ultimatum on Tuesday, allowing the Schober government only four hours to reply. Rather than submit to such humiliation, Schober had resigned. Despite deep suspicion in Paris, Norman had not offered his help in order to circumvent the French demands, of which he learned to his fury only later. And the Austrians resigned before learning of the Bank of England loan.[10]

Until this time Norman, like most British observers, saw the crisis as simply a European one. He was aware of German exchange weakness since mid-May, and mounting agitation from Berlin for a suspension of reparation payments. He agreed that these political debts were a poison which must be purged from the international financial system if it was to be restored to health. But while he feared that the east European countries might succumb to Communism thanks to French obstruction of reparation revision, he remained confident of Germany's survival. One reason, no doubt, was that the German bankers and business leaders he met were competent and reasonably cautious. Another was that Germany was a large, economically advanced country, and size seemed crucial to survival in an age of mass production. Third and most important, it also seemed of superior 'moral' character, with a government ready to mete out repeated doses of retrenchment and a population disciplined enough to take them. As he explained that spring to various audiences in the United States: 'Germany had made great progress during the last six months... Political uncertainty has been largely dissipated .... the budget and taxation have been adjusted to present needs; and unemployment ... has been placed upon an improved economic basis.... In conclusion ... international payments by Germany were likely to continue on schedule.'[11] Partly because of warnings from the United States against any hope of further war debt concessions, but also because of their exaggerated confidence in Germany's self-discipline, Norman and Treasury experts advised MacDonald to avoid discussion of the reparations question when Chancellor Brüning paid an official visit on 5 June. The visit had been planned since March simply as a good will gesture to strengthen Brüning's hand in his struggle against political extremism. On the eve of his arrival reports from Berlin confirmed further cuts in public spending, serious civil unrest, and official word that Germany could not pay reparations beyond the autumn. Nevertheless the visit was deliberately kept informal, with a courtesy call on the King, and lunch at Chequers with G.B. Shaw and John Galsworthy, whose books were enjoying great popularity in Germany, and the Poet Laureate, John Masefield, as well as Norman and Vansittart. Despite the desperate situation, MacDonald virtually ignored Brüning's attempt to win British support for a reparations initiative through the offer of commercial concessions, and after a few more well-publicised receptions bade him farewell, convinced he had scored another diplomatic triumph.[12]

Nervousness in the mark, evident since the Kreditanstalt failure, turned into panic following the announcement that reparation payments would probably be suspended. Although issued to appease victims of the latest round of wage and spending cuts, Brüning had planned to force the issue as early as March. Unfortunately he had not taken Hans Luther, the Reichsbank President, into his confidence, and the Reichsbank now found itself confronted with a massive flight of capital which undercut its reserves.[13] On 13 June, Henry Stimson, the American Secretary of State, telephoned MacDonald about the crisis and to ask if the United States could help, perhaps by a temporary suspension of intergovernmental claims. MacDonald, after consulting Vansittart, Leith Ross, and Norman, left him with the impression that Britain would wait and see if the Reichsbank's decision to raise its discount rate from 5 to 7 per cent would be enough to restore confidence. The impression was corrected next day when Harrison called from New York to find Norman deeply pessimistic about the German situation. Thereafter Norman repeatedly urged American intervention, until 20 June, when President Hoover responded. Alive at last to the calamitous impact a German crash would have on his country's financial system in view of the huge volume of dollar loans at risk, Hoover announced America's readiness to join in a one-year moratorium on inter-governmental debts.[14]

News of the proposal caused elation in London. Germany, dangerously overburdened by foreign financial claims, was to gain at least temporary relief. Moreover the United States at last seemed to have acknowledged the integral connection between reparations and war debts. Hoover himself was given credit for a major act of statesmanship, the value of which has been accepted to this day. Yet the moratorium, impressive from an isolationist United States perhaps, was merely a gesture. For anything to be made of it, two major obstacles needed to be cleared away. First, a large-scale source of new capital was essential to still the doubts now raised about the soundness of European currencies. A temporary moratorium meant the prospect of a resumption of reparation demands – moreover, augmented by the postponed charges – within just twelve months. This was certain to impel investors to continue their efforts to divest themselves of German and European assets, unless more substantive measures were taken. The time had passed when central bank cooperation could stem the tide. What was needed was concerted action, at the official level, by the three major creditor powers, the United States, Britain, and France. The second requirement was an easing of tension in Europe, and for this Britain and the United States would have to accept a share of responsibility for European security. With such a commitment a pacific settlement of Franco-German differences could be envisaged; without it the vicious cycle of German revisionist claims and hostile French reaction was bound to continue, undermining confidence in Europe and leaving it prone to the disruption of hot money movements. By itself the Hoover moratorium changed nothing. Its only immediate consequence was to dramatise the gulf that divided France from her former allies.

To the British and Americans the moratorium had come in the nick of time to save the international financial system. To the French it was merely a desperate attempt by the Anglo-Saxon powers to save their commercial banking systems, which had tied up hundreds of millions of pounds in Germany, and to do so by demanding that France, whose banks had wisely refrained from heavy investment in Germany, should now jeopardise her financial stability by foregoing reparations. To the British and Americans, France stood to gain as much as anyone from the avoidance of an international financial collapse, and could well afford to forego reparations since her coffers were bursting with gold and surplus loan capital. In France the dominant fact was that, barely five years after the 'Poincaré miracle' had cut short runaway inflation and restored national finances, she was facing the prospect of a serious budget deficit and so more than ever needed reparations payments. Unfortunately no one in London or Washington recognised how different the moratorium seemed from Paris, nor how disturbed the French were by the loss of budgetary equilibrium, and no one was prepared even to mention the security issue. Thus when the French refused to participate in the moratorium unless exception was made for unconditional reparations as in the Young Plan, annoyance in Britain and America knew no bounds. 'France', MacDonald wrote in his diary, 'has been playing its usual small minded and selfish game over the Hoover proposal. Its methods are those of the worst Jews. To do a good thing for its own sake is not in line with France's official nature. So Germany cracks while France bargains.'[15]

Shortly after the moratorium offer, Norman took the lead in arranging a $100 million short-term credit for the Reichsbank from the BIS and central banks of France, the United States, and Britain. Amidst continuing uncertainty this did little to halt the decline in reserves. Desperate for further help, Hans Luther, the Reichsbank President, flew to London on Thursday 9 July. His reserves had reached the legal limit of 30 per cent, he warned Norman. Without help, he would have to start printing money, and this could trigger 'an internal flight from the mark', a total collapse of the exchanges, and drag down 'most of the countries of Central Europe and involve obvious risks of social and political disorders. London as the financial centre with the greatest commitments in Germany would be very seriously affected.'

Only the day before Norman had told Harrison he was ready to help arrange a central bank credit for the Reichsbank of $500 million or even $1 billion. Now he abruptly abandoned any such idea. It was not that he doubted Luther's scenario: on the contrary, he feared the outcome would be even more catastrophic. But precisely because of the magnitude of the threat, he now believed further central bank assistance would be useless, perhaps worse than useless. The problem was political, not financial. Not until governments agreed to remove the burden of reparations would Germany stop needing constant injections of short-term credits, which made her so vulnerable to hot money movements. Further credits would only increase her liabilities, while enabling politicians to evade their responsibilities.[16]

Luther left London empty-handed on Friday 10 July, flying to Paris in time for lunch with Moret and senior Regents at the Bank of France. The gathering was cordial but unproductive. The Board of Regents was dominated by François de Wendel, who was anti-German and abhorred the idea of giving aid to Germany, and Baron Edmond de Rothschild, who was pro-British and wanted French financial aid to go first to Britain and other non-German victims of the crisis. They did not accept Luther's claim that the capital fleeing Germany was mostly foreign, nor that having raised interest rates Germany could do no more to help itself. Comparing the situation to their franc crisis of 1926, they believed Germany must make yet heavier sacrifices. But they agreed that having the means to save the mark from collapse offered France a unique opportunity for 'certaines satisfactions politiques indispensables' from Germany, and so was a matter for government decision. The Finance Minister Flandin, who arrived later, linked the crisis to Germany's provocative, revisionist policies; financial assistance would be given only if 'the political atmosphere in Berlin improved'. Since Luther was not in a position to deal with the political issues, German ministers should come to Paris at once to discuss the changes France had in mind.[17]

Luther then turned to the BIS at Basle, where central bankers met him on Sunday, July 12. During talks that day and the next, all agreed that the German economy was fundamentally sound, and most were sympathetic to Luther's appeal. Moret still insisted on an improvement in the political climate, however, and Norman shocked the others by suggesting Germany should declare a moratorium on foreign debt if this was the only way to make politicians see reason on reparations. In the end the existing $100 million credit was renewed, but only, at Norman's insistence, for a fortnight. The larger credit Luther sought was refused.[18]

That same Monday morning the collapse of the giant Darmstädter und National (Danat) Bank was announced in Berlin, along with the closing of the Bourse and a two-day national bank holiday. The German Ambassador, Konstantin von Neurath, called on Arthur Henderson at the Foreign Office to appeal for British financial aid. Henderson again deprecated German failure to 'make some gesture', such as renouncing the customs union scheme or halting construction of the pocket battleship now on the stocks, which would make it easier for France to open her coffers. Neurath pointed out unpublicised acts, such as a 50 million mark reduction in military spending; the difficulty was that more obvious concessions would be politically suicidal, as the Nazis' striking electoral success had made clear. It scarcely affected the issue, however, since Britain had already lent a dangerously large amount to Germany and Austria, and could lend no more.[19]

What remained for Britain to do? Norman persuaded Snowden and the Treasury that only radical political action could save the situation. American statesmen, anxious to avert the collapse of the international financial system but too fearful of isolationist sentiment at home to involve themselves in European affairs, now constantly urged their British counterparts to take the lead: first to press the French to accept the moratorium, then to convene an international conference where some means of restoring Germany could be devised without leaving her to face France alone. On 1 July Henderson secured Cabinet approval to arrange such a conference, and on the 7th missions in the chief western capitals were told to sound out governments on their willingness to attend.[20] Henderson spent much of the next two weeks trying to persuade the French to settle their differences with Germany in London, warning that each day's delay increased the threat of Communism in Germany. The French Premier, Pierre Laval, more realistically predicted a victory for Hitler. Nevertheless he resisted attending a conference in London, fearing he would find himself alone to face German and 'Anglo-Saxon' demands for revision of reparations, and that, whatever the result, the French electorate would suspect him of trading away French interests. Henderson did eventually win French agreement to attend, conceding only that Brüning and his Foreign Minister Curtius should hold preliminary talks in Paris before proceeding to London. But whether his efforts were of any real value is more than doubtful.[21]

Throughout July signals from London remained disturbingly contradictory. Norman and Leith Ross made no secret of their view that the conference must deal with basic issues affecting Germany's financial stability. As Norman told Harrison, Snowden and MacDonald had made it clear to him that the 'fundamental reason' for holding the conference 'was to discuss a readjustment of all the economic difficulties arising out of reparations and other political considerations [including] the Young Plan, the Versailles Treaty and war debts as well'. However, the French were opposed to such wide-ranging revision, and Stimson had made clear that he would walk out of any conference that broached controversial European issues. MacDonald and Snowden therefore assured Stimson that they intended no such thing: the conference would deal solely with measures for relieving the immediate crisis. Unfortunately, here too the way forward seemed barred. Stimson was unwilling to entertain requests for financial aid to Germany beyond the $260 million the United States had already provided (temporarily) through the moratorium.[22] Britain had nothing to offer but her good offices – that 'comfortable exertion of influence' Vansittart had derided in his Old Adam paper to the Cabinet in the spring. The only power with *anything* to offer was France, and it was inconceivable that France would rescue Germany on terms set by any other power than itself.

The sterling crisis and the collapse of the Labour government

Sir Clive Wigram, private secretary to George V, on 11 July wrote to the King who was on board the royal yacht at Cowes, warning of ominous developments. Germany was hovering on the brink and 'If there is a collapse ... the repercussions in this country will be awful. We are sitting on top of a volcano and the curious thing is that the Press and the City have not really understood the critical situation.'[23] Part of the explanation for the calm may have been the strength of the Bank of England's reserves, which had benefited from the flight of capital from the continent as well as seasonal factors to stand at £164 million on 8 July, comfortably above the 'Cunliffe minimum' and the low point reached in the winter.[24] Yet even as Wigram was writing, pressure across the sterling–franc exchange again roused angry comment in the City. The *Daily Mail* that day captioned its report of trading, 'New French Gold Raid.' The *Financial Times* also saw political motives at work: 'It is not without significance that whenever an international or Franco-British conference is arranged ... the Paris rate of exchange definitely develops a strong tendency.' The City editor of the *Daily Herald* encouraged the same francophobic suspicion. And when the Paris Bourse reopened after the *fête nationale* of the 14th and sterling fell sharply below gold export point, press criticism of France intensified. According to Arthur Wade, City editor of the *Evening Standard*, 'We know that this movement is due to withdrawal of ... funds controlled by the Bank of France and the Treasury. ... French authorities regard shipments of gold as moves in the diplomatic game.'

The accusations were as misplaced as ever, but in the crisis atmosphere rumours of French machinations persisted. They were consistent with the evidence: France, having tried to blackmail Austria into abandoning the customs union with Germany, and obstructing the Hoover moratorium until Germany was brought to her knees, was now sabotaging the pound in order to force Britain to give up diplomatic support for Germany. French financial policy, it seemed, was thus serving her militaristic ambition to dominate the Continent.

In fact the French, so far from orchestrating an attack on sterling, were concerned only to shore it up, the statesmen because of Britain's vital importance as an ally, the financial authorities because of the crucial role sterling played in the international monetary system. During the summer French commercial banks ran down their London balances, while French Treasury balances in London declined only modestly, from £3.4 million on 30 June to £2.4 million on 30 September; the Bank of France's sterling balances, amounting to about £64 million, were maintained and even slightly increased.[25] As early as 18 July Regents of the Bank of France agreed it was desirable to aid Britain, and Moret repeatedly made known their readiness to help the British defend their exchange rate.[26] What help they did give, however, was ignored, or suspected as proof of growing French influence, and not only in the narrowly nationalistic press. MacDonald and his Cabinet suspected that the run on sterling was a French plot, and even Norman and his colleagues at the Bank seem to have agreed.[27]

A clear indication of other factors at work was that, for much of the summer, sterling was weak not just against the French franc but against the Swiss franc, the Dutch gilder, and the dollar. The spreading financial crisis, which forced Dutch and Swiss bankers to run down London balances, goes some way to explain the pressure on sterling. There were also seasonal factors – the Bank had lost gold every summer since 1925 – and there was a secular decline in the balance of payments. Important as these were, they do not wholly account for the sudden rush of selling that began on 15 July and continued for the next two months.[28] Some was speculative selling: an outrush of hot money created, despite strenuous denials, by British nationals as well as foreigners. As early as February Norman had had to dissuade Lord Bearsted, financier and chairman of Shell, from bearing the pound. During the summer Moret, and sources close to Morgan Grenfell and the Federal Reserve Bank of New York reported a British flight of capital.[29] Even *The Bankers' Magazine* admitted that sterling was being sold not only by foreigners but 'to our shame, be it said, by Britishers'.[30] The claim that it was the foreigner who was undermining sterling diverted criticism from the City, but like the alleged French conspiracy, it did not square with the evidence.

Nor is there much doubt some selling was due to pessimistic talk in official British circles. During July J.H. Thomas, Snowden's private secretary Donald Fergusson, and Norman's colleague Sir Charles Addis were all heard in public to say that sterling might soon be forced off the gold standard.[31] Later MacDonald blamed Henderson, claiming he had loosed a similar rumour in Paris, and French ministers confirmed this had shaken confidence in sterling in the nervous Paris market. MacDonald managed to forget that he had telephoned Henderson in Paris, and on an open line urged him to advance the London conference by a day because of serious developments that threatened a moratorium.[32] But whatever was said or denied it was common knowledge that the City had huge short-term liabilities, while much of its short-term credits were tied up in Central Europe. The Macmillan Committee report, published on 13 July, confirmed this in harsh statistical terms.[33] Hence, as Wigram warned the King, a German collapse would have an awful effect on the City and on sterling.

The London conference lasted from Monday 20 July to the 23rd. The statesmen seemed frantic with worry and began almost at once to justify their inability to do anything more. MacDonald pointed out that Britain held relatively more short-term credits in Germany than any other country, and indicated that it was now up to Germany to take the necessary steps to secure French funds. Neither the Germans nor the French were however prepared to make the necessary concessions. Brüning pointed to the extreme deflation already imposed on his people and warned that they could stand no more. Flandin stated that while French bankers held only 5 per cent of German short-term liabilities, they were at least not running them down, an assertion that Brüning confirmed. Laval, speaking to British delegates, added that France had also contributed a good deal indirectly to Germany's support by leaving large balances on deposit in third markets; in other words, it was French money in London which British bankers had used to keep Germany afloat. French Ministers also pointed out that they alone had advanced a concrete proposal: a large long-term loan to Germany, guaranteed by the three principal creditor powers.

The French proposal got nowhere. Henry Stimson, the American Secretary of State, who was participating in the conference, refused to contemplate a government guarantee for any loan, British Ministers were becoming uncomfortably aware that they were scarcely less in need of assistance than the Germans, and the French themselves continued to insist upon unspecified political concessions which the German delegates would not discuss. MacDonald suggested that France might assume liability for some of Britain's short-term commercial credits to

Germany. Flandin refused: he could not dictate to French banks, and they were not prepared to risk more capital without appropriate guarantees. Snowden then suggested that the Finance Ministers present should examine the possibility of collective central bank action. Emile Francqui, the Belgian delegate, warned against simply returning the ball to the central bankers' court. But delegates for the other creditor countries leapt at the suggestion.[34]

As the conference went on, frustration in the British delegation became acute. Henderson was abruptly rebuffed by von Bülow when he again urged the Germans to contribute to political appeasement; angrily Henderson accused them of 'fiddling while Rome was burning'. Foreign Office officials pointed out that since the moratorium proposal the United States had 'taken no action whatever'. Others directed their anger at the French for trying to impose on Germany what MacDonald called 'slave conditions'.[35] Tempers were short because of awareness that Britain was helpless. As Vansittart cynically commented:

> We are no longer on very strong ground for advising the German Government … seeing that there is at present little chance of anything of real value being done – least of all by us.… The best and most we can go for is … something for the shop window, since the financiers produce even smaller mice.[36]

At the third session MacDonald presented the draft statement prepared by the Finance Ministers. They recommended that the central bankers renew their existing $100 million credit to Germany for another three months, rediscount commercial bills in the Reichsbank portfolio, and make concerted efforts to discourage private lenders from further running down their credits to Germany. Snowden, who had almost certainly been speaking with Norman, then threw the meeting into confusion by condemning this attempt to lean on the central banks and private lenders. Instead, he demanded that the interested powers must break the vicious circle by agreeing to abandon reparations and war debts: 'We cannot shirk hard facts indefinitely. We may, like an ostrich, bury our heads in the sand so as to try to hide for a time, but the blast will continue to blow and we shall have to face it sooner or later.'

Stimson, visibly angered by this slight, read out Snowden's own words of the previous day calling on the central banks for help. As he reminded the others, he had agreed to attend the conference on the clear assurance that the war debt–reparation issue was avoided. MacDonald sided with Stimson, affirming that the conference must remain within the bounds of the agreed agenda. In the end the conference agreed to recommend that commercial short-term creditors participate in a 'standstill' on withdrawals, that the central banks maintain their credit to the Reichsbank, and that the BIS set up an expert committee to investigate Germany's credit requirements and the possibility of converting a portion of existing credits into long-term loans.[37] But that was all. The politicians, shaken by the slump and carried along on the flood-tide of nationalism it was creating throughout the world, had lost the capacity to work together. Despite Francqui's and Snowden's warnings, they had hurled the ball back to the central bankers' court – back, in other words, where it had been two weeks before.

On the evening of 22 July Norman called on Snowden at 11 Downing Street to warn of serious weakness in the pound. In little over a week the Bank had lost £15 million in foreign exchange, or nearly a quarter of its free reserves. The following day when the conference ended and the world learned that the politicians had failed to devise any solution for the crisis, pressure on the pound would intensify. Already forward sales of sterling had reached ominous proportions, and Norman intended to recommend a 1 per cent increase in Bank rate when the Committee of Treasury met next morning. He was sending Kindersley to Paris on the 25th to arrange a short-term credit for the Bank, and would discuss a larger long-term loan with J.P Morgan Jr when the American banker arrived in London on the weekend. The politicians, by failing in their responsibilities, left him no choice. Snowden mentioned the report of the Committee on National Expenditure or May Committee, which was soon to be published showing a large budget deficit for the coming year. Norman warned of the need to forestall a deficit if sterling was not to be further endangered, a sentiment with which Snowden wholly agreed.

Next day Hopkins added a further warning on behalf of Treasury officials. The May report would soon confirm a prospective deficit on the national accounts of £120 million, which, he admitted, 'may exaggerate the position' somewhat, since almost half of it (£50 million) represented repayment of past debt. But he had no doubt that with the trade balance in a parlous state and sterling under constant pressure, attempts to explain away the figures would do no good; there must be immediate concrete proposals for balancing the budget. When Norman met Morgan to discuss a loan Hopkins was sure the American's first question would be, 'Will steps be first taken about the dole and the budgetary position?'[38]

Hopkins was half right. Meeting at Norman's home on Sunday afternoon, Morgan and his two senior London partners, Sir Edward Grenfell and Eric Whigham, almost immediately discussed the budget, but it was Norman, not Morgan, who raised the subject. Norman, on the verge of another nervous collapse, complained bitterly that the government paid no attention to his warnings against excessive spending and seemed to be 'looking forward to an indefinite period of unbalanced budgets and obtaining necessary cash by short-term borrowing'. Morgan, who evidently had favoured a British government loan, was naturally disturbed. He now suggested that the government, before approaching its American bankers (his own firm) should prepare a plan showing how it intended to confront the budgetary problem. Norman agreed, saying he had Snowden's permission to discuss the situation candidly and report back. By this, one may assume, the Chancellor shared his anxiety for immediate and drastic budgetary reform, and would not be displeased to be able to tell his Cabinet colleagues that the bankers made this a condition for any loan.[39]

The British bankers may appear to have been not a little self-serving. Having lent vast sums of borrowed money to Germany – and not as in pre-war times in the form of self-liquidating trade bills but mainly as unsecured bank credits – they then attempted, when repayment of those credits became doubtful, to restore confidence in the pound by pressuring their government into vigorous retrenchment.[40] Yet by their own lights they doubtless felt they had done no wrong. Their task had been to restore London as the financial engine of the postwar world economy. The government's task was to keep the budget balanced and avoid obstructing the impact of world market forces on domestic wages and prices. The bankers had done all they could, it was up to the politicians to do the rest. The principal difficulty was unemployment insurance, known derisively as the dole. Not only had it become a major charge on the budget as the slump drove up the numbers of unemployed and undercut its premium basis, but at present levels of benefit it allegedly blocked any further reduction in wages, making it impossible for Britain to compete in world markets. Norman, the Bank of England's economic adviser Professor Henry Clay, the financier Robert Brand – almost everyone in the City agreed on the need to put this right, however awkward it was to say so with a Labour government in office. Aside from Amery, Maxse, and a few others on the radical right, they could also count on the support of opposition parties, members of the FBI, Fleet Street, the Treasury, and every other conservative interest.

Their anxiety for retrenchment was only too understandable when the pound threatened to go the way of the schilling and the mark. If their aggressiveness betrayed a certain desperation, it was perhaps because many of them faced severe personal loss. At the end of July a standstill agreement was adopted whereby London banks and acceptance houses left some £70 million tied up in Germany.[41] Already Lazard Brothers was virtually bankrupt and kept afloat only by means of a £3 million lifeline from the Bank of England.[42] Sir Robert Kindersley,

Lazards chairman, was 'a ruined man', Sir Charles Addis noted dourly in his diary.[43] The British Overseas Bank was in similar straits and so, by all the evidence, were Schroeders, Seligmans, Helbert Wagg, Barings, and many other financial houses.[44] But the bankers only behaved as could be expected in the midst of a severe exchange crisis. What was surprising was the willingness of senior Labour ministers to encourage the attack on social expenditure – that and the frequency with which defenders of the pound, in their desperation to force the government to accept its responsibilities, undermined the very confidence they were seeking to restore. The May Committee's overdrawn picture of deficits in the public account is the best-known instance. Norman's discouragement of an American long-term loan is another. There were more.

On Saturday 25 July, Kindersley flew to Paris to discuss temporary financial assistance with Clément Moret, who was only too ready to help. By Sunday afternoon arrangements were in hand for a £25 million support credit. At Moret's suggestion a similar credit was arranged the following week through the Federal Reserve Bank of New York.[45] On Thursday 30 July, Snowden told the House of approaching budgetary problems, while declaring his readiness to impose harsh sacrifices to maintain 'the proud and sound position of British credit'.[46] Meanwhile the Bank's Committee of Treasury approved a further 1 per cent increase in Bank rate to 4½ per cent. All seemed secure for the steadying of the exchanges, when the May report the next day confirmed a prospective £120 million budget deficit.[47] In Hopkins' words, this 'flashed round the world'. On Saturday, with Parliament in recess and the markets closed, the Bank announced the French and American central bank credits and a £15 million increase in the sterling fiduciary issue. Monday 3 August was a bank holiday, and sterling remained above gold export point when the markets reopened on Tuesday. The government, however, had still done no more than promise to form an Economy Committee to examine the Budget deficit before dispersing for the summer recess. This was too much for Norman and his colleagues, who, frustrated by the need to borrow abroad, and particularly from Paris, decided upon a drastic handling of the credits 'to make the British government understand the seriousness of their position'.[48]

Governor Moret was deeply concerned at hostile references to French financial manipulation by the British press. He was sure the rundown of London balances by French commercial banks was prompted not by lack of confidence in sterling, let alone malevolent political designs, but simply the need for liquidity in face of withdrawals from Paris, due to the worsening situation in Germany. He therefore insisted on sharing the Bank credit with all the leading Paris banks as a way of demonstrating their solidarity with London and countering press speculation. Bank of England officials, however, did not appreciate his motives. Rather than being grateful, they were annoyed; the only result they could see was to ensure that any drawing they made on their credit would signal their exchange position to the Paris market. To restore secrecy they asked Moret to call up the whole of the credit immediately. Then, to jolt their own government into retrenchment, they called Moret on Wednesday 5 August and, over his protests, ordered him to suspend intervention in sterling trading.

The Bank of France had purchased £2 million sterling on Tuesday and further small purchases at the start of exchange dealings next morning. At mid-morning the Bank's broker was obliged to say that he was no longer a buyer of sterling. The result was pandemonium as dealers, suspecting the worst, rushed to sell sterling, and for the first time since the end of July the sterling–franc exchange fell to gold import point in Paris. This led to weakness against the dollar and other currencies, and to anxious inquiries from the Bank of France and the Federal Reserve Bank of New York. The Bank of England hastily reversed its policy and called on the Bank of France to intervene in support of sterling. But by then the damage was done. Some £2.5 million in reserves were lost before sterling was restored above gold import point in Paris. More important, the psychological effect of the central bank credit was gratuitously and irretrievably lost.[49] Perhaps it did not matter. Perhaps London's exposure to the liquidity crisis in Central Europe and Britain's own yawning deficit in international payments made a renewed run on sterling only a matter of time. But one cannot be sure.

On 20 July the crisis took another victim when Norman collapsed from nervous exhaustion and had to be carried home from the Bank. He did not return for the balance of the crisis, and the Bank came under the control of Sir Ernest Harvey and Edward Peacock. Harvey, the Deputy Governor, was a permanent official. He had joined the Bank forty-six years earlier as a clerk straight from public school. He had made central banking his whole life, indeed had lived in the Bank before the war and one of his children was born there. Utterly dedicated to the Bank's interest, but a quiet, cautious man, he had been content to work within the long shadows cast by Cunliffe and Norman, and now allowed Peacock to play the leading role. Peacock, tall and dignified in appearance and decisive in judgment, was a son of the manse from Glengarry County in Ontario, a one-time school teacher who had made a career in merchant banking in London since 1907. A director of the Bank of England from 1921 to 1924, he returned in 1929 as the Barings representative, succeeding Lord Revelstoke. He was also Revelstoke's successor as financial adviser to the King, a most useful position for maintaining pressure on the government.

In the aftermath of the Paris exchange fiasco, French and American central bankers renewed their deprecation of the pessimistic rumours freely circulating in London, and urged the British to make liberal use of the new credits to combat speculative selling. Bank of England officials refused. Instead they continued to allow their gold reserves to be run down, hoping to make the politicans act.[50] On Thursday 6 August, Harvey reported to Snowden from the Bank's Committee of Treasury. All the directors present that morning agreed that the situation was 'extremely grave. However black the Governor may have painted the picture in his discussions with you, his picture cannot have been more black than theirs today.' Time was running out. The Bank had lost £60 million in gold and foreign exchange, practically exhausting its free reserves. The bankers could do no more while the budget deficit undermined foreign confidence in sterling. A further rise in Bank rate would be taken as a sign of weakness in present circumstances. And whereas Governor Moret would have arranged a long-term loan a few weeks ago, that was now out of the question since Moret regarded Britain's predicament as similar to that of France in 1926 when Poincaré halted the run on the franc by stringent reforms. Moret, like every other foreign authority, now awaited such action from the British.[51]

That Moret believed the British were living beyond their means is certain: this was accepted wisdom in official French circles. Nonetheless Harvey's claim that he could get no help from foreign central bankers was contradicted by all the evidence. During late July Governor Harrison, with Moret's endorsement, had repeatedly urged Norman to take up a large long-term loan as well as short-term credits. It was Norman, not the foreign bankers, who was 'dubious' of such a step while the politicians left the budget unbalanced.[52] On 7 August Moret urged the Bank of England to reconsider a loan, and Harrison again supported the idea.[53] On 11 August Walter Layton reported from BIS headquarters in Basle that Emile Moreau, the Bank of France's nominee on the German standstill inquiry and chairman of the Banque de Paris et des Pays Bas, was worried by the weakness of sterling and utterly at a loss to know why Britain was not taking up a loan in Paris. He was sure that 'the one and only foreign loan which would be really popular would be an English loan – but that it ought to be raised *now*'.[54] That same day in London Leith Ross met Escallier and Bizot, whom Flandin had sent over to see what cooperation was possible; among other things the French Treasury officials discussed a British loan in Paris, which they were confident could be arranged. Leith Ross dismissed the idea. In fact the Treasury, like the Bank, regarded a loan as a way of putting off disagreeable financial reforms, which could only increase the final reckoning.[55]

Snowden at least was ready to act. As he wrote to MacDonald on 7 August, the budget deficit would be huge. The trade situation was grim and the prospects worse. The burden of supporting the unemployed, with 3 million out of work in 1931 and probably 4 million in 1932, was financially intolerable. Revenue sources had already been taxed to the point of diminishing returns. Unless they were to start printing money the only thing to do was to convene the Cabinet Economy Committee forthwith and begin serious retrenchment.[56] MacDonald hurried back from Lossiemouth, heard Snowden's report, from Harvey and Peacock heard the latest on the exchange position, and in the evening of the 11th issued a statement to the press confirming that the Economy Committee would hold its first meeting the very next day, and that he was determined to balance the budget.[57] With MacDonald's permission, Harvey met the Liberals' representative, Sir Herbert Samuel, and the Conservative leaders to inform them of the grave situation. Baldwin was persuaded to break off his holiday in Aix-en-Provence and met Grenfell, the Conservative MP and Morgans partner, amidst the dust covers of his London house where Harvey and Peacock called later in the day. He trusted the bankers' advice, but could not hide his annoyance at having his vacation interrupted and at once returned to France, leaving Neville Chamberlain as Conservative representative.[58] It was a different story with other Opposition leaders, who used the bankers' warnings to negotiate with their Labour opponents.

Earlier in the summer, before the sterling crisis began, Amery had met his old friend Jack Seely on the train to Cowes and learned that Seely had been 'colloquing a good deal with JRM[acDonald] and the King on the subject of a National Government'. Amery encouraged the idea. With MacDonald drawn into a Conservative-dominated alliance he saw a possible arrangement whereby workers were offered high wages and industry preferential tariffs while the economy was boosted by a reflationary bimetallic monetary system. Thus would his dream of a Greater British Empire be realised.[59] For months he had laboured to forge a producers' alliance under the imperial banner. By August he had at last secured the agreement of the FBI, NFU, Chambers of Commerce, and other representative bodies, on the thorniest issue, agricultural policy.[60] It depressed him to hear talk of retrenchment when what was needed was a large scheme for expanding demand behind Empire tariff walls. Chamberlain seemed to have been driven off course by the bankers.[61]

The difference between Amery and Chamberlain was that Amery identified Britain's fate with leadership of the Empire, whereas Chamberlain worried about the future of capitalism itself. On the 12th Chamberlain met MacDonald and Snowden, who were ready to do whatever was necessary to balance the budget, in spite of the prospect of an even larger deficit than that predicted by the May Committee.[62] Chamberlain gloated over this opportunity to drive the Labour Party – 'the enemy' as he persisted in calling it[63] – onto the rocks of retrenchment, destroying it, or forcing it to jettison its socialist policies. Yet he saw the advantage of salvaging MacDonald and perhaps Snowden and a few others from the wreckage to head a national government which would be able to reconcile working-class voters to the harshest measures. Then and only then could Britain take up her imperial mission.

Everyone and everything seemed to conspire to bring about a national government. For Snowden and MacDonald the crisis underlined the need for the all-party cooperation they had been looking for since the start of the year, and they regularly talked of, or encouraged talk of, a national government. Conservative and Liberal leaders were equally receptive, not least because it would cause a rift in the Labour Party. Wigram, the King's secretary, kept pressing for a national government, and so did Geoffrey Dawson, editor of *The Times* and a regular in Court and Conservative circles.[64] Conservative and Liberal newspapers daily reminded readers of the awful calamity awaiting the country in the absence of immediate retrenchment. And the bankers frightened everyone of influence with warnings about declining reserves and the constantly reiterated claim that only savage retrenchment would restore foreign confidence in sterling.[65]

At the first session of the Economy Committee Snowden gave the Treasury's new estimate of the 1932 deficit as £170 million, not the £120 million of the May Committee prediction. The committee adjourned until early the next week to prepare proposals. This time Henderson led off with an appeal to remember the party's commitment to welfare, particularly the welfare of the unemployed. MacDonald and Snowden brushed this aside, saying that temporary sacrifices were necessary to save the pound, and Henderson, never at home in economic debate, fell silent.[66] A revenue tariff was proposed but was opposed by Snowden and several others. The only alternative seemed to be deflationary adjustments in Exchequer income and expenditure. The committee adopted the face-saving formula of 'equality of sacrifice', whereby reductions in services which benefited chiefly the working class would be matched by increased taxation on middle-class incomes. They failed to agree on a reduction in the standard rate of unemployment benefit, but did agree on economies totalling £78.6 million of which fully £43.5 million was to come from the dole. On the revenue side they approved an increase of £88 million in taxation including a new tax on fixed income securities. In the tradition of confidentiality, however, they left details of tax changes to the Chancellor, which, given Snowden's susceptibilities, was a risky thing to do. Almost at once the Treasury informed him that a tax on rentier income was administratively impracticable, and that other measures such as a further reduction in the dole and indirect taxes on consumption goods should be adopted in its place. Snowden, it appears, was ready to accept this extraordinary piece of special pleading, yet he said nothing about it to his colleagues.[67] Thus they drafted their report on 18 August, believing it fulfilled the principle of equality of sacrifice.[68]

All next day the Cabinet debated the committee's report. Apprised of the Treasury's new estimate of the budget deficit and the gravity of the sterling crisis, Ministers agreed to the proposed £88 million in additional taxation as well as £29 million in economies on education, roads, the armed forces, health, and other services, and £28.5 million from the unemployment insurance scheme. But again Ministers baulked at more radical measures. Johnston, Lansbury, and Greenwood stood out against a reduction in the standard rate of unemployment benefit, while the problems in transferring responsibility for £20 million in transitional benefits from the Exchequer to local authorities were left to a subcommittee chaired by Margaret Bondfield.

In his summary of the committee's work Snowden had not mentioned the revenue tariff proposal, but Henderson raised it and, on forcing a vote, found fifteen of the twenty-one Ministers were in favour.[69] At this Snowden launched into a tirade, particularly against his former ally Graham: 'William, there will be a free trade candidate next time in Central Edinburgh.'[70] As usual he had his way, threatening that he and several more would otherwise resign. After eleven hours the Cabinet adjourned, having agreed to £57 million in economies and provisionally to another £20 million. This was a vast amount, in fact over 20 per cent of total welfare spending,[71] but still not enough to balance the budget or satisfy their critics.

The following day, Tuesday 20 August, revealed the government's dilemma. In the morning Opposition leaders called at Downing Street to hear the retrenchment proposals. MacDonald and Snowden, who gave them to understand that Cabinet had approved £78.5 million in economies, indicated that they quite agreed with Chamberlain and Samuel who were unimpressed: too much new taxation, not enough from the dole.[72] The rest of the day was largely given over to meetings with elements of the Labour movement. The Consultative Committee of the Parliamentary Labour Party and the National Executive Committee were content with a statement from MacDonald, and left matters in his hands. The TUC General Council were not so pliant. For two years they had pressed ministers to break the habit of responding to every weakening of the exchanges by retrenchment, and recognise other options. On the Macmillan Committee, the Prime Minister's Economic Council, and elsewhere they had asked for consideration of a modest tariff, Empire preferences, devaluation, abandonment of the gold standard – anything but another turn of the deflationary screw, which only forced other countries to act likewise, leaving everyone worse off. Again, ministers spoke of nothing else. Snowden, who attended reluctantly out of jealousy for his authority and disdain for working-class advice, tried to impress them with the seriousness of the financial crisis. Citrine stated that the TUC was not prepared merely to be informed of the government's intentions and would be submitting their own proposal. Bevin complained that MacDonald and colleagues kept Tory papers like the *Daily Mail* better informed than the *Herald*, or themselves. Despite denials, the council was sure the bankers were leading the government by the nose.[73]

That evening Bondfield's sub-committee on transitional benefits reported to Cabinet. They had failed to find the anticipated £20 million saving. Not only that: they ruled out as impractical the 'premium' from employed workers agreed in Cabinet the previous day, so that economies on unemployment insurance now reached only £20 million. Snowden was incensed. Pointing to the fall in the cost of living since benefits were set by the first Labour government and warning of the dire results if confidence in sterling was not soon restored, he demanded further economies. Several options were considered including a 5 per cent reduction in standard benefit.[74] But no decision had been reached when members of the Economy Committee had to leave to meet the TUC delegation.

Citrine, speaking for the delegation, repeated their opposition to mere deflation and proposed alternatives: increased public works, a tax on fixed income securities, temporary suspension of sinking fund payments, and possibly a revenue tariff. Snowden was exasperated: 'if sterling went the whole international financial structure would collapse, and there would be no comparison between the present depression and the chaos and ruin that would face us in that event. There would be millions more unemployed and complete industrial collapse.' His figure for unemployment had risen from 5 million to 10 million since morning, but the delegation refused to be frightened. Bevin coolly suggested that the effects of going off gold might not be all bad. Snowden would not discuss it, and the meeting ended.[75] MacDonald later recorded his loathing for these TUC leaders with their 'usual pompous and self-important (of the type produced by inferiority complex) attitude'.[76]

He next called in Harvey, who had been keeping up the Bank's pressure on him by daily reports on the sterling exchange position. Harvey was not encouraging. He insisted that 'from the point of view of the foreign interests concerned' there must be 'very substantial economies ... on Unemployment Insurance'.[77] Next morning MacDonald described this meeting to the Cabinet and appealed for further sacrifices. Snowden spoke angrily of the TUC delegation: the TUC had 'no real appreciation of the seriousness of the situation; the statements made appeared to be based on a pre-crisis mentality'. The Cabinet agreed the TUC must be told their advice could not be heeded. They approved a means test for unemployment insurance benefit and further cuts in education, but this saving of £2 million was as far as they could agree. Reduction in the standard benefit divided them 'almost equally'. Snowden opposed the revenue tariff proposal. The only additional initiative was the temporary suspension of £47.5 million from the sinking fund provision.[78] With this modest list MacDonald and Snowden set out to get the bankers' and opposition leaders' support.

Harvey, of course, dismissed it as utterly inadequate. He told them J.P. Morgan and Company, the government's financial agents in America, were willing to arrange a banking credit only on assurance of adequate reforms. He claimed 'foreign lenders regarded the heavy financial burdens on industry of the Unemployment Insurance Scheme as impairing the security of their loans'. Nor would he endorse suspension of sinking fund payments: 'any attempt of this kind to camouflage the true position would at once be detected'.[79]

Opposition leaders reacted similarly, and Snowden and MacDonald 'let it be quite apparent' that they too regarded the savings as inadequate. The Opposition leaders insisted that, if further economies could not be found, the government should resign or recall Parliament and face the consequences. After adjourning for consultation among themselves, Samuel and Chamberlain met MacDonald alone at Downing Street. They agreed to return after the Cabinet meeting next morning to hear the government's final proposal. If MacDonald was prepared to go on without his colleagues, they were prepared to work under him, they both assured him. MacDonald promised to bear their offer in mind.[80]

That Saturday morning Snowden tried to frighten colleagues into further economies by painting a grim picture of the calamity that would follow suspension of the gold standard. He betrayed his long-smouldering hostility towards the Labour movement: 'he had no doubt whatever, if he was compelled to choose between retaining the Labour movement in its present form and reducing the standard of living of workmen by 50 per cent, which would be the effect of departing from the gold standard, where his duty would lie.... The position could only be rectified by resolute facing of this Unemployment Insurance question.' Even then the Cabinet refused MacDonald's proposed £20 million saving, including a 10 per cent reduction in the standard unemployment insurance benefit. Only after Snowden and Thomas weighed in against resisters did they retreat a step, authorising MacDonald to inquire 'for informational purposes only' if the additional cuts would satisfy their political and financial critics.[81]

Opposition leaders, while pleased at the reduction of the dole, cautiously left the adequacy of the proposals to the bankers.[82] Harvey was less pleased. The American and French central bank credits of July were now almost used up, and to ride out the storm he believed both a loan and further credits were needed. But the tables were turned: before, he had been pressuring the politicians, and now they were forcing him to make an awkward choice. To make matters worse, MacDonald had asked him to approach the Americans for help without telling them the full extent of the prospective budget deficit. This was tantamount to issuing a false prospectus, which to a banker like Harvey was the worst kind of sin.[83]

Next morning, Sunday 23 August, MacDonald called on the King to warn that opposition in the Cabinet might make it impossible for him to carry on beyond that evening. The King had cut short his stay at Balmoral on account of the crisis and Wigram had just passed on Geoffrey Dawson's urging to do everything possible to see that a Labour government secured sacrifices from the working class.[84] Peacock, the King's financial adviser, had also called on Wigram that morning to warn that the future of sterling could be measured in hours, not days, and entreat him to bring the pressure of the Crown on the politicians to secure retrenchment.[85] Thus the King coolly and skilfully encouraged MacDonald to remain: he was 'the only man who could carry the country through'.[86]

A few hours later, senior Morgan partners met in New York to decide on the British request for help. Their predicament was acute. The Cabinet wanted a reply by 7 p.m. in order to decide the future of the government before the markets opened on Monday morning. But this in New York was 2 p.m., which left scarcely enough time to find out how much could be raised, especially since key directors of many leading banks and bond houses were on holiday and the New York market itself was badly demoralised. In London the bankers had constantly claimed that a loan would depend on restoring *foreign* confidence in British finances, but deliberations here contradicted this: American bankers were only concerned with *London* financial opinion. They had to depend on Harvey for this information, and to their frustration he refused to give a forthright opinion.[87]

Ten days earlier Norman had recovered sufficiently from his nervous breakdown to embark on the Canadian Pacific liner, the Duchess of York, wearing a blue velvet beret and calling himself 'Mr Montague'.[88] On this Sunday evening Harrison telephoned him at the Château Frontenac in Québec to ask his opinion of the British government's economy measures. Norman, in another breathtaking example of brinkmanship, dismissed them as wholly insufficient.

> Norman felt that the program was inadequate; that we must not fool ourselves now; that any inadequate program would cause trouble in a year or so and that it is essential that we must force an economic adjustment now and not in a year or so from now; that the program, in his judgment, must be sufficiently drastic to place the cost of output and wages on a competitive basis with the rest of the world and unless that were done he was certain that the program would not be adequate; that if the Government attacked the situation courageously ... then, in his judgment, they would not need a credit at all.[89]

Harrison, who thought Norman still far from well, could not agree. With the Franco-American credit almost exhausted, the pound would be forced off the gold standard before the budget adjustments Norman wanted could work their effect on wages and prices.

The Morgan partners evidently shared this opinion, for George Whitney telephoned Sir Edward Grenfell, who was waiting with Harvey at the Bank of England. Whitney advised that a public loan was out of the question until Parliament had acted on budget reform and the New York market had been canvassed, but a private credit of $100–150 million, on the security of 90-day Treasury bills renewable for up to a year, would be 'less difficult' to arrange, provided Paris offered equivalent support and the Bank of England and the City gave 'sincere approval' to the reforms.[90]

Harvey rushed to Downing Street with the message. MacDonald emerged from the Cabinet room, seized the message, read it, asked Harvey to wait, and hurried back into the room.[91] The Cabinet, having hung about for two hours to hear the bankers' reply, now found themselves in a dilemma: accept the economies they themselves had proposed, and face the censure of their party's supporters, or reject them, refuse the offer of financial help, and make way for others to deal with the crisis. Nervous, ill-tempered discussion resumed for another half-hour as MacDonald made one last effort to persuade them to acquiesce in retrenchment. A majority were prepared to endorse the crucial 10 per cent reduction in unemployment benefit. But as discussion went round the table Henderson, who had held back in Cabinet deliberations, abruptly announced that he would resign rather than accept the reduction. Graham, Greenwood, Johnston, and Lansbury sided with him and others expressed their dissatisfaction. Belatedly, Addison proposed the abandonment of the gold standard, thereby removing any need for foreign assistance. Snowden brutally denounced the proposal, no one came forward in support, and the matter was dropped. Henderson suggested suspending sinking fund payments. Snowden and MacDonald claimed, perhaps too confidently, that the bankers and opposition leaders would not hear of it.[92] With no agreement possible, MacDonald announced his intention to submit his resignation to the King, and with Harvey set off for Buckingham Palace.[93]

MacDonald may have thought this was the end of his political career, and certainly he acted as if it were. Neither his political opponents nor the bankers appear to have liked or respected him much, but they were determined to keep him in office. In present circumstances the pull he exerted on Labour supporters made him an invaluable asset. The King was dining with Wigram and Peacock when MacDonald arrived at the Palace. The advisers retired, and MacDonald offered his resignation to the King. The King heard him out, but urged that rather than take a hasty decision he should sleep on it for a night, and with Harvey and Peacock, MacDonald returned to Downing Street.[94] They went in by the garden door to avoid the journalists and onlookers at the front. Sitting exhausted in the semi-darkness of the Cabinet room, still strewn with papers from the recent meeting, MacDonald spoke dejectedly of his inability to command support within his own party. The bankers pointed to Snowden, the only Minister present, as one supporter he could count on, and assured him he could play a role of more importance than ever. Meanwhile Grenfell, who had been dining with Harvey at the Bank, set off to find Neville Chamberlain. Chamberlain was preparing to retire, unaware that anything more could be done that evening. By 11 p.m. however both he and Samuel were at Downing Street, appealing to MacDonald to carry on as head of a national government. MacDonald, exhausted, left his decision for the morning when they would all go to the Palace. The bankers slipped back out through the garden, seen but not identified by lingering journalists.[95]

The contradictions of retrenchment

Monday 24 August seemed briefly to mark the turning-point in the crisis. At 10 a.m. the King invited MacDonald to form a national government, and leaders of the three main parties quickly agreed on terms for an alliance during 'the present financial emergency'.[96] At noon MacDonald told the Labour Cabinet the startling news. *The Times* that morning had inadvertently revealed that the Franco-American credit had been exhausted, which intensified the run on sterling. Reserves fell by £9 million, a record for one day.[97] By afternoon, with news of the formation of a non-party government, the exchanges became firmer. Almost at once Paris and New York were approached for new credit, this time to the government rather than the Bank of England.

Leith Ross and Siepmann, who flew to Paris on Tuesday in a chartered Moth, found French officials anxious to help, although cautious about the practical arrangements. The British asked for a £40 million credit; the French commercial banks offered £20 million firm and £20 million more by public subscription. The British officials, believing that the banks could provide the whole amount, were disappointed, and anxious about the American credit, which had been offered on the condition of equal French participation.[98] The French bankers were annoyed that the Americans, with their vastly greater resources, were unwilling to put up more than them. British officials were also annoyed at Morgans for taking advantage of Britain's vulnerable position by using it to justify high interest charges.[99] In fact, nervousness in New York due to the domestic depression and the German standstill made it difficult to form a syndicate large enough to handle the credit, and when New York learned that only half the French credit would be offered firm, the Morgans syndicate threatened to break up.[100] By now rumours were widespread and delay meant disaster, but on the evening of the 28th a compromise was reached. Drawings on the American credit would be limited to the French banking credit and public subscription. The announcement came none too soon. As Harvey informed the Cabinet on 3 September, the Bank had lost £130 million since the crisis began, and with the obligation to repay the £50 million central bank credits in gold if requested, only £80 million in free reserves remained.[101]

A week later Snowden introduced what he immodestly called 'the most momentous Budget ever introduced to the House of Commons in peacetime'. It was certainly among the most severe. It included tax increases of £82 million, economies of £70 million including a 10 per cent reduction in the standard benefit from unemployment insurance, and a temporary reduction of £20 million in the sinking fund provision.[102] The press at home and abroad praised MacDonald and Snowden for so courageously facing up to their unpopular duty, but Commons approval of the budget was by now a foregone conclusion. For this reason many now found it possible to think of other issues, and began to realise that the expected budget deficit was not the only, probably not even the most important, cause of sterling weakness.

Meeting with the Cabinet on 3 September, Harvey listed four other possible reaons for the continued run on sterling. One was the lack of confidence in all major currencies, including the Dutch florin, the Swiss and French francs, and the dollar, which was stimulating widespread hoarding of gold. Another was ordinary trade commitments, a seasonal source of weakness for the pound. Third, there was the probability that Britain's balance of payments had become adverse, a factor 'which many people appeared to think might be of importance'. The difficulty here was to know what it amounted to. The foreign exchanges had been relied upon to signal the approach of a deficit, whereupon the Bank was expected to use the weapons at its disposal to restore the balance. The Board of Trade compiled figures on merchandise trade, but the Bank had only begun systematically to collect statistics on the equally important 'invisible' or financial items for the Macmillan Committee, and as yet they were far from accurate. There was finally the possibility of a domestic flight from sterling. Lord Reading, Foreign Secretary in the new government and director of several large City-based companies, declared that 'many institutions and firms are ... selling sterling securities and investing in dollars, francs and guilders. ... They proceed upon the argument that as trustees for shareholders they are bound to take this action unless the Government makes it illegal.'[103] Harvey denied knowledge of British sterling selling 'on any large scale', but others corroborated Reading's claim which, if true, was scarcely surprising.[104]

Besides these factors and the tendency for all speculative currency movements to generate their own momentum, several developments contributed to nervousness. One was the evident anger within the Labour Party and TUC at MacDonald's desertion from Labour ranks, and at the alleged 'bankers' ramp' which had wrecked the Labour government. In face of repeated denunciations in the *Daily Herald*, it was open to question whether the retrenchment measures would not bring a wave of industrial unrest that would nullify their effect on sterling.[105] Government supporters inevitably talked of this threat, but scarcely less unsettling was the mounting evidence that, if the government was united on retrenchment, it was irreconcilably divided on other measures, and likely to throw the country into the renewed uncertainty of a general election.

On 8 September Parliament reconvened. Baldwin spoke of the serious external trade deficit as well as the budgetary deficit, but said that, in view of the controversy it would stir up, the trade deficit must await an end to the present emergency. On the other hand Churchill called for an immediate election to secure a mandate for 'a national policy' of a tariff and protection for agriculture. Amery followed with similar advice, and with fellow backbenchers expressing impatience at their leaders' collusion with free trade opponents, the tariff question reopened, much to the embarrassment of government leaders. MacDonald (as well as Henderson, who was now leader of the Labour opposition), was ready to accept a moderate degree of protection; Snowden was not. For the Liberals, Walter Runciman, although in his own words 'a hard-bitten free trader', was prepared to accept restrictions on luxury imports such as were imposed during the war, and Simon, agreeing that the external deficit was of far greater moment that the 'temporary unbalancing of the budget', would go further and accept a general tariff. Samuel would accept none of them.[106] Baldwin and his Conservatives thus faced the likelihood of splitting the government or at least forcing several important resignations which would reduce its all-party character if they adopted protection, and a rebellion within their own party if they did not. Their banking advisers strongly discouraged any thought of forcing a general election before the pound was out of danger, but from the Conservative leaders' standpoint there seemed more and more to be said for ending the uncertainty and at the same time securing a mandate for protection by going to the country.

Another sign that internationalism was on the way out – and another source of weakness for the pound, which Harvey did not mention – was increasingly open discontent with the gold standard. One form it took was renewed interest in bimetallism. This emerged early in July when Amery, as chairman of the new FBI–Empire Economic Union joint currency committee, placed it on the agenda.[107] Lord Hunsdon, the one financier prominent in the EEU, then wrote a letter to *The Times* on remonetising silver, which loosed a flood of comment, most of it favourable. On 1 September the China Association sent invitations to a meeting to discuss the issue. The hope was that remonetisation would increase world liquidity and stimulate trade, particularly with China and India, important British markets where silver had long served as a store of value and, until recently, an important part of their currency. The meeting was scheduled for the boardroom of Messrs Mathieson and Company in the City, but such was the response that the venue was transferred to the School of Oriental Studies, Finsbury Circus.[108]

Most sympathisers on the silver issue probably saw it as a way of reforming the gold standard and removing its deflationary tendency, not as an alternative monetary system. As the summer crisis wore on, however, others spoke out for more direct action. Thomas Jenkins, a leading Manchester industrialist, wrote to the FBI, calling for the devaluation of sterling rather than more deflation. Roy Glenday, the FBI's chief economist, regarded devaluation as perhaps undesirable because of the international repercussions, but accepted that it was probably inevitable.[109] Writing to MacDonald on 5 August, Keynes also accepted the near inevitability of devaluing sterling or going off the gold standard. Unlike Glenday, however, he saw it as an opportunity to form a 'new Currency Union' of the Empire and all other countries prepared to break free of the constraints of gold parities and join in a coordinated programme of reflation. There were 'far more people than you might expect, even in the City [who] are now in favour of something of this sort at the bottom of their hearts'.[110] Jay Crane, an official of the Federal Reserve Bank, who spent most of August in London, reported on the 24th:

> Even at the Bank of England one hears men like Siepmann and Rodd admit quite frankly that the only way out is for England and most other European countries to go off the gold standard temporarily, leave France and the United States high and dry, and then return to gold at a lower level. Discussions along this line have undoubtedly been an important reason for the lack of confidence in sterling on the part of countries like Holland, Switzerland and Belgium, which were heavy sellers of sterling during the crisis.[111]

Meantime the government mounted a massive propaganda campaign to promote acceptance of its retrenchment measures. The King's offer, prompted by MacDonald, to make a show of relinquishing part of the Civil List, was taken up. The difficult question was how much he should forego. Too little would not persuade his subjects to make sacrifices of their own; too much might invite speculation about the opulence of his life-style, as well as curtailing 'the spectacular effect of His Majesty's appearances in public', just when they were needed most as an instrument of social control. Eventually the Cabinet settled on £50,000, a cut of about 10 per cent in his public income and the same percentage as the unemployed were facing.[112] This was given headline treatment in the national press. Meanwhile MacDonald was filmed holding a letter posted from Germany during the period of hyper-inflation, and explaining that the 80,000 million marks in postage stamps had once been worth £4,000,000,000.[113] Sir Henry Page Croft similarly brandished worthless German notes, and Neville Chamberlain warned that 'whatever happened in Germany, it would have been far worse here if there had been a break in the pound'.[114] A few impatient voices were raised from Labour's ranks, denying that conditions were anything like those which brought the destruction of the German currency, but they received scant attention.[115] The press issued daily warnings that the abandonment of the gold standard meant a vicious circle of currency depreciation, spiralling food costs, uncontrollable wage demands, industrial unrest, economic collapse, and mass starvation. Some private firms also took advantage of the situation, to persuade workers to accept lower wages.[116] The public was duly frightened. Yet it is at least possible that this constant harping on imminent catastrophe did more to accelerate the flight from sterling than to strengthen it.

Not everyone in a position of influence was impressed. The Cabinet Secretary, Sir Maurice Hankey, asked Lord D'Abernon to broadcast an account of Germany's experience of hyper-inflation in all its grim detail. To his surprise, D'Abernon refused. Like Keynes, he found it ludicrous to worry about inflation at a time of vast underused capacity and millions of unemployed, and deplored attempts to orchestrate national hysteria. Although as yet unwilling to say so in public, he opposed any further defence of the gold standard. Professor Henry Clay, the Bank of England economist, was drafted to broadcast in his place.[117]

In Whitehall and Westminster the strain was showing. Treasury officials privately fulminated against the French for strangling Germany with unsupportable reparation demands, and the Americans for encouraging a standstill agreement that committed British banks to leave huge credits tied up in Germany, then cutting and running with a large fraction of their own funds.[118] In Paris to negotiate the government credit on 26 August, Leith Ross had taken it on himself to raise the issue of reparations with Flandin, indicating that only a revision of intergovernmental debt would save the world from worse trouble.[119] Flandin was decidedly cool, but this did not deter MacDonald from speaking to Stimson along the same lines.[120] Some elements of the press called loudly for an immediate conference to reconstruct the world economy. Feelings in the Foreign Office also ran high. Officials there accepted that Britain's influence in the world had long depended on her command of financial resources, and with this role undermined she found herself in a humiliating position *vis-à-vis* other powers and particularly nationalist France. They directed their frustration against the Treasury for a policy of confrontation with France, something they regarded as foolhardy in present circumstances.[121] In Parliament Labour spokesmen joined with Liberals in calling for reform of the world monetary and financial system, frequently in language tainted by nationalism and even xenophobia. Hugh Dalton referred to reckless overlending to Germany by City banking firms, 'many of them semi-foreign in character and foreign in origin, many of them manned by people whose names are not common British names'. Lieutenant-Commander Kenworthy spoke of the present government going 'cap in hand again to Wall street and Paris; ... When will the dictation end?' The usually mild-mannered internationalist Pethick-Lawrence shrilly proclaimed, 'this government has been formed for the express purpose of placing the neck of this country underneath the foot of foreign finance. ... The Government calls itself a national Government, but to me as an Englishman the position seems pitiably unpatriotic.'[122] The Labour Party might be internationalist, but this was the language of Beaverbrook and the *National Review*.

Five days after the introduction of the budget news reached London of a mutiny in the Atlantic Fleet at Invergordon. Ratings at this northerly port had read in their newspapers that retrenchment measures included a sharp reduction in their already meagre pay. Nothing had been done to prepare them for this blow nor to assist their families to adjust to it. When a few leaders from below deck demanded negotiations with the Admiralty, there was overwhelming support. Fleet manoeuvres were cancelled. The term 'mutiny' was disputed: official sources shunned it. But the irony of the situation was obvious. The budget, designed to restore confidence in Britain's finances, contained cuts in public sector pay so onerous as to induce unrest in the senior service, which sent shock waves throughout the financial system. The mutiny cannot be said to have undermined the effect of the budget, however, for the budget had already been discounted by the markets. During the four days Monday 7 September through budget day, Thursday the 10th, the Bank's reserve losses averaged £2.4 million per day. During the three-day trading period after the introduction of the budget and before news of the mutiny, daily average losses rose to £3 million.[123] Nor did the mutiny have an immediate impact on the exchanges: on 15 September, when the press reported the event, reserve losses were £2.8 million, less than on the two previous days. The following day they rose to £3.9 million, somewhat larger than on budget day, but on Thursday the 17th they soared to £6.22 million.[124] The figures suggest that no factor was decisive in weakening the pound but each contributed to it: criticism of retrenchment, talk of an early election, the mutiny, and more fundamental factors such as the worsening balance of payments and the financial crisis on the continent. Harvey stressed that the acute situation in Holland and Switzerland was forcing nationals of these countries to repatriate balances from London.[125] It did not help the situation, and certainly infuriated the bankers, that MacDonald, Thomas, and other Ministers repeatedly gave the latest figures on the Bank's reserves to cronies in the Commons smoking room, from whence they became known to speculators in the City and elsewhere.[126]

On Monday 14 September Harvey warned Snowden that with £20 million of the £80 million government credit used up, the gold standard could not be maintained for more than a month.[127] By the afternoon of the 17th £30 million of the credit had been drawn down and free reserves stood at £55 million. Harvey revised his earlier projection to 'ten days at the most'.[128] Since mid-summer Bank directors had been pondering whether to raise Bank rate again and restrict credit further, but reluctantly concluded that doing so would cause more harm than good by demonstrating their ineffectualness.[129] A Cabinet committee attended by senior Ministers and Bank and Treasury officials examined other possible means of holding the exchange. Lord Reading proposed calling up privately held domestic and foreign securities, to be used in the last resort as collateral for further loans. But aside from Reading, no one was prepared to interfere with private holdings, especially as the Treasury dismissed sterling securities as of no international value in a crisis, and pointed out that a voluntary appeal during the First World War had brought in only £56 million when the portfolio of foreign securities was greater than the present £3–4,000 million.[130]

The adoption of import restrictions was considered and set aside. As Sir Philip Cunliffe-Lister, President of the Board of Trade, pointed out, prohibitions (or quantitative restrictions) were ruled out by the Anglo-German commercial treaty whose provisions extended to other countries by the most-favoured-nation clause. A prohibitive duty on luxury items raised no legal difficulties but would raise a storm of opposition from exporting countries, especially France, and as exemptions of perhaps three months must be allowed for existing contracts, such a duty would be little use in the present crisis. And duties on non-luxury goods required a complicated system of exemptions and drawbacks. The Conservatives might press for protection, but conditions were not right, and a Cabinet which included the free traders Samuel and Snowden would never agree. Nor was there time to go to the country for a mandate.

Exchange controls were discussed and rejected. Disputing Reading's claim that Britons were responsible for a sizeable portion of sterling sales, the bankers claimed they were doing as much as was possible or necessary by means of 'moral suasion' through the clearing banks and the Stock Exchange. Harvey and Peacock could see only three alternatives: for the government to announce that it was prepared to take whatever action was necessary, including adoption of a tariff; to seek another foreign credit; or to abandon the gold standard. The bankers clearly preferred the first alternative, but divisions within the Cabinet ruled it out. No one was prepared openly to advocate the third, so the only choice was further foreign assistance. Something might be done, Peacock suggested, if the French and Americans were made to realise how much they stood to lose if Britain was toppled from the gold standard.[131]

On Thursday 17 September Bank of England reserves declined nearly £7.5 million before late in the day when the Bank learned of serious financial difficulties in Amsterdam. Those who had urged efforts to secure new foreign credits now hesitated,[132] but next afternoon MacDonald cabled to Stimson and Snowden to Flandin, reminding them of the grave situation all would face if sterling collapsed, and appealing as a matter of 'extreme urgency' for further assistance.[133]

MacDonald, who had motored down to Chequers to await replies, had to be recalled at once to Downing Street. At 9.30 p.m. Harvey, Peacock, and several Treasury officials reported that, with trading continuing in New York, the Bank's reserve losses were mounting out of control. That day they exceeded £17 million; the American credit was exhausted and only £15 million remained of the French credit. Harrison had confirmed that conditions in New York were too uncertain for raising further credits, and there could be no authorisation for government help until Congress reconvened in December. Moret, who had taken it on himself to increase his sterling balances, was prepared to offer further help. But the bankers were reluctant to become more beholden to the French, and doubtful that any Paris loan would be large enough. They therefore paid scant heed to Moret's offer, and MacDonald, who shared their hostility towards the French, was also content to let the offer pass.

From this point discussion turned to the question of when to suspend the gold standard. Harvey showing signs of distress, seemed uncertain how to proceed. After saying that the Bank would continue to sell gold through the half day trading on Saturday and as long as possible on Monday morning, he advised that the Bank must suspend sales on Monday morning with the press duly warned. This was accepted. All further agreed that the financial system should be kept functioning as normally as possible, with emergency powers in reserve. The clearing bankers, scheduled to meet the next morning, would advise on the need for a bank holiday. The crucial question was whether the public could be kept calm and not start a run on the banks or trigger panic sales of sterling securities. It was decided the Prime Minister should ask Sir Josiah Stamp about setting up a committee of advisers, chosen for their ability to reassure the public, particularly the working class, that contrary to everything said before, a dip in sterling did not spell runaway inflation.[134]

Earlier that morning Francis Osborne, the minister at the Washington Embassy, drove to Stimson's suburban home to deliver MacDonald's appeal for help. Stimson phoned Hoover (who already knew of the appeal through a leak in London),[135] and a Cabinet meeting was hastily arranged. At 11 p.m. Osborne was summoned to the White House for the verdict. As Stimson emotionally explained, they had examined every possible means, even reducing Britain's war debt obligations, but could see no way of helping in the brief time that remained. He was deeply distressed to admit it, but the United States was helpless to save Britain being forced off the gold standard.[136]

In Paris, Ronald Campbell, the Chargé d'Affaires, delivered Snowden's message to Laval, Flandin being in Geneva. Shortly before noon the next day Laval called in Campbell to report that Moret had 'spontaneously volunteered to seek a long-term loan, the details of which he was already discussing with Stimson'. Laval wished it to be made clear to London that however long the odds he would do everything possible to help. He had lent his personal support for the loan, but was waiting for Flandin's return before committing the government. The Credit Lyonnais, to whom Moret turned, was doubtful about raising more than £8 million: the Paris banks were having serious trouble of their own. Moret insisted that a loan of £15–25 million was possible, but in the event it was too little, too late. On Sunday the talks were broken off.[137]

When Harvey phoned Harrison in New York to ask him to avoid any serious break during Saturday's half-day of trading so that suspension could be orderly, Harrison repeatedly urged him to carry on. But Harvey was resigned. The Bank had lost nearly £18 million in reserves on Friday, another £8½ million in London that morning, and expected to lose the £6 million remaining from the French tranche of the government credit in the next few hours' trading in New York, especially as Americans had been the main sellers of sterling in recent days. The Bank would have lost £200 million since the crisis began and with no end in sight it was fruitless to waste more assets trying to hold the exchanges any longer.[138]

At Downing Street on Saturday afternoon Harvey and Peacock informed MacDonald of their latest plans. The Stock Exchange, which had slumped badly that morning, would be closed on Monday 'to give 24 hours to steady people's nerves'. Power to declare a bank holiday should be held in reserve in case of serious trouble, but closing joint stock banks was a serious matter, and earlier that day they had agreed to remain open on Monday and carry on as if nothing had happened. The British banks could be counted on to restrain clients from action damaging to sterling; the difficulty lay with the foreign banks in the country, and the central bankers wanted secret powers to impose, if needed, controls rationing access to foreign exchange. Samuel, who arrived with Baldwin midway through the meeting, disagreed. He was sure that the very existence of such powers would frighten sterling holders into selling, and create just the predicament they were trying to avoid. Harvey admitted he was only feeling his way, and agreed to consult further with banking representatives.[139]

Shortly afterwards Harvey, Leith Ross, Fisher, Stamp, and Keynes gathered in Fisher's room at the Treasury to resume the discussion. It was Keynes who now advocated exchange controls. Direct measures for curbing imports and expanding exports, he argued, threatened to weaken the world's debtor countries and reduce Britain's invisible receipts, nullifying their intended effect on the balance of payments. Instead of seeking recovery through further deflation or protectionism, both of which were self-defeating, he looked for coordinated international reflation. One approach might be to seek barter agreements with the Dominions, Germany, Argentina, and other producer countries, offering them prices substantially above world levels provided the proceeds were applied against their British debts. Another was to hold an international currency conference to secure agreement on greatly increasing world liquidity, with the threat that in the absence of agreement Britain would invite the Dominions and other like-minded countries to join her in a new currency and credit system. In either case, Britain would have to provide an energetic lead, requiring exchange controls to avert a paralysing attack on sterling. Stamp supported Keynes, but Leith Ross again insisted that controls would cause 'a complete breakdown of our trading business and would be more damaging to sterling than a free market', and Harvey, who only wanted controls as a last resort, agreed. Thus the bill suspending the gold standard provided for exchange controls only as an emergency measure, and found no place in subsequent policy planning.[140]

That evening and all day Sunday Ministers and officials rushed to complete arrangements for minimising the shock from news of Britain's suspension of gold payments. MacDonald, flanked by Baldwin, Snowden, and Samuel, called in editors of the national press to inform them and explain that this was forced on them by foreign developments, and that now the country's finances were on a sound footing, there was of course no reason for inflation.[141] Thomas cabled Empire governments to play up by minimising their recourse to authorised grant-in-aid funds or the London capital market, and to shoulder a share of Empire defence which now rested almost entirely upon Britain.[142] Fisher called on de Fleuriau, the French Ambassador and Dawes, the American, who in turn secured the cooperation of French and American banks in the City. The Bank of England approached City-based Swiss banks for their support.[143] In New York Harrison met leading American bankers at his home, while Tom Lamont of J.P. Morgan & Co. spoke to newspaper editors.[144] In Paris Flandin, who had offered to close the Bourse on

Monday, was requested to do so. This caused no little embarrassment when it turned out that his advisers, who had known nothing of his offer, warned that to close the Bourse might so panic already nervous rentiers as to make its reopening exceedingly difficult. In a compromise solution the Bourse remained open but sterling and sterling securities were not quoted, and secret instructions were given to refuse execution of orders in sterling by British nationals.[145] Diplomatic moves also led to the temporary closure of the Bourses in Berlin, Brussels, Copenhagen, The Hague, Rome, and Vienna, while in Switzerland trading was restricted as in France.[146] A meeting of the Cabinet on Sunday afternoon gave approval to these arrangements, while a hundred miles to the north at Sandringham the Privy Council gathered to receive the King's signature on emergency proclamations in case a bank holiday became necessary.[147]

In one of the most secret operations of the weekend, Harvey and Peacock met TUC leaders to appeal for their cooperation. The first meeting was at the Bank of England, the second at Brooks', Peacock's St James's club. The trade unionists were embarrassed to be seen in this haven of privilege, and insisted on a private room. But according to Peacock, the meetings were friendly enough. To promote accord, the bankers insisted there was no truth to the claim of a 'bankers' ramp' forcing the country to retrench. As they were leaving Peacock recalled Bevin saying, 'Well, I think you have made your case. But (and here he winked), don't expect me to say so in public.'[148]

The road to imperial protectionism

A mood of quiet apprehension prevailed on Monday 21 September. The morning papers, excepting only the *Daily Express*, relied for their editorial opinion on the government's statement of the evening before, which declared the suspension a tragedy but stressed the basic soundness of the country's finances. (The *Daily Express* declared it a victory for common sense.)[149] While the Stock Exchange remained closed, the banks reopened without any rush of withdrawals. From overseas first reports indicated no sharp break in confidence. Snowden's speech introducing the Gold Standard (Amendment) Bill in the Commons during the afternoon was also intended to reassure the world: although the situation was serious, this 'temporary' suspension was happily due to 'an exchange crisis and not because of any disorder in our own internal finances'. Since the government had balanced the budget 'and therefore removed the danger of having to print paper, which leads to uncontrolled inflation', the country could 'face the position with calmness'.[150]

Experts closest to the scene, including Peacock, Harvey, and H.D.

Henderson, did not expect the pound to collapse amidst a vicious spiral of currency depreciation, rising import prices, wage demands, and speculative attacks on sterling – contrary to hysterical warnings officially delivered before the break. Their best guess was that the pound would slump, then recover on profit taking, and subsequently remain only fractionally depreciated.[151] This is precisely what did happen. Nevertheless until they could be sure, there was bound to be extreme nervousness, mingled with a feeling of injustice and national humiliation. As Peacock put it[152] and Snowden repeated in his Commons speech, no one could accuse Britain of not playing the game: it was other powers that had flouted the rules and forced her into default. Saying nothing about domestic price levels, the City's precarious reliance on foreign short-term balances, or the domestic flight from sterling, he now credited Britain with leading the world back to financial and monetary stability in the postwar years, and blamed others for allowing their disproportionate share of war payments to produce a serious maldistribution of monetary gold stocks, which in turn led to a financial crisis and the collapse of international trade. Now that sterling had been forced off the gold standard, perhaps it would

> bring home to those who have hitherto been reluctant to enter into a discussion on the matter the pressing necessity of concerted action.... I think we are entitled to look for some recognition on the part of other creditor countries of their responsibility for the present situation.... Much more could be said, but I will only add this: America and France taken together have now acquired three-quarters of the entire gold in the world and have buried it in their vaults, where it is largely sterilised and useless for the purpose of promoting international trade.

Many others besides Snowden expressed exasperation and deep disappointment with the United States. Nigel Law, a bill broker, spoke privately of the City's reaction to reports that the Chase Manhatten Bank, America's largest bank, might be in trouble. The City welcomed the news, he explained, not out of *schadenfreude* but from the conviction that only something as immediate as this would bring home to Americans the need for concerted action.[153] Beaverbrook, though no friend of the gold standard, was deeply affected by Britain's symbolic loss of standing. Telephoned by a New York banker on the morning the suspension was announced, Beaverbrook roared into the receiver, 'You want my advice, do you? Well, you'll get nothing from me. It was you who did this – you and your banking friends in Paris. You worked for it and you got what you wanted. But I'll see you in hell before I give you any help.'[154] Keynes expressed something of the same annoyance when he commented privately, 'A week ago the pound looked the dollar in the face. Today it is kicking it in the arse.'[155]

But as usual it was France that came in for the worst abuse. Cecil, in Geneva for the Twelfth League Assembly, accused the French delegation of acting contemptuously towards Britain because of her temporary weakness, and reported proudly on a sharp exchange between Salter and Flandin, when Salter, repeating Snowden's explanation, aroused angry protestations from Flandin.[156] A few weeks later Sir Charles Mendl, a permanent official at the British Embassy in Paris, wrote to a friend of his visit to London. 'The feeling in London of intense "gallophobia" really frightened me. I have never seen anything like it, and lunching at one of our new Under-Secretaries' ... someone alluded to the "lousy French" which drew my goat and I was quite offensive.'[157] The feeling was particularly strong in the City, strong enough for de Fleuriau, the French Ambassador, to voice his concern to the Foreign Office and mount a quiet campaign to counter it.[158]

The idea of an international monetary conference, raised by the Macmillan Committee report in July then revived during the final run on the pound, received the government's endorsement in Snowden's speech of 21 September. During the next few weeks the necessity for a conference was affirmed by, among others, Walter Layton of *The Economist* and *News Chronicle*, Sir Herbert Samuel, Keynes, *The Statist*, and spokesmen for the League of Nations Union, Association of British Chambers of Commerce, and the Labour Party.[159] France, however, remained opposed, as did the United States, and a spirit of defeatism ruled out any initiative at the League of Nations.[160] Failure to make the world a more stable, peaceful place was underlined in the midst of the Twelfth League Assembly when the Japanese, bent on carving out an exclusive economic bloc for themselves and taking advantage of the turmoil in Europe, invaded Manchuria. The almost total lack of results from scores of attempts to foster collective economic action had made regulars to the League cynical. 'Conference,' according to Salter, had become 'an indecent word' at Geneva.[161]

For all the talk, however, it was obvious Britain too had turned its back on an international solution. Keynes in the press and Samuel in the Cabinet claimed that depreciation of the pound removed the need for a tariff and strengthened Britain's negotiating position *vis-à-vis* other creditor powers, and this was probably true.[162] But with the gold standard gone and not the remotest possibility of restoring it in the present grim uncertainties, the pressure to strike out in a new direction became overwhelming. Abandonment of the gold standard, the lynch-pin of economic internationalism, was accompanied by an almost complete ban on foreign lending. In October the government went to the country for a 'doctor's mandate' for economic recovery, a term well understood to include the possibility of tariff protection. Prompted by Conservative Central Office and enthusiastically led by MacDonald and Snowden, National candidates revived fears that their Labour opponents would send the pound the way of the rouble and the Reichsmark.[163] The result was a landslide victory for the National candidates, who received 14½ million votes and obtained 497 seats (472 of them going to Conservatives); the 6.6 million votes that went to Labour secured only 46 seats in the new Parliament.

The next month royal assent was given to an Abnormal Importations Act, granting the President of the Board of Trade discretionary powers to impose duties on a wide range of commodities, and that same day the Board placed duties of 50 per cent on 23 classes of goods.[164] In December a similar Horticultural Products Act was passed empowering the Minister of Agriculture to levy duties on imported fruit and vegetables.[165] Meanwhile sanitary restrictions were plied with increasing severity – their unchanged 'scientific' basis notwithstanding – upon a number of imported foodstuffs.[166] Then on 4 February 1932 Neville Chamberlain, as Chancellor of the Exchequer, introduced an Import Duties Bill which sanctioned a 10 per cent general tariff with temporary exemption for Empire goods, and included provision for an Import Duties Advisory Committee (IDAC) to recommend further duties or reductions.[167] Introduced with an emotional reference to Joseph Chamberlain's valiant struggle for Tariff Reform thirty years earlier, and adopted despite an open split between National Conservatives and National Liberals, the act came into effect on 1 March. Barely six weeks later the IDAC's first report, calling for import duties of 20 per cent on manufactured goods and 25–30 per cent on luxury goods, was implemented. In a further step to insulate the domestic economy from external pressures, the budget in June gave formal recognition to the exchange equalisation account, which placed £150 million in the hands of the Bank of England in order to iron out short-run exchange fluctuations and discourage the return to what now was accepted as the overvalued rate of £4.86.[168] The following month Chamberlain led a delegation to the Imperial Economic Conference at Ottawa, where a series of agreements was reached with the Dominions, establishing substantial intra-imperial preferences at the cost of raising barriers against imports from the rest of the world.

With this the era of economic internationalism ended, and a chapter of history closed.

Conclusion

Montagu Norman learned of the collapse of the gold standard when he reached Liverpool docks on the morning of 23 September 1931. The blow to the prestige of the Bank and the shattering of his plans for world capitalism came as a deep shock to him. He suffered another near breakdown, and sought medical advice before facing re-election for another two-year term as Governor.[1]

Yet the break with internationalism was not as complete and decisive as it must have seemed at the time. Leaders of the industrial community, having united in demands for relief from further deflationary pressures and an active trade policy, were driven apart again by the political crisis brought on by the slump. TUC leaders lined up behind the shrunken but shrilly anti-capitalist Labour Party. Industrialists, appeased by the introduction of trade protectionism, united behind the Tory-dominated National government that controlled Parliament for the balance of the decade on the promise of keeping socialism in check. Meanwhile spokesmen for the City found their voices again and discouraged monetary and financial experimentation. Having split over the question of cheap money in the winter of 1931, the Bank and the Treasury also united against monetary initiatives at the Ottawa Conference in the summer of 1932.[2] In 1933 Britain joined France in promoting currency stabilisation, while Franklin Roosevelt torpedoed the World Economic Conference by signalling new reflationary experiments. Subsequently the path was obstructed by the approaching war. But after 1945 British strategy was governed by the pursuit of a special relationship with the United States, for which the Americans, as the new world leaders, made multilateralism a condition: albeit haltingly and in conjunction with a half-hearted European commitment, Britain moved back towards a posture of economic internationalism.

Towards the end of the long period of postwar economic growth, between 1945 and 1973, academic interest turned increasingly to the idea of a corporate bias in British politics, with its suggestion of a tripartite decision-making process involving industrial capital, organised labour, and party political leaders.[3] However, since the onset of the latest world crisis its appeal has faded. Once again Conservative governments have loudly proclaimed their devotion to industrial recovery while subordinating their economic strategy to the attainment of narrow monetary targets. The City has re-established itself as the great mercantile and financial clearing-house of the world, and the CBI has been snubbed and disregarded just as its predecessors the FBI and NUM were treated in the 1920s. Once again worried talk is heard of de-industrialisation, a decline in the industrial spirit, and the failure of the educational system to supply the trained recruits required for modern high-technology industry. And once again the party system and economic disparities reveal the division between the North and South or South-East, which defines in an approximate way the industrial, and mercantile–financial communities. It may be said therefore that British capitalism reached a crossroads in the inter-war years without, however, permanently changing course.

But this is as much a study of international history as of purely British affairs, and the final observations are reserved for the wider scene. In recent years American scholars have given prominence to the role of the United States in restoring European stability after the First World War. The acute dollar shortage in Europe did of course make American loans or relief from war debt demands a matter of great importance, and on several occasions access to the American capital market was effectively used to promote European cooperation. But taking other aspects of European–American relations into account, nothing has been added to alter the longstanding view of America's role as faltering and contradictory: helpful in alleviating the war debt–reparation problem, but distinctly unhelpful on security issues or commercial relations and in allowing the Wall Street boom to undermine the international payments system. Britain was far more consistent in promoting multilateral trade and payments for most of the period. Unfortunately British influence was ambiguous for other reasons.

In the first place Norman and his allies in the City, Fleet Street, and Westminster, having won the battle for the gold standard in 1925, faced increasingly stiff domestic opposition to their form of internationalism after the coal crisis in the same year and especially after the general strike in 1926. It was not internationalism itself that was objectionable to most critics: rather it was the intensity with which it was pursued despite the divergent policies among Britain's main industrial competitors. Discontent in the industrial community led the government to back away from League-sponsored multilateral trade reform in the latter part of the decade, and instead move tentatively towards a policy of protection. A similar decline in leadership was evident in international monetary and financial relations.

As early as 1926 Norman feared the possibility of an international financial crisis; by 1928 he and other financial experts were virtually certain of one in the absence of decisive action by the major central banks. The Young Plan and the BIS were both products of this concern. Neither met the immediate problem of large and growing imbalances in banking liquidity. Rather than supporting Strakosch and Salter in their efforts to bring public pressure on the other central banks, however, Norman actively discouraged them and sought instead to limit deliberations to private and informal contacts among the central bankers themselves. This was an understandable response to the situation. American and French central bankers had grown hostile towards all proposals for expanding international liquidity and felt little sympathy for the worsening plight of the Bank of England. Norman, aware of this and shaken by domestic criticism of the gold standard, was anxious to avoid drawing further attention to the central bankers' failure to deal with the situation. He had spent ten years struggling to free the Bank of England and other central banks from public influence. He was not going to expose them to further censure now. But cajoling his foreign colleagues brought no result: London no longer possessed sufficient prestige or influence decisively to affect conditions in New York or Paris, and nothing Norman could do alone had the slightest chance of staving off the crisis.

A second source of ambiguity was illustrated most vividly when the second Labour government in 1929 sought to reinvigorate British international leadership, only to obstruct the second-best solutions available. Confronted with a general retreat towards protectionism, the government sought to hold the line against the discriminatory regional or bilateral schemes for salvaging trade that surfaced at this time. It may be doubted whether, even combined with a reflationary monetary policy, any useful purpose would have been served by entering into closer imperial economic arrangements, given the strong protectionist leanings of the Dominions. Nor was any French-led scheme on the lines of the Briand plan likely to succeed, given the change in German leadership following Stresemann's death and tensions elsewhere on the continent. But one cannot be sure. Despite resort to protectionism, the desire for economic cooperation in Europe was strong, and Britain's importance both as a political counterweight in the Franco-German balance and as far-and-away the largest import market placed her in a uniquely influential position. It was just possible therefore that a scheme along the lines of the Oslo Convention would, with British backing, have saved Europe and the world from the worst of the crisis. As it was, British policy failed utterly in its purpose. By September 1930 it was clear that the alternative to discriminatory trade relations was not equitable if reduced access to foreign markets and international peace, but autarky, nationalist extremism, and possibly another European war. Once again, as in the pursuit of the gold standard, the best was the enemy of the good.

Another aspect of international history that deserves comment is the hostility British authorities displayed towards the United States and France, particularly as the crisis developed. British feelings towards the United States, though intense, were generally kept from public view. If American trade made deep inroads into traditional British markets, American commercial and financial policies dislocated the international payments system, and American naval expansion plans threatened to upset the military balance, this was regrettable but largely unavoidable in view of America's burgeoning strength. Britain could not bully the United States into more responsible behaviour, and the need for her friendship made it too dangerous even to try. Perhaps partly through a process of transference, open hostility was concentrated instead on France. Not only did France offer numerous sources of dissatisfaction, but many of them seemed attributable simply to Gallic ill-will. Anglo-French relations in fact rested on mutual dependence, since both countries sought stability and peace in Europe and each required the other to hold the line against violent upheaval. Yet British authorities preferred to believe that it was only the French who in their weakness required foreign support, and that without French obstruction the German problem could be resolved. French insistence on a different national viewpoint thus appeared to be wilful obstruction of the path to peace, disarmament, and economic reconstruction, and the German problem became overshadowed by the French problem. Resentment had already reached a dangerous level when in 1931 French opposition to the Hoover moratorium endangered the gold standard, the keystone of the international capitalist system Britain had sacrificed so much to rebuild since the war. In reaction, British hostility knew no bounds; nothing Moret or Laval could do would persuade their British counterparts of French good will. This was a tragedy of the first order, for it meant that the three great democratic powers entered the period of fascist aggression thoroughly estranged from one another.

If 1931 marked the transition from a postwar to a pre-war period, in a very real sense the shape of events in the latter period were prefigured by developments in the 1920s. Britain's effort to set the example for economic internationalism, while not without effect in Europe, imposed a severe cost on Britain and brought its own reaction in increasing British interest in regional or continental economic blocs. The challenge from America's largely self-contained economy, the Bolsheviks' organisation of the Russian Empire, weakness and division in Europe, and centrifugal tendencies in the British Empire became all the more starkly apparent with every internationalist initiative. When progress towards multilateralism was halted in 1929, British and foreign support for limited economic blocs swiftly increased. But the new blocs that emerged differed from those anticipated by British imperialists. Germany pursued hegemony in *Mitteleuropa*, Japan extended its domination of Korea to Manchuria and China, and Mussolini sought to turn the Mediterranean into an Italian lake, while France was politically marginalised and the British Dominions proved resistant to integration into an Empire bloc, just as internationalist critics warned. By the time British authorities set aside the imperial dream as well as rigid principles of internationalism, the chance to influence the fate of Europe was nearly lost and six years of war were necessary to re-establish it. The peculiar character of Britain's capitalist system was only one factor in these developments. Nevertheless the central place Britain occupied in international political and economic relations at this time ensured it an importance that later events and the historian's common aversion to 'systems' have largely obscured.

Notes

Introduction

1 See in particular Carl Parrini, *Heir To Empire. United States Economic Diplomacy, 1916–1923* (Pittsburgh, 1969), Frank Costigliola, *Awkward Dominion. American Political, Economic, and Cultural Relations with Europe, 1919–1933* (Ithaca, 1984), and the extreme, almost conspiratorial account in Stephen A. Schuker, 'American Foreign Policy and the Young Plan', in *Konstellationen Internationaler Politik 1924–1932*, ed. Gustav Schmidt (Bochum, 1983), 122–30; also Melvyn P. Leffler, *The Elusive Quest: America's Pursuit of European Stability and French Security*, (Chapel Hill, 1979), and Werner Link, *Die amerikanische Stabilisierungspolitik in Deutschland, 1921–32* (Dusseldorf, 1970). The impression given in all these works is that of the United States leading the way after the First World War in rebuilding an 'open world economy' in face of an unhelpful and often obstructive Britain: a version of history that exaggerates the coherence of American intentions and actions, and seriously misrepresents British policy. As this study shows, British bankers and statesmen were deeply worried about the impact of American economic expansion upon the Empire, but remained committed to multilateralism and strenuously resisted a retreat into imperial protectionism. As for the American contribution, it is true that certain leading east coast bankers participated actively in European financial reconstruction, but they did so independently of and largely in spite of narrowly nationalistic administrations in Washington. To some extent, it seems, exponents of this revisionist history have adopted the outlook of American businessmen of the 1920s, notably their unalterable suspicion of the Old World (and particularly Britain whose power they greatly exaggerated), and their innocence about America's own ambitions. Thus anything Britain did in the international arena is regarded as self-evidently designed to regain Britain's 'financial leadership', while any American initiative is seen as a contribution to an 'open world economy'.

2 Stephen A. Schuker, *The End of French Predominance in Europe: The Financial Crisis of 1924 and the Adoption of the Dawes Plan* (Chapel Hill, 1976): Jacques Bariéty, *Les Relations franco-allemandes après la première guerre mondiale* (Paris, 1977); Denise Artaud, *La question des dettes interalliées et la reconstruction de l'Europe (1917–1929)*, tomes 1–11 (Paris, 1978); Walter A. MacDougall, *France's Rhineland Diplomacy, 1914–24: The Last Bid for a*

Balance of Power in Europe (Princeton, 1978); Marc Trachtenberg, *Reparation in World Politics: France and European Economic Diplomacy, 1916–1923* (New York, 1980).

3 On English nationalism see Tom Nairn, *The Break-up of Britain. Crisis and Neo-Nationalism*, 2nd edn. (1981), ch. 1.

4 Sir Henry Clay, *Lord Norman* (1957), Andrew Boyle, *Montagu Norman. A Biography* (1967).

1 The politics of economic internationalism

1 Sir John Clapham, *An Economic History of Modern Britain*, ii (Cambridge, 1967), 389; J.M. Keynes, *The End of Laissez Faire* (1926), 26 and passim.

2 Karl Polanyi, *The Great Transformation* (Boston, 1957), chs. 11–21.

3 Clapham, *An Economic History of Modern Britain*, i, 63.

4 *Ibid.*, 486.

5 Boyd Hilton, *Corn, Cash, Commerce: The Economic Policies of the Tory Governments, 1815–1830* (Oxford, 1977), 48, 56; Clapham, *An Economic History of Modern Britain*, i, 523; Frank W. Fetter, *Development of British Monetary Orthodoxy, 1797–1875* (Cambridge Mass., 1965), passim.

6 At the end of the First World War the interpretation of the gold standard mechanism changed from an emphasis upon the role of Bank rate in drawing in gold from abroad to its impact upon domestic activity and price-levels: an implicit recognition of Britain's diminished place in the world economy. See the description in UK, Committee on Currency and Foreign Exchanges after the War, *First Interim Report*, 1918, Cd. 9182, 3–4.

7 E.J. Hobsbawm, *Industry and Empire* (1968), ch. 6 and passim; P.J. Cain and A.G. Hopkins, 'The Political Economy of British Expansion Overseas, 1750–1940,' *The Economic History Review*, 2nd ser., 33/4 (November 1980), 485.

8 Bernard Semmel, *Imperialism and Social Reform, English Social–Imperial Thought* (1960), 94 and passim. The best study of the earlier part of the era remains Elie Halévy, *History of the English People, Epilogue, 1895–1905* (Harmondsworth, 1939).

9 Public Record Office, Foreign Office papers (hereafter FO), 368/1855, 20345/-, memorandum by F.H. Pierson, 'The Need for a Permanent Intelligence Bureau', 1916.

10 J.A. Venn, *The Foundations of Agriculture Economics together with an Economic History of British Agriculture during and after the Great War*, 2nd ed. (Cambridge, 1933), 480; Richard Jebb, *Empire in Eclipse* (1926), 122. There was no dissent when Lloyd George told the House of Commons on 23 February 1917, 'The war at any rate has taught us one lesson, that the preservation of our essential industries is as important a part of national defence as the maintenance of our Army and Navy.' Quoted in National Farmers' Union No. 1, 'The Nation's Food Supply' (March 1920). See also Keith Middlemas, *Politics in Industrial Society. The Experience of the British System since 1911* (1979), 123 and passim; Kenneth O. Morgan, *Consensus and Disunity: The Lloyd George Coalition Government, 1918–1922* (Oxford, 1979), 18, 27.

11 Jamie Camplin, *The Rise of the Plutocrats. Wealth and Power in Edwardian England* (1978), 26–27, renews the claim that industrialists replaced land-

owners as the dominant element in the ruling elite, although his choice of subjects rather belies the claim.

12 Stephen Blank, *Industry and Government in Britain: The Federation of British Industry in Politics* (Farnborough, 1973), 14.

13 A.R. Ilersic and P.F. Liddle, *The Parliament of Commerce: The Story of the Association of British Chambers of Commerce, 1860–1960* (1960), 168–69.

14 FO 369/912, 63184/f.63184, Crowe minute, 5 April 1916.

15 *The Times*, 16 July 1924, 22.

16 In the words of the London Chamber's secretary, his organisation was 'the dominant partner in the Chamber of Commerce movement'. London Chamber of Commerce papers (hereafter LCC), MS. 16,650/1, statement, 1 December 1930. The Chamber was founded in 1881, the same year as northern manufacturers formed the National Fair Trade League, Canadian manufacturers convened a meeting with their British counterparts to form the British and Intercolonial Tariff Trade Union Association, and controversy occurred over the pending Anglo-French trade treaty. It was intended primarily to wage the City's battle against protectionism. Steven R.B. Smith, 'The Centenary of the London Chamber of Commerce', *London Journal*, 8/2 (1982), 156–70.

17 United Kingdom, Committee on Finance and Industry (hereafter Macmillan Committee), *Minutes of Evidence*, i (1931), Q.2493; Federation of British Industries papers (hereafter FBI), FBI/S/Walker/100/2, Nugent to Rylands, 13 January 1919, Nugent to Pollock, 27 May 1919, Nugent to Allard, 17 June 1919.

18 Roland Nugent, the FBI's first director, and Roy Glenday, its longtime economic adviser, were both seconded from the Foreign Office's Commercial Department, Blank, *Industry and Government*, 15.

19 FBI/S/Walker/100/2, Nugent to Walker, 17 June 1919; *British Industries*, 28 October 1924, 621.

20 Blank, *Industry and Government*, 15–21; Wyn Grant and David Marsh, *The Confederation of British Industry* (1977), 17–22; Robert F. Holland, 'The Federation of British Industries and the International Economy, 1929–39,' *Economic History Review*, 2nd ser., 34 (1981), 287–301.

21 W.D. Rubinstein, 'The Victorian Middle Classes: Wealth, Occupation, and Geography', *Economic History Review*, 2nd ser. 30/4 (November 1977), 622 f.2; J.A. Clifton, 'Competition and the Evolution of the Capitalist Mode of Production,' *Cambridge Journal of Economics*, 1 (1977) 143.

22 See below, pp. 152–53.

23 On the CLA, see *The Times*, 24 June 1927, 9; Macmillan Committee, *Evidence*, i, memorandum, 31 December 1929. On the Central and Associated Chambers of Agriculture, see *Annual Reports*; W. Philip Jeffcock, *Agricultural Politics, 1915–1935, Being a History of the Central Chamber of Agriculture during that Period* (Ipswich, 1937). The statistics are from Venn, *The Foundations of Agricultural Economics*, 113.

24 Peter Self and Herbert J. Storing, *The State and the Farmer* (1962), 39; National Farmers' Union, '1908–1929' (1930).

25 Henry Pelling, *A History of British Trade Unionism*, 3rd edn (1976), table 302–03, 169, 172.

26 Ross M. Martin, *TUC: The Growth of a Pressure Group, 1868–1976* (Oxford, 1980), 219.

27 Labour Party, 'Party Constitution and Standing Orders' (1918), 7.
28 'Labour and Protection', *The Free Trader*, June 1923, 136–39; Halévy, *History of the English People. Epilogue*, iii, 112–13.
29 Henry Pelling, *A Short History of the Labour Party*, 5th edn (1976), 39.
30 *Ibid.*, 46, 50, 52, 56.
31 *Ibid.*, 48–49.
32 Richard Lyman, *The First Labour Government, 1924* (Princeton, 1957), 7.
33 Catherine Ann Cline, *Recruits to Labour: The British Labour Party, 1914–1931* (Syracuse, NY, 1963), 66.
34 F.W. Pethick-Lawrence, *Fate Has Been Kind* (1943), 34, 61.
35 See his *Towards the Peace of Nations: A Study in International Politics* (1928), a lengthy and impassioned appeal for Britain to 'lead the world ... along new paths of constructive peace and international righteousness'. xi. See also *Memoirs*. i. *Call Back Yesterday, 1887–1931* (1953), 59, 112, 121, 122. His orthodox views on trade and fiscal policy are evident in 'Will Capital Leave the Country?' ILP (1924), and 'Some Reflections on the Budget', *Labour Magazine*, May 1929, 14–15.
36 The portrait is drawn from the MacDonald papers and diaries, David Marquand, *Ramsay MacDonald* (1977); Mary Agnes Hamilton, *J. Ramsay MacDonald* (1929); Egon Wertheimer, *Portrait of the Labour Party*, 2nd edn (1930); and other sources.
37 John Scanlon, *Pillars of Cloud* (1936), 90, 92.
38 Runciman papers, 244, Free Trade Union papers.
39 Philip Snowden, 'The Menace of the Trusts and How to Deal with It', ILP (1919); see also his 'Socialism Made Plain', ILP (1920); 'Twenty Objections to Socialism', ILP (1920); 'Wages and Prices' (1920); *Labour and the New World* (1921), 153.
40 Viscount Snowden, *An Autobiography*, ii (1934), 723.
41 *Socialist Review*, January 1928, 3.
42 *The Times*, 23 November 1923, 14.
43 Lloyd George papers, G/18/8, Ethel Snowden to Lloyd George, 22 December 1923. See also Beatrice Webb diary, 43, 6 July 1929, and 23 September 1929.
44 Basil Fuller, *The Life Story of the Rt. Hon. J.H. Thomas. A Statesman of the People* (1943), 208.
45 H.R.S. Philpott, *The Right Hon. J.H. Thomas (Impressions of a Remarkable Career)* (1932), 138. See also Lyman, *The First Labour Government*, 279.
46 Pelling, *A Short History of the Labour Party*, 32; Mary Agnes Hamilton, *Arthur Henderson* (1938).
47 Arthur Henderson, 'Labour's Peace Terms', Labour Party (1918); Henderson, 'Labour and an After-War Economic Policy' (1917); 'Peace Terms', Labour Party (1919).
48 G.D.H. Cole and Raymond Postgate, *The Common People, 1746–1946*, 4th edn (1966), 451.
49 Rubinstein, 'The Victorian Middle Classes', 618.
50 *Ibid.*, 610.
51 Steen Eiler Rasmussen, *London, The Unique City* (1934), chs. 2–3. See also J.E. Neale, *The Elizabethan House of Commons* (New Haven, 1950), 384–87; B.W. Hill, 'The Change of Government and the "Loss of the

City", 1710–1711', *Economic History Review*, 2nd ser., 24/3 (1971), 395; Lucy S. Sutherland, 'The City in Eighteenth-Century Politics', in *Essays Presented to Sir Lewis Namier*, ed. R. Pares and A.J.P. Taylor (1956). Lord Balogh explained the influence of the City in terms of its capacity to wield 'the extra-constitutional veto of a financial confidence crisis'. (Thomas Balogh, 'The Apotheosis of the Dilettante: The Establishment of Mandarins', in *The Establishment*, ed. Hugh Thomas (1959), 112.) There is something in this charge, as the present study illustrates, but the readiness of the country to tolerate such action must be understood in terms of the City's place as the repository of the wealth and economic wisdom of the mercantile–financial community.

52 P.G.M. Dickson, *The Financial Revolution in England: A Study in the Development of Public Credit, 1688–1756* (1967), 9.

53 Leland Hamilton Jenks, *The Migration of British Capital to 1875* (1963), 6–8, 16–17.

54 R.E. Pumphrey, 'The Introduction of Industrialists into the British Peerage: A Study in Adaptation of a Social Institution', *American Historical Review*, 65/1 (October 1959).

55 A.S.J. Baster, *The International Banks* (1935), 1; *The Times*, 'The City of London' (1927); Paul H. Emden, *Money Powers of Europe in the Nineteenth and Twentieth Centuries* (1938), 377–87; Stanley D. Chapman, *The Rise of Merchant Banking* (1984), 3–4.

56 The phrase is from S.G. Checkland, 'The Mind of the City, 1870–1914', *Oxford Economic Papers*, new ser., 9/3 (October 1957), 261. On social change, Chapman, *The Rise of Merchant Banking*, 178, comments, 'Among the numerous honours of the late Victorian and Edwardian age, the ranks of the "steel barons" and "beerage" look thin compared with the City nobility.' See also Juffef Cassis, 'Les Banquiers anglais, 1890–1914: étude sociale', Ph.D. dissertation, University of Geneva (1982).

57 Thus despite their prominence in merchant banking, only three Jews were elected directors of the Bank of England from its establishment in 1694 to 1945. Paul Emden, *Jews of Britain* (1945), 496.

58 Balogh, 'Apotheosis of the Dilettantes', 112; Checkland, 'The Mind of the City', 262; Rubinstein, 'The Victorian Middle Classes', 602–23; D.W. Rubinstein, 'Wealth, Elites, and the Class Structure of Modern Britain', *Past and Present*, 77 (August 1977), 99–126. The economic and social ascendancy of the City merchants goes far to explain the decline described in Martin J. Wiener, *English Culture and the Decline of the Industrial Spirit, 1850–1980* (Cambridge, 1981). See also Nairn, *The Break-Up of Britain*, 23 and passim; Ralf Dahrendorf, *On Britain* (1982), ch. 9.

59 W.O. Aydelotte, 'The Business Interests of the Gentry in the Parliament of 1841–47', in G. Kitson Clark, *The Making of Victorian England* (1962), appendix, 290–305; F.M.L. Thompson, *English Landed Society in the Nineteenth Century* (1963), 305–08; Avner Offner, *Property and Politics, 1870–1914* (1981), 110–12.

60 Cain and Hopkins, 'The Political Economy of British Expansion Overseas', 481.

61 T.F. Lindsay and Michael Harrington, *The Conservative Party, 1918–1970* (1974), 9–10, 19; Halevy, *Epilogue*, i, 22–24, 36ff. The importance of finance and related activities did not diminish during the interwar years:

see J.M. McEwen, 'Unionist and Conservative Members of Parliament, 1914–1939', Ph.D. dissertation, University of London (1959) 42–44.

62 Michael Pinto-Duschinsky, *British Political Finance, 1830–1980* (1981), 33 and passim.

63 See the well-informed description of Conservative finances in *The Times*, 2 October 1924, 15. The importance of the City as a source of political finance is indicated by the fact that in the spring of 1929 City magnates provided two-thirds of the Conservative Party's expenses for the forthcoming general election, most of it in £5,000 donations at a single fund-raising lunch. J.C.C. Davidson papers, Davidson to Neville Chamberlain, 6 January 1929, and 'General Election, May 1929: Income and Expenditure Account and Schedules'; PRO 30/69/1753, MacDonald diary, 30 April 1929. To gauge the magnitude of these sums, it may be pointed out that the Unionist Party in the St George's (Westminster) division was regarded as particularly well-heeled in 1930 and able to contribute to other constituencies, having an income of £2,000. Gillian Peele, 'St George's and the Empire Crusade', *By-Elections in British Politics*, eds. Chris Cook and John Ramsden (1973), ch. 4.

64 Lloyd George chose Austen Chamberlain as Chancellor in the Tory-dominated postwar Coalition government despite his preference for Churchill, Worthington-Evans, or Sir Auckland Geddes, because, Chamberlain understood, 'the pressure of the City had been too strong'. Sir Charles Petrie, *The Life and Letters of the Rt. Hon. Sir Austen Chamberlain*, ii (1940), 137. Baldwin in 1924 evidently chose Churchill after the City had made known its opposition to Sir Robert Horne. Keith Middlemas and John Barnes, *Baldwin* (1969), 280.

65 Baster, *The International Banks*, tables 5 and 6; R. Bruce Lockhart, *Your England* (1955), 106; Boyle, *Montagu Norman*, 137; Paul Ferris, *The City*, rev. edn (Harmondsworth, 1965), 14; Richard Spiegelberg, *The City: Power without Responsibility* (1973), 12–16.

66 Spiegelberg, *The City*, 74; Clay, *Lord Norman*, 291–324. Sir Josiah Stamp, the former civil servant and chairman of the LMS Railway, was the token industrialist. Sir Charles Addis of the Hong Kong and Shanghai Banking Corporation was the first banker as opposed to merchant. R.J. Truptil, *British Banks and the London Money Market* (1936), 27.

67 Walter Bagehot, *Lombard Street*, 9th edn (1888), 224.

68 Boyle, *Montagu Norman*, 198.

69 Federal Reserve Bank of New York papers (hereafter FRBNY), Benjamin Strong papers, 1000.9, Siepmann to Steward, 8 July 1928.

70 Clay, *Lord Norman*; Boyle, *Montagu Norman*; Francis Williams, *A Pattern of Rulers* (1965), 195–221; Sir Lawrence Jones, *Georgian Afternoon* (1958), 122–25; and *The Memoirs of Lord Chandos* (1962), 143.

71 Emile Moreau, *Souvenirs d'un Gouverneur de la Banque de France* (Paris, 1954), 137.

72 Graham Murdock and Peter Golding, 'The Structure, Ownership and Control of the Press, 1914–76', in *Newspaper History from the Seventeenth Century to the Present Day*, eds. George Boyce, James Curran, and Pauline Wingate (1978), ch. 7; Alan J. Lee, *The Origins of the Popular Press, 1855–1914* (1976); Colin Seymour-Ure, 'The Press and the Party System between the Wars', in *The Politics of Reappraisal, 1918–1939*, eds. Gillian Peele and Chris Cook (1975).

73 Thomas W. Lamont papers (hereafter TWL). 111–15, Grenfell to Lamont, 29 October 1923.

74 Stephen Koss, *The Rise and Fall of the Political Press in Britain*, ii, *the Twentieth Century* (1984), 3.

75 Harold Herd, *The March of Journalism* (1952), 185; Stephen Koss, *Fleet Street Radical: A.G. Gardiner and the Daily News* (1973), 243; J.M. McEwan, 'Lloyd George's Acquisition of the Daily Chronicle in 1918', *Journal of British Studies*, 22/1 (Fall 1982), 129. The paper passed through the hands of a succession of financiers and merchants during the 1920s, including Lloyd George's crony, Sir Henry Dalziel, Sir Thomas Catto and Sir David Yule, and Mr William Harrison. Francis Williams, *Dangerous Estate: The Anatomy of Newspapers* (1957) 182.

76 Lord Burnham, who owned the *Daily Telegraph* until 1928, had followed a similar path. First a Liberal MP, then a Unionist MP, he remained a lifelong internationalist, chairing several international labour conferences at Geneva in the 1920s and participating in many other international gatherings over the years.

77 *The History of the Times, The 150th Anniversary and Beyond, 1912–1948*, part 2 (1952), 773–75. The board was ostensibly concerned exclusively with the finances of the paper, but the evidence suggests that Brand for one did not hesitate to intervene on the editorial side when the situation required it. Of Dawson, the official history records, 'He had no foreign languages, no knowledge of economics, and no interest in the Reparation question', *Ibid.*, 794.

78 Brand papers, 95(i), Brand to Astor, 30 October 1922; *ibid.*, Brand to Lazard Frères et Cie., Paris, 26 November 1922; *ibid.*, Brand to Astor, 30 October 1923; *ibid.*, C.H. Kent to Brand, 19 October 1925. According to Jacques Rueff, the French Financial Attaché in London for part of the interwar period, Brand was the real influence behind *The Times*. France, Ministère des Finances (hereafter MAE), F30/803, Rueff to Germain Martin, 29 March 1934.

79 See below, ch. 2. The *Morning Post* published the anti-semitic forgery, 'Protocols of the Elders of Zion' shortly after the war. Richard Griffiths, *Fellow Travellers of the Right: British Enthusiasts for Nazi Germany, 1933–9* (Oxford, 1983), 60–61.

80 Cox was a former Liberal MP and Secretary of the Cobden Club, and 'a somewhat extreme individualist'. *The Times*, 2 May 1936, 9.

81 Norman managed to give most of the City editors the impression that they alone were privy to his thoughts. See Andrew Boyle on Mill, *Montagu Norman*, 217; TWL 103/11, Leffingwell to Lamont, 16 March 1926, on Edward Hilton Young; FRBNY, Strong papers, 1116.7, Strong to Jay, 10 November 1927, on Kiddy; C.S. Addis diary, 28 January 1928, on Hobson; Edward Lysaght, *Brendan Bracken* (1979), 102, on Hobson; and Francis Williams' account of his own 'exclusive' access to Norman while City editor of the *Daily Herald* in the late 1920s, in *Nothing So Strange* (1970), 95.

82 John E. Kendle, *The Round Table Movement and Imperial Union* (Toronto, 1975), 167–68, 206; Walter Nimocks, *Milner's Young Men: The 'Kindergarten' in Edwardian Imperial Affairs* (Durham NC, 1968), 192, 206. Kendle suggests that Brand was too busy to play an active role in the

Round Table after the war. Brand's papers suggest otherwise. Brand wrote a touching preface and edited *The Letters of John Dove* (1938).

83 Stephen King-Hall, *Chatham House* (1937), 18, 22–23, and appendix 4. The Institute's initial funds came from the financier Sir Abe Bailey.

84 Donald Birn, *The League of Nations Union, 1918–1945* (Oxford, 1981), 93; Lord Robert Cecil, Add. MS. 51080, Cecil to Baldwin, 9 August 1927; 'A Speech by Lord Robert Cecil on a League of Nations Policy', League of Nations Union (1922); Cecil, *The Way of Peace, Essays and Addresses* (1928), 2, 72–79, 179; Cecil, *A Great Experiment* (1941), appendix 1; Cecil, *All the Way* (1949), 175.

85 Sir Arthur Salter, *Memoirs of a Public Servant* (1961), 25–26, 129; Erin E. Jacobsson, *A Life for Sound Money. Per Jacobsson, His Biography* (Oxford, 1979), 49.

86 George L. Ridgeway, *Merchants of Peace. Twenty Years of Business Diplomacy through the International Chamber of Commerce, 1919–1938* (New York, 1938), 14, 74, 129, 141; Charlotte M. Leaf, *Walter Leaf, 1852–1927* (1932), 278.

87 Of the 72 recruits to the Foreign Office between 1871 and 1907, 22 had attended Eton and 11 Harrow. Of the 111 recruits between 1857 and 1901, only one listed his father's occupation as 'business'. Ray Jones, *The Nineteenth-Century Foreign Office* (1971), 63, table 2, 62, table 1.

88 Sir Francis Oppenheimer, a former Commercial Attaché, wrote of Lord Hardinge, the Permanent Under-Secretary, that 'in the spirit of the Old Diplomacy, [he] saw in trade and commerce something sordid – something unworthy of the Diplomatic Service'. *Stranger Within* (1960), 305. Sir Roger Casement, a retired Consul-General, similarly complained, 'The Foreign Office entirely controls the Consular Service, but nobody in the Foreign Office has ever been a consul or knows anything about the duties of a consul.' United Kingdom, *Fifth Report of the Royal Commission on the Civil Service*, Minutes of Evidence, 29 April 1914 – 16 July 1914, Cd. 7749, Q38,599. See also the critical remarks of C.E. Musgrave, Secretary of the London Chamber of Commerce, Sir Francis Hurst, editor of *The Economist*, Sir Edwin Peers, and the Association of Chambers of Commerce, in ibid., QQ.38,862, 38,877, 40,595, 40,658, 40,655, appendix lxxxix, 321, appendix xc, 326; D.C.M. Platt, *The Cinderella Service: British Consuls since 1825* (1971), 92, 108–09, 231–39; Frank Ashton-Gwatkin, *The British Foreign Service* (Syracuse, NY, 1951), 20.

89 John Connell, pseud. (John Henry Robertson), *The 'Office'. A Study of British Foreign Policy and its Makers, 1919–1951* (1951), 12.

90 See below, ch. 11. The union of interests has been symbolised, and no doubt reinforced, by the regular departure of senior Foreign Office and diplomatic personnel for lucrative posts in the City. On recent examples, see Richard Kellett, *The Merchant Banking Arena, with Case Studies* (1967), 97, 100.

91 The leading advocate was Victor Wellesley who, like his more senior supporter, Sir Eyre Crowe, had been profoundly influenced by his intimate knowledge of Germany. Having grown up in Germany and observed German commercial expansion at first hand as a Commercial Attaché, Wellesley formed the conviction that the basis of Germany's military prowess rested with its 'really scientific organisation', failure to apprehend

which had been responsible for Britain's lack of preparedness in 1914. FO 368/1855, 141670/2049, Wellesley memorandum, 28 June 1917; CAB 27/57, MTC 3rd minutes, Wellesley evidence to Cave committee, 28 May 1919. On the anticipated difficulties in the postwar era, see FO 368/2036, 62458/14578, Wellesley memorandum, 9 March 1918.

92 United Kingdom, *Memorandum by the Board of Trade and the Foreign Office with respect to the Future Organisation of Commercial Intelligence*, Cd. 8715, 17–30.

93 FO 800/89, Runciman to Grey, 29 August 1916; CAB 23/3, WC 216(10), 15 August 1917; FO 368/2036, 62458/14578, Wellesley memorandum, 9 March 1918; FO 368/2253, 93604/79699, Wellesley to Crowe, 7 June 1919. On the earlier contest, see Jones, *The Nineteenth-Century Foreign Office*, ch. 4.

94 CAB 27/58, G-237, Report of the Conference on Unemployment and the State of Trade, 14 March 1919.

95 Sir Hubert Llewellyn Smith, *The Board of Trade* (1928), 69; Sir Frank Lee, *The Board of Trade* (1958), 11; Sir Sydney Chapman, *Autobiography* (n.d.), passim.

96 Henry Roseveare, *The Treasury, Evolution of a British Institution* (1969), 249; D.C. Watt, *Personalities and Politics* (1965), 104; Sir Horace P. Hamilton, 'Sir Warren Fisher and the Public Service', *Public Administration*, 29/2 (Spring 1951), 7, 32.

97 Kathleen Burk, 'The Treasury: From Impotence to Power', in *War and the State: the Transformation of British Government, 1912–1919*, ed. K. Burk (1982), 84–107.

98 Thus Sir Thomas Heath, the former Joint Permanent Secretary, writing in 1927, deliberately omitted from his description of the Treasury all its recently acquired responsibilities. For, so far as most members were concerned, these were temporary burdens. As before their overriding task was the maintenance of Treasury control: the granting or withholding of assent to 'any measure increasing or tending to increase public expenditure'. Heath, *The Treasury* (1927), 1; Roseveare, *The Treasury*, 148.

99 Sir Andrew McFadyean, *Recollected in Tranquillity* (1964), 45.

100 Balogh, 'Apotheosis of the Dilettante'; Max Beloff, 'The Whitehall Factor: The Role of the Higher Civil Service, 1919–1939', in *The Politics of Reappraisal, 1918–1939*, eds. Gillian Peele and Chris Cook (1975), ch. 9.

101 Geoffrey Ingham, *Capitalism Divided? The City and Industry in British Social Development* (1984), 130–33, 140–42, 173, 181.

102 Among the members of the finance division who went into the City after the war were O.T. Falk, Dudley Ward, Harry Siepmann, and their superiors Sir John Bradbury, Sir Basil Blackett, and Sir Otto Niemeyer. Keynes was also active in the City at this time.

103 T188/2, 'Foreign Exchanges after the War', 19 July 1918. Membership of the committee and members' occupations are given in T185/1, 81.

104 Cunliffe Committee, *First Interim Report*, Cd. 9182, 3, 5. A *Final Report* was later issued, but it did no more than recur to the arguments set out in the interim report.

105 Morgan, *Consensus and Disunity*.

106 *Ibid.*, 46, 76; Rowland, *Lloyd George*, 506–07; Lindsay and Harrington,

The Conservative Party, 28; Maurice Cowling, *The Impact of Labour: The Beginning of Modern British Politics* (Cambridge, 1971), 24 and passim.

107 CAB 27/58, G-237, G.T.-6924, 4th minutes, 24 February 1919.

108 Susan Howson, *Domestic Monetary Management in Britain, 1919–38* (Cambridge, 1975), 11.

109 See the near hysterical discussions in Thomas Jones, *Whitehall Diary*, i, *1916–25*, ed. Keith Middlemas (1969), 17 January, 2 February 1920.

110 Sir Bernard Mallet and C. Oswald George, *British Budgets, Second Series, 1913–14 to 1920–21* (1929), 181–87 and 368.

111 Howson, *Domestic Monetary Management*, 14.

112 Bonar Law and Milner kept up their rearguard action for some time longer. See for instance, CAB 27/71, F.C. 1st minutes, 24 July 1919, and 2nd minutes, 11 August 1919.

113 CAB 27/71, F.C. 1st minutes, 24 July 1919.

114 A.C. Pigou, *Aspects of British Economic History, 1918–1925* (1947), 139.

115 CAB 27/71, F.C. 3rd minutes, 20 August 1919.

116 *Hansard*, House of Commons Debates, 5th series, vol. 123, columns 43–46 (hereafter HC Deb. 5 s., 123, cols. 43–46, etc).

117 The words were Lloyd George's, in CAB 27/71, FC 1st minutes, 24 July 1919. Kenneth Morgan, in a spirited attempt to exonerate Lloyd George from responsibility for the slump, accuses Austen Chamberlain of fuelling the speculative boom of 1919–20 by 'grossly mistaken budgeting for large surpluses', then recognising the inflationary consequences and adopting the Treasury–Bank of England advice of monetary restriction. In fact, Chamberlain's budgets in 1919 and 1920 were both severely deflationary: in a mere two years, government spending was cut by 54 per cent, which turned a deficit of £1.6 billion into a surplus of £231 million. It was not Chamberlain but Lloyd George who displayed inconsistency on economic policy. Morgan further claims that the slump could not have been caused by the increase in Bank rate to 7 per cent in 1920 because by then signs of a world slump were already apparent. This ignores two things: first, that the adoption of a 7 per cent rate was only the last step in the policy authorised eight months earlier to make money both dear and tight; and second, that Britain, as the world's greatest trader and lender, was bound to exert an important influence on economic conditions overseas. Morgan, *Consensus and Disunity*, 256–59.

118 *The Economist*, Banking Supplement, 10 May 1920, 16.

119 Mallet and George, *British Budgets, Second Series*, 368.

120 Richard Jebb, *Empire in Eclipse* (1926), 122; Pigou, *Aspects of British Economic History*, 139–44; Royal Institute of International Affairs, *British Tariff Policy* (1932), 7–10; Board of Trade papers (hereafter BT), S.O.T./12, memorandum 2 July 1929.

121 Ian M. Drummond, *Imperial Economic Policy, 1917–1939: Studies in Expansion and Protection* (1974), 67, 94, and passim.

122 Edith H. Whetham, 'The Agricultural Act, 1920, and its Repeal – the "Great Betrayal"', *Agricultural History Review*, 22 pt. 1 (1974), 36–49.

123 Several of the best-known British firms, such as Austin and Wolseley, were forced to the wall: Roy Church, *Herbert Austin. The British Motor Car Industry to 1941* (1979), 43, 105.

2 *Crucified on a cross of gold*

1 The negotiations are summarised in Michael L. Dockrill and J. Douglas Gould, *Peace without Promise. Britain and the Peace Conferences, 1919–23*(1981), ch. 2. The condemnation of the 'Carthaginian peace' was most sensationally presented in J.M. Keynes, *The Economic Consequences of the Peace* (1919).
2 See above, p. 32.
3 Between 1919 and 1922 Lloyd George attended thirty-three international conferences, most of them dealing wholly or in part with reparations. C.J. Lowe and M.L. Dockrill, *The Mirage of Power*, vol. ii, *British Foreign Policy, 1914–22* (1972), 335.
4 FBI/C/65, Credits and Currency Committee, 21 October 1920.
5 *Ibid.*, 30 June 1921.
6 *Bulletin of the Federation of British Industries*, 19 July 1921, 438.
7 *Ibid.*, 4 October 1921, 579.
8 United Kingdom, *Report of the Committee on Financial Facilities*, Cd. 9227. See also T176/5, Pt. 2, Niemeyer to Meiklejohn, 5 October 1921.
9 FBI/C/65, Credits and Currency Committee, 13 October 1921.
10 Clay, *Lord Norman*, 180–85.
11 *Ibid.*, 136; *The Economist*, 16 October 1920, 579.
12 Sir William Goode, 'The General Financial Position of Austria', *The Commercial Supplement. Reconstruction in Europe*, 15 June 1922, 143; Clay, *Lord Norman*, 180–85; Philip Cottrell, 'Austria Between Diplomats and Bankers, 1919–1931', 18–22, Paper presented to the Conference on the 1931 Crisis and its Aftermath, Clare College, Cambridge, 14–16 April 1982; K.W. Rothschild, *Austria's Economic Development between the Two Wars* (1947), 14–32.
13 J. Saxon Mills, *The Genoa Conference* (1922), ch. 10 and appendix 5; Stephen V.O. Clarke, *The Reconstruction of the International Monetary System: The Attempts of 1922 and 1933* (Princeton, 1973), 13–14; R.G. Hawtrey. *Monetary Reconstruction*, 2nd edn (1926), ch 6.; United Kingdom, *Papers Relating to the International Economic Conference, Genoa, April–May 1922*, Cmd. 1667; Carole Fink, *The Genoa Conference. European Diplomacy, 1921–1922* (Chapel Hill, 1984), 232–42.
14 Clay, *Lord Norman*, 137–38 and passim.
15 FRBNY, Strong papers, 1116.3, Norman to Strong, 24 February 1922. Strong replied on 9 March, affirming his own objection to 'the extreme views which I understand Mr Hawtrey holds.'
16 Norman applauded Addis's speech as 'an antidote to the policy of the inflation-mongers', FRBNY, Strong papers, 1112.2, Norman to Strong, 11 November 1921.
17 Addis diary, 1 April 1922.
18 FRBNY, Strong papers, 1116.3, Norman to Strong, 23 June 1922; *ibid.*, Strong to Norman, 14 July 1922.
19 FRBNY, Strong papers, 1116.3, Norman to Strong, 31 October 1922.
20 Clay, *Lord Norman*, 185–92; Sir Arthur Salter, *Slave of the Lamp. A Public Servant's Notebook* (1967), 97–98; Salter, *Memoirs of a Public Servant*, 175–77; F.P. Walters, *A History of the League Nations*, i (1952), 208–10; W.M. Hill, *The Economic and Financial Organisation of the League of Na-*

tions: a Survey of Twenty-five Years Experience (Washington, 1946), 27–28.

21 H.R.G. Greaves, *The League Committees and World Order* (1931), 76.

22 R. Bruce Lockhart, *Your England*, 108, refers to Strakosch as 'a cold intellectual, more English than the English in manner, and apparently devoid of all emotion,' which is probably as unfair as it is unflattering. On Strakosch's financial interests see BoE, Norman diary, 15, 23 January 1924, 25, 30 June 1925, etc.

23 Clay, *Lord Norman*, 181; Boyle, *Montagu Norman*, 147; Jacobsson, *A Life for Sound Money*, 55; Salter, *Slave of the Lamp*, 72.

24 BoE, Norman diary, 11, 24 January, 31 March 1924; Clay, *Lord Norman*, 148.

25 UK, *Dispatch to the Representatives of France, Italy, Serbo-Croat-Slovene State, Roumania, Portugal and Greece respecting War Debts*, 1 August 1922, Cmd. 1737.

26 FRBNY, Bank of England cables, 1922–23, Norman to Lubbock, no. 98, 19 January 1923; Boyle, *Montagu Norman*, 156, 162.

27 Keith Middlemas and John Barnes, *Baldwin* (1969), 135–36, discounts Norman's influence on the decision. Per Jacobsson, one of Norman's few close friends, concluded years later that it was a mistake for the British government to have sent Norman with Baldwin. Erin E. Jucker-Fleetwood, 'Montagu Norman in the Per Jacobsson Diaries', *National Westminster Bank Review* (November 1968), 59. See also P.J. Grigg, *Prejudice and Judgment* (1948), 101; Artaud, *La Question des dettes interalliées*, i, 522.

28 Carl Bergmann, *The History of Reparations* (1927), 82.

29 Boyle, *Montagu Norman*, 155.

30 FRBNY, Bank of England cables, 1922–23, Norman to Strong, no. 85, 27 February 1923, and no. 86, 3 March 1923.

31 *Ibid.*, Norman to Strong, no. 7, 22 May 1923. See also Hawtrey, *Monetary Reconstruction*, 147–48; Clay, *Lord Norman*, 145–56.

32 FRBNY, Bank of England cables, 1922–23, Strong to Norman, no. 33, 8 May 1923.

33 T176/13, Pt. 2, Baldwin to Norman, 23 June 1923.

34 FRBNY, Bank of England cables, 1922–23, Norman to Strong, no. 15, 2 July 1923.

35 FBI/C/1, Grand Council, 18 July 1923.

36 H.D. Henderson, *The Inter-War Years and Other Papers* (Oxford, 1955), 5–8.

37 *The Nation*, 11 August 1923, 4.

38 Keynes, *The End of Laissez-Faire*, 34.

39 Keynes, *A Tract on Monetary Reform* (1923), 172.

40 United Kingdom, *Imperial Economic Conference, Record of Proceedings and Documents, 1924*, Cmd. 2009; L.S. Pressnell, '1925: The Burden of Sterling', *Economic History Review*, 2nd ser., 31/1 (February 1978), 77–78.

41 *The Times*, 10 October 1923, 10; 15 October 1923, 21; 16 October 1923, 21; 17 October 1923, 13, 17, 19. *The Bankers' Magazine*, January 1924, 12.

42 FBI/C/4, Grand Council, 17 October 1923; *Bulletin of the Federation of British Industries*, 30 October 1923, 663–66.

43 *The Times*, 26 October 1923, 17.

44 Middlemas and Barnes, *Baldwin*, ch. 10; Davidson papers, 'Political Gen-

eral, 1926–29', 24 September 1929-; Lindsay and Harrington, *The Conservative Party*, 54; W.A.S. Hewins, *The Apologia of an Imperialist*, ii (1929), 278–79; Keith Feiling, *The Life of Neville Chamberlain* (1947), 108f; Lord Baldwin, *A Memoir* (1947), 8; Austen Chamberlain papers, 35/3/12, Gilmour to Austen Chamberlain, 18 October 1923, Austen to Neville Chamberlain, 29 October 1923; Neville Chamberlain diary, 10 October 1924, 7 October 1927.

45 J.R. MacDonald, *Socialism: Critical and Constructive* (1921), 206–07. See also MacDonald, *History of the ILP* (1921), 18, 20.

46 HC Deb., 5 s., 161, col. 2472.

47 *Daily Mail*, 10 January 1924, 8; On ILP proposals see *New Leader*, 2 November 1923, 8, 16 November 1923, 8.

48 Quoted in Lyman, *The First Labour Government, 1924*, 81–82.

49 FRBNY, Strong papers, 1116.4, Norman to Strong, 30 January 1924.

50 Morgan Grenfell & Co. (hereafter MGC), Box P.651, Norman to Chairman, Bankers' Clearing House, 1 January 1924.

51 *Daily Mail*, 1 January 1924, 9, and 3 January 1924, 6.

52 Neville Chamberlain diary, 2/21, 18 November 1923. See also Neville Chamberlain papers, 18/1/422, Neville to Ida Chamberlain, 12 January 1924.

53 Marquand, *Ramsay MacDonald*, 308.

54 Boyle, *Montagu Norman*, 166.

55 Neville Chamberlain diary, 2/21, 22 January 1924.

56 Boyle, *Montagu Norman*, 170; Snowden, *An Autobiography*, ii, 615.

57 Per Jacobsson diary, 23 December 1928, 10 April 1932; Moreau, *Souvenirs*, 212; Sweet-Escott, 'Gallant Failure', 75; *The Times*, 8 February 1971.

58 T176/5, Pt. 1, Niemeyer minute, March 1924.

59 Reginald McKenna, *Post-War Banking Policy* (1928), 74–87; *The Bankers' Magazine*, March 1924, 480. On McKenna's subsequent reassertion of opposition, see below ch. 2, p. 69, 73.

60 MacDonald on 18 February 1924 in HC Deb. 5 s., 169, col. 1309, and Snowden on 19 February 1924 in *ibid*, col. 1529.

61 Brand papers, 67, Brand to Weill, 26 March 1924.

62 *Ibid.*, Brand to Keynes, 30 June 1924.

63 McDougall, *France's Rhineland Diplomacy, 1914–1924*, 145, 203–04, 287, 297–98, 358, 366; Schuker, *The End of French Predominance in Europe*, 171–73; Trachtenberg, *Reparation in World Politics*, 301, 303, 333.

64 United States Department of State, *Foreign Relations of the United States* (hereafter *FRUS*), 1923, II, Chilton aide-mémoire to Hughes, 13 October 1923.

65 *Ibid.*, Hughes aide-mémoire to Chilton, 15 October 1923.

66 Quoted in McDougall, *France's Rhineland Diplomacy, 1914–1924*, 345.

67 As General Dawes wrote, 'It should not be forgotten that this is a European plan, created chiefly by Europeans, with the blessing of the American experts. In saying this, however, I should qualify it ... by saying that Young has been a most constructive element in its development at all times.' Charles G. Dawes, *A Journal of Reparations* (1939), 180. Salter and Stamp were the actual authors of the plan.

68 Harold G. Moulton, *The Reparation Plan* (New York, 1924).

69 Jacques Bariéty, *Les Relations franco-allemandes après la première querre*

mondiale (Paris, 1977), 754 and passim; Hjalmar Schacht, *Confessions of the Old Wizard* (Boston, 1956), 179–87; Clay, *Lord Norman*, 212.

70 FO 371/9740, C6331/70/18, Niemeyer memorandum, 14 April 1924; FO 371/9744, C7637/70/18, minutes of meeting at the Treasury, 10 April 1924.

71 TWL, 176–8, Lamont to J.P. Morgan & Co., 17 April 1924; *ibid.*, 176–9, Lamont to Morgan, 29 April 1924; *ibid.*, 176–8, Morrow minute, 'The Dawes Report', 1 May 1924.

72 TWL, 176–14, memorandum 'D', 15 July 1924.

73 Stuart Crocker papers, Young Plan diary, 11 February 1929; TWL, 176–77, Lamont to J.P. Morgan & Co., 20 July 1924.

74 UK, *Proceedings of the London Reparation Conference, July and August 1924*, Cmd. 2270, i, 283–90.

75 TWL, 176–26, Lamont to Morgan Grenfell & Co. for Norman, 14 August 1924; *ibid.*, Morgan Grenfell & Co. to Lamont, 14 August 1924; *ibid.*, Whigham to Lamont, 14 August 1924.

76 Schuker, *The End of French Predominance in Europe*, 114; Costigliola, *Awkward Dominion*, 126.

77 US gold reserves reached a peak of $4,527 million or £931 million (£1 = $4.86) in November 1924. Bank of England reserves were approximately £150 million. World monetary gold stocks were perhaps £2,070 million. *Federal Reserve Bulletin*, various issues; statement by Snowden, 3 July 1924, in HC Deb. 5 s., 175, col. 1494; *The Commercial*, 24 July 1924, 100; *The Economist*, Supplement, 'Gold and the Price Level', 5 July 1930.

78 Clay, *Lord Norman*, 146.

79 FRBNY, Strong papers, 1000.5, Strong to Jay, 23–28 April 1924.

80 Strong described Norman, Revelstoke, and Addis as the 'real ones here'. FRBNY, Strong papers, 1000.5, Strong to Jay, 11 April 1924. On Norman, Addis, and their relationship, see FRBNY, Strong papers, 1112.2, Norman to Strong, 18 December 1921; Addis diary, 11, 13, 18, 25 June 1924; Addis papers, Sir Charles to Eba Addis, 26 October 1924 and 27 February 1929. Addis wrote of the weekly meetings of the Committee of Treasury, on 18 June 1924, 'The gold standard question is turning into a duel between the Governor and me. The others say little and scarcely understand the question and its bearings.' Despite his occasional displays of impatience, Addis took the lead in resisting the efforts of other directors to remove Norman from the Governorship, in 1924, 1926, 1927 and 1928. Addis papers, PP MS. 14/454, 28 September 1926; *ibid.*, 14/455, Addis submission to Special Committee, 23 February 1927; *ibid.*, 14/456, Addis minute to Court, 24 May 1928; *ibid.*, Addis address to Court, 18 October 1928.

81 See for instance Addis's public statements in *The Bankers' Magazine*, January 1924, 19–31; *The Times*, 15 April 1924, 19. Addis lumped Hawtrey with the advocates of a managed currency, and was pleased when Hawtrey affirmed his support for the gold standard if operated on the basis of the Genoa resolutions: Addis diary, 14 and 17 April 1924.

82 Addis diary, 25 October 1924.

83 Addis diary, 18 June 1924.

84 Boyle, *Montagu Norman*, 197. See also the bitter anti-American remarks of Norman's confidant, Lord Revelstoke, quoted below, ch. 5, p. 184.

85 BoE, Norman diary, 12 April 1924; FRBNY, Bank of England cables,

Norman to Strong, no. 87, 3 June 1924; FRBNY, Strong papers, 1116.4, Norman to Strong, 16 June 1924.

86 *Ibid.*

87 HC Deb. 5 s, 170, col. 1613; Clay, *Lord Norman*, 149; T160/197, F7528, Norman to Niemeyer, 16 April 1924.

88 D.E. Moggridge, *British Monetary Policy, 1924–1931: The Norman Conquest of $4.86* (Cambridge, 1972), 52–53; Hawtrey, *Monetary Reconstruction*, 146.

89 Norman found the tone of the report too sensational, but scarcely regretted its effect upon City opinion. FRBNY, Strong papers, 1116.4, Strong to Norman, 3 June 1924; *The Bankers' Magazine*, June 1924, 858–59.

90 *Nation and Athenaeum*, 24 May 1924, 272, and 28 June 1924, 422.

91 *Westminster Bank Review*, June 1924, 3–4; reprinted in *The Bankers' Magazine*, August 1924, 146–49.

92 T160/197, F7528/02/1, Leaf evidence to the Chamberlain/Bradbury Committee, 4 July 1924, 147.

93 *New Statesman*, 21 June 1924, 305; J.M. Keynes, 'The Policy of the Bank of England', *National and Athenaeum*, 19 July 1924, 500.

94 *The Bankers' Magazine*, April 1924, 146.

95 *The Times*, 20 June 1924, 22. See also Hobson, *The Commercial*, 19 June 1924, 858, and 3 July 1925, 14.

96 BoE, Norman diary, 13 June 1924.

97 *The Times*, 24 June 1924, 21.

98 See p. 53 above. McKenna was dissatisfied with monetary policy because his clients were on the verge of bankruptcy, Norman recorded in his diary on 28 May 1923. See also Boyle, *Montagu Norman*, 161.

99 *The Economist*, 28 June 1924, 1289; *The Statist*, 28 June 1924, 1160.

100 ILP, *Report of the Annual Conference*, 1924, 27, 105.

101 *New Leader*, 20 June 1924, 8.

102 *Ibid.*, 30 January 1925, 11, and 8 May 1925, 8.

103 *Forward*, 17 January 1925, 9.

104 See for instance *Forward*, 10 January 1925, 1, and 14 January 1925, 1. For other instances of anti-semitism, see issues of 19 March 1927, 16 June 1928, and 22 September 1928.

105 *New Leader*, 16 January 1925, 2.

106 *Ibid.*, 4 July 1925, 2.

107 Quoted in Semmel, *Imperialism and Social Reform*, 79.

108 His attacks on the 'money power' began after the war in the *National Review*, September 1920, 71. Instances of Strachey's increasingly strident criticism are in *The Spectator*, 19 January 1924, 78; 22 February 1924, 150; 28 June 1924, 1029; 5 January 1925, 5, and regularly thereafter.

109 Macmillan Committee, *Evidence*, i, 255.

110 Allan Nevins and Frank E. Hill, *Ford, Expansion and Challenge, 1915–1933* (New York, 1957), 612 and passim. See also Henry Ford, *Today and Tomorrow* (New York, 1926), 27–33.

111 John L. Finlay, *Social Credit, The English Origins* (Montreal, 1972), 8–14, 23–25.

112 *NUM Journal*, August 1924, 128, and June 1925, 92; *National Review*, March 1925, 63–76, and June 1925, 525–36; FBI/S/Walker/25/2, Peyton to Dibben, 9 June 1925, Dibben to Glenday, 24 June 1925.

113 R.R. Enfield, *The Agricultural Crisis, 1920–1923* (1924), 15, 147–52.
114 *59th Annual Report of the Council of the Central and Associated Chambers of Agriculture*, 9 December 1924, 18.
115 FBI/C/1, Grand Council, 9 July 1924.
116 *The Times*, 16 July 1924, 22; Association of British Chambers of Commerce (hereafter ABCC), MS. 14,480, i, minutes of Finance and Taxation Committee, 30 September 1924.
117 FBI/EA/Glenday/9, Committee on National Debt, 23 July 1924; British Industries, 5 August 1924, 445–46.
118 HC Deb. 5s., 175, col. 1964.
119 T176/5, Pt. 1, Hawtrey memorandum to Niemeyer, 26 April 1924; T176/5, Pt. 2, Hawtrey memorandum to Niemeyer, 4 July 1924.
120 T160/197, F7528, Norman to Niemeyer, 16 April 1924.
121 T160/197, F7528/01/1, Chamberlain/Bradbury Committee, 27 June 1924.
122 Moggridge, *British Monetary Policy*, 38.
123 T160/197, F7528/02/1, Chamberlain/Bradbury Committee, 27 June 1924, 3–4, 8, 12–13, 17, 18, 30.
124 *Ibid.*, 41–55.
125 *The Bankers' Magazine*, June 1924, 866–72.
126 T160/197, F7528/02/1, Chamberlain/Bradbury Committee, 3 July 1924, 77.
127 ABCC, MS. 14,480/1, Finance and Taxation Committee, 28 June 1924.
128 FBI/EA/Glenday/9, Committee on Bank Rate, 15 July 1924.
129 *Ibid.*, Committee on National Debt, 23 July 1924, statement by Armstrong.
130 FBI/EA/Glenday/4, Glenday to Butler, 18 August 1931.
131 FBI/EA/Glenday/9, Committee on National Debt, 23 July 1924; FBI/EA/Glenday/11, Rylands to Nugent, 31 December 1929.
132 T160/197, F7528/02/3, Chamberlain/Bradbury Committee, 30 July 1924, 36. Written evidence in T160/197, F7528/01/1, FBI memorandum, 29 July 1924.
133 McKenna, *Post-War Banking Policy*, 1–19, 20–36.
134 T160/197, F7528/02/2, Chamberlain/Bradbury Committee, 10 July 1924, 47, 52, 59, 61.
135 *Ibid.*, 11 July 1924, 106–21.
136 T160/197, F7528/01/1, Bradbury to Farrer, 24 July 1924.
137 FRBNY, Bank of England cables, Norman to Strong, no. 95, 19 July 1924; *New Leader*, 8 August 1924, 6; *Westminster Bank Review*, January 1925.
138 The developments are summarised in William Adams Brown Jr, *England and the New Gold Standard, 1919–1926* (New Haven, 1929), 174, 207–26; Clarke, *Central Bank Cooperation*, 93–99.
139 Labour Party, *Report of the 24th Annual Conference, 1924*, 160, 165–66.
140 *The Times*, 11 October 1924; 11, 14 October 1924; 10, 20 October 1924, 20.
141 FRBNY, Strong papers, 1116.4, Strong to Norman, 4 November 1924. The best account of Strong's activities is in Lester V. Chandler, *Benjamin Strong, Central Banker* (Washington DC, 1958), 300 and seq.
142 Boyle, *Montagu Norman*, 179; Martin Gilbert, *Winston S. Churchill*, Companion Volume V, Part 1 (1980), 305.
143 MGC, B.G. Loan 5, J.P. Morgan to Grenfell, 11 February 1925; FRBNY, Bank of England Revolving Credit, C261.1, Strong minute, 11 January 1925; TWL, 103–13, Leffingwell to Lamont, 8 March 1929.

144 Addis diary, 8, 9, 21 January 1925.
145 FRBNY, Bank of England cables, Lubbock to Norman no. 54, 9 January 1925.
146 *Ibid.*, Lubbock to Norman, no. 59, 9 January 1925. Sir Warren Fisher subsequently echoed Niemeyer's misgivings: T172/1500A, Fisher to Niemeyer, 12 January 1925.
147 Neville Chamberlain diary, 5 November and 1 December 1924; Robert Rhodes James, *Victor Cazalet. A Portrait* (1976), 98; Middlemas and Barnes, *Baldwin*, 280.
148 Middlemas and Barnes, *Baldwin*, 281–83; Amery, *My Political Life*, 299–300, 510. The City, although not Baldwin, may have been influenced by the fact that Churchill was acquainted with several prominent financiers, loudly defended free trade, and relied upon income from investments, mostly foreign investments. Gilbert, *Churchill*, Companion Volume V, Part 1, 9, 15 n. 2, 81.
149 Boyle, *Montagu Norman*, 179.
150 McKenna, *Post-War Banking Policy*, 101–03.
151 T172/1499B, Churchill to Niemeyer, 6 February 1925.
152 A.J.P. Taylor, *Beaverbrook* (Harmondsworth, 1974).
153 Beaverbrook papers, C/47, Beaverbrook to Boothby, 1 May 1925. Churchill later wrote that the encounter took place 'I think at the end of February'. But the direct personal attack on Niemeyer in the *Express* papers at the end of January points to the previous month. *Ibid.*, C/85, Churchill to Beaverbrook, 2 November 1925. See also Charles Kenneth Young, *Churchill and Beaverbrook: a Study in Friendship and Politics* (1966), 74, 79; *The Times Business News*, 20 March 1969.
154 *Daily Express*, 28 January 1925, 1.
155 T175/9, Churchill memorandum, 29 January 1925. See also the excellent summary of the correspondence by Robert Skidelsky in *The Times Business News*, 20 March 1969.
156 See statement by Addis to the Chamberlain/Bradbury Committee, T160/197, F7528/02/1, 27 June 1924, 46; and the Niemeyer–Norman exchange over the Dominions' readiness to return to the gold standard before Britain, in *ibid.*, F7528/02/3, 28 January 1925, 69.
157 T175/9, Niemeyer and Norman memoranda, 2 February 1925.
158 HC Deb. 5 s., 180, col. 361.
159 T172/1499B, Churchill to Niemeyer, 6 February 1925.
160 *Ibid.*, Churchill to Niemeyer, 22 February 1925.
161 *Ibid.*, Treasury memorandum, March 1925. Niemeyer confidently advised the Australian government to expect a British announcement of resumption within two months — although the Chancellor had not as yet taken any decision. Pressnell, '1925', 79.
162 FRBNY, Strong papers, 1112.2, Addis to Strong, 14 April 1925.
163 FRBNY, Bank of England cables, Strong to Norman, no. 32, 18 February 1925; Addis diary, 23 February 1925.
164 *Daily Herald*, 5 March 1925, 4; *Daily Mail*, 5 March 1925, 8; FBI/C/5, Executive Committee of Grand Council, 11 March 1925; T172/1499, Nugent to Churchill, 17 March 1925; *NUM Journal*, April 1925, 44; T172/1500B, McConechy (Manchester Association of Importers and Exporters, representing directors of the Manchester Ship Canal and leading

textile firms in the city) to Churchill, 1 April 1925. See also the critical articles in the *Empire Citizen*, October 1924, 178, and November 1924, 194. The journal, created during the war to strengthen patriotism among the working class, claimed a circulation of 100,000; see Middlemas, *Politics in Industrial Society*, 132. See also the articles on the 'money power' by Sir Oswald Stoll in *The Referee*, 4 January 1925, 1; and the indirect criticism in the *Morning Post*, 16 April 1925, 8, and 25 April 1925, 6.

165 The Treasury papers, which do not contain all the protests, show that Niemeyer went far out of his way to belittle or demean critics of an early return to gold. See in particular his comments to Churchill on St Loe Strachey, 'an exporter', Keynes, Stamp, the Manchester Association of Importers and Exporters, and Darling, in T172/1499B.

166 FRBNY, Bank of England Revolving Credit, C261.1, Norman to Strong, no. 87, 21 March 1925; *ibid.*, Strong to Norman, no. 48, 24 March 1925; FRBNY, Strong papers, 1116.5, Norman to Strong, 15 April 1925; *ibid.*, Strong to Norman, 27 April 1925.

167 Grigg, *Prejudice and Judgement*, 182–84; Gilbert, *Churchill*, Companion Volume V, Part 1 436.

168 MGC, B.G. Loan 5, Grenfell to Morgan, no. 25/458, 31 March 1925. Norman typically proposed that the American credits should be kept a secret. Strong rejected the suggestion, arguing that this would only result in greater embarrassment when their existence was discovered.

169 BoE, Norman diary, 19 March 1925; T172/1499B, Niemeyer minute, 20 March 1925.

170 HC Deb. 5 s., 183, col. 60 and passim.

171 *The Observer*, 3 May 1925, 2.

172 Labour Party papers, TUC–Labour Party Joint Research and Information Department, Advisory Committee, Monthly Report, March and April 1925.

173 Hugh Dalton, 'Churchill and the Golden Calf', *Lansbury's Labour Weekly*, 2 May 1925, 3; Ellen Wilkinson, 'The Cross of Gold', *Lansbury's Labour Weekly*, 16 May 1925, 9.

174 FRBNY, Strong papers, 1116.5, Norman to Strong, 5 May 1925; Sayers, *The Bank of England*, i, 150.

175 HC Deb. 5 s., 183, cols. 657–66.

176 *Ibid.*, cols. 234–36, 397–400, 644, 693, 833.

177 *Ibid.*, cols. 192, 683.

178 FBI/D/Nugent/5, Nugent to Lennox Lee, 20 March 1929. Brown, typical of later commentators, accepted that British industrialists generally were 'agnostic' towards the return to gold, and quoted Lord Inchcape as representative of industrial opinion. See W.A. Brown Jr, *England and the New Gold Standard*, 244–47. Inchcape was not an industrialist at all, but a City-based shipowner and banker and a confidant of Norman. See Clay, *Lord Norman*, 146. Brown himself was related to the Browns of Brown Brothers Shipley, the banking firm in which Norman had been a partner.

179 A complete list of the 'thieves' – there were 42 – was published in the *Bulletin of the Federation of British Industries*, 2 January 1919, 1. Some of the names changed in later years, but their Conservative allegiance did not.

180 *The Economist*, 2 May 1925, 846.

181 Pressnell, '1925', 67. At least one official later regretted the decision; see Sir

Ralph Hawtrey, 'The Return to Gold in 1925', *The Bankers' Magazine*, August 1969, 61–69.

182 For calculations, see Ross E. Catterall, 'Attitudes to and the Impact of British Monetary Policy in the 1920s', *Revue Internationale d'Histoire de la Banque*, 12 (1976), 40. Real interest rates reached 8 per cent under the Thatcher government – and unemployment again soared to crisis levels.

183 Brand papers, 83B, 'The Gold Standard', draft of article for the *Round Table*, March 1925.

3 'Normalcy'

1 Middlemas and Barnes, *Baldwin*, ch. 1, 2.

2 *New Leader*, 5 June 1925, 2.

3 *The Times*, 1 May 1929, 18. Baldwin's daughter was married to the merchant banker Captain R. Gordon Munro of Helbert Wagg & Co.

4 Quoted in Middlemas and Barnes, *Baldwin*, 2; James (ed.), *Memoirs of a Conservative*, 173.

5 *The Times*, 3 October 1924, 17. See also *ibid*, 27 October 1924, 8.

6 *Ibid*, 3 October 1924, 17; 13 October 1924, 7; 24 October 1924, 9.

7 CAB 24/169, C.P.–169(24), memorandum by Wood, 24 November 1924; *ibid*, C.P.–519(24), Ryland to Wood, 2 December 1924, Wood to Ryland, 2 December 1924; CAB 24/171, C.P.–93(25), memorandum by Wood, 19 February 1925.

8 CAB 23/49, 67(24)11, 17 December 1924.

9 CAB 24/174,C.P.–377(25), memorandum by Wood, 31 July 1925.

10 Baldwin papers, 27, Churchill to Baldwin, 24 December 1924; Swinton papers, 270, 2/5, Churchill to Cunliffe-Lister, 30 December 1924.

11 UK, *Safeguarding of Industries, Procedures and Enquiries*, 1925, Cmd. 2327.

12 HC Deb. 5 s., 180, cols. 703–20.

13 *Ibid.*, col. 747.

14 *Ibid.*, cols. 720–23.

15 *Ibid.*, cols. 796–97.

16 *Glasgow Evening Standard*, 21 February 1925, 4. See also *ibid.*, 28 February 1925, 4; 7 March 1925, 4; 14 March 1925, 4; 28 March 1925, 4. *Forward*, 21 February 1925, 2. *Lansbury's Labour Weekly*, 28 February 1925, 5; 7 March 1925, 3. HC Deb. 5 s., 181, col. 221; *Daily Mail*, 27 February 1925, 9.

17 The *Daily Mail* reported that Arthur Henderson 'leans strongly' towards a policy of prohibiting sweated imports, but omitted to add that he opposed unilateral action, 28 February 1925, 9.

18 *Daily Herald*, 4 March 1925, 1; Labour Party, *Report of the 25th Annual Conference, 1925*, 91.

19 *Daily Herald*, 7 March 1925, 1.

20 *Morning Post*, 2 April 1925, 7; Independent Labour Party, *Report of the Annual Conference, 1925*, 165.

21 TUC, General Council, 9, Item 226, 25 March 1925; *ibid.*, General Council 10, item 239, 8 April 1925.

22 *The Times*, 19 December 1924, 8.

23 *Ibid.*, 14 May 1925, 9.

24 *Forward*, 21 February 1925, 2; *Daily Herald*, 4 March 1925, 1.

25 *Daily Mail*, 7 March 1925, 9; *Daily Herald*, 10 March 1925, 6; *New Leader*, 13 March 1925, 3; HC Deb. 5 s., 183, col. 118.
26 Iron and Steel Trades Confederation papers, 62, International Steelworkers' Federation meeting, minutes, 4–5 January 1925; *ibid.*, International Metalworkers' Conference, Cologne, minutes, 1 March 1925. See also interview with Brownlie in the *Daily Herald*, 10 March 1925, 6; statement by Sir Nicholas Grattan Doyle in HC Deb. 5 s., 181, col. 2195.
27 HC Deb. 5 s., 181, col. 841.
28 *Ibid.*, col. 2184; see also comment by James Maxton in *ibid.*, col. 2224.
29 CAB 24/172, C.P.–198(25), International Labour Policy Committee Report, 7 April 1925.
30 CAB 23/173, C.P.–215(25), memorandum by Steel-Maitland, 27 April 1925.
31 See below, p. 243.
32 HC Deb. 5 s., 182, col. 2225; *ibid.*, 183, col. 471.
33 *Liberal Magazine*, July 1925, 388, 419.
34 HC Deb. 5 s., 184, col. 2387; *The Times*, 13 June 1925, 14.
35 *Daily Express*, 12 June 1925, 1. See also (Conservative Party) *Gleanings and Memoranda*, July 1925, 41–45.
36 *Sunday Pictorial*, 14 June 1925, 6.
37 *Liberal Magazine*, July 1925, 388.
38 *Daily Herald*, 20 June 1925, 2. See also statements by Tom Johnston and John Beckett in the *New Leader*, 26 June 1925, 5, 7.
39 HC Deb. 5 s., 184, col. 2428.
40 *Glasgow Eastern Standard*, 27 June 1925, 7. *Lansbury's Labour Weekly*, 17 June 1925, 7; 25 July 1925, 10; 22 August 1925, 8–9.
41 *New Leader*, 19 June 1925, 3.
42 In February Brailsford praised the merits of the international division of labour and assured readers that 'in the long run there can be no import without an equivalent export'. *New Leader*, 20 February 1925, 8. By October he was arguing that 'We must cure ourselves of the obsession which in every emergency looks overseas for fresh markets. The new markets can be created at home.' *Ibid.*, 16 October 1925, 10.
43 *The Times*, 24 July 1925, 10.
44 Davidson papers, 1924, Thomas speech, 19 June 1924. See also *Report of the Proceedings at the 57th Annual Trades Union Congress, 1925*, 553–55.
45 *New Leader*, 19 June 1925, 2.
46 *Daily Herald*, 20 July 1925, 1.
47 Baldwin papers, 28, Graham to Amery, 29 August 1925. See also Amery diary, 24 June 1925.
48 Labour Party, 'Sweated Imports and International Labour Standards' (1925).
49 *New Leader*, 2 October 1925, 2.
50 Labour Party, *Report of the 25th Annual Conference, 1925*, 266, 269–71.
51 Middlemas and Barnes, *Baldwin*, 323–29; James, *Memoirs of a Conservative*, 218–29.
52 CAB 23/49.
53 See for instance Beaverbrook's signed article, 'George Washington and Winston Churchill', in the *Sunday Express*, 10 May 1925, 8. Also *ibid.*, 17 May 1925, 8; 14 June 1925, 8; 12 July 1925, 8.

54 *Daily Chronicle*, 11 July 1925, 3.
55 *The Times*, 13 July 1925, 9. See also Churchill's speech in *ibid*, 16 July 1925, 16.
56 *The Economic Consequences of Mr Churchill* (1925), also reprinted as ch. 5 of *Essays in Persuasion* (1931).
57 *British Industries*, 30 July 1925, Supplement, viii.
58 FRBNY, Bank of England cables, Norman to Strong, no. 41, 22 May 1925; FRBNY, Strong papers, 1116.5, Norman to Strong, 26 May 1925; *ibid.*, Strong memorandum, 22 July 1925; Norman interview with Royal Commission on Indian Currency and Finance, *Minutes of Evidence*, QQ. 13690, 13740, 29 March 1926.
59 FRBNY, Bank of England cables, Strong to Norman, no. 91, 23 May 1925; Clarke, *Central Bank Cooperation*, 105, 142, f108.
60 T176/13, Pt. 2, Niemeyer to Norman, 21 July 1925; *ibid.*, Norman to Niemeyer, 24 July 1925. Norman and Strong had spent ten days in Berlin before retiring to Spa, and were about to set off for Biarritz when Churchill's call came; TWL, 111–16, Grenfell to Lamont, 29 July 1925.
61 Middlemas and Barnes, *Baldwin*, 378–79; Addis diary, 26, 28, 29 July, 4 August 1925; FRBNY, Strong papers, 1000.6, Strong to Case, 1 August 1925.
62 HC Deb. 5 s., 187, cols. 1462–69. Churchill was so embarrassed and annoyed by Stamp's criticism that he refused to speak to him for a year. Yet his respect for Stamp was if anything enhanced, for he appointed him to represent Britain in the Young Plan negotiations in 1929. That year Churchill asked Stamp if he still thought Britain had returned to gold too soon. When Stamp replied yes, Churchill acknowledged, 'Then that is a severe condemnation of me.' Stamp papers, memorandum on the Paris negotiations, n.d.
63 *The Times*, 8 August 1925, 11.
64 *Ibid.*
65 *The Commercial*, 23 July 1925, 12.
66 S.S. Hammersley, *Industrial Leadership* (1925), 51, 70, 215–19. See also remarks by Lord Aberconway, the Liberal peer and chairman of John Brown and the Sheepbridge Coal and Iron Company, in *The Times*, 29 September 1925, 20.
67 *NUM Journal*, October 1925, 145.
68 Keynes was guest speaker at the Manchester branch of the FBI: *The Commercial*, 15 October 1925, 393. He was disowned in 'FBI and Currency Policy: A Restatement', *ibid.*, 29 October 1925, 458. But see the references to the importance of monetary policy in *British Industries*, Economic Supplement, 30 October 1925, ii.
69 *Daily Herald*, 1 May 1925, 4.
70 *Ibid.*, 8 August 1925, 5.
71 Labour Party, *Report of the 25th Annual Conference, 1925*, 262–66.
72 *The Commercial*, International Banking Supplement, 23 July 1925, 262–66.
73 T176/13, Pt. 2, Norman to Niemeyer, 19 September 1925.
74 *Annual Conference Reports of the National Union of Conservative and Unionist Associations*, Minutes of Annual Conference, Brighton, 8th and 9th October 1925.
75 T176/17, Pt. 1, Churchill to Niemeyer, 21 July 1925; *ibid.*, N.E. Young

Memorandum to members of Overseas Loan Sub-Committee, 7 August 1925; *ibid.*, Young memorandum, 14 July 1925; CAB 24/175, C.P.–432(25), statement by Sir Felix Schuster in 'Trade Outlook', memorandum by Cunliffe-Lister, 15 October 1925; BoE, Norman diary, 17 September 1925.

76 T176/17, Pt. 2, Norman to Niemeyer, 24 July 1925.

77 FRBNY, Strong papers, 1116.5, Norman to Strong, 8 May 1925. See also comments by Norman's kindred spirits, Courtney Mill in *The Times*, 23 May 1925, 28; and Oscar Hobson in the *Manchester Guardian*, 28 May 1925, 5; Pressnell, '1925', 81.

78 T176/17, Pt. 1, Norman to Niemeyer, 11 May 1925.

79 *Ibid.*, Niemeyer to Churchill, 13, 27 May 1925; *ibid.*, Norman minute, 27 May, Churchill minute, 28 May 1925; *ibid.*, Leith Ross to Fergusson, 8 June 1925; *ibid.*, Norman to Churchill, 9 June 1925.

80 CAB 23/50, 28(25)6, 10 June 1925; T176/17, Pt. 2, Treasury telegram to representatives in the Dominions, 15 June 1925. Niemeyer's memorandum of 13 May 1925 is also in the Baldwin papers, 3, 139–41.

81 T176/17, Pt. 1, Bruce to Amery, 18 June 1925.

82 T176/13, Pt. 2, Norman to Niemeyer, 4 July 1925.

83 BoE, Norman diary, 11 June 1925.

84 *Ibid.*, 29 June 1925; T176/17, Pt. 1, Norman to Sir Joseph Cook, 30 June 1925.

85 T176/17, Pt. 1, Chapman to Niemeyer, 24 June 1925; CAB 24/174, C.P.–366(25), 'Unemployment Policy and Trade Revival', memorandum by Cunliffe-Lister, 27 July 1925.

86 T176/17, Pt. 2, Amery to Churchill, 16 October 1925; *New Leader*, 30 October 1925, 7; *National Review*, May 1925, 380, and January 1926, 795–96.

87 HC Deb., 5 s., 186, col. 90.

88 FBI/EI/Glenday/34, memorandum by Glenday and A.L. Please, with introduction by Nugent, July 1925.

89 T172/1499B, Niemeyer memorandum, 19 September 1925. In May he put the balance at £30 million, see T176/17, Pt. 1, Niemeyer to Churchill, 13 May 1925.

90 BoE, Norman diary, 29 September 1925.

91 T176/17, Pt. 2, First Draft Overseas Loan Sub-Committee Report, 2 October 1925.

92 T176/17, Pt. 2, Amery to Churchill, 16 October 1925; Amery diary, 19 October 1925; *Morning Post*, 23 October 1925, 6; *Daily Express*, 31 October 1925, 3.

93 T176/17, Pt. 2, Churchill to Amery, 20 October 1925.

94 *The Times*, 4 November 1925, 19. See also Baldwin's speech in Aberdeen on 5 November 1925, in Conservative Party, *Gleanings and Memoranda*, December 1925, 616.

95 Amery diary, 27–28 December 1925. Sir Maurice Hankey, the Secretary to the Cabinet and CID and another advocate of disengagement, was equally enthusiastic. See Hankey papers, 4/17, Hankey to Austen Chamberlain, 19 October 1925. On the origins and making of the treaties, see Jon Jacobsson, *Locarno Diplomacy, Germany and the West, 1925–1929* (Princeton, 1972).

96 FBI/C/73, Merchandise Marks Committee, 2 December 1924; *Morning*

Post, 12 June 1925, 13; Conservative Party, *Gleanings and Memoranda*, August 1925, 158.

97 CAB 24/173, C.P.–292(25), 'Safeguarding of Industries, Application from the Iron and Steel Industry', memorandum by Cunliffe-Lister, 15 June 1925; Baldwin papers, 28, Churchill to Baldwin, 12 June 1925; *ibid.*, 160, Churchill to Baldwin, 19 June 1925; CAB 24/174, C.P.–305(25), 'The Iron and Steel Industry', memorandum by Salisbury, 23 June 1925; CAB 23/50, 30(25)4, 31(25)2.

98 CAB 24/175, C.P.–482(25), 'Summary of Evidence and of Memoranda Submitted to the Committee of Civil Research', circulated by Baldwin, 16 November 1925.

99 CAB 23/51, 60(25)7, 18 December 1925.

100 HC Deb., 5 s., 189, col. 1945.

4 Conflict over commerce

1 Asa Briggs, *The Age of Improvement*, 400; Richard H. Heindel, *The American Impact on Britain, 1898–1914* (1940), chs. 7, 9.

2 See for instance Gilbert Frankau, 'My Unsentimental Journey', serialised in the *Morning Post*, starting 20 September 1926, and William A. Robson, 'Letter from America', *English Review*, November 1924–26, a more thoughtful series. See also Walton Newbould's account of his seven-month tour through the 'Western World', serialised in *Forward*, 1927–28. Not every tourist was impressed: see Arthur Pugh's reports in *Man and Metal*, January–September 1928. Other visits are reported in HC Deb. 5s., 213, cols. 469–72, 479, 491; *ibid.*, 217, col. 2187.

3 *National Review*, December 1926, 555–62; quoted in Robert Rhodes James, *Victor Cazalet. A Portrait* (1976), 106. America attracted serious observers from other countries as well, see Gustav Stolper, *The German Economy, 1870 to the Present*, rev. edn (1967), 97; Earl R. Beck, *Germany Rediscovers America* (Tallahassee, 1968).

4 *The Times*, 2 November 1925, 15; 25 November 1925, 18; 1 December 1925, 16. *The Economist*, 14 November 1925, 793. *National Review*, December 1925, 490. CAB 24/180, C.P.–235(26), 'Inquiry into Industrial Relationships in America', memorandum by Steel-Maitland, 11 June 1926.

5 Recent studies dismiss the rumours as baseless, but there were strong grounds for believing that Lloyd George would have abandoned free trade had it been politically feasible. John Campbell, *Lloyd George. The Goat in the Wilderness, 1922–1931* (1977), 47–49; Peter Rowland, *Lloyd George* (1975), 602–03; *The Free Trader*, February 1921, 2, and August 1923, 169.

6 *NUM Journal*, October 1924, 151.

7 HC Deb. 5s., 182, col. 781.

8 *The Times*, 5 August 1925, 6.

9 Sir Ernest Petter, *The Disease of Unemployment* (1925); Petter, 'Industry's Rights and Wrongs', *Nineteenth Century and After*, January 1926, 57–67; *National Review*, February 1926, 803; HC Deb. 5s., 181, col. 131.

10 *Morning Post*, 25 May 1925, 13. Inge had earlier aroused fears of the 'yellow peril': *The Times*, 25 February 1921, 12.

11 *Spectator*, 13 February 1926, 260, and 27 March 1926, 573.

12 *National Review*, March 1926, 27.

13 *Ibid.*, and May 1926, 351–53.
14 CAB 24/180, C.P.–235(26), 'Inquiry into Industrial Relationships in America', memorandum by Steel-Maitland, 11 June 1926.
15 CAB 23/53, 4(26)3, 16 June 1926.
16 Sir Oswald Mosley, *My Life* (1968), 185–86, 200. Robert Skidelsky, *Mosley* (1975), 305, claims that Mosley was alone among English politicians in 'discovering' the secret of American economic success. The striking feature of the time is the large number of English politicians who made the discovery.
17 *Daily Herald*, 11 August 1925, 2; Oswald Mosley, *Revolution by Reason* (1925). See also the work of Mosley's collaborator, John Strachey, *Revolution by Reason* (1925).
18 ILP, *Report of the Annual Conference*, 1926, 76; Robert E. Dowse, *Left in the Centre. The Independent Labour Party, 1893–1940* (1966), 133–34.
19 H.N. Brailsford *et al.*, *The Living Wage* (1925), 8–9.
20 *New Leader*, 1 October 1926, 9. Precisely the same theme is developed in J. Walcher, *Ford oder Marx. Die praktische Lösung der sozialen Frage* (Berlin, 1925).
21 *New Leader*, 26 March 1926, 3; 2 March 1926, 3; 9 August 1926, 11.
22 League of Nations (hereafter LN), *The United States in the World Economy. The International Transactions of the United States during the Interwar Period*, by Hal B. Lary (Washington DC, 1943), 122–23.
23 On American concessions on interest payable see Benjamin D. Rhodes, 'Reassessing Uncle Shylock: the United States and the French War Debt, 1917–1929', *Journal of American History*, 55 (March 1969), 787–803, and Joan Hoff Wilson, *Herbert Hoover, Forgotten Progressive* (Boston, 1975), 183. The concessions are summarised in H.C. Moulton and Leo Pasvolsky, *World War Debt Settlements* (New York, 1927), ch. 8. On the severe limits of these concessions see Artaud, *La Question des dettes interalliées*, 5 and passim.
24 George Peel, *The Economic Impact of America* (1928), 5; Paul Studenski and Herman E. Kroos, *Financial History of the United States*, 2nd edn (New York, 1963), 327, 342–43. Tariff levels may be measured in different ways to give different results. Compare the measurement of protection under the Fordney–McCumber tariff in Herbert Hoover, *Memoirs*, ii (New York, 1952), 297, with those in *The Statist*, 6 July 1929, 21, and *The Economist*, 27 July 1929, 160–61. But there were few who would have disagreed with the claim by Sir Arthur Salter, head of the League of Nations Economic and Financial Section, that it was one of the four highest tariffs in the world: *International Affairs*, November 1927, 354.
25 Cleona Lewis, *America's Stake in International Investments* (Washington DC, 1938), 454. The (gross) figure includes portfolio and direct long and short-term investments. Net private foreign investment was just under $9,000 million. See also LN, *The United States in the World Economy*, 21.
26 Frank A. Southard, *American Industry in Europe* (New York, 1931), xiii–xiv; Mira Wilkins, *The Maturing of Multinational Enterprize: American Business Abroad from 1914 to 1970* (Cambridge Mass. 1974), ch. 7; Robert L. Heilbroner, 'None of Your Business', *New York Review*, 20 March 1975, 6; John H. Dunning, *American Investment in British Manufacturing Industry* (1958); Lewis, *America's Stake in International Investments*, table 6; Costigliola, *Awkward Dominion*, chs. 5, 6.

27 Bernard Auffray, *Pierre de Margerie (1861–1942) et la vie diplomatique de son temps* (Paris, 1976), 481. See also Fernand L'Houillier, *Dialogues franco-allemands, 1925–1933* (Strasbourg, 1971), ch. 1.

28 Carl H. Pegg, *Evolution of the European Idea, 1914–1932* (Chapel Hill, 1983), 68, 77, and passim. The roster of French supporters of these organisations reads like a who's who of French politics and big business. How many of those who lent their names actually believed in the possibility of a united Europe may be disputed. It is significant nevertheless that so many thought it desirable to identify with the European movement.

29 *Journal officiel de la République française. Débats parlementaires* (hereafter JO), Chambre des Députés, 28 January 1925, 332, 354.

30 L'Houillier, *Dialogues*, 31–42; Jean Schlumberger and Robert Mayer, *Emile Mayrisch, Précurseur de la construction de l'Europe* (Lausanne, 1967), 31–40.

31 France, Ministère des Affaires Etrangères (hereafter France, MAE), carton 1253, 1, Laboulaye to Massigli, 5 June 1929; *ibid.*, carton 1263, Seydoux note, 4 June 1927; *ibid.*, circular despatch, 15 March 1927; Morinosuke Kajima, Jacques de Launay, Vittorio Pons, and Arnold Zurcher, *Coudenhove-Kalergi, le pionnier de l'Europe unie* (Lausanne, 1971), x; *The Diaries of a Cosmopolitan. Count Harry Kessler, 1918–1937* (1971), 259.

32 Richard Coudenhove-Kalergi, *An Idea Conquers the World* (1953), 146.

33 *The Times*, 2 December 1925, 16.

34 Antonina Vallentin, *Stresemann*, trans. Eric Sutton (1931), 232. Briand's remarks are not included in the German record of the meeting, but Stresemann anticipated that he would raise the threat of American financial domination, see Germany, Auswärtiges Amt, *Akten zur deutschen auswärtigen Politik 1918–1945*, Band 1, 2 (Bonn, 1949), Stresemann memorandum, no. 159, 26 October 1926.

35 Gustav Stresemann, *His Diaries, Letters and Papers*, iii, ed. and trans. Eric Sutton (1940), 504.

36 Jacobson, *Locarno Diplomacy*, 72–74, 373–74. Jacobson overstates the solidity of their positions in Parliament and government. On Briand see Artaud, *La Question des dettes interalliées*, 728, 835, and passim. On Stresemann see Erich Eyck, *Geschichte der Weimarer Republik*, Band 2, 4. Auflage (Erlenbach–Zürich, 1972), 44–48.

37 In March 1928 even Poincaré appealed to Stresemann to join in saving Europe from 'American mammonism and Russian Bolshevism'. Quoted in Jacobsson, *Locarno Diplomacy*, 194.

38 Walter Lipgens, 'Europäische Einigungsidee 1923–1930 und Briands Europaplan im Urteil der deutschen Akten', 1. Teil, *Historische Zeitschrift*, 203 (1966), 69–70.

39 Jules Laroche, *La Pologne de Pilsudski: souvenirs d'une ambassade, 1926–1935* (Paris, 1953), 101ff; Paul Binoux, *Les Pionniers de l'Europe* (Paris, 1972), part 2; Lipgens, 'Europäische Einigungsidee,' 71; Edgar Stern-Rubarth, *Three Men Tried: Austen Chamberlain, Stresemann, Briand and their Fight for a New Europe* (1939); Georges Soutou, 'L'Alliance franco-polonais (1925–1933) ou comment s'en débarrasser?' *Revue d'histoire diplomatique*, 2–4 (1980), 335.

40 Lipgens, 'Europäische Einigungsidee', 57–58; Reinhard Frommelt, *Paneuropa oder Mitteleuropa. Einigungsbestrebungen im Kalkül deutscher Wirtschaft und Politik 1925–1933* (Stuttgart, 1977).

41 Conflict between the British and American 'empires' became a prominent Comintern theme at its third world congress in 1921: Leon Trotsky, *Europe and America: Two Speeches on Imperialism* (New York, 1971); Jane Degras, *The Communist International, 1919–1943*, Documents, i, 1919–22 (1956), 235.
42 Jean Freymond, *Le IIIe Reich et la réorganisation économique de l'Europe, 1940–42* (Leiden, 1974), 19–23 and passim.
43 UK, Committee on Industry and Trade, *Survey of Overseas Markets* (1925). The main findings are summarised in the *Round Table*, September 1926, 690–703.
44 *The Times*, 24 July 1925, 10; *NUM Journal*, August 1925, 115, October 1925, 145.
45 *The Free Trader*, October 1925, 224.
46 The EIA held its first organisational meeting on 8 April 1925 in the offices of the British Commonwealth Union. EIA papers, 221/1/2/1, minutes of Consultative Committee, 1st meeting, 8 April 1925. Sir Robert Horne was invited to be chairman but he declined mainly out of concern for the free trade sympathies of his constituency where he had gone down to defeat in the tariff election of 1923: *ibid.*, 2nd meeting, 23 June 1925.
47 *Annual Conference Reports of the National Union of Conservative and Unionist Associations*, minutes of the annual conference, Brighton, 8–9 October 1925. See also *ibid.*, minutes of the annual conference, Scarborough, 7–8 October 1925.
48 *National Review*, August 1926, 821.
49 Amery diary, 20 October 1926.
50 *Ibid.*, 4 November 1926.
51 *Morning Post*, 18 November 1926, 12. *The Times*, 4 December 1926, 14; 17 December 1926, 19; 24 February 1927, 7; 29 March 1927, 11; 9 April 1927, 14; 24 May 1927, 18; 9 June 1927, 7; 8 August 1927, 9; 16 March 1928, 16; 19 April 1928, 18; 17 July 1928, 9; 22 September 1928, 7. Amery, *The Empire in the New Era. Speeches Delivered During an Empire Tour, 1927–1928* (1928), 7–12 and passim; Amery, *My Political Life*, ii, 472.
52 Robert Boothby, *I Fight to Live* (1947), 110.
53 Robert Boothby, John De V. Loder, Harold Macmillan, and Oliver Stanley, *Industry and the State: A Conservative View* (1927), 109, 110, 114.
54 *Morning Post*, 12 November 1926, 10; Stanley Bruce, 'The Problem of Economic Welfare', *Nineteenth Century and After*, December 1926, 795–802. George Ferguson, the Premier of Ontario, spoke out against 'the danger of Canada being over-Americanised', and affirmed, 'The inevitable destiny of Canada was to be a great imperial unit in the British Empire and to that end he would devote himself.' But other Canadian politicians were more concerned to keep at arms length from Britain. *The Times*, 24 January 1927, 12.
55 *United Empire*, January 1927, 43–44; ibid., May 1926, 274; Sir Hugo Cunliffe-Owen, 'Industry and the Empire Crusade. A Statement to Manufacturers' (n.d.).
56 As Lloyd George observed, Mond bolted before the scheme was even debated let alone adopted by the Liberal Party. Edward Hilton-Young, the financial journalist, who defected at the same time, also pointed to the land scheme as the sole reason for his decision, although as early as 1924 he had

come to look upon Baldwin as his 'spiritual godfather'. Campbell, *Lloyd George*, 99, 113, 128; Roy Douglas, *The History of the Liberal Party, 1895–1970* (1971), 192–93; Lloyd George papers, G/10/14, Hilton-Young to Asquith and Lloyd George, 11 February 1926; Kennet papers, 4/1, Baldwin to Hilton-Young, 14 March 1924; *ibid.*, 78/14a, Hilton-Young to Copeman, 6 June 1926.

57 W.J. Reader, *Imperial Chemical Industries, a History*, i (1970), 465; L.F. Haber, *The British Chemical Industry, 1900–1930* (Oxford, 1971), 296–99.

58 *Morning Post*, 13 October 1926, 12.

59 *Ibid.*, 23 December 1926, 12; Haber, *The British Chemical Industry*, 299.

60 *National Review*, January 1927, 672.

61 *Morning Post*, 19 February 1927, 8.

62 *The Times*, 16 February 1927, 16.

63 LN, *Commercial Policy in the Interwar Period: International Proposals and National Policies*, L.N.11.1942.11.A.6 (Geneva, 1942), 37–38 and passim.

64 *The Free Trader*, December 1925, 265.

65 *Round Table*, June 1926, 476–501. See also *The Times*, 20 April 1926, 12; John A. Hobson, 'The Economic Union of Europe', *Contemporary Review*, September 1926, 290; A. Mackenzie Livingstone, in *The Free Trader*, November 1926, 283; *New Leader*, 22 October 1926, 2; F.W. Hirst, *Safeguarding and Protection in Great Britain and the United States* (1927); Lord Gainford in *The Times*, 19 January 1928, 17; F.C. Goodenough in *ibid.*, 20 January 1928, 21.

66 International Chamber of Commerce, 'Progress in Economic Restoration' (Paris, 1925); *ibid.*, 'Resolutions Passed at Third Congress' (Paris, 1925), *The Times*, 22 June 1926, 13; 23 June 1926, 15; and 24 June 1926, 13.

67 Achille Loria, 'Le Réaction protectionniste', *Revue Economique Internationale*, May 1925, 229–42; Margaret S. Gordon, *Barriers to World Trade. A Study of Recent Commercial Policy* (New York, 1941), 18–19; LN, *Commercial Policy in the Interwar Period*, 37–38.

68 LN, *Official Journal*, 6th Assembly, 1925, 81.

69 William E. Rappard, *Post-War Efforts for Freer Trade*, Geneva Studies ix, 2 (March 1938), 26.

70 Louis Loucheur, *Carnets secrets, 1908–1932* (Paris, 1962), appendix.

71 *The Commercial*, 29 October 1925, 459. See also Loucheur, 'Situation de la France et de la Belgique dans l'Europe nouvelle de l'après guerre', *Revue Economique Internationale*, June 1925, 441–59.

72 *Liberal Magazine*, January 1926, 33. This ironically was also Mond's main argument the last time he spoke in the House as a Liberal. HC Deb. 5s., 189, col. 1478.

73 Brand papers, 95i, Brand to Dawson, 2 December 1925.

74 Sir Arthur Salter, *The United States of Europe and other Papers* (1933), 33–43; *The Times*, 4 May 1927, 17.

75 Leaf, *Walter Leaf, 1852–1927*, 314; *Morning Post*, 21 October 1926, 13.

76 *The Free Trader*, November 1926, 262–83.

77 ABCC, MS. 14, 476/11, Executive Council, 3 November 1926. See also *Shipping World*, 10 November 1926, 4.

78 *The Economist* published the 180 names, claiming the list included 'more than 200', 23 October 1926, 659–60, 668–70; *The Times*, 20 October 1926, 17.

79 *NUM Journal*, December 1926, 432; *National Review*, December 1926, 543–44.
80 *The Times*, 1 December 1926, 8; *Morning Post*, 1 December 1926, 12. Lloyd George's derisive comment is probably explained by the current feud within the Liberal Party. Lloyd George was then organising preparations for a radical new economic strategy. The authors of the petition deplored his new ideas; Sir Charles Mallet, the historian, was shortly to write a hostile biography of Lloyd George.
81 *International Affairs*, March 1927, 69–81.
82 Layton later expressed regret that the conference was treated in London as 'a victory for the British thesis as against the French thesis'. *International Affairs*, November 1927, 361.
83 *Round Table*, December 1926, 17.
84 Barker warned (p. 24), 'The advance of the United States is so fast that unless there is soon a change, England may rapidly sink to the position of another Belgium or Holland and the Dominions and Colonies may drift towards the United States. Most men are unaware that the decline and fall of great States is more frequently brought about by economic causes than by defeat in war. Nations are born in war and die in peace.' The diagnosis if not the prescription anticipated exactly Hitler's musings a year later. Thomas Greenwood, a regular contributor to the *Empire Review*, did not hesitate to equate the Soviet and American threats: they 'aim both, consciously or unconsciously, at the disruption of the British Empire – the former with a subversive propaganda, the latter with financial imperialism': September 1929, 192. See also the hostile observations in *Blackwood's Magazine*, December 1925, 869–78, and Hugh P. Vowles, 'Some Fruits of Americanism', *National Review*, January 1927, 702–08.
85 On aspects of commercial rivalry see Artaud, *La Question des dettes interalliées*, i, 504; CAB 24/174, C.P.–364(25), memorandum by Austen Chamberlain, 22 July 1925; CAB 24/189, C.P.–292(27), 'Memorandum Respecting the Future of Anglo-American Relations', Foreign Office, 17 November 1927; Michael J. Hogan, *Informal Entente: The Private Structure of Cooperation in Anglo-American Economic Diplomacy, 1918–1928* (1977), ch. 9; Ludwell Denny, *America Conquers Britain* (New York, 1930); *Morning Post*, 20 November 1926, 10; Barker, *America's Secret*, ch. 14; FO 371/12962, C3504/29/37, Crowe to Chamberlain, 7 May 1928; FO 371/12728, A5499/108/51, 'Treasury 2% Stamp Tax and Latin American Loans', memorandum by Hadow, 24 August 1928. On the naval dispute see below, ch. 5, pp. 147–48.
86 HC Deb. 5s., 203, cols. 2039–44, 2051–52, 2085, 2088; *ibid.*, 204, cols. 277, 294, 308.
87 Sir Alfred Mond, *Industry and Politics* (1927), 276.
88 *The Times*, 5 May 1927, 18.
89 Board of Trade papers (hereafter BT) 11/35, C.R.T.2107/28, Report of the British Representatives to the World Economic Conference, 24 May 1927; *The Free Trader*, July 1927, 144.
90 LN, *Report and Proceedings of the World Economic Conference held at Geneva, May 4th to 23rd, 1927*, 1927.II.52i.4., 72, 107, 112; *The Times*, 11 May 1927, 13; Rappard, *Post-War Efforts for Freer Trade*, 45.
91 LN, *Reports and Proceedings*, 130–32; summary of speeches in FO

371/12659, W4247/53/98, Cavendish Bentinck to Chamberlain, no. 52LNCC, 7 May 1927.

92 LN, *Report and Proceedings*, 13–16.

93 *Ibid.*, 48.

94 Heinrich Liepmann, *Tariff Levels and the Economic Unity of Europe*, trans. H. Stenning (1938), passim.

95 LN, *Report and Proceedings*, 50; *The Times*, 12 May 1927, 13.

96 LN, *Report and Proceedings*, 62, 75–77; *The Times*, 18 May 1927, 15.

97 FBI/EA/Glenday/5, Committee on Geneva Conference Agenda, 27 January 1927; FBI/EA/Glenday/36, Committee recommendations, 31 March 1927.

98 Labour Party, *Report of the 27th Annual Conference, 1927*, 141– 43; BT 11/35, C.R.T.2107/28, Report of the British Representatives, 24 May 1927.

99 *The Times*, 21 October 1926, 13. But see also *The Statist*, 9 April 1927, 603.

100 LN, *Report and Proceedings*, 1927.II.52ii., 147.

101 *Ibid.*, 148, 150, 151.

102 *Ibid.*, 168.

103 *The Times*, 17 May 1927, 13; BT 11/35, C.R.T.2107/28, Report of the British Representatives, 24 May 1927.

104 LN, *The World Economic Conference, Geneva, May 1927. Final Report*, 1927.II.46.

105 Compare the *Nation and Athenaeum*, 30 April 1927, 103, and *ibid.*, 4 June 1927, 294. See also *The Times*, 4 May 1927, 17, and *ibid.*, 30 May 1927, 15; *The Economist*, 28 May 1927, 1108; Sir Arthur Salter, *The Economic Consequences of the League* (1927), 8, 14.

106 *The Times*, 1 February 1927, 13.

107 CAB 23/52, 16(26)2, 15 April 1926; CAB 24/186, C.P.–149(27), 'Agriculture and Safeguarding of Industries', memorandum by Guinness, 12 May 1927.

108 *National Review*, June 1927, 448; T172/1576, Churchill statement to deputation from the Conservative Party Agricultural Committee, 14 July 1927.

109 CAB 24/186, C.P.–149(27), Guinness memorandum, 12 May 1927.

110 Peter Self and Herbert J. Storing, *The State and the Farmer* (1962), 39.

111 *The Times*, 20 May 1927, 9; and 28 May 1927, 9.

112 *Ibid.*, 16 June 1927, 19; 1 July 1927, 18; 11 July 1927, 20; 25 July 1927, 19. *Annual Register, 1927*, 74.

113 CAB 24/188, C.P.–201(27), 'Position of the Heavy Steel Industry', memorandum by Cunliffe-Lister, 15 July 1927.

114 *Morning Post*, 31 October 1927, 8; J.C. Carr and W. Taplin, *History of the British Steel Industry* (Oxford, 1962), ch. 41.

115 T172/1530, Page-Croft for EIA deputation to Churchill, 27 March 1928; *Iron and Coal Trades Review*, 3 August 1928, 172.

116 UK, *Committee on Industry and Trade, Final Report*, 1929, Cmd. 3282, 268.

117 On the composition of the committee see *The Times*, 30 July 1924, 12; 31 July 1924, 9. *Morning Post*, 31 July 1924, 6. According to *The Economist*, 2 August 1924, 187, 'Industrial capital is well represented by Sir Norman Hill, Sir Alan Smith, Mr Pybus, and the chairman, and banking by Sir Harry Goschen.' In fact, Sir Norman Hill was a spokesman for the shipping interests, and Mr Pybus, a 'company director', was a prominent

Liberal and City-based financier. Leaving them aside, 'industrial capital' was represented by only two men on a committee of eighteen.

118 FBI/EA/Glenday/36, FBI-Reichsverband conversations, 3 December 1926.

119 FBI/EA/Glenday/15, Nugent to Docker, 20 November 1924; *ibid.*, Nugent to Muspratt, 17 November 1926; FBI/C/31, meeting of international Trade Relations Committee, 7 September 1927; FBI/C/1, Grand Council, 12 October 1927; FBI/C/5, Executive Committee, Director's report on meeting with President of the Board of Trade, 13 December 1927.

120 James, *Memoirs of a Conservative*, 182.

121 *Morning Post*, 17 December 1928, 11; CAB 24/204, C.P.–124(29), 'Safeguarding of Industries. Report of the Woollen and Worsted Committee', memorandum by Cunliffe-Lister, 13 June 1929.

122 *Yorkshire Post*, 2 March 1928, 6.

123 *Morning Post*, 3 December 1928, 10, 11 and 7 December 1928, 12.

124 *Ibid.*, 20 December 1928, 10, 12; Baldwin papers, 29, Pugh to Baldwin, 31 December 1928, 125, copy in CAB 24/201, C.P.–20(29).

125 CAB 23/55, 32(27)9, 19 May 1927; *The Times*, 21 May 1927, 14.

126 *The Times*, 24 June 1927, 11; 20 June 1927, 13; 22 July 1927, 9; 25 July 1927, 19.

127 CAB 23/55, 42(27)5, 20 July 1927; CAB 23/57, 15(28)11, 21 March 1928.

128 CAB 23/60, 4(29)2, 6 February 1929; Amery diary, 6 February, 1, 9 May 1929.

129 Baldwin papers, 28, Amery to Baldwin, 10 April 1927; Neville Chamberlain diary, 2/22, 1 July, 21 July, 4 August 1927; Amery diary, 7 May, 4, 9, 10, 11, 23 July, 2 August 1928; *The Times*, 30 July 1928, 7, 13 and 3 August 1928, 7; Gilbert, *Churchill*, Companion Volume 5, Part 1, 1314, 1316; CAB 23/58, 43(28)2.

130 BT 55/58, S.O.I./12, memorandum, 2 July 1929.

131 LN, *World Economic Conference*, 1927, 11.50 (Geneva, 1927); *The Free Trader*, August–September 1927, 166; HC Deb. 5s., 208, col. 1827; *ibid.*, 209, cols. 519, 521.

132 LN, *Quantitative Trade Controls. Their Causes and Nature*, (Geneva, 1943), 7–26.

133 Chapman, *Autobiography*, 236–38; Ministry of Agriculture and Fisheries (hereafter MAF), 40/5, SS12620, Report of the British Delegation to the International Conference for the Abolition of Import and Export Prohibitions held in Geneva in October and November 1927, 30 November 1927. The convention and other relevant documents are in FO 371/14943, W6/6/98.

134 MAF 40/5, SS12620, minutes by Thomson, 30 August, 3, 10 October 1927; *ibid.*, Fountain to Howell Thomas, 25 October 1927, Howell Thomas minute, 27 October 1927, Guinness to Cunliffe-Lister, 27 October 1927, Hamilton to Chapman, n.d.; FO 371/17661, C1964/873/22, Thomas to Under-Secretary of State, 9 February 1928; MAF 40/6, TAY 13783, Franklin to Pinsent, 29 August 1928.

135 The history and politics of the issue are examined in Robert Boyce, 'Insects and International Relations: Canada, France, and British Agricultural "Sanitary" Import Restrictions between the Wars', *International History Review*, 9/1 (February 1987), 1–27.

136 The size of the French peasantry and its potential for influencing parliamentary decisions has led to exaggerated estimates of its actual political role during the Third Republic. Not until the later 1920s did it begin to realise its political potential. See FO 371/16388, W3670/63/50, Cahill memorandum, 1 April 1932; Gordon Wright, *Rural Revolution in France. The Peasantry in the Twentieth Century* (1964), 14; but also Boyce, 'Insects and International Relations'.

137 Great Britain, Foreign Office, *Documents on British Foreign Policy, 1919–1939* (hereafter DBFP), Ser.1A, vol. iv, French note in Phipps to Chamberlain, 2 April 1928. On the level of duties as they affected France see Liepmann, *Tariff Levels*, 246.

138 T172/1713, Chapman to Graham, 1 March 1930.

139 Britain derived twice as much revenue from duties on imports from France as France derived from duties on imports from Britain, see FO 371/15684, W11768/11768/50, note of conversation with M. Rollin, 7 October 1931. Taking revenue from import duties as a percentage of the total value of merchandise imported for domestic consumption, the United Kingdom (9.60% in 1925) was substantially more protective than France (3.30%): see LN, *Tariff Level Indices*, annex ii. But this was not a wholly satisfactory measure of protection: in certain instances duties were so high as to discourage trade altogether.

140 André Mertens, 'L'Accord commercial franco-allemand du août 1927', *Revue Economique Internationale*, October 1927, 23–45; DBFP, Ser. 1A, 4, French note in Phipps to Chamberlain, 2 April 1928; Alfred Sauvy, *Histoire économique de la France entre les deux guerres*, iv (Paris, 1975), 20, 23; F.A. Haight, *A History of French Commercial Policies* (New York, 1941), 133–38; Pierre Guillan, 'La Politique douanière de la France dans les années vingt', *Relations Internationales*, 16 (Paris, 1978), 315–31.

141 B.R. Mitchell and Phyllis Deane, *Abstract of British Historical Statistics* (Cambridge, 1962), 326. The figure £37.5 million excludes re-exports. The contemporary official estimate placed the average deficit at £32.9 million per annum: UK, *Statistical Abstract for the United Kingdom*, 1932, Cmd. 3991, 322–23, 326–27. Interestingly, British exports to France were mostly raw materials and foodstuffs, coal being the most important single item, whereas French exports to Britain were mostly manufactures. Tourism probably added another £30 million per annum to Britain's bilateral deficit. See FO 371/16388, W3670/63/50, Cahill memorandum, 1 April 1932.

142 Sauvy, *Histoire économique de la France*, iv, ii, accepts Bernard Nogaro's estimate that the French tariff provided over-all protection of 8.77 per cent in 1913. He estimates that the comparable figure after the signing of the Franco-German commercial treaty in August 1927 was about 15 per cent, although after subsequent agreements with Belgium and Switzerland this figure was reduced to about 12 per cent. On the other hand a contemporary analysis, based on revenue from import duties, placed French protection at 8.81 per cent in 1913 and only 3.30 per cent in 1925: see LN, *Tariff Level Indices*, annex ii. The free trader Walter Layton commented in 1927, 'One could imagine what would have happened had French commercial policy been as imperialistic as French political policy during recent years. It is only fair to recognise that it had been relatively liberal since the end of the war.' *International Affairs*, November 1927, 362.

143 CAB 24/187, C.P.–174(27), 'Trade Outlook', memorandum by Cunliffe-Lister, 10 June 1927. See also the *Chamber of Commerce Journal*, 5 January 1929, 84–85, and 5 June 1929, 10.
144 DBFP, Ser. 1A, vol. iv, Chamberlain to Crewe, no. 59, 9 January 1928. See also *ibid.*, Chamberlain to Crewe, 20 March 1928.
145 *Ibid.*, Phipps to Chamberlain, 29 March 1928.
146 CAB 24/193, C.P.–89(28), 'Trade Outlook', memorandum by Cunliffe-Lister, March 1928; CAB 24/195, C.P.–1579(28), 'Trade Outlook', memorandum by Cunliffe-Lister, 17 May 1928.
147 HC Deb. 5s., 216, col. 839.
148 FBI/EA/Glenday/36, minutes of FBI–Reichsverband conversations, 3 December 1926; BT 11/35, C.R.T. 2107/28, report of FBI–Reichsverband meeting, 12 July 1927.
149 DBFP, Ser.1A, vol. iv, Lindsay to Chamberlain, 24 March 1928.
150 *Ibid.*, Graham to Chamberlain, 4 April 1928.
151 Jacques Rueff, *Combats pour l'ordre financier* (Paris, 1972), 72–73.
152 LN, *Official Journal*, Resolutions of Council, 16 June 1927.
153 Chapman, *Autobiography*, 238.
154 FRUS, 1929, I, memorandum by McClure, 988–89; Joseph M. Jones Jr, *Tariff Retaliation: Repercussions of the Smoot-Hawley Bill* (Philadelphia, 1934), 159–63; Haight, *A History of French Commercial Policies*, 133–38; Julius Klein, *Frontiers of Trade* (New York, 1929), 278; *The Economist*, 2 February 1929, 221, 22 June 1929, 1393.
155 United States Bureau of the Census, *Historical Statistics of the United States, Colonial Times to 1957* (Washington DC, 1960), 550, 552, (U125, U143). Sauvy estimates the deficit on total French commodity trade during the 1920s at 35.3 billion francs, and the deficit on commodity trade with the United States alone at 34.7 billion: *Histoire économique de la France*, i, annexe ix, 477, 489.
156 LN, *Commercial Policy in the Interwar Period*, 118.
157 *The Statist*, 6 July 1929, 21.
158 Southard, *American Industry in Europe*, 121–22.
159 SdN, E/P.C./1st Session/P.V.1(1), Economic Committee, Meeting of Rapporteurs on Commercial Policy, first meeting, 22 March 1928, 4–5.
160 See articles 1 and 2 of model draft treaty in FO 371/11862, W10343/10343/50.
161 SdN, E/P.C./1st Session/P.V.3(1), Economic Committee, Meeting of Rapporteurs on Commercial Policy, third meeting, 23 March 1928, 20; SdN, R2727, E395, Report by Chapman, 31 March 1928.
162 SdN, E/P.C./1st Session/P.V.1(1), Economic Committee, Meeting of Rapporteurs on Commercial Policy, first meeting, 22 March 1928, 5; *ibid.*, third meeting, 23 March 1928, 22.
163 *Ibid.*, third meeting, 23 March 1928, 8.
164 LN, C,357.M.III.1928.II, Report of Economic Committee to Council, June 1928; LN, C.20.M.14.1929.II, Report of Economic Committee to Council, January 1929; LN, C.155.M.61.1929.II, Report of League Economic Committee to Council, April 1929.
165 LN, C.217.M.73.1928.II, Report of the Economic Consultative Committee on its First Session, 14–19 May 1928, 7.

166 LN, C.130.M.45.1929.II, Report of the Economic Consultative Committee on the period May 1928 to May 1929, 8–9.
167 *The Times*, 8 May 1929, 15.

5 The scramble for gold

1 FRBNY, Strong papers, 1116.5, Norman to Strong, 8 May 1925: 'We rather prepared for a mountain and have (so far) brought forth a mouse!'
2 See above ch. 3, pp. 91–92.
3 FRBNY, Strong papers, 1116.5, Norman to Strong, 21 August 1925; *ibid.*, Strong to Norman, 23 August 1925; *ibid.*, Bank of England cables, Strong to Norman, no. 51, 18 September 1925; *ibid.*, Norman to Strong, no. 16, 19 September 1925; *ibid.*, Strong to Norman, no. 53, 21 September 1925; *ibid.*, Norman to Strong, no. 18, 22 September 1925; *ibid.*, Jay to Norman, no. 54, 22 September 1925; *ibid.*, Strong papers, 1116.5, Strong to Norman, 25 September 1925.
4 *Ibid.*, Bank of England cables, Strong to Norman, no. 78, 14 October 1925.
5 *Ibid.*, Norman to Strong, no. 56, 15 October 1925; *ibid.*, Norman to Strong, no. 59, 19 October 1925; *ibid.*, Norman to Strong, no. 25, 30 November 1925.
6 BoE, Norman diary, 3 December 1925; Clay, *Lord Norman*, 292; Grigg, *Prejudice and Judgement*, 193.
7 Gilbert, *Winston S. Churchill*, Companion Volume 5, pt. 1, 685.
8 HC Deb. 5s., 194, cols. 1696–97.
9 *The Times*, 6 February 1926, 7, and *ibid.*, 12 March 1926, 16.
10 FBI/S/Walker/25/2, Glenday to Dibben, 25 June 1925; *ibid.*, Tennyson to Johnston, 24 February 1926.
11 LCC papers, MS. 16, 623, Financial Section, vol. 2, minutes, 11 November 1925, 24 January 1926.
12 Terence O'Brien, *Milner, Viscount Milner of St James's and Cape Town, 1854–1925* (1979), 364, 367.
13 *The Times*, 24 July 1925, 23.
14 Sir Ernest Petter, 'The Disease of Unemployment' (1925). The title is borrowed from Milner's *Questions of the Hour*, rev. edn. (1925), 30. See also Petter, 'Industry's Rights and Wrongs', *Nineteenth Century and After*, January 1926, 57–67, and references to Petter's views in the *National Review*, February 1926, 803–08; HC Deb. 5s, 191, col. 131.
15 J.F. Darling, *Economic Unity of the Empire* (1926).
16 Vincent C. Vickers, *Economic Tribulation* (1941), 11; FBI/S/Walker/25/2, Vickers to Nugent, 2 July 1927. Vickers had been a member of the Bank's Court but resigned in 1919 on grounds of ill-health. Besides his connection with the Bank, he was a director of the London Assurance Company and later became a Lieutenant of the City of London. But his chief attachment remained to industry and the land, as his criticism of the Bank suggested.
17 Jeffcock, *Agricultural Politics, 1915–1935*, 21; J. Taylor Peddie, *The Dual System of Stabilisation* (1930), viii. See also Peddie, *The Flaw in the Economic System: The Case Against the Gold Standard* (1928); Peddie, *The Producers' Case for Monetary Reform. Is Great Britain now a Second-Rate Power?*, 3rd edn (1929); British Economic Federation, 'Agriculture and

Industry', Report of a Conference held at the Surveyors' Institute, Great George Street, SW1, on Wednesday, October 17th, 1928 (1928).

18 McKenna, *Post-War Banking Policy*, 132–35.

19 T160/384, F9780/1.

20 *Ibid.*

21 FBI/S/Walker/25/2, March 1927; *New Leader*, 17 December 1926, 3.

22 *British Industries*, Economic Supplement, 30 April 1927, i-iv.

23 Baldwin papers, 28, Amery to Churchill, 6 December 1926; *ibid.*, Amery to Baldwin and Churchill, 10 April 1927.

24 T175/11, Niemeyer to Churchill, 9 May 1927; *ibid.*, Churchill to Niemeyer, 9 May 1927.

25 Lord Moran, *Winston Churchill* (1966), 303. See also *The Times Business News*, 21 March 1969; Boyle, *Montagu Norman*, 263; Christopher Hassall, *Edward Marsh* (1959), 570. Some indication of Churchill's feelings about the gold standard experience is revealed in his later calls for reflation: see *The Times*, 8 May 1932, 16, and 16 May 1932, 11. Despite their strained relations, Churchill allowed Norman and his colleagues prior knowledge of his budget plans – an interesting comment on their confidentiality: see Addis diary, 17 April 1928.

26 Boyle, *Montagu Norman*, 230.

27 HC Deb. 5s, 208, col. 99.

28 BoE, Norman diary, 8 November 1925; FRBNY, Strong papers, 1116.5, Norman to Strong, 4 March 1926; *ibid.*, 20 May 1926; *ibid.*, 25 October 1926; *ibid.*, Strong papers, 1116.6, Strong to Norman, 26 November 1926. Norman had similarly refused to do business with the Czech government until it set up an independent central bank: *ibid.*, Norman to Strong, 15 November 1924.

29 MGC, Belgian Government Loan, 1926/1, J.P. Morgan & Co. to J.P. Morgan and Whitney (London), no. 25/2328, 9 October 1925; FRBNY, Bank of England cables, Norman to Strong, no. 98, 11 November 1925; *ibid.*, no. 26, 30 November 1925; *ibid.*, Anderson to Strong, no. 19, 24 November 1925; *ibid.*, Strong papers, 1117.1, Anderson to Strong, 27 November 1925; *ibid.*, Strong to Anderson, 7 December 1925.

30 Raymond Philippe, *Le Drame financier de 1924 à 1928* (Paris, 1931), passim; TWL, 113–5, N.D. Jay to Charles Whigham, 15 June 1926; Artaud, *La Question des dettes interalliées*, ii, 504; André Neurisse, *Histoire du franc*, 2nd edn. (Paris, 1967), 60–65; Martin Wolfe, *The French Franc between the Wars, 1919–1939* (New York, 1951), ch. 2; D.W. Brogan, *The Development of Modern France, 1870–1939* (1940), 591–96. On talk of a *coup d'état* see FRBNY, French situation, C261.1, Strong to Harrison, 21 July 1926. The most thorough analysis of the French dilemma is in Charles S. Maier, *Recasting Bourgeois Europe: Stabilization in France, Germany, and Italy in the Decade after World War I* (Princeton, 1975), ch. 8 and passim.

31 FRBNY, Bank of England Revolving Credit, C261.1, Norman to Strong, 29 October 1926.

32 Moreau, *Souvenirs*, 246.

33 *Ibid.*, foreword by Jacques Rueff.

34 Jean Noel Jeanneney, 'L'Influence des milieux financiers sur la politique extérieure de la France dans les années 1920s', *Les Relations financières internationales, facteurs de solidarités ou de rivalités?* (Bruxelles, 1979), 75.

35 René Girault, 'Economie et politique internationale: diplomatie et banque pendant l'entre-deux-guerres', *Relations Internationales*, 21 (Spring 1980), 7 and passim.
36 Jacques Bariéty, 'Finances et relations internationales: A propos du "plan de Thoiry" (September 1926)', *Relations Internationales*, 21 (Spring 1980), 53–57; Soutou, 'L'Alliance franco-polonaise (1925–1933), ou comment s'en débarrasser?', 306–07.
37 Emile Moreau, 'Le Relèvement financier et monétaire de la France (1926–1928)', pt. 2, *Revue des Deux Mondes*, 15 March 1927, 309–11; Boyle, *Montagu Norman*, 228; Chandler, *Benjamin Strong*, 371–74; Clarke, *Central Bank Cooperation*, 117–18; Clay, *Lord Norman*, 230–31.
38 Banque de France, Délibérations du Conseil Général, procès verbal (hereafter BdeF, CG), 14 April 1927; Clay, *Lord Norman*, 232; Moreau, 'Le Relèvement financier', 309, 311; Moreau, *Souvenirs*, 251–55. The *Financial News*, 31 March 1927, encouraged the rumour that the Bank of England had used the French gold deposit and would have to buy it in; *The Times*, *Morning Post*, *Statist*, and most other British papers denied it. In fact, neither central bank was embarrassed by repayment of the credit: see France, MF, F30/12639, note by Pouyanne, 4 April 1927, and 'The French Purchases of Gold in London', *The Banker*, July 1927, written by Pouyanne, as confirmed in MGC, bundle 242.
39 Moreau, *Souvenirs*, viii–ix, 163, 164, 182, 184, 438; MGC, Belgian Government Loan, 1926/2, Lamont to J.P. Morgan & Co., no. 26/4724, 21 May 1926; Moreau, 'Le Relèvement financier', pt. 2, 309–11; Jacques Rueff, 'Sur un point d'histoire: le niveau de la stabilisation Poincaré', *Revue d'Économie Politique*, 62/2 (1959), 169–78.
40 Moreau, *Souvenirs*, 308, 315, 317, 320; FRBNY, Strong papers, 1116.7, Norman to Strong, 22 May 1927; *ibid.*, Bank of England general, C261, Norman to Strong, no. 40, 25 May 1927.
41 FRBNY, French situation, C261.1, Quesnay, minutes of meeting, 27 May 1927; *ibid.*, Bank of England general, C261, Norman to Strong, no. 43, 30 May 1927.
42 FRBNY, Harrison papers, Bank of France cables, Strong to Moreau, no. 15, 26 May 1927; *ibid.*, Moreau to Strong, no. 16, 31 May 1927; *ibid.*, Strong to Moreau, no. 19, 1 June 1927.
43 Sayers, *The Bank of England*, iii, appendix 17; Moreau, *Souvenirs*, 372.
44 Chandler, *Benjamin Strong*, 375–77.
45 The total of US foreign capital issues in 1926 was $1,629 million, in 1928 $1,498 million, and in 1929 $790 million. *Federal Reserve Bulletin*, various.
46 Clarke, *Central Bank Cooperation*, 121, 128–29.
47 Hélène Carrère d'Encausse and Stuart Schram, *Marxism and Asia* (1969), 31.
48 E.H. Carr, *Socialism in One Country, 1924–1926*, iii (1964), 669.
49 Peter Lowe, *Britain in the Far East: A Survey from 1819 to the Present* (1981), 128.
50 Bridgeman papers, diary, August 1927; Stephen W. Roskill, *British Naval Policy between the Wars*, i (1968).
51 *The Statist*, 2 July 1927, 17; Gilbert, *Winston S. Churchill*, Companion vol. 5, pt. 1, 1031–35.
52 Cecil papers, Add. MS. 51073, Cecil to Churchill, 26 July 1927; *ibid.*, Add.

MS. 51080, Cecil to Baldwin, 9 August 1927; *ibid.*, Add. MS. 51079, Cecil to Sir Austen Chamberlain, 10 August 1927.

53 See above, 98–99.

54 Robert Liefmann, *Cartels, Concerns and Trusts* (1932), 149–58 and passim.

55 FO 371/14378, C6268/6268/18, Cahill memorandum, 4 February 1929.

56 Jacques Seydoux, *De Versailles au Plan Young* (Paris, 1932), 24; CAB 24/193, C.P.–89(28), 'Trade Outlook', memorandum by Cunliffe-Lister, March 1928.

57 *The Times*, 15 March 1928, 15. See also Seydoux, *De Versailles au Plan Young*, 31; L'Houillier, *Dialogues franco-allemands*, 35–36.

58 Brand, ed., *The Letters of John Dove*, 292.

59 Clay, *Lord Norman*, 323; Hugh Quigley, *Towards Industrial Recovery* (1927); *The Economist*, 29 January 1927, 199, and 5 March 1927, 464; *The Statist*, 19 February 1927, 283, and 9 April 1927, 603; HC Deb. 5s., 214, col. 1962.

60 *Morning Post*, 28 January 1928, 4. The banker was F.C. Goodenough, chairman of Barclays Bank: see *The Economist*, 21 January 1928, 121; also the *National Review*, March 1928, 46–47.

61 BEAMA *Trade Survey*, June 1928, 3.

62 *National Review*, June 1928, 510. See also *Bradford Chamber of Commerce Journal*, October 1928, 66.

63 Central and Associated Chambers of Agriculture, *Annual Report, 1927*, 10–13.

64 Charles Dampier-Whetham, *Politics and the Land* (1927), 3–4 and passim; *The Times*, 2 May 1927, 21, 5 December 1927, 20, 19 December 1927, 11; Taylor Peddie, *The Flaw in the Economic System*; Sir Daniel Hall, 'The Economic Position of Agriculture', *Contemporary Review*, February 1928, 139; *The Times*, 16 January 1928, 17.

65 *Journal of the Farmers' Club*, Pt. 2, March 1928, 21–29. *The Times* published a six-paragraph summary of Dampier-Whetham's address but not a word of the discussion that followed it, 6 March 1928, 11. See also Dampier-Whetham's address at the Surveyors' Institute, *The Times*, 3 April 1928, 9.

66 *The Times*, 7 March 1928, 11.

67 Cecil papers, Add. MS. 51164, Bledisloe to Cecil, 30 January 1924; *ibid.*, Bledisloe, 'A New Agricultural Policy for Great Britain', n.d. (? 1926).

68 Kitson's organisation was created in the summer of 1926. It was only the latest of several such bodies he had backed since 1905. See *National Review*, August 1926, 956. Peddie's organisation was created in 1927. Other organisations included the Agricultural and Industrial Union, the League of the British Commonwealth, and Hammersley's producers' group formed in 1928 or early 1929.

69 EIA, MSS. 221/1/3/1, minutes of Executive Committee, 1 February 1926; *ibid.*, minutes of Provisional Executive Committee, 19 April 1926.

70 *The Farmer and Stock Breeder*, 26 March 1928, 700; 9 April 1928, 813; 16 April 1928, 865; 23 April 1928, 924.

71 *Labour Magazine*, April 1929, 568–71.

72 TUC, T211/262.017, Mond to Citrine, 23 November 1927 and 20 December 1927. Details of their occupations are given in G.W. McDonald and Howard F. Gospel, 'The Mond–Turner Talks, 1927–1933: A Study in Industrial Cooperation', *Historical Journal*, xvi, 4 (1973), 807–29.

73 *Report of the Proceedings at the 59th Annual Trades Union Congress, 1927*, 387–96.
74 TUC, G.C.6, 1927–28, item 86, 23 November 1927.
75 *Industrial Review*, March 1928, i. The rationale for the talks is set out in TUC, T211/262.02, notes of joint conference, 8 November 1928.
76 TUC T210/262.01, Milne-Bailey to Blanco White, 23 January 1928; *ibid.*, T211/262/08, special General Council meeting, 24 January 1928; Hawtrey papers, 10/15, Blanco-White to Hawtrey, 9 February 1928.
77 TUC, T210/262.02, minutes of joint conference, 21 March 1928; *ibid.*, G.C. 15, 1927–28, item 194, 28 March 1928; *The Times*, 18 April 1928, 18.
78 'Gold and Industry', *Industrial Review*, May 1928, 9. Original in T172/1500B, Mond and Turner to Churchill, 12 April 1928.
79 T172/1500B, Grigg to Churchill, 13 April 1928.
80 FRBNY, Bank of England general, C261, Harrison to Crane, 18 February 1928.
81 *The Times*, 19 April 1928, 22.
82 Brand papers, 92(2), Brumwell to Brand, 6 May 1928; *ibid.*, Brand to Dawson, 7 and 14 May 1928.
83 *The Times*, 19 April 1928, 22.
84 *Ibid.*, 25 April 1928, 22.
85 *Ibid.*, 12.
86 FBI/S/Walker/25/2, Rylands to Nugent, 26 April 1928; *ibid.*, Nugent to Rylands, 27 April 1928.
87 *British Industries*, 15 June 1928, 215; T175/1500B, Corcoran to Churchill, 21 May 1928; BEAMA *Trade Survey*, June 1928, 2; T160/384, F9780/1, Sir Auckland Geddes, Lord Denbeigh, Frank Farrell, and others to Prime Minister, 25 April 1928.
88 HC Deb. 5s., 217, col. 706.
89 *Ibid.*, col. 721, 732, 748, 806.
90 *Ibid.*, 722.
91 T172/1500B, Churchill minute, 14 April 1928.
92 HC Deb. 5s., 217, col. 808.
93 *Ibid.*, col. 804–06.
94 FRBNY, French situation, C261.1, R.B. Warren minute, 25 August 1926. Quesnay admitted that 'some people' were worried by the scissors effect of the divergent price levels, see *ibid.*, Warren minute, 26 August 1926. See also MGC, Belgian Government Loan 1926/2, Lamont to New York, no. 26/4724, 21 May 1926.
95 FRBNY, Strong papers, 1012.3, Strong to Jay, 4 August 1927.
96 UK, *Royal Commission on Indian Currency and Finance*, iii, appendixes, v, *Minutes of Evidence*, Q.13,696, appendix 82, 92. FRBNY, Bank of England general, C261, Strong to Anderson, no. 84, 16 January 1926; *ibid.*, Bank of England cables, Strong to Norman, no. 20, 5 March 1926.
97 TWL, 103–12, Leffingwell to Lamont, 12 July 1927.
98 BoE, Norman diary, 24 June 1927.
99 Strong's sterling balances reached a total of £12.35 million before the recovery of the sterling exchanges in the autumn of 1927 enabled him to dispose of them at a comfortable profit. FRBNY, Bank of England general, C261, Strong to Harding, 5 October 1927.
100 BoE, Niemeyer papers, OV9/257, Norman to Lubbock, 19 July 1927; *ibid.*,

Strong to Young, 21 July 1927; *ibid.*, Niemeyer to Salter, 29 July 1927; MGC, TWL/3, Lamont to Grenfell, 20 April 1923.

101 One can make too much of the influence of personality on the outcome of these events, but it is worth noting the contrasting tone of the Norman–Strong correspondence. Strong's letters to Norman are studded with mock familiar phrases such as 'old scout', 'old Boy', 'dear old queer duck', 'Old Dear' (31 December 1927), and 'Old Chap' (3 March 1928), and end typically, 'My best regards to you, Sincerely yours...'. In 1928 Strong deliberately avoided Norman when he travelled to Europe for the last time. Norman on the other hand usually included in his letters gushing expressions of concern about Strong's health and future plans and reproaches for not writing more often. Returning to London in January 1925 after two weeks in New York – where Britain's return to gold was settled – Norman discovered Strong's velvet jacket in his trunk. 'What am I to say to you? I will keep the jacket – at any rate until you come again – and I will wear it when I want to look nice or to recall 270 Park Avenue'. In November 1925 he began, 'I ... only write again because I keep thinking about you all the time'. In February 1927 he appealed for a letter: 'I wish greatly to know what is happening to your pulse, & sleep & pins & breathing ... & not a word have I heard for 4 weeks!' In September 1927, after learning that Strong's son Phil would probably marry, he wrote, 'We (not you alone) must consider carefully what line of life you are going to choose'. Strong's death in November 1928 left him grief-stricken. 'My thoughts are like a torrent but my powers of expression are dry', he wrote to Benjamin Strong Jr. 'Death leaves a gap & we may as well acknowledge it: in my case it cannot now be filled or grow over'. It is difficult to believe that Norman's emotional attachment did not add to his already exaggerated faith in Anglo-American financial cooperation. FRBNY, Strong papers, 1116.7, Norman to Strong, 24 January 1925, 23 November 1925, 26 February 1927, 18 September 1927; *ibid.*, Norman to Benjamin Strong Jr, 10 November 1928.

102 BoE, Norman diary, 25 November 1927.

103 FRBNY, Strong papers, 1116.7, Norman to Strong, 28 November 1927.

104 *Ibid.*, Strong papers, 1012.3, Strong to Jay, 4 August 1927.

105 Harold L. Reed, *Federal Reserve Policy, 1921–1930* (New York, 1930), 137.

106 FRBNY, Strong papers, 1012.3, Strong to Jay, 21 July 1927.

107 See for instance, *ibid.*, Strong papers, 1116.7, Strong to Norman, 30 August 1927; *ibid.*, Bank of England general, C252, Strong to Harrison, 24 December 1927; Per Jacobsson diary, 7 July 1928.

108 *Ibid.*, Strong papers, 1116.8, Strong to Norman, 27 March 1928. See also *ibid.*, Bank of England general, C252, Strong to Harrison, 24 December 1927.

109 The indelible character of the lesson was demonstrated during controversy over French monetary policy in the 1960s. Jacques Rueff, de Gaulle's chief financial adviser, made constant reference to the malfunctioning of the gold exchange standard in the 1920s when he had been a Ministry of Finance official stationed first in Geneva and later in London. See Jacques Rueff and Fred Hirsch, *The Role and Rule of Gold: An Argument* (Princeton NJ, 1965); Rueff, *The Monetary Sin of the West* (1971).

110 FRBNY, Strong papers, 1000.9, Strong memorandum, 27 May 1928; BdeF, CG, 23 August 1928; statement by Marcel Netter, Quesnay's suc-

cessor as directeur d'études économiques at the Bank of France, quoted in Jean Bouvier, 'A propos de la stratégie de l'encaisse (or et devises) de la Banque de France du juin 1928 à l'été 1932', unpublished paper presented to the Conference on the 1931 Crisis and its Aftermath, Clare College, Cambridge, 14–16 April 1982.

111 Moreau, *Souvenirs*, 431.

112 *Ibid.*

113 Baring Brothers & Company archives, D.P.P., 2.4.4., Revelstoke papers (hereafter BB & Co), Revelstoke diary, 4 March 1929.

114 According to Norman's deputy, Moreau felt the British and Americans were 'leaving him out in the cold'. FRBNY, Strong papers, 1117.1, Lubbock to Strong, 28 February 1928.

115 *Ibid.*, Strong papers, 1000.9, memorandum on Bank of England – Bank of France relations, 24 May 1928.

116 BoE, Norman diary, 26, 27 January 1928.

117 Moreau, *Souvenirs*, 488–89.

118 FRBNY, Bank of England general, C261, Norman to Strong, no. 246, 29 December 1927; BoE, Niemeyer papers, OV9/331, minutes, 31 January 1928, 7, 10 February 1928. Norman was infuriated that Niemeyer should have taken his wife with him to New York, believing that this destroyed his chances of developing close personal relations with Strong. Strong, who was ill at the time, confirmed that her presence made no difference. FRBNY, Strong papers, 1116.8. Norman to Strong, 3 January 1928; *ibid.*, Strong to Norman, 3 March 1928.

119 *Ibid.*, Strong papers, 1117.1, Lubbock to Strong, 28 February 1928; Moreau, *Souvenirs*, 506–09; Addis diary, 28 February 1928.

120 FRBNY, Harrison papers, Bank of France cables, Moreau to Strong, no. 12, 27 February 1928; Moreau, *Souvenirs*, 511.

121 Clay, *Lord Norman*, 265.

122 FRBNY, Strong papers, 1116.8, Harrison to Norman, 23 April 1928; *ibid.*, Strong papers, 1000.9, memorandum on Strong-Lubbock conversation, 12 June 1928; Clay, *Lord Norman*, 265; Moreau, *Souvenirs*, 566; Chandler, *Benjamin Strong*, 417–18.

123 FRBNY, Strong papers, 1116.7, Norman to Strong, 9 October 1927; *ibid.*, Strong papers, 1117.1, Anderson to Strong, 11 February 1926; Addis diary, 13 October, 28 December 1927.

124 Addis papers, PP MS. 14/456, minute to the Bank's Court, 31 May 1928. See also FRBNY, Strong papers, 1000.9, memorandum of discussions with the Bank of France, 27 May 1928; *ibid.*, Strong to Stewart, 8 July 1928. At each attempt to oust Norman Addis agreed that it was desirable to restore the practice of rotating the Governorship, but not before the challenges facing the Bank were overcome. After the downfall of the gold standard, however, Addis abandoned his defence. 'Norman more autocratic and extravagant than before his holiday. Will brook no opposition', he wrote in his diary on 7 October 1931. '[Norman] is a dear man, but I think the time has come for him to go', he recorded six days later.

125 *Ibid.*, Strong papers, 1117.1, Lubbock to Strong, 28 February 1928; Addis diary, 22, 24, 27, 28 February 1928; BoE, Norman diary, 28 February – 11 April 1928.

126 Sayers, *The Bank of England*, iii, appendix 18; Moreau, *Souvenirs*, 544–46.

Pouyanne pointed to the Yugoslav government's failure to satisfy the claims of French holders of pre-war Serbian debt. BoE, Norman diary, 26 January 1928.

127 Clay, *Lord Norman*,261.

128 FRBNY, Strong papers, 1000.9, memorandum on Bank of England--Bank of France relations, 24 May 1928; *ibid.*, memorandum of discussions with the Bank of France, 27 May 1928.

129 *Ibid.*, Strong papers, 1117.1, Lubbock to Strong, 16 June 1928.

130 Strong's hostility notwithstanding, the Stable Money Association was supported by men of considerable standing in conservative circles. Among its founders were the financiers John G. Winant, Simon Guggenheim, Bernard Baruch, and Otto Kahn, and the industrialists Alfred P. Sloan Jr, Pierre DuPont, James Rand, W.C. Procter, and Owen Young. *Bulletin of the Stable Money Association*, October 1928, 8–9. The association also obtained permission to accord the title of honorary vice-president to a number of prominent foreigners, among them Sir Herbert Holt, Edouard Benes, Alberto Pirelli, Oscar Rydbeck, K.A. Wallenberg, C.E. ter Meulen, Gerald Vissering, Alexander de Popovics, Sir Josiah Stamp, Sir Henry Strakosch, Max Lazard, and most remarkably Emile Moreau. *Ibid.*, December 1929, 47. Moreau's motives for becoming vice-president of the French section are unclear. While accepting the association's main objective, namely stable price levels, he explicitly rejected the method it promoted, of a 'managed' gold standard.

131 FRBNY, Strong papers, 1116.8, Strong to Norman, 27 March 1928.

132 Addis diary, 22, 23 February 1928.

133 BoE, Niemeyer papers, OV9/262, Strakosch to Salter, 9 May 1928.

134 See above, ch. 2, p. 42.

135 SdN, R2957, Draft Resolution proposed by Mr Layton, 16 May 1928,in SdN, vol. 1536, Gold Delegation of the Financial Committee, i, 1st Session, August 1929.

136 FRBNY, Strong papers, 1116.8, Harrison to Norman, 23 April 1928; *ibid.*, Strong papers, 1000.9, Strong–Salter conversation, 25 May 1928; BoE, Niemeyer papers, OV9/262, minute of conversation, 25 May 1928.

137 T160/384, F9780/1, Sir Auckland Geddes, Frank Farrell, D.A. Bremner and others to Prime Minister, 25 April 1928.

138 FRBNY, Strong papers, 1116.8, Norman to Strong, 11 April 1928.

139 BoE, Niemeyer papers, OV9/257, minute of conversation with Schacht, n.d.; *ibid.*, Niemeyer to Marcus Wallenberg, 13 June 1928.

140 LN, Report of the Financial Committee, 4 June 1929, L.N.C.281.1928.II.

141 BoE, Niemeyer papers, OV9/262, minute of Salter–Moreau conversation, 25 June 1928; Moreau, *Souvenirs*, 600–01.

142 Per Jacobsson diary, 7 July 1928; FRBNY, Strong papers, 1000.9, Strong to Harrison, 6, 8 July 1928. Strong made an exception for Jacobsson, whom he described as an earnest and sensible fellow.

143 FRBNY, Strong papers, 1000.9, Strong to Stewart, 8 July 1928; *ibid.*, Strong papers, 1117.2, Strong to Stewart, 20 July 1928.

144 *Federal Reserve Bulletin*, 1928–29.

145 The (approximate) foreign exchange figures are compiled from data in FRBNY, Strong papers, 1000.9, memorandum of discussions with the Bank of France, 27 May 1928, and BdeF, CG, 10 January 1929, 2 May

1929, et seq. The gold reserve figures are from the annual report of the Bank of France in the *Federal Reserve Bulletin*, March 1929, 206.

146 Annual Report of the Bank of France, 1929, *Federal Reserve Bulletin*, March 1930, 113.

147 BdeF, CG, various dates.

148 Sir Henry Strakosch, 'Gold and Price Level', *The Economist* Supplement, 5 July 1930, annex c.

149 T175/34, Lindsay to Hopkins, 11 April 1929.

150 Sayers, *The Bank of England*, iii, appendix 17.

151 T176/16, Hawtrey to Hopkins, 12 July 1928; FRBNY, Bank of England general, C261, Lubbock to Harrison, 3 August 1928.

152 *The Banker*, September 1928, 204.

153 FRBNY, Bank of England cables, Norman to Harrison, no. 166, 6 September 1928.

154 BB & Co, Revelstoke diary, 24 January 1929; FRBNY, Bank of England general, C261, Norman to Lubbock, no. 41, 7 February 1929; *ibid.*, Harrison to Norman, nos. 58, 68, 104, 19 February – 27 March 1929.

155 BoE, Norman diary, 15, 27 November 1928.

156 BoE, Niemeyer papers, OV9/262, Salter to Strakosch, 23 November 1928.

157 SdN, Council resolution (2), 14 December 1928, in vol. 1536, Gold Delegation of the Financial Committee, i, 1st Session, August 1929, documents.

158 BoE, Norman diary, 17 December 1928.

159 BoE, Norman diary, 25 February 1929. As Norman told Sir Robert Vansittart of the Foreign Office, his difference with Moreau 'had all been concerned with the League [loan issue]: that on banking questions Moreau and I had no differences'. BB & Co, Norman to Revelstoke, 12 March 1929.

160 SdN, Salter papers, S123, Salter to Strakosch, 23 November 1928.

161 *The Economist*, 14 July 1928, 61.

162 *The Commercial*, Annual Review, 31 January 1929, 27.

163 *Daily Express*, 21 March 1928, 1, 12 April 1928, 4, 14 April 1928, 4, 18 April 1928, 4. *Sunday Express*, 11 November 1928, 14. See also *Daily Mail*, 22 September 1928; 'Bank of England Reform', *Empire Review*, November 1928, 361–62.

164 *British Industries*, Economic Supplement, 30 April 1927 and subsequent issues.

165 *New Leader*, 13 July 1928, 4, 9; *ibid.*, 3 August 1928, 4, 28 September 1928, 9.

166 *The Times*, 1 November 1928, 16. See also Josiah Stamp, *Papers on Gold and the Price Level* (1931), 3–7.

167 HC Deb. 5s., 222, col. 352–53.

168 *Manchester Guardian*, 16 November 1928, 12.

169 *The Times*, 14 November 1928, 12.

170 See statement by Hammersley on the activities of the Master Cotton Spinners' Association in *The Times*, 10 July 1928, 16; also W.H. Waller, *The Gold Standard and the Effect of our Return on the Cotton Trade and other Industries of the Nation. A Series of Letters* (Manchester, 1929); statement by T. Driver in British Economic Federation, 'Agriculture and Industry', 17; *The Times*, 21 December 1928, 16; B. Bowker, *Lancashire under the Hammer* (1928); Ernest E. Canney, *Lancashire Betrayed. Essays on Cotton Trade Politics* (Deansgate and Manchester 1929).

171 BEAMA, *Trade Survey*, December 1928, 4–12.
172 *The Times*, 5 December 1928, 21; *Daily Express*, 5 December 1928, 1; *The Economist*, 8 December 1928, 1050; *Sunday Times*, 16 December 1928; *The Bankers' Magazine*, January, 1929, 14–20; *National Review*, January 1929, 792. The first issue of BEAMA's *Trade Survey*, in December 1926, roundly condemned the return to gold (pp. 5–6), but this passed unnoticed in the press.
173 The quotation is from the *Daily Express*, 8 February 1929.
174 See statements in *ibid.*; *Daily Mail*, 8 February 1929; CAB 24/202, C.P.–84(29), 'Trade Survey', memorandum by Cunliffe-Lister, 22 March 1929.
175 *Annual Register*, 1929, 3; *The Times*, 17 January 1929, 9.
176 Jeffcock, *Agricultural Politics*, 137. *The Times*, 25 February 1929, 18; 26 February 1929, 11; 27 February 1929, 9.
177 Baldwin papers, 25, 'The Agricultural Position', 7 March 1929.
178 CAB 24/196, C.P.–39(28), 'The Steel Trade: A Matter of Concentration', memorandum by Worthington-Evans, 16 July 1928; CAB 24/197, C.P.–255(28), 'Iron and Steel', memorandum by Steel-Maitland, 23 July 1928; CAB 24/202, C.P.–57(29), 'Government Assistance to Rationalisation', memorandum by Cunliffe-Lister, 24 February 1929.
179 CAB 23/58, 36(28)5, 4 July 1928; Amery diary, 10 July 1928; CAB 23/58, 40(28)2.
180 CAB 24/179, C.P.–168(26), 'International Regulation of Hours of Work', memorandum by Steel-Maitland, 20 April 1926; CAB 24/188, C.P.–206(27), 'Washington Hours Convention', memorandum by Steel-Maitland, 18 July 1927; CAB 24/201, C.P.–17(29), 'Washington Hours Convention', memorandum by Steel-Maitland, 28 January 1929.
181 Gilbert, *Winston S. Churchill*, Companion Volume 5, pt. 1, 1128; CAB 24/192, C.P.–8(28), 'A Plan to Relieve and Encourage Manufacturing Producers', by Churchill, 20 January 1928; CAB 24/194, C.P.–116(28), 'The Leak in the Revenue', memorandum by Amery, 2 April 1928.
182 FO 371/12853, C2598/12/17, Bateman minute, 3 April 1928; FO 371/12962, C1836/29/37, Crewe to Chamberlain, no. 806, 7 May 1928; *British Industries*, 15 May 1928, 201; T175/34, Lindsay to Hopkins, 11 April 1929.
183 *Bradford Chamber of Commerce Journal*, March 1929, 244.
184 BEAMA *Trade Survey*, December 1928, 13–17; *The Times*, 22 January 1930, 9.
185 Lord Strathspey, 'Keep British Capital in the British Empire', *Empire Review*, July 1926, 12–15; *Morning Post*, 4 September 1926, 8; *National Review*, December 1928, 517, January 1929, 691. On frustration among industrialists see also FBI/S/Walker/25/2, McCausland to Walker, 9 November 1926; FBI/S/Walker/105/3, Muspratt to McKenna, Beaumont Pease and others, 3 February 1927; FBI/EA/Glenday/11, Hersee to Walker, 21 July 1930. *Forward*, 19 March 1927, 1; 3 September 1927, 1; 16 June 1928, 1; 22 September 1928, 1; 12 January 1929, 1. See also M. Philips Price, *The Economic Problems of Europe. Pre-War and After* (1928), 179.
186 Liberal Party, *Britain's Industrial Future. Report of the Liberal Industrial Inquiry* (1928), 44. *Nation and Athenaeum*, 23 July 1927, 538; 30 July 1927,

566, 567; 8 September 1928, 722; 16 February 1929, 679; 23 February 1929, 710. See also Hugh Quigley, 'Power Finance and Imperial Preference: The Example of Canada', *World Power*, October 1929, 319; *The Times*, 4 October 1929, 20.

187 FO 371/14094, W1847/1846/50, Sir E. Crowe to Wellesley, 4 February 1929.

188 FO 371.12018, A1458/351/35, Harvey to Chamberlain, no. 10, 24 January 1927; FO 371/11956, A6753/5125/51, Vansittart to Treasury, 28 November 1927; FO 371/12728, A5499/108/51, 'Treasury 2% Stamp Tax and Latin American Loans', memorandum by Hadow, 24 August 1928. See also FO 371/11457, A1668/1668/51, Baring Brothers memorandum, Revelstoke to Treasury, 26 March 1928; FO 371/12853, C2598/12/17, Bateman minute, 3 April 1928; FO 371/12962, C1836/29/37, Crewe to Chamberlain, no. 806, 7 May 1928.

189 FO 371/14094, W1846/1846/50, 'Foreign Trade, Finance, and the Foreign Office', memorandum by Chamberlain, 16 February 1929; *ibid.*, Sargent minute, 18 March 1929.

190 FO 371/11956, P998/998/50, 'Treasury Policy with regard to Foreign Loans', 12 October 1927; FO 371/13705, C416/47/92, Upcott to Vansittart, 15 January 1929.

191 T175/34, Lindsay memorandum to Hopkins, 11 April 1929; BB & Co, Revelstoke diary, 4 March 1929; Clay, *Lord Norman*, 286–88.

192 CAB 24/201, C.P.–37(29), 'Unemployment', memorandum by Steel-Maitland, 16 February 1929.

193 CAB 23/58, 35(28)3, 27 June 1928; Amery diary, 27 June 1928; Gilbert, *Winston S. Churchill*, Companion vol. 5, pt. 1, 1306–07; HC Deb. 5s., 225, col. 547.

194 CAB 24/202, C.P.–53(29), 'Unemployment', memorandum by Churchill, 25 February 1929.

195 Baldwin papers, 30, Amery to Baldwin, 11 February 1929.

196 Sauvy, *Histoire économique de la France*, i, annex iv and passim; Shepard B. Clough, *France, a History of National Economics, 1789–1939* (New York, 1939), 313; LN, *The United States in the World Economy*, 150.

197 *The Times*, 6 July 1926, 17, described France's condition as 'false prosperity' brought about by the depreciation of the franc. See also the more favourable judgment in the FBI's *British Industries*, 15 February 1927, 70; 16 May 1927, 215; 15 November 1927, 483. Austin Harrison, 'European Tendencies', *Contemporary Review*, January 1927, 18; Sisley Huddleston, 'France's True Economic Condition', *Contemporary Review*, June 1927, 704–12; B.S. Townroe, 'Industrial Evolution in France', *Contemporary Review*, July 1927, 46–51. See also United Kingdom, Board of Trade, *Report on the Economic Conditions in France to March 1923*, by Robert Cahill (1923).

198 UK, Board of Trade, *Report on the Economic Conditions in France in 1928*, by Robert Cahill (1928).

199 *The Times*, 29 November 1928, 15. See also *Morning Post*, 29 November 1928, 10, 11; *National Review*, January 1929, 790–96; *Chamber of Commerce Journal*, 4 January 1929, 7; *The Statist*, 12 January 1929, 56.

200 HC Deb. 5s., 209, col. 802, 913; *ibid.*, 214, col. 1949.

201 Geoffrey Jones, *The State and the Emergence of the British Oil Industry* (1981), 219–31; Francis Delaisi, *Le Pétrole* (Paris 1922); Ludwell Denny, *We Fight for Oil* (New York, 1927).

202 Hogan, *Informal Entente*, 191–207.
203 *European Finance*, 14 January 1929, 9; Denny, *America Conquers Britain*, 190–92.
204 *The Commercial*, 3 January 1929, 16, and 7 February 1929, 156; *The Statist*, 2 February 1929, 188.
205 *European Finance*, 1 February 1929, 77; *The Times*, 29 January 1929, 20, and 6 February 1929, 21.
206 *The Times* Annual Financial and Commercial Review, 5 February 1929, vi; *The Economist*, 16 February 1929, 352; *New Statesman*, 22 June 1929, 354; *Daily Telegraph*, 27 June 1929, 2; *The Economist*, 31 August 1929, 403.
207 HC Deb. 5s., 214, col. 1960; *British Industries*, 15 May 1928, 201, and 15 September 1928, 312; CAB 24/197, C.P.–267(28), 'Trade Outlook', memorandum by Cunliffe-Lister, 10 August 1928.
208 *The Times*, 29 November 1928, 13. United Kingdom, Board of Trade, *Report on Economic Conditions in France in 1928*, 100. *European Finance*, 18 January 1929, 43; 25 January 1929, 52; 28 March 1929, 220. *The Times*, 13 March 1929, 15. *New Statesman*, 11 May 1929, 28. *The Commercial*, 28 March 1929, 369; 28 November 1929, 660.
209 *The Times*, British Motor Number, 20 March 1928; The Society of British Motor Manufacturers and Traders Ltd., *The Motor Industry of Great Britain, 1929*, 110–11; *The Statist*, 2 February 1929, 494.
210 See for example HC Deb. 5s., 214, cols. 1944, 1962; *ibid.*, 218, col. 959; *ibid.*, 226, col. 1816. *European Finance*, 28 March 1929, 220. J.P. Castley, 'The Empire's Foreign Cars', *Empire Review*, June 1929, 371–76. *The Times*, 9 October 1929, 10; 17 October 1929, 17; 18 October 1929, 17. *The Commercial*, 19 September 1929, 315.
211 HC Deb. 5s., 217, col. 1535 and passim; *ibid.*, 218, col. 857 and passim; Hogan, *Informal Entente*, ch. 6; Denny, *America Conquers Britain*, ch. 14.
212 CAB 24/193, C.P.–77(28), 'Electrical Development and American Capital', memorandum by Ashley, 9 March 1928; CAB 23/57, 14(28)5, 13 March 1928; T172/1626, Ashley to Churchill, 15 March 1928, Churchill minute, 18 March 1928.
213 CAB 24/194, C.P.–145(28), 'Electrical Development and American Capital, Report', 30 April 1928; CAB 23/57, 27(28)1, 4 May 1928.
214 Denny, *America Conquers Britain*, 146–47.
215 *The Commercial*, 21 February 1929, 226; *New Statesman*, 23 February 1929, 648.
216 HC Deb. 5s., 223, cols. 1007–08.
217 *The Economist*, 18 May 1929, 111.
218 R. Jones and O. Marriott, *Anatomy of a Merger. A History of GEC, AEI, and English Electric* (1970), chs. 5–6.
219 *The Commercial*, 21 March 1929, 342; *The Economist*, 8 June 1929, 1292, 15 June 1929, 1350, 22 June 1929, 1388. Beaverbrook, for all his anxiety about America, 'the devouring Republic', deplored Hirst's readiness to interfere with the freedom of capital: see *Daily Express*, 14 November 1928, 1, and 11 March 1929, 1.
220 FRBNY, Bank of England general, C261, Harrison to Norman, no. 83, 12 March 1929; *ibid.*, Norman to Harrison, no. 70, 15 March 1929, no. 71, 16 March 1929, no. 73, 21 March 1929; Clay, *Lord Norman*, 289.

221 *Daily Telegraph*, 5 July 1929, 4.
222 *The Commercial*, 16 May 1929, 578, and 30 May 1929, 632; *Daily Telegraph*, 22 June 1929, 2.
223 BB & Co, Revelstoke to Peacock, 8 March 1929; *ibid.*, Revelstoke diary, 9 March 1929.
224 Quoted in Middlemas and Barnes, *Baldwin*, 375.
225 John A. Spender, *The America of To-day* (1928), 238–39; *The Times*, 10 October 1928, 15, 20 October 1928, 13; *Nation and Athenaeum*, 20 October 1928, 98; *The Economist*, 10 November 1928, 812; *Blackwood's Magazine*, January 1929, 136.
226 CAB 24/198, C.P.–344(28), 'Anglo-American Relations', memorandum by Cushendun, 14 November 1928.
227 CAB 24/199, C.P.–358(28), 'Anglo-American Relations', memorandum by Churchill, 19 November 1928.
228 Baldwin papers, 109, Howard memorandum, 17 October 1928.
229 CAB 24/198, C.P.–344(28), 'Anglo-American Relations', memorandum by Cushendun, 14 November 1928. See also CAB 24/199, C.P.– 364(28), 'Anglo-American Relations', memorandum by Cushendun, 24 November 1928; CAB 24/196, C.P.–232(28), statement by Sir Austen Chamberlain in minutes of 236th meeting of CID, circulated to the Cabinet by order of the Prime Minister, 13 July 1928.
230 CAB 24/199, C.P.–367(28), 'Anglo-American Relations', memorandum by Amery, 26 November 1928.
231 Middlemas and Barnes, *Baldwin*, 374–75.
232 Herbert C. Hoover, *The New Day. Campaign Speeches of Herbert Hoover, 1928* (Stanford Cal., 1928).
233 *New Statesman*, 10 November 1928, 146; John B.C. Kershaw, 'The American Presidential Election and the Future of British and European Trade', *Financial Review of Reviews*, January–March 1929, 51– 60; *The Times*, 14 March 1929, 17; *Daily Express*, 16 March 1929, 1; speech by Eden in HC Deb. 5s., 227, col. 331; *Round Table*, March 1929, 261.
234 S.K. Ratcliffe, 'President Hoover and Europe', *Contemporary Review*, August 1929, 137–45; Ignatius Phayre, 'America's Bid for World Trade, 1. The Strategy', *Quarterly Review*, January 1930, 172–73. An accurate description of competition in Latin American markets is given in David Joslin, *A Century of Banking in Latin America* (1963), 216–33.
235 *The Commercial*, 21 February 1929, 237; *The Statist*, 23 February 1929, 313.
236 FO 371/14094, W1846/1846/50, 'Foreign Trade, Finance, and the Foreign Office', memorandum by Chamberlain, 16 February 1929.
237 *Ibid.*
238 FO 371/13510, A1397/12/45, Wellesley minute, 19 February 1929, Chamberlain minute, 23 February 1929, Cunliffe–Lister minute, 1 March 1929.
239 *The Times*, 5 March 1929, 15.
240 Jones, *Whitehall Diary*, ii, 177. According to Norman it was Sir Auckland Geddes, the chairman of Rio Tinto, who approached Baldwin, 'and had frightened him about the danger of acquisition by foreigners of: Rhodesian Copper Companies, Public Utility Companies, Overseas Banks, Shipping Companies, and had pointed out the danger of US control'. BB & Co., Revelstoke diary, 9 March 1929. But by all accounts Norman did his share

of the frightening. During Baldwin's second government Norman normally spoke with the Prime Minister once or twice a week: *ibid.*, Revelstoke diary, 10 March 1929.

241 France, MF, F30/807, Chalendar, 'Rapport sur la situation financière de la Grande Bretagne', 21 February 1929.

242 Norman discussed with Edward Hilton-Young, the financial journalist, the City's 'subservience' to the New York market, and found him in agreement that it was best left unmentioned in the press. BoE, Norman diary, 13 December 1926.

243 BB & Co, Revelstoke diary, 14 February 1929.

244 FRBNY, Bank of England general, C261, Norman to Lubbock, no. 41, 7 February 1929; *ibid.*, Norman to Harrison, no. 47, 18 February 1929.

245 TWL, 178–19, Leffingwell to J.P. Morgan Jr, 2 March 1929.

246 TWL, 103–13, Leffingwell to Lamont, 8 March 1929.

247 MGC, British Government Loan 5, Grenfell to Leffingwell, 6 March 1929.

248 BB & Co, Revelstoke diary, 10 March 1929. See also MGC, British Government Loan 5, Norman to Harrison, 12 March 1929; TWL, 173– 1, Lamont diary, 12 March 1929: 'Long talk with M. Norman at Plaza Athenée re desperate monetary conditions'.

249 TWL, 103–13, Leffingwell to Grenfell, 6 March 1929; *ibid.*, Leffingwell to Lamont, 8 March 1929.

250 TWL, 178–18, J.P. Morgan Jr to New York, 11 March 1929.

251 FRBNY, Bank of England general, C261, Norman to Harrison, no. 108, 10 May 1929.

252 Sayers, *The Bank of England*, iii, appendix 30.

253 The defeat for the pro-safeguarding Conservative candidate in the Middlesbrough by-election in March 1928 was a severe setback for imperial protectionists, especially in view of the fact that it occurred in an iron and steel manufacturing town. See *The Times*, 8 March 1928, 14. Barely four months later, however, Henry Bell, president of the Free Trade Union, warned members that protectionism was gaining ground in the country and was certain to figure prominently in the next general election. 'Free Trade opinion has perhaps a year within which to reassemble its forces.' *The Free Trader*, August 1928, 156.

254 *The Times*, 15 April 1929, 8–9, 1 May 1929, 18, 17 May 1929, 9.

6 *The second Labour government at The Hague*

1 TWL, 103–12, Leffingwell to Lamont, 12 July 1927. See also above, ch. 5, p. 158.

2 Jacobsson, *Locarno Diplomacy*, 143–45.

3 See above, ch. 5, pp. 159, 161.

4 Gilbert, *Winston S. Churchill*, Companion Volume 5, Pt. 1, Churchill to Fisher. 14 September 1928, 1337–39; CAB 24/197, C.P.–281(28), Churchill memorandum, 28 September 1928.

5 Jacobsson, *Locarno Diplomacy*, 216; CAB 23/59, 47(28)4, 17 October 1928.

6 CAB 24/198, C.P.–311(28), Churchill memorandum, 19 October 1928.

7 CAB 23/59, 48(28)3, 29 October 1928.

8 J. Harry Jones, *Josiah Stamp, Public Servant: The Life of the first Baron Stamp of Shortlands* (1964), 53.

9 Stamp contributed the foreword to the English edition of Fisher's *The Money Illusion* (1930).
10 Owen D. Young papers, R31, Andrew Mellon to Young, 9 April 1929; *ibid.*, Henry Stimson to Young, 16 April 1929; *ibid.*, green box, minutes of meeting between Elihu Root, Young, Gilbert, and Lamont, 9 April 1929.
11 T160/268, F11150/02/2, Stamp to Hopkins, 15 April 1929. See also Charles G. Dawes, *Notes as Vice President, 1925–1929* (Boston, 1935), 74; Clay, *Lord Norman*, 239.
12 Stuart Crocker papers, Young Plan diary, 22 February, 3 June 1929. On Young's career and role at the experts' conference see Josephine Y. Case and Everett N. Case, *Owen D. Young and American Enterprise* (Boston, 1982).
13 Crocker papers, Young Plan diary, 18 March, 17 April 1929; Erich Eyck, *A History of the Weimar Republic*, ii (Cambridge, Mass., 1964), 187.
14 Crocker papers, Young Plan diary, 6–7, 53. See also the account in BB & Co, Revelstoke diary, 9 March 1929.
15 TWL, 179–1, New York cable to Lamont, 26 March 1929: 'Money twenty per cent'. On German bank borrowing, see Gerd Hardach, 'The 1931 Crisis in Germany', paper presented to the Conference on the 1931 Crisis and its Aftermath, Clare College, Cambridge, 14–16 April 1982.
16 French authorities threatened to provoke withdrawals and French commercial balances were undoubtedly withdrawn. But as on similar occasions, the evidence suggests that the French state had little control over private institutions. The withdrawal of balances was due simply to commercial estimates of risk. Crocker papers, Young Plan diary, p. 147; TWL, 178–22, Lamont to New York, 27 April 1929.
17 Werner Link, *Die amerikanische Stabilisierungspolitik in Deutschland 1921–32* (Düsseldorf, 1970), 464; Eyck, *A History of the Weimar Republic*, ii, 187.
18 Crocker papers, Young Plan diary, 26 April 1929.
19 *Ibid.*
20 *Ibid.*, 4 May 1929.
21 Link, *Die amerikanische Stabilisierungspolitik*, 466–67; Eyck, *A History of the Weimar Republic*, i, 187–90; Jacobsson, *Locarno Diplomacy*, 262–63; Crocker papers, Young Plan diary, 6 May 1929.
22 Crocker papers, Young Plan diary, 24 April 1929.
23 PREM 1/83, Stamp memorandum, 4 July 1929.
24 Stamp papers, memorandum on the Paris negotiations, n.d.; PREM 1/83, Stamp memorandum, 4 July 1929.
25 PREM 1/83, Stamp memorandum, 4 July 1929.
26 TWL, 103–13, Lamont to Leffingwell, 26 February 1929. The idea of dividing the annuity probably originated with Schacht, see Crocker papers, Young Plan diary, 18 February 1929.
27 CAB 24/195, C.P.–157(28), Cunliffe–Lister memorandum, 17 May 1928; CAB 24/195, C.P.–194(28), Cunliffe–Lister memorandum, 19 June 1928; CAB 29/116, British Delegation, Financial Note no. 7A, 'British Coal Trade and the Young Plan', n.d.
28 FO 371/14378, C6268/6268/18, Cahill memorandum, 4 February 1929.
29 A good description of the spill-over effect of payments-in-kind in one industry is given in BEAMA, *Trade Survey*, December 1928, 17–24.

30 FO 371/14378, C6268/6268/18, Waley memorandum, 6 August 1928.
31 See representations in T160/209, F7800/4; T160268, F11150/02/1, Fryer memorandum, 27 March 1929; T160/389, F11300/4, FBI resolution, 10 July 1929; *The Nation and Athenaeum*, 17 August 1929, 642. The Board of Trade's attitude was of course the same as Stamp's: see T160/268, F11150/02/1, Hamilton to Hopkins, 18 March 1929.
32 UK, *Report of the Committee of Experts on Reparations, June 1929*, Cmd. 3343.
33 PREM 1/83, Stamp memorandum, 4 July 1929. See also Stamp's statement on the importance of the Bank proposal in the *Daily Telegraph*, 8 June 1929, 11, and the dinner in his honour: *The Times*, 3 July 1929, 12, *The Economist*, 6 July 1929, 6.
34 TWL, 180–11, J.A.M. de Sanchez memorandum, n.d. (? May 1929).
35 Crocker papers, Young Plan diary, 43; Young papers, R35, Young to Kellogg, 2 March 1929. Francqui was the Minister responsible for Belgium's return to gold in 1926. In 1929 he was chairman of the Société Nationale de Crédit à l'Industrie, the state-supported institution created to promote the reconstruction of Belgium's private industry.
36 TWL, 180–11, J.A.M. de Sanchez memorandum, n.d.
37 Young papers, R33, Committee of Experts, annex 3, 'Bank for International Settlements Provision Plan', prepared by W.W. Stewart, Shepherd Morgan, and W. Randolph Burgess in consultation with Pierre Quesnay and Hjalmar Schacht, 6 March 1929.
38 Young papers, R34, record of meeting no. 14, 11 March 1929.
39 Cmd. 3343.
40 Young papers, R35, 'Capital of the Office of International Payments. Aim of the Institution, its profits, its risks, its losses', by Pierre Quesnay, 2, 3, and 5 March 1929.
41 FO 371/13598, C4710/1/18, memorandum by Pinsent and Rowe-Dutton, 26 June 1929.
42 Young papers, R31, Edwin C. Wilson for Stimson to Young, 16 April 1929; *The Times*, 17 May 1929, 11.
43 HC Deb. 5s., 227, cols. 119–21, 313; *Sunday Express*, 21 April 1929, 14.
44 *Yorkshire Post*, 8 May 1929, 10; *Daily Mail*, 8 May 1929, 13; *The Observer*, 12 May 1929, 16; *Sunday Express*, 12 May 1929, 14; *Labour Magazine*, October 1929, 268.
45 HC Deb. 5s., 227, cols. 2310–11.
46 *Daily Herald*, 18 May 1929, 1, and 28 May 1929, 2; *Daily Telegraph*, 25 May 1929, 8; Snowden, *An Autobiography*, ii, 755.
47 *The Economist*, 3 August 1929, 207.
48 See for instance Frank Wise in *New Leader*, 9 August 1929, 3; Walton Newbould in *Forward*, 24 August 1929, 11; Vickers, *Economic Tribulation*, 38.
49 T160/268, F11150/02/3, Stamp to Hamilton, 15 April 1929; FO 371/13598, C4898/1/18, Carr memorandum, 17 June 1929, Sargent minute, 22 June 1929; FBI/C/1, minutes of Executive Committee, 10 July 1929.
50 *The Bankers' Magazine*, June 1929, 855–59, and July 1929, 14–26.
51 *The Nation and Athenaeum*, 15 June 1929, 360; *The Times*, 10 June 1929, 12; *The Commercial*, 13 June 1929, 694; *The Economist*, 15 June 1929,

1332–34; *The Banker*, July 1929, 10–14; *Chamber of Commerce Journal*, 14 June 1929, 587, and 21 June 1929, 604.
52 Siegfried, *England's Crisis*.
53 Labour Party, *Labour and the Nation*, rev. edn. (1929), 13, 20, 11, 37, 46, 43.
54 Harold Nicolson, *King George the Fifth. His Life and Reign* (1952), 435.
55 PRO 30/69/8/1, MacDonald diary, 4 June 1929; Reginald Bassett, *Nineteen Thirty-One: Political Crisis* (1958), 27–28; Gregory Blaxland, *J.H. Thomas. A Life for Unity* (1964), 20–21; Clement Attlee, *As It Happened* (1954), 74; Mary Agnes Hamilton, *Arthur Henderson*, 236, 238; Snowden, *An Autobiography*, ii, 597.
56 Arthur Henderson, 'Labour and an After-war Economic Policy' (1917). See also his 'The League of Nations and Labour' (1918); 'Labour's Peace Terms' (n.d. ? 1918); 'The Peace Terms' (1919).
57 Arthur Henderson, 'Socialism as a World Force', *Labour Magazine*, September 1928, 198–203.
58 Thomas N. Graham, *Willie Graham* (1948); C.R. Attlee, 'William Graham: An Appreciation', *Labour Magazine*, February 1932, 450–51; Mary Agnes Hamilton, *Remembering My Good Friends* (1944), 109–33; Snowden, *An Autobiography*, ii, 655, 657.
59 Snowden, *An Autobiography*, ii, 745–46.
60 HC Deb. 5s., 194, col. 1882.
61 Labour Party, *Report of the 28th Annual Conference 1928*, 231–32.
62 *The Economist*, 15 June 1929, 1331–32.
63 James McNair, *Maxton: The Beloved Rebel* (1955), 188.
64 *Daily Telegraph*, 29 May 1929, 11.
65 *Chamber of Commerce Journal*, 31 May 1929, 525.
66 *The Economist*, 20 April 1929. 848.
67 *Ibid.*, 8 June 1929, 1279.
68 *Ibid.*, 22 June 1929, 1393, and 13 July 1929, 64; *European Finance*, 26 July 1929, 79–80; André Siegfried, 'European Reactions to American Tariff Proposals', *Foreign Affairs*, October 1929, 13–19; Lucien Romier, *Who Will be Master, Europe or America?*, trans. Matthew Josephson (1929); Edouard Herriot, *The United States of Europe*, trans. Reginald Dingle (1930), Jones, *Tariff Retaliation*, passim.
69 *Daily Telegraph*, 11 June 1929, 9.
70 France, MAE, 1253/no. 1, French army intelligence report, 1 August 1929; Germany, *Akten zur deutschen auswärtigen Politik 1918–1945*, Series B, Bd.xi, no. 19, Aufzeichnung des Dolmetschers P. Schmidt, 11 June 1929; Lipgens, 'Europäische Einigungsidee 1923–1930', 73.
71 *The Times*, 6 July 1929, 13; *Daily Herald*, 15 July 1929, 3.
72 *Daily Herald*, 12 July 1929, 1.
73 Amery diary, 13 July 1929; Beaverbrook papers, C/52, Beaverbrook to Borden, 8 September 1929.
74 Amery diary, 4 July 1929; Austen Chamberlain papers, 5/1/478, Austen to Hilda Chamberlain, 13 July 1929.
75 *Ibid.* The phrase is Austen's, but it summed up Neville's opinion equally well: see Neville Chamberlain diary, 2/22, 26 July 1929, 4 November 1929.
76 HC Deb. 5s., 229, cols. 110, 723.
77 Austen Chamberlain papers, 5/1/478, Austen to Hilda Chamberlain, 13 July 1929; Amery diary, 9, 11 July 1929.

78 Croft papers, 1/2, Amery to Page Croft, 6 June 1929; Amery diary, 1, 2, 10, 19 July 1929.
79 Middlemas and Barnes, *Baldwin*, 534.
80 CAB 24/204, C.P.–188(29), Passfield memorandum, 2 July 1929.
81 *The Times*, 3 July 1929, 15. See also *ibid.*, 19 July 1929, 15.
82 HC Deb. 5s., 229, cols. 225–26, 276–77, and 230, col. 1055.
83 *Ibid.*, 229, col. 60, 230–33, 813–14.
84 CAB 24/205, C.P.–209(29), Graham memorandum, 15 July 1929; FO 371/13537, A4956/139/45, Craigie, Lindsay, Wellesley minutes, 12 July 1929, Henderson minute, n.d.; CAB 23/61, 29(29)5, 17 July 1929.
85 HC Deb. 5s., 229, cols. 60–61.
86 FO 800/280, Sargent memorandum, 17 June 1929.
87 T160/392, F11300/03/3, Tyrrell to Henderson, no. 1034, 18 July 1920, and Tyrrell to Henderson, no. 1077, 26 July 1929.
88 T160/389, F11300/4, Howard to Henderson, no. 1135, 14 June 1929; *ibid.*, Howard to Henderson, no. 1179, 20 June 1929.
89 FO 800/280, Sargent memorandum, 17 June 1929. Henderson concurred, see *ibid.*, Henderson to Tyrrell, 24 June 1929.
90 T160/388, F11300/3, Fisher to Snowden, 19 June 1929.
91 *Ibid.*, Hopkins memorandum, 19 June 1929.
92 France, MF, F30/930, de Chalendar to Farnier, 20 June 1929. The authoritative *Revue Politique et Parlementaire*, June 1929, 506, also confidently discounted Snowden's pre-election demands for better British terms.
93 Sir Frederick Leith Ross, *Money Talks. Fifty Years of International Finance* (1969), 106.
94 T160/388, F11300/3, Leith Ross to Grigg, 24 June 1929; T172/1694, Leith Ross to Grigg, 11 July 1929. During the Young Plan negotiations in the spring Churchill promised Stamp he would 'sit on Leith Ross's head if he gets troublesome'. But after the Conservatives' defeat in the general election and Snowden's assumption of responsibility for the reparations issue, Churchill climbed on Leith Ross's shoulders, as it were, to crow the shortcomings of the Young Plan. Stamp papers, memorandum on the Paris negotiations, n.d.
95 CAB 24/204, C.P.–175(29), Snowden memorandum, 24 June 1929.
96 CAB 23/61, 27(29)6, 17 July 1929.
97 MacDonald papers, PRO 30/69/1/254, Lindsay to Vansittart, 31 July 1929.
98 CAB 29/108, H. 2nd meeting, 6 August 1929.
99 *Ibid.*, 3rd meeting, 7 August 1929.
100 Leith Ross, *Money Talks*, 124. See also FO 371/13602, C6130/1/18, Phipps to Sargent, 7 August 1929. Leith Ross exaggerated the official French balances in London. Hopkins more accurately put them at about £100 million. T176/13, Pt. 2, Hopkins to Grigg, 19 August 1929.
101 *Samuel H. Montagu & Company Weekly Bulletin Letter*, various issues; *The Economist*, 31 August 1929, 391; *New Statesman*, 21 September 1929, 724.
102 Moreau described his embarrassment to the regents at a meeting of the Conseil Général on 1 August. Two weeks later he informed them that the Bank of France had received 1,843,702,000 francs gold (£15 million) between 1 July and 8 August. Practically all of it was received in the form of bars from Paris banks which had purchased them in London when the sterling exchange made the transaction worthwhile; the Bank of France had

done nothing to encourage the movement from sterling into gold. Among the banks mainly involved were the Banque Lazard, which had presented 1,109,527,000 francs gold, and the Banque Monroë and the Guaranty Trust Company, which had presented 210,627,000 and 136,896,000 francs gold respectively. B deF, CG, 1 and 16 August 1929.

103 FO 371/13605, C6184/1/18, minutes of first meeting of Financial Committee, 8 August 1929.

104 CAB 24/205, C.P.–238(29), 'The Hague Conference, 1929', 23 August 1929; T172/1694, Waley to Snowden, 10 August 1929; Hankey papers, 8/27, Sir Maurice to Robin Hankey, 5 September 1929.

105 Hankey papers, 4/21, Hankey to Jones, 1 August 1929; Charles G. Dawes, *Journal as Ambassador to Great Britain* (New York, 1939), 42–44; Dalton diary, 10–29 August 1929; Webb, *Beatrice Webb's Diaries, 1924–32*, 214; MacDonald diary, PRO 30/69/8/1, 11 August 1929.

106 BoE, Norman diary, 9, 10, 19 August 1929.

107 FO 371/13605, C6428/1/18, Snowden to MacDonald, 10 August 1929; *ibid.*, MacDonald to Snowden, 11 August 1929; *ibid.*, MacDonald to Snowden, 11 August 1929.

108 FO 371/13605, C6283/1/18, Snowden to MacDonald, no. 7, 12 August 1929.

109 Grigg, *Prejudice and Judgement*, 229.

110 CAB 24/205, C.P.–238(29), 'The Hague Conference, 1929', 23 August 1929; CAB 29/109, First meeting of delegates from the six inviting powers, 21 August 1929.

111 CAB 24/205, C.P.–239(29), 'The Hague Conference, 1929', 31 August 1929.

112 Dalton diary, 31 August 1929. But see also the very different view of Graham's role in Hankey papers, 8/27, Sir Maurice to Robin Hankey, 5 September 1929.

113 Hankey papers, 4/21, Snowden to MacDonald, 23 August 1929.

114 CAB 24/206, C.P.–256(29), 'The Hague Conference, 1929', 23 September 1929.

115 Jones, *Whitehall Diary*, ii, 201–02; Hankey diary, 8/1, 24 August 1929.

116 Hankey papers, 8/27, Sir Maurice to Robin Hankey, 5 September 1929.

117 Jones, *Whitehall Diary*, ii, 203.

118 CAB 24/205, C.P.–238(29), 'The Hague Conference, Synopsis (continued) from 24 August 1929 to the end of the first stage', 31 August 1929. See also FO 371/13608, C6859/1/18, Waley to Sargent, 3 September 1929.

119 CAB 29/109, H(D), 3rd meeting, 27 August 1929.

120 CAB 24/206, C.P.–263(29), 'The Hague Conference: The Political Discussions', memorandum by Henderson, 3 October 1929.

121 Grigg, *Prejudice and Judgement*, 228.

122 *The Statist*, 17 August 1929, 245. *Daily Herald*, 2 September 1929, 1; 6 September 1929, 1; 20 September 1929, 2.

123 *Daily Herald*, 3 September 1929, 1. The address is printed in full in *The Bankers' Magazine*, October 1929, 574–82.

124 T172/1694, Leith Ross memorandum, 26 August 1929.

125 *New Leader*, 16 August 1929, 1; 23 August 1929, 8; 30 August 1929, 3. Tom Johnston, the editor of *Forward*, defended Snowden from Brailsford's criticism but published Sir Leo Chiozza Money's 'In Criticism of Mr Snowden', 31 August 1929, 8.

126 *The Nation and Athenaeum*, 17 August 1929, 643; 24 August 1929, 670–71; 31 August 1929, 698–99. *Observer*, 4 August 1929, 10. *The Economist*, 10 August 1929, 265–66; 17 August 1929, 299–300; 31 August 1929, 383–84.
127 Phipps papers, 2/8, Sargent to Phipps, 9 September 1929; Stamp papers, Addis to Stamp, 19 August 1929.
128 *Sunday Times*, 4 August 1929, 14; *Morning Post*, 5 September 1929, 9; *The Bankers' Magazine*, October 1929, 482.
129 *The Statist*, 17 August 1929, 245.
130 Jones, *Whitehall Diary*, ii, 208.
131 Snowden later admitted that a breakdown had been possible two weeks after the conference began: *An Autobiography*, ii, 802, 809.
132 Georges Suarez, *Briand*, vi, *L'Artisan de la paix, 1923–1932* (Paris, 1952), 301. See also Jacobsson, *Locarno Diplomacy*, 330, 363, and 386; Eyck, *A History of the Weimar Republic*, ii, 208–09.
133 Dalton diary, 10–19 August 1929. See also *The Nation and Athenaeum*, 17 August 1929, 643.
134 CAB 24/204, C.P.–175(29), 'German Reparations. Experts' Report', memorandum by Snowden, 24 June 1929; Hankey papers, 1/40, 'The Bank for International Settlements', 27 July 1929.
135 Clay, *Lord Norman*, 364–65.
136 Boyle, *Montagu Norman*, 247. Norman dismissively commented to the Macmillan Committee that the Young Plan had included in its outline of the proposed Bank for International Settlements 'certain vague references to all sorts of things which might be done towards rebuilding the world. How these are ever to be carried out I have not the slightest idea, what they precisely mean I do not know.' Macmillan Committee, Evidence, ii, Q9188. See also the cool reception of Francis Rennell Rodd, BoE, Niemeyer papers, OV9/289, Rodd to Norman, 13 July 1929.
137 T172/1656, Lamont to Snowden, 20 August 1929.
138 CAB 29/116, British Delegation, Financial Note No. 3, 'The Bank for International Settlements', 1 December 1929.
139 *Ibid.*
140 *Ibid.* See also T172/1694, 'Note of Discussions with the French Treasury, November 5th–11th', 1929, by Leith Ross; *ibid.*, 'Note of Interview between the Chancellor of the Exchequer and M. Francqui', by Leith Ross, 14 November 1929.
141 France, MF, B12612/no. 53,821, Chalendar to Massigli, 14 October 1929; *ibid.*, B12612, no. 54,074, Chalendar to Ministry, 28 November 1929; FO 371/13609, C8498/1/18, Hopkins to Leith Ross, no. 256, 9 November 1929.
142 Sayers, *The Bank of England*, iii, appendix 17.
143 Clay, *Lord Norman*, 251, 252; T176/13, Pt. 2, Harvey to Hopkins, 26 July 1929.
144 TUC, G.C. 17. 1928–29, item 260, 24 July 1929.
145 According to *The Commercial*, 10 October 1929, 408 'Industry has been virtually unanimous in demanding the investigation into banking, financial and credit policy of the country'.
146 *Board of Trade Journal*, 28 February 1929, 279.
147 S.S. Hammersley *et al.*, 'Petition to the Rt.Hon. J. Ramsay MacDonald, MP, 27 July 1929', Another original in T172/1651, Hammersley *et al.* to Prime Minister, 2 October 1929. See also HC Deb. 5s., 229, cols. 330–35.

148 MacDonald diary, PRO 30/69/8/1, 11 August 1929.
149 T176/13, Pt. 2, Hopkins to Grigg, 16, 19 August 1929.
150 *The Times*, 2 October 1929, 19. See also protests in the *Daily Express*, 27 September 1929, *Daily Herald*, 28 September 1929, and in T160/384, F9780/1.
151 *Sunday Express*, 29 September 1929, 12.
152 *Report of the Proceedings at the 61st Annual Trades Union Congress, 1929*, 198; *Daily Herald*, 30 October 1929, 4.
153 Labour Party, *Report of the 29th Annual Conference, 1929*, 234.
154 Clay, *Lord Norman*, 363.
155 *Daily Telegraph*, 4 October 1929, 12.

7 *Free trade: the last offensive*

1 F0371/14133, W8694/5754/98, Summary of interview, 31 August 1929.
2 Carlton, *MacDonald versus Henderson*, chs. 4, 5.
3 HC Deb. 5s., 229, cols. 48–49.
4 FO 371/14133, W8509/5754/98, A.W.A. Leeper memorandum, 30 August 1929.
5 *Morning Post*, 12 July 1929, 13.
6 *The Times*, 1 November 1929, 9. See also Amery's address at Chatham House, 'The British Empire and the Pan-European Idea', *International Affairs*, January 1930, 1–22.
7 *The Commercial*, 12 September 1929, 13.
8 *The Statist*, 14 September 1929, 373.
9 *The Economist*, 13 July 1929, 64; 20 July 1929, 107–08; 14 September 1929, 463; 21 September 1929, 526.
10 *New Statesman*, 21 September 1929, 701–2.
11 *Daily Herald*, 13 July 1929, 4.
12 Cecil papers, MS.51, 107, Noel Baker to Cecil, n.d. (13 August 1929?); *New Leader*, 30 August 1929, 1–2; Fernand Vanlangenhove, *L'Élaboration de la politique étrangère de la Belgique entre les deux guerres mondiales* (Bruxelles, 1979), 89.
13 LN, *Official Journal*, Records of the Tenth Assembly, Plenary Meetings, 1929, 52.
14 *Ibid.*, 70; Lipgens, 'Europäische Einigungsidee,' 79.
15 LN, *Official Journal*, Records of the Tenth Assembly, 1929, Plenary Meetings, 36.
16 *Ibid.*, 79–81.
17 France, MAE, 1253/no.1, Note pour Massigli, 2 September 1929, *ibid.*, Resumé de l'échange de vues qui a eu lieu à l'issue du déjeuner offert le 9 septembre par M. Briand aux représentants des états européennes à la SdN; *ibid.*, série Y, no. 639, Claudel to Briand, no. 424, 13 September 1929; *l'Europe Nouvelle*, 28 September 1929, 1287.
18 LN, *Official Journal*, Records of the Tenth Assembly, Second Committee, 1929, 12.
19 *Ibid.*, 14.
20 *Ibid.*, 25–27.
21 *Ibid.*, 13–14.
22 *Ibid.*, 20, 22, 27, 32–33.

23 LN, Report of the Second Committee to the Assembly, A.68.1929.11, 23 September 1929.
24 Hill, *The Economic and Financial Organisation of the League of Nations*, 41–45.
25 LN, Supplementary Agreement, 11 July 1928, C.13.M.10.1929.11, (C.I.-A.P.33(2)); LN, Third International Conference for the Abolition of Import and Export Prohibitions and Restrictions, Proceedings of the Conference, C.176.M.81.1931.11., 9.
26 Charles Kruszewski, 'The German–Polish Tariff War and its Aftermath,' *Journal of Central European Affairs*, 3/3 (1943), 294–325. According to Peter Kruger, 'La Politique extérieure allemande et les relations franco-polonaises (1918–1932),' *Revue d'histoire diplomatique*, 2–4 (1981), 286, the commercial war was largely non-political, and not prosecuted by the Germans in the effort to secure Polish concessions on the corridor.
27 FO 371/14119, W11534/94/98, Campbell to Henderson, no. 160, 6 December 1929; *ibid.*, W11535/94/98, Salter to Noel Baker, 6 December 1929; Soutou,' L'Alliance franco-polonaise (1925–1932) ou comment s'en débarrasser?' 334.
28 *Ibid.*, Howard Smith minute, 9 December 1929.
29 *Ibid.*, Campbell to Henderson, no. 165, 10 December 1929; *ibid.*, W11720/94/98, Erskine to Hendemon, no. 69, 12 December 1929.
30 FO 371/14943, W82/6/98, Chapman memorandum to Henderson, 2 January 1930.
31 LN, Third International Prohibitions Conference, annex, 56– 57; United Kingdom, International Convention for the Abolition of Import and Export Prohibitions and Restrictions, with Supplementary and Protocol, 1930, Cmd. 3502.
32 FO 371/14943, W5254/6/98, Broadmead to Henderson, 21 May 1930; FO 371/14944, W6105/6/98, Dalton minute, 7 July 1930.
33 See for example HC Deb. 5s., 235, cols. 12–14, 1122; *ibid.*, 237, cols. 296–97, 1650; *ibid.*, 238, cols. 17–19, 40–41; *ibid.*, 240, cols. 941–43, 1168, 2153–54.
34 Carlton, *MacDonald versus Henderson*, 114–17.
35 Passfield papers, Beatrice Webb diary, 28 July 1929. See also *ibid.*, 9 November and 2 December 1929; MacDonald diary, PRO 30/69/8/1, 17 and 27 November 1929.
36 Thomas Johnston, *Memories* (1952), 103. See also Mosley, *My Life*, 231; *Beatrice Webb's Diaries, 1924–32*, 212. *The Economist*, 15 February 1930, 351–52, and *The Banker*, March 1930, 356, gave the new body a cool reception on account of its size and composition. Susan Howson and Donald Winch, *The Economic Advisory Council* (Cambridge, 1977), make out a case for taking the EAC seriously in its smaller reconstructed form after 1931, but offer no reason for doing so before this.
37 Mosley used *Lansbury's Labour Weekly*, 30 April 1927, 5, to criticise Snowden for his defence of the gold standard. See also the articles by 'ZZ' advocating a floating exchange, in *Lansbury's Labour Weekly*, 11 June 1927, 8, 2 July 1927, 11, and 16 July 1927, 4.
38 Lansbury became an enthusiast for H.D. Henderson's plan for national reconstruction in 1930. See the wrongly dated memorandum in Lansbury papers, 19, d.81–86, 22 July 1929.

39 CAB 24/209, C.P.–31(30), Mosley memorandum, 16 January 1930.
40 Liberal Party, 'We Can Conquer Unemployment' (1929).
41 CAB 24/201, C.P.–27(29), 'Unemployment,' memorandum by Joynson-Hicks, 7 February 1929.
42 Robert Skidelsky, *Politicians and the Slump: The Labour Government of 1929–1931* (Harmondsworth, 1970), 119–23.
43 See below, p. 311. See also Leslie Hannah, *The Rise of the Corporate Economy* (1972), 55–56, 73–74; Boyle, *Montagu Norman*, 250.
44 *The Times*, 11 January 1920, 7.
45 See documents in BT 56/17, CIA/820; CAB 23/63, 3(30)6, 16 January 1930, appendix; Citrine papers, 1/6, 'Economic Council, 9 December 1929.' Reminiscent of recent times, Snowden and Norman looked for a 'superman' to rationalise the steel industry and briefly thought they had found one – in the United States. BoE, SMT 2/51, Snowden to Norman, 13 September 1929.
46 HC Deb. 5s., 235, cols. 409–10. See also Milne-Bailey, 'The Economic Advisory Council,' *Labour Magazine*, May 1930, 19–20.
47 Cf. Marquand, *Ramsay MacDonald*, 500, who suggests that Ministers could not have expected that 1929 would witness yet another bout of recovery and setback. Unemployment ceased falling and began to rise in July 1929, one month after the government took office.
48 *The Statist*, 16 November 1929, 865; Amery diary, 21 November and 18 December 1929.
49 TUC, T211/262.02, notes of the joint conference, 8 November 1928; *Industrial Review*, 12 March 1929, 9. See also Labour Party papers, G.C. and E.C., 1.1929–1930, minutes of joint meeting, 23 October 1929; *ibid.*, 27 November 1929.
50 Amery diary, 13 July 1929.
51 Lord Beaverbrook, 'Empire Free Trade' (1929), 4. See also Beaverbrook's rare appearance in the upper House, in HL Deb. 5s., 17, cols. 546–62.
52 *The Times*, 13 November 1929, 16.
53 *Ibid.*, 15 November 1929, 11.
54 Lloyd papers, 7/19, Study Circle on Imperial Economic Cooperation, 2nd Meeting, 28 October 1929.
55 *Annual Conference Reports of the National Union of Conservative and Unionist Associations, 1929*, 21 November 1929.
56 Amery diary, 24 November 1929, 27 and 30 January 1930, 2 February 1930, 5 and 7 March 1930; Neville Chamberlain papers, 7/2/42, Amery to Chamberlain, 21 January and 21 February 1930; Beaverbrook papers, C/5, Amery to Beaverbrook, 21 February 1930.
57 *The Times*, 6 February 1930, 9.
58 *Ibid.*, 5 March 1930, 9.
59 Neville Chamberlain diary, 2/22, 8 December 1929; Thomas papers, U1625/043, Cunliffe-Lister to Gower, 7 January 1930, memorandum, 1930, replies from Stewart, Balfour, Peacock. McGowan, Duckham, Pigott, Lewis, 10 January – 14 February 1930.
60 *Ibid.*
61 *The Times*, 7 February 1930, 14, and 28 November 1929, 24; *Iron and Coal Trades Review*, 24 January 1930, 173.
62 *The Times*, 10 December 1929, 13; *Chamber of Commerce Journal*, 10

January 1930, 30, and 14 February 1930, 66. See also opposition to the tariff truce expressed by *inter alia* the Nottingham Chamber of Commerce, *The Times*, 22 February 1930, 9; *The Times*, 15 February 1930, 11; FBI/C/5, vol. 11, minutes of the Executive Committee, 11 December 1929; *The Times*, 3 March 1930, 9.

63 *The Times*, 28 May 1929, 17. See also comments by *The Economist*, 4 May 1929, 976, and *The Times*' endorsement of the tariff truce proposal on 11 September 1929, 13, 13 January 1930, 13, and 20 February 1930, 15.

64 LN, Preliminary Conference of Governments as Proposed in Section 2 of the Resolution on the Economic Work of the League adopted by the Tenth Assembly, C.26.M.7.1930.11, 7 January 1930.

65 FO 371/14950, W194/17/98, Tyrrell to Henderson, no. 22, 6 January 1930.

66 SdN, Work of the 58th Council, 14 January 1930, C/58th Session/P.V.3(1).

67 FO 371/14365, C1002/230/18, Tyrrell to Vansittart, 28 January 1930.

68 FO 371/14365, C1234/230/18, Tyrrell to Vansittart, 11 February 1930.

69 FO 371/14951, W1602/17/98, Tyrrell to Henderson, no. 26, 13 February 1930.

70 FO 371/14951, W999/17/98, Fountain to Foreign Office, C.R.T.324/30, 28 January 1930; FO 371/14365, C230/230/18, Howard Smith minute, 7 February 1930.

71 FO 371/14950, W63/17/98, Fountain to Foreign Office, C.R.T.4269/29, 2 January 1930.

72 CAB 24/209, C.P.–43(30), Graham memorandum, 8 February 1930.

73 CAB 23/63, 10(30)10, 12 February 1930.

74 HC 5s., 235, cols. 210–11. See also the hostile questions in HC 5s., 234, cols. 832, 1668; *ibid.*, 235, cols. 20–21, 385.

75 CAB 24/211, C.P.–130(30), 'League of Nations Preliminary Conference with a view to Concerted Economic Action,' memorandum by Graham, 22 April 1930.

76 LN, Proceedings of the Preliminary Conference with a view to Concerted Economic Action, 17 February – 24 March 1930, C222.M.109.11, 22 April 1930.

77 *Ibid.*, 78.

78 *Ibid.*, 82–84, 90, 86.

79 *Ibid.*, 99, 106–07, 92, 93–94.

80 *Ibid.*, 96, 108–09, 114.

81 *Ibid.*, 153.

82 *Ibid.*, 162.

83 *The Times*, 1 March 1930, 11; Chapman, *Autobiography*, 260.

84 T172/1713, Chapman to Graham, 1 March 1930; *ibid.*, Snowden to Graham, 6 March 1930.

85 LN, Proceedings of the Preliminary Conference, 278, 279–80.

86 *Ibid.*, 282.

87 *Ibid.*, 284.

88 *Ibid.*, 291.

89 *Ibid.*, 306.

90 T172/1713, Chapman to Graham, 8 March 1930.

91 FO 371/14953, W2469/17/98, Chapman to Graham, no. 11, 10 March 1930. See also MAF 43/12,HH5172, minutes by Dale, 30 January 1930,

and Barnaby, 4 March 1930, on the renewed controversy over French cherry exports.

92 HC Deb. 5s., 236, cols. 278–398, especially 300–03. See also *ibid.*, cols. 2–14, 1097–98, 1132.

93 *Manchester Guardian*, 10 March 1930.

94 LN, Proceedings of the Preliminary Conference, 166–67, 124–25.

95 *Ibid.*, 198, 220, 221–23, 226, 229.

96 *Ibid.*, 361–63.

97 LN, Commercial Convention, Protocol and Final Act, C.203.M.96.11, 15 April 1930.

98 LN, Proceedings of the Preliminary Conference, 142–43.

99 *The Times*, 26 March 1930, 17; HC Deb. 5s., 237, cols. 253, 1057–61; *ibid.*, 238, cols. 19, 40–41, 1969, 2004–07; *ibid.*, 240, cols. 941–43, 1168, 2153–54; *ibid.*, 241, cols. 444–45, 2454–56, 2478–84.

100 FO 371/14952, W3103/17/98, Tyrrell to Henderson, no. 319, 25 March 1930.

101 *The Times*, 25 March 1930, 16.

8 The challenge of regionalism

1 FO 371/12900, C2116/652/18, Tyrrell minute, 20 March 1928.

2 FO 371/14234, W7294/6739/98, memorandum, 24 July 1929.

3 FO 371/11246, C10417/10417/62, Tyrrell minute, 2 October 1926.

4 Winfried Gosmann, 'Die Stellung der Reparationsfrage in der Aussenpolitik des Kabinetts Brüning', *Internationaler Beziehungen in der Weltirtschaftskrise 1929–1933*, eds. Josef Becker and Klaus Hildebrand (Munich, 1980), 238–40; Eyck, *A History of the Weimar Republic*, ii, 213 and passim.

5 Frommelt, *Paneuropa oder Mitteleuropa*, 73 and passim.

6 Hans-Jürgen Schröder, 'Die deutsche Südosteuropapolitik und die Reaktion der angelsächsischen Mächte 1929–1933/34', *Internationaler Beziehungen in der Weltwirtschaftskrise 1929–1933*, eds. Josef Becker and Klaus Hildebrand (Munich, 1980), 343–50; Gosmann, 'Die Stellung der Reparationsfrage', 240–45; Lipgens, 'Europäische Einigungsidee', 82–86.

7 T160/392, F11300/03/3, Tyrrell to Henderson, no. 1034, 18 July 1929; *ibid.*, Tyrrell to Henderson, no. 1077, 26 July 1929.

8 FO 800/284, Tyrrell to Henderson, 30 October 1929. The personal and tactical reasons for Tardieu's decision are discussed in John M. Sherwood, *Georges Mandel and the Third Republic* (Stanford, 1972), 111.

9 FO 371/14365, C230/230/18, Tyrrell to Henderson, no. 3, 8 January 1930; *ibid.*, C1002/230/18, Tyrrell to Vansittart, 28 January 1930. See also La Roche, *La Pologne de Pilsudski*, 69–70.

10 FO 371/14365, C1032/230/18, Tyrrell to Vansittart, 30 January 1930; *ibid.*, C1570/230/18, Tyrrell to Henderson, no. 179, 17 February 1930; FO 371/14951, W1602/17/98, Tyrrell to Henderson, no. 26, 13 February 1930.

11 FO 371/14365, C2355/230/18, Graham to Henderson, no. 187, 14 March 1930.

12 *Ibid.*, C1358/230/18, Rumbold to Sargent, 13 February 1930; *ibid.*, C2545/230/18, Rumbold to Henderson, no. 190, 14 March 1930. See also *ibid.*, C1753/230/18, Rumbold to Sargent, 28 February 1930.

13 *European Finance*, 28 February 1930, 136. Plans were also under way for a

Franco-German Institute and a Franco-German Chamber of Commerce in Cologne: see L'Houillier, *Dialogues franco–allemands*, 93.

14 FO 371/14365, C2356/230/18, Rumbold to Henderson, no. 214, 21 March 1930.

15 FO 371/14366, C3438/230/18, Rumbold to Henderson, no. 333, 29 April 1930.

16 DBFP, 2nd Ser. Vol. 1, no. 303, Rumbold to Henderson, no. 347, 2 May 1930.

17 FO 800/281, Tyrrell to Henderson, 28 March 1930; FO 371/14365, C2841/230/18, Tyrrell to Henderson, no. 411, 11 April 1930.

18 BT 11/234, C.R.T.7094/30, Board of Trade memorandum, 5 April 1930.

19 FO 371/14980, W5193/451/18, Bentinck to Howard Smith, 6 May 1930.

20 France, MAE, 1253/no.2, de Margerie to Briand, no.444–49, 19 May 1930; FO 371/14981, W5336/451/98, Rumbold to Henderson, no. 408, 20 May 1930. Serruys spoke at Heidelberg the day before the Berlin Congress, see L'Houillier, *Dialogues franco-allemands*, 98; Pegg, *Evolution of the European Idea*, 140.

21 UK, Despatch to His Majesty's Ambassador in Paris enclosing the Memorandum of the French Government on the Organisation of a System of European Federal Union, Cmd. 3595. The memorandum was drafted by Léger after consultation with Serruys and others. Fouques-Duparq, one of Léger's senior colleagues, sought to include more thorough discussion of the economic issues, but this was resisted. France, MAE, 1253/no.1, Fouques-Duparq, to (illegible), 14 April 1930; *ibid.*, note by Fouques-Duparq, n.d.; Rueff, *Combats pour l'ordre financier*, 23.

22 Lipgens, 'Europaische Einigungsidee,' 333. As a Foreign Office official commented, 'Opinion in most countries realises that the attitude of His Majesty's Government will be decisive.' FO 371/14982, W5919/451/98, minute by Mallet, 10 June 1930.

23 FO 371/14365/, C1570/230/18,A.W.A. Leeper minute, 24 February 1930; FO 371/14366, C3439/230/18,A.W.A. Leeper minute, 8 May 1930.

24 FO 371/14980, W5111/451/18, Sargent minute 23 May 1930; FO 371/14366, W5585/451/18,A.W.A. Leeper memorandum, 30 May 1930.

25 FO 800/281, Note on Monsieur Briand's memorandum, Noel Baker to Henderson, n.d.; FO 371/14981, W5585/451/98, Noel Baker, 26 May 1930.

26 FO 800/281, League of Nations Union memorandum, 23 May 1930; *ibid.*, League of Nations Union memorandum to Henderson, 20 June 1930; *ibid.*, Henderson to Gilbert Murray, 27 June 1930.

27 FO 371/14982, W5805/451/98, Salter letter and memorandum to Noel Baker, 23 May 1930.

28 *Ibid.*, Selby to Noel Baker, 28 May 1930, (illegible) to Howard Smith, 2 June, Howard Smith minute, 5 June 1930. On the coal conference see 'Disappointments at the ILO,' *Industrial Review*, July 1930, 15–16.

29 Lipgens, 'Europäische Einigungsidee,' 328.

30 FO 371/14917, W6464/6464/17, Tyrrell to Henderson, 25 June 1930.

31 FO 800/281, Tyrrell to Henderson, 28 June 1930. The French Ambassador also appealed directly to Henderson, see France, MAE, 1253/no. 2, de Fleuriau to Briand, no.285, 27 June 1930.

32 FO 800/281, Tyrrell to Henderson, 5 July 1930. On Franco-Italian friction see John W. Wheeler-Bennett, *Disarmament and Security since Locarno, 1925–1931* (1932), 216.

33 CAB 27/424, Committee on the proposed European Federal Union, 14 July 1930.
34 CAB 23/64, 41(30)8, 16 July 1930; FO 371/14983, W7204/451/98, Vansittart to de Fleuriau, 16 July 1930.
35 *Report of the Proceedings at the 61st Annual Trades Union Congress, 1929*, 64–65.
36 FBI/EA/Glenday/11, Nugent to Lennox Lee, 14 January 1930.
37 *Chamber of Commerce Journal*, Supplement, 30 May 1930; *ibid.*, 6 June 1930, 663–69.
38 *Daily Herald*, 29 May 1930; *Labour Magazine*, June 1930, 73.
39 TUC, T310/263.14, minutes of joint FBI–TUC committee, 15 May 1930; FBI/S/Walker/102/22, minutes of meeting, 26 May 1930.
40 TUC, 'Commonwealth Trade. A New Policy' (1930).
41 Beaverbrook papers, C/5, Beaverbrook to Gwynne, 19 February 1930.
42 *Ibid.*, C/19, Elibank memorandum, n.d.; Amery diary, 3 March 1930.
43 James, *Memoirs of a Conservative*, 342–43; Neville Chamberlain diary, 2/22, 22 June 1930.
44 *The Times*, 14 June 1930, 12.
45 *Chamber of Commerce Journal*, 6 June 1930, 674.
46 Amery diary, 23 June 1930.
47 *Ibid.*, 24 June 1930; *The Times*, 25 June 1930, 10.
48 *The Bankers' Magazine*, August 1930, 175–79. See also *The Times*, 10 July 1930, 19.
49 Runciman papers, WR221, Benn to Runciman, 8 July 1930; *The Bankers' Magazine*, August 1930, 180–85.
50 Baldwin papers, 31, Amery to Baldwin, 4 July 1930; Amery diary, 4 July 1930.
51 John Evelyn Wrench, *Geoffrey Dawson and our Times* (1955), 282; *The Times*, 4 July 1930, 14.
52 *The Times*, 5 July 1930, 15; *The Observer*, 6 July 1930, 16; *Sunday Express*, 6 July 1930, 1; *The Nation and Athenaeum*, 12 July 1930, 462.
53 Amery diary, 7 July 1930; *The Times*, 8 July 1930, 14.
54 Austen Chamberlain papers, 5/1/508, Austen to Ida Chamberlain, 7, 19 July 1930.
55 Amery diary, 20 July 1930.
56 *Ibid.*, 30 July, 7, 8 August 1930; Neville Chamberlain diary, 2/22, 30 July 1930; Neville Chamberlain papers, 7/2/45, Chamberlain to Amery, 6 August 1930.
57 Austen Chamberlain papers, 5/1/510, Austen to Ida Chamberlain, 4 August 1930.
58 *Manchester Guardian*, 4 August 1930, 9; 5 August 1930, 12.
59 *The Observer*, 31 August 1930, 12.
60 *The Times, 2* September 1930, 14; Manchester Guardian, 18 October 1930, 9. Lloyd George gave repeated cause to doubt his commitment to free trade, as when in Parliament on 29 January 1930 he declared in favour of anti-dumping legislation. But see claims to the contrary in Rowland, *Lloyd George*, 672; Campbell, *Goat in the Wilderness*, 262.
61 Skidelsky, *Politicians and the Slump*, 309.
62 *Report of the Proceedings at the 62nd Annual Trades Union Congress, 1930*, 71.
63 *Ibid.*, 258–86.

64 *British Industries*, 20 October 1930, 233–34.
65 FBI/S/Walker/102/22, Lithgow to MacDonald, 25 September 1930. See also FBI–TUC memorandum in *Industrial Review*, October 1930, 10–11.
66 FBI/C/32, Lithgow to National Council of Industry, EEU, EIA, NUM, Association of British Chambers of Commerce, NFU, and others, September 1930; FBI/C/2/1931A, minutes of coordinating committee, 17 June 1931.
67 FBI/S/Walker/78/4, Walker to Dawes, 23 February 1931.
68 *The Times*, 19 and 20 September 1930; *Industrial Review*, October 1930, 9; Andrews and Brunner, *Lord Nuffield*, 25.
69 Skidelsky, *Politicians and the Slump*, 309–12; Campbell, *Goat in the Wilderness*, 277; Brand papers, 31, Brand to Keynes, 30 January 1931.
70 *Manchester Guardian*, 26 September 1930,6.
71 Jones, *Whitehall Diary*, ii, 235.
72 Thomas papers, U1625/C114, Balfour to Cunliffe-Lister, 19 January 1930.
73 MacDonald papers, PRO 30/69/1/243, Buxton letter, 25 October 1930.
74 CAB 23/63, 14(30)1, 11 February 1930.
75 *Ibid.*
76 MacDonald papers, PRO 30/69/1/4 ii, Snowden to MacDonald, 24 February 1930.
77 Labour Party, 'The Menace of Protection,' by Philip Snowden (1930).
78 CAB 23/63, 17(30)1, 26 March 1930.
79 *The Times*, 11 January 1930.
80 MacDonald papers, PRO 30/69/1/243, Buxton memorandum, 17 April 1930.
81 *Ibid.*, Addison to MacDonald, 17 and 30 April 1930; *ibid.*, Snowden to MacDonald, 28 April 1930; CAB 24/211, C.P.–139(30), Snowden memorandum, 2 May 1930; Marquand, *Ramsay MacDonald*, 560.
82 MacDonald papers, PRO 30/69/2/10, MacDonald to Molteno, 18 November 1930; *ibid.*, PRO 30/69/2/11 Pt.1, MacDonald to Norman, 29 June 1931.
83 MacDonald diary, PRO 30/69/8/1, 10 July 1929.
84 *Ibid.*, 15 and 27 November, 12 and 24 December 1929, 22 May 1930.
85 *Ibid.*, 20 November 1929, 29 April 1930.
86 *Ibid.*, 25 September, 3 and 5 December 1929.
87 Marquand, *Ramsay MacDonald*, 405.
88 On the fate of Mosley's memorandum see Skidelsky, *Oswald Mosley*, 195–97.
89 CAB 24/211, C.P.–134(30), Report of the Unemployment Policy Committee, 1 May 1930.
90 MacDonald diary, PRO 30/69/8/1, 19 May 1930.
91 Thomas papers, U1625/C114, MacDonald to Mosley, 19 February 1930; *ibid.*, U1625/C102, MacDonald to Thomas, 21 February 1930.
92 Skidelsky, *Politicians and the Slump*, 208–13.
93 *Ibid.*, 209.
94 MacDonald diary, PRO 30/69/8/1, 29 May 1930.
95 Passfield papers, Beatrice Webb diary, 31 May 1930.
96 MacDonald diary, PRO 30/69/8/1, 16 May 1930.
97 Marquand, *Ramsay MacDonald*, 545–46.
98 MacDonald papers, PRO 30/69/6/33, MacDonald to Newbold, 2 June 1930.

99 *Ibid.*, 30/69/1/455, 'Industrial Reconstruction Scheme,' memorandum by H.D. Henderson, 30 May 1930.
100 Henderson, *The Inter-War Years*, 39–42.
101 Jones, *Whitehall Diary*, ii, 262.
102 FO 371/14952/17/98, Fountain to Foreign Office, C.R.T.2146/30, 8 May 1930.
103 MacDonald papers, PRO 30/69/1/243, Attlee memorandum, 9 June 1930; MAF 40/16, 'Agricultural Policy. Note of Discussion in Dr Addison's Room at the House of Commons at 4.30 p.m. on Monday 23rd June 1930.'
104 CAB 23/64, 33(30)12,24 June 1930.
105 HC Deb. 5s., 240, col. 1397.
106 Austen Chamberlain papers, 5/1/508, Austen to Hilda Chamberlain, 30 June 1930; Baldwin papers, 31, Smithers to Fry, 6 July 1930.
107 Austen Chamberlain papers, 5/1/508, Austen to Hilda Chamberlain, 14 July 1930.
108 Baldwin papers, 31, Smithers to Fry, 6 July 1930. See also *ibid.*, Craig to Baldwin, 28 July 1930; Amery diary, 9 and 16 July 1930.
109 *The Times*, 5 July 1930, 16.
110 Snowden, *An Autobiography*, ii, 923–24.
111 *The Times*, 14 July 1930, 14.
112 Labour Party, 'The Truth about Protection: The Worker Pays,' Philip Snowden (1930); *The Times*, 17 July 1930, 12; MacDonald diary, PRO 30/69/8/1, 17 July 1930.
113 MacDonald papers, PRO 30/69/1/243, Attlee memorandum, 9 June 1930.
114 CAB 24/213, C.P.–234(30), Addison memorandum, 9 June 1930.
115 CAB 24/213, E.A.C(H.) 97, Report of Committee on Agricultural Policy, 7 July 1930.
116 CAB 24/213,C.P.–250(30), Snowden memorandum, 17 July 1930.
117 CAB 58/2, E.A.C./7th Mtg., 24 July 1930.
118 FO 371/14936, W10320/7399/50, A.W.A. Leeper minute, 7 October 1930.
119 CAB 23/64, 48(30), 31 July 1930.
120 Marquand, *Ramsay MacDonald*, 560.
121 HC Deb. 5s., 244, col. 891.
122 MacDonald papers, PRO 30/69/1/4 Pt. 2, Snowden to MacDonald, 24 February 1930.
123 CAB 23/65, 49(30)1, 6 August 1930.
124 *Daily Herald*, 11 August 1930, 3; *The Observer*, 31 August 1930, 12.
125 Dawes, *Journal as Ambassador to Great Britain*, 230.
126 MacDonald papers, PRO 30/69/2/10, MacDonald to Thomas, 31 August 1930. See also *ibid.*, Snowden to MacDonald, 4 September 1930; *ibid.*, PRO 30/69/1/420, Graham to MacDonald, 3 September 1930.
127 CAB 23/65, 50(30)2, 2 September 1930.
128 Binoux, *Les Pionniers de l'Europe*, 131; FO 371/14366, C5529/230/18, Tyrrell to Henderson, no. 784, 8 July 1930; *ibid.*, C6393/230/18, Campbell to Henderson, no. 930, 13 August 1930; DBFP, 2nd ser., no. 307, Rumbold to Henderson, no. 545, 3 July 1930; *ibid.*, no. 319, Rumbold to Henderson, no. 744, 5 September 1930.
129 France, MAE, 1253/no. 3, Note by Fouques-Duparq, 4 July 1930; FO 800/282, Henderson to Briand, 1 August 1930, Briand to Henderson, 12 August 1930.

130 France, MAE, 1253/no. 4, 'Conférence tenue à Geneve sur l'organisation d'un régime d'union fédérale européenne,' 8 September 1930; FO 371/14984, W9214/451/98, Cadogan to Henderson, no. 45L.N., 9 September 1930. See also Suarez, *Briand*, iv, 341–43; Bariéty, 'Idee européenne et relations franco-allemandes,' 581.
131 Cecil papers, MS.51,081, Cecil to Henderson, 9 September 1930; *ibid.*, Cecil to Henderson, 12 September 1930; Dalton diary, 7 September – 1 October 1930. On Venizelos's Europeanism, see *European Finance*, 27 June 1930, 263.
132 Cecil papers, MS.51,081, Cecil to MacDonald, 18 August 1930. The French were aware of Cecil's hostility, see France, MAE, 1253/no. 3, note by Fouques-Duparq, 1 July 1930; Cecil interview in *Le Petit Journal*, 7 September 1930, quoted in Rolo, *Britain and the Briand Plan*, 22.
133 LN, *Official Journal*, 1930, Special Supplement, no. 84, Records of the Eleventh Ordinary Session of the Assembly, Plenary Minutes, 37–39.
134 FO 371/14984, W9423/451/98, Campbell to Henderson, no. 1035, 15 September 1930.
135 LN, Records of the Eleventh ... Assembly, Plenary Minutes, 117–18, 126; FO 371/14984, W9910/451/98, Henderson to Vansittart, no. 59, 29 September 1930.
136 LN, Records of the Eleventh ... Assembly, Plenary Minutes, 50, 52, 59, 61, 102, 86.
137 *Ibid.*, 40, 69–71.
138 FO 371/14936, W9119/7399/50, Broadmead to Henderson, no. 438, 2 September 1930.
139 LN, *Review of World Trade, 1931 and 1932*, 11.A.25., 9.
140 LN, *Official Journal*, 1930, Special Supplement no. 86, Records of Eleventh Ordinary Session of the Assembly, Minutes of the Second Committee, 23, 29, 48, 19, 43–46.
141 *Ibid.*, 32, 35, 36, 40, 47, 49, 54–55.
142 *Ibid.*, 83.
143 Coudenhove-Kalergi, *An Idea Conquers the World*, 114; Dalton diary, 7 September – 1 October 1930; Ralph T. White, 'Regionalism vs. Universalism in the League of Nations. A Study of Pan-Europeanism and the League Secretariat between 1925 and 1930, based on material in the League Archives at Geneva', *Annales d'Etudes Internationales*, 1 (1970), 88–114.
144 LN, Assembly Resolutions regarding the Economic Work of the League of Nations, Report by the Representative of Germany, 1 October 1930, C.578.1930.11.
145 LN, Records of the Eleventh ... Assembly, Minutes of the Second Committee, 56.
146 LN, Records of the Eleventh ... Assembly, Plenary Minutes, 183–86.
147 CAB 24/214, C.P.–298(30), Thomas memorandum, September 1930. To the joint FBI–TUC appeal for action at the conference, MacDonald replied that the government was working on 'concrete proposals to this end.... The ideas we have in mind cover everything you suggest and have been worked out in great detail.' FBI/S/Walker/102/22, MacDonald to Lithgow, 26 September 1930. Events soon demonstrated the emptiness of MacDonald's assurance.

148 *NFU Record*, September 1930, 290. See also *Daily Herald*, 15 September 1930.
149 CAB 23/65, 52(30)1, 17 September 1930.
150 CAB 23/65, 55(30)1, 24 September 1930.
151 MacDonald diary, PRO 30/69/8/1, 9 October 1930.
152 CAB 32/80, 2nd Plenary Session, 8 October 1930. Blaxland, *J.H. Thomas*, 240. On the merits of the offer, see Ian M. Drummond *Imperial Economic Policy, 1917–1939* (1974), 155.
153 CAB 23/65, 56(30)7, 9 October 1930.
154 MacDonald diary, PRO 30/69/8/1, 9 October 1930.
155 Amery diary, 27 October 1930.
156 *NFU Record*, November 1930, 57. See also *NFU Yearbook for 1931*, 445, 449. On MacDonald's state, see Austen Chamberlain papers, 5/1/516, Austen to Ida Chamberlain, 4 October 1930.
157 Drummond, *Imperial Economic Policy*, 160.
158 CAB 24/216, C.P.–366(30), Thomas memorandum, 27 October 1930.
159 CAB 23/65, 64(30), 28 October 1930.
160 MacDonald diary, PRO 30/69/8/1, 28 October 1930.
161 CAB 23/65, Committee on Existing Imperial Preferences, conclusions, 29 October 1930.
162 MacDonald diary, PRO 30/69/8/1, 12, 13 November 1930.
163 *Ibid.*
164 FO 371/14953, W12060/17/98, Jenkins to Foreign Office, C.R.T.4365/30, 14 November 1930; FO 371/15688, W232/1/98, Chapman report to Foreign Office, 8 January 1931.
165 *Ibid.*
166 FO 371/15688, W232/1/98, A.W.A. Leeper minute, n.d.
167 HC Deb. 5s., 248, cols. 47–48.
168 *Daily Herald*, 7 July 1930, 6; Labour Party, *Report of the 30th Annual Conference*, 1930, 200–04.
169 Amery diary, 9 October 1930; Neville Chamberlain diary, 2/22, 19 October 1930.
170 Beaverbrook papers, C/19, Baldwin to Beaverbrook, 21 October 1930. Beaverbrook to Baldwin, 22 October 1930.
171 Amery diary, 30 October 1930; Henry Page Croft, *My Life of Strife*(1948), 187–88; Randolph S. Churchill, *Lord Derby: 'King of Lancashire'*(1959), 584–86.
172 Skidelsky, *Politicians and the Slump*, 308–09.
173 Dowse, *Left in the Centre*.
174 Skidelsky, *Politicians and the Slump*, 301f.
175 *The Times*, 8 December 1930, 7.
176 Amery diary, 11 October 1930; Campbell, *Goat in the Wilderness*, 276. Morris contributed £50,000 to Mosley's New Party: Mosley, *My Life*, 345. On Petter's frustrations, see the *National Review*, November 1930, 984–87, and *ibid.*, December 1930, 1039–48.
177 Skidelsky, *Politicians and the Slump*, 231.
178 CAB 24/216, C.P.363(30), Report of the EAC Committee of Economists, 24 October 1930.
179 CAB 24/215, C.P.–330(30), Balfour to MacDonald, 1 October 1930.
180 Harold Nicolson, *King George the Fifth*, 448.

181 Marquand, *Ramsay MacDonald*, 574–75.
182 *The Times*, 8 September 1930, 14.
183 HC Deb. 5s., 244, col. 704.
184 Marquand writes, 'but there is no reason to believe that he thought seriously about taking part in a National Government until the question was revived in very different circumstances nine months later.' This is an extraordinary claim. By Marquand's own evidence it is obvious that MacDonald was doing everything possible to telegraph his availability for a National Government to other Party leaders. See Marquand, *Ramsay MacDonald*, 574–75, 578–81.
185 PRO 30/69/8/1, MacDonald diary, 14 January 1931.
186 CAB 24/214, C.P.–283(30), 'The Problems of British Industry', Attlee memorandum, 29 July 1930; CAB 24/216, C.P.–390(30), Note by Lansbury, 22 November 1930; CAB 27/534, T.P.C.(30), 2nd Mtg., Minutes, 2 December 1930, statements by Hartshorn, Thomas, Graham.
187 CAB 23/66, 9(31)5, 21 January 1934.

9 The gold standard undermined

1 Labour Party, *Report of the 29th Annual Conference, 1929*, 230.
2 FBI/S/Walker/25/3, Dibben to Nugent, 4 October 1929; FBI/C/82, vol. 175, first meeting of Committee on Industry and Finance, 23 October 1929; *ibid.*, second meeting, 13 November 1929; T172/1651, Hammersley to Snowden, 17 October 1929; *ibid.*, Leith Ross to Hopkins and Grigg, 19 October 1929. On the importance of the membership see also *The Commercial*, 10 October 1929, 409, G.D.H. Cole, 'The Problem of the Bank Rate,' *New Statesman*, 12 October 1929, 4.
3 *New Leader*, 8 November 1929, 3.
4 Brand papers, 27, 'Memorandum on the Economic Crisis', by Walton Newbold, 30 January 1930.
5 Marquand, *Ramsay MacDonald*, 458.
6 Brand papers, 27, minutes of meeting, 10 January 1930, 3. On Macmillan compare E.P. Thompson's portrait of a more recent bencher in 'The Report on Lord Radcliffe', in *Writing by Candlelight* (1979).
7 Brand papers, 27, minutes of meeting, 10 January 1930, 7.
8 *Ibid.*, 10.
9 T200/4, minutes of meeting, 20 February 1930, 60.
10 *Ibid.*, minutes of meeting, 28 February 1930, 71.
11 *Ibid.*, 73, 75.
12 *Ibid.*, 86, 88, 89.
13 *Ibid.*, minutes of meeting, 6 March 1930, 115–19, 122; *ibid.*, 7 March 1930, 128–32.
14 Brand papers, 27, 'Memorandum on Currency Reform', 3 January 1930.
15 *The Commercial*, 29 May 1930, 489.
16 Macmillan Committee, *Evidence*, i, 347–56.
17 *Ibid.*, QQ.2873, 2888.
18 Macmillan Committee, *Evidence*, ii, 134–38.
19 FBI/EA/Glenday/11, Nugent to Lee, 10 February 1930; FBI/EA/Glenday/4, Nugent to Amery, 29 November 1930.
20 FBI/EA/Glenday/4, Rylands to Nugent, 31 December 1930;

FBI/S/Walker/100/2, Butler to Walker, 1 October 1929; *ibid.*, Walker to Butler, 2 December 1929.

21 FBI/C/1, vol. 2, minutes of Executive Committee of Grand Council, 12 March 1930.

22 FBI/EA/Glenday/11, Lithgow to Walker, 5 March 1930.

23 *Ibid.*, Hewit to Nugent, 6 March 1930; *ibid.*, Walker to Lee, 10 March 1930; *ibid.*, Nugent to Snow, 14 March 1930.

24 Macmillan Committee, *Evidence*, i, Q.3121.

25 *Ibid.*, QQ.3213, 3233.

26 FBI/C/82, vol. 175, minutes of Finance and Industry Committee, 8 April, 19 June 1930; FBI/EA/Glenday/11, Hewit to Nugent, 3 June 1930.

27 Macmillan Committee, *Evidence*, ii, QQ.8462, 8469, p. 240 no. 14.

28 TUC, *Report of the 63rd Annual Trades Union Congress, 1931*, 271–75.

29 Macmillan Committee, *Evidence*, ii, 323–25.

30 *Ibid.*, i, 223–24.

31 *Journal of the Farmers' Club*, Pt. 1, February 1931, 2–17.

32 Macmillan Committee, *Evidence*, ii, 225–27.

33 *Ibid.*, i, QQ.2498, 2594, 2575.

34 *Ibid.*, ii, p. 112 no. 16, QQ.7041, 7045.

35 Manchester Chamber of Commerce *Monthly Record*, 31 March 1930, 74–80.

36 T172/1722, Manchester Chamber of Commerce to Prime Minister, 15 September 1930. See also *The Economist*, 20 September 1930, 520; *Cotton Gazette*, 21 September 1930, 911; *Chamber of Commerce Journal*, 24 October 1930, 439; *ibid.*, 21 November 1930, 538; T172/1722, Joint Committee of Cotton Trade Organisations to MacDonald, 17 November 1930.

37 Addis diary, 31 March 1930.

38 Macmillan Committee, *Evidence*, i, QQ.3360–61, 3490, 3328, 3332, 3345.

39 *Ibid.*, ii, Q.7770.

40 Royal Institute of International Affairs, *The International Gold Problem, Collected Papers* (1931).

41 *Ibid.*, first meeting, 5 December 1929. See also Macmillan Committee, *Evidence*, i, 239–54; Stamp, *Papers on Gold and the Price Level*, 8–44.

42 Strakosch was ably assisted by two other experts and publicists: Dr Thomas (later Lord) Balogh, who was in his employ during 1930, and Mr Joseph Kitchin, the managing director of the Union Corporation. Macmillan Committee, *Evidence*, ii, 23 May 1930; *The Economist* Supplement, 'Gold and Price Level', 5 July 1930.

43 *The Banker*, April 1930, 78; Sayers, *The Bank of England*, iii, appendix 17.

44 The 16,000 shares were oversubscribed by a remarkable 158 times. See BdeF, GC, 22 May 1930; Paul Einzig, 'Co-operation and the International Bank', *The Banker*, June 1930, 272–75; *The Economist*, 24 May 1930, 1160.

45 T160/403, F19437, Hawtrey memorandum, 'French Monetary Policy', 14 January 1931; *Federal Reserve Bulletin*, various; *The Economist* Supplement, 5 July 1930, annex B, p. 10.

46 SdN, vol. 1461, Gold Delegation, first session, 4th meeting, 27 August 1929.

47 *Ibid.*, first session, 6th meeting, 29 August 1929.

48 *Ibid.*, second session, 3rd meeting, 11 June 1930.

49 LN, *Interim Report of the Gold Delegation of the Financial Committee*, C.375.M.161. 1930.

50 Charles Rist, 'La Question d'or', *Revue d'Economie Politique*, November–December 1930, 1489–1518; T188/158, Leith Ross to McKenna, 1 November 1930; BoE, OV9/264, Strakosch to Niemeyer, 1 September 1930; Clay, *Lord Norman*, 370; *Chase Economic Bulletin*, 29 September 1930; *The Economist*, 20 December 1930, 1157–58.
51 BoE, OV9/264, Strakosch to Niemeyer, 1 September 1930.
52 BoE, OV9/258, Niemeyer to Strakosch, 25 October 1930.
53 *Daily Mail*, 16 August 1930, 8.
54 T160/430, F12317/1, Leith Ross to Waley, 30 May 1930.
55 George Glascow, 'Foreign Affairs', *Contemporary Review*, December 1929, 768–92; *ibid.*, June 1930, 783; *ibid.*, August 1930, 241; *The Observer*, 20 July 1930, 2; Paul Einzig, 'Co-operation and the International Bank', *The Banker*, June 1930, 272–75; *Daily Herald*, 20 May 1930, 7; *ibid.*, 21 July 1930, 10.
56 J. Henry Schroder & Co., *Quarterly Review*, July 1930, 1–11; *Sunday Express*, 27 July 1930, 6; *Daily Mail*, 21 July 1930, 10; *European Finance*, 1 August 1930, 72; *The Economist*, 9 August 1930, 269; *The Times*, 9 August 1930, 16; *ibid.*, 16 August 1930, 16; *ibid.*, 23 August 1930, 15.
57 Brand papers, 28, Leith Ross to Brand, 21 July 1930.
58 MacDonald papers, PRO 30/69/1/257, Leith Ross memorandum to Grigg for Snowden and MacDonald, 28 July 1930. Bellerby, the only prominent academic economist advocating devaluation at this time, was an Oxford man.
59 CAB 58/10, EAC(H) 81, Report of Committee on Economic Outlook, 4 April 1930; CAB 58/10, EAC(H) 83, Note by Snowden, 8 April 1930; CAB 58/2, EAC/4th Mtg, Conclusions, 8 May 1930; CAB 58/2, EAC/5th Mtg, 19 June 1930.
60 CAB 52/2, EAC/7th Mtg, 24 July 1930.
61 T172/1722, Leith Ross memorandum, 24 September 1930; *ibid.*, Snowden to Leith Ross, 25 September 1930; *ibid.*, Grigg to Usher, 26 September 1930.
62 MacDonald papers, PRO 30/69/1/258, 'Monetary Policy and its Effect on Unemployment', 20 October 1930.
63 MacDonald papers, PRO 30/69/2/10, MacDonald to Marley, 23 October 1930. MacDonald also denied Marley's memorandum, proceeded to single out aspects of it for criticism.
64 T200/5, minutes of meeting, 23 October 1930, 5, 24–25.
65 CAB 58/2, EAC/9th Mtg, Conclusions, 7 November 1930.
66 T200/5, minutes of meeting, 7 November 1930, 167–81.
67 Addis diary, 7 November 1928, 20 December 1929.
68 T200/6, minutes of meeting, 20 November 1930, 31, 37.
69 CAB 58/10, EAC(H) 81, Report of Committee on Economic Outlook, 4 April 1930.
70 *The Times*, 14 July 1930, 20; 27 August 1930, 16; 4 October 1930, 11; 7 October 1930, 10 and 19; 14 November 1930, 10.
71 France, MF, B12612/no. 53, 778, Chalendar to Farnier, 3 October 1929; *ibid.*, F30/1389, Chalendar to Farnier, 10 September 1930; BdeF, GC, 27 November 1930.
72 T160/430, F12317/1, Leith Ross memorandum, 3 January 1931.
73 France, MF, F30/1411, note by Lacour-Gayet, 23 October 1930; *ibid.*, B12614/no. 57, 840, Rueff to Farnier, 17 February, 4 December 1930.

74 France, MF, B12625/no. 59, 020, Farnier note to Germain-Martin, n.d. (? 2 January 1931); FO 371/15641, W629/56/17, Leith Ross to Howard Smith, 16 January 1931.
75 France, MF, F30/1411, Farnier to Moreau, 24 September 1930.
76 *Ibid.*, Laboulaye to Escallier, 23 December 1930.
77 T160/430, F12317/1, Leith Ross to Hopkins, 17 November 1930; FO 371/14919, W12605/12605/17, Vansittart minute, 24 November 1930.
78 France, MF, B12613/no. 56, 743, Rueff to Farnier, 29 July 1930; FO 371/15640, W56/56/17, Leith Ross to Vansittart, 2 December 1930; T160/430, F12317/1, Leith Ross note of interview with Pouyanne and Rueff, 4 December 1930.
79 BdF, GC, 11 December 1930; T160/430, F12317/1, Leith Ross note of interview with Pouyanne, 16 December 1930.
80 T160/430, F12317/2, Waley minute, 30 January 1931. See also *ibid.*, Leith Ross to Fergusson, 17 February 1931.
81 T188/22, Leith Ross note of conversations on 2–3 January 1931.
82 *The Times*, 3 January 1931, 16; BdF, CG, 27 November 1930.
83 BdF, GC, 27 November 1930, statement by Moreau; T160/430, F12317/1, Tyrrell to Wellesley, 7 January 1931.
84 *Ibid.*, Leith Ross note, 16 January 1931.
85 Paul Einzig, *The Fight for Financial Supremacy* (1931), 110–13; *The Banker*, February 1931, 130; *The Economist* Banking Supplement, 9 May 1931, 9.
86 T160/430, F12317/2, Leith Ross to Bizot, 23 January 1931; *ibid.*, Bizot to Leith Ross, 2 February 1931.
87 FO 371/15712, W645/102/98, Leith Ross to Niemeyer, 16 January 1931; LN, Report of the Financial Committee, C.143.M.44.1931.11, 27 January 1931.
88 LN, *Second Interim Report of the Gold Delegation of the Financial Committee*, C.75.M.31.1931.11, 20 January 1931; *The Economist*, 31 January 1931, 217.
89 FO 371/15641, W1485/56/17, Leith Ross to Cahill, 2 February 1931.
90 *Federal Reserve Bulletin*, March 1931, 146–50; *The Times*, 2 February 1931, 17.
91 T160/430, F12317/2, Bizot to Leith Ross, 2 February 1931.
92 T188/22, Note of meeting on 20–21 February 1931; FO 371/15641, W2171/56/17, Leith Ross to Howard Smith, 23 February 1931; France, MF, B12614/no. 57, 840, Rueff to Farnier, 17 February 1931.
93 T160/404, F557/011, Leith Ross to Hopkins and Snowden, 2 February 1931; *ibid.*, Hopkins to Fisher, 3 February 1931; *ibid.*, Fisher to Snowden, 7 February 1931.
94 FO 371/15213, C404/11/18, Rumbold to Henderson, no. 47, 16 January 1931.
95 T188/22, note of meeting on 22–23 February 1931.
96 *Financial Times*, 26 February 1931; *Financial News*, 26 February 1931; *The Banker*, April 1931, 6; *The Economist*, 28 February 1931, 436.
97 *The Economist*, 7 March 1931, 483; *Financial Times* Banking Supplement, 30 March 1931, 3.
98 *The Economist*, 22 November 1930, 952; Edgar Vincent D'Abernon, *The Path to Recovery* (1931). Snowden, perhaps expecting him to be intensely anti-inflationist after his experience as Ambassador in postwar Germany, had sought D'Abernon as chairman of the Macmillan Committee: T160/426, F11548, D'Abernon to Snowden, 17 October 1929.

99 T175/53, Rennie Smith to Snowden, 15 September 1930; *The Times*, 20 November 1930, 8.
100 LCC, Ms. 16, 650/1, A. deV. Leigh to E.H.D. Skinner, 20 November 1930.
101 *Ibid.*, Skinner to Leigh, 22 November 1930; *ibid.*, statement for Lord Herbert Scott, 1 December 1930.
102 *Ibid.*, J.E. Sealy to Leigh, 28 January 1931.
103 Clay, *Lord Norman*, 370.
104 CAB 23/66, 6(31)3, 14 January 1931.
105 Runciman papers, WR244, 'National Economy', Liberal Council pamphlet, January 1931; *The Bankers' Magazine*, March 1931, 434–41; Friends of Economy, *Annual Report* (1932).
106 *The Economist*, 7 February 1931, 285.
107 HC Deb. 5s., 248, cols. 446–47.
108 MacDonald diary, PRO 30/69/8/1, 15, 17 February 1931; Amery diary, 12 February 1931; Austen Chamberlain papers, 5/1/530, Austen to Ida Chamberlain, 16 February 1931; M. Philips Price, *My Three Revolutions* (1969), 266.
109 HC Deb. 5s., 248, cols. 731–33.
110 Skidelsky, *Oswald Mosley*, 242, 247; MacDonald papers, PRO 30/69/5/178, Oliver Baldwin to Henderson, 26 February, Cynthia Mosley to MacDonald, 3 March 1931; Brown, *So Far*, 159.
111 Price, *My Three Revolutions*, 266.
112 Middlemas, *The Clydesiders*, 253.
113 Skidelsky, *Politicians and the Slump*, 335–36.
114 PREM 1/94, Clark to Thomas, no. 13, 4 February 1931.
115 T175/53, Leith Ross to Hopkins and Snowden, 6 February 1931. See also *ibid.*, Snowden to Crombie, 22 September 1930, and Snowden to Rennie Smith, 24 September 1930.
116 T175/53, Waley minute to Fergusson and Leith Ross, 14 February 1931; *ibid.*, Thomas to Snowden, 16 February 1931; *ibid.*, Snowden to Thomas, 17 February 1931; *ibid.*, telegram to Clerk, no. 217, 17 February 1931, MacDonald repeated the message directly to Ambassador Dawes. FRUS, 1931, I, Dawes to Stimson, no. 49, 20 February 1931.
117 CAB 23/66, 16(31)16, 4 March 1931.
118 FRUS, 1931, I, Dawes to Stimson, no. 67, 5 March 1931.
119 FO 371/15487, F2205/672/10, Lindsay to Henderson, no. 642, 8 April 1931; *ibid.*, F3566/672/10, Lindsay to Henderson, no. 937, 8 June 1931; FRUS, 1931, I, Stimson to Dawes, no. 137, 20 May 1931; *ibid.*, Dawes to Stimson, no. 158, 21 May 1931.
120 FO 371/15675, W2222/2222/50, Sargent minute, 1931.
121 *Ibid.*, Leith Ross to Sargent, 24 February 1931.
122 Addis diary, 15 April 1931; T160/394, F11324, Harvey to Leith Ross, 16 April 1931.
123 T160/394, F11324, Leith Ross to Harvey, 20 April 1931; *ibid.*, Leith Ross to Hopkins, 21 April 1931; *ibid.*, Hopkins to Leith Ross, 20 April 1931; *ibid.*, Leith Ross minutes to Hopkins, 21, 25 April 1931.
124 T160/398, F12377, Leith Ross to Hopkins and Snowden, 30 January 1931; *ibid.*, Leith Ross to Rowe-Dutton, 24 February 1931; FO 371/15676, C3191/3191/50, Leith Ross to Vansittart, 5 February 1931.
125 Clarke, *Central Bank Cooperation*, 179–80; France, MF, B12614/no. 57,

840, Rueff to Germain Martin, 15 February 1931. The Reichsbank sought a loan from Morgans, was refused, and turned to Lee Higginson & Co., which arranged a credit of $100–150 million. Besides British, Swiss, and Austrian houses, Paribas also participated: see MGC, Box P.655, Luther to Morgan & Cie., 14 January 1931, and subsequent correspondence; Gosmann, 'Die Stellung der Reparationsfrage', 251–52.

126 FRBNY, Harrison–Norman correspondence, Norman to Harrison, 3 March 1931.

127 T160/398, F12377, Waley to Leith Ross, 11 March 1931; *ibid.*, Leith Ross minute, 20 March 1931; *ibid.*, Leith Ross to Fergusson and Waley, 16 April 1931; *ibid.*, Pinsent to Waley, 1 May 1931.

128 American financiers also resisted the Francqui plan: TWL, 173–3, Lamont and Carter to J.P. Morgan & Co., 4 May 1931.

129 BdeF, CG, 23 April, 7 May 1931; Clay, *Lord Norman*, 371.

130 CAB 58/2, EAC/12th Mtg, 12 March 1931.

131 D'Abernon sent a collection of his speeches on the currency question to MacDonald the previous month. MacDonald papers, PRO 30/69/3/34, MacDonald to D'Abernon, 24 March 1931.

132 CAB 58/2, EAC/13th Mtg. 16 April 1931.

133 Amery diary, 26 February, 2, 5 March 1931; Churchill, *Lord Derby*, 586; Gillian Peele, 'St George's and the Empire Crusade', *By-Elections in British Politics*, eds. Chris Cooke and John Ramsden (1973), ch. 4.

134 Churchill, *Lord Derby*, 587; Middlemas and Barnes, *Baldwin*, 601; Taylor, *Beaverbrook*, 398–403.

135 Neville Chamberlain papers, 7/2/52, Amery to Chamberlain, 16 April 1931; *ibid.*, Chamberlain to Amery, 17 April 1931.

136 *The Economist*, 16 May 1931, 1037–38; *New Statesman and Nation*, 30 May 1931, 526, and 27 June 1931, 59; *The Banker*, July 1931, 11; Price, *My Three Revolutions*, 266.

137 PREM 1/93, H.D. Henderson to MacDonald, 6 June 1931; *ibid.*, MacDonald to Norman, 18 June 1931.

138 MacDonald papers, PRO 3/69/2/11 Pt. 1, Norman to MacDonald, 25 June 1931. Sprague made the same remarks to the Macmillan Committee in Norman's presence. Macmillan Committee, *Evidence*, ii, 18, 19 February 1931. Courtney Mill meanwhile kept up a running battle with D'Abernon in *The Times*, see correspondence in Hawtrey papers, 10/71.

139 MacDonald papers, PRO 30/69/2/11 Pt. 1, MacDonald to Norman, 29 June 1931.

140 CAB 58/12, EAC(H)144, Henderson to MacDonald, 26 June 1931; see also *ibid.*, Keynes memorandum, 16 July 1931.

141 Clarke, *Central Bank Cooperation*, 202.

142 PREM 1/95, MacDonald to H.D. Henderson, 29 June 1931.

10 The Austro-German customs union crisis

1 T160/430, F12317/1, Leith Ross to Hamilton, 13 January 1931.

2 SdN, CEUE/2nd Session/PV 1, provisional minutes of first meeting, Geneva, 16 January 1931.

3 *Ibid.*, CEUE/2nd Session/PV 2, 16 January 1931; *ibid.*, CEUE/2nd Session/PV 4, 17 January 1931.

4 *Ibid.*, CEUE/2nd Session/PV 4, 17 January 1931.
5 *L'Europe Nouvelle*, 24 January 1931, 121–23; Vanlangenhove, *L'Elaboration de la politique étrangère de la Belgigue entre les deux querres mondiales*, 116; Belgium, *Documents diplomatiques belges*, ii, no. 220, Vanlangenhove memorandum, 20 November 1930; Ole Karup Pedersen, *Denrigsminister P. Munch opfattelse af Danmarks stillung i international politik* (Copenhagen, 1970), ch. 2.
6 SdN, CEUE/2nd Session/PV 5, 19 January 1931.
7 *Ibid.*, CEUE/2nd Session/PV 6, 20 January 1931.
8 *Ibid.*, CEUE 12, note by the Secretary-General, 'Resolutions adopted at the 2nd Session of the Commission (January 16th–21st 1931)', C.114.M.41.1931, 22 January 1931.
9 FO 371/15693, W966/7/98, Ovey to Henderson, no. 26, 19 January 1931; *ibid.*, W1420/7/98, minutes by A.W.A. Leeper, Carr, and others, 9–10 February 1931.
10 *Ibid.*, W1420/7/98, Howard Smith to Shackle, 12 February 1931.
11 FO 371/15694, W1649/7/98, Chapman to Howard Smith, 12 February 1931; *ibid.*, minutes by Howard Smith, Dalton, and others, 13 February 1931.
12 FO 371/15694, W2276/7/98, Tyrrell to Henderson, no. 224, 26 February 1931; *ibid.*, W2408/7/98, Tyrrell to Henderson, no. 240, 2 March 1931.
13 HC Deb. 5s., 247, cols. 2–3, 774–76; also *ibid.*, 248, cols. 47–48, 1925–26; *ibid.*, 249, cols. 1861–62; *ibid.*, 250, cols. 205–06; *ibid.*, 251, cols. 9–10.
14 *Ibid.*, 247, col. 1610.
15 MAF 40/9, SG5904A, Henderson to Drummond, 5 March 1931; *ibid.*, Drummond to Henderson, 5 March 1931.
16 FO 371/15689, W4295/1/98, 'Report of the United Kingdom Delegate to 2nd Session of 2nd International Conference on Concerted Economic Action, 16–18 March 1931', 14 April 1931; *ibid.*, Chapman to Graham, 16 March 1931; *ibid.*, Graham to Chapman, 16 March 1931; LN, *Official Journal*, 'Report by Colijn to 63rd Session of Council, 22 May 1931', 1466–67.
17 CAB 27/333, C.P.–52(31), Agricultural Development Committee, interim report, 20 February 1931.
18 CAB 23/66, 16(31)8 and 9, 4 March 1931.
19 CAB 58/2, EAC/12th Mtg, 12 March 1931.
20 CAB 24/220, C.P.–90(31), memorandum by Graham, 10 April 1931; CAB 23/66, 24(31)3, 22 April 1931.
21 CAB 24/220, C.P.–89(31), memorandum by Snowden, 13 April 1931.
22 CAB 23/66, 22(31)8, 23(31)1, 15 April 1931.
23 CAB 58/2, EAC/13th Mtg, 16 April 1931.
24 CAB 23/66, 23(31)8, 15 April 1931.
25 Schröder, 'Die deutsche Südosteuropapolitik', in Becker and Hildebrand, *Internationale Beziehungen*, 346–50; Jacques Bariéty, 'Der Tardieu-Plan zur Sanierung des Donauraums (Februar-Mai 1932), in *ibid.*, 365–68; Jürgen Gehl, *Austria, Germany, and the Anschluss, 1931–1938* (1963), 13–14; F.G. Stambrook, 'The German–Austrian Customs Union Project of 1931: A Study of German Methods and Motives', *Journal of Central European Affairs*, 21/1 (April 1961), 15–44.
26 DBFP, 2nd ser, vol. 2, no. 2, note by Vansittart, 21 March 1931; FO 371/15159, C2216/673/3, Phipps to Henderson, no. 103, 30 March 1931; *ibid.*, C2270/673/3, Rumbold to Henderson, no. 237, 1 April 1931.

27 See for instance, *The Economist*, 28 March 1931, 659; *The Statist*, 28 March 1931, 469; *New Leader*, 3 April 1931, 9.
28 FO 371/15159, C2170/673/3, note by Law Officers of the Crown to the Foreign Secretary, 31 March 1931.
29 FO 371/15160, C2468/673/3, Fountain to Under-Secretary of State, C.R.T. 1665/31, 14 April 1931; *ibid.*, C2482/673/3, Graham to Henderson, 13 April 1931.
30 FO 371/15159, C2274/673/3, Rumbold to Henderson, no. 254, 3 April 1931. See also *ibid.*, C2273/673/3, report by Thelwall in Rumbold to Henderson, no. 253, 3 April 1931; *ibid.*, C2538/673/3, Rumbold to Henderson, no. 271, 13 April 1931.
31 FO 371/15160, C2418/673/3, Phipps to Henderson, no. 125, 8 April 1931.
32 *Ibid.*, C2460/673/3, Sargent memorandum, 14 April 1931.
33 *Ibid.*, C2701/673/3, Noel Baker memorandum, 18 April 1931.
34 *Ibid.*, C2702/673/3, Busk memorandum, 23 April 1931.
35 *Ibid.*, C2631/673/3, Campbell to Vansittart, 19 April 1931.
36 *Ibid.*, C2703/673/3, Sargent memorandum, 22 April 1931. A copy of the original memorandum by Francois-Ponçet is in France, MF, F30/1384, 'Mémoire sur l'Anschluss économique', n.d.
37 FO 371/15160, C2790/673/3, Sargent memorandum, 23 April 1931.
38 *Ibid.*, C2804/673/3, Cadogan minute, 25 April 1931; FO 371/15161, C2922/673/3, Henderson to Rumbold and Phipps, 30 April 1931, Henderson minute, 2 May 1931.
39 CAB 23/66, 22(31)7, 15 April 1931.
40 FO 371/15162, C3223/673/3, Palairet (Bucharest) to Henderson, no. 167, 6 May 1931; *ibid.*, C3260/673/3, Phipps (Vienna) to Henderson, no. 166, 7 May 1931; *ibid.*, C3322/673/3, Chilston (Budapest) to Henderson, no. 85, 9 May 1931; *ibid.*, C3376/673/3, Russell (The Hague), no. 167, 12 May 1931.
41 FO 371/15160, C2706/673/3, Rumbold to Henderson, no. 292, 17 April 1931.
42 FO 371/15676, W4802/3191/50, Waley to Sargent, 27 April 1931. The French record of the conversation is in France, MF, F30/B12657, 'Echanges de vues avec les représentants de la Trésorerie britannique au cours des travaux de la sous-commission européenne', 24 April 1931.
43 FO 371/15161, C2982/673/3, Sargent minute, 30 April 1931.
44 *Ibid.*, C2969/673/3, Drummond to Cadogan, 30 April 1931.
45 *Ibid.*, C2885/673/3, Clutterbuck to Sargent, 30 April 1931.
46 *The Economist*, 24 January 1931, 156, hailed the Oslo Convention as a major event. The six signatory countries, Belgium, Denmark, Luxembourg, the Netherlands, Norway, and Sweden, carried out £1,150 million or 9 per cent of the world's trade. They were 'treading ... the very road on to which Britain has been trying to lead the other nations. Does this not provide a conspicuous opportunity for Britain to throw the whole weight of the influence she still wields ... into the scale of fiscal sanity?... We profoundly hope that our Government is alive to its importance, and is prepared to lend it all the encouragement in its power.'
47 FO 371/15689, W5150/1/98, Board of Trade memorandum to Henderson, C.R.T. 1554/31, 2 May 1931.
48 CAB 24/221, C.P.–115(31), Henderson memorandum, 5 April 1931.
49 CAB 23/67, 27(31)2, 6 May 1931.

50 T188/19, Leith Ross minute, 2 May 1931.
51 France, MF, F30/B12657, Briand to de Fleuriau, nos. 623–40, 30 April 1931; FO 371/15161, C2966/673/3, de Fleuriau memorandum, 4 May 1931.
52 FO 371/15160, C3142/673/3, Leith Ross note, 7 May 1931; France, MF, F30/B12657, Rueff to Flandin, no. 58, 318, 7 May 1931.
53 FO 371/15161, C3180/673/3, Tyrrell to Henderson, no. 534, 7 May 1931.
54 Suarez, *Briand*, vi, 357; FO 371/15161, C3173/673/3, Tyrrell to Henderson, no. 542, 8 May 1931.
55 FO 800/283, Tyrrell to Henderson, 8 May 1931.
56 FO 371/15161, C3183/673/3, Sargent aide mémoire to de Fleuriau, 11 May 1931.
57 FO 371/15162, C3201/673/3, Sargent memorandum, 11 May 1931.
58 France, MF, F30/1394, Bizot memorandum, 'Echanges de vues avec M. Boissard sur le problème du blé et du crédit agricole', 15 February 1931; FO 371/15730, W 6262/4884/98, Waley to A.W.A. Leeper, 28 May 1931.
59 FO 371/15730, W4837/102/98, minutes by A.W.A. Leeper, Cadogan, and others, 29–30 April 1931; *ibid.*, W5688/4884/98, A.W.A. Leeper memorandum, 15 May 1931.
60 *Ibid.*, W5641/4884/98, Henderson to Snowden, no. 26LN, 14 May 1931.
61 *Ibid.*, Vansittart to Henderson, no. 29, 14 May 1931; *ibid.*, Snowden to Henderson, no. 30, 15 May 1931.
62 PREM 1/105, MacDonald minute, 15 May 1931.
63 FO 371/15162, C3404/673/3, Harding to Vansittart, 16 May 1931.
64 PREM 1/105, Thomas to MacDonald, 16 May 1931.
65 PREM 1/106, Vansittart to MacDonald, 20 May 1931; *ibid.*, Vansittart to Selby, 19 May 1931; FO 371/15730, W5383/4884/98, Vansittart to Henderson, no. 36, 18 May 1931.
66 FO 800/284, Henderson to Tyrrell, 16 May 1931.
67 SdN, CEUE/3rd Session/PV 4, 16 May 1931.
68 *Ibid.*, LNC.341.1931, 16 May 1931.
69 *Ibid.*, CEUE/3rd Session/PV 3, 16 May 1931. The French proposals are set out in *ibid.*, LNC.388.M.151.1931, 16 May 1931.
70 FO 371/15162, C3425/673/3, Patteson to Vansittart, no. 39LN, 18 May 1931.
71 SdN, CEUE/3rd Session/PV 5, 19 May 1931.
72 *Ibid.*, CEUE/3rd Session/PV 6, 20 May 1931.
73 *Ibid.*, CEUE/3rd Session/PV 7, 21 May 1931.
74 *Ibid.*, LNC.380.M.156.1931, VII, 22 May 1931; FO 371/15696, W6357/7/98, Leith Ross to Vansittart, 27 May 1931.
75 CAB 24/221, C.P.–125(31), Vansittart memorandum, 14 May 1931.
76 CAB 23/67, 29(31)10, 20 May 1931.

11 The collapse of economic internationalism

1 FO 371/15697, W9109/7/98, Layton to Noel Baker, 15 July 1931.
2 UK, *Report of the Committee on Finance and Industry*, 1931, Cmd. 3987.
3 CAB 58/12, E.A.C.(H.)144, Henderson to MacDonald, 26 June 1931; *ibid.*, Keynes memorandum, 16 July 1931.
4 CAB 23/67, 36(31)3, 1 July 1931; CAB 23/67, 38(31)9, 15 July 1931; CAB 23/67, 40(31)18, 30 July 1931.

5 Hans Kernbauer, 'The Policy of the Austrian National Bank before and during the 1931 Crisis' (unpublished paper presented to the Conference on the 1931 Crisis and its Aftermath, 14–16 April 1982, Clare College, Cambridge), 1.
6 *Ibid.*, 12.
7 France, MF, F30/12657, Rueff to Flandin, 4 June 1931.
8 FRBNY, Austria, C.261.1, J.P. Morgan & Co. to Morgan Grenfell, 31/2208, 19 May 1931; *ibid.*, Norman to Harrison, no. 143/31, 25 May 1931; *ibid.*, Norman to Harrison, no. 152/31, 28 May 1931; BoE, ATM 14/10, Thompson–McCausland memorandum, 7.
9 MGC, 'Private Telegrams no. 50', Morgan Grenfell & Co. to J.P. Morgan & Co., 25 May 1931.
10 FRBNY, Harrison papers, 3115.2, Harrison minute, 18 May 1931; France, MF, F30/B12657, Rueff to Flandin, no. 54,544, 18 June 1931; *ibid.*, Berthelot to de Fleuriau, no. 70,501, 20 June 1931; BoE, OV28/69, Rodd memorandum, 20 June 1931.
11 FRBNY, Harrison–Norman correspondence, Harrison to Stimson, 21 April 1931. Even in June Norman assured Hambros Bank that Germany was still 'a good bet in the long run'. BoE, Norman diary, 10 June 1931.
12 FRUS, 1931, vol. 1, MacDonald to Stimson, no. 177, 8 June 1931; Gosmann, 'Die Stellung der Reparationsfrage', 254–55; Eyck, *A History of the Weimar Republic*, ii, 311.
13 Hardach, 'The 1931 Crisis in Germany', 7; Edward W. Bennett, *Germany and the Diplomacy of the Financial Crisis, 1931* (Cambridge Mass. 1962), 48–49.
14 FRBNY, Harrison papers, 3115.2, Harrison minutes, 15, 18, 20 June 1931. MacDonald claimed to have inspired the Hoover moratorium, although the idea had been in the air for most of the spring: MacDonald diary, PRO 30/69/8/1, 21 June 1931.
15 MacDonald diary, PRO 30/69/8/1, 5 July 1931.
16 FRBNY, Harrison papers, 3115.2, Harrison minutes, 23, 24 June, 9 July 1931.
17 BdeF, CG, 9, 15 July 1931; FRBNY, Harrison papers, 3125.2, Harrison minute, 11 July 1931; Hardach, 'The 1931 Crisis in Germany', 9–10.
18 FRBNY, Harrison papers, 3013.1, Harrison minutes, 14, 21 July 1931. De Fleuriau, the French Ambassador, complained to the Foreign Office that Norman had made it generally known at Basle that in his opinion 'it was much better that there should be complete bankruptcy on the part of Germany as this would raise the whole question of reparations and revision of the Treaty of Versailles, including the Polish Corridor'. FO 371/15187, C5283/172/62, Vansittart minute, 16 July 1931.
19 FO 371/15186, C5115/172/62, Henderson to Newton, no. 759, 13 July 1931.
20 FO 371/15183, C4553/172/62, Lindsay to Henderson, no. 374, 28 June 1931; CAB 23/67, 36(31)2, 1 July 1931; FO 371/15185, C4860/172/62, Foreign Office to Tyrrell, no. 178, 7 July 1931.
21 Henderson is credited with playing a maverick role during his visit to Paris which 'has probably no parallel in the history of British foreign policy', Carlton, *MacDonald versus Henderson*, 222. MacDonald credited himself with another diplomatic coup by drawing the foreign statesmen to London.

'It was a risky throw, but it has come off'. MacDonald diary, PRO 30/69/8/1, 19 July 1931.

22 FRBNY, Harrison papers, 2013.1, Harrison minutes, 17, 21 July 1931; FRUS, 1931, vol. 1, Stimson memoranda, 15, 17 July 1931. On the 'incoherence' of the American policy towards the inter-governmental debt issue at this time, see Franz Knipping, 'Der Anfang vom Ende der Reparationen: Die Einberufung des Beratenden Sonderausschusses im November 1931', *Internationaler Beziehungen in der Weltwirtschaftskrise 1929–1933*, eds. Josef Becker and Klaus Hildebrand (Munich, 1980), 235–36.

23 RA, G.V. M2329/2, Wigram to King, 11 July 1931.

24 Sterling had however fallen to a discount on the forward exchange markets elsewhere in Europe, a reflection no doubt of nervousness at the large but indeterminate sterling commitments in Austria and Germany. Clarke, *Central Bank Cooperation*, 202; 'City News', *The Times*, 13, 14 July 1931.

25 BdeF, CG, 23 July, 21 September, 5 December 1931. French Treasury balances are set out in France, MF, F30/897, Rueff to Ministry, various dates. See also FRUS, 1931, vol. 1, Atherton to Castle, 24 July 1931; MGC, bundle 55, Pesson-Didier to J.P. Morgan & Co., no. 87570, 14 July 1931.

26 BdeF, CG, 18 July 1931.

27 Lord Tyrrell undertook a personal investigation shortly after the run on sterling began, from which he concluded that Paris had not been a major seller of sterling, and what selling had occurred was motivated chiefly by the desire of French banks to increase their liquidity. FO 371/15187, C5298/172/62, Tyrrell to Vansittart, no. 174, 16 July 1931. But such was the suspicion of French financial manipulation within the Cabinet that Tom Johnston went to Paris in August to confront French Ministers with the allegations. Flandin and Laval strenuously denied them. Johnston, *The Financiers and the Nation* (1939), 198. See also RA, G.V. M1329/10, Wigram to Rumbold, 3 August 1931; Boyle, *Montagu Norman*, 263. Much of the misunderstanding arose because British critics wilfully refused to distinguish official French balances from commercial balances, on the wholly unfounded assumption that the latter were manipulated at will by French officials. Thus, in a droll exchange, the 'socialist' MacDonald assured an approving Stimson that so long as he was Prime Minister British capitalism would remain pure and untainted by the political interference that occurred in France. FRUS, 1931, vol. 1, Stimson memorandum, 31 July 1931.

28 On continental withdrawals see Willard Hurst, 'Holland, Switzerland and Belgium and the English Gold Crisis of 1931', *Journal of Political Economy*, 40/5 (October 1932), 638. D.E. Moggridge, 'The 1931 Financial Crisis – a New View', *The Banker*, August 1970, 832–39, advances the view that the decline in the balance of payments is enough to explain why sterling was forced off the gold standard. In fact, the weakness of the balance of payments had been the subject of anxious comment early in 1931 (see for instance the *Financial Times*, 26 February 1931, and the *Empire Review*, April 1931, 415), and became the most widely accepted explanation of sterling weakness in the two weeks preceding the collapse of the gold standard. Hot money movements were nonetheless important. Suffice it to note that throughout the first six months of 1931 the balance of payments was declining while sterling reserves were rising.

29 BoE, Norman diary, 5 February 1931. Not long afterwards Norman informed Harrison that investors were 'alarmed' at the state of Britain's public finances and had made 'large transfers of funds from England to America'. FRBNY, Harrison–Norman correspondence, Harrison to Stimson, 21 April 1931. See also BdeF, CG, 13 August 1931; MGC, Bundle 223, J.P. Morgan & Co. to Morgan Grenfell & Co., no. 31/2491, 29 September 1931; FRBNY, Bank of England Credit 1931, C261.1, George J. Seay to Harrison, 27 August 1931; Dalton diary, 20 August 1931.
30 October 1931, 492.
31 Dalton diary, 16–17 July, 28 August 1931.
32 FRUS, 1931, vol. 1, Stimson memorandum, 31 July 1931; MacDonald papers, PRO 30/69/6/34, MacDonald to Robert Lowy, 14 October 1931; T188/21, Leith Ross memorandum, 13 August 1931; FO 371/15188, C5432/172/62, Henderson memorandum, 20 July 1931.
33 Cmd. 3987, 112–13. Clay, *Lord Norman*, 396, explains why the figures published in the Macmillan Report exaggerated London's liquidity problem. See also BdeF, CG, 16 July 1931, where Moret linked sterling's weakness to the City's over-commitment in Germany.
34 CAB 29/136, minutes of the London conference, 1931.
35 MacDonald diary, PRO 30/69/8/1, 22 July 1931.
36 FO 371/15189, C5610/172/62, Foreign Office memorandum, 22 July 1931.
37 CAB 29/136, London conference, 4th meeting, 23 July 1931.
38 T175/51, Hopkins to Snowden, 24 July 1931.
39 MGC, bundle 'German Crisis 1931', J.P. Morgan to J.P. Morgan & Co., 29 July 1931.
40 Morton, *British Finance, 1930–1940*, 33–36.
41 Brown, *The Gold Standard Reinterpreted*, ii, 1046.
42 Addis diary, 18 July 1931. Years later Sir Robert Brand described his efforts to arrange the Standstill agreement as if it was a selfless act, although it almost certainly saved his firm Lazard Brothers and himself from bankruptcy. Brand, 'A Banker's Reflections on Some Economic Trends', *Economic Journal*, 63/252 (December 1953), 765.
43 Addis diary, 17 July 1931.
44 Sweet Escott, 'Gallant Failure', 56. Paul Reynaud, the right-wing deputy who represented the financial district of Paris, asked the British Commercial Attaché if it was not true that Baring Brothers was on the brink of collapse. FO 371/15190, C5667/172/62, Cahill to Selby, 20 July 1931. French Treasury officials subsequently heard from a representative of Mendelssohns that 'Germany was ruined and that Schroeders, Barings, and other London houses would have to close their doors'. T188/21, Leith Ross minute, 13 August 1931. Sir Edward Grenfell wrote to Thomas Lamont that the assets of British acceptance houses tied up in Germany were 'a good deal less than I anticipated'; but were still 'unpleasantly large' and a threat to the solvency of many of them. TWL, 111–23, Grenfell to Lamont, 18 July 1931. However, the magnitude of British commitments was not fully known at the time. A qualified British observer wrote, 'The Accepting Houses, which constitute the major part of the Court of the Bank of England, are many of them more or less insolvent'. MacDonald papers, PRO 30/69/1/260, Keynes to MacDonald, 5 August 1931.
45 BoE, ATM 14/10, Thompson–McCausland memorandum, 11–12.

46 HC Deb., 5s., 255, col. 2514.
47 UK, *Committee on National Expenditure Report, 1931*, Cmd. 3920.
48 FRBNY, Harrison papers, 3125.2, Harrison minute, 8 August 1931. Siepmann similarly explained to Moret that 'it appeared necessary to them to give a serious warning to the government and to the public'. This in plain language is of course 'the extra-constitutional veto of a financial confidence crisis' that Lord Balogh described (see 378 n 51), or as it was known in 1931, a 'bankers' ramp'.
49 BdeF, CG, 27, 30 July, 5 August, 4 September 1931; T160/444, F12901, Lefaux (Bank of England) memorandum, n.d.; *Financial Times*, 6 August 1931; *News Chronicle*, 6, 7 August 1931; *Financial News*, 6 August 1931.
50 BoE, ATM 14/10, Thompson–McCausland memorandum, 17–18; FRBNY, Harrison papers, 3125.2, Harrison minutes, 8 August 1931.
51 MacDonald papers, PRO 30/69/1/260, Harvey to Snowden, 6 August 1931.
52 FRBNY, Harrison papers, 3125.2, minutes of Harrison–Lacour Gayet conversations, 6, 7 August 1931; Clarke, *Central Bank Cooperation*, 210.
53 FRBNY, Harrison papers, 3125.2, minutes of Harrison–Lacour Gayet conversations, 6, 7 August 1931.
54 T160/431, F12414/01/1, Layton to Snowden, 11 August 1931.
55 T188/21, Leith Ross memorandum, 13 August 1931.
56 MacDonald papers, PRO 30/69/1/260, Snowden to MacDonald, 7 August 1931.
57 BoE, ATM 14/10 Thompson–McCausland memorandum, 20–21.
58 PRO 30/69/8/1, MacDonald diary, 11 August 1931; Samuel papers, A/78.3, Samuel to Lloyd George and others, 15 August 1931; BoE, ATM 14/10, Thompson–McCausland memorandum, 24.
59 Amery diary, 4 July 1931. On Seely's activities see also Stevenson, *Lloyd George, a diary*, 18 February 1934.
60 Empire Economic Union, 'Report of a Joint Committee on Agricultural Policy', May 1931.
61 Amery diary, 15 August 1931; Beaverbrook papers, BBK C6, Amery to Beaverbrook, 26 August 1931.
62 Feiling, *Neville Chamberlain*, 191; Swinton papers, 174/2/1, Lloyd to Cunliffe-Lister, 14 August 1931.
63 Gwynne papers, 17, Neville Chamberlain to Gwynne, 13 August 1931.
64 RA, G.V. M2329/2, Wigram to King, 11 July 1931; *ibid.*, M2329/10, Wigram to Rumbold, 3 August 1931; Wrench, *Geoffrey Dawson and Our Times*, 291.
65 BoE, ATM 14/10, Thompson–McCausland memorandum, 21, 22.
66 MacDonald diary, PRO 30/69/8/1, 17 August 1931; CAB 23/67, 41(31), 19 August 1931; Dalton diary, 20 August 1931.
67 Barbara C. Malament, 'Philip Snowden and the Cabinet Deliberations of August 1931', *Society for the Study of Labour History Bulletin*, 41 (Autumn 1980), 31.
68 CAB 23/67, 41(31), 19 August 1931.
69 CAB 23/67, 42(31)2, 20 August 1931; Dalton diary, 20 August 1931; RA, G.V. K2330(1)14, Wigram–Duff conversation, 20 August 1931.
70 Dalton diary, 27 August 1931.
71 Sir Bernard Mallet and C. Oswald George, *British Budgets, third series, 1921–22 to 1932–33* (1933), table iii, 558–59.

72 Neville Chamberlain papers, 1/26/446, Neville to Hilda Chamberlain, 21 August 1931.
73 Labour Party, E.C. vol. 60, 240; Lord Citrine, *Men and Work* (1964), 281.
74 CAB 23/67, 42(31)2, 20 August 1931.
75 Citrine affirmed that it was he who proposed the recommendation of a revenue tariff during the private deliberations of the TUC leaders. Bevin at the last moment had second thoughts, but Citrine was sure the proposal would be approved by their conference and put it to Ministers when they met again that evening. Citrine papers, 7/4, notes on 'Ernest Bevin' by Francis Williams, 7 November 1952.
76 MacDonald diary, PRO 30/69/8/1, 21 August 1931.
77 CAB 23/67, 43(31)1, 21 August 1931.
78 *Ibid.*
79 CAB 23/67, 44(31)1, 22 August 1931; BoE, ATM 14/10, Thompson–McCausland memorandum, 29.
80 Samuel papers, A/78.7, memorandum, 23 August 1931; MacDonald diary, PRO 30/69/8/1, 22 August 1931.
81 CAB 23/67, 44(31)1, 22 August 1931.
82 CAB 23/67, 45(31), 22 August 1931.
83 Neville Chamberlain diary, 2/22, 22 August 1931.
84 Wrench, *Geoffrey Dawson and Our Times*, 291.
85 RA, G.V. K2330(1)6, Peacock to Wigram, 23 August 1931.
86 MacDonald diary, PRO 30/69/8/1, 23 August 1931.
87 MGC., bundle 'Gold Standard 1931', diary of events, 23 August 1931; BoE, ATM 14/10, Thompson–McCausland memorandum, 35; FRBNY, Harrison papers, 3115.2, memorandum, 24 August 1931.
88 *Daily Mail*, 24 August 1931.
89 FRBNY, Harrison papers, 3115.2, minute and memorandum, 24 August 1931.
90 MGC, bundle 'Gold Standard 1931', diary of events, 23 August 1931; CAB 23/67, 46(31)1, 23 August 1931.
91 MGC, bundle 'Gold Standard 1931', diary of events, 23 August 1931; BoE, ATM 14/10, Thompson–McCausland memorandum, 37.
92 CAB 23/67, 46(31)1, 23 August 1931; Dalton diary, 27 August 1931, 3 November 1931; Malament, 'Philip Snowden and the Cabinet Deliberations of August 1931', 32.
93 CAB 23/67, 46(31)1, 23 August 1931.
94 BoE, ATM 14/10, Thompson–McCausland memorandum, 37; MGC, bundle 'Gold Standard 1931', diary of events, 23 August 1931. Peacock later declared that the crisis had not been mentioned over dinner, and that instead, like two farmers at a cattle sale, he and the King had spent their time discussing grain prices. Norman Rose, *George V* (1983), 375. This may be so, but it is worth noting that Peacock could not remember the presence of a second guest, Wigram, and it seems almost inconceivable that the three did not discuss the crisis at some stage in the evening, especially as Peacock himself was almost desperate for the King to intervene.
95 BoE, ATM 14/10, Thompson–McCausland memorandum, 37.
96 Samuel papers, A/78. 11a, memorandum, 24 August 1931.
97 FRBNY, Harrison papers, 3115.2, Harrison to Harvey, no. 307/31, 24 August 1931; PREM 1/97, daily reports from Comptroller of Bank of

England to Duff, July–September 1931. Addis diary, 24 August 1931, records the figure as £10 million for the day.

98 Leith Ross, *Money Talks*, 138; FO 371/15679, W10,007/9770/50, Campbell to A.W.A. Leeper, 1 September 1931. Failure to keep the French informed of the true financial position was probably once again the source of British difficulties.

99 TWL, 110–12, Carter to Lamont, 31 August 1931.

100 FO 371/15679, W9994/9770/50, Campbell to Vansittart, 28 August 1931; CAB 24/223, C.P.–230(31), Snowden memorandum, 15 September 1931; MGC, bundle 'Gold Standard 1931', diary of events, 25–28 August 1931.

101 CAB 23/68, 53(31), 3 September 1931.

102 Snowden, *An Autobiography*, ii, 967; HC Deb. 5s., 256, cols. 302–03.

103 FO 800/226, Reading to MacDonald, 10 September 1931; CAB 27/462, F.S.C.(31), 1st Mtg., 14 September 1931.

104 MGC, bundle 'Gold Standard 1931', diary of events, 31 August 1931; MacDonald papers, PRO 30/69/1/260, Rowe, Swann & Co. circular, 3 September 1931; RA, G.V. K2330(2)/76, Peacock to Wigram, 11 September 1931; PRO 30/69/5/180, MacDonald to King, 14 September 1931; France, MF, F30/930, Rueff to Flandin, no. 59, 056, 20 September 1931. Two weeks after Harvey's statement to Ministers, Siepmann acknowledged to French bankers that 'losses of foreign balances were being augmented by an export of national capital'. BdeF, CG, 22 September 1931.

105 *The Times*, 27, 28 August 1931; *Daily Mail*, 28 August 1931; HC Deb. 5s., 256, cols. 44, 111; TUC, *Proceedings of the 63rd Annual Trades Union Congress*, 1931, 399.

106 HC Deb. 5s., 256, cols. 331, 726, 729–30.

107 FBI/C/65, Empire Currency Committee, first meeting, 2 July 1931.

108 *The Times*, Amery letter, 23 July 1931, Horne letter, 24 July 1931, Dampier letter, 28 July 1931, Wardlaw-Milne, Boothby, and others, 29 July 1931; *Financial Times*, 25 July 1931; *Daily Herald*, 4 August 1931; *Evening Standard*, 20 August 1931; FBI/EA/Glenday/4, Barnby to Glenday, 31 August, Glenday to Barnby, 7 September, Gull to Locock, 14 September 1931.

109 FBI/EA/Glenday/4, Jenkins to Butler, 12 August, Glenday to Butler, 18 August 1931.

110 MacDonald papers, PRO 30/69/1/260, Keynes to MacDonald, 5 August 1931. Keynes subsequently wobbled, and encouraged MacDonald to try to save the pound by severe deflation. *Ibid.*, Keynes to MacDonald, 12 August 1931.

111 FRBNY, C.261.1, Austria, Crane memorandum, 16 September 1931.

112 CAB 23/68, 53(31)1, 3 September 1931. MacDonald, only too well aware of the influence of the Crown among Labour supporters, had proposed the gesture, RA, G.V. K2330(1)/2, MacDonald to Wigram, 19 August 1931.

113 Eric Estorick, *Sir Stafford Cripps* (1949), 98.

114 *The Scotsman*, 12 September 1931. See also MacDonald's statement in HC Deb. 5s., 256, col. 21; and *Liberal Magazine*, September 1931, 391.

115 HC Deb. 5s., 256, cols. 333, 363.

116 See for example, CAB 21/350, Sir Eric Geddes (chairman, Dunlop Rubber Co.) to employees, 14 September 1931.

117 Hankey diary, 1/7, 9 September 1931; MacDonald papers, PRO

30/69/5/180, D'Abernon to MacDonald, 9, 12 September 1931; *New Statesman and Nation*, 19 September 1931, 354.
118 FO 371/15195, C6784/172/62, Hopkins memorandum, 28 August 1931; CAB 27/462, F.S.C.(31) 2nd meeting, 17 September 1931, Leith Ross statement to Ministers.
119 T188/21, Leith Ross memorandum, 1 September 1931.
120 Baldwin papers, 44, MacDonald to Baldwin, 5 September 1931; MacDonald papers, PRO 30/69/2/11 Pt. 1, MacDonald to Stimson, 15 September 1931.
121 FO 371/15187, C5176/172/62, Vansittart minute, 12 August 1931; FO 371/15195, C6784/172/62, Sargent minute, 29 August, Vansittart minute, 31 August 1931.
122 HC Deb. 5s., 256, cols. 386, 407, 787.
123 PREM 1/97, Comptroller of Bank of England to Duff, daily reports, September 1931. Snowden later claimed that 'The Budget had the immediate effect of restoring confidence abroad. For some days after its introduction the withdrawals of foreign deposits from London fell sharply.' *An Autobiography*, ii, 976. This was wishful thinking.
124 Alan Ereira, *The Invergordon Mutiny. A Narrative History of the last great Mutiny in the Royal Navy and how it forced Britain off the Gold Standard* (1981), gives an excellent account of the event but attributes too much to it in claiming that it forced Britain off the gold standard.
125 CAB 27/462, F.S.C.(31), 2nd meeting, 17 September 1931.
126 MGC, bundle 'Gold Standard 1931', diary of events, 14–21 September 1931.
127 CAB 27/462, F.S.C.(31), 1st meeting, 14 September 1931.
128 CAB 27/462, F.S.C.(31), 2nd meeting, 17 September 1931.
129 MGC, bundle 223, Morgan Grenfell & Co. to J.P. Morgan & Co., no. 31/5012, 20 September 1931.
130 CAB 27/462, F.S.C.(31)2, note by Treasury, 12 September 1931. The government's American financial advisers were not so discouraging: MGC, bundle 223, J.P. Morgan & Co. to Morgan Grenfell & Co., no. 31/2491, 29 September 1931.
131 CAB 27/462, F.S.C.(31), 2nd meeting, 17 September 1931.
132 CAB 23/68, 59(31), 17 September 1931.
133 PREM 1/97, MacDonald to Stimson, 18 September 1931; T188/286, Snowden to Flandin, 18 September 1931.
134 MacDonald diary, PRO 30/69/8/1; 18 September 1931; PREM 1/97, note of a meeting between MacDonald, Harvey, and Peacock, 18 September 1931.
135 T188/286, Osborne to MacDonald, no. 577, 19 September 1931.
136 FO 371/15681, W11646/10755/50, Osborne to Reading, no. 1495, 25 September 1931.
137 FO 371/15681, W11075/10755/50, Campbell to Reading, no. 1024, 22 September 1931; T188/286, Leith Ross to Hopkins and Waley, 23 September 1931.
138 FRBNY, Harrison papers, 3117.1, Harrison minute, 19 September 1931; MGC, bundle 223, J.P. Morgan & Co. to Morgan Grenfell & Co., no. 31/2454, 19 September 1931; *ibid.*, no. 31/2461, 20 September 1931.
139 PREM 1/97, F.S.C.(31), 3rd mtg., 19 September 1931.

140 Leith Ross, *Money Talks*, 140; *New Statesman and Nation*, 19 September 1931, 329; CAB 58/18, E.A.C.(EI)4, J.M. Keynes, 'The Balance of International Payments, Draft Report', 21 September 1931.
141 Beaverbrook papers, C/27, Baxter (enclosure) to Beaverbrook, 30 April 1934.
142 FO 800/226, J.H. Thomas letter, 19 September 1931.
143 PREM 1/97, Fisher to Snowden and MacDonald, 20 September 1931.
144 MGC, bundle 'Gold Standard 1931', diary of events, 20 September 1931; TWL, 96/14, Egan to Lamont, 19 September 1931.
145 FO 371/15681, W11075/10755/50, Campbell to Reading, no. 1024, 22 September 1931; BdeF, CG, 24 September 1931.
146 FO 371/15680, W10767/10755/50, Campbell to Foreign Office, no. 216, 21 September 1931.
147 CAB 23/68, 60(31), 20 September 1931; PREM 1/97, F.S.C.(31), 3rd mtg., Hankey statement, 19 September 1931.
148 BoE, ATM 14/10, Thompson–McCausland memorandum, 39f.
149 MGC, bundle 'Gold Standard 1931', diary of events, 21 September 1931.
150 HC Deb. 5s., 256, cols. 1291–99.
151 PREM 1/97, notes of a meeting between MacDonald, Harvey, and Peacock, 18 September 1931; T172/1746, H.D. Henderson, 'The Balance of Payments', 18 September 1931.
152 PREM 1/97, notes of a meeting between MacDonald, Harvey, and Peacock, 18 September 1931.
153 FO 371/15195, C6974/172/62, Law to O'Malley, 9 September 1931.
154 Beaverbrook papers, C/27, Baxter (enclosure) to Beaverbrook, 30 April 1934.
155 Dalton, *Call Back Yesterday*, i, 290.
156 LN, *Official Journal*, 12th Assembly, Work of the Second Committee, 23 September 1931, 60–66; Cecil papers, 51,082, Cecil to Reading, 21 September 1931; Cecil papers, 51,107, Cecil to Noel Baker, 25 September 1931.
157 Phipps papers, vol. 1, 2/21, Mendl to Phipps, 20 November 1931.
158 FO 800/226, Selby to Vansittart, 2 October 1931; France, MF, F30/12625, de Fleuriau to Briand, no. 581, 18 November 1931.
159 Samuel papers, A81.3, memorandum, 24 September 1931; League of Nations Union, II, 11, minutes of Executive Committee, 181, 25 September 1931; Labour Party, 'Labour and the Crisis', by Arthur Henderson (1931); ABCC, MS. 14476/12, minutes of Executive Council, 7 October 1931.
160 T160/403, F12666, Leith Ross to Rowe-Dutton, 12 October 1931; MacDonald papers, PRO 30/69/1/5 iii, Stimson to MacDonald, 25 September 1931.
161 Dalton diary, 30 September 1931.
162 CAB 58/18, E.A.C.(EI)4, Keynes memorandum, 21 September 1931; CAB 24/233, C.P.–243(31), Samuel memorandum, 24 September 1931.
163 *The Times*, 25 September 1931; Dalton diary, 12 October 1931; Hargrave, *Professor Skinner*, 190; Jones, *Georgian Afternoon*, 163. MacDonald, who had repeatedly produced worthless German banknotes in order to frighten voters from the Labour Party, later accused the trade unions of unfair tactics. 'The intimidation by the Trade Unions was indescribable, but he hoped he had smashed forever Trade Union tyranny in the North East of

England and he meant to do all he could to smash it all over England.' RA, G.V., K2331(1)/46, Wigram memorandum, 28 October 1931.
164 HC Deb. 5s., 260, col. 1420.
165 *Ibid.*, 260, col. 1539.
166 *Ibid.*, 257, col. 979.
167 *Ibid.*, 261, col. 288.
168 *Ibid.*, 264, col. 1425.

Conclusion

1 Boyle, *Montagu Norman*, 268–69, 277.
2 T175/57, Pt. 1, Hopkins minute, 16 February 1932; Sayers, *The Bank of England*, 1, 448.
3 The most detailed and influential study is Keith Middlemas, *Politics in Industrial Society. The Experience of the British System since 1911* (1979), but see also the criticism of the literature in Leo Panitch, 'Recent theorizations of corporatism: reflections on a growth industry', *British Journal of Sociology*, 31/2 (June 1980).

Bibliography

MANUSCRIPT SOURCES

Individuals

Sir Charles Addis papers (School of Oriental and African Studies, University of London)
1st Viscount Addison (Christopher Addison) papers (Bodleian Library, Oxford)
Leopold S. Amery papers (private hands, London)
1st Earl Baldwin (Stanley Baldwin) papers (Cambridge University Library)
1st Baron Beaverbrook (William Maxwell Aitken) papers (House of Lords Record Office)
George Blumenfeld papers (House of Lords Record Office)
Andrew Bonar Law papers (House of Lords Record Office)
1st Baron Brand (Robert H. Brand) papers (Bodleian Library, Oxford)
1st Viscount Bridgeman of Leigh (William Clive Bridgeman) papers (Churchill College, Cambridge)
Viscount Cecil of Chelwood (Lord Robert Cecil) papers (British Library, Add. Mss.)
Arthur Neville Chamberlain papers (University Library, Birmingham)
Sir Austen Chamberlain papers (University Library, Birmingham)
Sir Sydney Chapman papers (British Library of Political and Economic Science)
1st Baron Citrine (Walter MacLennan Citrine) papers (British Library of Political and Economic Science)
1st Baron Croft (Henry Page Croft) papers (Churchill College, Cambridge)
1st Viscount D'Abernon (Edgar D'Abernon) papers (British Library, Add. Mss.)
1st Lord Dalton (Hugh Dalton) papers (British Library of Political and Economic Science)
1st Viscount Davidson (J.C.C. Davidson) papers (House of Lords Record Office)
Geoffrey Dawson papers (Bodleian Library, Oxford)
King George V papers (Royal Archives, Windsor)
1st Earl Lloyd George (David Lloyd George) papers (House of Lords Record Office)
Sir Percy James Grigg papers (Churchill College, Cambridge)
H.A. Gwynne papers (Bodleian Library, Oxford)

1st Baron Hankey (Maurice P.A. Hankey) papers (Churchill College, Cambridge)
Sir Patrick Joseph Henry Hannon papers (House of Lords Record Office)
George Harrison papers (Federal Reserve Bank of New York)
Sir Ralph Hawtrey papers (Public Record Office, Kew)
Arthur Henderson papers (Public Record Office, Kew)
Sir Richard Valentine Nind Hopkins papers (Public Record Office, Kew)
Per Jacobsson diary (British Library of Political and Economic Science)
1st Baron Kennet (Edward Hilton Young) papers (Cambridge University Library)
Thomas W. Lamont papers (Baker Library, Harvard Business School, Cambridge Mass.)
George Lansbury papers (British Library of Political and Economic Science)
Sir Frederick Leith Ross papers (Public Record Office, Kew)
Edward Mayow Hastings Lloyd papers (British Library of Political and Economic Science)
James Ramsay MacDonald papers (Public Record Office, Kew)
1st Baron Melchett (Alfred Moritz Mond) papers (private hands, Norfolk)
Sir Otto Ernst Niemeyer papers (Public Record Office, Kew; Bank of England)
1st Baron Norman of St Clere (Montagu Norman) diary (Bank of England)
1st Baron Passfield (Sidney James Webb) papers (British Library of Political and Economic Science)
Sir Frederick Phillips papers (Public Record Office, Kew)
Sir Eric Phipps papers (Churchill College, Cambridge)
1st Baron Ponsonby of Shulbrede (Arthur Ponsonby) papers (Bodleian Library, Oxford)
1st Marquess of Reading (Rufus Isaacs) papers (House of Lords Record Office)
1st Viscount Runciman of Doxford (Walter Runciman) papers (University of Newcastle Library)
Sir Arthur Salter papers (League of Nations Archives, Geneva)
1st Viscount Samuel (Herbert Samuel) papers (House of Lords Record Office)
1st Viscount Sankey (John Sankey) papers (Bodleian Library, Oxford)
Sir Orme Sargent papers (Churchill College, Cambridge)
1st Baron Stamp of Shortlands (Josiah Stamp) papers (private hands, London)
Benjamin Strong papers (Federal Reserve Bank of New York)
Bickham Sweet-Escott papers (British Library of Political and Economic Science)
1st Earl of Swinton (Philip Cunliffe-Lister) papers (Churchill College, Cambridge)
J.H. Thomas papers (Kent County Record Office)
Beatrice Webb diary (British Library of Political and Economic Science)
1st Viscount Weir (William Douglas Weir) papers (Churchill College, Cambridge)
Sir Laming Worthington-Evans papers (Bodleian Library, Oxford)
Owen D. Young papers (Van Hornesville, NY)

Institutions

Association of British Chambers of Commerce (Guildhall Library, London)
Bank of England
Bank of France

Baring Brothers & Co. Ltd.
Empire Industries Association (Modern Records Centre, University of Warwick Library)
Federal Reserve Bank of New York
Federation of British Industries (Modern Records Centre, University of Warwick Library)
France, Ministère des Affaires Etrangères; Ministère de Commerce; Ministère des Finances
Independent Labour Party (British Library of Political and Economic Science)
Iron and Steel Trades Confederation (Modern Records Centre, University of Warwick Library)
Labour Party
League of Nations (United Nations Archives, Geneva)
League of Nations Union (British Library of Political and Economic Science)
London Chamber of Commerce (Guildhall Library, London)
Morgan Grenfell & Co. Ltd.
National Union of Manufacturers (Modern Records Centre, University of Warwick Library)
Trades Union Congress
United Kingdom: Cabinet; Premier; Foreign Office; Treasury; Board of Trade; Ministry of Agriculture and Fisheries; Dominions and Colonial Office

PRINTED SOURCES

Official publications

Belgium. *Documents diplomatiques belges, 1920–1940*, tome ii, ed. Charles Visscher et Fernand Vanlangenhove (Bruxelles, 1964)
France. *Journal Officiel de la Republique Française*, Débats Parlementaires.
Documents diplomatiques français, 1932–(Paris, 1972-)
Germany. *Akten zur deutschen auswärtigen Politik 1918–1945*, Series B, Band I–XI (Göttingen, 1966-)
League of Nations. *Official Journal*, 1920–32.
International Economic Conference. Tariff Level Indices. L.N.1927.II.34.
Report and Proceedings of the World Economic Conference held at Geneva, May 4th to 23rd, 1927. 2 vols. L.N.II.52.1–2.
World Economic Conference. 27.II.50 (Geneva, 1927).
The World Economic Conference, Geneva, May 1927, Final Report. L.N.1927.
International Convention for the Abolition of Import and Export Prohibitions and Restrictions, 8 November 1927. C.559.M.20.1.II (C.I.A.P. 19(1) 1927).
International Convention for the Abolition of Import and Export Prohibitions and Restrictions, Supplementary Agreement, 11 July 1928. C.13.M.10.1929.II.(C.I.A.P.33(2).).
Report of the Economic Consultative Committee on its First Session, 14–19 May 1928. C.217.M.73.1928.II.
Report of the Financial Committee, 18 December 1928. C.613.M.190.1928.II.
Report of the Consultative Committee on the Application of the Recommen-

dations of the International Economic Conference, 1 April 1929. C.130.M.45.1929.II.
Third International Conference for the Abolition of Import and Export Prohibitions and Restrictions. Proceedings of the Conference. C.176.M.81.1931.II.
Preliminary Conference of Governments as Proposed in Section 2 of the Resolution on the Economic Work of the League adopted by the Tenth Assembly. C.26.M.7.1930.II., 7 January 1930.
Commercial Convention, Protocol, and Final Act, C.203.M.96.1930.II., 15 April 1930.
Proceedings of the Preliminary Conference with a view to Concerted Economic Action, 17 February – 24 March 1930, C.222.M.109.1930.II., 22 April 1930.
Assembly Resolutions regarding the Economic Work of the League of Nations. Report by the Representative of Germany. L.N.C.578.1930.II., 1 October 1930.
Proceedings of the Second International Conference with a view to Concerted Economic Action (1st session), Geneva, November 17 – 28, 1930. C.149.M.48.1931.II.B.
Provisional Minutes of Meetings of the Second Session of the Commission of Enquiry for European Union, Geneva, 16–20 January, 1931. C.E.U.E./2nd Session/P.V.1–6.
Note by the Secretary-General. Resolutions Adopted at the Second Session of the Commission (January 16th – 21st, 1931), 22 January 1931. C.114.M.41.1931, C.114.M.41.1931.VII.C.E.U.E.12.
Proceedings of the Second International Conference with a view to Concerted Economic Action (2nd session), Geneva, March 16–18, 1931. C.269.M.124.1931.II.B.
Provisional Meetings of the Third Session of the Commission of Enquiry for European Union, 16–21 May, 1931, C.E.U.E./3rd session/P.V.1–7.
The French Plan. C.338.M.151. Geneva, 16 May 1931.
Balance of Payments, 1930. L.N.1932.II.A.26 (Geneva, 1932).
Commercial Policy in the Interwar Period: International Proposals and National Policies. L.N.II.1942.II.A.6. (Geneva, 1943).
Quantitative Trade Controls. Their Causes and Nature, by Gottfried Haeberler and Martin Hill. L.N.II.1943.A.5. (Geneva, 1943).
The International Currency Experience. Lessons of the Interwar Period, by Ragnar Nurkse. L.N.II.1944.A.4. (Princeton NJ, 1944).

United Kingdom. Parliamentary Papers, 1916. Recommendations of the Economic Conference of the Allies. Cd. 8271
1918. Final Report of the Committee on Commercial and Industrial Policy after the War. Cd. 9035.
1918. Committee on Financial Facilities, Report. Cd. 9227.
1919. Committee on Currency and Foreign Exchanges after the War, First Interim Report. Cd. 9182.
1922. Reparation. Agreement between the Allies for the Settlement of Certain Questions as to the Application of the Treaties of Peace and Complementary Agreements with Germany, Austria, Hungary and Bulgaria, Signed at Spa, July 16, 1922. Cmd. 1615.
1922. International Economic Conference, Genoa. Resolutions of the Finan-

cial Commission recommending certain Resolutions for Adoption by the Conference. Cmd. 1650.
1922. Papers Relating to the International Economic Conference, Geneva, April – May 1922. Cmd. 1667.
Dispatch to the Representatives of France, Italy, Serb-Croat-Slovene State, Roumania, Portugal and Greece at London respecting War Debts. Cmd. 1737.
1924. Imperial Economic Conference. Record of Proceedings and Documents. Cmd. 2009.
1924. Reports of the Expert Committees appointed by the Reparation Commission. Cmd. 2105.
1924–25. Report of the Committee on the Currency and Bank of England Note Issues. Cmd. 2393.
1924–25. Court of Inquiry concerning the Coal Mining Dispute, Report. Cmd. 2478.
1925. Safeguarding of Industries, Procedures and Enquiries. Cmd. 2327.
1928–29. Memoranda on Certain Proposals Relating to Unemployment. Cmd. 3331.
1929–30. Report of the Committee of Experts on Reparations. Cmd. 3343.
1929–30. International Convention for the Abolition of Import and Export Prohibitions, with Supplementary and Protocol. Cmd. 3502.
1929–30. Dispatch to His Majesty's Ambassador in Paris enclosing the Memorandum of the French Government on the Organisation of a System of European Federal Union, 28 May 1930. Cmd. 3595.
1930–31. Report of the Committee on Finance and Industry. Cmd. 3987.
1930–31. Committee on National Expenditure, Report. Cmd. 3920.
1931. Committee on Finance and Industry, Minutes of Evidence, 2 vols.
1932. Statistical Abstract for the United Kingdom. Cmd. 3991.
Board of Trade Journal, 1919–.
Board of Trade, 1925. Committee on Industry and Trade. *Survey of Overseas Markets.*
Board of Trade, 1928. Report on Economic Conditions of France in 1928, by Robert Cahill.
House of Commons Debates, 5th series.
House of Lords Debates.
1926. Royal Commission on Indian Currency and Finance, vol. 3, appendices, vol. v. minutes of evidence.
United States. Bureau of the Census, *Historical Statistics of the United States, Colonial Times to 1957* (Washington DC, 1960).
Department of Commerce. *The United States in the World Economy. The International Transactions of the United States during the Interwar Period,* by Hal B. Lary (Washington, DC, 1943).
State Department, *Foreign Relations of the United States.*

Newspapers
Daily Express
Daily Herald
Daily Mail
Daily Telegraph
Evening Standard

Financial News
Financial Times
Journée Industrielle
Manchester Guardian
Morning Post
News Chronicle
The Observer
Sunday Express
Sunday Times
The Times

Periodicals

Annual Conference Reports of the National Union of Conservative and Unionist Associations
The Banker
The Bankers' Magazine
Blackwood's Magazine
British Industries
Bulletin of the British Engineers Association
Bulletin of the Stable Money Association (New York Public Library)
Chamber of Commerce Journal
CLA (Central Landowners Association) *Journal*
The (Manchester Guardian) *Commercial*
Conservative Gleanings and Memoranda
Contemporary Review
The Co-ordinator
Cotton Gazette
Economic League. Notes for Speakers
The Economist
European Finance
Farmer and Stockbreeder
Federal Reserve Bank of New York, Annual Reports
Federal Reserve Bulletin
Fortnightly Review
Forward
The Free Trader
Independent Labour Party, *Reports of the Annual Conferences, 1919–*
Industrial Review
International Affairs
Iron and Coal Trades Review
J. Henry Schroder Quarterly Review
Journal of the Farmers' Club
Journal of the Royal Agricultural Society
Labour Bulletin
Labour Magazine
Labour Monthly
Labour Party, *Reports of the 19th – 32nd Annual Conferences, 1919–32*
Lansbury's Labour Weekly
Liberal Magazine

Liverpool Steam Ship Owners' Association, Annual Reports
Man and Metal
Manchester Chamber of Commerce Monthly Record
NFU Record
Nation and Athenaeum
National Review
National Union of Manufacturers Journal
New Clarion
New Leader
New Statesman
Nineteenth Century and After
Political Quarterly
Revue d'Economie Politique
Revue Politique et Parlementaire (Paris)
Round Table
Samuel H. Montagu & Co Weekly Bullion Letter
Socialist Review
The Spectator
The Statist
TUC, *Reports of the Proceedings at the 55th – 64th Annual Trades Union Congresses, 1923–32.*
United Empire

Memoirs, biographies, etc.

(Unless otherwise indicated, place of publication is London)

Amery, Leo S. *My Political Life*, vol. ii, *War and Peace, 1914–1929*, vol. iii, *The Unforgiving Years, 1929–1940* (1953, 1955).
Attlee, Clement R. *As It Happened* (1954).
'William Graham: An Appreciation', *Labour Magazine*, February 1932, 450–51.
Auffray, Bernard. *Pierre de Margerie (1861–1942) et la vie diplomatique de son temps* (Paris, 1976).
Bagehot, Walter. *The Collected Works of Walter Bagehot*, vol. ix, ed. Norman St John Stevas (1978).
Baldwin, Stanley. *A Memoir* (1947).
Barnes, John and Keith Middlemas. *Baldwin. A Biography* (1969).
Barnes, John and David Nicholson (eds.). *The Leo Amery Diaries, vol. 1, 1869–1929* (1980).
Blaxland, Geoffrey. *J.H. Thomas. A Life for Unity* (1964).
Bolitho, Hector. *James Lyle Mackay. First Earl of Inchcape* (1936).
Bonnet, Georges. *Vingt ans de vie politique, 1918–1938. De Clemenceau à Daladier* (Paris, 1969).
Boothby, Robert. *I Fight to Live* (1947).
Recollections of a Rebel (1978).
Boyd, Charles W. (ed.). *Mr Chamberlain's Speeches*, vol. ii (1914).
Boyle, Andrew. *Montagu Norman. A Biography* (1967).
Brand, Lord. 'A Banker's Reflections on Some Economic Trends', *Economic Journal*, 63/252 (December 1953), 763–77.
Briand, Aristide. *Discours et écrits de politique étrangère*, ed. Achille Elisha (Paris, 1965).

Brockway, Fenner. *Inside the Left* (1943).
Towards Tomorrow. The Autobiography of Fenner Brockway (1977).
Brüning, Heinrich. *Memoiren 1918–1934* (Stuttgart, 1970).
Bullock, Allan. *The Life and Times of Ernest Bevin*, vol. i, *Trade Union Leader, 1881–1940* (1960).
Campbell, John. *Lloyd George. The Goat in the Wilderness, 1922–1931* (1977).
Case, Josephine Young and Everett Needham Case. *Owen D. Young and American Enterprise* (Boston, 1982).
Cecil of Chelwood, Viscount. *The Way of Peace, Essays and Addresses* (1928).
All the Way (1949).
A Great Experiment (1941).
Centre de Recherches Européennes. *Emile Mayrisch. Précurseur de la construction de l'Europe* (Lausanne, 1967).
Chamberlain, Sir Austen. *Down the Years* (1935).
Peace in Our Time. Addresses on Europe and the Empire (1928).
Chandler, Lester V. *Benjamin Strong, Central Banker* (Washington DC, 1958).
Chandos, Oliver Lyttleton, Viscount. *The Memories of Lord Chandos* (1962).
Channon, Sir Henry. *Chips. The Diaries of Sir Henry Channon*, ed. Robert Rhodes James (1967).
Church, Roy. *Herbert Austin. The British Motor Car Industry to 1941* (1979).
Churchill, Randolph S. *Lord Derby, 'King of Lancashire'* (1959).
Citrine, Walter. *Men and Work* (1964).
Clay, Sir Henry. *Lord Norman* (1957).
Cobden, Richard. *Political Writings*, vol. i, 2nd edn (1868).
Colvin, Ian. *Vansittart in Office* (1965).
Coote, Colin. *A Companion of Honour. The Story of Walter Elliot* (1965).
Coudenhove-Kalergi, Richard, Count. *An Idea Conquers the World* (1953).
Croft, Henry Page, Lord. *My Life of Strife* (1948).
Cross, Colin. *Philip Snowden* (1966).
Sir Samuel Hoare. A Political Biography (1977).
Cross, J.A. *Lord Swinton* (Oxford, 1982).
Current, Richard N. *Secretary Stimson. A Study in Political Statecraft* (New Brunswick, NJ, 1954).
Curtius, Julius. *Sechs Jahre Minister der deutschen Republik* (Heidelberg, 1948).
D'Abernon, Viscount. *Portraits and Appreciations* (1931).
Dalton, Hugh. *Memoirs*, vol. ii, *Call Back Yesterday, 1887–1931* (1953).
Dawes, Charles G. *Journal as Ambassador to Great Britain* (New York, 1939).
Journal of Reparations (1939)
Notes as Vice President, 1928–1929 (Boston, 1935).
Dayer, Roberta A. 'The Young Charles Addis: Poet and Banker', in *Eastern Banking. Essays in the History of the Hong Kong and Shanghai Banking Corporation*, ed. Frank A.A. King (1983), 14–31.
Donoghue, Bernard and George W. Jones. *Herbert Morrison. Portrait of a Politician* (1973).
Edge, Walter E. *A Jerseyman's Journal. Fifty Years of American Business and Politics* (Princeton NJ, 1948).
Einzig, Paul. *In the Centre of Things* (1960).
Montagu Norman. A Study in Financial Statesmanship (1932).
Feiling, Keith. *The Life of Neville Chamberlain* (1946).
Forbes, John Douglas. *J.P. Morgan Jr, 1867–1943* (Charlottesville, VA, 1981).

François-Poncet, André. *The Fateful Years. Memoirs of a French Ambassador in Berlin, 1931–1938*, trans. by Jacques Leclercq (New York, 1949).
Fuller, Basil. *The Life Story of the Rt. Hon. J.H. Thomas. A Statesman of the People* (1943).
Gilbert, Martin. *Winston S. Churchill.* Companion Volume 5, Part 1. Documents. *The Exchequer Years, 1922–1929* (1980).
Graham, Thomas N. *Willie Graham* (1948).
Gregory, Sir Theodore. 'Lord Norman: A New Interpretation', *Lloyds Bank Review*, 88 (April 1968), 31–51.
Grigg, Percy James. *Prejudice and Judgement* (1948).
Halperin, Vladimir. *Lord Milner and the Empire* (1952).
Hamilton, Sir Horace P. 'Sir Warren Fisher and the Public Service', *Public Administration*, 29/2 (Spring 1951), 3–38.
Hamilton, Mary Agnes. *Remembering My Good Friends* (1944).
Up-Hill All the Way (1954).
Hargrave, John. *Professor Skinner, alias Montagu Norman* (1940).
Harrod, R.F. *The Life of John Maynard Keynes* (1951).
Herriot, Edouard. *Jadis* (Paris, 1952).
Hewins, W.A.S. *The Apologia of an Imperialist. Forty Years of Empire Policy*, vol. ii (1929).
Hoover, Herbert. *The Memoirs of Herbert Hoover*, vol. iii (New York, 1952).
The State Papers and other Public Writings of Herbert Hoover, vol. ii, ed. William Starr Myers (New York, 1934).
Hymans, Paul. *Memoirs*, 2 vols. (1958).
Jacobsson, Erin E. *A Life for Sound Money. Per Jacobsson. His Biography* (Oxford, 1979).
James, Robert Rhodes. *Victor Cazalet. A Portrait* (1976).
(ed.). *Memoirs of a Conservative. J.C.C. Davidson's Memoirs and Papers, 1910–37* (1969).
Jeanneney, Jean-Noel. *Francois de Wendel en Republique: l'argent et le pouvoir, 1914–1940* (Paris, 1976).
Johnston, Thomas. *Memories* (1952).
Jones, J. Harry. *Josiah Stamp, Public Servant. The Life of the first Baron Stamp of Shortlands* (1964).
Jones, Sir Lawrence. *Georgian Afternoon* (1958).
Jones, Thomas. *A Diary with Letters, 1931–50* (1954).
Whitehall Diary, vol. i, *1916–25*, vol. ii, *1926–30*, ed. Keith Middlemas (1969).
Jucker-Fleetwood, Erin E. 'Montagu Norman in the Per Jacobsson Diaries', *National Westminster Bank Review* (November 1968), 52–71.
Kajima, Morinosuke, Jacques de Launay, Vittorio Pons, and Arnold Zurcher. *Coudenhove-Kalergi. Le Pionnier de l'Europe unie* (Lausanne, 1971).
Kenworthy, James M. *Soldiers, Statesmen – and Others. An Autobiography* (1933).
Kessler, Harry. *The Diaries of a Cosmopolitan. Count Harry Kessler, 1918–1937*, trans. and ed. by Charles Kessler (1971).
Keynes, John Maynard. *Collected Writings*, vols. xix–xxi, ed. Sir Austin Robinson and Donald Moggridge (1981–82).
Essays in Biography, 2nd edn (1951).
Koss, Stephen. *Fleet Street Radical. A.G. Gardiner and the Daily News* (1973).

Laroche, Jules. *La Pologne de Pilsudski. Souvenirs d'une ambassade, 1926–1935* (Paris, 1953).
de Launay, Jacques. *Emile Mayrisch et la politique du patronat* (Bruxelles, 1965).
Leaf, Charlotte. *Walter Leaf, 1852–1927. Some Chapters of Autobiography, with a Memoir by Charlotte Leaf* (1932).
Leger, Alexis Saint-Leger. *Briand* (New York, 1943).
Leith Ross, Sir Frederick. *Money Talks. Fifty Years of International Finance* (1969).
Lockhart, Robert H. Bruce. *Comes the Reckoning* (1947).
Your England (1955).
Loucheur, Louis. *Carnets secrets, 1903–1932*, présenté et annoté par Jacques de Launay (Paris, 1962).
Lysaght, Charles Edward. *Brendan Bracken* (1979).
McFadyean, Sir Andrew. *Recollected in Tranquillity* (1964).
McLeod, Ian. *Neville Chamberlain* (1961).
McNair, James. *Maxton. The Beloved Rebel* (1955).
Miller, J.D.B. *Richard Jebb* (1956).
Milner, Lord. *Questions of the Hour*, rev. edn (1925).
Monick, Emmanuel. *Pour Mémoir* (Paris, 1970).
Moran, Charles Wilson, 1st Baron. *Winston Churchill. The Struggle for Survival, 1940–1965* (1966).
Moreau, Emile. *Souvenirs d'un Gouverneur de la Banque de France* (Paris, 1954).
Mosley, Sir Oswald. *My Life* (1968).
Nevins, Allan, and Frank Ernest Nevins. *Ford. Expansion and Challenge, 1915–1933* (New York, 1957).
Nicolson, Harold. *Diaries and Letters, 1930–1939*, ed. Nigel Nicolson (1966).
King George the Fifth. His Life and Reign (1952).
Noel, Léon. 'Souvenirs de la Conférence de la Haye (5–30 août 1929)', *Revue d'histoire diplomatique*, 3–4 (1983), 231–55.
O'Brien, Terence H. Milner. *Viscount Milner of St James's and Cape Town, 1854–1925* (1979).
Oppenheimer, Sir Francis. *Stranger Within* (1960).
Paton, John. *Left Turn*, vol. ii (1936).
Pedersen, Ole Karup. *Udenrigsminister P. Munchs opfattelse af Danmarks stillung i international politik* (Copenhagen, 1970).
Pethick-Lawrence, Frederick. *Fate has been Kind* (1943).
Petrie, Sir Charles. *The Life and Letters of the Rt. Hon. Sir Austen Chamberlain*, vol. ii (1940).
Phillpott, H.R.S. *The Rt. Hon. J.H. Thomas, Impressions of a Remarkable Career* (1932).
Price, M. Philips. *My Three Revolutions* (1969).
Reid, James MacArthur. *James Lithgow, Master of Work* (1964).
Reynaud, Paul. *Au coeur de la mêlée* (Paris, 1951).
Rose, Kenneth. *King George V* (1983).
Rose, Norman. *Vansittart. Study of a Diplomat* (1978).
Roskill, Stephen. *Hankey. Man of Secrets*, vol. ii, *1919–1931* (1974).
Rowland, Peter. *Lloyd George* (1975).
Rueff, Jacques. *Combats pour l'ordre financier* (Paris, 1972).
De l'aube au crépuscule, autobiographie (Paris, 1977).
Salter, Sir Arthur. *Memoirs of a Public Servant* (1961).
Slave of the Lamp. A Public Servant's Notebook (1967).

Samuel, Herbert Viscount. *Memoirs* (1945).
Schacht, Hjalmar H.H. *Confessions of the Old Wizard* (Boston, 1956).
Schlumberger, Jean, Robert Meyer, and Henri Rieben. *Emile Mayrisch, précurseur de la construction de l'Europe* (Lausanne, 1967).
Selby, Sir Walford. *Diplomatic Twilight, 1930–1940* (1953).
Seydoux, Francois. *Mémoirs d'Outre-Rhin* (Paris, 1975).
Shinwell, Emmanuel. *I've Lived Through it All* (1973).
Simon, John Viscount. *Retrospect* (1952).
Skidelsky, Robert. *Oswald Mosley* (1975).
Slocombe, George. *A Mirror to Geneva* (New York, 1938).
Snowden, Philip Viscount. *An Autobiography*, 2 vols. (1934).
Soulié, Michel. *La vie politique d'Edouard Herriot* (Paris, 1962).
Stevenson, Frances. *Lloyd George. A Diary*, ed. A.J.P. Taylor (1971).
Stimson, Henry L. and McGeorge Bundy. *On Active Service in Peace and War* (New York, 1948).
Stresemann, Gustav. *His Diaries, Letters and Papers*, vol. iii, ed. and trans. by Eric Sutton (1940).
Suarez, Georges. *Briand*, vol. vi, *L'Artisan de la paix, 1923–1932* (Paris, 1952).
Swinton, Viscount. *I Remember* (1950).
Taylor, A.J.P. *Beaverbrook* (1972).
Thomas, J.H. *My Story* (1937).
Turner, Ben. *About Myself, 1863–1930* (1930).
Vallentin, Antonina. *Stresemann* (1931).
Vansittart, Robert, Lord. *The Mist Procession* (1955).
Vickers, Vincent Cartwright. *Economic Tribulation* (1941).
Warren, Harris Gayford. *Herbert Hoover and the Great Depression* (New York, 1959).
Webb, Beatrice. *Beatrice Webb's Diaries, 1924–32*, ed. Margaret Cole (1956).
Our Partnership (1948).
Wedgewood, Josiah. *Memoirs of a Fighting Life* (1941).
Wellesley, Sir Victor. *Diplomacy in Fetters* (1945).
Willert, Sir Arthur. *Washington and other Memories* (Boston, 1972).
Williams, Lord Francis. *Ernest Bevin* (1952).
A Pattern of Rulers (1965).
Winkler, Henry R. 'Arthur Henderson', in *The Diplomats*, eds. Gordon A. Craig and Felix Gilbert (Princeton, 1953).
Wise, Leonard. *Arthur Kitson* (1946).
Woolf, Leonard. *Downhill All the Way. An Autobiography of the Years 1919–1939* (1967).
Wrench, John Evelyn. *Geoffrey Dawson and Our Times* (1955).
Young, Charles Kenneth. *Churchill and Beaverbrook. A Study in Friendship and Politics* (1966).

Contemporary studies – books

Aberconway, Henry Viscount. *The Basic Industries of Great Britain* (1927).
Amery, Leopold S. *Empire and Prosperity* (1930).
The Empire in the New Era. Speeches Delivered during an Empire Tour, 1927–1928 (1928).
Austin, Bertram and W. Francis Lloyd. *The Secret of High Wages: The New Industrial Gospel*, 2nd edn, Foreword by W.T. Layton (1926).

Baker, Philip Noel. *The League of Nations at Work*, 2nd edn (1927).
Barker, J. Ellis. *America's Secret. The Causes of her Economic Success* (1927).
Benham, F.C. *Go Back to Gold* (1932).
Bergmann, Carl. *The History of Reparations* (1927).
Bonnamour, Georges. *Le Rapprochement franco-allemand* (Paris, 1927).
Boothby, Robert, John de V. Loder, Harold Macmillan, and Oliver Stanley. *Industry and the State. A Conservative View* (1927).
Bowker, B. *Lancashire under the Hammer* (1928).
Brailsford, H.N., John A. Hobson, A. Creech Jones, and E.F. Wise. *The Living Wage* (1926).
Canney, Ernest E. *Lancashire Betrayed* (Deansgate and Manchester, 1929).
Cassel, Gustav. *The Crisis in the World's Monetary System* (1932).
Cordier, A.W. *European Union and the League of Nations* (Geneva, 1931).
Croft, Sir Henry Page. *The Crisis* (1931).
Dalton, Hugh. *Towards the Peace of Nations. A Study in International Politics* (1928).
Dampier-Whetham, Cecil. *Politics and the Land* (1927).
Darling, J.F. *Economic Unity of the Empire* (1926).
The 'Rex': a New Money to Unify the Empire (1930).
Delaisi, Francois. *Le Pétrole* (Paris, 1922).
Dell, Robert. *The Geneva Racket, 1920–1939* (1942).
Denny, Ludwell. *America Conquers Britain* (New York, 1930).
We Fight for Oil (New York, 1927).
D'Ormesson, Wladimir. *Confiance en Allemagne?* (Paris, 1928).
Einzig, Paul. *The Bank for International Settlements* (1930).
Bankers, Statesmen and Economists (1935).
Behind the Scenes of International Finance (1932).
The Fight for Financial Supremacy (1931).
Elliot, Walter. *Toryism and the Twentieth Century* (1927).
Enfield, R.R. *The Agricultural Crisis, 1920–1923* (1924).
Fisher, Irving. *The Money Illusion* (1930).
Germain-Martin, Louis. *Le Problème financier, 1930–1936* (Paris, 1936).
Greaves, H.R.G. *The League Committees and World Order* (1931).
Greenwood, Arthur. *The Labour Outlook* (1929).
Gregory, Theodore E. *Gold, Unemployment and Capitalism* (1933).
The Return to Gold (1925).
Hammersley, S.S. *Industrial Leadership* (1925).
Hawtrey, R.G. *The Art of Central Banking* (1932).
The Gold Standard in Theory and Practice (1931).
Monetary Reconstruction, 2nd edn (1926).
Heath, Sir Thomas L. *The Treasury* (1927).
Henderson, Sir Hubert Douglas. *The Inter-War Years. A Selection from the Writings of Hubert Douglas Henderson*, ed. Henry Clay (1955).
Herriot, Edouard. *The United States of Europe*, trans. Reginald Dingle (1930).
Hirst, Francis W. *Safeguarding and Protection in Great Britain and the United States* (1927).
Jebb, Richard. *Empire in Eclipse* (1926).
Jenks, Sir Maurice. *The Tyranny of Gold* (1933).
Johnston, James. *A Hundred Commoners* (1931).
Johnston, Thomas. *The Financiers and the Nation* (1934).

Jouvenal, Bertrand de. *Vers les Etats Unis d'Europe* (Paris, 1930).
Keynes, John Maynard. *The Economic Consequences of Mr Churchill* (1925).
The Economic Consequences of the Peace (1919).
The End of Laissez-Faire (1926).
A Tract on Monetary Reform (1923).
A Treatise on Money (1930).
Essays in Persuasion (1931).
Klein, Julius. *Frontiers of Trade* (1929).
Liberal Party. *Britain's Industrial Future. The Report of the Liberal Industrial Inquiry* (1928).
Lloyd George, David. *The Truth about Reparations and War Debts* (1932).
Loveday, Alexander. *Britain and World Trade. Quo Vadimus and other Economic Essays* (1931).
McCurdy, The Rt. Hon. Charles A. *Empire Free Trade* (1930).
MacDonald, James Ramsay. *History of the ILP* (1921).
McKenna, Reginald. *Post-War Banking Policy* (1928).
Melchett, Lord. *Imperial Economic Unity* (1930).
Modern Money. A Treatise on the Reform of the Theory and Practice of Political Economy (1932).
Mills, J. Saxon. *The Genoa Conference* (1922).
Mirkine-Guezevitch, B. and Georges Scelle (eds.). *L'Union européene* (Paris, 1931).
Mosley, Oswald. *Revolution by Reason* (1925).
Moulton, H.G. and Leo Pasvolsky. *War Debts and World Prosperity* (1932).
World War Debt Settlements (New York, 1927).
Moye, Marcel and Bertrand Nogaro. *Le Régime douanière de la France* (Paris, 1931).
Nearing, Scott and Joseph Freeman. *Dollar Diplomacy. A Study in American Imperialism* (1926).
Peddie, J. Taylor. *The Dual System of Stabilisation* (1930).
The Flaw in the Economic System: The Case Against the Gold Standard (1928).
The Producers' Case for Monetary Reform. Is Great Britain now a Second-Rate Power? 3rd edn (1929).
Peel, Rt. Hon George. *The Economic Impact of America* (1928).
Pethick-Lawrence, Frederick. *Why Prices Rise and Fall*, 2nd rev. edn (1923).
Petter, Sir Ernest. *The Disease of Unemployment and the Cure* (1925).
Philippe, Raymond. *Le Drame financier de 1924 à 1928* (Paris, 1931).
Price, M. Philips. *The Economic Problems of Europe. Pre-War and After* (1928).
Rappard, William E. *Uniting Europe. The Trend of International Cooperation since the War* (New Haven, 1930).
Richardson, John H. *Economic Disarmament. A Study on Economic Co-operation* (1931).
Riedl, Richard. *Exceptions to Most-Favoured-Nation Treatment. Report presented to the International Chamber of Commerce* (1931).
Romier, Lucien. *Who Will be Master, Europe or America?* trans. Matthew Josephson (1929).
Royal Institute of International Affairs. *British Tariff Policy* (1932).
Memorandum on the Most-Favoured-Nation Clause as an Instrument of International Policy (1933).
The International Gold Problem. Collected Papers (1931).

Salter, Sir Arthur. *The United States of Europe and other Papers*, ed. with notes by W. Arnold Foster (1933).
and others. *The Economic Consequences of the League* (1927).
Seydoux, Jacques. *De Versailles au Plan Young* (Paris, 1932).
Siegfried, André. *America Comes of Age* (1927).
England's Crisis (1930).
Smith, Sir Herbert Llewellyn. *The Board of Trade* (1928).
Snowden, Philip. *Wages and Prices* (1920).
Labour and the New World (1921).
Stamp, Sir Josiah. *Papers on Gold and the Price Level* (1931).
Tryon, George C. *A Short History of Imperial Preference* (1931).
Vienot, Pierre. *Incertitudes allemandes* (Paris, 1929).
Walcher, J. *Ford oder Marx. Die praktische Lösung der sozialen Frage* (Berlin, 1925).
Waller, W.H. *The Gold Standard and the Effect of our Return on the Cotton Trade and other Industries of the Nation. A Series of Letters* (Manchester, 1929).
Wardlaw-Milne, J.S. *The ABC of £sd. The Plain Man's Guide to the Money Problem* (1931).
The GHQ of £sd (1932).
Wertheimer, Egon. *Portrait of the Labour Party*, 2nd edn (1930).
Winslow, E.M. *The League and Concerted Economic Action* (Geneva, 1931).

Contemporary studies – articles and pamphlets

'Agriculture and Industry', Report of a Conference held at the Surveyors' Institution, Great George Street, SW1, on Wednesday, 17 October, 1928 (1928).
Beaverbrook, Lord. 'Empire Free Trade: The New Policy for Prosperity' (1929).
Benn, Captain Wedgwood. 'Safeguarding Whom? The Profiteer or the Worker?', The Labour Party (1929).
Bidwell, Percy Wells. 'The American Tariff: Europe's Answer', *Foreign Affairs*, October 1930, 13–26.
Butler, Harold Beresford. 'The International Economic Conference', Paper read before the Manchester Statistical Society, 24 February, 1927 (Manchester, 1927).
Churchill, W.S. 'The United States of Europe', *Saturday Evening Post*, 15 February 1930, 25.
Cunliffe-Owen, Sir Hugo. 'Industry and the Empire Crusade: A Statement to Manufacturers' (n.d. ? 1927).
D'Ormesson, Wladimir. 'Une fédération européenne, est-elle possible?', *Revue de Paris*, 15 October 1929, 749.
Empire Economic Union. 'A Plan of Action' (1932).
'Report of a Joint Committee on Agriculture Policy' (1931).
Fay, H. Van V. 'Commercial Policy in Post-War Europe: Reciprocity versus Most-Favoured-Nation Treatment', *Quarterly Journal of Economics*, 41/3 (May 1927), 441–70.
Federation of British Industries. 'Industry and the Nation' (March 1931).
Friends of Economy. 'First Annual Report to 1st November 1931' (1932).
Hammersley, Samuel Schofield. 'Petition to the Rt. Hon J. Ramsay MacDonald, MP, 27 July 1929' (1929).

Henderson, Arthur. 'Labour and an After-War Economic Policy' (1917).
'Labour's Peace Terms' (n.d.? 1918).
'The League of Nations and Labour' (1918).
'The Peace Terms', The Labour Party (1919).
'This Year is Disarmament Year', Labour Party (1931).
Herriot, Edouard. 'Pan-Europe?' *Foreign Affairs*, January 1930, 237–47.
Hoover, Herbert C. 'What Herbert Hoover Stands For', Republican National Committee (Washington DC, 1928).
Hurst, Willard. 'Holland, Switzerland and Belgium and the English Gold Crisis of 1931', *Journal of Political Economy*, 40/5 (October 1932), 638–60.
International Chamber of Commerce. 'Progress in Economic Restoration' (Paris, 1925).
'Resolution Passed at Third Congress' (Paris, 1925).
Kershaw, John B.C. 'The American Presidential Election and the Future of British and European Trade', *Financial Review of Reviews*, January–March 1929, 51–61.
Labour Party. 'Wages, Prices and Profits' (1922).
'Unemployment, Peace and the Indemnity' (n.d. ? 1922).
'Labour and the War Debt. A Statement of Policy for the Redemption of War Debt by a Levy on Accumulated Wealth' (n.d. ? 1922).
'Unemployment Relief' (n.d. ? 1922).
'Labour and the European Situation' (1923).
'No Surrender' (1924).
'Labour and the Nation. Supplement on Banking and Currency' (1928).
'Wealth or Commonwealth. Labour's Financial Policy' (1929).
'Labour and the Nation', rev. edn (1929).
'Party Constitution and Standing Orders, Approved by the Annual Conference at Brighton, 1929' (1930).
'The Labour Government's Record of Achievement' (1930).
'The Prime Minister Looks Back – and Ahead' (1931).
'Labour's Call to the Nation' (1931).
Labour Party and Trades Union Congress. 'Why It Happened' (October 1931).
League of Nations Union. 'A Speech by Lord Robert Cecil on League of Nations Policy' (1922).
Loria, Achille. 'La Réaction protectionniste', *Revue Economique Internationale*, May 1925, 229–42.
Loucheur, Louis. 'Situation de la France et de la Belgique dans l'Europe nouvelle d'après-guerre', *Revue Economique Internationale*, June 1925, 441–59.
MacDonald, James Ramsay. 'The Conscription of Wealth' (n.d.? 1917).
Martin, William. 'The Tariff Truce', *Svenska Handelsbanken Index*, 5 (1930), 45–49.
Melchett, Lord. 'International Industry and the Young Plan' (1929).
Mertens, André. 'L'Accord commercial franco-allemand du 17 août 1927', *Revue Economique Internationale*, October 1927, 23–45.
Mond, Sir Alfred. 'Industry and Politics' (1927).
Moreau, Emile. 'Le Relèvement financier et monétaire de la France (1926–1928)', pt. 2, *Revue des Deux Mondes*, 15 March 1927, 299–319.
Nightingale, Robert T. 'The Personnel of the British Foreign Office and Diplomatic Service, 1851–1929', *American Political Science Review*, 24/2 (May 1930), 310–31.

Ohlin, Bertil. 'A European Customs Union?', *Svenska Handelsbanken Index*, August 1929, 5–9.
'A Road to Freer Trade', *Svenska Handelsbanken Index*, May 1929, 2–9.
Pethick-Lawrence, Frederick. 'The Capital Levy. How the Labour Party would settle the War Debt', Labour Party (n.d.? 1921).
'Socialism and Finance', Independent Labour Party (n.d.? 1924).
Rist, Charles. 'La Question de l'or', *Revue d'Economique Politique*, November–December 1930, 1489–518.
Salter, Sir Arthur. 'Economic Policy: The Way to Peace and Prosperity', *Problems of Peace*, 2nd ser. (Geneva, 1928), 104–23.
'The First Results of the World Economic Conference', *Problems of Peace*, 3rd ser. (Geneva, 1929), 75–95.
Siegfried, André. 'The Passing of England's Economic Hegemony', *Foreign Affairs*, July 1928, 525–40.
'European Reactions to American Tariff Proposals', *Foreign Affairs*, October 1929, 13–19.
Simon, Sir John. 'Safeguarding Examined', Speech delivered at the Liberal Summer School on 4 August, 1928 (1928).
Snowden, Philip. 'The Chamberlain Bubble. Facts about the Zolverein with an Alternative Policy', Independent Labour Party (1903).
'The Menace of the Trusts, and How to Deal with It', Independent Labour Party (1919).
'Socialism Made Plain', Independent Labour Party (1920).
'Twenty Objections to Socialism', Independent Labour Party (1920).
'The Big Business Budget', TUC and Labour Party (1923).
'The Tory Government's Pitiable Confession of Incapacity', Labour Party (1926).
'The Menace of Protection', Labour Party (1930).
'The Truth about Protection – The Worker Pays', Labour Party (1930).
Spender, John A. 'The America of To-day' (1928).
Strachey, John. 'Revolution by Reason. An Account of the Financial Proposals Submitted to the Labour Movement by Mr Oswald Mosley' (1925).
Taussig, Frank W. 'The Tariff Bill and our Friends Abroad', *Foreign Affairs*, October 1929, 1–12.
Trotsky, Leon. 'Europe and America. Two Speeches on Imperialism' (New York, 1971).
Trades Union Congress. 'Commonwealth Trade. A New Policy' (1930).
Villiers, Brougham (pseud.). 'Tariffs and the Worker', Labour Party (1920).

Secondary studies – books and theses

Aaronovitch, Sam. *The Ruling Class. A Study of British Finance Capital* (1961).
Acres, W. Marston. *The Bank of England from Within, 1694–1900*, 2 vols. (1931).
Aldcroft, Derek H. *The Inter-War Economy: Britain, 1919–1939* (1970).
and Peter Fearon, eds. *Economic Growth in Twentieth-century Britain* (1969).
Amery, Julian. *Joseph Chamberlain and the Tariff Reform Campaign, 1901–1903* (1969).
Armitage, Susan M.H. *The Politics of Decontrol of Industry: Britain and the United States* (1969).
Arndt, Heinz Wolfgang. *The Economic Lessons of the Nineteen Thirties* (1944).

Artaud, Denise. *La Question des dettes interalliées et la reconstruction de l'Europe (1917–1929)*, 2 vols. (Paris, 1978).
Ashton-Gwatkin, Frank T.A. *The British Foreign Service* (Syracuse NY, 1950).
Bagehot, Walter. *Lombard Street*, 9th edn (1888).
Balogh, Thomas. *Studies in Financial Organisation* (Cambridge, 1947).
Bariéty, Jacques. *Les Relations franco-allemandes après la première guerre mondiale* (Paris, 1977).
Bassett, Reginald. *Nineteen Thirty One. Political Crisis* (1958).
Baster, A.J.S. *The International Banks* (1935).
Beck, Earl R. *Germany Rediscovers America* (Tallahassee, 1968).
Becker, Joseph, and Klaus Hildebrand (eds.), *Internationale Beziehungen in der Weltwirtschaftskrise 1929–1933* (Munich, 1980).
Bennett, Edward W. *Germany and the Diplomacy of the Financial Crisis, 1931* (Cambridge Mass., 1962).
Beyen, J.W. *Money in a Maelstrom* (1951).
Binoux, Paul. *Les Pionniers de l'Europe. L'Europe et le rapprochement franco-allemand: Joseph Caillaux, Aristide Briand, Robert Schuman, Konrad Adenauer, Jean Monnet* (Paris, 1972).
Birn, Donald S. *The League of Nations Union, 1918–1945* (Oxford, 1981).
Bishop, Donald G. *The Administration of British Foreign Relations* (Syracuse NY, 1962).
Blank, Stephen. *Industry and Government in Britain. The Federation of British Industries in Politics, 1945–65* (Farnborough, 1973).
Bracher, Karl Dietrich. *Europe in der Krise. Innengeschichte und Weltpolitik seit 1917* (Frankfurt am Main, 1979).
Brand, Carl F. *The British Labour Party. A Short History*, rev. edn (Stanford, 1974).
Brandes, Joseph. *Herbert Hoover and Economic Diplomacy. Department of Commerce Policy, 1921–1928* (Pittsburgh, 1962).
Bridges, Lord. *The Treasury* (1963).
Briggs, Asa. *The Making of Modern England, 1783–1867: The Age of Improvement* (New York, 1965).
Brogan, Dennis W. *The Development of Modern France, 1870–1939* (1940).
Brown, Kenneth D. (ed.). *Essays in Anti-Labour History: Responses to the Rise of Labour in Britain* (1974).
Brown, William Adams Jr. *England and the New Gold Standard, 1919–1926* (New Haven, 1929).
The International Gold Standard Reinterpreted, 2 vols. (New York, 1940).
Butler, Harold Beresford. *The Lost Peace. A Personal Impression* (1941).
Camplin, Jamie. *The Rise of the Plutocrats. Wealth and Power in Edwardian England* (1978).
Camrose, Viscount. *British Newspapers and their Controllers* (1947).
Carlton, David. *MacDonald versus Henderson. The Foreign Policy of the Second Labour Government* (1970).
Carr, J.C. and W. Taplin. *History of the British Steel Industry* (Oxford, 1962).
Carter, Gwendolin M. *The British Commonwealth and International Security: The Role of the Dominions, 1919–1939* (Toronto, 1947).
Cassel, Gustav. *The Downfall of the Gold Standard* (Oxford, 1936).
Cassis, Juffef. 'Les Banquiers anglais, 1890–1914: Etude sociale', Ph.D. Thesis, University of Geneva (1982).

Chandler, Lester V. *America's Greatest Depression, 1929–1941* (1970).
American Monetary Policies, 1928–1941 (New York, 1971).
Chapman, Stanley D. *The Rise of Merchant Banking* (1984).
Chastenet, Jacques. *Histoire de la troisième république, vol. v. Les années d'illusions, 1918–1931* (Paris, 1960).
Clapham, Sir John. *An Economic History of Modern Britain*, vols. i, ii (Cambridge, 1967).
Clarke, Stephen V.O. *Central Bank Cooperation, 1924–1931* (New York, 1967).
Clarke, William M. *The City in the World Economy* (1967).
Cline, Catherine Anne. *Recruits to Labour: The British Labour Party, 1914–1931* (Syracuse NY, 1963).
Cole, G.D.H. *British Trade and Industry. Past and Future* (1932).
and Raymond Postgate. *The Common People, 1746–1946*, 4th edn (1961).
Connell, John (pseud. of John Henry Robertson). *The 'Office'. A Study of British Foreign Policy and its Makers, 1919–1951* (1958).
Cowling, Maurice. *The Impact of Labour, 1920–1924: the Beginning of Modern British Politics* (Cambridge, 1971).
Dahrendorf, Ralf. *On Britain* (1982).
Dickson, P.G.M. *The Financial Revolution in England. A Study in the Development of Public Credit, 1688–1756* (1967).
Dockrill, Michael L. and J. Douglas Gould. *Peace without Promise. Britain and the Peace Conferences, 1919–23* (1981).
Douglas, Roy. *The History of the Liberal Party, 1895–1970* (1971).
Dowse, Robert E. *Left in the Centre. The Independent Labour Party, 1893–1940* (1966).
Drummond, Ian M. *British Economic Policy and the Empire, 1919–1939* (1972).
Imperial Economic Policy, 1917–1939. Studies in Expansion and Protection (1974).
Dulles, Eleanor Lansing. *The Bank for International Settlements at Work* (New York, 1932).
Dunning, J.H. *American Investment in British Manufacturing Industry* (1958).
and C.J. Thomas. *British Industry. Change and Development in the Twentieth Century* (1961).
The Economist, 1843–1943 (1943).
Emden, Paul H. *Jews of Britain* (1945).
Money Powers of Europe in the Nineteenth and Twentieth Centuries (1938).
Ereira, Alan. *The Invergorden Mutiny. A Narrative History of the last great Mutiny in the Royal Navy and how it forced Britain off the Gold Standard in 1931* (1981).
Eyck, Erich. *A History of the Weimar Republic*, 2 vols., trans. Harlan P. Hansen and R.G.L. Waite (Cambridge MA, 1962–64).
Feaveryear, Sir Albert. *The Pound Sterling. A History of English Money*, 2nd edn (Oxford, 1963).
Feinstein, Charles H. *National Income. Expenditure and Output of the United Kingdom, 1855–1965* (Cambridge, 1972).
Feis, Herbert. *Diplomacy of the Dollar. First Era, 1919–1932* (Baltimore, 1950).
Europe. The World's Banker, 1870–1914 (New Haven, 1930).
Ferrell, Robert H. *American Diplomacy in the Great Depression* (1957).
Ferris, Paul. *The City*, rev. edn (Harmondsworth, 1965).

Fetter, Frank Whitson. *Development of British Monetary Orthodoxy, 1797–1875* (Cambridge MA, 1965).
Fink, Carole. *The Genoa Conference. European Diplomacy, 1921–1922* (Chapel Hill, 1984).
Finlay, John L. *Social Credit. The English Origins* (Montreal, 1972).
François-Poncet, André. *De Versailles à Potsdam. La France et le problème allemand contemporain, 1919–1945* (Paris, 1948).
Freymond, Jean. *Le IIIe Reich et la réorganisation économique de l'Europe, 1940–1942* (Leiden, 1974).
Friedman, Milton and Anna Jacobson Schwartz. *A Monetary History of the United States, 1867–1960* (Princeton, 1963).
Frommelt, Reinhard. *Paneuropa oder Mitteleuropa. Einigungsbestrebungen im Kalkül deutscher Wirtschaft und Politik 1925–1933* (Stuttgart, 1977).
Gayer, Arthur D. and Carl T. Schmidt. *American Economic Foreign Policy: Postwar History. Analysis and Interpretation* (New York, 1939).
Gehl, Jurgen. *Austria, Germany, and the Anschluss, 1931–1938* (1963).
Gordon, Margaret S. *Barriers to World Trade. A Study of Recent Commercial Policy* (1941).
Gordon, Michael R. *Conflict and Consensus in Labour's Foreign Policy, 1914–1965* (Stanford, 1969).
Grant, A.T.K. *A Study of the Capital Market in Britain from 1919–1936*, 2nd edn (1967).
Grant, Wyn, and David Marsh. *The Confederation of British Industry* (1977).
Gwatkin, Frank Ashton. *The British Foreign Service* (Syracuse NY, 1951).
Haber, L.F. *The British Chemical Industry, 1900–1930* (Oxford, 1971).
Haight, Frank Arnold. *A History of French Commercial Policies* (New York, 1941).
Halévy, Elie. *History of the English People. Epilogue, 1895–1905*, 3 vols. (Harmondsworth, 1939).
Hancock, Sir William Keith. *Survey of British Commonwealth Affairs, vol. ii. Problems of Economic Policy, 1918–1939* (1940).
Hannah, Leslie. *The Rise of the Corporate Economy* (1972).
Heindel, Richard Heathcote. *The American Impact on Great Britain, 1898–1914. A Study of the United States in World History* (Philadelphia, 1940).
Herd, Harold. *The March of Journalism. The Story of the British Press from 1622 to the Present Day* (1952).
Hill, William Martin. *The Economic and Financial Organisation of the League of Nations: A Survey of Twenty-five Years' Experience* (Washington DC, 1946).
Hilton, Boyd. *Corn, Cash, Commerce. The Economic Policies of the Tory Governments, 1815–1830* (Oxford, 1977).
Hindle, Wilfrid. *The Morning Post, 1772–1937. Portrait of a Newspaper* (Westport CT, 1974).
Hodson, H.V. *Slump and Recovery, 1929–1937. A Survey of World Economic Affairs* (1938).
Hogan, Michael J. *Informal Entente. The Private Structure of Cooperation in Anglo-American Economic Diplomacy, 1918–1928* (1977).
Holland, Robert F. *Britain and the Commonwealth Alliance, 1918–1939* (1981).
Howson, Susan. *Domestic Monetary Management in Britain, 1919–38* (Cambridge, 1975).

Ilersic, A.R., and P.F. Liddle. *The Parliament of Commerce: The Story of the Association of British Chambers of Commerce, 1860–1960* (1960).
Imlah, Albert H. *Economic Elements in the 'Pax Britannica': Studies in British Foreign Trade in the Nineteenth Century* (Cambridge MA, 1958).
Ingham, Geoffrey. *Capitalism Divided? The City and industry in British social development* (1984).
Jacobson, Jon. *Locarno Diplomacy. Germany and the West, 1925–1929* (Princeton, 1972).
Jacobsson, Per. *Monetary Problems – International and National*, ed. Erin E. Jucker-Fleetwood (1958).
Jeffcock, W. Philip. *Agricultural Politics, 1915–1935. Being a History of the Central Chamber of Commerce during that Period* (Ipswich, 1951).
Jenks, Leland Hamilton. *The Migration of British Capital to 1875* (1963).
Johnson, Paul Barton. *Land Fit for Heroes. The Planning of British Reconstruction, 1916–1919* (1968).
Jones, Geoffrey. *The State and the Emergence of the British Oil Industry* (1981).
Jones, Joseph Marion Jr. *Tariff Retaliation. Repercussions of the Hawley-Smoot Bill* (Philadelphia, 1934).
Jones, R. and O. Marriott. *Anatomy of a Merger. A History of GEC, AEI, and English Electric* (1970).
Jones, Ray. *The Nineteenth-Century Foreign Office* (1971).
Kellett, Richard. *The Merchant Banking Arena, with Case Studies* (1967).
Kendle, John E. *The Round Table Movement and Imperial Union* (Toronto, 1975).
Kennedy, Paul. *The Reality Behind Diplomacy. Background Influences on British External Policy, 1865–1980* (1981).
Kindleberger, Charles P. *The World in Depression, 1929–1939* (1973).
King-Hall, Stephen. *Chatham House* (1937).
Koss, Stephen. *The Rise and Fall of the Political Press in Britain*, vol. ii: *the Twentieth Century* (1984).
de Launay, Jacques. *Major Controversies of Contemporary History*, trans. J.J. Buckingham (1965).
Lee, Alan J. *The Origins of the Popular Press, 1855–1914* (1976).
Lee, Sir Frank. *The Board of Trade* (1958).
Leffler, Melvin P. *The Elusive Quest. America's Pursuit of European Stability and French Security, 1919–1933* (Chapel Hill, 1979).
Lewis, Cleona. *America's Stake in International Investments* (Washington DC, 1938).
L'Houillier, Fernand. *Dialogues franco-allemands, 1925–1933* (Strasbourg, 1971).
Liefmann, Robert. *Cartels, Concerns and Trusts* (1932).
Liepmann, Heinrich. *Tariff Levels and the Economic Unity of Europe*, trans. H. Stenning (1938).
Lindsay, T.F. and Michael Harrington. *The Conservative Party, 1918–1970* (1970).
Link, Werner. *Die amerikanische Stabilisierungspolitik in Deutschland 1921–32* (Dusseldorf, 1970).
Lowe, C.J. and M.L. Dockrill. *The Mirage of Power*, vol. ii, *British Foreign Policy, 1914–22* (1972).
Lowe, Marvin, E. *The British Tariff Movement* (Washington DC, 1942).

Lyman, Richard. *The First Labour Government, 1924* (Princeton, 1957).
McCord, Norman. *Free Trade. Theory and Practice from Adam Smith to Keynes* (Newton Abbot, 1970).
McDougall, Walter A. *France's Rhineland Diplomacy, 1914–1924: The Last Bid for a Balance of Power in Europe* (Princeton, 1978).
McElwee, William. *Britain's Locust Years, 1918–1940* (1962).
McEwen, J.M. 'Unionist and Conservative Members of Parliament, 1914–1939', Ph.D. Thesis, University of London (1959).
McKibbin, Ross. *The Evolution of the Labour Party, 1910–1924* (1974).
Maier, Charles S. *Recasting Bourgeois Europe: Stabilization in France, Germany, and Italy in the Decade after World War I* (Princeton, 1975).
Mallet, Sir Bernard, and C. Oswald George. *British Budgets, Second Series, 1913–14 to 1920–21* (1929).
British Budgets, Third Series, 1921–22 to 1932–33 (1933).
Martin, Ross M. *TUC: The Growth of a Pressure Group, 1868–1976* (Oxford, 1980).
Meyer, Richard Hemming. *Bankers' Diplomacy: Monetary Stabilization in the Twenties* (1970).
Middlemas, Keith. *The Clydesiders* (1965).
Politics in Industrial Society. The Experience of the British System since 1911 (1979).
Miller, Kenneth E. *Socialism and Foreign Policy. Theory and Practice in Britain to 1931* (The Hague, 1967).
Mitchell, B.R. and Phyllis Deane. *Abstract of British Historical Statistics* (Cambridge, 1962).
Moggridge, D.E. *British Monetary Policy, 1924–1931: The Norman Conquest of $4.86* (Cambridge, 1972).
The Return to Gold, 1925. The Formation of Economic Policy and its Critics (Cambridge, 1969).
Morgan, E.V. *Studies in British Financial Policy, 1914–1925* (1952).
Morgan, Kenneth O. *Consensus and Disunity. The Lloyd George Coalition Government, 1918–1922* (Oxford, 1979).
Morton, Walter A. *British Finance 1930–1940* (Madison, 1943).
Mowat, Charles Loch. *Britain Between the Wars, 1918–1940* (1968).
Nairn, Tom. *The Break-Up of Britain. Crisis and Neo-Nationalism*, 2nd edn (1981).
Nimocks, Walter. *Milner's Young Men: The 'Kindergarten' in Edwardian Imperial Affairs* (Durham NC, 1968).
Offer, Avner. *Property and Politics, 1870–1914* (Cambridge, 1981).
Orde, Anne. *Great Britain and International Security, 1920–1926* (1977).
Pegg, Carl H. *Evolution of the European Idea, 1914–1932* (Chapel Hill, 1983).
Pelling, Henry. *A History of British Trade Unionism*, 3rd edn (1976).
A Short History of the Labour Party, 5th edn (1976).
Perrot, Marguerite. *La Monnaie et l'opinion publique en France et en Angleterre de 1924 à 1936* (Paris, 1965).
Phillips, Gregory D. *The Diehards: Aristocratic Society and Politics in Edwardian England* (1979).
Pigou, A.C. *Aspects of British Economic History, 1918–1925* (1947).
Pinto-Duschinsky, Michael. *British Political Finance, 1830–1980* (1981).
Platt, D.C.M. *The Cinderella Service. British Consuls since 1825* (1971).

Pollard, Sidney (ed.). *The Gold Standard and Employment Policies between the Wars* (1970).
Ramsden, John. *A History of the Conservative Party*, vol. iii, *The Age of Balfour and Baldwin, 1902–1940* (1978).
The Making of Conservative Party Policy: The Conservative Research Department since 1929 (1980).
Rappard, William E. *Post-War Efforts for Freer Trade* (Geneva, 1938).
The Quest for Peace since the World War (Cambridge Mass. 1940).
Rasmussen, Steen Eiler. *London, the Unique City* (1934).
Reader, William Joseph. *Imperial Chemical Industries, a History*, vol. i (1970).
Reed, Harold. L. *Federal Reserve Policy, 1921–1930* (New York, 1930).
Richardson, John Henry. *British Economic Foreign Policy* (1936).
Economic Disarmament. A Study on International Cooperation (1931).
Ridgeway, George L. *Merchants of Peace: 24 Years of Business Diplomacy through the International Chamber of Commerce* (New York, 1938).
Romasco, Albert U. *The Poverty of Abundance. Hoover, the Nation, the Depression* (New York, 1965).
Roseveare, Henry. *The Treasury. The Evolution of a British Institution* (1969).
Roskill, Stephen W. *Naval Policy between the Wars, vol. 1. The Period of Anglo-American Antagonism, 1919–1929* (1968).
Rothschild, K.W. *Austria's Economic Development between the Two Wars* (1947).
Royal Institute of International Affairs. *British Tariff Policy* (1932).
Rubinstein, W.D. *Men of Property* (1981).
Sauvy, Alfred. *Histoire économique de la France entre les deux guerres*, 4 vols. (Paris, 1965–75).
Sayers, Richard S. *The Bank of England, 1891–1944*, 3 vols. (Cambridge, 1976).
Central Banking after Bagehot (1957).
Scally, Robert J. *The Origins of the Lloyd George Coalition: the Politics of Social Imperialism, 1900–1918* (Princeton, 1975).
Scanlon, John. *Pillars of Cloud* (1936).
Schuker, Stephen A. *The End of French Predominance in Europe. The Financial Crisis of 1924 and the Adoption of the Dawes Plan* (Chapel Hill, 1976).
Self, Peter, and Herbert J. Storing. *The State and the Farmer* (1962).
Semmel, Bernard. *Imperialism and Social Reform. English Social-Imperial Thought, 1895–1914* (1960).
Skidelsky, Robert. *Politicians and the Slump. The Labour Government of 1929–1931* (Harmondsworth, 1970).
Southard, Frank A. *American Industry in Europe* (New York, 1931).
Spiegelberg, Richard. *The City: Power without Responsibility* (1973).
Stegmann, D., B.-J. Wendt, and P.C. Witt (eds.). *Industrielle Gesellschaft und politisches System. Beiträge zur politischen Sozialegeschichte. Festschrift für Fritz Fischer* (Bonn, 1978).
Stern-Rubarth, Edgar. *Three Men Tried. Austen Chamberlain, Stresemann, Briand and their Fight for a New Europe* (1939).
Stolper, Gustav. *The German Economy, 1870 to the Present*, rev. edn (1967).
Strange, Susan. *Sterling and British Policy* (1971).
Tennyson, Sir Charles. *Stars and Markets* (1957).
Thomas, Hugh (ed.). *The Establishment* (1959).
Thompson, F.M.L. *English Landed Society in the Nineteenth Century* (1963).
The History of the Times, vol. iv pt. 2, 1921–1948 (1952).

The Times. *The City of London* (1927).
Trachtenberg, Marc. *Reparation in World Politics. France and European Economic Diplomacy, 1916–1923* (New York, 1980).
Truptil, R.J. *British Banks and the London Money Market* (1936).
Tucker, William Rayburn. *The Attitude of the British Labour Party towards European and Collective Security Problems, 1920–1939* (Geneva, 1950).
Vanlangenhove, Fernand. *L'Élaboration de la politique étrangère de la Belgique entre les deux guerres mondiales* (Bruxelles, 1979).
Venn, J.A. *The Foundations of Agricultural Economics together with an Economic History of British Agriculture during and after the Great War*, 2nd edn (Cambridge, 1933).
Wálter, F.P. *A History of the League of Nations*, 2 vols. (1952).
Watt, D.C. *Personalities and Policies. Studies in the Formulation of British Foreign Policy in the Twentieth Century* (1965).
Whetham, Edith. *The Agrarian History of England and Wales*, vol. viii, *1914–39* (Cambridge, 1978).
Wicker, Elmus R. *Federal Reserve Monetary Policy, 1917–1933* (New York, 1966).
Wiener, Martin J. *English Culture and the Decline of the Industrial Spirit, 1850–1980* (Harmondsworth, 1985).
Wilkins, Mira. *The Maturing of Multinational Enterprise: American Business Abroad from 1914 to 1970* (Cambridge Mass. 1974).
Williams, Francis. *Dangerous Estate. The Anatomy of Newspapers* (1957).
Fifty Years' March. The Rise of the Labour Party (1949).
Winch, Donald. *Economics and Policy. A Historical Study* (1969).
Wolfe, Martin. *The French Franc between the Wars* (New York, 1951).
Wright, Gordon. *Rural Revolution in France. The Peasantry in the Twentieth Century* (1964).
Zuylen, Baron von. *Les Mains libres. Politique extérieure de la Belgique, 1914–1940* (Bruxelles, 1950).

Secondary studies – articles and conference papers

Aldcroft, Derek H. 'The Impact of British Monetary Policy, 1919–1939', *Revue Internationale d'Histoire de la Banque*, 3 (1970), 37–65.
Atkin, John. 'Official Regulation of British Overseas Investment, 1914–1931', *Economic History Review*, 2nd ser., 23/2 (August 1970), 324–35.
Auboin, Roger. 'The Bank for International Settlements, 1930–1935', *Princeton Studies in International Finance*, no. 22 (1955).
Aydelotte, W.O. 'The Business Interests of the Gentry in the Parliament of 1841–1847', in G. Kitson Clark, *The Making of Victorian England* (1962), appendix, 219–305.
'The Balance of Payments in the Inter-war Years: Further Details', *Bank of England Quarterly*, 14/1 (March 1974), 24–26.
Balogh, Thomas. 'The Apotheosis of the Dilettante: The Establishment of Mandarins', *The Establishment*, ed. Hugh Thomas (1959), 81–126.
Bariéty, Jacques. 'Communication', *Bulletin de la Société d'Histoire Moderne*, 2 (1969).
'Finances et relations internationales: A propos du "plan de Thoiry" (September 1926)', *Relations Internationales*, 21 (Spring 1980), 51–70.
'Idee européenne et relations franco-allemandes, 1929–1932', *Bulletin de la faculté des lettres de Strasbourg* (March 1968), 571–84.

'Industriels allemands et industriels français à l'époque de la République de Weimar', *Revue Allemagne*, 4/2 (April–June 1974).

Barker, Rodney. 'Political Myth: Ramsay MacDonald and the Labour Party', *History*, 61 (1976), 46–56.

Beloff, Max. 'The Special Relationship: an Anglo-American Myth', in *A Century of Conflict, 1850–1950: Essays for A.J.P. Taylor*, ed. Martin Gilbert (1966), 151–71.

'The Whitehall Factor: The Role of the Higher Civil Service, 1919–1939', in *The Politics of Reappraisal, 1918–1939*, eds. Gillian Peele and Chris Cook (1975), ch. 9.

Blank, Stephen. 'Britain: The Politics of Foreign Economic Policy, the Domestic Economy, and the Problem of Pluralistic Stagnation', *International Organisation*, 31/4 (Autumn 1977), 674–721.

Booth, Alan. 'Corporatism, Capitalism and Depression in Twentieth-century Britain', *British Journal of Sociology*, 33/2 (June 1982), 200–23.

Bouvier, Jean. 'A propos de la stratégie de l'encaisse (or et devises) de la Banque de France de juin 1928 à l'été 1932', Paper presented to the Conference on the 1931 Crisis and Its Aftermath, Clare College, Cambridge, 14–16 April 1982.

Boyce, R.W.D. 'Britain's First "No" to Europe: Britain and the Briand Plan, 1929–30', *European Studies Review*, 10 (1980), 17–45.

'Insects and International Relations: Canada, France, and British Agricultural "Sanitary" Restrictions between the Wars', *International History Review* 9/1 (February 1987), 1–27.

Burk, Kathleen. 'The Treasury: from Impotence to Power', in *War and the State: The Transformation of British Government, 1912–1919*, ed. K. Burk (1982), 84–107.

Cain, P.J. and A.G. Hopkins. 'The Political Economy of British Expansion Overseas, 1750–1940', *Economic History Review*, 2nd ser., 33/4 (November 1980), 463–90.

Catterall, Ross E. 'Attitudes to and the Impact of British Monetary Policy in the 1920s', *Revue Internationale d'Histoire de la Banque*, 12 (1976), 29–53.

Chapman, Stanley D. 'The International Houses: The Continental Contribution to British Commerce, 1800–1860', *Journal of European Economic History*, 6/1 (Spring 1977), 5–48.

Checkland, S.G. 'The Mind of the City, 1870–1914', *Oxford Economic Papers*, new ser., 9/3 (October 1957), 261–78.

Clarke, Stephen V.O. 'Making Economic Policy in a Changing Environment, 1929–31', Paper presented to the Conference on the 1931 Crisis and Its Aftermath, Clare College, Cambridge, 14–16 April 1982.

'The Reconstruction of the International Monetary System: The Attempts of 1922 and 1933', *Princeton Studies in International Finance*, no. 33 (Princeton, 1973).

Clegg, H.A. 'Some Consequences of the General Strike', *Transactions of the Manchester Statistical Society* (1953–54), 1–29.

Clifton, J.A. 'Competition and the Evolution of the Capitalist Mode of Production', *Cambridge Journal of Economics*, 1 (1977), 140–58.

Conze, Werner. 'Brünings Politik unter dem Druck der grossen Krise', *Historische Zeitschrift*, 199 (1964), 529–50.

Costigliola, Frank C. 'Anglo-American Financial Rivalry in the 1920s', *Journal of Economic History*, 37/4 (December 1977), 911–34.

'The Other Side of Isolationism: The Establishment of the First World Bank', *Journal of American History*, 59/3 (December 1972), 602–20.

Cottrell, Philip L. 'Austria Between Diplomats and Bankers, 1919–1931', Paper presented to the Conference on the 1931 Crisis and Its Aftermath, Clare College, Cambridge, 14–16 April 1982.

d'Ormesson, Wladimir. 'Une tentative prématurée', *Revue de Paris*, February 1962, 18–27.

Dowse, Robert E. 'The Left-Wing Opposition During The First Two Labour Governments', *Parliamentary Affairs*, 14/1 (Winter 1960–61), 80–93, and 14/2 (Spring 1961), 229–43.

Falkus, M.E. 'United States Economic Policy and the "Dollar Gap" of the 1920s', *Economic History Review*, 2nd ser., 24/4 (November 1971), 599–623.

Fleury, Antoine. 'Un sursaut antiprotectionniste dans le contexte de la crise économique de 1929: le projet d'une trève douanière plurilatérale', *Relations Internationales*, 39 (Autumn 1984), 333–54.

Gegenmüller, Ernst. 'Botschafter von Hoesch und der deutsche–österreichische Zollunionplan von 1931', *Historische Zeitschrift*, 195 (1962), 581–95.

Girault, René. 'Economie et politique internationale: diplomatie et banque pendant l'entre-deux guerres', *Relations Internationales*, 21 (Spring 1980), 7–22.

'L'Europe centrale et orientale dans la stratégie des hommes d'affaires et des diplomats français', in *Les Relations financières internationales, facteurs de solidarités ou de rivalités?*, Centre d'études européennes (Bruxelles, 1979), 119–32.

Gospel, Howard F. 'Employers' Labour Policy: A Study of the Mond–Turner Talks, 1927–33', *Business History*, 21/2 (July 1979), 180–97.

Gregory, Sir Theodore. 'The "Norman Conquests" Reconsidered', *Lloyds Bank Review*, new ser., 46 (October 1957), 1–20.

Guillen, Pierre. 'La Politique douanière de la France dans les années vingt', *Relations Internationales*, 16 (Winter 1978), 315–31.

Hardach, Gerd. 'The 1931 Crisis in Germany', Paper presented to the Conference on the 1931 Crisis and Its Aftermath, Clare College, Cambridge, 14–16 April 1982.

Harrison, Royden. 'Labour Government: Then and Now', *Political Quarterly*, 41/1 (January–March 1970), 67–82.

Hauser, Oswald. 'Der Plan einer deutsch–österreichische Zollunion von 1931 und die europäische Föderation', *Historische Zeitschrift*, 179 (1955), 45–92.

Hawtrey, Sir Ralph. 'The Return to Gold in 1925', *Bankers' Magazine*, August 1969, 61–67.

Hill, B.W. 'The Change of Government and the "Loss of the City", 1710–1711', *Economic History Review*, 2nd ser., 24/3 (August 1971), 395–413.

Holland, R.F. 'The Federation of British Industry and the International Economy, 1929–39', *Economic History Review*, 2nd ser., 34 (1981), 287–301.

Howson, Susan. 'The Origins of Dear Money, 1919–20', *Economic History Review*, 2nd ser., 27 pt. 1 (February 1974).

Hume, L.J. 'The Gold Standard and Deflation: Issues and Attitudes in the Nineteen-Twenties', *Economica*, new ser., 30/119 (August 1963), 225–42.

Jeanneney, Jean-Noel. 'L'Influence des milieux financiers sur la politique extérieure de la France dans les années 1920', *Les Relations financières interna-*

tionales, facteurs de solidarités ou de rivalités?, Centre d'études européennes (Bruxelles, 1979), 65–77.

Kernbauer, Hans. 'The Policy of the Austrian National Bank Before and During the 1931 Crisis', Paper presented to the Conference on the 1931 Crisis and Its Aftermath, Clare College, Cambridge, 14–16 April 1982.

Kruger, Peter. 'La Politique extérieure allemande et les relations franco-polonaises (1918–1932)', *Revue d'histoire diplomatique*, 2–4 (1981), 264–94.

Kruszewski, Charles. 'The German–Polish Tariff War and its Aftermath', *Journal of Central European Affairs*, 3/3 (1943), 294–325.

Leffler, Melvin P. 'Political Isolationism: Economic Expansionism or Diplomatic Realism? American Policy Towards Western Europe', *Perspectives in American History*, 8 (1974), 413–61.

Lipgens, Walter. 'Europäische Einigungsidee, 1923–30 und Briands Europaplan im Urteil der deutschen Akten', *Historische Zeitschrift*, 203 (1966), 46–89, 316–63.

Lowe, Rodney. 'The Erosion of State Intervention in Britain, 1917–24', *Economic History Review*, 2nd ser., 31/2 (May 1978), 270–86.

McDonald, G.W. and F. Howard Gospel. 'The Mond–Turner Talks, 1927–1933: A Study in Industrial Cooperation', *Historical Journal*, 16/4 (1973), 807–29.

McEwen, J.M. 'Lloyd George's Acquisition of the *Daily Chronicle* in 1918', *Journal of British Studies*, 22/1 (Autumn, 1982), 127–44.

Maier, Charles S. 'Between Taylorism and Technocracy: European Ideologies and the Vision of Industrial Productivity in the 1920s', *Journal of Contemporary History*, 5/2 (1970), 27–61.

Malament, Barbara C. 'Philip Snowden and the Cabinet Deliberations of 1931', *Society for the Study of Labour History Bulletin*, 41 (Autumn 1980), 31–33.

März, Eduard and Fritz Weber. 'The Antecedents of the Austrian Crash', Paper presented to the Conference on the 1931 Crisis and Its Aftermath, Clare College, Cambridge, 14–16 April 1982.

Milward, Alan S. 'The Economic Effects of the Two World Wars on Britain', (1970).

Moggridge, D.E. 'British Controls on Long-term Capital Movements, 1924–1931', *Essays on a Mature Economy: Britain after 1840*, ed. Donald N. McCluskey (London, 1971), 113–35.

'The 1931 Financial Crisis – a New View', *The Banker*, August 1970, 832–39.

Mouton, Marie-Renée. 'Société des Nations et reconstruction financière de l'Europe: la conférence de Bruxelles (24 septembre – 8 octobre 1920)', *Relations Internationales*, 39 (Autumn 1984), 309–31.

Murdock, Graham and Peter Golding. 'The Structure, Ownership and Control of the Press, 1914–76', in *Newspaper History from the Seventeenth Century to the Present Day*, eds. George Boyce, James Curran, and Pauline Wingate (1978), ch. 18.

Panitch, Leo. 'Recent Theorizations of Corporatism: Reflections on a Growth Industry', *British Journal of Sociology*, 31/2 (June 1980).

Peele, Gillian. 'St George's and the Empire Crusade', in *By-Elections in British Politics*, eds. Chris Cook and John Ramsden (1973), ch. 4.

Platt, D.C.M. 'Some Drastic Revisions in the Sum and Direction of British Investment Overseas, 31 December 1913', Paper presented to the Seminar on the City and the Empire, Institute of Commonwealth Studies, London, 3 May 1983.

Pollard, Sidney. 'The Great Disillusion', *Society for the Study of Labour History Bulletin*, 16 (1968), 33–41.

'Nationalisation of Banking', in *Ideology and the Labour Party*, eds. David Rubinstein and David Martin (1979).

'Trade Union Reactions to the Economic Crisis', *Journal of Contemporary History*, 4/4 (October 1969), 101–15.

Pressnell, L.S. '1925: The Burden of Sterling', *Economic History Review*, 2nd ser., 31/1 (February 1978), 67–88.

Pumphrey, R.E. 'The Introduction of Industrialists into the British Peerage: A Study in Adaptation of a Social Institution', *American Historical Review*, 65/1 (October 1959), 1–16.

Rappard, William E. 'Post-War Efforts for Freer Trade', *Geneva Studies*, 9/2 (March 1938), 7–67.

Renshaw, Patrick. 'Anti-Labour Politics in Britain, 1918–27', *Journal of Contemporary History*, 12/4 (October 1969), 3–19.

Rubinstein, W.D. 'The Victorian Middle Classes: Wealth, Occupation, and Geography', *Economic History Review*, 2nd ser., 30/4 (November 1977), 602–23.

'Wealth, Elites and the Class Structure of Modern Britain', *Past and Present*, 76 (August 1977), 99–126.

Ruge, Wolfgang and Wolfgang Schumann. 'Die Reaktion des deutschen Imperialismus auf Briands Europaplan 1930', *Zeitschrift fur Geschichtswissenschaft*, 20/1 (1972), 40–70.

Seymour-Ure, Colin. 'The Press and the Party System between the Wars', in *The Politics of Reappraisal*, eds. Gillian Peele and Chris Cook (1975), ch. 10.

Smith, Steven R.B. 'The Century of the London Chamber of Commerce', *London Journal*, 8/2 (1982), 156–70.

Soutou, Georges. 'L'Alliance franco-polonaise (1925–1933), ou comment s'en débarrasser?', *Revue d'histoire diplomatique*, 2/4 (1980), 295–348.

Stambrook, F.G. 'The German–Austrian Customs Union Project of 1931: A Study of German Methods and Motives', *Journal of Central European Affairs*, 21/1 (April 1961), 15–44.

Sutherland, Lucy S. 'The City in Eighteenth-century Politics', in *Essays Presented to Sir Lewis Namier*, eds. R. Pares and A.J.P. Taylor (1956).

Thompson, F.M.L. 'Britain', in *European Landed Elites in the Nineteenth Century*, ed. David Spring (Baltimore, 1977), 22–44.

Tomlinson, B.R. 'Britain and the Indian Currency Crisis 1930–32', *Economic History Review*, 2nd ser., 32/1 (February 1979), 88–99.

Wallace, W.V. 'The Management of Foreign Economic Policy in Britain', *International Affairs*, April 1974, 251–67.

Whetham, Edith. 'The Agricultural Act, 1920 and its Repeal – the "Great Betrayal"', *Agricultural History Review*, 22, pt. 1 (1974), 36–49.

White, Ralph T. 'Regionalism vs. Universalism in the League of Nations. A Study of "Pan-Europeanism" and the League Secretariat between 1925 and 1930, based on material in the League Archives at Geneva', *Annales d'Etudes Internationales*, 1 (1970), 88–114.

Williams, David. 'The Evolution of the Sterling System', in *Essays in Money*

and Banking in Honour of R.S. Sayers, eds. C.R. Whittlesey and J.S.G. Wilson (1968).
'London and the 1931 Financial Crisis', *Economic History Review*, 15/3 (April 1963), 512–28.
'Montagu Norman and Banking Policy in the Nineteen Twenties', *Yorkshire Bulletin of Economic and Social Research*, 11/1 (July 1959), 38–55.
'The 1931 Financial Crisis', *Yorkshire Bulletin of Economic and Social Research*, 15/2 (November 1963), 92–110.
Winkler, Henry R. 'The Emergence of a Labour Foreign Policy in Great Britain, 1918–1929', *Journal of Modern History*, 28 (1956), 247–58.

Index